QuarkXPress® Unleashed

QuarkXPress®
Unleashed

Power Techniques to Make You a Virtuoso

Brad Walrod

New York

QuarkXPress® Unleashed: Power Techniques to Make You a Virtuoso

Cover design by Amy King
Cover illustration by Ron Chan
Chapter opener artwork by Elyse Chapman
Book composed and produced by High Text Graphics

Published in the United States by Random House, Inc., New York, and simultaneously in Canada by Random House of Canada, Limited. Manufactured in the United States of America.

First Edition

0 9 8 7 6 5 4 3 2 1

ISBN 0-679-79164-7

New York Toronto London Sydney Auckland

Contents

2 Typography

3 Page Layout

6 Tables

7 Automating DTP

8 Scripting

Appendixes

Foreword

This book is not for the faint of heart. It delves deeply into the tricks and techniques used by the real professionals—the people who have to meet a deadline no matter what it takes.

Brad Walrod has an extensive background in typography and production. As a typesetter who lives and dies by his ability to make QuarkXPress perform miracles on time and under budget, he is eminently qualified to write about QuarkXPress (and most other Macintosh prepress software, for that matter).

QuarkXPress Unleashed pulls no punches. It gives you many no-nonsense production hints that help you automate tasks that are tedious to do in any WYSIWYG product. If you thought the days of code-based editing were gone, Brad gives you good reason to think again. Using sophisticated searching and editing techniques, he shows you how to make an arduous process much less time-consuming. His focus on solving real-world problems is something that is truly unique and extraordinarily useful.

And the best part of all is that you don't need to go out and buy lots of specialized software to do all this fancy stuff. Most of the tools you need are included with the book.

Peruse its pages. If you're an intermediate to high-end user of QuarkXPress, chances are there's something in here that will save you time and money. Chances are there's something that will prevent a missed press deadline. All in all, *QuarkXPress Unleashed* is a book you should have in your library.

Tim Gill
Founder, Chairman, Senior VP of Research and Development
Quark, Inc.

Acknowledgments

When first approached by my editor, Mike Roney, to write this book, I was asked if I'd like a co-author. I gave many answers to that question—some more subtle than others—letting him know that I really wanted to do it myself. Such naiveté must come only from first-time authors! During the year it took to write this book, I received an amazing amount of help from a lot of people. Some were friends before I started the book. Others, especially the folks at Quark and Random House, became friends as we worked on the book.

It was the first time I had a chance to work professionally with Kip Shaw and Mike Arst, whose knowledge and talent I was already familiar with. Who better to act as technical editors—Kip, officially, and Mike, informally (but no less diligently)? They kept me honest to the point of pain. I'd like to publicly apologize to them for not once answering the questions they included in each chapter's feedback, including the ever-present "3.3? Don't you mean 3.2?"

I had already worked professionally with Jeff Cheney and Ben Ko, and semi-professionally with Elyse Chapman, before starting the book. Jeff's knowledge of Quark's EfiColor XTension and Apple Events support was of incalculable value when it came time to produce those sections of this book. Ben's unique ideas and constant support throughout the production of the book were a crutch I would not have wanted to be without. And Elyse's beautiful chapter opener artwork and "tip" and "disk" icons greatly enhance the appearance of the book. Her patience with my picky changes deserves a nod, too.

Jon Hodges' contributions to the Typography chapter, Sam Merrell's insights into the Graphics chapter, and Lenny Bergson's help with the color plates should not be overlooked, either!

Many people at Quark helped with this project. First and foremost, I'd like to thank Tim Gill, both for his kind Foreword and for his personal interest in the success of the book. Ralph Risch, the product manager for QuarkXPress for the Macintosh, was very generous with his time and suggestions. His assistant, Elizabeth Jones, and two other members of the 3.3 development team, Michael Johnson and Becky Lefebvre, kept me up to date on product changes and they answered innumerable questions. Michael Reuter, Quark's on-line technical support representative, chased down answers for some of my more bizarre questions. The generosity of Mark Niemann-Ross, Kathleen Erramouspe, and Tom Brinkman greatly enhanced the reference material, and I thank Dave Shaver, John Cruise, and Kelly Kordes for reviewing selected sections for accuracy.

Other vendor representatives that gave freely of their time and materials are William Buckingham, Tami Stodghill, Jim Wiegand, and Robin Riley, all from XChange; Michael Kim, of Datastream Imaging Systems; Karen Wilson, formerly of 21st Century Media; ArtBeat's Phil Bates; Dynamic Graphics' Steve Justice; and Tony Jackson of Taco Clipart Company.

My new friends at Random House include Mike Roney, editor, Jean Davis Taft, managing editor, and Niki DiSilvestro, production manager. Through Random House, I had the good fortune to meet copy editor Jodi Beder, proofreader Lynn Contrucci, and Dennis Beach, the wizard at R. R. Donnelley who figured out how to get QuarkXPress almost-but-not-quite-3.3 files to impose on their system. Each of these folks spent more time taking weight off my shoulders than putting it on, and I appreciate that.

I'd be remiss if I didn't also thank two friends and clients, Betty Binns and Beth Umland. Both went well beyond the call of duty to keep my regular production work away from me during the crucial last few months of writing. And when they could hold out no longer, they batched jobs together and took pains to reduce the number of passes. It's also their work that adorns many of this book's illustrations!

First a friend, then a client, and now my agent, Richard Kendall helped to take care of the business end of things while I wrote this book, and I'm very glad I had the opportunity to work with him again.

Finally, this book is dedicated to my father, Jerry Walrod, and my mother, Betty Bitterman. Their unconditional support and encouragement over the years can never be repaid, but can always be honored.

Introduction

This book is designed for professionals who want to save time and money, as well as folks just getting into the business who want to create pages professionally. When wearing my typesetting hat—which has fit comfortably on my head for the past 15 years—I tend to gravitate toward large and complex jobs, the better to sink my teeth into. This is not to say that I enjoy the dreary drudge work that often accompanies such jobs. Instead, I'm constantly searching for faster and more efficient ways to accomplish complex tasks.

In some cases, I need look no farther than QuarkXPress, since many of its options are well suited for a variety of work. The key is to know which options to use for a particular task, as well as which settings are appropriate for each option. QuarkXPress is very customizable, and I discuss many of its built-in features—and their various uses—in these pages. My goal is to show you the time-saving tips and techniques I've learned over the years, either on my own or with help from others.

TIP Tips and techniques are often woven into the text and at other times are called out by the use of the "tip" icon shown here. Some tips talk about undocumented or possibly ignored features, while others may make brief mention of an XTension.

Another mission of this book is to show you how to further customize QuarkXPress for the unique requirements of any job you may encounter. Today's off-the-shelf publishing software is used to produce a wide variety of projects, under the same—if not worse—budget constraints that have always existed. Publishing programs shouldn't exist in a vacuum, nor should they try to be all things to all people. To make tools like QuarkXPress more effective, you need to integrate various utilities into the production stream, but with an eye toward simplifying tasks, not complicating them further. Commercial and shareware utilities and XTensions are covered at great length in this book.

When wearing my training hat—which also fits comfortably on my head, albeit for slightly fewer years—I've fallen into a pattern of teaching that strikes a chord in me and that has seemed to work for my QuarkXPress students, both in individualized and classroom settings. I find that I generally:

- Review the basics of a particular subject
- Introduce new concepts, with an overview of their features
- Illustrate the use of the concepts with real-world examples
- Compare each concept's ease of use with its learning curve

I follow this model in all of the chapters, including a general discussion, tips and techniques gleaned from experience, and profiles and comments on third-party XTensions that will make certain jobs easier.

A good example of this method in action is the first chapter, **Text Preparation**. In it, I discuss text massaging—the act of cleaning up a client's files so that you can import them into a QuarkXPress document with a minimum of hassle. I first review some of the search-and-replace capabilities in QuarkXPress and Microsoft Word, and then I introduce utilities that are worth learning even for simple or small jobs, especially if those jobs are repeat business. One of the utilities covered in this chapter is Torquemada the Inquisitor, a search-and-replace program. I show a few jobs that benefit from Torquemada's use, and I consider at what point I would switch from using QuarkXPress' built-in Find/Change command to utilizing a third-party utility such as Torquemada.

The next chapter, **Typography**, is an extensive discussion of the typographic features available in QuarkXPress. The chapter culminates in a number of examples from jobs I've set in which lines are improperly spaced, and I've included specific—and ordered—instructions on how such lines can be fixed. This chapter, more than any other, makes use of Encyclofont to illustrate the Command (⌘), Option (⌥), Shift (⇧), and Control (⌃) keys that are used in many keyboard shortcuts.

The theme of problem solving on real jobs is certainly carried over into the **Page Layout** chapter, where I discuss how to build a page from the ground up. I illustrate how decisions made at the creation of a document have repercussions throughout it's life. There are sections on master pages, templates, libraries, and anchored boxes, as well as a discussion on vertical justification.

You'll see the focus of the book shift back to the interaction between various programs when you get to the **Graphics** chapter. Here's where I try to make sense of some of the commonly used graphics formats, such as Encapsulated PostScript (EPS), Tagged Image File Format (TIFF), and PhotoCD (sometimes referred to as PCD). I talk about what QuarkXPress can and can't do with images in these formats, as well as what it can and can't do *well*. The book starts to get more deeply into XTensions at this point, as I discuss XTensions for both gathering and generating information on graphics used in your files. There are also sections on color manipulation and illustration creation XTensions. The chapter concludes with a discussion on the EfiColor XTension.

The issue of getting all of these pages that have been laid out with type and graphics off the screen and onto paper—either laser bond or rolls for an offset web press—is the goal of the **Output** chapter. I review some of the proofing devices available and take a look at some useful XTensions that concentrate on printing. A good chunk of the chapter is given over to trapping, including how to use QuarkXPress' trapping controls. That's followed by a list of specifications you'll need from a printer before starting a job, as well as what the printer will require from you once your part of the project is over. Finally, I cover how to initiate, nurture, and maintain that most important relationship in desktop publishing—the one between you and your service bureau.

The **Tables** chapter starts off with a necessarily brief description of QuarkXPress' built-in table-making commands. The remainder is devoted to four third-party table-making XTensions, starting with the one that's easiest to use but which offers the fewest features, and ending with the one with the most features and the sharpest learning curve. Don't stop me in the street and ask me what table XTension you need; the answer to the question lies in knowing both the complexity of the tables you need to create and the capabilities of the people who will need to create them. The chapter tries to convey what kinds of tables can best be made with each XTension, as well as how difficult it will be to make each kind of table.

The **Automating DTP** chapter is perhaps the crown jewel of this book. If I can be allowed to slip my typesetting hat back on for a moment, I'd be hard pressed to think of a large or complex job that wouldn't benefit from at least one—if not all—of the utilities and XTensions discussed in this chapter. From Mark My Words, which automates so much of the massage required to bring formatted word processing files into QuarkXPress documents, to Xdata, which can be used to merge databases—or any structured files—with Quark XPress, there's a wealth of information here. In between, there are a handful of powerful utilities and XTensions that can be used on their own or in combination with each other to make large jobs flow smoothly, maintain consistency across files, and retain their recoverability. Let's face it: Some jobs have to be done the right way, or they have to be done again. These utilities can take much of the pain out of doing a job right the first time, and every time.

The **Scripting** chapter offers a glimpse into the future, or perhaps into the past, for us ex-programmers. QuarkXPress' support for Apple Events is truly impressive. Up to now, I've discussed how you can automate specific desktop publishing tasks. Scripting allows real inter-application communication; this means that you can set up procedures for individual utilities and then run a script that passes files through a number of utilities, opens a QuarkXPress document, creates the required text and picture boxes, imports text and graphics, and even saves, prints, and makes a backup of the file. The bulk of this chapter is an annotated script that should give you a feel for what it takes to write a moderately complex script, as well as serve as a reference when you start writing your own scripts.

The Appendixes provide a wealth of resource materials, starting in **Appendix A** with an overview of the features first introduced in QuarkXPress 3.2. I've found that people tend to know well the features they learned when they first started using a program, but the more upgrades they've been through, the farther behind they are in knowing the full capabilities of the program. By covering the new features in 3.2—as well as 3.3, in **Appendix B**—and in some cases describing the ramifications of the new features, I hope to prevent my readers from falling into that nasty trap.

Appendix C is an overview of the various coding languages available for importing massaged files into QuarkXPress, including Quark's own markup language, XPress Tags. Two XTensions, Xtags and ProTagsXT, are also documented here. Note that ProTagsXT is so new that I didn't have a chance to cover its extensive features in the **Automating DTP** chapter, but I was able to include a piece of its documentation in this appendix.

Appendixes D to **F** list all of the Quark Authorized Training Consultants, Quark Authorized Service Bureaus, and Quark and third-party XTensions. The lists are current as of about a month before this book was printed; the problem with such lists is that they are out of date the minute ink hits paper. Still, you should be able to use them as a starting point whenever you're looking for a trainer or consultant, a service bureau, or an XTension to make your jobs run smoother.

Don't forget to take a look at the disk in the back of the book. It contains free, shareware, and demonstration versions of most of the utilities and XTensions mentioned throughout the book. Assuming I haven't overlooked any, you should see a disk icon next to any paragraphs that refer to something on the disk. Wherever possible, I've mentioned the disk file at the start of a discussion; that way you'll know that you can pop the disk in and follow along. General disk installation instructions can be found in **Appendix G**.

I hope that the following pages help you to unleash the power of QuarkXPress!

Brad Walrod

1

Text Preparation

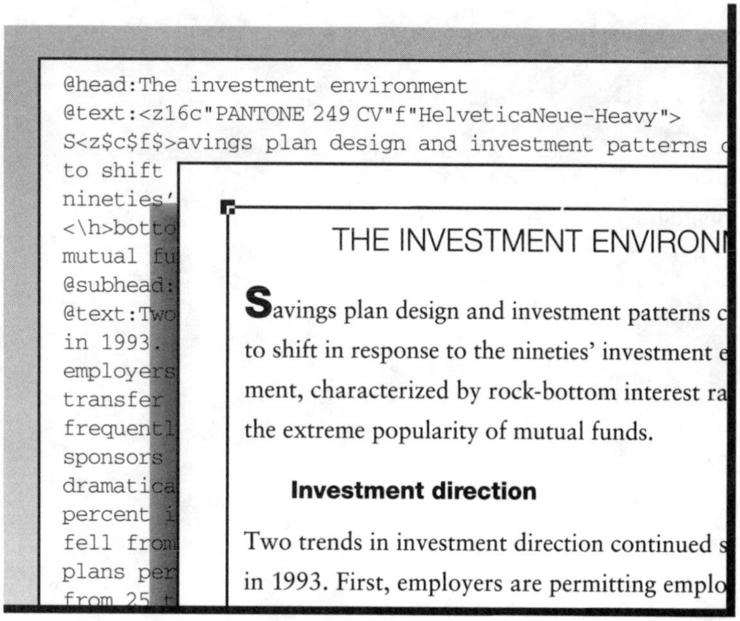

```
@head:The investment environment
@text:<z16c"PANTONE 249 CV"f"HelveticaNeue-Heavy">
S<z$c$f$>avings plan design and investment patterns c
to shift
nineties'
<\h>botto
mutual fu
@subhead:
@text:Two
in 1993.
employers
transfer
frequentl
sponsors
dramatica
percent i
fell from
plans per
from 25 t
```

THE INVESTMENT ENVIRONI

Savings plan design and investment patterns c
to shift in response to the nineties' investment e
ment, characterized by rock-bottom interest ra
the extreme popularity of mutual funds.

Investment direction

Two trends in investment direction continued s
in 1993. First, employers are permitting emplo

CHAPTER 1 CONTENTS

FIGURES

Although QuarkXPress is primarily a page layout tool, it has a full-featured word processor built in. This is especially helpful when it comes time to edit a job, but you can also use it to directly enter all the text for your file. For small jobs with few pages and little type, this is fine. However, in production environments or when working with clients who have their own computers, you're going to need to be able to import text into your QuarkXPress documents.

In this chapter I'll discuss the various ways that files may be presented to you, as well as what to do once you have them. Although I think of the following as just the basics, there's a chapter's worth of stuff to discuss. Later on in the book—in both the **Automating DTP** and **Scripting** chapters—I'll build on these basics, taking file "massaging" to an advanced level.

Sucking in the files

Files may be presented to you in any number of ways. They may be plain text files or extensively formatted; they may have been typed on a Macintosh or a PC; they might even come to you with XPress Tags in them. In each case, you'll have to decide whether further processing is necessary before importing into QuarkXPress.

Formatted files

QuarkXPress can recognize the formatting of some Mac word processor files and translate that formatting into its own style of coding. The filters that come with the program determine which word processing files it can read. These filters are XTensions: add-on modules that customize your personal copy of the program.

Many of these filters can be found in a folder called Other XTensions inside your QuarkXPress folder (Figure 1.1). You were asked

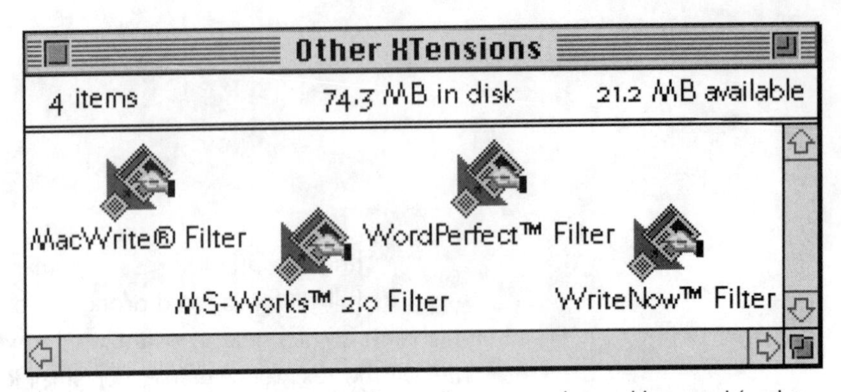

Figure 1.1 Other XTensions During the installation procedure, seldom-used (as determined by you) word processing filters will be moved into this folder. You won't be able to access these filters while in QuarkXPress unless you move them out of the Other XTensions folder and into the main QuarkXPress folder or XTension folder.

which XTensions you wanted to use when you installed the program; the ones you didn't want ended up in this folder. While there, they'll have no effect on your copy of the program, since to be active they must reside loose in the same folder as the program. I keep only the MS Word and XPress Tags filters loose in my QuarkXPress folder, with the rest of the filters—which I seldom need—tucked away in the Other XTensions folder.

I usually don't find it very useful to import formatted text from word processors, as there always seem to be so many differences between the way a file was typed and the way it needs to be typeset. My clients, for example, tend to style text as bold or underlined for emphasis, whereas the proper typesetting convention is to style emphasized text as italic.

TIP QuarkXPress' word processing filters can come in handy when you have a file for which you don't have the creating application and you'd like to edit the text in another word processing program. If you import a word processing file into QuarkXPress using the appropriate filter, you can then export it using **File→Save Text**. I usually choose to export files using either the ASCII Text or XPress Tags options, depending on which one gives me the more useful text file to work with. I prefer to use XPress Tags, since it produces codes that can be searched and replaced. If the original file is formatted to death, however, ASCII Text can be the better choice, since exporting in this manner will automatically strip all the formatting from the file.

PC files

If you're bringing files into your Macintosh that originated on an IBM PC–compatible computer, you'll have two hurdles to cross. The first is getting your Macintosh to physically recognize the PC floppy disk; the second is finding a program that can logically understand the contents of the files on the disk. The Superdrive floppy disk drives available on most Macintosh computers these days take care of the first hurdle, allowing you to read PC disks as long as you have software that allows the floppies to mount.

The Apple File Exchange program can be used to mount the floppies, and since it comes with the Mac's system software, it's certainly the cheapest solution. However, you need to have the program running in order to mount the floppies and copy files to or from them. Much easier to use is a small System extension from Dayna called DOS Mounter. With this extension, you can slip a PC floppy right into the drive and watch it mount just like a Mac disk. You can then drag files to and from the floppy disk, as usual. AccessPC, from Insignia Solutions, offers a similar solution.

If you have both Macs and PCs on a network, you won't have to worry about mounting floppy disks, but you'll still need to translate the file formats.

Format translators

If your favorite word processor's files can't be read directly into Quark XPress, there are programs available that translate between native word processing formats. Dataviz' MacLink Plus can convert a dizzying number of Mac and PC file formats, both word processing and graphics.

If you have Microsoft Word or WordPerfect—and if you've been keeping it up to date—then you already have a tool for converting file formats. Both programs come with a good selection of translators. I regularly use MS Word to open up PC WordPerfect files, since I don't own WordPerfect for the Mac but all my PC-using clients seem to like WordPerfect.

XPress Tags

There's a very powerful feature of QuarkXPress that a lot of folks don't make use of, either because they don't know about it or because they're intimidated about the time necessary to learn how to use it. I'm talking about XPress Tags. I'd like to offer some suggestions on getting started with tags; talk about common, everyday use of tags; and show examples of using tags for character styling. In the **Automating DTP** chapter, we'll talk about working with XPress Tags and databases.

XPress Tags are bits of code that you can add to plain text (ASCII) files before importing them into QuarkXPress. You can use tags to pre-apply style sheets to paragraphs, as well as to make character style changes. You can even use them to *define* style sheets in your word processor files, but you'd have to be a bit masochistic to do so when it's so much easier to make a style sheet in QuarkXPress.

Getting started with XPress Tags

Let me show you what the next paragraph looks like as XPress Tags. If you're going to be following along on your own computer, don't forget to place the XPress Tags Filter file into your QuarkXPress folder if it's not already there; if you still have an old Style Tags Filter, move that into the Other XTensions folder.

After creating a style sheet and typing in a little text, keep your text box active and choose **File→Save Text**. There are as many file format options available under the pop-up menu as there are filters in your QuarkXPress folder (Figure 1.2). In this case, we're going to choose the XPress Tags option. Name and save the file.

To see what the file you just created looks like, make a text box and choose **File→Get Text**. Both Convert Quotes and Include Style Sheets should be turned off for the purposes of this test, since you won't want tick marks converted or tags interpreted; usually you'll want both of these options to be turned on when working with XPress Tags. Here's what I got in my file:

```
<v1.60><e0>
@text=[S"","text"]<*J*h"Standard"*kn0*kt(2,2)
*ra0*rb0*d0*p(132,26,0,15,0,0,g,"U.S. English")
```

```
*t(30,0," ")Ps100t0h100z13k0b0c"Black"
f"ClearPrairieDawn-Plain">
@text:After creating a style sheet and typing
in a little text, keep your text box active
and choose <B>File<Bf"Symbol">Æ<Bf"ClearPrairie
Dawn-Plain">Save Text<B>. There are as many file
format options available under the drop-down
menu as there are filters in your Quark<\d>
XPress folder (Figure 1.2). In this case, we're
going to choose the XPress Tags option. Name
and save the file.
```

Let's ignore everything above the line that starts with **@text:**, since that's just the style definition created when the text was saved. I've made bold all the parts that we will be talking about. The **@text:** command is the name of the style sheet used for that paragraph. A style sheet tag needn't appear at the start of every paragraph, as a style sheet will carry from paragraph to paragraph until a new one is called.

The other codes I want to point out are **<B>**, **<f"...">**, and **<\d>**. The **<B>** command applies the bold style to any characters following

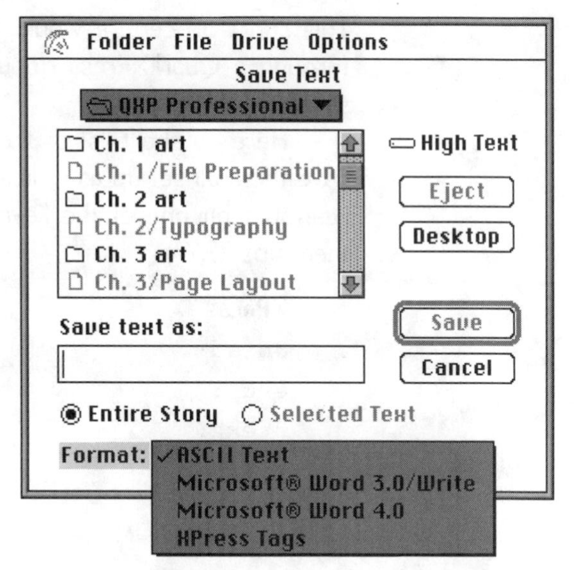

Figure 1.2 Save Text Your choices when using the Save Text command depend on which word processing filters you have in your QuarkXPress folder. Note that the Microsoft Word filter handles more than one version of that program's files.

it until turned off with another **<B>**. The **<f"...">** command changes the typeface, and in the sample paragraph I've changed faces twice: once to change to the Symbol font to access the "→" character, and once to change back to this book's text face, Clear Prairie Dawn.

In the example, you can see how XPress Tags can be ganged together into one command, since both the command that toggles the bold styling on and off and the command to change faces appear together (**<Bf"Symbol">**). The last command, **<\d>**, is a discretionary return that allows the word "QuarkXPress" to break in the middle without hyphenating (as discussed in the **Typography** chapter).

Daily use of XPress Tags

One of the best reasons to pre-apply your coding in a word processor file is that you can often search for something that's already in a file and change it into something that QuarkXPress can use. For example, say the client religiously typed two extra carriage returns before every subhead and one extra return after the subhead. You could search for three returns and replace them with one return and an XPress Tag for the subhead style sheet. Then search for two returns and replace them with one return and the tag for the text style sheet. This short procedure would be a heck of a lot quicker than going through a QuarkXPress document and applying the different style sheets by hand.

Here's a short list of the XPress Tags I use every day. In fact, I have them all set up as QuicKeys macros in Microsoft Word so that I can just hit one of the keypad characters on my keyboard to call them up.

XPress Tag	Meaning
`@head:`	Main head style sheet
`@sub:`	Secondary head style sheet
`@text:`	Ordinary text style sheet
`<I>`	Change to/from the italic character style
`<B>`	Change to/from the bold character style
`<\n>`	New line command (Shift-Return)
`<\f>`	En space/figure space (Option-Space)

Whenever I need an exception to this set, I do one of the following:

- Perform a search-and-replace.
- Add a QuicKeys macro.
- Type it in once and copy and paste it where needed.
- Type it in manually whenever necessary.
- Just forget about it altogether until I get the file into QuarkXPress.

As you can see, there are a lot of options. The point is to do whichever gives you the most flexibility and saves you the most time.

Character styling with XPress Tags

Whether or not to use XPress Tags for character styling is a judgment call. I tend to use the abovementioned <B> and <I> tags when a client has given me a file that has italics and bold already styled, since I know I'm going to lose that styling when I save the file as text. Much of the time it's easier to go through a file and insert the codes around phrases that are already italic and bold (since you can see them) than to look for them later in a QuarkXPress document.

TIP The XPress Tags filter won't work with native word processor files, so you have to save the files as plain text. WordLess Plus—discussed below—can take care of converting formatted Microsoft Word files into text and changing all the character styling to XPress Tags. It will also flag any paragraph styling, such as style sheets, that were used.

Sometimes, however, you'll have a large number of instances where characters need more than just a single style change. Here are the tags necessary to create a square bullet in a size, font, and color that differ from the paragraph's style sheet:

XPRESS TAG	MEANING
`<z8.5>`	Change size to 8½ points
`<z$>`	Return to point size in current style sheet
`<f"ZapfDingbats">`	Change font to Zapf Dingbats
`<f$>`	Return to font in current style sheet
`<c"PANTONE 286 CV">`	Change color to PANTONE 286 CV
`<c$>`	Return to color in current style sheet

The above can all be combined into two strings of commands, shown below with the letter "n" in the middle (the key you need to type in Zapf Dingbats to get a square bullet):

```
<z8.5f"ZapfDingbats"c"PANTONE 286 CV">n<z$f$c$>
```

Now, I would certainly never type all that, but recently I was working on a job that required a number of changes to one of the Bundesbahn Pi fonts (to get a number knocked out of a square box). I typed each of the numbers inside square brackets and then searched and replaced all the square brackets with the proper XPress Tags. It worked like a charm!

Another way of handling instances of many characters that need to be set in a different face or size is to stick with simple XPress Tags and then use **Edit→Find/Change** or **Utilities→Font Usage** in QuarkXPress to set the proper face and size (Figure 1.3). For example, if you're using the typeface Berkeley Old Style in the Medium weight for your text and you want the Black weight to be used for important phrases, the <B> tag won't be accurate (since applying the bold style to Berkeley Medium gives you Berkeley Bold, not Black).

You can still use the <B> tag in your word processor files, though. You'll just have to remember to go to Font Usage under the Utilities menu and change all the text in Berkeley Old Style Medium with the applied Bold style to plain Berkeley Old Style Black.

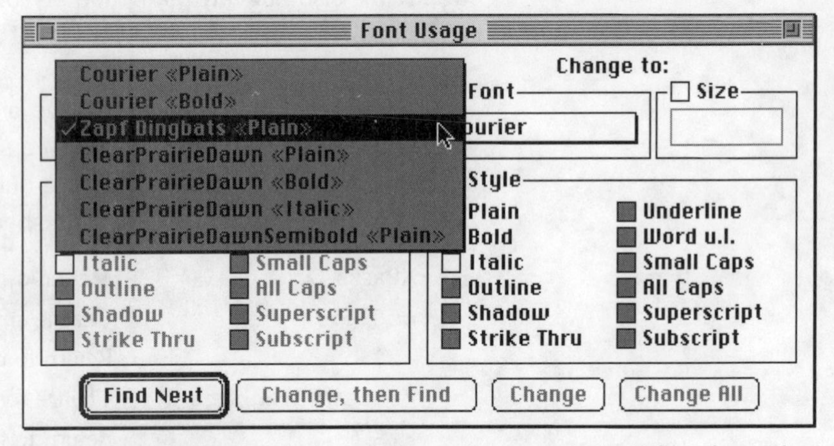

Figure 1.3 Font Usage If I had used XPress Tags to apply the Bold style to Clear Prairie Dawn but I really wanted the Semibold weight once the file was in QuarkXPress, I could use Font Usage to change all or selected occurrences of the style.

Using WordLess Plus to create XPress Tags

If you have styled MS Word files, or can convert your files to MS Word format, there's a great utility that will translate your Word files into plain text files containing XPress Tags. Called WordLess Plus, it was written by Greg Swann, a man who will be mentioned often in this book. It has a simple drag-and-drop interface, and never overwrites your original files.

If your files have Word style sheets applied, WordLess Plus will append XPress Tags to the starts of the paragraphs. If the files just have local formatting, WordLess Plus will create the appropriate XPress Tags for this, too. It's a free utility, and it's available on the disk in the back of this book. Depending on how the files were styled, you may need to do some search and replacing at this point, but luckily, that's what we're going to talk about next.

Seek out and destroy

Although the above heading is meant as a joke, as with any good comedy, there's an element of truth in it. Search-and-replace routines are often necessary in job preparation, but they must be done with a clear head and a watchful eye, as one can do a lot of damage to a file's contents. Following a few safety precautions will keep you from committing any permanent damage, however, and this section—along with its high-end counterpart in the **Automating DTP** chapter—should save you a lot of time.

TIP The most important thing to remember when running search-and-replace routines on your files is that you should always save to a backup copy of the original file. Yes, you may end up with a dozen copies of the same file, and at some point you'll need to pick which files to keep and which ones to throw away. But by saving copies of the files at each stage of processing, you should never have to redo any manual work; and automated work will be recoverable, since you can always go back to an older version of a file.

One change at a time

It's entirely possible that in some jobs you'll be able to just do a few search-and-replaces with the tools built into QuarkXPress or a word processing program. For example, if the only thing keeping you from bringing an MS Word file into QuarkXPress is the fact that it's littered with extra carriage returns, you can use the Replace command in Word to fix this pretty easily (Figure 1.4).

Keep changing all the double carriage returns to single returns until Word reports that there were no changes made. And if you already have the text in a QuarkXPress document, you could similarly search and replace them there (Figure 1.5).

TIP Each time you repeat this translation in QuarkXPress, you'll want to hold down the Option key so that the search starts over at the start of the story or document. If you have no more than a hand-

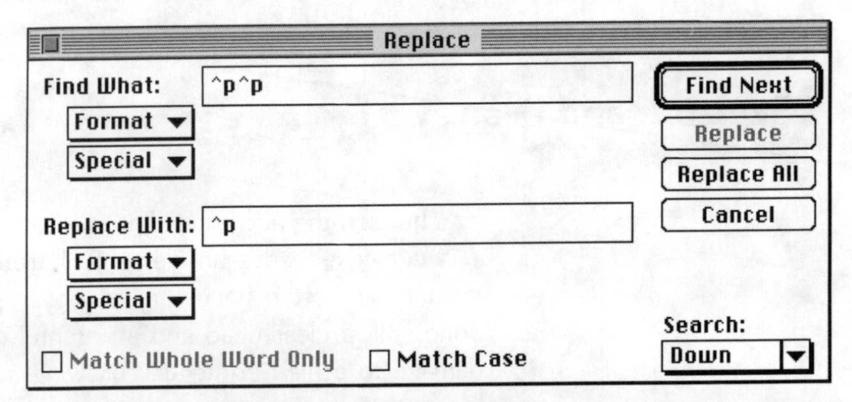

Figure 1.4 Translating in MS Word You can simply run this translation in MS Word to get rid of extra carriage returns, each one signified by the combination of the "^" (Shift-6) and "p" characters.

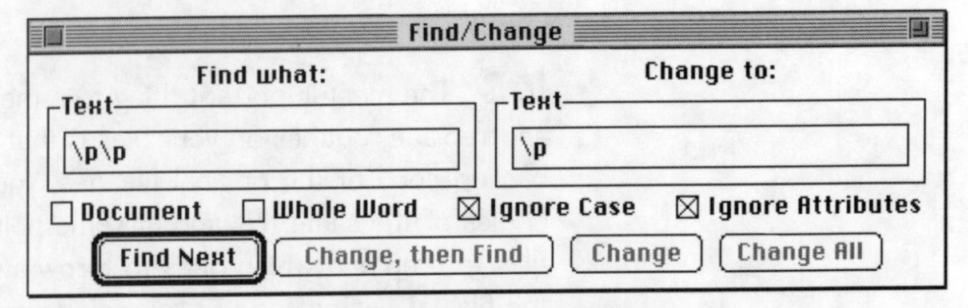

Figure 1.5 Translating in QuarkXPress To get rid of extra carriage returns after your text is in QuarkXPress, use **Edit→Find/Change**. You can either type the "\" preceding the "p" shown above or just type Command-Return to get the same thing.

ful of simple translations like this to do, and if you have only a couple of files to process, this method is not only sufficient but preferred, since it's so easy.

Other translations that I do on almost every job include changing double spacebands to single spacebands and stripping out spacebands before and after em dashes (or double hyphens).

Batch translations

There are a number of batch translation utilities available for both Macintosh and PC computers. If you're generating text files on PCs, it might be wise to do the translations there; it depends on whether you want to do the translations closer to the text-entry stage or the page-layout stage. I prefer to do the translations on the computer on which I'll be doing the page layout, since that way I can easily tweak a translation if I see a problem after flowing text into a QuarkXPress document.

The theory behind batch translation programs is that they allow you to build tables of search-and-replace translations that can be saved and then applied to any number of files. Generally, you'll start by picking a file that's representative of much of your project, build and test your translations on that file, and then customize the translations as variations crop up in subsequent files, as they always do.

TIP I'm also a strong believer in applying a translation table only to the files I'm working on in a given session, since that saves me from having to retranslate dozens of files after I discover changes in the way the files were typed. The alternative to retranslating files can be even worse: I'd have to make a bunch of manual changes in my Quark XPress files for the duration of the job and hope I caught everything. If you translate the files only when you need them, you can avoid these headaches.

In their simplest form, batch translation programs group together and remember the search-and-replaces that you would otherwise need to do by hand and remember from file to file. That alone could save you a lot of time and prevent you from missing any changes that you might forget to make. But they can also be made much more complex, "masking" out patterns of characters for the insertion of codes and condensing slight variations in searches into one powerful replacement string. I'll talk about these more robust features in the **Automating DTP** chapter; for now, let's take a look at simpler uses of the batch translation program included on this book's disk.

Torquemada the Inquisitor

This strangely named utility, written by Greg Swann, offers a great way to get started with batch translations. Very simple to use for simple translations, its learning curve only starts to rise sharply when you move into complex translations.

Adding codes

This first example comes from a book project I did in which the client requested that lines not break before or after certain combinations of abbreviations and their attendant values.

The first and third columns of the table in Figure 1.6 show strings of characters that I want the program to search for; their replacements are shown in the second and fourth columns. Each Torquemada translation table can hold up to 20 strings of translations. This first table has only 16 translations, with the first pair doing nothing but

Spaces

	======·SPACES·======	p.·	p.<\!s>
·cm	<\!s>cm	pp.·	pp.<\!s>
·in.	<\!s>in.	pl.·	pl.<\!s>
		no.·	no.<\!s>
		nos.·	nos.<\!s>
		No.·	No.<\!s>
H·	H<\!s>	Nos.·	Nos.<\!s>
W·	W<\!s>	fig.·	fig.<\!s>
D·	D<\!s>	figs.·	figs.<\!s>
L·	L<\!s>	vol.·	vol.<\!s>

Open Set... ⌘O | Save Set... ⌘S | Clear All ⌘K | Wildcards ⌘? | OK

Figure 1.6 Simple batch translation table This Torquemada the Inquisitor translation table looks for abbreviations followed or preceded by spacebands. It replaces the spacebands with the XPress Tag for a nonbreaking spaceband. (The raised period indicates a spaceband in Torquemada translation tables.)

holding the name of the table—unnecessary in this case, but you'll see later how I use this method to name different sections of the same table. There are also three blank translations that do nothing.

Whenever possible, I like to leave room in a table for growth. In fact, this table kept growing as I found more and more abbreviations that needed to be kept with their preceding or following values.

Once a translation table—or set, to use Torquemada's terminology—has been defined and saved, it can be applied to any text file. Just hit "OK," tell the program to start translating, pick a text file, and set the process in motion. Torquemada creates a new file with the letters ".TQM" appended to the original file name.

Code bursting

This next example shows how easy it is to use translation tables to add awkward XPress Tags to text files. The first translation, which can't be fully seen without scrolling through Torquemada's tiny windows, changes every occurrence of a left bracket to the following string of XPress Tags:

```
<z18c"PANTONE 286 CV"f"HelveticaNeue-Heavy">
```

I've added left and right brackets around letters that will become stick-up caps when brought into QuarkXPress, where the caps will be a different size, font, and color. Instead of changing them all by hand, I created one in QuarkXPress, chose **File→Save Text** to see what XPress Tags would be needed to generate them, and then pasted the XPress Tags into my Torquemada translation table.

The right bracket gets changed to `<c$z$f$>`, which reverts the color, size, and font back to whatever is used in the current style sheet. I'd never want to type all those codes by hand, but pasting into a translation table keeps me from having to apply all the specs by hand (Figure 1.7).

The third translation in this table looks for all instances of the XPress Tag that calls out the "sub" style sheet and adds a callout for the "par" style sheet followed by the fleuron character (*ƒ*) and a car-

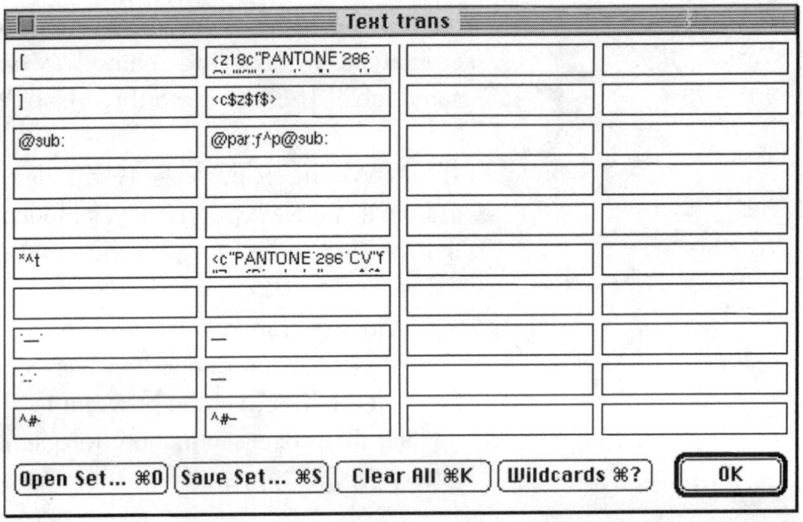

Text trans

Find	Replace
[	<z18c"PANTONE 286
]	<czf$>
@sub:	@par:f^p@sub:
*^t	<c"PANTONE 286 CV"f
˙—˙	—
˙--˙	—
^#-	^#–

Open Set... ⌘O | Save Set... ⌘S | Clear All ⌘K | Wildcards ⌘? | OK

Figure 1.7 Adding verbose XPress Tags In this Torquemada translation table, I'm replacing a few key characters with XPress Tags. Note that there are more characters being replaced than can be shown in these small windows, but you can scroll through the window to see them all.

riage return (^p). The par symbol looks like the flag that hangs on those poles seen on golf courses, and the designer on this project wanted one of them above each subhead. In this case, the "par" style sheet in QuarkXPress will call the appropriate font; the fleuron character represents the par symbol in that font.

Fourth, I'm looking for any asterisks followed by tabs (^t), as this is the way I indicated places where square bullets needed to be added to the file. Here's the replace side of that translation:

```
<c"PANTONE 286 CV"f"ZapfDingbats">n<c$f$><\f>
```

This time I'm adding both the before and after codes for a special character into one translation, since I know that the codes will always be applied to the same character. I'm creating a blue square bullet (the "n" in Zapf Dingbats), changing back to the style sheet specs, and following it with an en space (<\f>).

The next two translations just look for em dashes or double hyphens with spacebands on either side and change them both to closed (no spaces) em dashes. And lastly, we have our first instance of wildcards, which warrants its own subhead.

Wildcards

Using wildcards to "mask" a particular type of character that falls within a larger pattern of characters is a very powerful capability of Torquemada (Figure 1.8). We'll stick to simple examples in this chapter, though. The last translation shown in the "Text trans" translation table uses a wildcard to look for any number followed by a hyphen and replaces it with the same number followed by an en dash.

TIP I'd have to say that I use the wildcard for numbers more than any other. I'm always needing to change hyphens to en dashes in number ranges, take away periods after numbers and insert en spaces, or change fonts in numbered lists.

There are also a handful of "untyped" wildcards, too, which are useful for looking for *any* character within a particular pattern. The example most commonly given for the use of untyped wildcards is probably in searching for swapped characters, such as an "i" before an "e" in the word "weird." You could use untyped wildcards to search for "w^1^2rd" and change any matches to the properly spelled "weird."

I've always thought that was a pretty lame example. A bit more useful—at least to the **QuarkXPress Unleashed** crowd—is the ex-

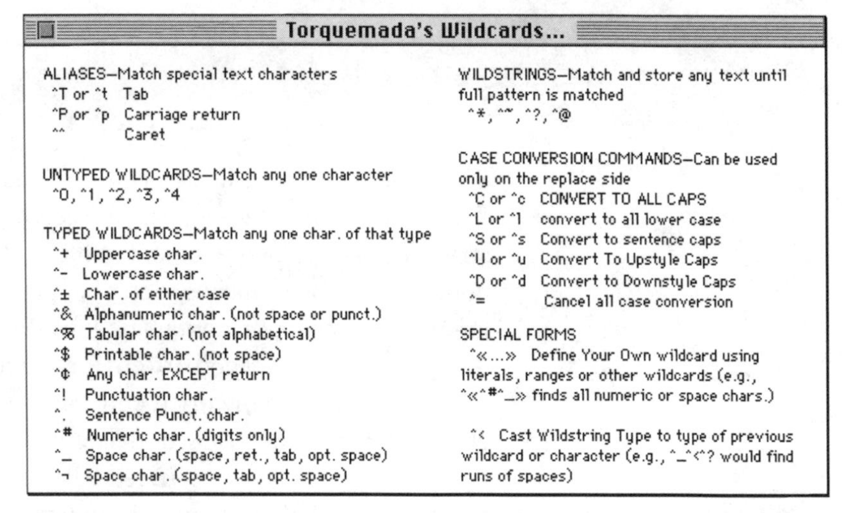

Figure 1.8 Torquemada's Wildcards... For now, just take a look at the many choices for wildcards that Torquemada offers. You might not know how you could ever use some of them, but rest assured that all of them have been requested by users of this program; feel free to blame me for the one called "Sentence Punct. char."

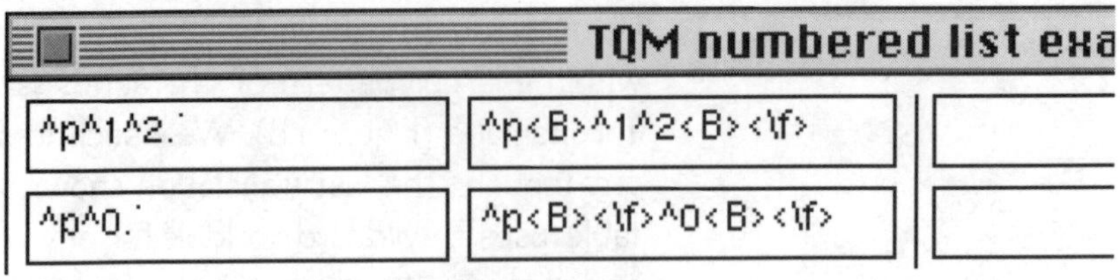

TQM numbered list exa

^p^1^2.˙	^p<B>^1^2<B><\f>
^p^0.˙	^p<B><\f>^0<B><\f>

Figure 1.9 Numbered lists This simple use of "untyped" wildcards shows how we can process patterns of information without having to identify each possible combination of characters (which in this case would be all the numbers between 0 and 99).

ample of reformatting single- and double-digit numbered lists (Figure 1.9). Admittedly, this would also convert lettered lists, but let's assume that the job in question doesn't have any of those.

I first look for any two characters following a carriage return and followed by a period and a spaceband. I change the numbers to bold, strip out the period, and change the spaceband to an en space.

After that, I look for the single-digit variety, choosing to add an en space in front of it (so that lists with both single and double digits align on the second character) in addition to the other style changes.

Producing a simple newsletter

I've been typesetting the Natural Resources Defense Council's monthly newsletter—*Earth Advocates Update*—for about three years (Figure 1.10). Over time, the method of production has changed considerably. By all means, don't be afraid to experiment with changing how you produce continuing jobs. By tinkering with this job over the years, I've managed to cut production time in half. This has allowed me to keep my price constant and offer faster service to the client while still effectively doubling my hourly rate.

Most of the tools discussed below were covered in greater detail earlier in this chapter. Some of the typesetting terms and page layout concepts will be covered in the next few chapters. For now, though, I just want to walk through a pretty simple job and try to show how all the pieces fit together.

NRDC

Earth Advocates

U P D A T E

July 1992 • NRDC, 40 West 20th Street, New York NY 10011

NRDC Defends America's Coastlines

BATTLES WORTH WINNING ARE RARELY won overnight. Indeed, many of NRDC's most important victories have required years of sustained effort. In these long sieges over precious natural resources, NRDC's primary weapons are litigation, lobbying, and education. And its chief allies are committed NRDC members who provide the support needed to stick with the fight.

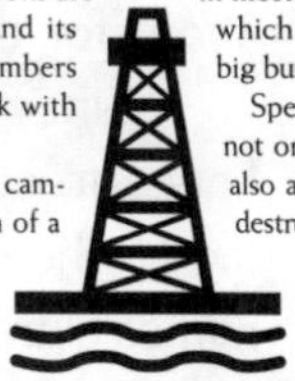

A good example of these prolonged campaigns is NRDC's fight for the adoption of a sane national energy policy, one it has now been waging for over a decade. America came one step closer to this goal last month when both houses of Congress overwhelmingly approved national energy legislation. Although neither bill addresses oil dependence or global warming, central energy policy concerns, NRDC did win important provisions that promote efficiency and renewable sources of energy and protect sensitive offshore areas from drilling. The House version of the Energy Bill contains particularly strong provisions in each of these areas.

The offshore drilling title is a major interim victory for NRDC's Water and Coastal Program, which has fought for over fifteen years to protect ecologically sensitive coastal and marine areas from oil development. The House bill would place a ten-year moratorium on new oil and gas leases off the entire East and West Coasts, Florida's Gulf Coast, and Alaska's Bristol Bay. Thereafter, it would impose rigorous requirements for environmental impact information before opening an area to drilling. It also would provide for the cancellation of existing leases, awarded to oil companies during the Reagan Administration, off the Florida Keys, North Carolina's Outer Banks, and in Bristol Bay.

Senior scientist Lisa Speer and senior attorney Sarah Chasis have fought offshore drilling together for nearly nine years. Speer, an energetic and intent woman, stresses the irreplaceable values of these areas. "From the rocky shoreline of Maine to the sunny beaches of Southern California, our coastlines are a scenic and recreational haven for millions of Americans."

These areas are also a haven to wildlife, providing critical habitat for a vast array of fish, migratory birds, and marine mammals. "Many people don't realize the economic value of keeping our coasts clean," Speer adds. "Bristol Bay, for instance, supports a world class fishery that generates a whopping billion dollars a year in revenues. And in most coastal states, tourism and recreation—which both depend on clean coastlines—are big business."

Speer explains that oil development brings not only the ever present danger of a spill but also air and water pollution, as well as habitat destruction, from the various industrial facilities required to develop, transport, and process the crude. "In Louisiana, for example, where offshore oil drilling is underway, coastal wetlands have sustained extensive damage from oil and gas pipelines," she says. "And the *Exxon Valdez* spill tragically illustrated the consequences of a major accident."

If anything has driven Speer in her long quest for coastal protections, it is her scientific knowledge informed by plain old pragmatism. "It just does not make any *sense* to drill in these areas," she says with a firm certainty. "Bristol Bay, for instance, is the biological crown jewel of the Outer Continental Shelf. And drilling in the area of

[over, please]

NRDC docket
HIGHLIGHTS

•

☞ ***NRDC Victory:*** **The punishment fit the crime in the recent settlement of three long-standing suits brought by the Citizen Enforcement Project against companies that violated their Clean Water Act discharge permits. Wyman Gordon, a Massachusetts company, will pay $15,000 to the United States and $135,000 for a project to improve fish habitat in the Blackstone River. Loewengart, a Pennsylvania tannery, will pay $45,000 to the Pennsylvania Conservancy to buy land for conservation along the Conococheague River. And Ward, a Pennsylvania electronics company with persistent PCB violations, will fund a study to improve its PCB detection limits and pay $3,000 to the Neuse River Foundation for water quality monitoring.**

printed on recycled paper

Figure 1.10 ***Earth Advocates Update*** The first page of this monthly newsletter, shown here without the color tints that will go behind the masthead and the sidebar.

Massaging the text

NRDC sends the text for the newsletter as a WordPerfect file saved to a 3.5-inch PC floppy disk. I just slip that floppy in the drive on my Macintosh, where DOS Mounter recognizes the format and mounts the floppy on my desktop. I drag the WordPerfect file from the floppy disk into the job folder set up for the newsletters.

Microsoft Word does a good job translating WordPerfect files into its own format, so I open up Word. I also have MacLink Plus, which does an equally good—but different—job of translating WordPerfect to Word, and it's only through experimentation that I've decided that I prefer the translation that Word gives me. I'll also need to be in Word for the next few steps, so it's more convenient to use Word for the translation.

Since DOS Mounter gives its own icon to the WordPerfect file, I need to open the file from within Word instead of just double-clicking on the file. After Word recognizes the Word Perfect file and automatically translates it, I'm left with a formatted document in an untitled window, so I save and then close it.

This is what a typical WordPerfect file would look like if we opened it on a Mac without translating it:

```
˘WPCÛ˚˘2S˘˘B P˘˘Z¶˘˘SCourier 10cpi#|x¤{Ùx¸6 X
 @…ì8«;X@¸¸¸¸¸¸¸˘¸˘˘˘¸˘˘¸HP LaserJet
IIPHPLASIIP.PRS¤x   @…áœ,8t0§!jX@--ä"†√√çff
†""†»X1√√çffç.∞∞∞»§1√√çffç.∞∞∞†"˚˘2x˘˘ Ö
6ïZÀS%#|xCourier 10cpiCourier 10cpi BoldCourier
10cpi ItalicHP LaserJet IIPHPLASIIP.PRS
¤x å @…áœ,8t0§ kêk˚ a8Documentg ¡Document
Style Style∫†ä¬Xe
```

Somewhere below all that gobbledygook I might actually find the text needed to set the job. Here's what the file looks like after MS Word has translated it:

Saving the Ancient Forests
of British Columbia

It is nearly impossible to picture the way North America looked <u>before</u> Europeans set foot on the continent. The political boundaries shown on modern maps are so familiar they seem to have always existed.

Back in the Finder, I drag and drop the newly saved MS Word file onto the WordLess Plus program icon. To be accurate, I'm actually dropping the file onto an alias icon placed along the bottom edge of my desktop. WordLess Plus will clear out any character and paragraph formatting that the clients did in their WordPerfect file and that was saved when the file was translated to MS Word format, replacing the styling with XPress Tags. The main reason I'm doing this on such a small file is to catch the italics imbedded in the text.

A second later, when WordLess Plus is finished doing its thing, I switch back to MS Word and open up the new file. If the file name was "EA/July/MS" before running it through WordLess Plus, it will now be called "EA/July/MS.WL+," since a new file was created using the original name with the characters ".WL+" appended to it. Here's what the file looks like now:

```
<v1.60><e0>
<B>Saving the Ancient Forests
of British Columbia<B>
It is nearly impossible to picture the way
North America looked <U>before<U> Europeans set
foot on the continent. The political boundaries
shown on modern maps are so familiar they seem
to have always existed.
```

At this point I'm going to manually insert some XPress Tags and do a few search-and-replaces in MS Word. Since I only have to add three or four tags and do the same number of replacements, I haven't bothered to set up a batch translation for this process. When I'm finished, the file looks like this:

```
<v1.60><e0>
@head:Saving the Ancient Forests
of British Columbia
@text1:It is nearly impossible to picture the
way North America looked <I>before<I> Europeans
set foot on the continent. The political
boundaries shown on modern maps are so familiar
they seem to have always existed.
```

The only XPress Tags I need at the start of the file are "@head:" for the headline, "@text1:" for the first paragraph of text, and "@text:"

(not shown) for the second paragraph of text. The subsequent paragraphs of text will use the same style as the second paragraph, so I don't have to go through the file and tag them all. Near the end I need to add a tag for the text that will go in the sidebar.

The search-and-replaces are simple, too: I change all instances of two spacebands to one spaceband, strip out all tabs, and convert the <U> tag (for underline) to <I> (for italic). Now the file is ready to be brought into QuarkXPress.

Laying out the page

Before opening the template for this job, I might as well open the fonts. I'm a Suitcase user, so I can access that program from the Apple menu, scroll through my list of font sets, and open the one that's named "NRDC/Earth Advocates" (Figure 1.11). I'm so glad they've added this feature to Suitcase, since I could never remember from month to month which Univers and which Futura font suitcases needed to be open, in addition to the Weiss and Cochin families.

Now I can open my template and get busy. The first thing I do after opening it is change the date. I've learned the hard way that I won't remember to change such stuff "later on." Then I click on the

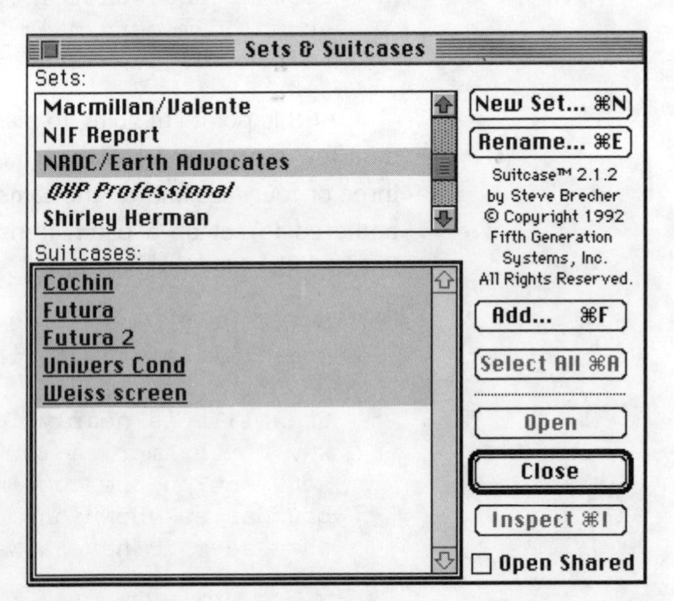

Figure 1.11 Sets & Suitcases This is the main window in Suitcase 2, a great utility from Fifth Generation. You can create sets of fonts for repetitive jobs so that the needed fonts can easily be opened and closed.

first text box in the story chain and choose **File→Get Text**. After turning on both the Convert Quotes and Include Style Sheets options, I bring in my text file.

TIP As of QuarkXPress 3.3, the Convert Quotes and Include Style Sheets check boxes in the **File→Get Text** dialog are no longer hard-wired so that they always revert to their default settings. I'm really glad that Quark decided to make these check boxes "sticky"; the options now remember the way each of us likes to work. Every power user I know has been asking since at least version 3.0 for these buttons to become sticky, so it's heartening to see that our pleas did not fall on deaf ears!

Kerning the headline

I like to kern the headline right away, as I may be printing the pages a couple of times and this way I'll get a chance to see my kerning on each printout and fine-tune it as necessary. Trusting the low-resolution computer screen for kerning decisions is really dangerous. Some would say that trusting your 300 dot-per-inch printer isn't too smart, either. To those people I say, "Buy me an imagesetter." Until one of them does, I tend to trust the laser printed output.

Let's look at the headline used in the issue that I showed a few pages ago to see how much kerning was needed. Note that although I tend to build in a negative tracking for large heads, the face used here—Cochin—has such large serifs that I avoid that action. Here it is without any kerning:

NRDC Defends
America's Coastlines

I definitely see a few problem areas. For starters, the space between the "D" and "C" is too large. Two characters with rounded sides facing each other often need to be closed up, since there's so much white space built into them. Below I've used a –7 kerning value. Now I look for characters with rounded sides facing characters with straight sides. I find a number of them, and most of them require –5 kerning values. Then I play for a while with that apostrophe before I settle on this:

NRDC Defends America's Coastlines

Don't be afraid to zoom in on your headlines while you kern them, as that will give you better effective resolution, but remember not to go nuts tightening stuff without printing it out once in a while. The larger screen view makes it easy to kern too much.

The balancing act

Now the balancing act starts. I have to make sure that all the lines of text look good within the designer's specifications, including those lines of text that are interrupted by oil wells (or whatever) on the front page and any photographs I'm instructed to leave space for. I also have to make sure that there are no column widows or orphans. A widow occurs when the last line of a paragraph falls at the top of a column; an orphan is the first line of a paragraph falling at the bottom of a column. I confess that I've left more than a few orphans in this job over the years due to the constraints of balancing the rest of the page.

I usually try to get the artwork sized and approximately in place before worrying about the type. Then as I fine-tune the type, I can make adjustments in the artwork in order to fix some of the type problems. It's not uncommon for me to tweak the text outset of an image or the vertical position of a photograph hole in order to gain or lose a line in a paragraph.

Of course, the worst possible situation is when I've gone nuts to get the balance just right and the client sends the job back with major corrections marked. The newsletter editor and I usually discuss this ahead of time and she tells me whether she has final approval on the copy (meaning I can go nuts making it look pretty) or if the text she's sending is a rough draft (meaning I probably won't even bother kerning the headline on the first pass). I highly recommend establishing a similar methodology with your clients; it's a real sanity saver.

2

Typography

CHAPTER 2 CONTENTS

FIGURES

Not only is QuarkXPress a great page layout program, but it's also a great typesetting tool. With the proper settings chosen in Typographic Preferences and other dialogs, and with a bit of practice, you can set type in QuarkXPress every bit as well as you can on most dedicated front-end systems, and more enjoyably due to the what-you-see-is-what-you-get (WYSIWYG) nature of Macintosh.

In the second half of this chapter, there are several examples showing the various ways that the program's commands can be used to create pleasant-looking paragraphs. But before the subtleties of typography can be discussed, we need to review the functions of the various commands and dialog box settings. We can't talk about how to use spaces, dashes, and returns to create the best possible page of type without completely understanding the way each of these works.

Typographic Preferences

There are a lot of options that need to be changed in the Typographic Preferences dialog box before you can begin setting professional-quality work in QuarkXPress. As we discuss recommended settings for each section, real-world use of the values will be given.

Superscript, Subscript, and Superior

Depending on the job, you'll be using the Superscript, Subscript, and Superior styles to create fractions, footnote references, and mathematical and chemical symbols. When speaking of fractions in this chapter, I'll be referring to solidus fractions (⁶⁄₈), as opposed to case fractions ($\frac{6}{8}$). Solidus fractions use a special slash character, called a virgule, that is accessed by typing Option-Shift-1 (⌥⇧1), and they are regularly found in text. Case fractions are more likely to be found in mathematics displays.

There are a number of ways to create solidus fractions. The approach taken for any given job will be partly determined by whether you want to create the fractions from the keyboard, from menus, or with XPress Tags. Other factors governing your choice of methods will be the overall look of the fractions, how easy it is to edit them, and (believe it or not) where the fractions are likely to fall on the page.

Making fractions using Superscript and Subscript

My favorite way to make fractions is to use the Superscript and Subscript styles. To do this, I need to edit the values used for these styles in **Edit→Preferences→Typographic** (Figure 2.1). The actual values will depend on the font used for a job, but I usually start with Superscript and Subscript settings defined as two-thirds of the cap height, offsetting the Superscript by 33% of the point size being used. The offset for the Subscript will generally be 0% when using this method, because I want the fraction's denominator to sit on the baseline.

To create a fraction from the keyboard using this method, you just need to type:

- Command for the Superscript style (⌘ ⇧ +)
- Numerator (6)

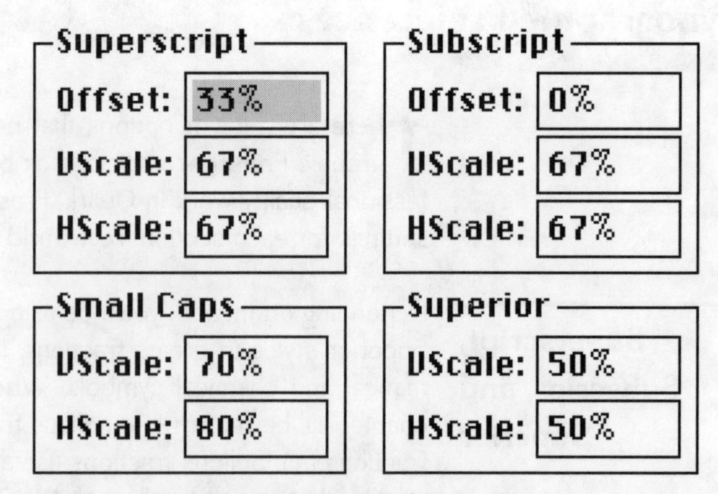

Figure 2.1 Superscript and Subscript method If you choose this method to create solidus fractions, you'll need to change the Typographic Preferences Superscript and Subscript scaling and offsets to approximately these values.

- Superscript command again, to turn off the style (⌘ ⇧ +)
- Virgule (⌥ ⇧ 1)
- Command for the Subscript style (⌘ ⇧ -)
- Denominator (8)
- Subscript command again (⌘ ⇧ -)

So, to get "6/8" you would type: (⌘ ⇧ +) 6 (⌘ ⇧ +) (⌥ ⇧ 1) (⌘ ⇧ -) 8 (⌘ ⇧ -). I've enclosed the commands in parentheses to make it easier to tell them apart; the parentheses are not actually typed. You can also pull down the **Style→Type Style** menu to access the Superscript and Subscript styles or to review their keyboard shortcuts.

TIP I realize that the above command line may look mondo bizarro, but it's important to learn the standard Mac keyboard shortcut character set in order to understand this and other technical documents. Partial lists of shortcuts will be given throughout the book, wherever necessary. The symbols used in these examples are: Command (⌘), Shift (⇧), and Option (⌥).

If you want to have your fractions typed correctly in a manuscript utilizing XPress Tags, "6/8" would be typed <+>6<+>/<->8<-> or <+>6<+><\#218><->8<->, depending on whether you want the virgule typed as a keyboard shortcut (⌥ ⇧ 1) or as its decimal value (<\#218>), the latter often being the better choice if the manuscript is being keyed on a PC (Figure 2.2).

Making fractions using Superior and Subscript-Superior

There is another nice way to make a fraction from the keyboard, using menus, or with XPress Tags. This method utilizes the Superior and Subscript styles, completely ignoring Superscript. It entails using the Superior style to set the numerator and applying both the Subscript and Superior styles for the denominator, as strange as that may sound. To use this method, the Subscript scaling should be set to 100%, with its offset amount left at the default at 33% of the point size; I recommend changing the Superior scaling to 60% (Figure 2.3).

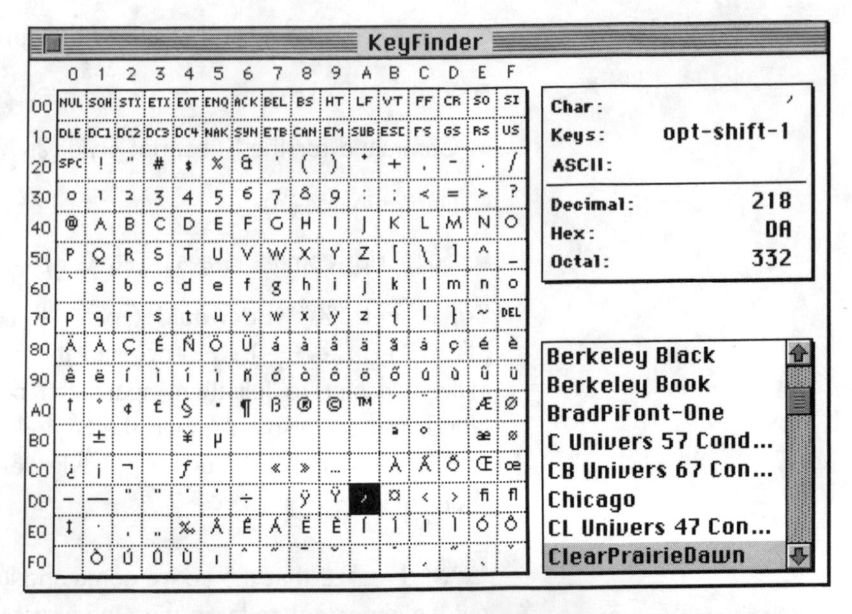

Figure 2.2 Keyfinder This desk accessory—part of Norton Utilities from Symantec—is great for looking up decimal values of characters that you want to access with XPress Tags. I used Keyfinder to determine that the virgule was decimal #218.

To get our popular "6/8" fraction, you would type:

- Command for the Superior style (⌘ ⇧ v)
- Numerator (6)
- Superior command again, to turn off the style (⌘ ⇧ v)
- Virgule (⌥ ⇧ 1)
- Command for the Subscript style (⌘ ⇧ -)
- Command for the Superior style (⌘ ⇧ v)
- Denominator (8)
- Subscript command again (⌘ ⇧ -)
- Superior command again (⌘ ⇧ v)

Using the above settings, the fraction would come out looking like this: 6/8. To achieve this look with XPress Tags, type: <v>6<v>/<-v>8<-v> or <v>6<v><\#218><-v>8<-v>.

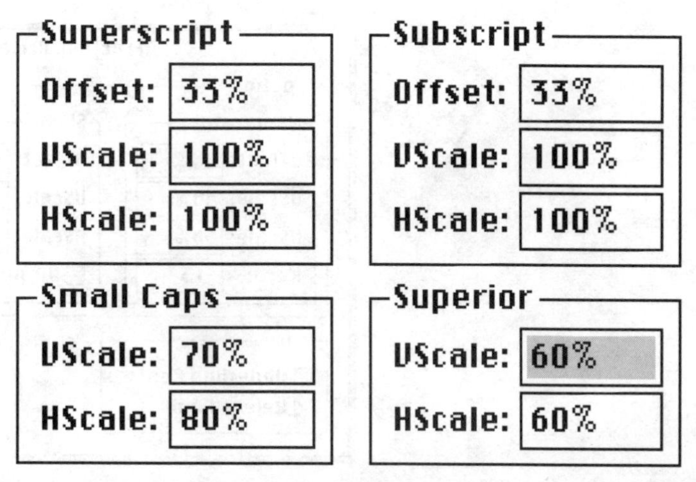

Figure 2.3 Superior and Subscript-Superior method The values defines for the Subscript and Superior scaling and the Subscript offset change dramatically when using this method. The Superscript values don't matter, in this case.

TIP There is no offset setting available for the Superior style. The top of a Superior character is always aligned with the top of the current font's ascender. There is a very real advantage to this: Characters using the Superior style will not push down all the text on a page when a Superior character ends up in the first line of a text box. Depending on your offset settings, it's quite likely that a fraction created with the Superscript/Subscript method will cause lines to move down, making it difficult to align columns and facing pages.

Making fractions using Make Fraction

This method of creating fractions is only available if you have obtained and loaded the FeaturesPlus XTension, available from Quark, Inc. as well as from many on-line services. Although in many ways it's the easiest method to use, it often requires the most amount of preparation; it's also the hardest one to edit if you or your clients don't like the fractions it produces (Figure 2.4).

Here's what our now infamous example looks like when produced with Make Fraction: $^6/_8$. The default settings for Make Fraction produce a fraction that top aligns with a font's ascender, like the Superior and Subscript-Superior method. It's important to note, though, that Make Fraction actually changes the point size of the

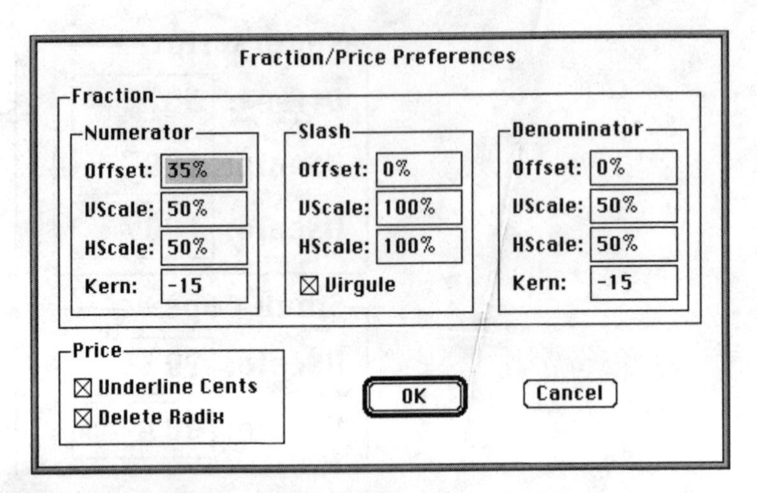

Figure 2.4 Make Fraction method When the FeaturesPlus XTension is loaded, this dialog box of preferences is added under the Edit menu. You'll probably need to fiddle with the kerning settings, at the very least.

numerator and denominator. It also automatically kerns the reduced characters closer to the virgule, which can be an advantage over the earlier two methods. Obviously, for the font used in this book, Make Fraction's default kerning values would need to be changed, since the fraction shown at the start of this paragraph is set too tight.

TIP When using either of the first two methods to make fractions, changes made to the offset and scaling values in **Edit→Preferences →Typographic** will globally change any occurrences of the Superscript, Subscripts, and Superior styles already in use. However, changing the Make Fractions defaults will only affect future uses of the command, so make sure you have a client's approval before setting a couple of thousand fractions this way!

There's no keyboard shortcut for this command, nor is there a way to use XPress Tags to code fractions created with this method.

Footnote references and chemicals

If you have a manuscript that contains both fractions and either footnote/endnote references or chemical symbols, the method used to create each character will depend on a number of things. If you have chemicals that need to have inferior characters, such as H_2O, you'd better either hope for only a few chemicals or a complete absence of fractions. Since I use the Superscript and Subscript method of making fractions, to create the chemical in the last sentence I had to style the "2" as Subscript and then manually increase the point size and add a baseline shift.

Had I been using the Superior and Subscript-Superior method of creating fractions in this document, I would have had to decrease the point size of the "2" instead. An inferior style has been sorely lacking from QuarkXPress since its inception, and I'm very thankful that (so far) I haven't run into a project that needed it extensively.

If you have both footnote/endnote references and fractions, I highly recommend the Superscript and Subscript method for the fractions and using Superior for the note references. In my experience, at least, it's more likely that the note references will be harder to find than fractions, hidden in the text, and capable of landing at the top of a column or page. If they are styled as Superior, at least they won't push the rest of the text down and throw off cross-column or cross-spread baseline alignment.

True vs. fake small caps

In a perfect world, all the fonts available to us on the desktop would offer true small caps, and they would be easy to use. Unfortunately, this is not a perfect world, at least not yet. To their credit, Adobe has been releasing a number of sets of true small caps to go with already released fonts, and newly released font families tend to have "expert sets" that include true small caps. Other font foundries have either been providing true small caps all along or are now jumping on Adobe's bandwagon.

For a font to be considered "true" small caps, it has to be designed that way, taking into account that the strokes for small cap characters need to be a little thicker to compensate for the fact that they'll often be sitting next to capital letters (Figure 2.5). Using the default values for small caps in **Edit→Preferences→Typographic** does not even approximate the way a true small cap font should look.

As much as I deplore stretching type, believing that it's an insult to the font designer, I have to recommend settings that do just that. If type is slightly stretched horizontally, its vertical strokes will get a little wider and thus better match the weight of any capital letters next to the small caps. I generally set the vertical scale for small caps at

MINION EXPERT SEMIBOLD (TRUE)

AABCDE FFGHIJ KKLMNO PPQRST UUVWXYZ

MINION SEMIBOLD (FAKE: 75/75)

AABCDE FFGHIJ KKLMNO PPQRST UUVWXYZ

MINION EXPERT SEMIBOLD (TRUE)

AABCDE FFGHIJ KKLMNO PPQRST UUVWXYZ

MINION SEMIBOLD (FAKE: 70/80)

AABCDE FFGHIJ KKLMNO PPQRST UUVWXYZ

Figure 2.5 Fake small caps settings Here's a comparison between Minion's expert set true small caps and the default and suggested settings for fake small caps.

70%, with the horizontal scale stretched to 80%. As with many of the **Edit→Preferences→Typographic** settings, I may change these values depending on the font in use.

TIP If you find that you're constantly struggling with an expert set of fonts in order to access its true small caps (or old style figures), keep in mind that it's not that hard to make a "composite" font that combines the capital letters from a regular font and the small caps from an expert font. Both Altsys' Fontographer and Ares' FontMonger can handle this, and both can be purchased from any mail order software house. Alternatively, if you don't want to take the time to learn one of these programs, consider contacting the manufacturers directly; I imagine that both of them can recommend freelancers who would be glad to modify some fonts for you for a reasonable price.

Leading

Auto leading

Since I believe that the only time auto leading is acceptable is when there's only one line of text in a box (and, thus, no leading is actually being used), I don't have any strong feelings about what value is used for auto leading. Here's why auto leading will get you into trouble: Even though it's supposed to be equal to the current point size plus 20% of that point size, the leading used for a given line will actually

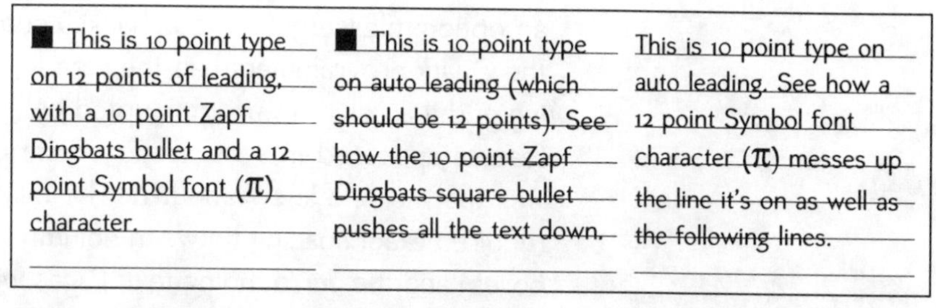

Figure 2.6 The evil auto leading In a professionally set job, the baselines of type won't be all over the place like they are here. Stick with fixed leading and you'll get exactly what you expect.

change if you mix fonts, styles, or sizes on a given line (Figure 2.6). In addition to the leading changing on the line containing the odd characters, it appears that the leading on the next line also changes—by an entirely different amount. Bottom line? Auto leading is bad news.

Leading mode

The leading mode can be set as Typesetting or Word Processing (Figure 2.7). The former measures leading as baseline to baseline (base to base); the latter measures from ascender to ascender. Probably the biggest difference you'll see if you try changing from one to the other is the way anchored text and picture boxes are spaced. Word Processing mode is really only useful for matching MS Word's leading and page breaks, which is what it was designed for.

Maintain Leading

This is a favorite option of mine. I often tell my college students that Maintain Leading could also be called the "Okay, Brad, we've made it

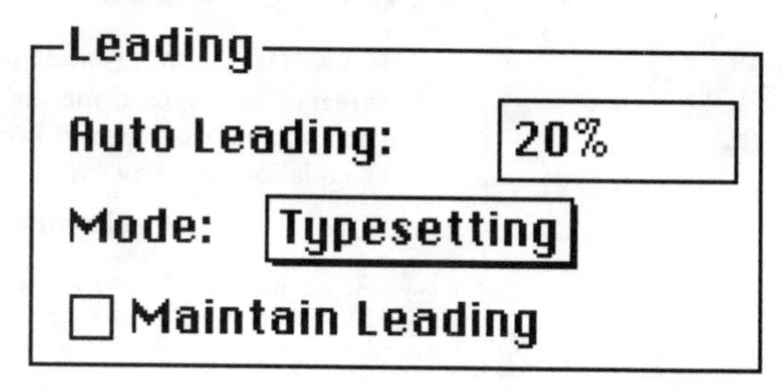

Figure 2.7 Leading mode All three leading choices can be found in **Edit→Preferences→Typographic**. I've never had occasion to change the leading mode from Typesetting to Word Processing.

an option; please get off our backs" command. It seems that one of the Quark programmers had the idea to snap text to an invisible leading grid if a column was interrupted by another item (Figure 2.8). This feature appeared in version 3.0 of the program—the only problem was that no one knew about it. The majority of my jobs at that time required exact spacing between column interruptions (such as picture boxes) and the surrounding text. Pages with illustrations at the tops or bottoms of columns weren't affected by this change, though.

I tried for months to find out why I could no longer apply a specific amount of text outset to the picture boxes and have the exact visual spacing required. Instead, all of the text below a picture box would snap to an invisible grid line. With Maintain Leading, the position of this grid line is determined by the leading in effect above the picture, such that the first line below the picture will be an even number of lines below the text appearing above the picture box. Eventually one of the technical support personnel tracked down the programmer who made this change, got him to confess to it, and convinced him to make it an explicit option in version 3.1, much to my relief (Figure 2.9).

The feature certainly does have its uses: If you're more concerned with having baselines of text align across columns than with holding to a specific visual space around graphics, you should certainly consider using it. In fact, it was specifically designed to help align baselines across magazine columns. Note that this is not the same as Lock to Baseline Grid. If you have a subhead with odd spac-

nounced plans to list the gnatcatcher as a "threatened" rather than "endangered" species. This status gives policymakers the flexibility to pursue

"It is NRDC's petitions and the threat of endangered species listing that have driven this rare collaborative process."

—Joel Reynolds

a compromise. Babbitt will issue a special rule allowing developers to build in some parts of the bird's habitat if they participate in a new state pro- will allow everyone to work together on planning for habitat protection.

At same time, NRDC has remained vigilant in defense of the threatened species and its habitat. When NRDC received word that a major developer was contemplating grading a huge section of the proposed right-of-way for the San Joaquin Hills Transportation Corridor in an effort to beat the March 17 deadline for listing the bird as a federal endangered species, Joel Reynolds quickly filed a supplemental request for emergency listing to halt the bulldozers.

"Thanks to the steadfast financial support of members, we have been able to defend the com-

Figure 2.8 Maintaining the leading In this example, I need to align baselines across columns. I could keep changing the Text Outset value for the pull-quote until I achieve alignment, but using Maintain Leading is easier.

About half the plan sponsors with GIC funds—243—have contracts maturing in 1992, totalling $5.4 billion; 204 of those plans are reinvesting a total of $3.6 billion of maturing proceeds in GICs and BDAs. The expected average maturity of these reinvestments is 3.8 years.

Rate of return

The average GIC rate of return by year-end 1991 was 8.29%, down sharply from 1990's 8.94%. Funds of all sizes experienced a similar drop in rate of return. The average return was 8.04% for the smaller GIC funds (under $10 million), increasing steadily with fund size to 8.96% among plans with more than $250 million in GIC assets. There are various reasons why larger funds realize higher returns:

■ Larger plans benefit from economies of scale. Contract expenses are lower as a per-

■ Large plans tend to have more experienced investment personnel in their benefits area.

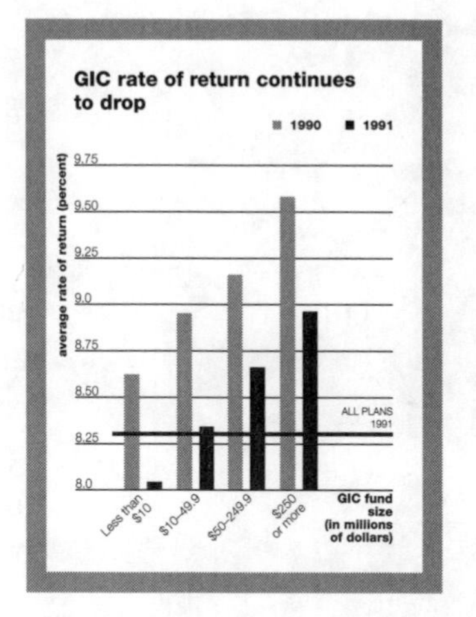

Apart from fund size, rate of return is affected by a variety of factors. These include:

Figure 2.9 Leaving the leading alone This job didn't require baselines to align across columns. Instead, an exact visual space of 18 points above and below each chart was expected, so I turned off the Maintain Leading option.

ing in one of your columns, text baselines still won't align. But in long, multi-column stretches of text interrupted only by other text and picture boxes, you might find that the Maintain Leading feature is more help than hindrance. Note that the feature doesn't distinguish between single- or multi-column layouts, and remember that your text outsets will not work predictably (to say the least).

Ligatures

In serif type, it's not uncommon for a lower case "f" to run into the following "i" or "l" character. Ligatures combine these characters into one good-looking character, and QuarkXPress offers a nice way to automatically access the "fi" and "fl" ligatures built into a font (Figure 2.10). Although you can still type these ligatures from the keyboard, it's much better to let the program generate them, since a manually generated ligature will mess up both the spell check and hyphenation routines.

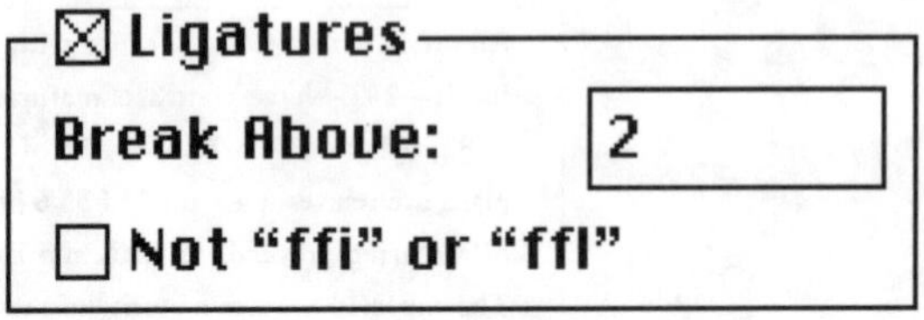

☒ Ligatures
Break Above: 2
☐ Not "ffi" or "ffl"

Figure 2.10 Ligature choices The Break Above value will depend a lot on the main font in use in a file.

The Break Above option controls how loose a line of type can get before QuarkXPress breaks a ligature pair into separate characters. If your hyphenation and justification settings allow for letterspacing, this option will make sure you don't end up with a tight ligature pair on a loosely spaced line. The value used will depend greatly on the main font being used in a document; fonts with wider lower-case "f" characters will require a higher value.

TIP You can simulate the effect that different Break Above values will have on a font by typing some "fi" and "fl" pairs into a flush left paragraph and applying tracking to the line. With a value of 2 (hundredths of an en space) for Break Above, for example, it will take a +3 track to break up the ligatures. If the "f" and "i" are crashing into each other when the ligature pair breaks up into separate characters, you will probably want to increase the Break Above value.

Since most fonts offer only the two most common ligature pairs, you're given an option to ignore an "fi" or "fl" pair when it falls after another "f." A type purist would balk at using "fi" and "fl" ligatures when the equally needed "ffi" and "ffl" ligatures (not to mention one for "ff" combinations) are not available. I'm not so bullheaded as to ignore the fact that a bad "fi" combination looks bad whether or not it's following an "f," so I usually allow QuarkXPress to make ligatures when the "fi" and "fl" pairs follow an "f" (Figure 2.11).

Fonts that come with expert sets tend to include ligatures for "ffi," "ffl," and "ff," in addition to the "fi" and "fl" available from all fonts. They need to be typed from the keyboard or replaced with **Edit→Find/Change**, but I hope you agree that they are worth the effort when you're setting an important job.

LIGATURES TURNED OFF

file officially or fly affluently

LIGATURES TURNED ON (NO FFI/FFL)

file officially or fly affluently

LIGATURES TURNED ON (YES FFI/FFL)

file officially or fly affluently

EXPERT SET LIGATURES

file officially or fly affluently

Figure 2.11 Ligature options The first three examples show the options available in most fonts. The fourth example shows an expert set which includes both "ffi" and "ffl" ligatures. The nonligatured "fl" combination doesn't look too bad in this font (Minion).

The rest of the Typographic Preferences

Accents for All Caps

If the Accents for All Caps option is turned on, QuarkXPress will stop removing accents from letters when the All Caps style is applied (Figure 2.12). This option is only available for documents created in version 3.2 or above; when an older file is opened, the option is grayed out in order to maintain flow compatibility with the older version.

Text with the Small Caps style applied to it will also retain its accents when this option is turned on. Be sure to check the style rules for whatever language you're working in, though. Accents are usually used when Spanish is capitalized; they come off in French and stay on in Quebecois.

Auto Kern Above

I consider the default for this option one of the more dangerous ones in QuarkXPress. At its default value of "10," type that's set smaller

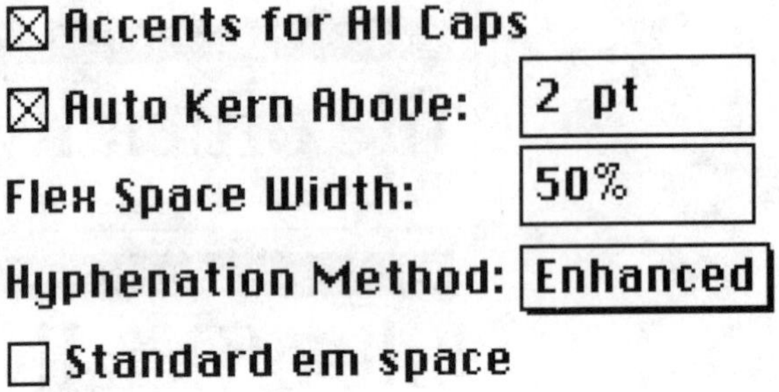

☒ Accents for All Caps
☒ Auto Kern Above: 2 pt
Flex Space Width: 50%
Hyphenation Method: Enhanced
☐ Standard em space

Figure 2.12 Miscellaneous options These options are all discussed in the next few pages.

than 10 point will not use the kern pair values built into the font. There's nothing quite like going to all the trouble to typeset a job beautifully and then getting the repro or film back from the service bureau with none of a font's kerning applied to the small type. Change this value from "10" to "2" and you can be assured of the best possible looking type in all sizes. In addition, if Auto Kern Above is not checked, any modifications in **Utilities→Tracking Edit** will be ignored.

Flex space width

The flex space width is defined as a percentage of the en space. I talk about it at length in the next section.

Hyphenation method

As of version 3.1 of QuarkXPress, the method used to hyphenate words has been greatly improved, mostly due to a much larger dictionary. You should only consider choosing Standard over Enhanced if you need to copy and paste text from a pre-3.1 document and maintain the same word breaks.

Standard em space

With the Standard em space option enabled in **Edit→Preferences→Typographic**, em spaces will be equivalent to the point size currently in use, rather than the double-zero width method that QuarkXPress employed exclusively prior to version 3.2. Two en spaces still have to be typed to get an em space, unfortunately. All kerning and tracking calculations are based on units of an em, so they will also be adjusted when this feature is turned on.

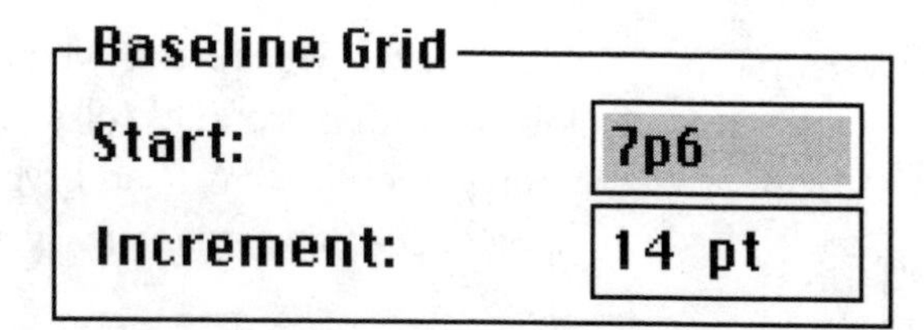

Figure 2.13 Baseline Grid settings If I was to use this feature in this book, I'd use these values, since they represent my first text baseline and my normal text leading.

Baseline Grid

I have to admit that I'm not the biggest fan of this feature. This is where the definition occurs for the Lock to Baseline Grid option in **Style→Formats**. Although text *can* be locked to the grid, perhaps its best use is when you want to snap a text or picture box to the grid. (You'll have to **View→Show Baseline Grid** to do this.) In either case, you'll probably want to make the Start value equal to the baseline position of the first line of text on your page and the Increment value equal to the regular text leading (Figure 2.13).

I definitely don't think that it should ever be turned on in a style sheet used for regular text. The reason for this is that it will yank your text down to snap to the grid all right, but it will leave a gap before the text, which as often as not is below a subhead (the absolute last place you want extra space to be added).

An argument could be stated for using the grid for subheads rather than text, but I think the best course of action for aligning baselines is making sure that spacing around heads adds up to an even increment of the leading applied to the surrounding text.

Spaces, dashes, and returns

QuarkXPress offers many different spaceband, dash, and return options. Learning to use the correct combinations of these characters is of paramount importance in making your work look more professional, as well as simplifying the task of editing jobs. At first, some of the following recommendations may seem like they're more trouble than they're worth. But whether you're working alone on your own jobs or with a group of folks editing each other's files, I guarantee that taking "the high road" and typing the best characters for the job will speed up editing dramatically and cut down on unfortunate mistakes.

Special spaces

Only two of the space characters in QuarkXPress will vary in width in justified text: the regular space and its nonbreaking variation, Command-Space (⌘ #). The rest are called—in typesetting lingo—relative spaces, meaning that they vary in width only relative to the point size and typeface that you are using, as well as any kerning and tracking that may be in effect.

The nonbreaking spaceband is useful for keeping related items together, such as "2.54 cm" and "FAS 106" (the latter being some kind of insurance law that crops up in a number of jobs I've done). Some folks also use it when setting European languages that require a space before punctuation marks, although I've also heard from a French typesetter that one-eighth of a normal space is proper in this case.

TIP All of the keyboard shortcuts for making nonbreaking spaces require the use of the Command key (⌘). If you find that none of your nonbreaking spaces are working, you may be getting bitten by a an undocumented feature that Apple has added to System 7. To switch between various keyboard layouts and scripts, Apple has appropriated the Command-Space shortcut, and *any* shortcut containing those two keys no longer works. Removing the extra layouts from the System file doesn't seem to help either, as I still can't get Command-Space to give me a nonbreaking space even after I removed the U.S.-System 6 layout from my System. As of Quark XPress 3.2, however, the Control key (⌃) key can be used instead of the Command key for all the nonbreaking spaces listed in this section.

En space/figure space

I imagine that the relative space most commonly used by most folks is the en space/figure space, accessed by typing Option-Space (⌥ #). QuarkXPress uses the width of the zero of the current font to determine the width of this space, which makes it handy to line up lists that include single- and double-digit numbers. This trick only works when all the numbers in a typeface use the same character

Old-style numbers	Lining figures
1, 2, 3, 4, 5, 6, 7, 8, 9, 0	1, 2, 3, 4, 5, 6, 7, 8, 9, 0
1. AutoLib	1. LogX™
2. AutoXTract™	2. MasterMenus™
3. ColorChange	3. Missing Link
4. Color Bundle	4. Navigator XT
5. Color Usage	5. Nouveau II
6. CopySet™	6. PageShot
7. Exposé	7. Picture Dæmon
8. FlexScale	8. Picture Tools
9. Fontasy	9. PressMarks™
10. Grid Master	10. Resize XT

Figure 2.14 Numbered lists Old-style numbers are wonderful for use in text, since they don't stick out as much as lining figures, which are often the same height as a capital letter. They wreak havoc with numbered list alignment, though. Either use lining figures for lists or set up tabs to get the periods and text to align properly.

width, but most do. You'll see variations in the character widths between numbers in faces that use old-style numbers, but seldom in faces using lining figures (Figure 2.14).

If you need to align the periods in a numbered list using old-style numbers, you'll need to use tabs, setting a right-aligned tab for the number and a left-aligned tab for the text. An en space should always be used after the period (or after the number, if you're not using a period) for each item of a numbered list, as the space there should be more than a regular spaceband, and it should be fixed (nonjustifying).

I haven't had much use for the nonbreaking en space (⌘ ⌥ #), since I'm usually using en spaces at the start of a line, but if you understand how a nonbreaking spaceband works, you'll understand this one, too.

Punctuation space

You may find that you occasionally need to leave enough space to clear the width of a period, and the punctuation space—typed

Shift-Space (⇧ #)—is, indeed, a space the width of a period in the currently selected typeface. Not surprisingly, a nonbreaking version is also available (⌘ ⇧ #). Nonbreaking punctuation spaces are especially useful in European-language typesetting. Sometimes large numbers are set with a space the size of a period or comma instead of with an actual punctuation character. For example, "DM. 1 234,56" contains a nonbreaking punctuation space between the "1" and "2."

TIP In many fonts—including those from Adobe—the widths of regular spacebands and punctuation spaces are the same. However, you can't reliably use a spaceband in place of a punctuation space, since a spaceband's size will change in justified text. A regular spaceband's size can also be redefined in a Hyphenation & Justification style, whereas the punctuation space will always be the size of a period.

Flex space

This is a wonderfully useful feature in QuarkXPress. The flex space is typed as Option-Shift-Space (⌥ ⇧ #), and it is defined as a percentage of an en space in **Edit→Preferences→Typographic**. You can use any value between 0% and 400%, meaning that you could actually use this as an em space by defining it as 200%. I often define it as 50% (the default) or 25% to create a half- or quarter-en space.

A nonbreaking version of the flex space is also available (⌘ ⌥ ⇧ #). In fact, I used a nonbreaking flex space defined as 50% for the spacing between all the symbols in the keyboard shortcuts in this section. And although I employed kerning around this book's em dashes to prevent them from running into the letters they were next to, small flex spaces—defined as 5 to 15% of the width of an en space—could also be used for this function.

Different dashes

For the most part, a hyphen should only be typed without a modifier key when it's used in compound words, such as "mother-in-law." I'll discuss the only exception to this rule in the **Paragraph and line editing** section of this chapter. *Any other use* of the hyphen key should be typed with one of the modifier keys mentioned below.

Nonbreaking hyphen

A nonbreaking hyphen is typed as Command-Equals (⌘ =). It should be used whenever a compound word or phrase shouldn't break apart, as in chemical or product names such as U-238 (for Uranium 238).

Discretionary hyphen

This type of hyphen remains invisible until it's needed, and should *only* and *always* be used when you want to override QuarkXPress' own computer-generated hyphenation. The discretionary hyphen is typed as Command-Hyphen (⌘ -), and if it's typed inside a word, the word will only be able to break at that point. If you type it at the start of a word (after the preceding spaceband, if any), then you will prevent the word from breaking at all.

Probably the biggest hassle with discretionary hyphens is finding the darn things when you're editing a job. If you're on the second or third pass of a job and you notice that a word is stubbornly refusing to break—either correctly or at all—you may need to place your insertion point at the end of the word and then hit the left cursor arrow (←) one letter at a time through the word. When you discover a spot within (or at the start of) the word that requires two hits of the left cursor arrow to get past a character, you've discovered the discretionary hyphen and you can delete it in the normal way.

En and em dashes

Whenever you are using a dash to represent the words "to" or "through," you need to use an en dash—typed Option-Hyphen (⌥ -). This is true for ranges of both numbers ("steps 1–15") and words ("Monday–Friday"). Parenthetical statements use an em dash—typed Option-Shift-Hyphen (⌥ ⇧ -).

Unfortunately, most typefaces available for the desktop have very wide en and em dashes with very small sidebearings (white space built into the left and right side of the character), which sometimes needs to be dealt with. Different clients will require different solutions to fix this problem. My personal favorite is to add 5 to 10 units of kerning to either side of the dashes. This would satisfy a client requesting a "hair space" around dashes, which just means that they don't want dashes to touch adjacent characters.

You could also define a flex space that suits your purpose or use a punctuation space, both useful for clients that want to really see some space. As for the widths of the dashes, about the only thing you can do is horizontally scale them, perhaps to 75%, or get a font creation program and modify the characters.

Random returns

Almost all files that come to me from new users of QuarkXPress have either too many returns in them or returns that are used incorrectly. How can you use a return incorrectly, you ask? To understand that, it's important to know just what happens when you hit the various return characters.

New paragraph

When you hit a regular return on the keyboard, you're actually asking for a new paragraph (↩) command. QuarkXPress defines a paragraph as any group of lines that ends with a new paragraph command, and will invoke any of a number of paragraph-level settings based on the position of that command. These settings include: first line indent, space before, space after, drop cap, keep with next, keep together, and rule above and below. New paragraph commands should never be used to create new line breaks unless you're prepared to live with the consequences of invoking such a "hard" command.

New line

A much better way of controlling your line breaks is the new line command, typed as a Shift-Return (⇧↩). Often referred to, in fact, as a "soft return," new line won't invoke any of the new paragraph settings, and it won't wipe out any special formatting established by the "indent here" command. If you want to insert new line commands in a text file with XPress Tags, the command is <\n>.

Discretionary new line

When rebreaking lines, it's not always appropriate to use a discretionary hyphen or a new line command. For example, note the way the word "QuarkXPress" breaks throughout this book. For reasons known only to Quark, Inc., they prefer not to hyphenate the name of their program. When the full name doesn't completely fit at the end of a line, the first half of the name stays at the end of one line and the second half goes down to the next line.

I could just use the new line command in the middle of the program name whenever it falls at the end of a line, but that means that I'll have to watch for occurrences of this at the copyediting stage of production, when I'll no doubt have lots of other things on my mind. By typing Command-Return (⌘ ↵) to get the discretionary new line command, I can be assured that any editing done earlier in a paragraph containing this word will not have an adverse effect. The new line command might leave me with a very loose line in the middle of a paragraph, whereas the discretionary new line command will simply be ignored if edits cause the name to appear in the middle of a line on the next editing pass.

You'll also want to use the discretionary new line command within phrases connected with a slash, such as "and/or." Nothing

KEYBOARD SHORTCUTS

Nonbreaking spaceband	⌘ #	Discretionary hyphen	⌘ -
En space/figure space	⌥ #	En dash (number ranges)	⌥ -
Nonbreaking en space	⌘ ⌥ #	Em dash (parenthetical)	⌥ ⇧ -
Punctuation space	⇧ #	New paragraph	↵
Nonbreaking punc. space	⌘ ⇧ #	New line	⇧ ↵
Flex space	⌥ ⇧ #	Discretionary new line	⌘ ↵
Nonbreaking flex space	⌘ ⌥ ⇧ #	New column	⌤
Nonbreaking hyphen	⌘ =	New box	⇧ ⌤

⌘ = Command; ⌥ = Option; ⇧ = Shift; # = Space; ↵ = Return; ⌤ = Enter

XPRESS TAGS

Nonbreaking spaceband	<\!s>	Discretionary hyphen	<\h>
En space/figure space	<\f>	En dash (number ranges)	<\#208>
Nonbreaking en space	<\!f>	Em dash (parenthetical)	<\#209>
Punctuation space	<\p>	New paragraph	<\#13>
Nonbreaking punc. space	<\!p>	New line	<\n>
Flex space	<\q>	Discretionary new line	<\d>
Nonbreaking flex space	<\!q>	New column	<\c>
Nonbreaking hyphen	<\!->	New box	<\b>

Figure 2.15 Spaces, dashes, and returns Here's a recap of all the keyboard shortcuts discussed in this section, along with their respective XPress Tags equivalents.

looks sillier than such a phrase breaking on its own as "and/-" and "or," which is something I see in newspapers all the time. The XPress Tags command for a discretionary new line is <\d>.

New column

When flowing text through a multi-column text box, the new column command—typed with the Enter key (⌤)—pushes any text following it into the next column. Hitting new paragraph commands until the text moves to the next column is a bad idea, as you'll need to adjust the number of new paragraph commands at the editing stage. The new column command does what you need with one keystroke and has a much smaller chance of messing up your layout later on. Type <\c> to get a new column in XPress Tags.

New box

The new box command is simply the new column command on steroids, and it's accessed by typing Shift-Enter (⇧⌤). Use this command if you have a multi-column box and need to push text through more than one column—all the way into the next box. Using multiple new column commands instead of a new box command is as bad as using multiple new paragraph commands. Text may legally use more columns of your layout at the editing stage than when you created it, and the new box command will let that occur without further adjustment. <\b> is the XPress Tags command for new box.

Hyphenation & Justification

In the early days of desktop publishing, a popular game for traditional typographers to play was to identify printed pieces that had been set on the desktop. It was, of course, too easy, but we were snobs and had fun doing it anyway. Things have certainly improved over the years, but it is unfortunately still easy to pick out some desktop work.

To properly set type in QuarkXPress, you'll need to both edit the Standard Hyphenation & Justification (H & J) style and make a few new styles of your own. If you make these changes and additions with no documents open, they will automatically be available to you in all new documents you create from then on.

Hyphenation options

Traditional type houses usually have a "shop standard" that describes their approach to typesetting. It states the general tightness or looseness to be used for word and letter spacing both text and headlines, especially when a client doesn't specify these things. By changing your Standard H & J style, you'll be defining your own shop standard. I think it's important to make these changes directly in the Standard style, since all your paragraphs and style sheets will use that H & J style by default; thus your job will be made easier and your type will look consistently spaced from file to file and job to job (Figure 2.16).

Smallest word that can hyphenate

Unless you work exclusively on display ads, you'll probably want to accept the default setting of Auto Hyphenation turned on, but the settings just beneath the Auto Hyphenation check box will change depending on what kinds of jobs you set. For example, if you work mostly on books with large line lengths (the width of the column or text box), you may want to continue restricting hyphenation to words of at least six characters.

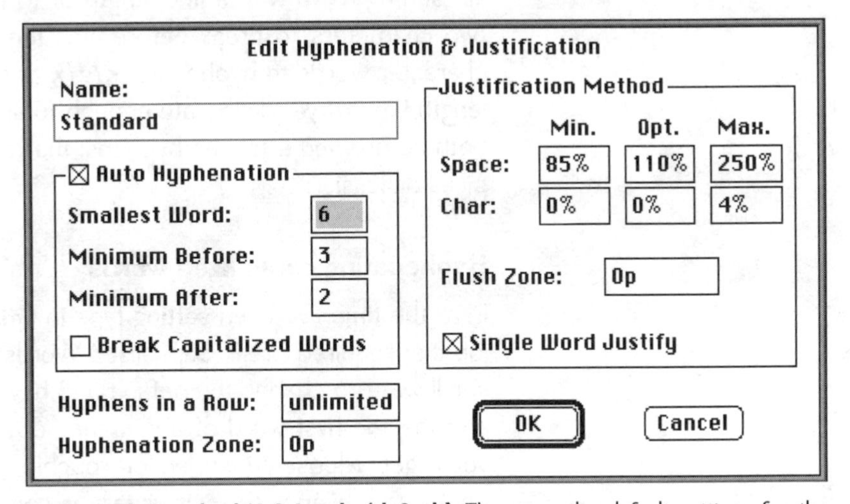

Figure 2.16 Standard H & J style (default) These are the default settings for the Standard H & J style as shipped by Quark. At the very least, you'll probably want to make some changes in the left-hand side of the dialog box.

Characters before and after hyphens

You can comfortably change the Minimum Before and Minimum After settings so that they are both set to three characters. This way you'll avoid having any two-letter suffixes breaking over to the start of a new line. Suffixes that count as their own syllable, such as "ly," aren't too obtrusive when they break over, but plural and past tense suffixes such as "es" and "ed" are often not pronounced as separate syllables and are awkward to read when broken to a new line. Since lines with longer lengths usually have plenty of spacebands and letters to use for space adjustment, you can completely avoid this readability problem with Auto Hyphenation settings of 6/3/3.

TIP In nonjustified copy, hyphenation settings that require a large number of letters before and after a hyphen will produce a rougher rag, since more characters of each breaking word will have to move down to the next line. A rough rag is one that exhibits more variance between line lengths; a tight rag is one in which the variance between the lengths of a paragraph's lines is minimal.

Magazine work may require much less luxurious settings, since every line may present a battle for (against?) good typography. When I'm setting a job with a line length of 16 picas or less, I usually allow two characters to break before *or* after a hyphen, and I allow five-character words to hyphenate (5/2/3 or 5/3/2). Note that at this line length I'm not yet desperate enough to allow two characters to break both before *and* after the hyphens; that comes with line lengths of 10 picas or less!

Hyphenating capitalized words

In all the time I've been setting type in QuarkXPress, I've only set one job that required Break Capitalized Words to be turned off. Generally, you'll want to change the default and have this option on. Otherwise, anytime the first word of a sentence doesn't fit at the end of a line, you'll get a loosely justified or roughly ragged line. This applies to books, too, even with their usually larger line lengths.

The only reason I've ever found for leaving this option off is when I wanted to avoid hyphenating proper nouns. I set a book for an art gallery that contained eight zillion—approximately—names of artists, and it would have been a real mess if we had allowed them to hyphenate. Luckily, the client was a big fan of rough rags.

Limiting the number of hyphens

Believe it or not, I've actually been involved in vicious debates about the Hyphens in a Row setting. Some people like the default setting of "unlimited," preferring to look through their pages and override excess hyphenation manually. I much prefer to let the computer do its best and then visually check for loose lines. Unless under extreme duress, I never allow more than two consecutive hyphenated lines.

The Bobzilla XTension offers a Line Check feature that allows you to set a number of criteria to search for, including loose lines and automatically hyphenated words (Figure 2.17). Line Check gives you a total count of problems and then allows you to move easily from one problem area to another, fixing as you go, if you wish. Bobzilla is included on the disk in the back of the book.

Line Check defines loose justification as any lines that have exceeded the Maximum word space value in the H & J style applied to a given paragraph. And even though QuarkXPress' hyphenation algorithms do a pretty good job, I like to do a commonsense assessment of the decisions it has made before showing a job to a client.

Setting the Hyphenation Zone

The Hyphenation Zone can be used to specify how rough the rag can get in nonjustified paragraphs. Before QuarkXPress will hyphenate a word, it checks to see if the second to last word on the line has entered the Hyphenation Zone—as measured from the right side of

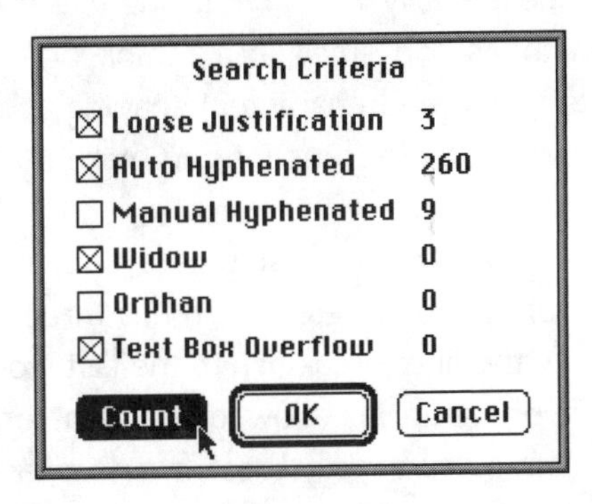

Figure 2.17 Line Check's search criteria Bobzilla's Line Check feature let's you count and search for any of these typography problems.

the column. If it has, the program decides that the line is long enough, thank you very much, and refuses to hyphenate the word.

The net result is that with a large enough Hyphenation Zone, you will end up with fewer hyphenated lines and a rougher rag. This procedure falls short of adequately controlling the look of the rag; for that, it would need to offer control of the lengths of lines not requiring hyphenation. As it stands, small words still get left within the zone, leaving far too many full lines in a paragraph.

Justification settings

In my role as a typesetter, I've found it difficult to set up a shop standard for the Justification Method section of an H & J style. This is due to the fact that so many different kinds of jobs cross my desk in a given week. Some jobs use narrow line lengths, and others are wide; some are justified, while others are set rag right (flush left); some use a point size that fits well into its line length, whereas some require point sizes completely out of balance with the line length.

Word spacing values

Your settings for Minimum, Optimum, and Maximum word and character spacing will have a major impact on how your type will look. I've found that I'm usually pretty happy with the spaceband size as defined in the font, so I change the default optimum word space setting from 110% to 100% most of the time. Please remember that my bias is toward text-size settings; if you're doing a bunch of display ads, this value should definitely be lowered further, since your spacebands will look too big at larger point sizes.

I often increase the minimum word space value from QuarkXPress' default of 85% to 95%. I like allowing the spacebands to get smaller, especially when I'm trying to set type that's too large in a line length that's too small, but I think 85% is too small. I'd rather not reduce word (and character) spacing at all, if possible, but it's amazing how much difference it can make in tight situations.

TIP QuarkXPress first sets a line using the optimum word and character space values. It then has three choices for determining how to justify the line: Break *before* the last word; break *after* the last word; or, if hyphenation is allowed, break at one of the allowable hyphenation points. It can only break *after* the last word if the minimum word or character space values are less than their respective optimum values; by default, they weren't, prior to QuarkXPress 3.2. It checks to see how much it has to expand or compress the spaces and characters in each of the three choices, and then it chooses the one which leaves the word space closest to the optimum value and which changes the character spacing the least.

If a line can't be properly justified using the values in your H & J style, any extra space will be added to the word spaces on a line, or between all the characters if there are no word spaces. A line in which the word or character space maximum is exceeded is flagged as a loose line by the Line Check feature of the Bobzilla XTension.

TIP Before starting a large or complicated job in which you expect to have problems making the type look good, I recommend running Bobzilla's Line Check feature on a sample file. This way you can experiment with different H & J settings to determine which ones will give you fewer loose lines and less auto hyphenation. The goal, of course, is to use H & J settings that will produce the fewest problems before requiring manual intervention.

Character spacing values

As of QuarkXPress 3.2, the maximum character space default was changed from an outrageous 15% to a satisfactory 4%. Invariably, text that had been letterspaced 15% (of the width of an en space) looked bad, so I'm glad this was changed. I tend to use 5% for the maximum character space in most of my jobs (Figure 2.18). And when I need to, I'm willing to change the minimum character space value to –2%. In 10 point type, 2% steals only one-tenth of a point from between each letter.

TIP Since the character space values are measured in the same units as kerning and tracking, you can easily see what kind of results you'll get with these settings by manually applying tracking to a sample line of text. If you start to get physically ill seeing your text tracked +5 units, then 5% might be too large a value for you to use for the maximum character space. I guarantee that if you do this test you will never again use a maximum value of 15%.

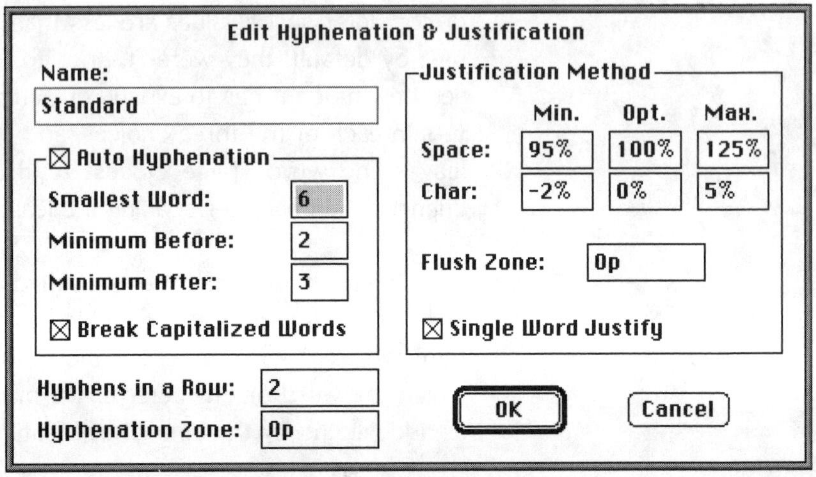

Edit Hyphenation & Justification

Name: Standard

☒ Auto Hyphenation
Smallest Word: 6
Minimum Before: 2
Minimum After: 3
☒ Break Capitalized Words

Hyphens in a Row: 2
Hyphenation Zone: 0p

Justification Method

	Min.	Opt.	Max.
Space:	95%	100%	125%
Char:	-2%	0%	5%

Flush Zone: 0p
☒ Single Word Justify

OK Cancel

Figure 2.18 Standard H & J style (custom) The job for which I set up this H & J style required a bit of flexibility in justification settings to accommodate a short line length and a desire for reasonable letterspacing.

Flush Zone and Single Word Justify

By default, the last line of a justified paragraph is set flush left. Flush Zones are useful in ad work where the last line of a paragraph needs to be justified if the last word on the line falls close to the full line length. This is where you define the meaning of "close." Flush Zones are also useful when you need to force break a paragraph with the New Column command. The New Column command acts like a New Paragraph command, setting the line it's on flush left. Also, the first line after the New Column command will have any new indents, spacing, and rules invoked in the current style sheet. Until QuarkXPress has a New Column command that acts like a New Line command, I'll keep using an H & J style with a large Flush Zone whenever I have to break a paragraph using the New Column command.

TIP As of version 3.2 of QuarkXPress, there's an alignment called Flush Justify. This handy way to justify the last line of a paragraph shouldn't be confused with the proper use of a Flush Zone. Flush Justify will justify the last line of a paragraph no matter what; a Flush Zone will only justify the line if the last word ends within the zone.

The Single Word Justify option refers to how the program will handle a line with no spacebands when trying to justify a paragraph.

When the option is turned on, the line will get as much character spacing as needed to fill the line length. If left off, the line will get no extra spacing and will be set flush left. Luckily, this situation doesn't crop up very often. I've only seen it when I've been trying to wrap justified text around an illustration.

Custom H & J styles

The only H & J style settings that ragged text will make use of are the ones for optimum word and character spacing. Although I rarely change these settings for regular text, I have created a custom H & J setting called Heads in which the word spacing is set at an optimum of 75%. This is a nice way for me to be sure that my larger headlines have proportionally smaller word spaces (Figure 2.19).

I've already mentioned that I have another H & J style, called Flush, which is identical to Standard with the exception that it has a large Flush Zone defined. I use this when I have to break columns manually and the break occurs mid-paragraph. It's set up to force the last line of the paragraph to justify.

My NoBreak H & J style is used in style sheets for subheads. These are generally heads that are close to or the same size as the text, so they use the same space settings, but hyphenation is not allowed.

These three H & J styles were created with no documents open, which means that they are available in all new documents I create. Once a document has been created, I'll sometimes make variations of the Standard H & J to accommodate text set in different sizes within the same document.

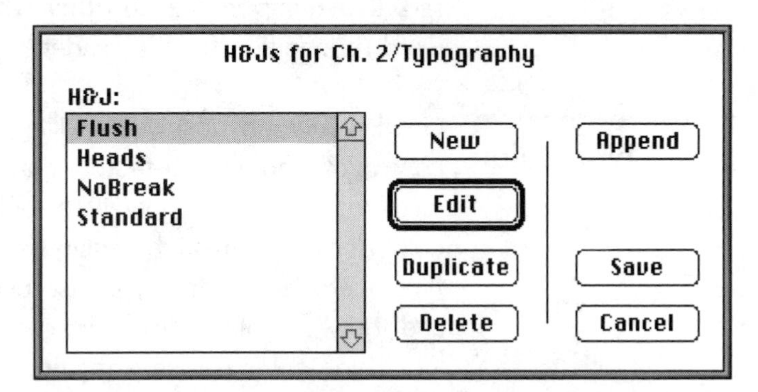

Figure 2.19 H & J style choices I always have these choices of H & J styles in all newly created documents, since I created the styles with no documents open.

Perhaps you'll want to add H & J styles called Tighter, Looser, 1Hyph, 2Hyphs, and 3Hyphs, all allowing easy switching between styles when editing a job. Also, be sure to see **Appendix A: New features in QuarkXPress 3.2** for information about how the Append and Delete features have been expanded for style sheets, colors, and H & Js.

Kerning and tracking

The kerning and tracking tools in QuarkXPress can help you set professional-quality type, but only if you understand how to use them properly. Discussions on manual kerning and tracking are interspersed throughout this chapter and the rest of the book, but in this section I'll be discussing how to use the table-editing tools in the Utilities menu.

Kerning refers to the adjustment of the way two characters fit together, and the value used for this adjustment is called the kern pair value. No typeface is designed so that every pair of characters has optically equal spaces between them, but kerning is used to create that effect.

Tracking tries to compensate for the optical problems that occur when you enlarge or reduce type size: Larger sizes require tightened letter spacing to maintain proper spacing proportions, while smaller sizes need to be loosened. Loosely spaced letters make it hard for the reader to recognize words. On the other hand, characters that bump into each other when spaced too tightly can impair word recognition for the reader.

Type color

Good typography involves a willingness to monitor and maintain tight control of a number of factors that affect type color—an all-inclusive term that describes how type looks when placed on a page. Type color derives from such design issues as the weight and shape of the typeface selected, the type size being used, the leading of the type, and the width of the text box or column in which it's set.

Type color is also affected by a myriad of technical concerns that we have already touched upon, such as justification mode and rules for hyphenation. But one of the key components in determining type color is a mixture of the aesthetic and the technical—it's the proper determination of letterspacing.

Type mass and usage

The amount of space desired around characters is determined by two factors: the weight—or mass—of the font being adjusted and the intended use for the font. A font has more mass as the character outlines get heavier. The bold typeface used in this book's heads and subheads has greater mass than the roman style used for the text. As a font gets heavier it usually loses interior white space, that space contained in what is called the character's counter. This is easy to see when comparing two weights of the same character in the same font: O/**O** or R/**R**, for example.

In general, as the interior white space decreases, the exterior white space—the space between letters—needs to diminish as well. Font foundries usually try to adjust for this by tightening a character's sidebearings. Sidebearings are the white spaces on either side of a character that are built into the character's width. You'll notice that when you set two letters together like "HI," there's a gap between them. The width of that gap is equal to the space contained in the letter H's right sidebearing added to the space in the letter I's left sidebearing.

Type usage is the other main consideration in determining letter fit. Most fonts are set up with sidebearings and kern pairs suitable for text setting when used in the 10, 11, or 12 point type range. When used in larger sizes, the font needs to be tracked tighter. This is because the interior white space of the characters increases proportionately while the exterior white space increases twice as much due to the fact that there are two sidebearings for each character pair. Likewise, when a font smaller than standard text size is used, it usually needs to be tracked looser.

Different types of typography also call for different spacing. In advertising typography, for instance, the type itself is often a design element in the advertisement. When an art director wants to darken or lighten the texture of an ad, the type color is manipulated and a font may be set very tightly or be tracked very loosely.

Font metrics

At its broadest definition, font metrics is simply the control of white space surrounding letters. It involves character widths and sidebearings, which can't be altered directly from QuarkXpress. And it is bound up with the issues of pair kerning and tracking, which *can* be effected through QuarkXPress. These twin concerns dictate that if we want to produce superior type, we need to use fonts that letter-space properly.

Fonts with good metrics are a pleasure to work with, while those with poor metrics can go from providing minor annoyance to major headaches depending on the extent of the metrics problem and the size of the job you're working on. Although purchasing fonts from large foundries is a good hedge against receiving a font with malformed characters or a bouncing baseline, it is not necessarily a guarantee for obtaining a well-spaced font. However, the large foundries do a fairly good job of defining balanced widths and sidebearings, a craft the older foundries like Linotype and Monotype have been practicing for decades.

The adjustment of widths and sidebearings is pretty much out of the scope of this book. If you want to start tinkering with widths you need a font editor such as Altsys' Fontographer. You should also spend some time understanding how the foundries set up their fonts. While adjusting widths can be a powerful tool that can significantly reduce your pair kerning chores, it is also extremely easy to completely destroy font spacing. Therefore, width manipulation should be approached with due consideration.

TIP A good source for more information on this topic is Walter Tracy's "Letters of Credit—A View of Type Design," published by David R. Godine (ISBN 0-87923-636-1). It's one of only a few treatises available on the arcane art of font spacing.

Built-in kerning pairs

It is in the area of pair kerning that the large foundries often run into trouble. Although well-balanced widths and sidebearings will go a long way toward ensuring that a font spaces correctly, there will always be problem character pairings—such as the "WA"—that need to be dealt with separately. In hot metal typesetting, the excess white space between two such characters was removed by shaving a letter so that portions of the letter overhung either the preceding or succeeding character. It was this overhang, called the letter's kern, from which today's term "kerning" is derived.

When photocomposition replaced hot metal, the same effect was achieved through pair kerning, whereby space between letters was automatically extracted or added by accessing a kerning look-up table. The foundries never provided these look-up tables with their proprietary systems—most type houses preferred to "roll their own" pairs. When they swung to the open PostScript platform, many font manufacturers did not have sets of kerning pairs to include with their fonts.

This resulted in strange circumstances, such as Monotype originally releasing a number of PostScript fonts with no kerning pairs at all. The early Adobe/Linotype releases usually had less than 120 pairs. And while some of the selections in the Adobe Originals collection come with close to 1,000 pairs, the bulk of the new offerings are in the 300 to 400 pair range. Eying a potential market niche, some small foundries—such as Treacyfaces, Red Rooster, and Carter & Cone—are offering fonts that have been painstakingly spaced and kerned. Most of their selections, however, are new designs; this doesn't provide much help if your project requires a traditional typeface.

Only you can be the judge of how many kerning pairs are needed to properly space a font. Figure 2.20 shows a list which contains slightly under 200 pairs, highlighting some of the more common ones that appear in kerning.

New Century Schoolbook was one of the first fonts released on the desktop; it contained 102 kerning pairs (Figure 2.21). Adobe Caslon, from the Adobe Originals collection, weighs in with 737 pairs. Badger, a Les Usherwood font offered by the Red Rooster type

(T	AW	Fe	LW	PA	T)	Tw	Vy	Y.	ca	r,	ta	yc
(V	AY	Fi	LY	Pa	T,	Ty	W,	Y:	e'	r-	tz	yd
(W	Av	Fo	Lv	Pe	T-	Tz	W.	Y;	ex	r.	v,	ye
(Y	Aw	Fr	Lw	Po	T.	T"	W:	YA	ev	rc	v.	ys
,"	Ay	Fu	Ly	Pr	T:	T'	W;	Ya	ew	rn	vc	yw
,'	Az	Fy	L"	Pu	T;	V,	WA	Ye	ey	rm	vg	"A
."	A"	Kv	L'	QU	TA	V.	Wa	Yi	ff	ro	w,	'A
.'	A'	Kw	OA	Qu	Ta	V:	We	Yo	f'	rt	w.	'd
AC	CA	Ky	OT	RC	Tc	V;	Wi	Yp	f"	ru	wc	'r
AG	DV	LC	OV	RT	Te	VA	Wo	Yq	ny	rv	we	's
AO	DW	LO	OW	RV	To	Va	Wr	Ys	n'	rw	wo	't
AQ	DY	LQ	OX	RW	Tr	Ve	Wu	Yu	ov	ry	xe	
AT	F,	LT	OY	RY	Ts	Vi	Wy	Yv	ow	rz	xo	
AU	F.	LU	P,	Ry	Tu	Vo	Y,	Yw	ox	r'	y,	
AV	FA	LV	P.	ST	Tv	Vu	Y-	az	oy	r"	y.	

Figure 2.20 Common kerning pairs For text work, you might be able to get by with a kerning list not much larger than this. If you're attempting to produce pairs for a tight-not-touching display setting, probably hundreds of additional pairs will be needed.

Sphinx of Black Quartz, Judge My Vow.
Sphinx of Black Quartz, Judge My Vow.
Sphinx of Black Quartz, Judge My Vow.
Sphinx of Black Quartz, Judge My Vow.

Figure 2.21 Kerning pairs galore Here are examples of New Century Schoolbook, Adobe Caslon, Badger, and Habitat, all using only their built-in kerning pairs. If done right, the more pairs that are built in, the less manual kerning will need to be done.

foundry, contains 1,520 pairs, while Joseph Treacy's TF Habitat—which includes a number of pairs involving accented characters—sports 2,536. Another weight in that family reportedly ships with 3,800 pairs, which could be a record among commercial fonts.

Kerning in QuarkXPress

When kerning a font, it's important to remember that less is usually more. It's not the number of kerning pairs a font has that determines how well it sets, but rather the quality of those pairs. For instance, there are several utilities out that will now "automatically" generate thousands of kerning pairs at a touch of a keystroke. Except in rare situations, the quality of such pairs is universally poor. Add pairs to address specific spacing problems—not simply to increase the number of pairs.

Take a look

Let's assume you wish to work on a serif face for text use. Run out some sample copy in text sizes to evaluate how it sets. If you're using laser output instead of high resolution repro, you might want to come up in size a bit to 18 point to get a more accurate picture of how the characters are letter fitting. Track the type tightly and look for letter combinations that appear too loose or too tight when compared to the overall type color.

In general, straight characters (the letters such as **h** and **m**, and the left or right side of letters like **p** and **d**) should have a fairly uniform amount of space between them when set next to another straight character. A straight character next to a round character (an **o** or an **e,** or the left or right side of letters like **q** and **b**) should have a little less space, while rounds next to rounds should have even less.

TIP Don't be fooled by looking at the gap between serifs—creating pairs by attempting to have a uniform amount of white space between serifs will almost certainly produce a poorly kerned font. Rather, look at the total volume of white space between letters and use that as a guide when kerning.

If the character widths have been fairly well set up, you should observe groups of characters that seem to kern fairly consistently. Unless you want to generate 2,000+ kerning pairs for the font, the idea is to try to stay within the framework of that built-in spacing, identifying problem characters—such as a straight letter that produces noticeably more or less space than other straights when positioned against similar letters. In general, in a font with good character widths you should find that your lower case letter pairs should be primarily confined to the three angled letters (**v**, **w**, and **y**) and the problem letters that don't fit into either the straight or round category (**a**, **f**, **g**, **s**, **t**, and **z**).

Sample documents

It's helpful in this evaluation to have a QuarkXPress document that lists some sample kerning pairs. There are several ways to generate such a list, the easiest being to steal one from another font. Simply go into **Utilities→Kerning Table Edit**, select a well-spaced font that you feel is similar to the one being worked on, and use the "export" feature to save the kerns as a text file.

TIP You can import the text file containing kerning pair information into Microsoft Excel, where it will come in as a two-column chart. The kerning pair will be in the first column and the kerning value will be in the second column. You can then delete the second column (if you're just interested in the character pairs) and save the first column back out as a text file. Then import the file into a QuarkXPress document to get a fast kerning pair list to use.

It's also important to have a document that contains sample text which uses the pairs on your list. This is because kerning pairs don't exist in a vacuum. They need to be balanced against a backdrop of other text. The sample file should include all upper and lower case letters next to such punctuation marks as the period, comma, hyphen, the open and close quote and parenthesis. Upper and lower case character combinations should be there, but go easy on the all-capped copy, since text set all caps should be rare. Again, your main problem letters will be the three slanted characters (**V**, **W**, and **Y**) as well as the **A**, **F**, **P**, **T** and **S**.

If you don't anticipate ever having to use the font for tabular work, you can include kerning pairs for the lining numerals. If you do plan to set numerals in tabs, you may at least want to kern the numerals against the hyphen and the en dash since these pairings frequently occur in text settings. But don't kern the figures against the period or comma, since they are also used in tabular work.

Using the Kerning Table editor

If, after evaluating your sample sheets, you are generally pleased with how a font is setting and only wish to modify a dozen or so problem letter combinations, QuarkXPress' built-in Kerning Table editor is up to the task.

As you page through your samples, make a note of the pairs you want to modify and how much kerning each needs to space properly. You do this by using the kerning/tracking tool on the Measurements palette. Once you have recorded the pairs, you can use the "Remove Manual Kerning" feature of the Features Plus XTension—included on the disk in the back of this book—to get rid of your manually kerned pairs and "zero out" your sample file.

Open the Kerning Table Edit utility and select the "Plain" variant of the font you wish to adjust (Figure 2.22). If you want to kern Helvetica Bold, select "B Helvetica «Plain»"; be sure not to select the bold-styled "Helvetica «Bold»." Choosing Edit opens the kerning table, where you can type in the pairs and corresponding kern values. If there is already a value entered, just add it to your value and enter the cumulative number. Select OK and then Save to complete loading the new pair values (Figure 2.23).

It's important to visualize exactly where the kerns you have just loaded reside. When you work on a QuarkXPress document, kerns can exist in one of three places: the font suitcase, the XPress Preferences file, and the document itself. By using **Utilities→Kerning Table Edit**, you have written your new kerns to the XPress Preferences file.

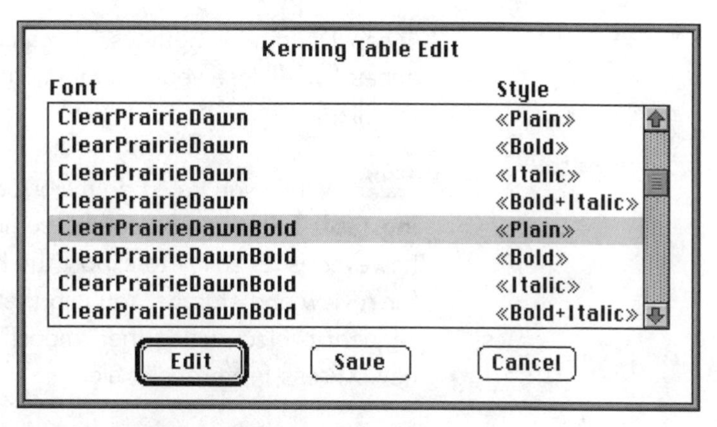

Figure 2.22 Kerning Table editor Be sure to choose the «Plain» style of bold, italic, or bold italic fonts, avoiding the styled variations.

Those kerns—as well as any kerns contained in the font suitcase—will be written to the document the next time you save it. This relieves you of the responsibility of sending along the XPress Preferences file when you send a document for service bureau output. Earlier versions of QuarkXPress required a file called XPress Data—the Preferences file forerunner—to be included with the document.

The new kerns will also be in effect on any new document you create, as long as you continue using the same XPress Preferences file. If you do not want to use the new kerns in subsequent documents, throw away the XPress Preferences file; QuarkXPress will generate a new preferences file next time it boots up. If you do trash the file, the next time you open the original document remember to select

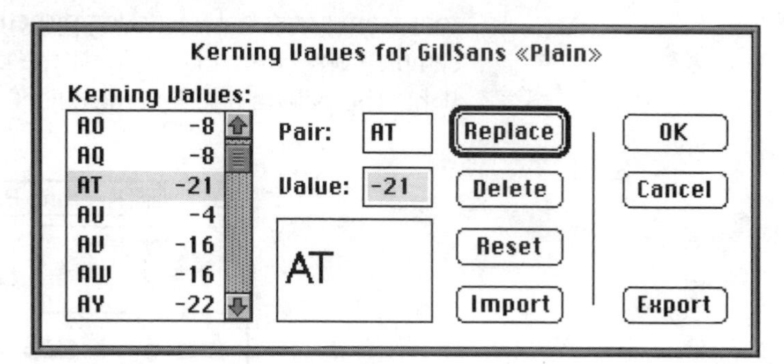

Figure 2.23 Entering the kern pair values When you enter this dialog and type two letters that already have a kern pair value, the scrolling list automatically jumps to that pair and displays its current value. New pairs can be created and given values, too.

"Keep Document Settings," because if you hit "Use XPress Preferences," you'll lose your custom kerns for good the next time you save the file.

TIP While you could do major pair kerning using **Utilities→Kerning Table Edit**, it's a bit cumbersome for heavy use. One nice feature, however, is its ability to export the kerns you've loaded into a text file for review and storage. You can then save the kerns for use in a subsequent project, using the "Import" command to reload them into a new XPress Preferences file.

The Kerning Palette XTension

If your kerning projects are going to be anything more substantial than adding a dozen or so kerns to a font, then I recommend investing in an industrial strength kerning tool such as the Kerning Palette XTension from Clearface, Inc.

The Kerning Palette, as its name suggests, provides a floating palette from which you can globally alter the kerning information of a document (Figure 2.24). I use the palette in two ways. First, it's great for use on one-shot jobs, where you have no interest in reworking an entire font—you just want to clean up some of the kerns that occur in the document. Since by default, the Kerning Palette is only changing the kerning that's in the document, not the tables in either the font suitcase or the XPress Preferences file, you don't have to worry that anything you do will affect subsequent jobs.

The second use for the palette is full-fledged font kerning. I have several files set up with sample pairs and text which I use to kern a font from scratch. By working directly in QuarkXPress, I can track my sample copy so that I can see if the pairs I create are too loose or too tight. The palette also lets me select a group of pairs at once and add

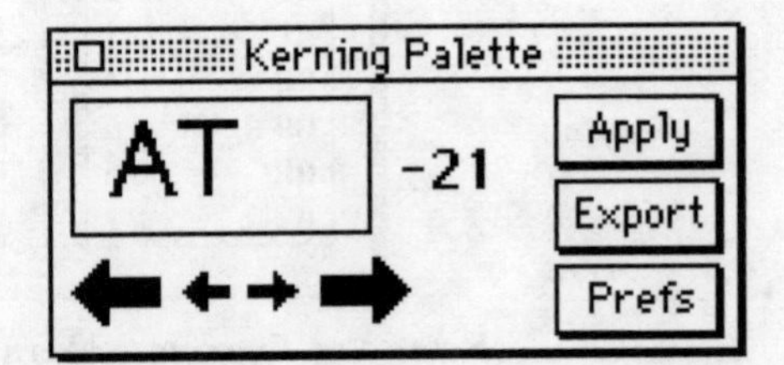

Figure 2.24 Kerning on demand The Kerning Palette is easy to use, but its simplicity masks a very sophisticated and full-featured kerning editor.

or subtract uniformly from whatever value they have loaded. For example, if I have two pairs, one with a –5 value and the other with +2, selecting them both and typing in a value of 2 changes them to –3 and +4, respectively. Once a font is kerned to my liking, the pairs can be applied to either the font suitcase or the XPress Preferences file; a new suitcase can be also created or you can export the kerns in text form (Figure 2.25). As far as I know, the Kerning Palette XTension is the only commercial utility that can tell you if an XPress Preferences file contains kerns for a given font.

Units to the em

In addition to understanding where kerning pairs reside, you should also have a firm grasp of what the kerning value you're entering for each pair means. Kerning, like tracking, is done in relative units. The Kerning Palette, by default, uses QuarkXPress' 200-to-the-em unit measure, although you can adjust the palette's unit value to whatever you wish. The palette can therefore accommodate typographers who have worked on pre-PostScript typesetting front end systems and are used to doing kerning in different fractions of an em, such as 18-, 27-, or 54-to-the-em.

A larger issue is how QuarkXPress defines an em space—not as the value of the point size you're in, but rather double the width of a zero. Such an arbitrary definition can wreak havoc when you go from

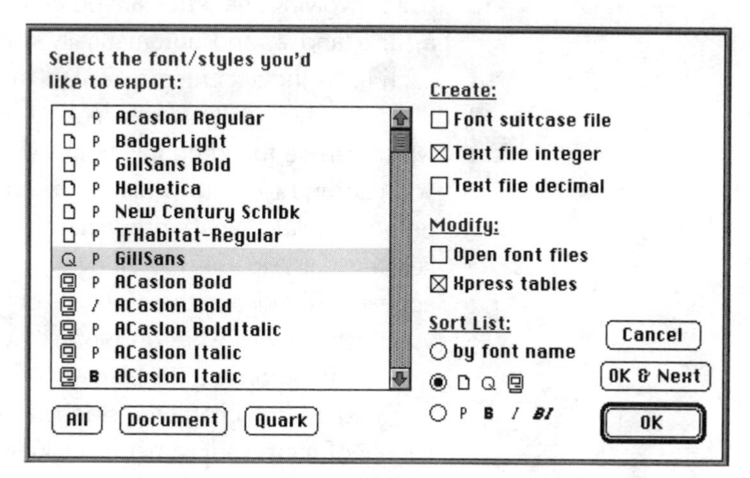

Figure 2.25 The export window The Kerning Palette lets you see where kerning data resides (the document, the XPress Preferences file, or the font suitcase).

kerning a narrow font to working on an expanded face; you might find you have to use 2 units of kerning in the narrow face to move approximately the same amount of space as the 1 unit you moved in the expanded font. The Kerning Palette allows you to redefine this "Quarkian" em to a more traditional em, although the best way to handle this is to simply toggle on the Standard em space feature in **Edit→Preferences→Typographic**.

Since the em definition affects kerning, tracking, and word spacing, you should decide early on which em you want to use. My recommendation is if your kerning projects are going to be modest, stick with the variable (Quarkian) em. If you will be doing a lot of pair kerning, a fixed em definition will pay off in the long run.

TIP The Kerning Palette allows you to define pair kerns involving word spaces, and as of version 3.3, QuarkXPress will finally recognize such pairs. You can also export those pairs to the font suitcase and use them in other applications.

Other kerning tools

There are a number of other kerning tools available on the market. KernEdit—available from Agfa—is a popular standalone kerning editor that has some nice support for inheritance linkages. This is especially helpful when doing work with accented characters, since most fonts don't kern diacritics. For instance, if you have a dozen kerning pairs involving the letter **a**, you can set up a group which includes **á**, **à**, **ä**, **â** and **ã**, and automatically create five dozen more pairs that each have the accented **a** kerned the same way as the base **a**.

Another utility worth looking at is Greg Swann's Pairing Knife, which can be found on this book's disk. Basically, you dump all the text you can find for your project into one giant text file and drag/drop it onto the utility. What's produced is a text file containing a list of all the kerning pairs in the file along with the number of times each pair appears. The idea is that if you're only going to do a handful of kerns, you might as well work on those that appear a lot in your job.

Fontographer 4.0 was mentioned before as a program in which you could alter character sidebearings. You can now also handle a variety of metric adjustments, including globally changing sidebearings on similar characters and a kerning pair inheritance setup with more features than KernEdit (Figure 2.26). One glaring lack, however, is an easy way to track type visually while performing pair kerning. There

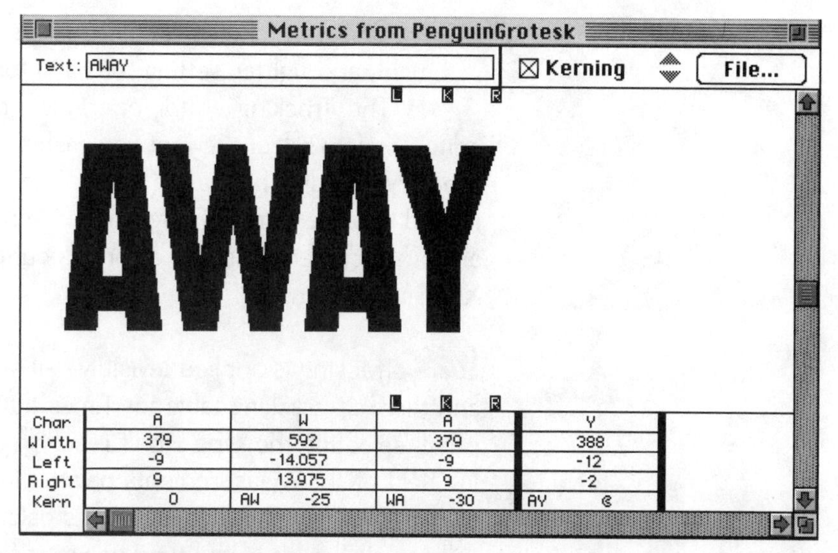

Figure 2.26 Altsys' Fontographer As of version 4.0, Fontographer sports a metrics window which lets you see at a glance such information as the character width, left and right sidebearings, and what the pair kerning values are to preceding or succeeding characters. Values shown are in thousandths of an em.

are several kludges you can use to simulate tracking, but this one feature gap is a major annoyance when working on font metrics in this program. Fontographer also has routines to automatically create widths and kerning pairs, although the results must be examined carefully on a font-by-font basis. Most likely, you'll want to use the results only as a starting point to begin your own kerning work.

Other font editors include Letraset's FontStudio and URW's Ikarus. URW also has an auto kerning utility of its own—called Kernus—which is interesting because it tries to even out sidebearings before working on pairs. It therefore creates both a new printer font and a font suitcase. All these programs have their afficionados, although Fontographer, which is available on both the Mac and PC platforms, is probably the leading font editing program at the moment.

Tracking

Once your pair kerns are perfected, it's time to work on tracking. Unfortunately, while QuarkXPress has some tremendously sophisticated type tools, its support for tracking is limited. In **Utilities→ Tracking Edit**, you're allowed to set only one track with four break points. Other typesetting front end systems, including Aldus' Page-

Maker, allow you to set multiple tracks so you can have a loose, normal, tight, and tighter setting for each font.

The Tracking editor operates similarly to the Kerning Table editor. Simply select the font you wish to track, hit Edit, plot your four break points and hit Save (Figure 2.27). The tracking information is loaded into the XPress Preferences file and will be applied to type on all new documents, as well as any document you open and click "Use XPress Preferences."

TIP Tracking is applied invisibly—if you set 12 point Times Roman and there's a tracking table for Times that includes a –3 tracking at 12 point, selecting the type won't result in a –3 appearing in the tracking field of the Measurements palette; instead, you'll see 0. Applying a –3 tracking via the Measurements palette to that same block of text will actually result in the type being tracked –6.

Tracking tables are a major headache to maintain because there are currently no third-party XTensions designed to manage them. It would be very nice to have an XTension that would print out any tracking tables contained in an XPress Preferences file—along with their corresponding break points—so you could easily load them into another copy of QuarkXPress. Ideally, it should also be able to write any tracking table contained in a document to the XPress Preferences

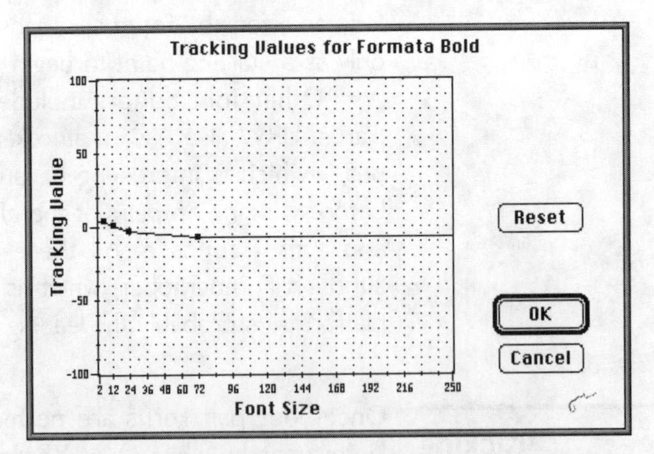

Figure 2.27 Tracking editor QuarkXPress' tracking support is limited to a single track with four break points. Since the bulk of your type will probably be in text sizes, don't hesitate to use three or even all four break points under 18 points if that's what it takes to produce proper fitting type.

file in use. Currently, the only way to move a tracking table is to re-create it by hand.

While the tracking table runs from 2 to 250 points, cluster your break points around the text sizes you most often use. I typically set my break points at 6, 12, or 18 points, with the final point at a large display size like 60 or 72 points. Realistically, given how often you use type larger than 72 points, you can probably hand kern it without too much sacrifice.

Pair kerning and tracking probably sounds like a lot of work—and it is! It's time-consuming and must be done at the start of a job, when you usually have a thousand other things to do. But like the time spent on templates and style sheets, work spent pair kerning and tracking a font will be rewarded in the long run. Plus, you will be doing your part to halt the slide to mediocracy that many typophiles have lamented since the start of the digital type revolution.

Page and column editing

Whether you work alone or pass files around a type shop or design studio, there is a concept of editing files that can't be stressed enough. I call it hard vs. soft editing, and it can mean the difference between frustrating, error-prone work and logical, safe editing habits.

It's common to have choices in the way you edit a file. Not unlike a number of other things in QuarkXPress, there are many ways to clean up and correct your files. A soft approach ensures the least amount of hassle on each subsequent pass of a job. Sometimes doing it the hard way, so to speak, will seem easier at the time, but that's only momentary gratification. Let's take a look at a couple of specific editing scenarios and discuss various ways to approach them.

Using style sheets to align baselines

It's not uncommon for a design spec to call for baseline alignment across the bottoms of columns and spreads. As mentioned in the **Page Layout** chapter, try to accomplish baseline alignment only after the majority of text edits have been made. I often give my clients what I call "paged galleys." That way they can see roughly how the text is flowing and how many pages will be needed—or how much text will need to be cut to get the number of pages wanted—before I do a lot of manual work fine-tuning the layout.

If at all possible, subhead spacing should add up to multiples of the text leading (Figure 2.28). This will go a long way toward ensuring baseline alignment. It's pretty simple when subheads are the same size as the text. If the subheads can use the same leading as the text, all you have to do is make sure that the Space Before and Space After settings in the **Style→Formats** dialog box add up to a multiple of the leading of the surrounding text. If your text and subheads use a leading of 12 points, your subhead could use a Space Before value of 16 points and a Space After value of 8 points, for example.

If the subheads use a leading that differs from the surrounding text, add its leading into the equation. With a text leading of 12 points and a subhead leading of 16 points, you might consider giving the subhead 16 points Space Before and 4 points Space After [16 before + 16 leading + 4 after = 36, or 3 × 12 (the text leading)]. Further complications arise when you have a two-line subhead that uses leading different from the text.

TIP For a large or often-repeated job, it's a good idea to prepare for multi-line subheads by making extra style sheets based on the subhead style sheet. Change the Space Before and After values in

to have been somewhat optimistic in setting 1992 premium levels. However, the actual per employee cost of an insured plan remained higher ($4,167) than that of a self-funded plan ($4,016).

EMPLOYEE CONTRIBUTIONS

The number of employers requiring employee contributions for single coverage rose from 55

common (16 and 15 percent of employers, respectively, use them). Employers in the Mid-Atlantic and New England regions, where a high percentage of employees are in unions, are most likely to use them (39 and 29 percent, respectively). Forty-two percent of respondents with at least half of their employees in unions had a basic hospitalization/major medical plan in 1992.

Figure 2.28 Adding up the space Even though the leading for the above subhead isn't the same as the surrounding text, I've maintained the baseline alignment by making sure all the subhead spacing adds up to an even number of text lines.

these new style sheets to reflect the values that will be necessary to get baseline alignment back on track when multi-line subheads appear. Don't apply the new style sheets until you need them, though, since you might end up with a page or column containing two or more multi-line subheads, in which case it may not be necessary to use the alternative spacing.

Manual spacing to align baselines

Here's the first example of hard vs. soft editing. If you need to add space around a subhead (or extract, or bulleted list, etc.) manually in order to align the baselines at the bottoms of pages, make sure you do so by adding the space via the **Style→Formats** dialog box, rather than hitting extra returns (Figure 2.29). First, extra returns can be more trouble than they're worth, since invoking the New Paragraph command with an extra return might do any number of things that you don't want, including adding more space above and below and calling out a paragraph rule. Getting rid of all that stuff often takes more time than doing it the "soft" way in the first place, and calling up the proper dialog box is as simple as typing Command-Shift-f (⌘ ⇧ f).

Second, even if you don't invoke a lot of extra stuff by hitting a return, you have still introduced a hard command that will possibly cause trouble on the next correction pass. New Paragraph commands,

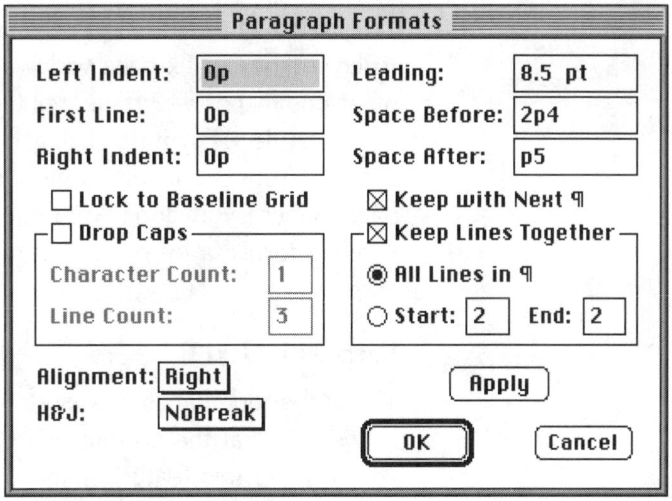

Figure 2.29 Manual editing This is the **Style→Formats** dialog box for a two-line version of the subhead shown in the last example. Since the text is on 12.5 points of leading, all I had to do was add 4 extra points to the Space Before value already in use to get the text baselines back in alignment.

for example, do not disappear when they fall at the tops and bottoms of columns, so it's entirely possibly that they'll have to be removed on the next pass, or worse, they won't be noticed and the job will be sent out incorrect.

TIP I hate to even mention this, but the Baseline Shift command shouldn't be used to align baselines. If just one of your lines scrolls up to the next page or column, it will no longer be positioned properly. In fact, a good rule of thumb to remember about baseline shift is this: If you're using it for more than a couple of characters at a time, you're probably doing something wrong.

Page widows and orphans

When the last line of a paragraph falls at the top of a page or column, you have what's called a page widow. This is almost always considered an unacceptable situation. The few times I have seen specs that allowed page widows, they came with the stipulation that the widow must be at least two-thirds the total line length. Generally, though, page widows are not allowed and need to be fixed. A page orphan happens when the first line of a paragraph falls at the bottom of a page or column. Subheads at the bottoms of pages or columns, detached from the following paragraph of text, are also considered to be page orphans.

Although you may find yourself using the Space Before and After settings to fix page widows and orphans, there are also some other commands worth mentioning. QuarkXPress offers two features in the **Style→Formats** dialog box that prevent page widows and orphans from occurring. Admittedly, they may create ragged-bottom pages where you don't want them, but they do prevent you from needing to use a lot of hard commands, as would otherwise be the case.

Keep with Next ¶

This is the tool that allows you to avoid page orphans caused by subheads sitting at the bottom of a page or column all by themselves. If you turn on this feature, either in individual cases or in your style sheets, your subheads will automatically be moved up to the next page or column when the following paragraph won't fit in the current page or column.

TIP As of version 3.3, Keep with Next ¶ is working properly. Files created prior to this version exhibited a problem wherein any multiple-line paragraph that needed to be kept with the following paragraph would instead break apart. Only the last line of the paragraph would be kept with the next paragraph, and the remainder of the first paragraph would be left at the bottom of the column. Also, more than two paragraphs couldn't be kept together, but this works now.

Keep Lines Together

The command that's used for preventing page widows and orphans is Keep Lines Together (Figure 2.30). You can choose to keep together all the lines in a paragraph, which is useful for subheads, or you can define the number of lines that can be kept together at the start and end of paragraphs. In most situations, you'll want to define both the start and end values as "2," which will prevent the first and last lines from splitting off from the rest of the paragraph.

TIP When you have a drop cap in a paragraph, it's important to remember to increase the number of start lines in the Keep Lines Together feature. It's usually a good idea to have twice as many lines

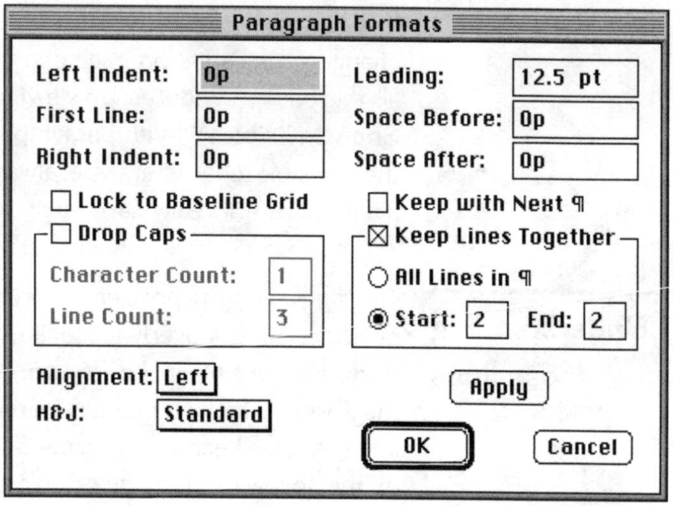

Figure 2.30 Page widows and orphans If you turn on the Keep Lines Together command and define start and end values of "2" and "2," page widows and orphans will not be allowed.

held together as there are lines in your drop cap. So if you have a three-line drop cap, define the start value as 6.

One method of getting rid of the space left by the program when it moves lines forward to avoid widows and orphans is to make facing pages a line short or long. If you do open up a text box so that an extra line fits, you must remember to adjust the facing page in the same manner. The same goes for closing up a text box to push lines forward. However, it's usually considered bad form for a spread that's one line long to follow or be followed by a spread that's one line short, the reason being that there's a good chance the reader will notice the change.

There are also paragraph-based methods of dealing with page widows and orphans, as well as the space left by their prevention, and they will be discussed in the next section.

Paragraph and line editing

Here's where the difference between hard and soft editing becomes most crucial. If you decide that you're not willing to change your habits on page and column editing, at least you can see all the bad procedures by viewing the invisible characters (**View→ Show Invisibles**). With paragraph and line editing, however, most of the invisible characters are always invisible, so sticking with good habits here will really save your sanity.

Understanding loose lines

The single biggest problem in producing justified type on any system most certainly is overly loose lines. The difference between a sophisticated and a simple H & J system is that the sophisticated system has the ability to look at an entire paragraph when making decisions about line breaks. There are systems in existence that can automate much of the following, but they don't offer some of the nice features of QuarkXPress. Someday we may have truly sophisticated H & J in this program; I guess that all we can do is keep asking.

TIP Before you can fix any paragraph and line problems in your file, you must be able to determine what's causing the problems. This process is a lot easier when you're the one who set up the job and can remember what restrictions you entered into the H & J styles. If you didn't do it or don't remember what you did, find out which H & J style a problem paragraph is using and go take a look at it. If you're new at this, write down the values so you can easily refer to them as you clean up the file.

When a line is too loose, there are three things you can do to fix it: Push characters down from previous lines, bring characters back from subsequent lines, or rewrite. The production of **Quark XPress Unleashed** is only the second time in 15 years of typesetting that I've had the luxury of being able to rewrite to fix loose lines. Usually I fix a line the best I can and leave it to the client to recognize the need for rewriting. In ad work, however, copy rewriting is a key component to ad design and is often the only way to produce superior typography.

H & J style limitations

Loose lines are generally caused by QuarkXPress' inability to fit on the current line all or part of the first word from the next line. This may be caused by the settings in the H & J style currently in use. If so, the problem could be:

- Auto hyphenation is turned off.
- The minimum word length is larger than the length of the word that needs to be hyphenated.
- The minimum number of characters allowed before or after a hyphen prevents an otherwise valid hyphenation.
- The word that needs to be hyphenated starts with a capital letter and that option is turned off.
- The maximum number of hyphens in a row has been met.

To determine if any of the above are causing the problem, check which H & J style is being used and then look to see what parameters it uses.

Words that just won't break

It's also possible that the first word on the next line won't break for reasons having nothing to do with the H & J style, such as:

- QuarkXPress doesn't think there is a valid hyphenation point in the word, or what it considers as a valid point is more restrictive than need be. Type "⌘ H" while your insertion point is inside the word to see what the program considers a valid hyphenation point.

- There is already a discretionary hyphen—possibly inserted on an earlier pass—in front of or within the word preventing the required break. Cursor through the word and look for spots that require an extra cursor to get past a character.

- There is a new line command at the end of the current, loose line. Turn on invisibles to see the new line command; if in justified alignment, you'll need to switch temporarily to left alignment to see any new line commands.

Fixing loose lines

Some solutions having to do with H & J styles and manually entered commands were just discussed, of course, but those are the easy ones. It gets a little trickier when you've already exhausted those solutions and still have nasty looking type. Besides, you can't change an H & J style every time you have a loose line. You can, however, override the H & J style or perform other manual intervention.

TIP The following examples are given in order of softest to hardest. The softest examples offer solutions that are less likely to cause problems on subsequent editing passes.

Discretionary hyphens

These can be used to selectively break the rules you've established in your H & J style. When your settings call for a minimum of three characters before and after a hyphen, for example, you can type a discretionary hyphen (⌘ -) after a two-letter prefix or before a two-letter suffix in order to let part of a word come up to the previous line (Figure 2.31).

Besides overriding the H & J style, discretionary hyphens can be used to override QuarkXPress' hyphenation decisions. Remember,

This was probably the first message thread we ever captured and uploaded to our libraries. And the version that's still there is about twice as long as what you're about to read. For space reasons, we've removed a number of branches of the thread that were either dated or didn't flow well with the rest of the discussion.	◀▶	This was probably the first message thread we ever captured and uploaded to our libraries. And the version that's still there is about twice as long as what you're about to read. For space reasons, we've removed a number of branches of the thread that were either dated or didn't flow well with the rest of the discussion.

Figure 2.31 Discretionary hyphen Although the current H & J style calls for a minimum of three characters before a hyphen, I manually placed a discretionary hyphen after the second character of "removed" to fix this loose line.

the program will use a hyphenation point that allows for the best possible spacing on a given line, regardless of the effect it has on the next line. You may choose to insert a discretionary hyphen at an earlier point in the word, or in front of the word, in order to move characters down to a subsequent loose line.

TIP When your H & J style allows space to be taken out from between words and characters, placing a discretionary hyphen *after* the point where a hyphenation has taken place will sometimes cause more letters to move up to the previous line. Other times, it just causes the whole word to move down to the next line. Don't be afraid to play with discretionary hyphens, but also don't forget to remove the ones you don't intend to use.

Discretionary returns

These can be used in instances where you want to control where a phrase is broken but where a hyphen—and hence a discretionary hyphen—isn't appropriate. Phrases with either an en dash (such as "Monday–Friday") or a slash (such as "and/or") can certainly be broken after the dash or the slash. Do so by inserting a discretionary return (⌘ ↵) after the character (Figure 2.32). If you insert a discretionary hyphen at those points the program will inappropriately generate its own computer hyphen.

QuarkXPress will also generate a computer hyphen when a discretionary hyphen is placed after an em dash. This is because a dis-

Paul Tower, formerly of Quark, Inc., made sure our forum members were taken care of by uploading many of the QuarkXPress "Freebies" files, including: the FeaturesPlus/Network XTensions, the Printer Calibration XTension, the Cool Blends XTension, some new PANTONE Color Sets, Quark's Multiple Master Utilities, Prepare for Service Bureau, PhotoShop Plug-In, the Bob XTension, and Son of Bob.	Paul Tower, formerly of Quark, Inc., made sure our forum members were taken care of by uploading many of the QuarkXPress "Freebies" files, including: the FeaturesPlus/ Network XTensions, the Printer Calibration XTension, the Cool Blends XTension, some new PANTONE Color Sets, Quark's Multiple Master Utilities, Prepare for Service Bureau, PhotoShop Plug-In, the Bob XTension, and Son of Bob.

Figure 2.32 Discretionary return By placing a discretionary return after the slash between "FeaturesPlus" and "Network," I've told the program that it's okay to break the phrase there but not to generate its own computer hyphen.

cretionary hyphen always produces a computer hyphen unless it's placed after a space character, at which point it prevents the following word from breaking. Use a discretionary return after an em dash, instead. I have also used discretionary returns in the middle of the word "QuarkXPress" so that it only breaks between the first and second half of the word and never hyphenates, as mentioned in the discussion on discretionary returns earlier in this chapter.

Tracking

When no amount of discretionary hyphen and discretionary return insertion helps to fix a loose line, it's time to consider manual tracking (Figure 2.33). One has to be careful with tracking, since it's easy to go overboard. As a rule, I never tighten a paragraph beyond –2

Many of the features of the above XTensions were answers to "wish list" items about which our members wrote to Quark. Direct online communications with vendors is one of the best ways to make sure your voice is heard and your vote counted.	Many of the features of the above XTensions were answers to "wish list" items about which our members wrote to Quark. Direct online communications with vendors is one of the best ways to make sure your voice is heard and your vote counted.

Figure 2.33 Tracking In this case I'm using tracking to kill two birds with one stone (I really hate that phrase). By tracking the entire paragraph I've gotten rid of both the paragraph widow and the loose line starting with "the best ways...."

units or loosen it beyond +2 units. The goal to keep in mind for both your H & J style settings and your manual use of tracking is not to grossly affect the color of the type. If you track too much, the area that's tracked will look appreciably darker or lighter than the surrounding text, and that's not good.

You may choose to track just one line instead of an entire paragraph, and it might not even be the line that's too loose. I usually won't track one line in a paragraph more than 1 unit in either direction, though, since I don't want the spacing to be noticeably different from the rest of the paragraph.

Word space tracking

Instead of tracking between all the letters in a line or paragraph, you can choose to track only the word spaces—but only if you're using Quark's Features Plus XTension (available on the disk in the back of the book). Rather than actually tracking the spacebands, the XTension kerns selected text between the first letter of each word and its preceding spaceband. Word space tracking is only available through keyboard shortcuts—the same keyboard shortcuts that have always worked for regular tracking, with the addition of the Control (⌃) key. Here are all the keyboard shortcuts for tracking:

	10 units	1 unit
Letterspaces	⌘ ⇧ [	⌘ ⌥ ⇧ [
Word spaces	⌘ ⌃ ⇧ [	⌘ ⌥ ⌃ ⇧ [

Word space tracking added by the Features Plus XTension does not show up in the Measurements palette as tracking. You can tell if you've used it in a paragraph only by clicking to the right of a spaceband. If a kern value shows in the Measurements palette, it's likely this paragraph has had word space tracking applied to it. You can remove these kerns—along with any other manual kerning done in the selected text—by choosing **Utilities→Manual Kerning**, a new option added to that menu by the Features Plus XTension.

TIP The preceding solutions are the softest approaches, since there's a good chance that discretionary hyphens, discretionary returns, and tracking won't cause you further problems when it's time to edit the paragraph again. The final two solutions should be used with caution, since they almost always cause problems when you come back for another editing session.

New line commands

What do you do when it's an entire word you need to move down to the next line and the word isn't already hyphenated? You use the new line (⇧↵) command (Figure 2.34). Actually, I'm presenting these solutions slightly out of order, since I will tend to use a new line command before tracking a paragraph. Even though it's a harder command, using new line is less likely to be noticed by the reader.

After scanning a paragraph for places to insert discretionary hyphens and returns, I look for lines ending in small words such as "a," "of," "an," "the," and "and." They needn't be on the line directly before the loose line, since knocking these small words down to the next line will often cause changes that ripple through the rest of the paragraph. A softer approach to this would be to replace the spaceband following a short word at the end of a line with a nonbreaking spaceband. That would force the small word to the next line without introducing the new line command at all.

One of the most prolific XTension developers is Dacques Viker of Vision's Edge. He regularly monitors the forum to get new ideas for XTensions, and he has uploaded his free XTensions for our members' use. They are: DocStamp XT, which inserts and updates the name of your document; the ViewLine and UtilitiesLine XTensions, which add dotted lines to out-of-control View and Utilities menus; and the Nudger Palette XTension, a new palette for easily moving items around on the screen.	◀▶	One of the most prolific XTension developers is Dacques Viker of Vision's Edge. He regularly monitors the forum to get new ideas for XTensions, and he has uploaded his free XTensions for our members' use. They are: DocStamp XT, which inserts and updates the name of your document; the ViewLine and UtilitiesLine XTensions, which add dotted lines to out-of-control View and Utilities menus; and the Nudger Palette XTension, a new palette for easily moving items around on the screen.

Figure 2.34 New line Note that I went all the way up to the second line to find a line ending with a small word. Inserting the new line command before the word "of" had a ripple effect through the rest of the paragraph.

TIP In many cases, it's not the actual number of characters being moved to another line that fixes a loose line, but rather the extra spaceband that now can be used to justify the line. I often count the spacebands on loose and tight lines to determine where I have the most chance for improving the paragraph spacing while doing the least amount of damage.

Hard hyphens

I really hate to even talk about this last solution, since judicious use of tracking can often create the same effect, but sometimes I actually insert a hard (normal) hyphen into the middle of a word that doesn't need to break (Figure 2.35). This pushes some of its letters to the next line, often fixing problems further down in the paragraph.

It's important to remember to also type a new line command after any hard hyphens you insert, since the combination will force any re-wrapping in subsequent passes to produce a short, ugly, easy-to-see line that will remind you to take out both commands. If you just type the hard hyphen, you will eventually end up printing a job that has a hard hyphen in the middle of a word, in the middle of a line. The addition of the new line command after each hard hyphen makes this hard formatting choice a lot more foolproof.

TIP This tip has nothing to do with loose lines and soft and hard solutions, but I figured we both could use a break. Those diamonds that I used in the examples to indicate which lines were being worked

In fact, one of the message
threads that follows this introduction
was started just six days after we
opened our doors! I picked it
because it highlights one of the key
strengths of any well-run forum: the
ability to partake in open and honest
dialogue between consumers and
vendors. (I also think it holds up well
over time.)

In fact, one of the message
threads that follows this introduc-
tion was started just six days after
we opened our doors! I picked it
because it highlights one of the key
strengths of any well-run forum: the
ability to partake in open and honest
dialogue between consumers and
vendors. (I also think it holds up well
over time.)

Figure 2.35 Hard hyphen Here I've added a hard hyphen in the middle of the word "introduction." I also added a new line command after the hard hyphen so that the hyphen doesn't end up in the middle of a line on subsequent correction passes.

on weren't produced with a pi font. Instead, I drew a half-point line and added arrowheads pointing in both directions. As nice as it would be to produce short, thin lines with proportionally sized arrowheads, QuarkXPress' limitations worked in my favor this time, since I quite like the diamond shapes it produced!

Paragraph widows

This type of widow is a little harder to define than the page widow. Essentially, it is a small word or a part of a word that sits alone as the last line of a paragraph. Some of my clients consider any partial word on the last line to be a widow; some will allow partial words, as long as the part of the word on the last line has at least four characters; and still others don't care if it's a full or partial word, as long as there are four or more characters. When in doubt, check with the client.

There are no QuarkXPress-based ways to prevent paragraph widows, so be prepared to look for them yourself. To get rid of them, use the same procedures outlined in the previous section. Either create more lines or reduce the number of lines through the use of the discretionary hyphen, discretionary return, tracking, word space tracking, new line, or hard hyphen commands.

The utility called XP8—discussed at length in the **Automating DTP** chapter and included on the disk—adds XPress Tags codes to text files being imported into QuarkXPress. Among its many talents, it can automatically insert discretionary hyphens before the last word of all the paragraphs in a file. This essentially prevents paragraph widows, although sometimes the second to last line of a paragraph will set too loose. As was discussed earlier, loose lines can be searched with the Bobzilla XTension.

3

Page Layout

CHAPTER 3 CONTENTS

FIGURES

I derive a genuine pleasure from bringing together the various elements that make up a page. From the scrap paper with hastily sketched pages surrounded by pica math to the pagination pass and all its frustrations—I enjoy my job. QuarkXPress provides a number of tools that both ease and add to the complexity of creating pages, depending on the type of page I'm trying to create. Almost all pages can use a grid structure, but not all require modifications to a master page or the creation of a template. Libraries can be handy in some cases, and an increasing number of jobs require anchored boxes that flow with text.

In the following pages, I illustrate different approaches to setting up new files, making use of master pages, editing templates, using libraries, anchoring boxes, and justifying pages. In each section, there are examples showing one of QuarkXPress' tools adding more work than it's worth, as well as examples of how certain tasks would be impossible without the same tool. In all cases, I try to recommend the best tool for a given job.

Creating pages

Many people spend far too *little* time in QuarkXPress' **File→New→Document** dialog box. Creating a solid base page is a little like creating a good foundation for a house. If you start your document with a solid structure, you can do almost anything to it without it tumbling down around you.

Take the time to type in the exact trim size of your publication, since everything else on the page will be placed in relation to the overall page area. Then figure out the size of the *type area*, which should be large enough to encompass all of the type on most of your pages. You can certainly break out of the type area for a special effect—such as a sash running diagonally across a page corner—but it will be your guide to consistent pages.

Calculating the type area

When setting books, magazine, or directories—anything that contains columns or pages of running text—it's important to make sure that the type area holds an exact number of lines of text. This will give you a visual cue as to how long or short your text is running. Not every job requires all columns and pages to line up at the bottom (thankfully!), but even when setting ragged-bottom pages you should be able to determine how far you are from the ideal length.

TIP I often sketch my page on a piece of paper before creating a new document, getting at least a rough idea of what my four margins and type area will be, but this isn't always necessary. Sometimes, in fact, it's more efficient to just make a new document and start experimenting. Each successive call to the New dialog box remembers the last set of figures you entered. Rather than switching to a master page and editing the Master Guides, I'll just hit Command-N (⌘ N) and modify the margin (usually) that needs adjustment, creating a new document to use for further experimentation.

The Nouveau II XTension allows you to save different document setups and reuse them whenever needed (Figure 3.1). You can name these setups and save them to the Nouveau Preferences file, as well as update and delete them at will.

Creating a grid structure

Whether or not you're going to have multiple columns of text, it's a pretty safe bet that you'll want to implement some sort of grid structure on your page. This is a tried-and-true method of maintaining consistency from page to page and helping your readers understand the logic of the design.

Establishing a grid structure in QuarkXPress is as simple as defining the number of columns and the gutter width in the **File→ New→Document** dialog box. This will automatically generate guides for you to use when creating text and graphic boxes on your pages. Do this even when you're not using an automatic text box, as the guides will still come in handy. Figure 3.2 illustrates three grid struc-

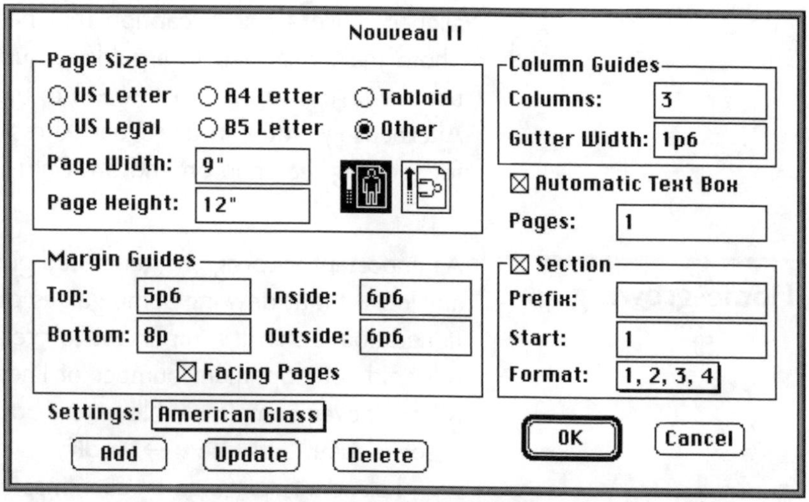

Figure 3.1 Nouveau II This XTension adds the capability to name new document settings and access them whenever you need them. You're also able to define the start of a new section when creating a new document.

tures: The first page uses a simple two-column grid; the second page has a three-column grid with a side area for illustrations or just white space, along with two columns of text; and the third page uses a five-column grid with a shaded sidebar straddling two of the grid columns, an illustration that straddles three of the grid columns, and three columns of text that also straddle three of the grid columns.

TIP I *always* leave **View→Snap to Guides** turned on, as there's not much point in setting up a grid if I'm going to be sloppy about using it. If I need something positioned close to a guide but not quite

Figure 3.2 Three grid structures The first page has a two-column grid; the second page shows a three-column grid; and the third page uses a five-column grid.

aligned—like a photo caption that needs to be two points from a photo that's snapped to a guide—I just switch to the Item tool and use the arrow cursors (↑←↓→) to move the item a point at a time. Alternatively, you can use QuarkXPress 3.2's new keyboard shortcut for toggling the snap on and off, Shift-Function-7 (⇧ F7).

Home-grown guides

As important as program-generated guides are, I can't imagine doing any job without drawing some guides of my own. For example, I mentioned above that it's important to create an automatic text box that will hold your optimum number of lines, but we all know that Quark XPress never completely fills a text box unless its Vertical Alignment is set to Justified in **Item→Modify**.

I place a ruler guide on each master page to show where the last baseline of each page should rest. This allows me to see approximately how far from the bottom of the type area the last baseline of text is resting on pages that are oddly spaced (due to subheads or other elements interrupting the text). I can also drag a guide down from the ruler and measure where the last baseline is. Then I subtract that number from the guide placed on the master page, and manually add space wherever appropriate to force that last baseline down to where it belongs.

TIP You can draw a ruler guide across an entire spread by clicking on the horizontal ruler, dragging down a ruler guide, and releasing the mouse on the pasteboard instead of within the page area. It would be handy to be able to draw one of these spread guides on master pages, but it won't show up on a document page unless drawn there. However, page guides drawn on a master page do appear on pages using that master page.

Whether used casually or with the greatest mathematical precision, having a "last baseline" guide at the bottom of each page will make it easier to create consistent pages. Ruler guides can be used for a lot of other things, too, such as aligning items on a page and indicating where the first line of text should rest on chapter-opening pages (Figure 3.3).

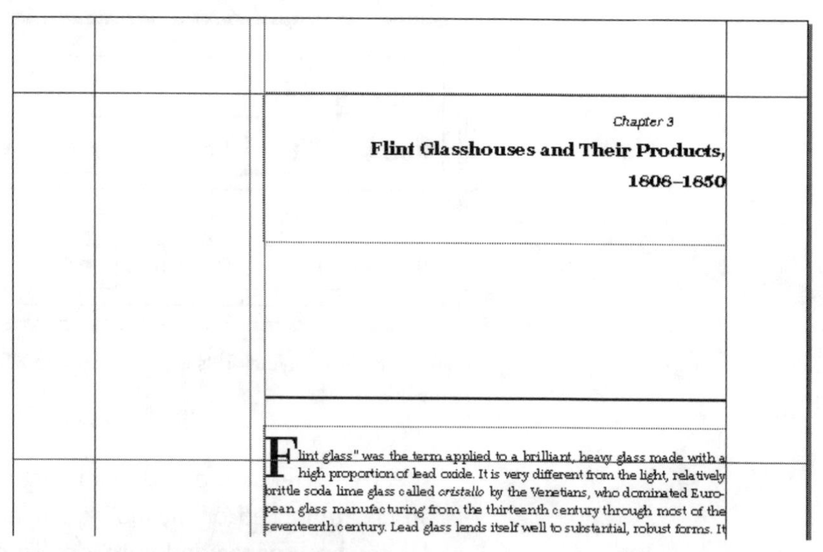

Figure 3.3 Ruler guides This page uses three ruler guides, all drawn originally on a master page. The horizontal guide marks the spot where the first baseline of text should rest; the two vertical ruler guides show where any side column illustrations should end and the text boxes begin.

Guide-creating XTensions

There are a number of XTensions on the market that help you create complete grid structures and individual guides. Grid Layout, Grid-Lock, Scitex Grids & Guides, and GuideLiner are all helpful; all allow precise placement of guides (something that's especially troublesome at odd views or if you have a shaky mouse hand); and all allow the assignment of different colors for guides that they generate. One thing nice about Grid Layout, by J. Michael Marriner and Robert Schwalbe, is the ability to define gutters to go between pairs of guides when creating a multi-column grid structure (Figure 3.4).

The Scitex Grids & Guides XTension is the most sophisticated of all these XTensions. You can define guides one at a time, specifying their numerical coordinates, color, and the view at which they appear. Complex grids can be created by specifying start and end points and the number of (or distance between) guides, and grids can be copied and pasted from page to page as well as saved and imported from other documents. You simply click on a guide to edit it, and it can be centered between another a pair of guides. You can also define guides along—or offset from—the edges of a text or picture box.

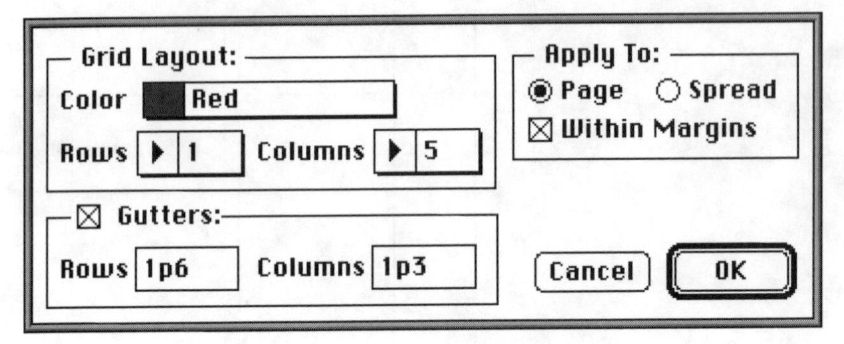

Figure 3.4 Grid Layout This is just one of the XTensions that allow you to create custom guides.

A free XTension called GuideLiner may be all you need, though. It can create locked or movable vertical guides, as well as horizontal guides for both pages and spreads. It's nice to be able to lock guides when distributing a template, for example. GuideLiner was written by Michael C. Kim, and it's included on the disk in the back of the book.

Master pages and templates

Every document you create in QuarkXPress uses at least one master page, whether or not you ask it to. On small jobs, you may want to completely ignore the master page, as I do. But on any jobs longer than one page, the proper use of master pages can save you a lot of time—especially at the corrections stage.

When you're producing multiple files for a large project, you'll want to be sure to work from a master template. A template can't accidentally be saved over itself, and it should contain all of a job's master pages, style sheets, hyphenation and justification information, and colors.

As mentioned in **Creating pages** (above), you can place helpful guides on a master page so that they appear on all pages using that particular master. You'll also want to draw any elements common to all or most of your pages, such as running heads or feet, folios (page numbers), and any decorative elements. The first couple of pages in a template may also contain guides and elements common only to those pages.

Multiple master pages

Having more than one master page is a necessity in many types of jobs. Sometimes the differences between masters are very minor. For example, in book work, it's not uncommon to use the current major heading as the running head or foot. I've found it convenient to pour the text into a document, create a new master page whenever I run into a new major head, and then apply the new master to the pages falling in that section. At other times, the differences between the pages in a document can be quite dramatic, as when they include a front page of a newsletter or a chapter opener in a book.

In the case of master pages with only minor differences between them, it's usually simplest to use the Document Layout palette to duplicate an already established master page and make minor changes manually. This saves you from having to set up from scratch—or copy from other master pages—the various elements already built into a standard page.

When it comes to drastically different master pages—for example, for part openers and chapter openers of a book—you will probably want to create completely new master pages. The layout will differ dramatically from that of a regular page in the document and may have none of the standard elements. Figures 3.5a–d show examples of duplicated and modified master pages.

Customizing master pages

When it's time to start creating all of these "exception" master pages, there are a few things you'll need to be aware of. First, the automatic box that you probably asked for when creating the new document will only appear on the A master and any masters that were made by duplicating it. If you create your new master pages from scratch, you will need to draw any necessary text boxes manually and link them to the automatic text chain yourself, if appropriate. All that entails is choosing the Linking tool, clicking on the master link in the upper left corner of your master page, and linking it to the newly drawn boxes.

TIP To help make matters simpler when dealing with multiple master pages, click on the master page name in the top half of the Document Layout palette and rename it. If your name starts with one,

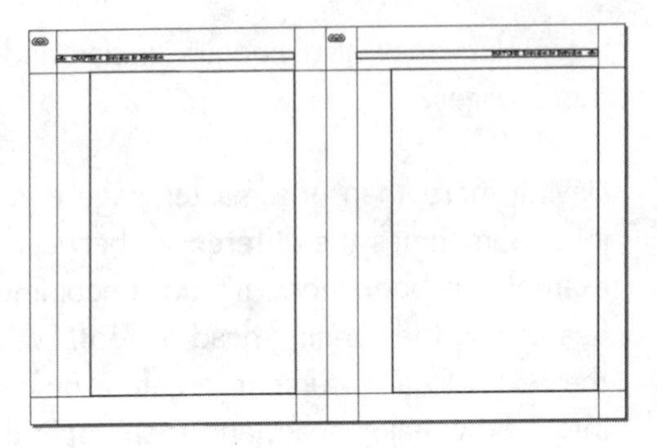

Figure 3.5a Master page for text This was the main master page used for flowing text in a book project I did recently.

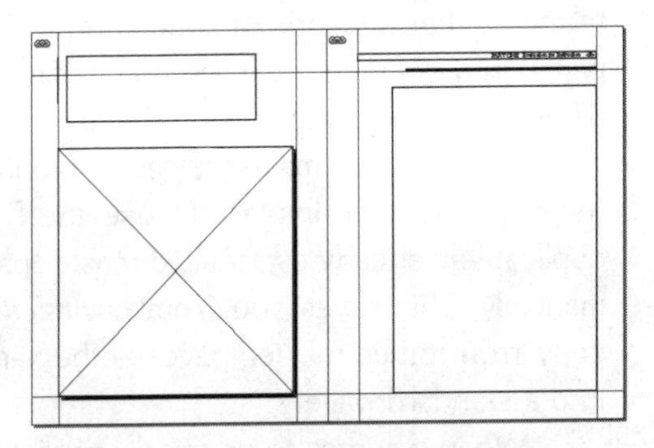

Figure 3.5b Master page for chapter opener Here's the chapter opening spread. Note that the recto (right page) is similar to the main text master page, but the verso (left page) is radically different and needed to be built from scratch.

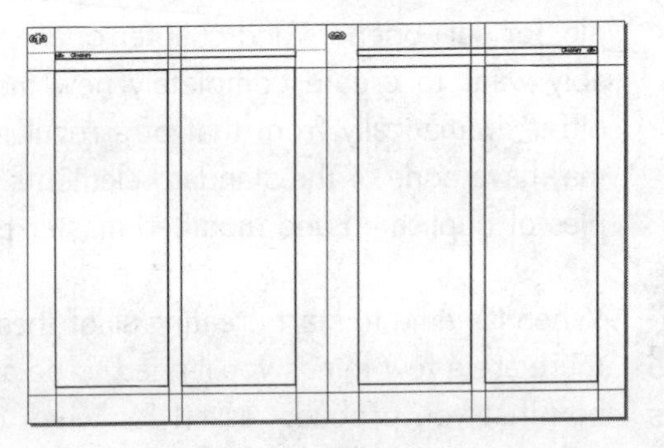

Figure 3.5c Master page for end matter Resource material at the end of each chapter needed to be set in a two-column layout, which was easily adapted from the main master page.

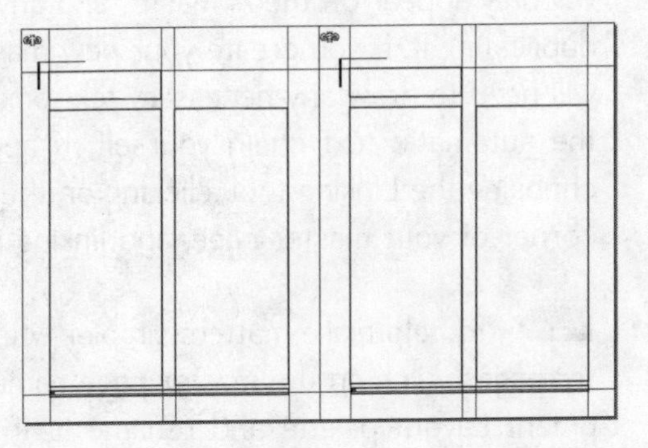

Figure 3.5d Master page for end matter opener Only one of these pages appeared in each chapter, depending on whether the end matter started on a recto or verso. It was further adapted from the end matter master page.

two, or three characters followed by a hyphen, those first few characters will be displayed on the icons for pages using that master page.

You'll probably need to do a bit of manual linking on the regular document pages, too, since text that's flowed into an automatic text chain using master page A, for example, will always create more of the same kind of page. Let's use Figures 3.5a–d to further explain this. If a file needs a chapter opener, a series of regular text pages, an end matter opener, and then a series of end matter pages, how would you actually produce the file?

Well, you could start by flowing all the text into the standard text page, since that's what most of the pages will need anyway. The only problem with this is that trying to apply a new master page to a page that already contains text—and expecting the text to reflow into the new layout—is often an invitation to disaster. You can try this method, as it sometimes works, but make sure you Save your document *before* experimenting.

Since I can usually be sure of how many exception pages will start a chapter, I place them in the Document Layout palette before flowing in the text. In our example, I can see that the chapter opener will be the first two-page spread in the file, so I drag a couple of those master pages to the top of the palette. Since this is a spread, I'll also need to make the first page start a new section, giving it an even starting page number so that it will stay on the left side.

TIP Since the folio on a right-hand page is always an odd number, QuarkXPress will insist on starting facing-page documents on a right-hand page unless you use the **Page→Section** command to change the first folio to an even number. As of version 3.3, a selected page's folio is displayed in the lower left-hand corner of the Document Layout palette. Clicking on the folio in the palette will get you into the Section dialog box quickly. Avoid using a number that's in use elsewhere in the document, since that can cause confusion when you are trying to print individual pages. Instead, use a very large number or—when dealing with front matter pages—a roman numeral.

When I've got my first two exception pages in place, I drag a regular text master page down below the opener pages in the palette, and then I manually link *all* of the text boxes of the opener spread through the first box of the regular text page. At this point, text flowed into the first page of the document will fill the opener pages, flow into the regular text page, and then continue to create more regular text pages until it runs out of copy (Figure 3.6).

But what about the end matter pages? You may be able to apply the end matter master page to the appropriate pages in the Document Layout palette and have the document pages automatically converted. Again, it's a hit-and-miss proposition. I wish I could tell you why this sometimes works and sometimes doesn't. After trying all sorts of permutations of complex and simple master pages using Keep and Delete Changes (**Edit→Preferences→General→Master Page Items**), I'm stymied as to why this works when it works. Since, above all, this is meant to be a practical book, I'd like to explain the way I usually add odd pages at the end of a file. Let's go through it step by step:

1 Save (⌘ S) the file, thus allowing you to choose **File→Revert to Saved** if you really mess up.

2 Select all the text in the file from the site of the insertion point to the end of the file by typing Command-Option-Shift-Down cursor (⌘ ⌥ ⇧ ↓), and then cut it.

3 Delete all the empty pages in the Document Layout palette (clicking on the first empty page and Shift-clicking on the last one really speeds this up).

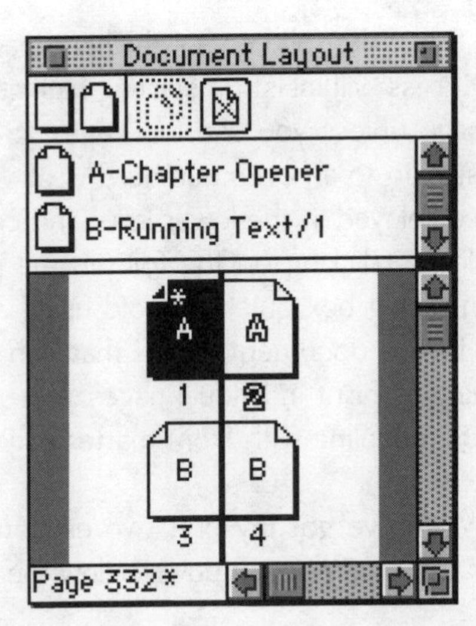

Figure 3.6 Document Layout palette The palette at the left is from a template that starts out with a chapter opening spread and is followed by regular text pages. The reason I named master page 2 "Running Text/1" is because there were a number of text master pages, each with a different running head to reflect section changes within the chapter.

4 Drag down the icon for the end matter opener and place it at the bottom of the Document Layout palette.

5 Add a couple of end matter text pages by dragging that icon down a few times.

6 Link them all together.

It should now be safe to Paste the text into this new chain of pages, starting at the top of the end matter opener page.

Stamping master pages

Many of us work in the world of letter-size laser printers, only outputting repro (resin-coated paper) or film at the very beginning of a job for samples and at the end for final output. In between, we're stuck with whatever we can image on those measly 8½ × 11 inches. A lot of the work I do ranges in size from 6 × 9 to 9 × 12 pages, and in all cases I want to help my clients and myself to identify a particular file name and version. This is especially important in the last stages of corrections when the client may spot something on an old proof and fax that to me for fixing.

The 6 × 9 stuff isn't much of a problem, since all I have to do is output it with registration marks. QuarkXPress will automatically add the name of the file, page number, and the time it was printed next to the top left crop mark. The closer I get to an 8½ × 11 page size, though, the harder it is to pull that off, even with Larger Print Area chosen in the **File→Page Setup** options. And with my 9 × 12 pages, I'm going to be using Manual Tiling to get the entire type area to show on the paper, so forget about registration marks.

TIP Using master pages and white space, I can usually work around this problem. I draw a text box—usually just outside the type area—and enter the name of the document, along with the words "page" or "galley" followed by the keyboard command for the current page number (⌘ 3). With this information imprinted on all pages of a document, I know that I'll be able to track down the page when a correction is needed. And when it's time to go for repro or film, I just go to the master page(s) and suppress the printout on any "stamping" boxes.

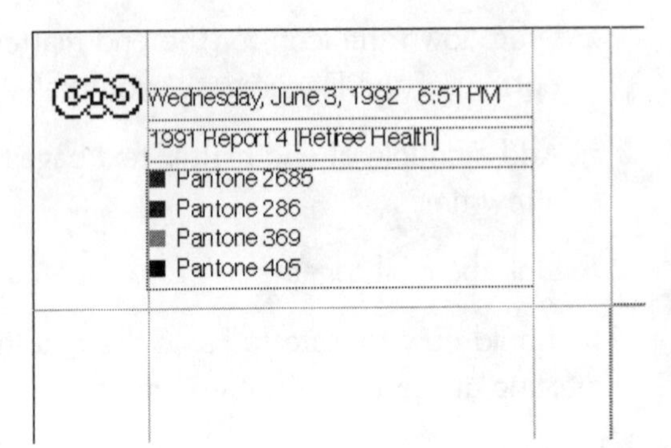

Figure 3.7 DocStamp and TimeStamp On this master page you can see both the DocStamp and TimeStamp XTensions in use, as well as a text box I created to show the PANTONE colors used in this document (which helps the client when I use the Print Colors as Grays option).

The DocStamp XTension, free from Dacques Viker of Vision's Edge and included on the disk in the back of this book, makes master page stamping even easier—some might say "idiot-proof." You draw your stamping box on the master page as described, but instead of typing in the document name, you tell the XTension to add a document stamp of its own (Figure 3.7). The stamp will be updated each time you save or open the file, so you can freely save under another name and not worry about having to go back to the master page and changing the information for each revision of the file.

The TimeStamp XTension, also from Vision's Edge, is a commercial product which adds a further enhancement to this process. TimeStamp allows you to stamp the date and time that the document was last saved. If you save the document before you print (which you should), this XTension essentially duplicates QuarkXPress' automatically produced time notification. With TimeStamp, you can also stamp the name of your Chooser device (which printer the job was output on) and the name of the day; you have five choices for the date format, and you can choose to leave the date off completely and just stamp the time. (I don't mind my clients knowing how late I work, but there are times that I'd prefer they didn't know I was working on the weekend.) TimeStamp includes DocStamp's features, too.

Converting files to templates

In the real world, the best time to commit to a template is after you've done a little work in a job. For example, I always set my sample pages or write and test my style and H & J sheets in a regular document—printing them out and fine-tuning them—before creating a template. On a book project, I may go so far as to set the first couple of chapters before committing to a template.

The reason for this is that no matter how many details you can keep in your head, you're bound to forget at least one—or the client will include at least one surprise. By doing some real work on the job, you'll discover areas that need to be adjusted. If you create a template at the very start of the job, real-world experience suggests that you'll be making a million small changes to your template. Continuously changing a template is a pain due to the very same reason we use them—a file name has to be given each time they're Saved.

If you follow the preceding suggestion, you'll find yourself with a live file that would make a pretty good template, if it didn't have all that text in it. The safest way to make your template from a live file is to duplicate the file in the Finder or do choose **File→Save As** (⌘ ⌥ S) before you begin. Then strip out all the text, along with any empty pages. You'll want to leave the first page, of course, and you may want to leave one or more other pages if they reflect special links between opening pages using different master pages. Choose **File→Save As** again, this time selecting Template instead of Document as the file type (Figure 3.8). QuarkXPress will automatically offer to make a preview of any templates it saves; as of version 3.2, you can specify that a preview is saved for a regular document, too.

It's usually a good practice to enter generic text for master page items that will change from file to file. In a book, the running head on the recto (right-hand) pages may be the chapter name, as it is in this book. If you typed in the name of the first chapter when you were setting up the job, you could leave that in the template, but that's a great way to accidentally end up with the first chapter's name at the top of the pages in the second and third chapters, too. In fact, I sent the

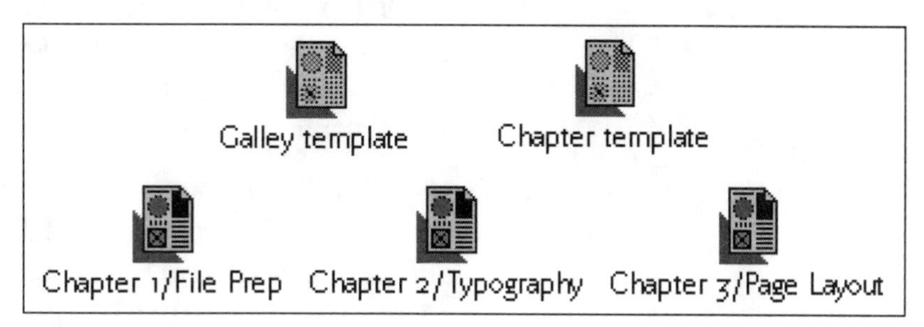

Figure 3.8 Templates and documents If you're viewing your job folder "by icon," you can easily see which files are templates; their icons are a ghost image of the regular document icons.

corrected and paginated version of the **Typography** chapter to Lynn, the proofreader, with "Text Preparation" as its recto running head. I should have re-read this chapter first, I guess.

To avoid ending up with the wrong text in the running head, I usually prefer to type in the words "chapter name." The text acts as a reminder to change the running head in each file. Even if I forget, I'll look less like an idiot to my clients if they see the generic text than if they see completely incorrect text at the top of the pages. Of course, if the book name goes at the top of most of the verso (left-hand) pages, I'll type it into the template and only change it on the files that require it, if any.

Editing the template

No matter how safe you play it, you're bound to run into something that wasn't considered when the template was created. At that point, you migt want to ask yourself: Will you ever see this exception again, and does it need to be added to the template? (Psychic powers should be a prerequisite in this business.) Here are a few examples of exceptions that you may run into. Each of them may require different solutions depending on the job and your work environment, but let me explain how I might treat them.

■ After having set up style sheets for plain text, hanging bulleted lists, and indented extracts in your template, you discover part way through the job that there is a bulleted list *inside of* an extract.

In this case, I'd probably create a new style sheet for a bulleted list that is both indented and hanging, and then I'd move that style sheet into the template. The quick and dirty method? Just make a copy of the paragraph that uses the new style sheet and paste it into the template; the new style sheet will be carried over. If you've made a number of new style sheets, then it might be worthwhile to use the Append function in the H & J styles dialog box.

■ The first few files in your job contain partial-page illustrations that all fit easily within the type area, but then you run into a full-page, broadside (turned sideways) illustration.

I could make a new master page without a running head (and possibly a different set of guides), but only if I thought this was going to happen often or if I was going to have to hand the job over to someone else to finish. It's much more likely that I would just cover the running head with the broadside table, or delete the running head text from that one page.

■ After you have produced letters pages for three issues of a magazine, all of a sudden the editor has taken to responding to the letters (in a different type style, of course).

Here I'd probably assume that I'll need the new style sheet in future issues, so I'd make it a part of the template.

■ In a special holiday issue of a newsletter, 10 extra contributor names need to be crammed into an already packed masthead.

Even though the text specs will require changes to accommodate extra contributors, I might not even change the style sheet in the current file, let alone move it to the template. I'd probably just change the specs by hand.

What this really all comes down to is this: Is the exception going to occur often enough that you would regularly need to make a manual change, or to remember what the heck you did last time? Your solution will almost always entail changing the template if you are handing the job over to someone else to produce. Otherwise, you need to decide whether or not it's worth the hassle.

Libraries and anchored boxes

QuarkXPress' Library feature is underutilized by most users of the program. If you find yourself leaving copies of things on the pasteboard or on a master page for future use; searching through a file, or files, looking for an element you've already used; or repeating the same box creation, styling, and alignment tasks over and over, you need to seriously consider using libraries to speed up your production.

Libraries are really only highly structured QuarkXPress documents. In fact, each open library takes away from the number of regular documents that you can have open at one time—a maximum of 25. Unlike regular documents, though, you can name the items in a library and see a thumbnail view of each. You also need to make sure that the Auto Library Save option is turned on in the **Edit→Preferences→Application** dialog box.

Using libraries

The most common use of libraries is for the storage of logos or other often-used items. You might have your own company's logo in a library that's placed on everyone's machine or on a file server. You could also place logos for a particular client in a library. For example, AT&T has a gazillion different logos that need to be used in different contexts. By placing them all in a library and then naming them, you'll have them all handy and you'll be able to refer to the names to help decide which to use in a given context.

The contents of a library aren't limited to artwork, though. Text boxes can be dragged into a library, too. While producing this book, I've been using a copy of the screen shot caption box that's stored in a library. The box contains a sample caption, already properly styled, so all I have to do is select the text and type over it when I'm writing a new caption.

Tons of time can be saved when you're working on a project that has common elements that relate to one another. The best example is a photograph, its caption, and the photo credit. Credit lines are often bottom- or top-aligned with a photo, and captions should start a consistent amount of space above or below the photo or other artwork. Having gone to the trouble of setting up this relationship once, why would you want to repeat the procedure over and over?

It's wise to group these elements when finished. Once grouped, they can be dragged into a library and named (Figure 3.9). You may want to create other versions of your group for eventualities that require the credit to be on the left instead of the right, or for photos that straddle two columns instead of one. This can be done while setting up the job; or you can create new groups as needed. But it's a good idea to start with a similar group already in the library, modify it, and drag the new group back into the library, naming it for easy finding next time you need it.

TIP Library elements are named by double-clicking on each one and typing in a name. Although you can sometimes tell what an element is just by the library's thumbnail view, the scaling that Quark

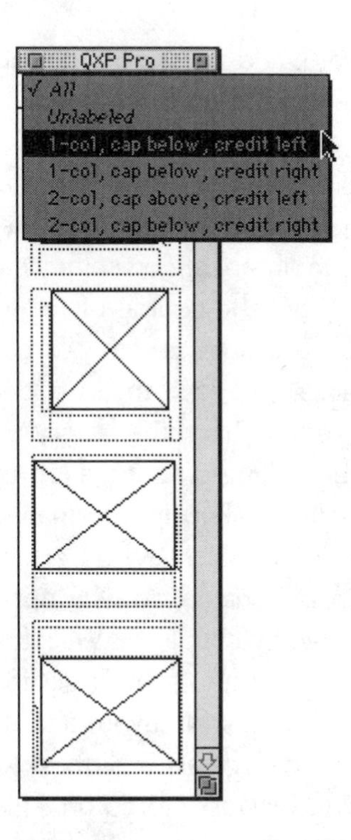

Figure 3.9 Grouped items in a library This small library contains four useful groups of items, all of which are graphic boxes with properly aligned text boxes for captions and credits. Note also how the list of elements is alphabetized, bearing no resemblance to the actual order shown in the main library window.

XPress uses for each library element differs. So it pays to give the element a descriptive name. Be careful what you name it, though, since more than one element in a library can use the same name!

Division and organization

Large companies—and even small studios—may find that libraries are a convenient way to split up the tasks involved in creating a large or complicated project. It's not uncommon for even a small brochure to contain complex illustrations, and the person laying out the pages in QuarkXPress may not be the same one creating the artwork. Libraries are a good way to send screen previews of illustrations to outsource (freelance) personnel who may not need the actual files but who do need the dimensions of the miscellaneous page elements.

One of my clients uses this procedure: High-resolution scans are made for all the photographs in a project, and then they are imported to a dummy QuarkXPress document. Each photo is dragged into a library and named. Only the screen previews and path names (the location on your hard disk) for the photos are retained, so the library itself is of a manageable size. They send me the library, the text files, and the template, and I paginate the job. When I give them the finished files, they put them back on their hard drive and are able to print them to an imagesetter at full resolution, since the path names for the photos will automatically find the original scanned photo.

Besides photos, they often give me Aldus FreeHand and Adobe Illustrator files in libraries. For some reason, these often need to be updated throughout the course of the job, so it's not uncommon for them to send me a library with corrected illustrations. When correcting the pages, all I have to do is delete the old picture box and drag the new version from the library.

If you are working on a large job that contains a lot of artwork, it makes sense to break it up into manageable chunks. You're probably already doing this anyway, by placing art in folders labeled, for example, by chapter name, so why not create libraries with the artwork broken down by chapters? Well, for one reason, it's a royal pain.

Manually creating lots of large libraries makes sense if you're sending out lots of files for layout and pagination, since it means you won't have to send large artwork files. And if you're working in a studio that has all its artwork stored on a file server, you should certainly consider making libraries to avoid the overhead of pulling the illustrations over the server. But if you're the only one who's going to touch a file, it probably doesn't make sense to use libraries to organize the artwork. It would add a layer of work that won't gain you any benefits.

TIP The AutoLib XTension from Vision's Edge can create libraries for you, in an automatic and painless manner. It can grab all the graphics in a selected folder, make a library, put all the graphics in boxes, and add them to the library. It will even use the file name of each graphic to name the items in the library for you!

Commercial libraries

Quark, Inc. sells collections of clip art that have already been put in libraries and named (Figure 3.10). The libraries come with the Adobe Illustrator files that were used to create them so you can edit the art, if necessary. The packages are Arts & Entertainment, Business, Calendar, Communications, Energy & Environment, Flags, Food & Nutrition, Health, Holidays, Home & Garden, Leisure, Maps, Medieval Illustrated Caps, Modern Illustrated Caps, Patterns, Publishing, Sports, and Travel.

Figure 3.10 Quark's Energy & Environment library Here are just a few of the many images that come with this library. I've used many of them for a newsletter I produce for an environmental organization.

I own the Energy & Environment and Flags packages, and have used them extensively. I even needed to combine art from the two packages when I wanted to add an atom to the center of the (then) U.S.S.R. flag, as shown in the chapter on **Graphics**.

Random extracts

It's common practice these days to allow a chunk of white space to remain on the sides of pages, and I heartily applaud this. Ample use of white space allows the eyes to relax and draws the brain to the contents of the page. White space is not sacrosanct, though. You can use it for placement of related graphics, subheads for the accompanying text, or even entire paragraphs of definitions. Just remember not to completely fill it up, or it won't be relaxing white space anymore!

If you're just going to be using side columns for random extracts or graphics, define your document or master pages with extra-large margins (left, right, inside, or outside). Let your automatic text box occupy only the type area that will be used for flowing text, even if your chapter opener will straddle both the text area and the white space (side column).

This method is simplest when use of the side column is rare. Assuming that there will be some extracts from the text or a few graphics in that area, go ahead and draw some vertical guides on your master pages so that you'll have something to use for alignment. I do a project every year that requires bar charts in the side columns of many pages, and I draw guides in four places: a couple of picas from the outside edge of the page; the required amount of offset

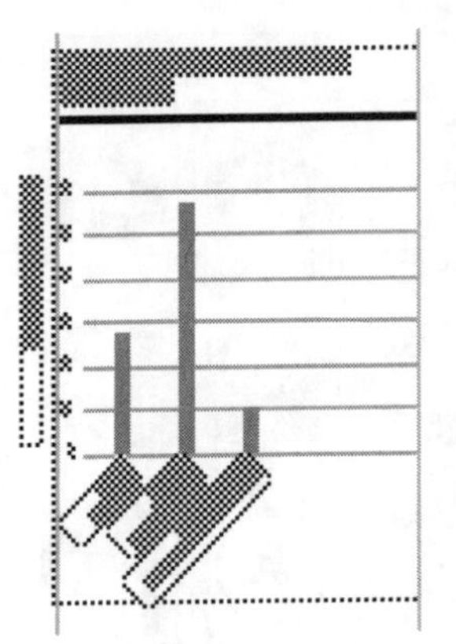

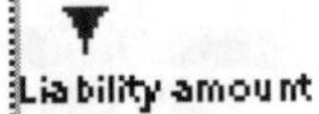

Figure 3.11 Side Column with random extracts The automatic text box flows independent of the graphic in the side column. The graphic is snapped to guides placed on the master page and vertically aligned by eye.

from both sides of the type area; and a couple of picas from the inside (binding) of the page (Figure 3.11).

Of course, you can also draw some horizontal guides if there will be consistency in the vertical placement of elements being positioned in the side columns. I eyeball the vertical placement most of the time.

Flowing anchored boxes

If you're in this business long enough, you're bound to run into a designer who specifies side heads that need to sit next to—and move along with—running text. Or maybe you *are* that designer. You can use the same setup as described above, drawing guides and, subsequently, new text boxes for each head. Then align the head boxes with the text, and manually move them each and every time the text reflows. This is not an optimal solution, obviously. What we want to do is set up the job in a way that allows maximum flexibility with a minimum of fuss at the editing stage.

Anchored boxes on the left

If you have one column of text and the heads are always to the left, as in this book, the solution is actually pretty easy. Just define one large text box that encompasses the text area and the side column, indenting all of your text (in style sheets, of course) to move it over the proper amount. Then create one extra style sheet that's pretty much the same as a normal text paragraph and remove the indent.

You may also end up adding extra space above it, or even a rule above it, but that's incidental.

Your heads will go in an anchored text box that gets pasted into the beginning of any paragraphs that don't have an indent. If you just have a few of these heads—and you probably don't, since then you would use the method described above under **Random extracts**—you could draw the box for them on the pasteboard, choose the Item tool, cut the box, go back to the Content tool, and paste the box into the text stream (Figure 3.12).

TIP Another method of using multiple text boxes is to create a library and drag a properly sized subhead box into it. Then whenever you need a box to paste into the text, all you have to do is click on its icon in the library, copy it, and paste it into the text stream. Note that I didn't say anything about changing tools: This procedure works perfectly well while remaining with the Content tool—and you don't have to draw a box of the appropriate width each time you need one. If you're typing the subhead yourself, be sure also to apply a style sheet to the beginning of the text box before adding it to the library, as it will save you time each time you use it.

For some projects, it's easy enough to resize anchored boxes so that they provide an indent for the entire paragraph to which they're attached. For **QuarkXPress Unleashed**, however, paragraphs with side heads have to break across pages. Instead of resizing the anchored boxes, I typed a Tab and an Indent Here command (⌘ \)

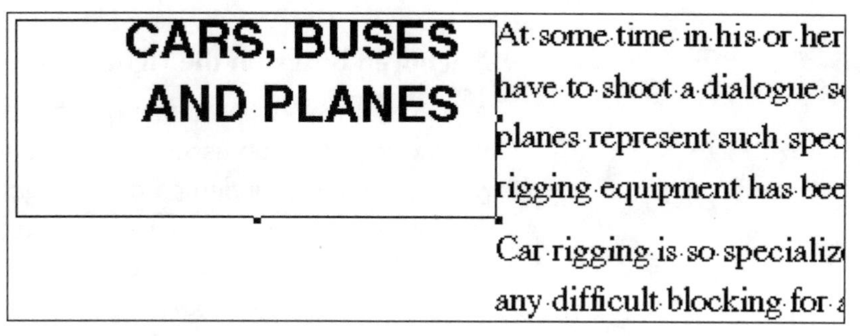

Figure 3.12 Side column with flowing sideheads The head shown here is in an anchored text box that's pasted into the beginning of a paragraph with no left indent. The style sheet for the head has a right indent to offset it from the text.

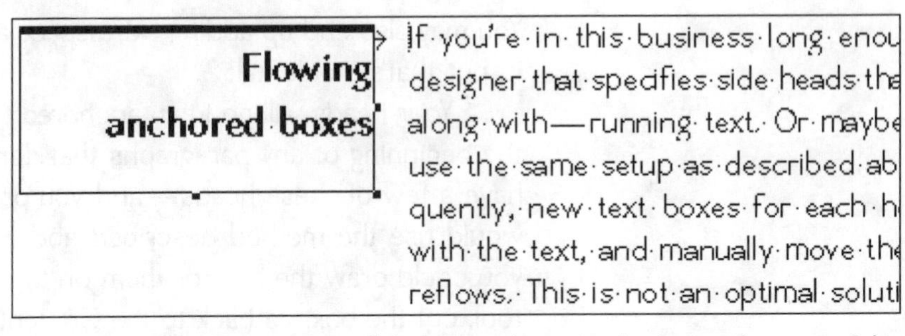

Figure 3.13 Indent Here command I suppose it's a tad redundant to show one of this book's subheads as an example, but the method used to produce them differed from the previous example. Here I'm using a Tab and Indent Here command.

(Figure 3.13). Even though I started writing this book in QuarkXPress 3.11, I had blind faith that by the time I paginated it—in version 3.3, as it turns out—the Indent Here command would honor indents in paragraphs breaking across pages. And so it does, as of version 3.3!

There are two more steps that you will invariably have to perform whether you use the library method or draw each box manually. You'll need to both change the alignment of the anchored text box and adjust its depth. By default, the alignment of the anchored text box will be set to the Baseline of the line of text you've pasted it into. You can change it by selecting the box and going to **Item→Modify** (⌘ M), or by clicking in the top left corner of the Measurements palette, which will show the icon for Ascent alignment. The depth of the box should be adjusted from the handle in the middle of the bottom of the box, since messing with the lower right-hand handle will risk changing the width of the box.

Anchored boxes on the right

A job requiring anchored text boxes to be placed on the right side of flowing text is set up essentially the same as above, except that most paragraphs will be indented on the right instead of the left. Also, the anchored boxes will need to be pasted somewhere *inside* the first line of the paragraph instead of at the beginning. Expect to have to try a few times to get the box where you want it!

It's not uncommon to have to use a New Line command (⇧ ↩) to move a piece of a word that insists on following your anchored item on the same line, and you may find that an option tab will be needed to move the item over to the right edge of your text box. If the type to the left of the anchored box is too close, you'll need to manually break those lines with the New Line command or add an outset to the anchored box using **Item→Runaround**. Unfortunately, once it's anchored, it's too late to add the outset.

TIP A quick and dirty way to get a copy of your anchored item is to select and duplicate it with **Item→Duplicate** (⌘ D). This will give you a non-anchored text or graphic box which you can then make changes to and paste back into the text. The way that text outsets are translated when an item is anchored to text is pretty strange: The left, bottom, and right outset values are ignored, and the top value is used for all four sides once anchored. When an anchored box is duplicated, all four sides will have the outset that was previously set for the top. (Don't holler at me; I didn't write the program, just the book.)

Anchored boxes on the inside or outside

The only reason I would smile upon the arrival of a job involving this kind of design would be the thought of how much money I'd make. If you're working for someone else, you'd probably smile at the hours of overtime you'll accrue. If you're on salary, you might want to start your vacation. (Make sure you stay out long enough for the job to get finished, of course.)

Actually, it doesn't have to be all that bad, but there are a few things you really need to do up front to preserve your sanity later on. Planning for the inevitable corrections pass on this kind of job, I would insist on producing what I call "paged galleys" the first time through. Paged galleys have the correct amount of type flowed into each page and usually include running heads and folios. The anchored boxes would all be inserted on the left for the paged galley stage of production. Moving them to the right on right-hand pages (if the job calls for outside placement), or to the right on left-hand pages (if the job calls for inside placement) comes after the majority of corrections that will reflow the text have been made.

Now, here's the tricky part: Make your automatic text box big enough to contain your text and *both* left- and right-hand anchored boxes (Figure 3.14). Give all your style sheets both left and right indents, and make a set of style sheets that remove one or the other.

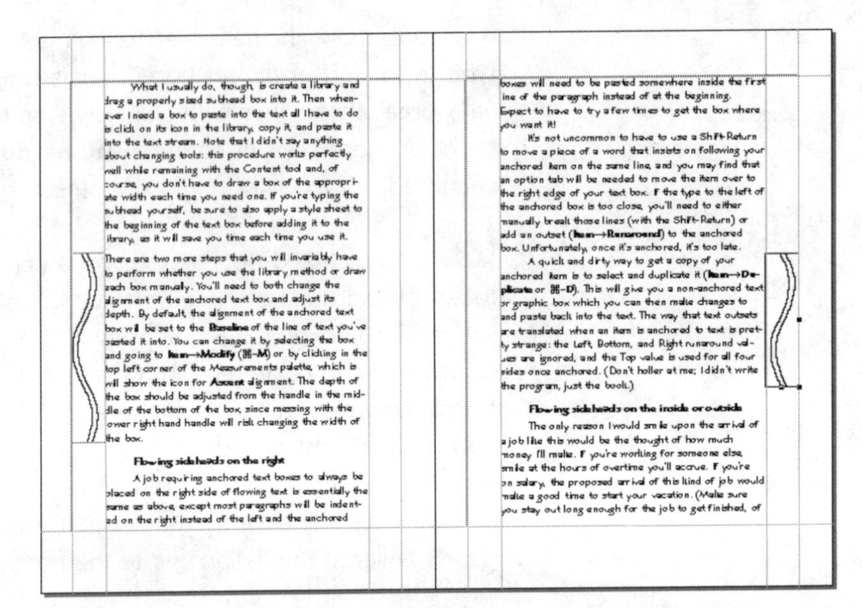

What I usually do, though, is create a library and drag a properly sized subhead box into it. Then whenever I need a box to paste into the text all I have to do is click on its icon in the library, copy it, and paste it into the text stream. Note that I didn't say anything about changing tools: this procedure works perfectly well while remaining with the Content tool and, of course, you don't have to draw a box of the appropriate width each time you need one. If you're typing the subhead yourself, be sure to also apply a style sheet to the beginning of the text box before adding it to the library, as it will save you time each time you use it.

There are two more steps that you will invariably have to perform whether you use the library method or draw each box manually. You'll need to both change the alignment of the anchored text box and adjust its depth. By default, the alignment of the anchored text box will be set to the **Baseline** of the line of text you've pasted it into. You can change it by selecting the box and going to **Item→Modify** (⌘-M) or by clicking in the top left corner of the *Measurements* palette, which is will show the icon for **Ascent** alignment. The depth of the box should be adjusted from the handle in the middle of the bottom of the box, since messing with the lower right hand handle will risk changing the width of the box.

Flowing sideheads on the right

A job requiring anchored text boxes to always be placed on the right side of flowing text is essentially the same as above, except most paragraphs will be indented on the right instead of the left and the anchored boxes will need to be pasted somewhere inside the first line of the paragraph instead of at the beginning. Expect to have to try a few times to get the box where you want it!

It's not uncommon to have to use a Shift-Return to move a piece of a word that insists on following your anchored item on the same line, and you may find that an option tab will be needed to move the item over to the right edge of your text box. If the type to the left of the anchored box is too close, you'll need to either manually break those lines (with the Shift-Return) or add an outset (**Item→Runaround**) to the anchored box. Unfortunately, once it's anchored, it's too late.

A quick and dirty way to get a copy of your anchored item is to select and duplicate it (**Item→Duplicate** or ⌘-D). This will give you a non-anchored text or graphic box which you can then make changes to and paste back into the text. The way that text outsets are translated when an item is anchored to text is pretty strange: the Left, Bottom, and Right runaround values are ignored, and the Top value is used for all four sides once anchored. (Don't holler at me; I didn't write the program, just the book.)

Flowing sideheads on the inside or outside

The only reason I would smile upon the arrival of a job like this would be the thought of how much money I'll make. If you're working for someone else, smile at the hours of overtime you'll accrue. If you're on salary, the proposed arrival of this kind of job would make a good time to start your vacation. (Make sure you stay out long enough for the job to get finished, of

Figure 3.14 Flowing sideheads on the outside The two paragraphs containing the artwork use two different style sheets that remove their left and right indents, respectively. All other paragraphs have both left and right indents in their style sheets.

Paragraphs requiring anchored boxes will at first use the style sheet that removes the left indent, but you'll change that when you need to move the anchored items on the final (we hope) pass of the job.

Vertical justification

The need to align the tops and bottoms of columns on a page or spread is not uncommon. You may need to align the text of multiple stories in a newsletter, side-by-side columns in a magazine, or facing pages in a book. Or you might need to stretch your text from the top to the bottom of a page for a cover page on a report. Let's talk about each of these examples, but remember: For your particular job, you might find that the solution I discuss for books is actually what you need in order to fix your magazine pages, or vice versa. Read through all the examples before deciding what might work best for a specific project.

Covering a cover page

QuarkXPress' built-in vertically justified alignment setting is the easiest way to spread text across the depth of a page. Instead of accepting the default Top alignment in the **Item→Modify** dialog box, you'll want to choose Justified and fill in a value for the interparagraph maximum (Figure 3.15).

TIP It's important to note that Justified Vertical Alignment often fails when another item interrupts the text flow in a justified box. For example, if you place a graphic box in the middle of a justified column of text, it will automatically revert to a top alignment. However, if the interruption *completely covers* the top or bottom of the column, vertical justification resumes. QuarkXPress can't do the math involved with vertically justifying text around objects, but if the objects leave no room in which to put text, there's no extra math involved and the program works as advertised. In fact, multiple objects can be placed at the tops and bottoms of justified columns; as long as they don't leave any empty space in the column, justification should work.

Gross amounts of space are frequently called for in the interparagraph maximum box in **Item→Modify**. This is because of the

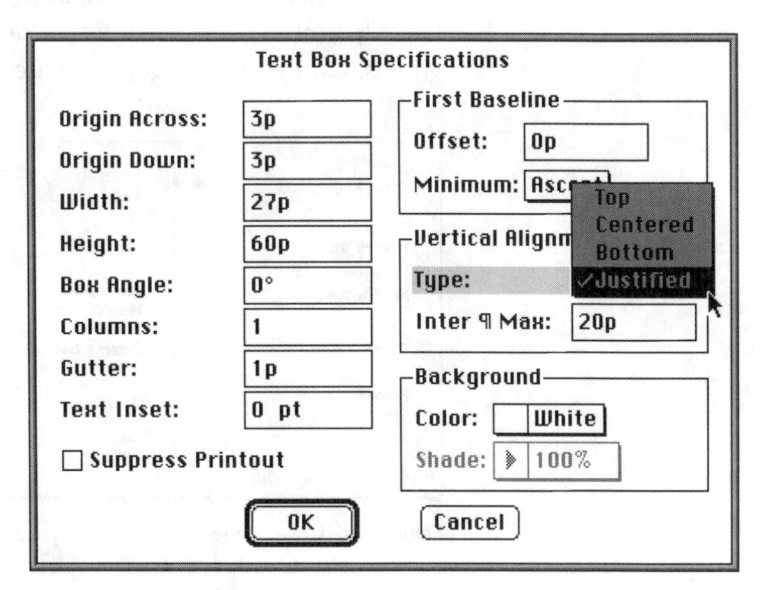

Figure 3.15 Vertical Alignment You can adjust the interparagraph maximum value when using the Justified option for text boxes.

way this alignment option works. When vertically justifying text, Quark XPress tries to add space between all the lines in the text box. This is commonly called "feathering" or "carding." If you have three lines of text on the cover of a report and you simply want the first line at the top of the page, the second line in the middle of the page, and the last line at the bottom of the page, you can ignore the interparagraph maximum setting, allowing all the extra space on the page to be divided evenly between all the lines. However, if you have blocks of text that you're trying to spread out on the page, then the interparagraph maximum setting comes in handy.

In Figure 3.16, there are three paragraphs on each page: the year, the name of the report, and the report number. Remember that Quark XPress defines a paragraph as any number of lines terminated with a New Paragraph command. The short lines of the second paragraph shown here could be created with a right indent or with New Line commands.

On the first page of the example, we see the results of choosing the Justified Vertical Alignment option without assigning any interparagraph maximum; the space is evenly divided between the lines. The second page shows what would happen if we defined a very large interparagraph maximum, such as 20 picas; the paragraphs are logically broken apart as all the extra space is placed between paragraphs. On the third page, there are two extra New Paragraph com-

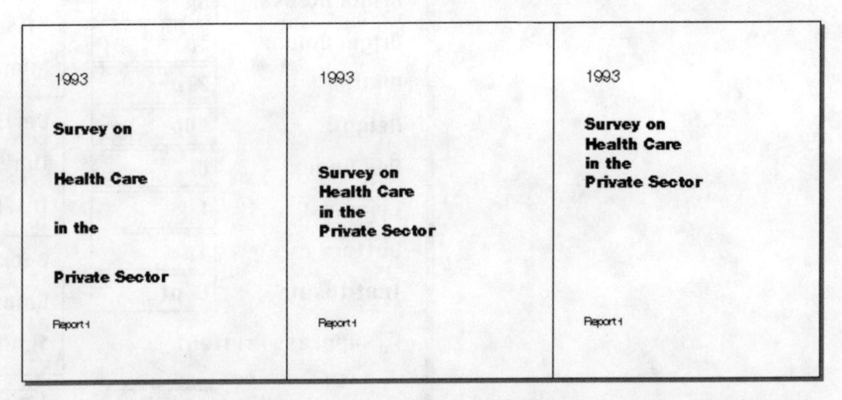

Figure 3.16 Cover pages The first two pages shown here have only two New Paragraph commands each: one after "1993" and the other after "Private Sector." Avoiding the excess use of New Paragraph commands is important when vertically justifying a page. The third page has two extra New Paragraph commands after "Private Sector."

mands after the report name. Although I don't believe in achieving space by adding extra New Paragraph commands, such a method works well in vertically justified text since it allows you to define and maintain proportions between text blocks.

TIP There shouldn't be a New Paragraph command at the end of a vertically justified text box, since that would cause the last paragraph to move up and a proportional amount of space placed at the bottom of the page. Of course, that might be what you want sometimes.

Aligning newsletter stories

For simple newsletters, you may also be able to use the Justified Vertical Alignment option. Feathering of text and adding space between paragraphs can both be used to achieve alignment of stories at the bottom of a page.

In the second cover page in the preceding example, the inter-paragraph maximum was set to a very large number in order to force all extra space in the column to go between the paragraphs. You can also use a more subtle amount, say, 3 to 6 points, to designate that the program add up to that amount between paragraphs before starting to feather. In cases where you have a handful of paragraphs in a column and are only a line or two short, no feathering would end up taking place. Instead, a little bit of space would be added between paragraphs.

If you don't want space between the paragraphs or the lines of a paragraph, then you'd better count on the kindness of subheads. Adjust their Space Before and After settings to align bottoms of columns. Any short columns that don't have any subheads will have to be left short unless you can pull off some other, nonvertical-spacing trick (as discussed in the **Typography** chapter), since you will have run out of options at this point. There really is a lot to be said for setting newsletters rag-bottom (also called bouncy-bottom), possibly adding a decorative rule across the bottoms of the pages to give it a clean, consistent look across pages.

Aligning magazine columns

It's a pretty good bet that you won't be able to get away with using QuarkXPress' Justified Vertical Alignment option in a magazine. Page after page of text with different leading (which is, after all, what feathering causes) or gapped paragraphs is going to be noticeable (and ugly). If you're setting a design-intensive magazine, you may be able to get away with rag-bottom pages, but I wouldn't count on it. All in all, this industry is pretty rigid on what is allowable and what is not.

Your first line of defense against problems at the bottoms of columns has nothing to do with page layout, but rather with type specs. Magazines are usually inundated with subheads, so make sure that their specifications are set up in a logical manner (Figure 3.17). Let's start with a simple example. If you're setting 10 point text on 12 point leading (usually indicated as 10/12), make sure that all the spacing in and around your subheads adds up to an even multiple of the text leading. If you have a one-line subhead that sets 12/14, whatever spacing you add above and below it should add up—with the leading—to a multiple of 12 (the text leading). Sixteen points of space above the head and 6 points below would add to the 14 point leading to produce a total of 36 points of overall spacing, or an even three lines of text.

The number of plans permitting only one or two transfers a year fell from 42 to 25 percent over the past two years.

Investment direction

In the past two years, the number of plans in which employees can direct the investment of all funds—their own and also their employers' contributions—has risen from 61 to 70 percent. The number of plans in which employees may direct only a portion of the money (usually their own contributions, as opposed to employer matching and profit-sharing contributions) has dropped from 30 percent to 20 percent.

Other provisions give employees greater control

Many sponsors have added plan provisions allowing participants some access to their savings plan funds. Most permit hardship withdrawals (89 percent). Almost half allow non-hardship,

Figure 3.17 Magazine column aligning In this example, we have 9 point type on 15 points of leading. The subheads are 8.5/11. One-line subheads have 2 picas of space before and 10 points of space after them, meaning that they take up 45 points of total space (24 + 11 + 10), or an even three lines worth of text leading. The two-line heads get an additional 4 points of space above them to make up for the second line of the head that adds 11 points of leading (28 + 11 + 11 + 10 = 60).

By following this method of determining your type specs, you're actually accomplishing two things: There's a much greater chance that your columns will fall into place at the bottom of the columns, and the baselines of your text will align across columns. Of course, all bets are off if the subhead falls at the top of the column. In that case, you'll probably have to add extra space below the subhead, or make up for the space lost from above the subhead somewhere else in the column.

You can also experiment with defining a baseline grid (**Edit→ Preferences→Typographic**) and then locking the text or the heads (or both) to the grid, but I usually find this too restrictive. Perhaps if it were a text-box level command instead of a document-wide command I wouldn't feel this way. In Figure 3.17, for example, locking everything to a 15 point grid would mess up the heads, since they only use 11 points of leading. Locking only the text to the grid would be okay, I guess, but then the heads would always have to be manipulated by hand, since the text below the heads would always be yanked down to the next grid line and the extra space caused by the heads would end up falling after the heads, instead of before them.

Aligning book pages

Book pagination differs from magazine pagination in that you usually don't have to worry about alignment of text baselines across spreads except at the tops and bottoms of pages. You'll still want to get the spacing in and around your heads to add up to even multiples of the text leading, though, since that will help a lot at the bottom of the page. The forces working against you in alignment of book pages are all the extra things that tend to crop up, such as extracts, bulleted lists, footnotes, and illustrations. It's all fine and dandy to have your head spacing add up properly, but the chance of all the spacing on these other elements adding up nicely is pretty slim.

It's rare to see extra space being added between paragraphs in a book to get the pages to align on the bottom, but that's one place that you might be able to use feathering. If you keep the the Vertical Alignment option's interparagraph maximum setting at zero, any extra space needed to fill a page will get added between the lines on a page. On a 36-line page that's only one line (of 12 point leading) short, so only one-third of a point would be added to each line; that shouldn't look bad at all. If you were two lines short, then two-thirds of a point would be added to each line.

TIP I can't stress enough how important it is to get a client's permission before deciding to feather a book. Most of the traditional book publishers I've worked with here in New York City would have a cow if they found out I feathered a page without their permission.

With books, it's also possible to set spreads a line short or long, meaning that our 36-line page would be reduced to 35 lines or expanded to 37 lines for the duration of the spread. It's important, though, to avoid having a short spread precede or follow a long spread, as your readers will notice a two-line jump.

Most of the books I typeset require that I take all the extra space on a page and split it up proportionally above elements that already have Space Before settings in their style sheets. If I have a head with 12 points of Space Before, a subhead with 6 points Space Before, and an extract with 3 points Space Before and After on a page that's one 12 point line short, I would add 6 more points before the head, 3 more points before the subhead, and 1.5 points both before and after the extract. Even with the easy numbers I used for this example, you can readily see how difficult this can be.

The Xstyle XTension, from Em Software, is absolutely essential for those times that you need to vertically justify a page manually. By just clicking in a paragraph you can get a complete report on all the spacing in effect, and you can edit that spacing, too (Figure 3.18). There's a demo version of Xstyle on the disk in the back of the book.

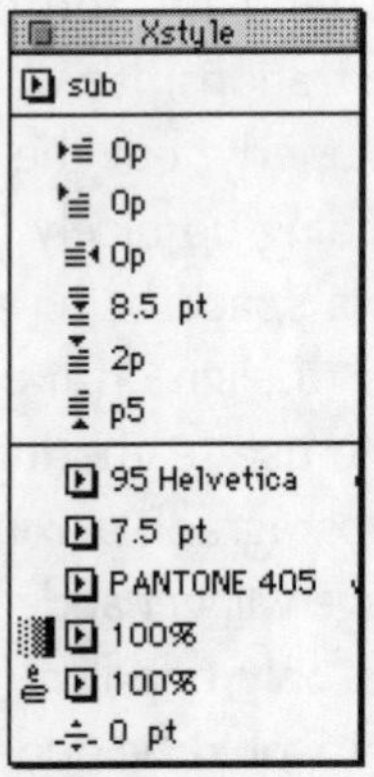

Figure 3.18 Xstyle's Character/Paragraph Settings palette The palette—shown above in its horizontal style and at left in its vertical style—displays and allows editing of paragraph and character attributes. Manual vertical justification of pages would be unbearable without this XTension.

4

Graphics

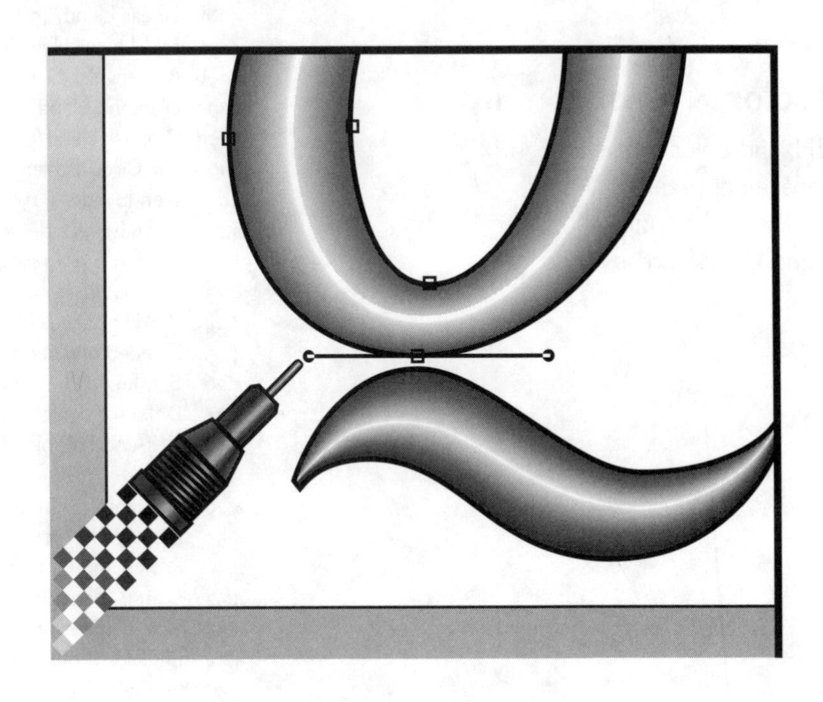

CHAPTER 4 CONTENTS

FIGURES

Graphics are a mystery to many QuarkXPress users. I certainly allowed them to remain a mystery to me for as long as possible. I believed that as long as graphics were generated in another program, all I needed to remember was that a graphics box had to be selected and the Contents tool chosen in order for **Get Picture** to show up under the **File** menu.

Eventually, the blinders fell away from my eyes and I realized that I needed to know a little bit about the different graphics I was bringing into my documents, if for no other reason than to understand why I could make changes to some graphics and not others. Along the way, I ran into a number of XTensions that made it easier (not to mention less mysterious) to work on graphics in QuarkXPress.

Let's begin with a discussion on TIFF, EPS, and PhotoCD images, followed by information on a number of XTensions—not the least of which is the EfiColor XTension from Quark.

Types of graphics

Macintosh graphics come in two distinct flavors: vector and raster. Vector-based graphics are also called object-oriented or draw images; raster-based graphics are often referred to as bitmapped or paint images.

Vector images are made in drawing programs such as MacDraw, Aldus FreeHand, and Adobe Illustrator, where objects are mathematically defined as a series of straight lines, arcs, and shapes (circles, squares). The big advantage to using vector graphics is that since they are composed of mathematical instructions, they keep looking better as the output resolution increases. They can also be scaled without loss of resolution.

Raster images, on the other hand, concern themselves with each individual pixel (picture element) of a graphic. Paint programs such as MacPaint and SuperPaint are used to create raster graphics. However, it's a lot more likely that you'll be dealing with raster graphics coming from scanners and image-manipulating programs such as Photoshop and ColorStudio.

Just to confuse matters slightly, it's also possible to have a hybrid file containing both types of graphics, vector and raster.

Whether working with vector or raster images, only a 72 dot-per-inch (dpi) preview is shown in a QuarkXPress graphics box. This preview is a PICT image, used only for printing when the original image is missing or when using a non-PostScript printer or fax/modem. Although PICTs can be either vector or raster (or a combination of the two), a PICT used as a preview is always raster.

TIP PICT previews are just pointers to the actual graphic being "imported" into QuarkXPress. This is why you must transport your images along with the document when sending a job to another user or a service bureau.

Encapsulated PostScript (EPS)

PostScript is a page description language developed by Adobe Systems, Inc., and all high-end DTP programs can interface with printer driver software that generates PostScript code. A PostScript printer has a built-in or attached interpreter that translates this code into the necessary instructions to output pages more or less like the pages seen on a monitor.

Encapsulated PostScript files created in drawing programs such as FreeHand and Illustrator—or QuarkXPress pages saved as EPS—are vector-based, although they may contain elements brought in from raster-based programs. EPS files can be opened with a word processing program; do so to see what the PostScript page description language looks like. They are plain text files, although they look more like a computer program than a book manuscript.

Encapsulation

The advantage of encapsulating a PostScript image is that the importing application doesn't have to understand or interpret the instructions contained in the image—it just passes the image on to the printer. The disadvantage is that once the image has been imported into QuarkXPress, its individual components cannot be modified. This is true of both vector- and raster-based EPS images. QuarkXPress can't tell one from the other, so all of the Style menu options normally available for imported raster graphics are unavailable, no matter which flavor of EPS you're using.

You can, however, perform matrix manipulations on the entire image, such as scaling, skewing, rotation, and reflection (**Style→Flip Horizontal** and **Flip Vertical**). Matrix manipulations don't actually change the image, but rather modify the image's coordinate system. If a graphic is flipped horizontally, for example, the x-axis of the image is swapped so that the image runs from the positive to the negative side of the axis, the opposite of a normal, nonflipped image (Figure 4.1). For raster-based images, it's much better to do major manipulations in an image-editing program, though, where all changes will be saved with the image. Any manipulations done in QuarkXPress will have to be processed for each pixel when the image is printed.

You can also pseudo-crop an image in QuarkXPress, since only the portion of an image viewable on the screen will be seen on the

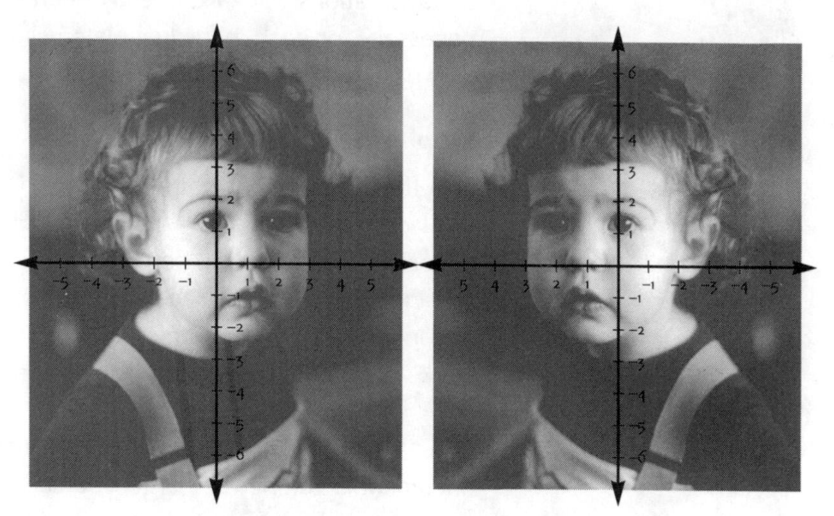

Figure 4.1 Matrix manipulations Actions such as scaling, skewing, rotation, and reflection act on the coordinate system of an image. In this case, my friend Colleen was flipped horizontally by swapping the positive and negative values on the x-axis.

printout. But the entire image is still being processed when it comes time to print. It's better to perform true cropping on any raster images in an image-editing program, where unwanted parts of the image will be permanently deleted.

Desktop Color Separation (DCS)

When saving full-color raster EPS files in image-editing software such as Photoshop, one of the options is DCS. The Desktop Color Separation option is important because it pre-separates the four plates needed for printing process colors: cyan, magenta, yellow, and black (CMYK). Saving with the DCS option forces the software to create five files, four EPS files for the CMYK plates and one PICT file to be brought into QuarkXPress as a preview.

Pre-separating full-color images means you have more files to keep track of, but it greatly speeds up printing. If an image-editing program is used to save a raster image as a TIFF file, as described below, the TIFF will have to be completely downloaded to the output device four times—once per plate. The raster image processor (RIP) of the output device will then have to extract the information it needs for each plate. If you have saved a raster image as a DCS EPS, though, the separations will have already been made and only the information necessary for each individual plate will need to be downloaded when that plate is printed.

Displaying EPS images

EPS files usually (but not always) carry a PICT preview image to aid in placing the image. Windows EPS files use a TIFF header. If you import an EPS file and it comes in as a gray box with the title, creator, and creation date, then the EPS was created without a PICT header. The image will still print fine to a PostScript printer, but it is harder to work with on the page, and it will not print to a non-PostScript printer.

TIP If you're working with numerous or large EPS files and your document is getting very large, you can go back to the application that created the EPS files and save them with either a black-and-white preview or no preview at all. This will reduce their size, and the type of preview will not affect how they print.

Sources for EPS images

There are a lot of companies that specialize in creating and selling packages of clip art, and those that cater to professional DTP users offer EPS images. For example, as "artistically challenged" as I am, I would never consider trying to draw a map by myself. In the past, I've purchased a number of map packages from a company called Cartesia (609-397-1611). They have maps of most of the industrialized nations, as well as maps of the world regions and various projections of globes. Cartesia has also produced maps of major U.S. metropolitan areas (Figure 4.2).

EPS images can also be purchased from Quark, as part of their QuarkLibraries packages. Each package contains disks full of EPS images, all conveniently placed into libraries and labeled, making it very easy to find and use an image. I've purchased both their Flags and Energy & Environment library packages, and have even combined elements from the two packages (Figure 4.3). Vector-based EPS clip art is made up of a lot of individual elements grouped together into

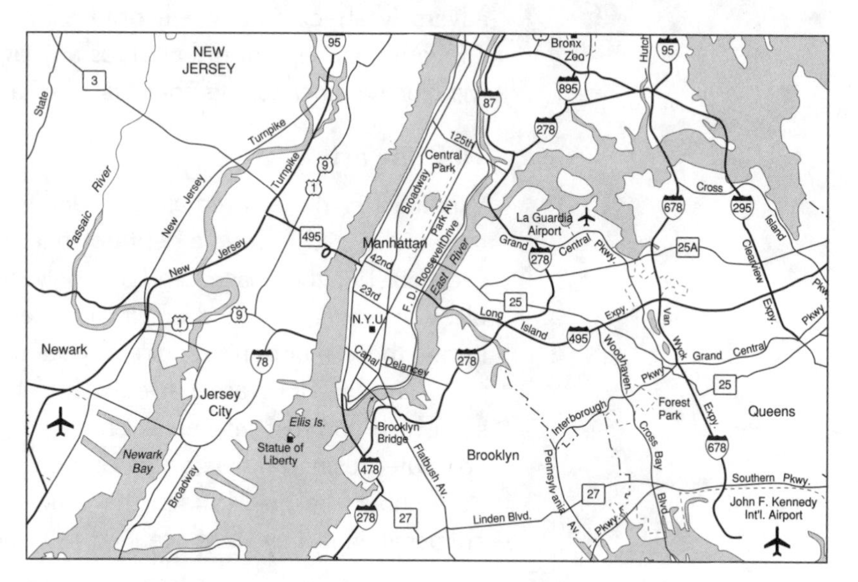

Figure 4.2 Cartesia maps This metropolitan New York City area map from Cartesia shows how detailed EPS images can be. The map has been pseudo-cropped (The Bronx and Staten Island are barely shown) and scaled to 75% of its original size. For what it's worth, I live near the square in the middle marking New York University (N.Y.U.).

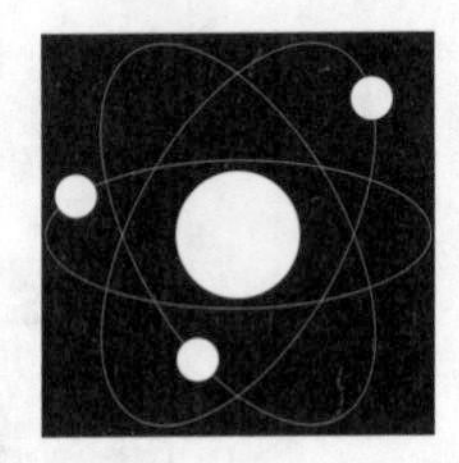

Figure 4.3 QuarkLibraries I combined elements from the flag of the former Soviet Union with the atom in the Energy & Environment library to create an illustration for an article on nuclear power.

one illustration, so if you have access to the drawing program that created or is compatible with an illustration, you can pick and choose which elements to use.

Tagged Image File Format (TIFF)

The Tagged Image File Format (TIFF) is always a raster image, never vector. Because TIFF files are raster, their printing resolution is directly related to the resolution at which they were created. Whereas a vector image can be scaled up or down, enlarging a TIFF image can adversely affect how well it prints. On the other hand, shrinking a TIFF often makes it print better, as any jagged edges on diagonal lines will blur together to give the illusion of a smoother edge.

TIFF line art

When a TIFF file is saved as black and white—without any shades of gray—it is said to have a depth of one bit (binary digit). That means each pixel of the image can have only one of two states: on or off, black or white. This kind of TIFF is often used for simple line drawings—those that don't require any subtle shading.

One-bit TIFFs are perfectly fine for cartoons. If you need to scan high-contrast images, such as pen-and-ink drawings, into the computer, using the line art or one-bit settings in the scanning software should be fine. In fact, the images should end up being much crisper than if they were scanned as grayscale.

TIP Line art images create the best possible output when they are scanned or saved at the resolution and size to be used on the final output device. There does, however, seem to be a threshold at about

600 dpi, above which the human eye can't perceive increased resolution in line art.

TIFF grayscale

When the bit depth of a TIFF is higher than one, it is said to be a grayscale TIFF. Grayscale TIFFs can be 4, 6, or 8 bits in depth, representing 16, 64, and 256 shades of gray, respectively. The most common bit depth for grayscale raster images is 8, and 256 shades is the maximum that PostScript can handle. Color TIFFs can be 24 or 32 bits in depth; 24-bit TIFFs contain 8 bits each for the colors red, green, and blue, and 32-bit TIFFs have 8 bits each for the process colors cyan, magenta, yellow, and black.

Eight bits is the maximum depth needed for production-quality grayscale images, since the human eye can perceive only around 250 shades of any one color—in this case, black. Eight bits isn't enough for full-color production, though, since the eye can perceive thousands of different colors at once.

TIP Keep in mind that the resolution of all grayscale raster images—whether TIFF or EPS—should really be twice the screen frequency being used on the final output. If you're outputting film at a 133-line screen, scanning or saving raster images in an image-editing program at any resolution higher than 266 dpi is just a waste of hard disk space. And if you know that the images are going to be scaled down, scanning at an even lower resolution will help save space and will not be detrimental to the final output.

Halftone cells

To determine how many shades of gray—for either a grayscale image or each plate of a color image—can be produced on an output device, you need to understand the concept of a PostScript halftone dot.

When traditional methods were used, a screen with line after line of holes was placed between a contone (continuous tone) photograph and the film being shot for the printing press. The line screen value was determined by how many of these lines of holes appeared in an inch. Today, a sheet of acetate covered with a dot pattern is used in lieu of a screen with holes.

If you're going to apply screens digitally, the first thing to determine is the line screen required for the printing press. (Some presses and papers can't handle a super-fine line screen, at least not without creating some pretty nasty-looking results.) Then divide the output device's resolution by the line screen, essentially creating a grid by overlaying the screen onto the film. By focusing on a 1-inch square of this grid, you have (mentally) created the halftone cell.

Counting the dots in the cell (or squaring one side of the grid) and adding one (for white), you can calculate the number of grays that can be produced at this particular line screen and output resolution. Remember, our goal is to get as close as possible to PostScript's maximum of 256 shades of gray, since that will produce the most photorealistic output. That equation again is:

$$(\text{resolution} \div \text{line screen})^2 + 1 = \text{no. of grays}$$

Figures 4.4a–c are representations of halftone cells at various line screens and output resolutions.

Displaying TIFF images

As mentioned in the introduction to this section, QuarkXPress uses a raster-based PICT preview to display any images brought into its graphic boxes. With EPS images, it uses the PICT preview that was made by the application that created the EPS. With TIFFs, however, QuarkXPress creates its own PICT preview. This means that the program can display any changes made to the TIFF, such as line art shading and grayscale contrast adjustments.

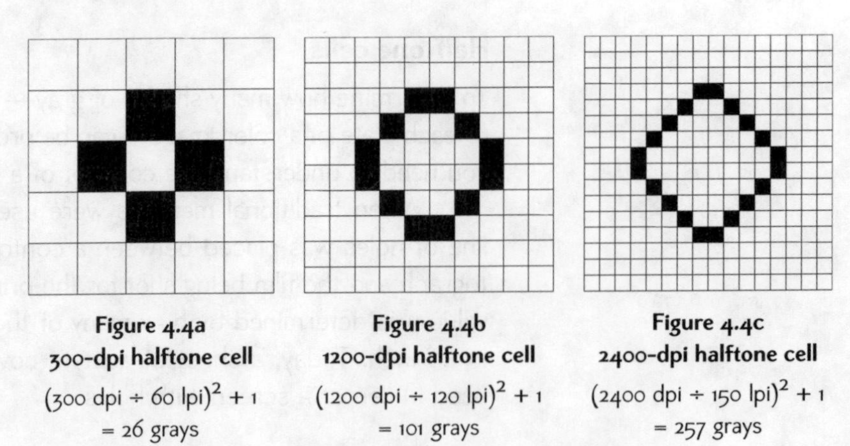

Figure 4.4a
300-dpi halftone cell
$(300 \text{ dpi} \div 60 \text{ lpi})^2 + 1$
= 26 grays

Figure 4.4b
1200-dpi halftone cell
$(1200 \text{ dpi} \div 120 \text{ lpi})^2 + 1$
= 101 grays

Figure 4.4c
2400-dpi halftone cell
$(2400 \text{ dpi} \div 150 \text{ lpi})^2 + 1$
= 257 grays

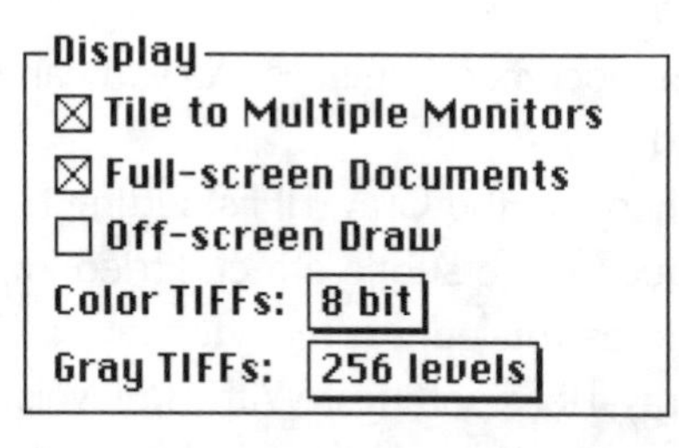

Figure 4.5 Display settings The TIFFs settings in the Applications Preferences dialog box can have a substantial effect on file sizes. If you don't need to see full-color images, keep the Color TIFFs setting at "8 bit."

With this convenience comes a potential problem, though. File sizes will vary dramatically depending on the settings used in the Display section of **Edit→Preferences→Applications** (Figure 4.5). In a perfect world, I'd leave this dialog's settings set at the highest resolution—"32 bit" for Color TIFFs and "256 levels" for Gray TIFFs. However, when those settings are used, it's possible to create relatively short documents that take up huge amounts of disk space.

TIP QuarkXPress compresses the screen previews that it creates when "8 bit" or "16 bit" Color TIFFs are requested. The previews are decompressed when files are opened and then recompressed when files are closed. When "32 bit" is chosen, TIFF previews are not compressed, ostensibly to avoid a substantial speed hit. I discovered this while preparing a six-page file with ten screen shots made on my color monitor. I was mortified to find that the file size was 3 megabytes, so I did some experimenting and found that I could get the file size down to 280k by simply changing the Color TIFFs setting from "32 bit" to "8 bit" and reimporting the graphics. For the sake of completeness, I also tested this with "16 bit" chosen, which produced a 360k file.

The Picture Tools XTension from Vision's Edge can be used to reduce the size of files created with the "32 bit" and "256 levels" settings in Application Preferences. Since any changes to these settings won't have any effect until all images have been reimported, the XTension's Forced Update feature really saves the day. Invoking the feature causes all images in a document to be reimported, retaining all changes you've made to the images since bringing them into Quark XPress. One thing to watch out for: Even though its submenu name is followed by an ellipsis (...), choosing Forced Update does not bring up a dialog box. Instead, the XTension immediately starts reimporting all of the document's images. As you can probably guess, I learned this the hard way.

Changing the Gray TIFFs setting from "16 levels" to "256 levels" has a much more subtle effect. I tried importing three grayscale TIFFs whose sizes totaled 2 megabytes into a QuarkXPress document using both Gray TIFFs settings. With "16 levels," the resulting file took 826k; changing the setting to "256 levels" and reimporting the graphics only increased the file size by 16%, to 958k. Of course, if you're using a lot of grayscale TIFFs, 16% can quickly add up. I was surprised to find that the TIFFs brought in at "16 levels" didn't look much worse than the higher resolution versions.

Sources for TIFF images

One excellent source for TIFF line art is Baseline Publishing (901-682-9676), distributors of 15 collections of FM Waves cartoons (Figure 4.6). Each image is scanned at 400 dpi, and the illustrators' tastes tend a bit toward the wacky, which possibly explains why I like them so much. In fact, last year I used a dozen images from their Business Cartoons collection for a calendar that I made for my clients.

There are a number of companies selling color TIFF photograph packages these days, but grayscale photographs are hard to come by. One source for grayscale TIFFs is Dynamic Graphics (309-688-8800); they sell subscription services that usually include a handful of different photographs each month (Figure 4.7).

An excellent source for color TIFF photographs is 21st Century Media (206-441-9355), whose PhotoDisc collections come on CD-

Figure 4.6 FM Waves cartoons This is one of my favorite images from Baseline Publishing's FM Waves Business Cartoons clip art collection. The image is only slightly reduced, to 85% of its original size.

Figure 4.7 Dynamic Graphics There are only a few grayscale photographs included each month in Dynamic Graphics' various subscription services. This one came as part of October 1993's Print Media Services collection. It's shown above scaled at 90% and severely cropped so as to focus on the biker.

ROMs in both TIFF and JPEG (Joint Photographic Experts Group) formats. Some beautiful marble-textured color clip art is available from ArtBeats (503-863-4429). Examples of 21st Century Media's and ArtBeats' selections are shown in this book's color plates, along with an image from Taco Clipart Company (402-344-7191).

Converting color TIFFs to grayscale

I'll often use color TIFF images from the PhotoDisc collection on jobs that are only being printed in black and white. Rather than just print a composite (nonseparated) page to the imagesetter, I ask my service bureau to do the conversion in Photoshop. There they can both see what the image will print like and make adjustments that improve the quality of the black-and-white output.

In the photo shown in Figure 4.8—which comes from a job I did while writing this chapter—the conversion from color to black and white caused immediate problems. The picture of the fishing boat looked both too dark and overexposed. Taking a look at the tone levels in Photoshop revealed the problem: The dynamic range of the picture was needlessly compressed. Out of a possible total of 256 shades of gray, only 197 are being used.

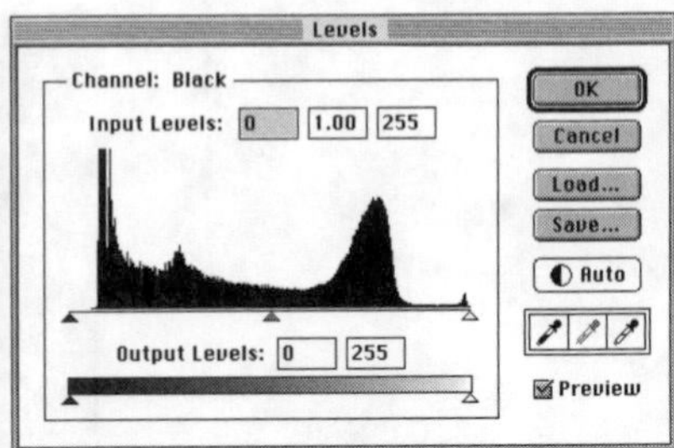

Figure 4.8 Color to black and white This is what the image looked like after simply converting from color to black and white. The various tones in the picture are nowhere near the sliders for those tones as shown at the bottom of the Photoshop histogram.

By moving the sliders in Photoshop's Levels dialog, I redefined the dynamic range to include only the tone levels used—or that I wanted to use—in this particular picture. The leftmost slider was moved directly beneath the darkest tone in the picture; the middle slider was placed below the picture's mid-tone peak; and the right-most slider was moved to the end of the high-tones that we were interested in (Figure 4.9).

There is actually some catchlight (sparkle) to the right of where we moved the slider, represented in the picture by the shiny surface in the water. By moving the slider to the left of the catchlight, we relegated these tones to pure white, at the same time lightening the objects that we wanted to define as the high-tones, such as the reflections off the fishing net.

The results from these few adjustments were that a lot of details began to show in the dark shadowed area, the broadside of the boat became truly reflective and luminous, the water regained its sparkle, and the sky brightened up.

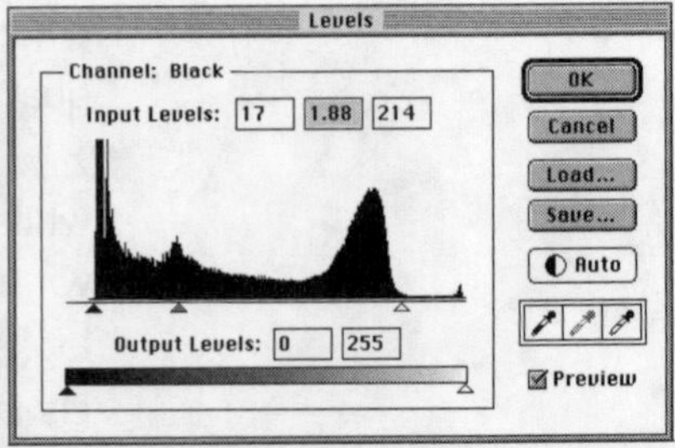

Figure 4.9 After making adjustments By editing the picture's histogram in Photoshop, the low-, mid-, and high-range tones were redefined so that each tone matched up with the corresponding use of tones in the actual picture.

PhotoCD (PCD)

Starting with version 3.2, QuarkXPress comes with a PhotoCD XTension that can be used to import Kodak PhotoCD (PCD) images. To be able to use the XTension, version 1.5 or above of Apple's QuickTime extension must also be loaded. PhotoCD is an exciting new technology that may prove to be some folks' introduction to the world of desktop color—mainly since it has the potential for being cheap and convenient.

When QuarkXPress imports a PhotoCD image, it creates its own TIFF preview. Unless you're going to adjust the colors on a calibrated monitor from within QuarkXPress, be sure to leave your Color TIFFs display setting in the Applications Preferences dialog box set to "8 bit." As discussed in the TIFFs section, the "32 bit" display setting may make a prettier picture on the screen, but it will also create an unnecessarily large file.

PhotoCD resolution

Each PhotoCD image file actually contains five or six different resolutions of the picture, depending on which format you use. QuarkXPress doesn't let you pick which resolution to use, but rather prints the resolution that makes most sense based on the output device chosen in the **File→Page Setup** dialog box. This way a low-resolution image will automatically be sent to a laser printer, offering relatively quick printing, and a version with higher resolution will be downloaded to an imagesetter.

PhotoCD Master is the most common format in use. It offers the following five resolutions, which must be created from 35mm film:

Base/16	128 × 192 pixels
Base/4	256 × 384 pixels
Base	512 × 768 pixels
Base × 4	1024 × 1536 pixels
Base × 16	2048 × 3072 pixels

The Base-divided-by-4 and Base-divided-by-16 resolutions are strictly thumbnail views. The Base resolution is for use on televisions. You can use the Base-times-4 resolution on desktop computers and, eventually, high-definition televisions (HDTV). The Base-times-16 resolution is the one that will be used by most people, since it is photographic resolution and will act as your digital negative.

The Pro PhotoCD Imaging Workstation (PIW) 4200 can be used to scan up to 4 × 5 inch original negatives or transparencies. It can also be used to scan 70mm and 120mm film. Pro PhotoCD Master adds the Base-times-64 resolution (Base × 64, or 4096 × 6144 pixels). But don't ask for the Pro PhotoCD Master format unless you really need the extra resolution, since the files it creates are quite large. Whereas a PhotoCD Master disk can contain roughly 100 images, Pro PhotoCD Master disks will hold only about 25 images.

Amateur vs. professional

The most important thing to remember about PhotoCD is that even though it can be used to inexpensively acquire amateur photographs, you'll be a lot better off starting with professional-quality photographs. Don't hold your breath waiting for 5 × 7 inch prints to be accepted by PhotoCD imaging centers, and rightly so. Prints are the output created from the original film, and they've already had algorithms applied to them based on the taste and skill of the film processor. A lot more detail is generally available in the film than what is shown on prints, and that detail may be important to you when you get the images on the computer.

Also, expect to have to edit PhotoCD images in an image-editing program. You may need to make the PhotoCD images sharper by using the unsharp masking feature in the software that opens the images. Please refer to the color plates in this book, which contain a PhotoCD image brought directly into QuarkXPress, along with the same image after professional photographer Sam Merrell messed with it a bit in Photoshop.

Graphics information XTensions

There are a number of XTensions available that gather and display information about graphics in QuarkXPress. One of them adds handy keyboard shortcuts, while another automates the creation of an image catalog; still another allows you to search and replace colors. All of the XTensions discussed in this section were written by Dacque Viker of Vision's Edge.

Picture Tools

I already mentioned one of Picture Tools' powerful features, Forced Update, back in the TIFF section of this chapter. This XTension has a few other features worth mentioning, too. QuarkXPress' Picture Usage dialog box allows the suppression of one or more picture boxes, but Picture Tools' Picture Suppress dialog box adds an extra level of convenience (Figure 4.10). The XTension allows all pictures in a document to be suppressed and unsuppressed at the touch of a button, and you can suppress both the picture *and* its frame. There's a demo version of Picture Tools on the disk in the back of the book.

Picture Tools also has a very useful Picture palette that—when opened to its full size—can tell you the name of the selected image, the date it was imported into the QuarkXPress document, its file size and type, and its current status: OK, modified, or missing (Figure 4.11). When the check box in the palette's corner is deselected, only the image's name is displayed.

And Picture Tools adds three useful keyboard shortcuts to Quark XPress, two of which can be defined by the user (Figure 4.12). My favorite is the Size Box to Picture command, which pretty much does what it says. By default, it will resize a graphic box based on the size

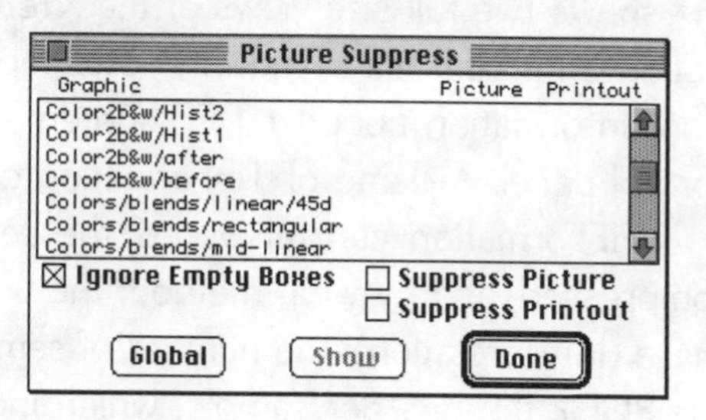

Figure 4.10 Picture Suppress This feature in Picture Tools is indispensible when doing high-resolution printouts of documents filled with FPO (for position only) images.

Figure 4.11 Picture palette Pictures Tools makes it easy to see useful info about any imported image. This is the info it displayed for Figure 4.10.

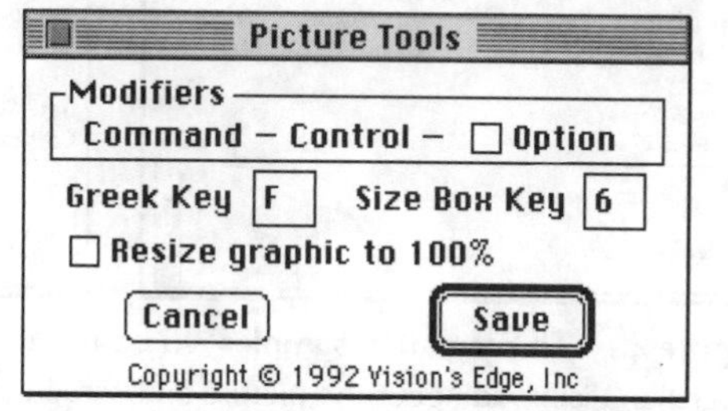

Figure 4.12 Picture Tools preferences The keyboard shortcuts that are used for greeking individual pictures and resizing boxes to fit their pictures can be changed here.

of the picture it contains. The command can resize the picture to 100% before resizing the graphic box, if you prefer. There's also a keyboard shortcut for "greeking" the currently selected picture box. This is very handy if you want to temporarily suppress the display of a picture when your work is taking forever due to interminable screen redraws of the picture.

The third keyboard shortcut allows you to scale both a graphic box and its contents from the keyboard. Whereas QuarkXPress' built-in shortcut for scaling graphics (Command-Option-Shift-< and >) scales only the picture in 5% increments, Picture Tools' keyboard shortcut (Command-Option-Control-< and >) scales both the picture *and* its box in 5% increments.

TIFFormation

The TIFFormation XTension lets a user see information that is sometimes saved in TIFF files by the applications that created them. Not all information is available for all TIFFs, but at the very least, all TIFFs will have their names, length and width, and X and Y resolutions displayed by this XTension. In fact, that's just the information you'll see if you choose to view the TIFFormation palette at its abbreviated size. Figure 4.13 shows two full-size views of the XTension; the first displays information on a TIFF file saved in Photoshop, and the other shows even more information about a TIFF screen shot made with the Capture control panel. A demo of TIFFormation can be found on the disk.

TIFFormation can tell you if the selected TIFF image has been compressed, and by what method; the way that color is stored in the image (Interpretation); the number of samples per pixel (1 is grayscale, 3 is RGB); the bits per sample, which indicates the number of grays

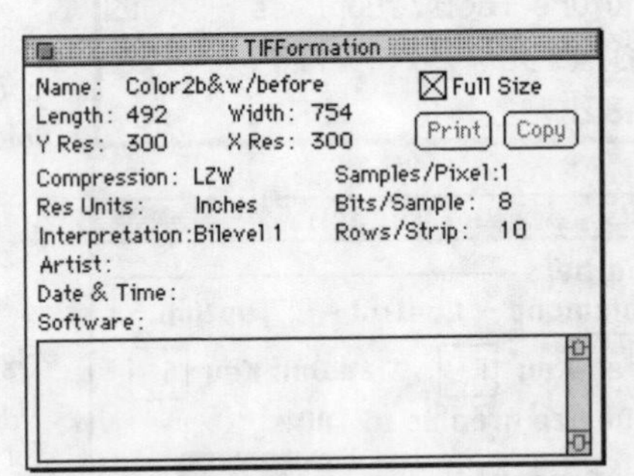

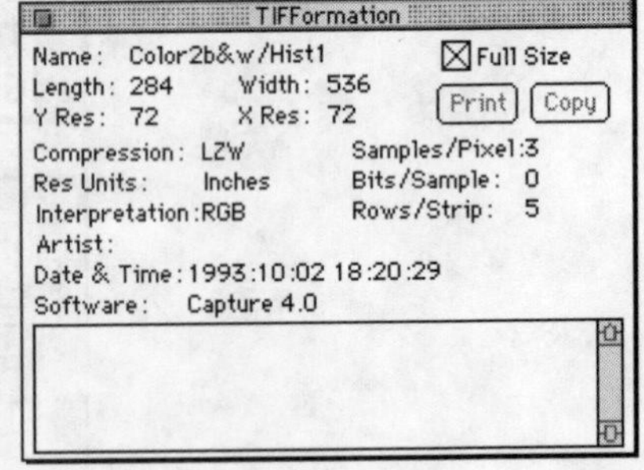

Figure 4.13 TIFFormation samples These two palettes show the information that the XTension displayed about the picture and screen shot shown in the "Converting color TIFFs to grayscale" discussion (in the TIFF section of this chapter).

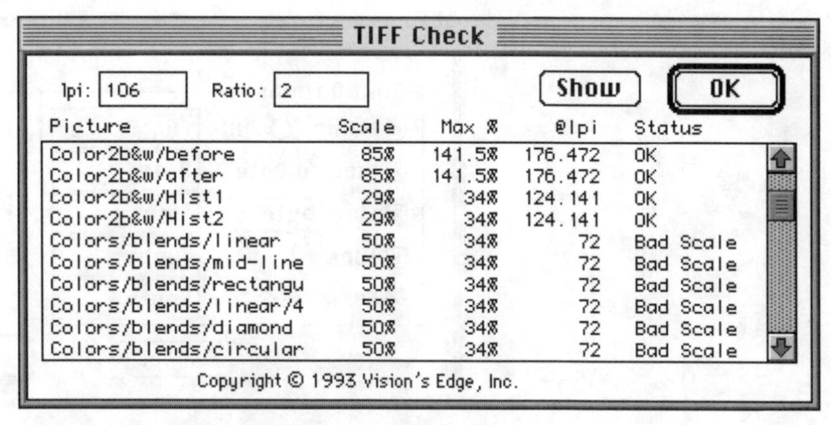

Figure 4.14 TIFF Check This portion of the TIFFormation XTension provides output-related information about each TIFF image in a document.

or colors; and the rows per strip, which refers to the way data is stored in the image. In addition, if the creating application records the artist's name, date and time, its own name, and any description information, that will be shown at the bottom of the palette.

Another powerful feature of TIFFormation is its TIFF Check dialog box (Figure 4.14). Here you'll find all the TIFFs used in the open document, any scale that you've applied, the maximum percentage at which the XTension believes each image will look good when printed, the lines per inch that would have to be used if an image is to be printed at 100%, and the status of the image based on the line screen and scaling currently in use.

When computing the values shown in TIFF Check, TIFFormation first uses the line screen present in the Page Setup dialog. However, that number can be modified at the top of the dialog box so that you can get immediate feedback for any changes you might want to make, including seeing how the images will print at a service bureau on a high-resolution device. The status column in TIFF Check will indicate a bad scale if the ratio between the selected lpi and the image's resolution (as shown in the main TIFFormation palette) is less than 2:1.

Exposé

This is a wonderful XTension for cataloguing artwork. In addition to automatically importing and sizing all the images in a selected folder, Exposé lets you customize which information should be included in a companion text box for each graphic. The file name or full path name, modified date, file size, file type, and list of fonts used in the image

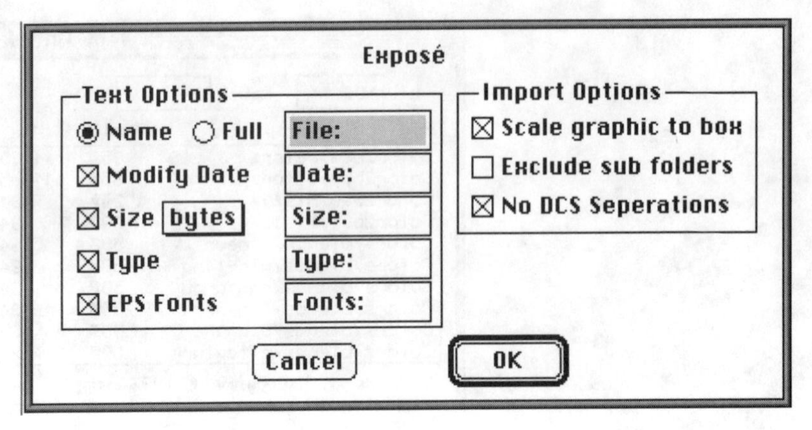

Figure 4.15 Exposé preferences All of the above Text Options, as well as the Import Options, can be customized for your purposes.

can all be collected, and the lead-in text to be used with each bit of information is editable in Exposé's preferences dialog (Figure 4.15).

Making a catalogue of images with Exposé is very easy. Start with a master page in a nonfacing pages document, creating one graphic box and one text box, grouped together. Choose the Identify Exposé Item that the XTension adds to the Utilities menu, and then duplicate (or step and repeat) the group around the page (Figure 4.16). The

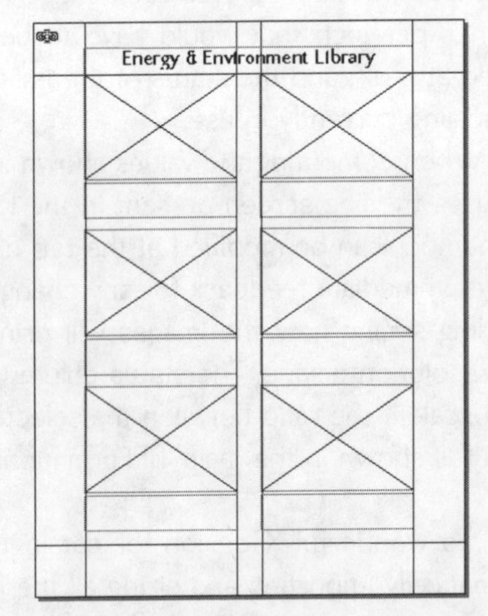

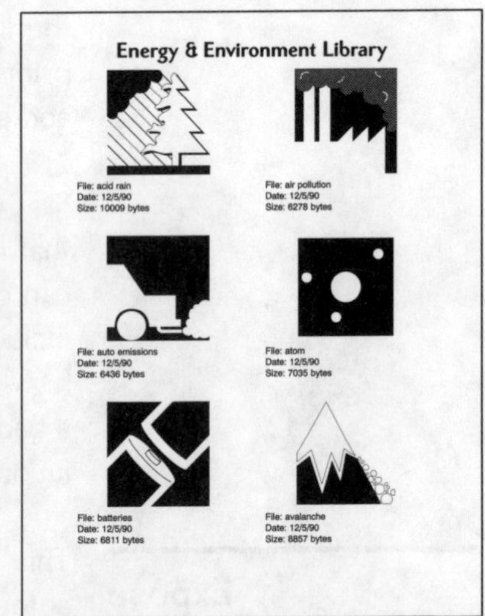

Figure 4.16 Exposé—before and after The catalogue template shown on the master page on the left was used to automatically create the page shown on the right.

XTension seems to be sensitive about the order in which you position the groups, though, so if you want a left/right top/down order, position groups in that order to begin with.

Return to a regular document page based on the master page that contains the Exposé groups, and choose the XTension. A prompt appears asking for the folder to be catalogued. Then just sit back and watch all the images in the folder come into the graphic boxes and all the image information come into the text boxes. While learning how to use this XTension I created a 20-page directory of Quark's Energy & Environment Library to send to the client of mine who always needs such illustrations in her jobs.

ColorChange

ColorChange compiles a list of all the colors in a document and allows search and replacement by color and/or shade (Figure 4.17). It's very useful for finding errant colors before printing separations, as well as selectively or globally replacing colors applied to frames, text, backgrounds, or pictures.

The No Hidden button tells ColorChange not to include hidden colors found in a file. This includes colors used in the Normal style sheet (which is always present in an empty text box), as well as the default frame color on items with a zero-width frame. A demo of ColorChange is available on the disk in the back of the book.

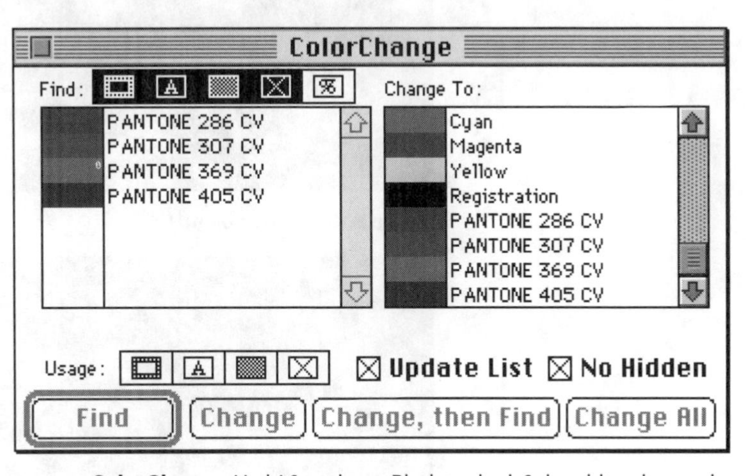

Figure 4.17 ColorChange Had I found any Black in the left-hand list shown above, I would have selectively replaced it with either Registration or PANTONE 405, since this client doesn't print a black plate.

Color-blending XTensions

There are also a number of XTensions that make working with colors in QuarkXPress both easier and more visually pleasing. Some add cooler blends to the program's Colors palette or add their own tools for customizing colors. Others let you convert type to its outlines so that you can work on it as a graphic.

Cool Blends

QuarkXPress has been able to create linear blends between two colors—or two percentages of the same color—since version 3.0. With blends, which are often called fountains, graduated fills, or dégredés, the goal is to create a smooth transition from one color to another over a fixed distance.

When a text or graphics box is selected and the background color icon is selected in the Colors palette, a drop-down menu gives a choice between Solid color or Linear blend. A linear blend starts at an item's side or corner—depending on the angle chosen—and ends at the opposite side or corner (Figures 4.18a–b).

Figure 4.18a Linear blend/0°

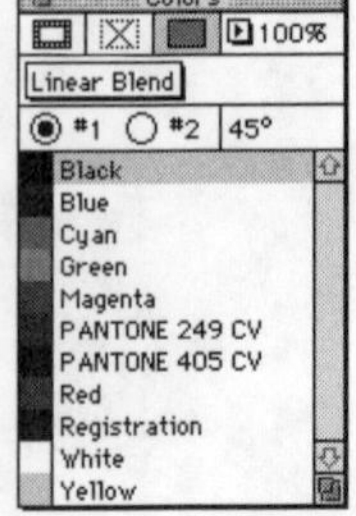

Figure 4.18b Linear blend/45°

Now, with the Cool Blends XTension loose in the QuarkXPress folder, there are also choices for Mid-Linear, Rectangular, Diamond, Circular, and Full Circular blends (Figures 4.19a–e). These are all radial blends, since they are generated from the center of the item rather than from its side or corner.

TIP One thing to keep in mind with all blends: The blend needs to be long enough for the output device to create at least as many halftone cells as there are steps in the blend. Referring back to the discussion on halftone cells, it was calculated that outputting a 150-line screen at 2400 dpi would give us the maximum number of shades

Figure 4.19a Mid-Linear blend/90°

Figure 4.19b Rectangular blend/90°

Figure 4.19c Diamond blend/90°

Figure 4.19d Circular blend/90°

Figure 4.19e Full Circular blend/90°

in PostScript: 256. Since all of the above examples go from 100% to 30% black, only 70 shades are being used in the blend. Seventy percent of 256 shades means that only about 180 steps need to print in this blend. And if those steps are divided into 150 lpi, it means that the blend should be at least 1.2 inches long (in the direction of the blend). Any less than that and the output device will have to skip steps due to the limitations of PostScript and its halftone cells. As equations, this looks like:

```
Shades used × shades possible = steps

Steps ÷ line screen = min. length of blend
```

BlendBuilder

BlendBuilder, from XTend, is an XTension that allows the blending of any two colors already present in QuarkXPress or in an individual document. Three models are available for blending: HSB (hue, saturation, and brightness), RGB, and CMYK. Blends created with BlendBuilder can be output as spot colors or as CMYK separations.

Just because BlendBuilder is creating new colors out of the HSB, RGB, or CMYK values being used for the original two colors, don't expect that you'll be able to blend two PANTONE colors and then out-

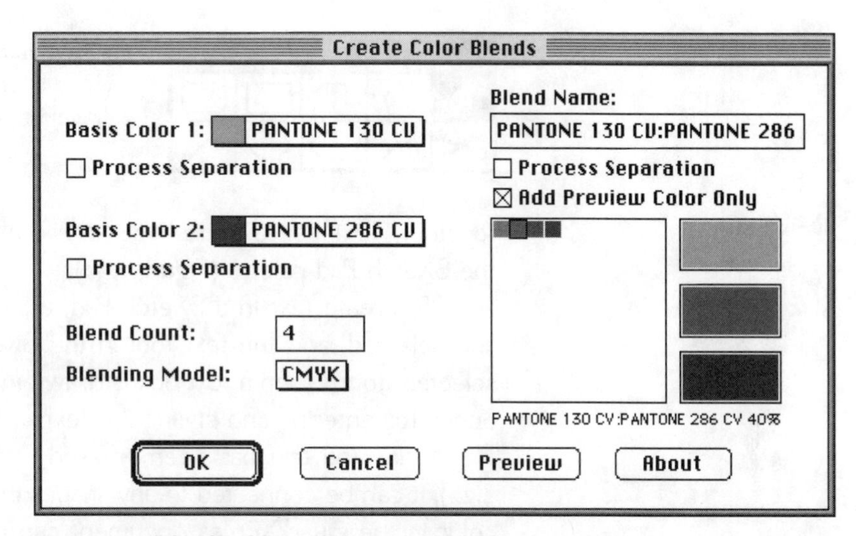

Figure 4.20 BlendBuilder Adjusting the blend count controls the number of colors shown in the preview window. Only the selected blend is added if Add Preview Color Only is chosen.

put percentages of each on two different spot color plates. Wouldn't that be great!

Instead, the XTension uses the Blend Count value that you assign and then mixes the colors incrementally, but always with percentages that add up to 100. In the large, square preview window shown in Figure 4.20, the first blend starts with 80% of the CMYK values stored in QuarkXPress for the PANTONE 130 CV color, then mixes that with 20% of the CMYK values of PANTONE 286 CV. The second blend, which I have selected, consists of 60% of the PANTONE 130 CV and 40% of the PANTONE 286 CV. It's using the CMYK values only because that's the Blending Model I chose.

SXetch Pad

SXetch Pad, from DataStream Imaging Systems, Inc., is an illustration XTension that lets you perform a number of tasks that formerly had to be done in stand-alone illustration programs. It allows you to create blends of many colors; turn text into outlines, so that the text can be worked on as a graphic; draw images, such as lines, arcs, and shapes; and connect text to an object, such as a squiggly line.

SXetch Pad adds a new tool, which is used to create a SXetch box, to the Tool palette. Each SXetch box can contain any number of text boxes and drawn images, and the text and images can be joined

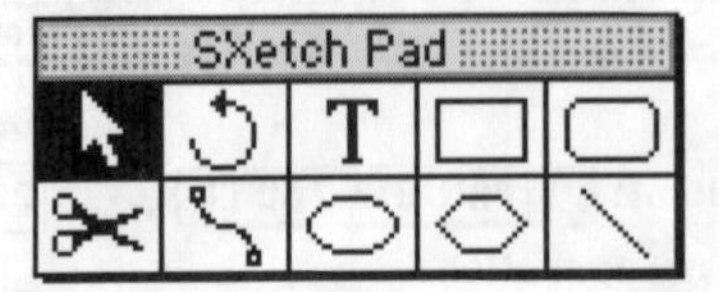

Figure 4.21 SXetch Pad palette The proper tool has to be chosen from this palette, which only appears when a SXetch box is selected.

together. Text boxes and shapes are created and manipulated with the SXetch Pad palette (Figure 4.21).

To create text in a SXetch Pad, a SXetch box has to be drawn and selected, and the text tool in the SXetch Pad palette has to be selected, too. When a text box is drawn in the SXetch box, a window opens for entering and styling the text.

Once the text has been entered into the type window (Figure 4.22), it can be connected to any shapes in the same SXetch box. Any color in the QuarkXPress document can be applied to the text, too, but for a blend of colors to be added to the text, the text must first be converted to outlines (Figure 4.23).

SXetch Pad offers the unique ability to mix any number of different colors into a blend. The blends window shows a sliding scale ranging from 100% to 0%, and any color in the document can be dragged over to any percentage level on the scale (Figure 4.24). If the scale is not completely filled with colors, only a portion of the selected elements will be filled, which may or may not be what you want.

Figure 4.22 SXetch box The outer handles on the above illustration belong to the SXetch box. The inner handles belong to a text box created with the SXetch Pad palette. The font is Farquarson, from the same designer who created this book's text face.

Figure 4.23 Text outlines Once the text is converted to outlines, each letter is a graphic element, and there is no longer a text box showing.

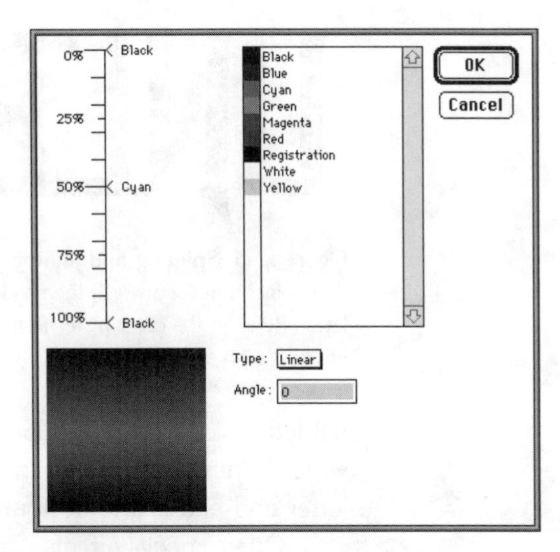

Figure 4.24 Building blends Any color that exists in the document can be blended into any other color. Here I've created a blend that starts at the top of an object as black, blending to cyan in the middle, and then back to black at the bottom.

Text can't be kerned in the SXetch Pad text box or in the type window, which is a real drawback. However, if the type is converted to outlines—so that it can be used as a graphic—then letters can be moved closer together or further apart. You can select one or more letters and move the selection one point at a time with the arrow keys—a nice touch.

One problem that crops up when blending colors in both upper and lower case text—or in a face with fancy letters like Farquarson—is that the shades of the blend aren't in the same place on each letter (Figure 4.25). This is because all the letters are considered separate objects, and each blend starts at the top and ends at the bottom of each object. By using the XTension's Split feature, individ-

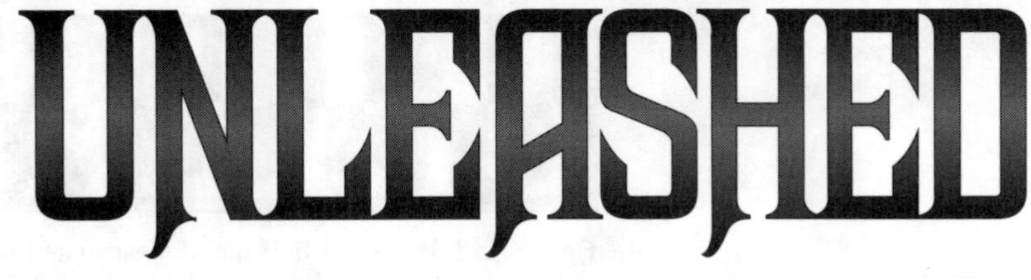

UNLEASHED

Figure 4.25 Blended and kerned text Here's what the text looks like after I converted it to outlines, kerned the letters together, and applied the blend. There's still a problem, though: The distribution of the blend differs depending on the height of the letter.

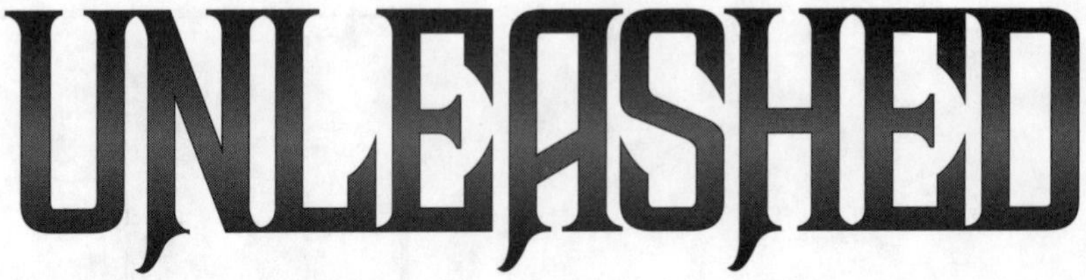

UNLEASHED

Figure 4.26 Splitting and joining If the elements of each letter are split apart and then joined into one word, the shades of the blend appear in the same place on each letter. Refer to the color plates in this book to see what the effect looks like going from black to cyan and back.

ual letters can be ungrouped and then joined together as an entire word. When that's done, the blend will start at the top of the tallest letter and end at the bottom of the deepest letter (Figure 4.26).

Other special effects can be performed on text with SXetch Pad's blending and outline conversion features. The XTension puts a frame around any text that's converted to outlines, and the frame can be treated as a stroke or line (as defined in Aldus FreeHand and Adobe Illustrator, respectively). The default color and thickness of text converted to outlines is black and one point. Both are editable. Other text effects can be performed by changing or removing the strokes and experimenting with the blend settings (Figures 4.27 and 4.28).

UNLEASHED

Figure 4.27 Different color stroke After converting this text—the lower case version of Farquarson—to outlines, I edited the "frame" around the characters so that it was 1.5 points thick and white. Then I changed the color of the SXetch box to cyan.

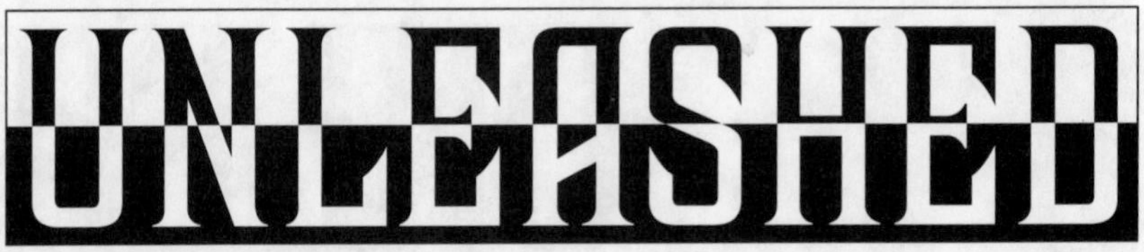

UNLEASHED

Figure 4.28 Half-and-half blend I eliminated the frame around the converted characters, creating a custom blend that was half black and half white, causing the text to become two-toned. Then a SXetch Pad rectangular shape was drawn, colored black, and moved to the back of the SXetch box.

The EfiColor XTension

Believe it or not, it's possible to understand color management and acquire the skills necessary to enjoy its benefits without earning a graduate degree in physics. In fact, this section of the book is an attempt to do just that—explain EfiColor without any in-depth discussion of color theory. If you wish to learn more about this subject, I encourage you to do so; it will add immeasurably to your understanding of the EfiColor XTension. The documentation that came with QuarkXPress 3.2, *Using the EfiColor XTension with QuarkXPress*, explains many of the key concepts in its "concept blocks." For a more complete discussion of color theory, I recommend the *Cachet Color Theory Guide* by William F. Schreiber. It's included with Cachet, as well as anything by Miles Southworth.

The EfiColor XTension is the product of two companies working together to produce a better solution than either of them could have produced independently. Before I explain the workings of this XTension, let's take a brief look at the history of electronic color publishing, at least as it relates to these two companies.

Quark, EFI, and color publishing

In the spring of 1987, QuarkXPress was the first Macintosh application to include the use of color. Coincidentally, this is also when the first Macintosh to support color, the Macintosh II, was introduced. QuarkXPress was also the first Macintosh application that was capable of generating both spot and process color separations. Unfortunately, it did not include the ability to separate continuous–tone (color bitmap) images.

However, this was soon overcome by a clever idea called Desktop Color Separation (DCS), which was discussed earlier in this chapter in the EPS section. The DCS specification was created and is still maintained by Quark. DCS provides a mechanism by which pre-separated continuous tone images can be imported into a QuarkXPress layout. On screen, a DCS image looks just like any other. But behind the scenes lie five separate files: a master file containing a PICT preview and the paths to the cyan, magenta, yellow, and black separation files. When QuarkXPress prints separations, these files are individually passed along to the printer, giving you full color separation capability. Each of these five DCS files is an EPS file, with special comments contained in the master file.

In August, 1990, Quark continued its leadership in color publishing by introducing automatic and manual color pair trapping in version 3.0. This capability was further enhanced by the trapping palette in version 3.1 (January 1992), which added the ability to set trapping for individual items. Along the way they also introduced the ability to create blends within QuarkXPress.

QuarkXPress 3.2 (July 1993) introduced us to color management with the addition of the EfiColor XTension. In the simplest terms, EfiColor does for color what Adobe Type Manager (ATM) does for fonts; it renders color more accurately, both on screen and on non-PostScript printers. QuarkXPress 3.2 also included support for the new DCS 2.0 specification, created specifically for high-fidelity (greater than four plates) color.

EFI's leadership in color publishing

When Efi Arazi, founder of Scitex, left that company, he took along several of his top engineers and started a new company called Electronics for Imaging (EFI). This new company was dedicated to creating an economical solution for producing high-quality color separations. The core technology on which EFI's color products are based was invented by Professor William F. Schreiber at MIT. On February 9, 1990, MIT granted EFI an exclusive license to this technology (U.S. Patent No. 4,500,919). EFI has subsequently sublicensed the technology to Kodak, Adobe, Scitex, Canon, Xerox, Toyo, JVC, and Minolta.

EFI's approach to color management was three-pronged. First, they created a hardware solution—the Fiery RIP (raster image processor) for the Canon Color Laser Copier. The Fiery RIP provided the quality and performance necessary to make the CLC into a viable solution for very short-run color printing. You may have seen advertisements for "Fiery prints," even though it's the CLC that does the actual printing; the Fiery just tells it what to print. The Fiery uses the same color transformation technology as all of EFI's products.

The second prong of EFI's attack on desktop color was an application solution—the Cachet color editor. Cachet introduced several key benefits of color management such as the Gamut Alarm, which warns the user when a selected color is outside of a printer's gamut (range of colors). Cachet also offers exceptional controls for creating color separations, and it introduced some revolutionary interface ideas like Edit by Reference and Multi-choice. These interface advances are particularly important for color applications because of the way our eyes work—we're great at comparing colors side by side, but terrible at being able to spot a particular color by itself.

The third prong is a system software solution—EfiColor. EFI chose not to wait for Apple to introduce color management hooks in the Macintosh operating system, so they forged ahead by creating an XTension that allows XPress to communicate with their EfiColor processor (the exact same one used by Cachet). Now that Apple has introduced its long-awaited color management solution, ColorSync, it's only a matter of time before EFI plugs EfiColor into the system, eliminating the need for the EfiColor XTension and making its benefits available to all applications.

Color management

Why do you need color management? What problems will it solve? What solutions does it promise? Is it worth the investment? Do you have a choice? The promise of color management is to provide WYSIWYG (what you see is what you get) color throughout the production process—on screen, color proofing, and in final output. Proper color management can save you the cost of separating color images more than once, as well as reduce the number of matchprints (laminated proofs made from separated negatives) necessary for each job. EfiColor does this by providing accurate color on low-cost color devices and eliminating much of the guesswork that's done without the benefit of display correction.

Without EfiColor, color produced on separate devices almost never matches. The color you see on your monitor doesn't match the original art that you scanned. Nor does it match what you get from your color printer, a matchprint, or the printed piece. In fact, it's rare that any of these even come close to matching, except for the matchprint and the printed piece. What you see is not what you get. And it's not even easy to predict what you'll get based on screen presentation, since sometimes an image appears different on the same screen over the course of a day.

The cause of this problem is that devices don't specify color meaning (the definition of a specific color), and they have independent gamuts. Typically, your scanner stores color information in terms of values of red, blue, and green (RGB) colorants. This is great because your monitor works with color in terms of RGB, too. But just because they use the same colorants doesn't mean that they have the same range of colors; 100% blue on your scanner may not match 100% blue on your monitor. This is because 100% blue has no color meaning; it does not define a specific color, but is rather a value relative to the device, and not absolute. When you go from your monitor to your printer, not only do you have to deal with their varying ranges of color, but also with the fact that they describe color in different terms. Instead of RGB, most color printers reproduce color using cyan, magenta, yellow, and black (CMYK). Suddenly the problem is much more complicated.

This problem can be overcome by defining color meaning for each device, then translating those color meanings between devices. Knowing the problem, the solution seems natural. We just need to define each device's range of colors in terms that we can compare and then make the appropriate adjustments to the color values to compensate for differences in the devices' gamuts.

How EfiColor works

EfiColor solves the problem of color management by translating color values on the fly. These translations are performed by the EfiColor processor, a system extension that resides inside the System folder. This is the same software used by EFI's color editing application, Cachet. The EfiColor processor translations are based on device profiles that define a device's range of colors in terms of a device-independent color space. In order for the system to work, you must have a profile for each device used in your production process. Each profile is stored as a text file inside a folder named "EfiColor db" that must be placed inside the System folder along with the EfiColor processor extension.

WYSIWYG color comes at a price—it takes a lot of processing time to perform these translations. The biggest lag is during the initialization of the translation tables; after that, things hum along fairly smoothly. And, as you'll see later, the XTension offers full control over exactly what elements you wish to have color-rendered and on which devices. You can eliminate the EfiColor XTension's effects either by turning the XTension off in its preferences dialog or by simply removing the XTension from your QuarkXPress folder (or XTension folder, starting with version 3.3).

An EfiColor profile is a detailed description of a device's range of colors, or gamut. A device's gamut depends on the specific technology used. It's also affected by the environment of the device and its consumables. Some inks will adhere to paper better or worse depending on the temperature and relative humidity of the air and of the paper. Profiles are created by averaging colorimeter readings from lots of printouts from several identical devices, thus defining their gamuts.

EfiColor's Rendering Styles gamut mapping is impossible to explain without some discussion of color spaces. When translating between the gamuts of different devices, there are several ways of compressing (adjusting) one gamut to fit another. Basically, there are three factors to consider. Do you wish to maintain hue or saturation, or both, for a limited range? In the case of continuous-tone images, it is usually advantageous to maintain the overall range of hues, thus compressing all values equally. In business graphics, such as bar charts, it is more important to maintain saturation, so that colors remain distinct. And with logos, you would usually want to maintain an exact hue, saturation, and brightness. EfiColor allows the user to specify how color should be rendered.

In solving the larger problem of color management, the solutions to several smaller problems come naturally. The benefit of being able to translate between color spaces goes beyond color matching to producing high-quality color separations with a variety of useful controls. An additional benefit is the ability to warn the user if a selected color is outside of the range of the selected output device, possibly preventing wasted output. This feature is known as the Gamut Alarm.

EfiColor and QuarkXPress

EfiColor works with QuarkXPress through the EfiColor XTension. This XTension provides controls to engage the EfiColor Processor. As mentioned before, the EfiColor Processor uses profiles, which are stored in the "EfiColor db" folder. To take advantage of the benefits of EfiColor color management in QuarkXPress, you must have Quark XPress 3.2 or greater, the EfiColor XTension, the EfiColor Processor, and EfiColor profiles for each of the devices on which you wish to render color. The EfiColor XTension, like all XTensions, must be placed in the QuarkXPress folder (or in the XTensions folder inside the QuarkXPress folder) in order for it to be loaded when QuarkXPress is launched. Both the EfiColor Processor and the "EfiColor db" folder must be placed in the System folder. If you installed or updated to QuarkXPress 3.2 or later with the default settings, then all of these files were copied to the appropriate places on your hard disk.

EfiColor Preferences

Let's take a look at **Edit→Preferences→EfiColor**. This dialog box, shown in Figure 4.29, gives us the controls to turn EfiColor correction on and off, to specify what types of colors are corrected, and to set the default profiles for RGB and CMYK color conversions. You can completely eliminate the effects of EfiColor simply by unchecking the "Use EfiColor" check box at the top of the dialog. This feature allows you to leave the EfiColor XTension in your QuarkXPress folder, even when you don't want EfiColor correction. That might not sound so wonderful, but it eliminates the irritating need to quit QuarkXPress, move the XTension around in the Finder, and restart QuarkXPress every time you want to turn it on or off.

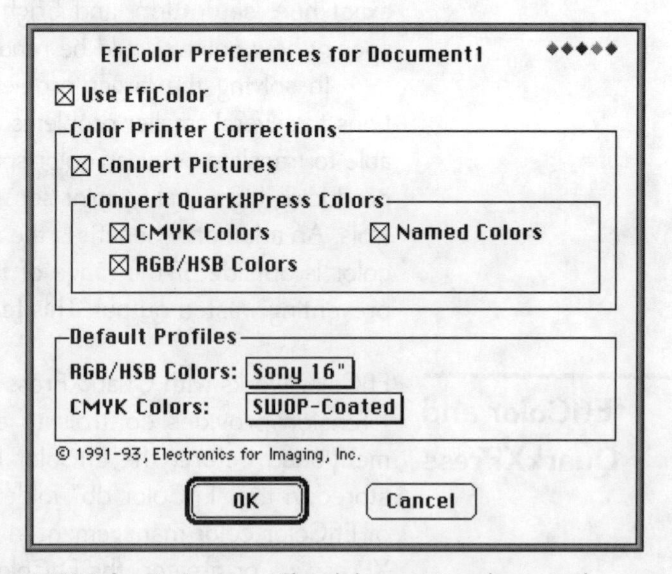

Figure 4.29 EfiColor Preferences This dialog contains the controls to completely turn EfiColor correction on or off, to specify what types of colors are corrected (by color model), and to set the default profiles for RGB and CMYK colors.

The middle section of the EfiColor Preferences dialog contains controls that determine what colors are rendered when printing or outputting to a PostScript file. These controls fall under the heading Color Printer Corrections, but this is a misnomer since they also control color correction when printing separations, almost always done on black-and-white devices. These controls are fairy straightforward. Each check box enables color correction for the specified item. Pictures are considered to be any imported continuous-tone image. If this box is checked, QuarkXPress will call on EfiColor to render all of the pictures in a document. QuarkXPress Colors are those defined in the Colors palette. The EfiColor XTension allows us to selectively control color correction based on the color model used to define the color (CMYK, RGB/HSB, or named). Named Colors include all of the color models defined by third-party vendors; in QuarkXPress 3.3, this includes all of the PANTONE choices, as well as the TRUMATCH, FOCALTONE, Toyo, and DIC matching systems.

At the bottom of the preferences dialog box are the default profiles for RGB and CMYK color. These profiles are used when rendering color if no other profile has been selected for an individual image. Next to each color model is a pop-up menu that lists all of the available profiles for devices that use that color model. Generally you want the default RGB profile to match your monitor and your CMYK profile should be your final output target. You'll see these defaults pop up later in other parts of the EfiColor interface.

TIP The EfiColor Preferences work just like all document preferences in QuarkXPress. If you change the settings while no documents are open, then the changes will affect all documents created thereafter. If you change the settings while a document is open, then the changes will only affect the active document.

Display Correction

The controls for EfiColor Display Correction fit naturally into Quark XPress' Application Preferences dialog. Your choices here are whether or not you want Display Correction turned on, and if so, what monitor you wish to correct for (Figure 4.30). The XTension comes with profiles for Apple, E-Machines, Seiko, Sony, SuperMatch (a.k.a. SuperMac), and Miro monitors. If your monitor isn't among these,

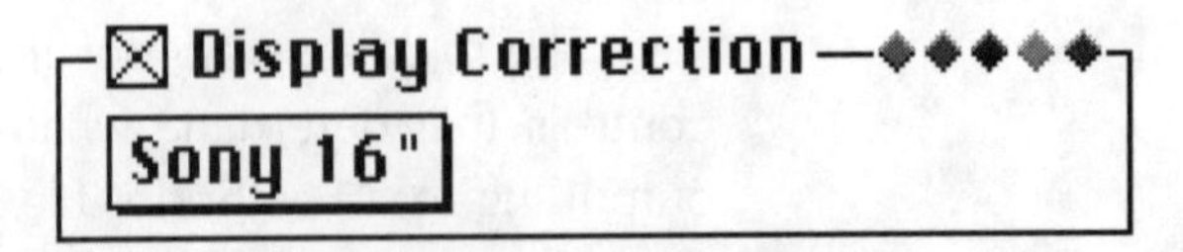

Figure 4.30 Display Correction EfiColor Display Correction is controlled through the **Edit→Preferences→Applications** dialog box. This setting, like all application preferences, is saved with the application, not the document.

check with the manufacturer or look for them on electronic bulletin boards, such as EFI's section in CompuServe's DTP Vendor Forum (GO DTPVENDOR), where the latest profiles are always available 24 hours a day. Monitor profiles are usually distributed for free.

Using Display Correction has an adverse effect on performance; it takes a lot of processor power to render color. For this reason you may want to work with this feature turned off most of the time and turn it on only when you wish to judge color on screen.

TIP The fact is, a fancy color monitor calibrator won't necessarily give you WYSIWYG color. There are numerous factors affecting the appearance of color on a computer monitor, such as the phosphors used in the picture tube, the coatings on the glass, colors surrounding the monitor (including the monitor frame itself), and the ambient room lighting. It is possible to measure and compensate for these factors, but it's a constant battle. Even if you do succeed in keeping your monitor calibrated and in using favorable room lighting, there are colors that your monitor can display but your color printer, matchprint device, and offset press can't reproduce.

Some manual labor required

There is one inherent problem that all color management solutions must overcome—the vast amount of unknown color that exists today. There are a lot of images for which color has no meaning; they contain colors that are defined in relative rather than absolute values. In order to render any color or color image, the color or picture must be assigned at least a profile—and preferably a rendering style as well. Some applications, like EFI's Cachet, can now embed profile and rendering style selections inside the image file. There they can later be read by the EfiColor XTension and automatically applied when displaying or printing the image, eliminating the need to manually select these settings. Let's hope that other applications adopt EFI's Metric Color Tag (MCT) standard so that we can have consistent color across applications as well.

An image's profile and rendering style are initially set in the **File→Get Picture** dialog box. Added to the bottom of the standard dialog box are two items: Profile and Rendering Style (Figure 4.31). When you select a color PICT or TIFF, the appropriate default profile will automatically be selected (depending on the color model), along with the Photographic Rendering Style. If the selected image file includes Metric Color Tags—which tell EfiColor what color meaning to apply to the values in the file—the "tagged" profile will automatically appear in the pop-up menu. If they're available on your system, they'll be underlined as well.

You can change either the profile or rendering style of an image by selecting another choice in the pop-up menu before importing the picture. After a picture has been imported, its profile and rendering style may be changed by selecting its picture box and then choosing **Style→Profile**. This will bring up a small dialog box with pop-up menus for the two values. If you have display correction enabled, you should be able to see notable differences depending on the profile

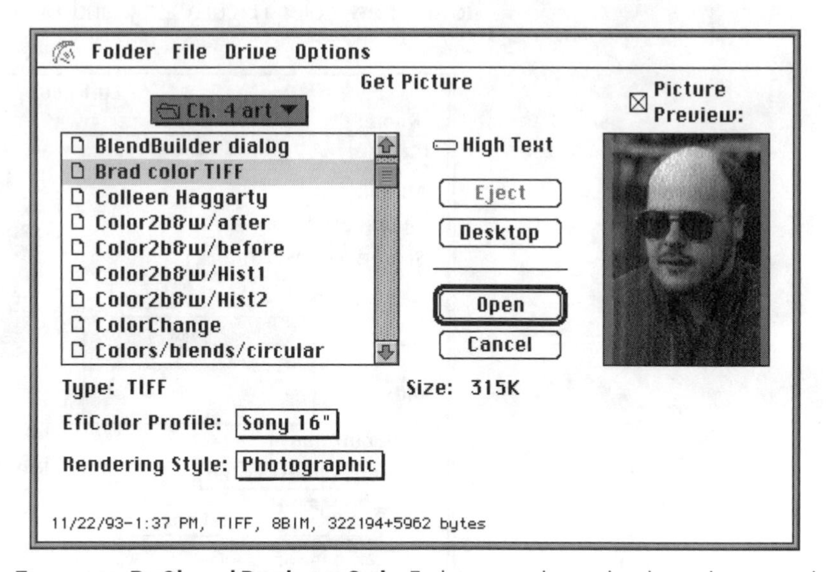

Figure 4.31 Profile and Rendering Style Each image to be rendered must be assigned an EfiColor Profile and Rendering Style. If a selected file contains Metric Color Tags, then the appropriate settings will be chosen automatically.

selection for any given image. The rendering style for a QuarkXPress process color is set in the **Edit→Color** dialog.

Auto Reality Check

Along with a pop-up menu for Rendering Style, the EfiColor XTension adds a very nice feature called the Gamut Alarm. The Gamut Alarm warns you of colors that are not reproducible on the selected target device (Figure 4.32, and also in color plates). This feature can be disabled simply by deselecting the Gamut Alarm checkbox. The target device may be changed by selecting another entry from the pop-up menu at the bottom of the dialog box.

The Gamut Alarm provides visual feedback in two forms. First, if the RGB color model is chosen and the Gamut Alarm is enabled, then EfiColor will draw a red outline on the color wheel. Colors within the outline represents the range of colors of the target device at that specific level of brightness. Colors outside the outline are "out of gamut," and if selected, will cause a small triangular icon with an exclamation mark on it to appear next to the color swatch. If a named color model, such as PANTONE, is chosen, out-of-gamut colors will appear with a slash through them and a warning icon will appear next to the new color (Figure 4.33, and in color plates).

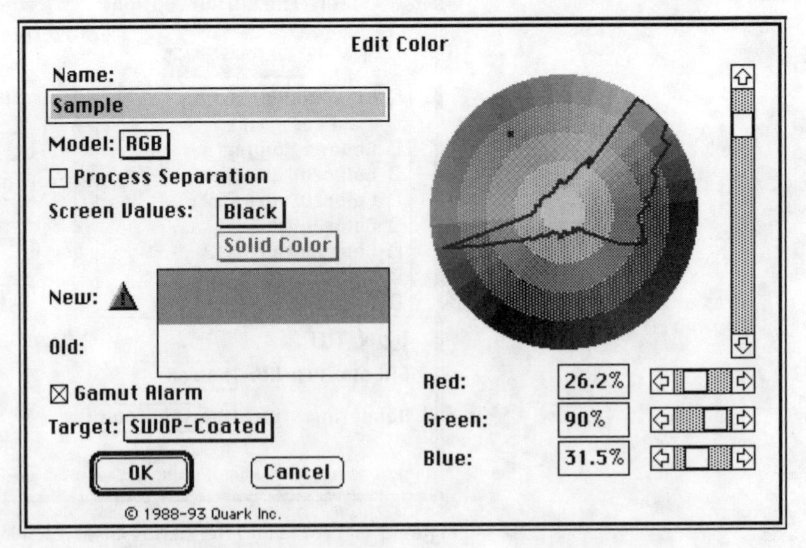

Figure 4.32 Gamut Alarm/RGB EfiColor warns you when you've selected a color outside of the limits of the selected target device.

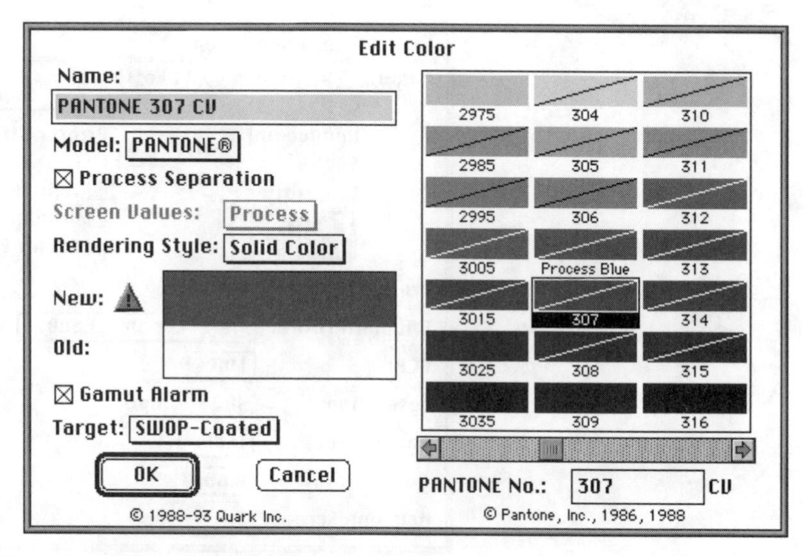

Figure 4.33 Gamut Alarm/PANTONE EfiColor puts a slash through this PANTONE color to tell us that it can't be accurately produced on the SWOP-Coated target device.

Printing with EfiColor

The EfiColor XTension includes several controls over the rendering of colors when proofing on a color printer or creating separations on a high-resolution black-and-white printer or imagesetter. EfiColor presents you with an appropriate choice of device profiles based on the Printer Type chosen in the **File→Page Setup** dialog box (Figure 4.34). If the selected printer is a color printer, then the pop-up list of profiles will include all of the available RGB or CMYK profiles, depending on the color model of the selected printer. If the printer is a high-resolution (greater than or equal to 600 dpi) black-and-white device, then the pop-up list of profiles will include all of the available CMYK profiles.

In addition, Gray Component Replacement (GCR) control is available when a separation profile—for example, SWOP-coated—is selected. GCR controls the amount of black to be used in the separation. There are several reasons for using as large amount of black as possible when creating separations. First, black ink is cheap. Second, the use of black reduces the total amount of ink on the page, speeding drying time. Third, putting as much imagery as possible on the black plate reduces the effects of misregistration. And fourth, because

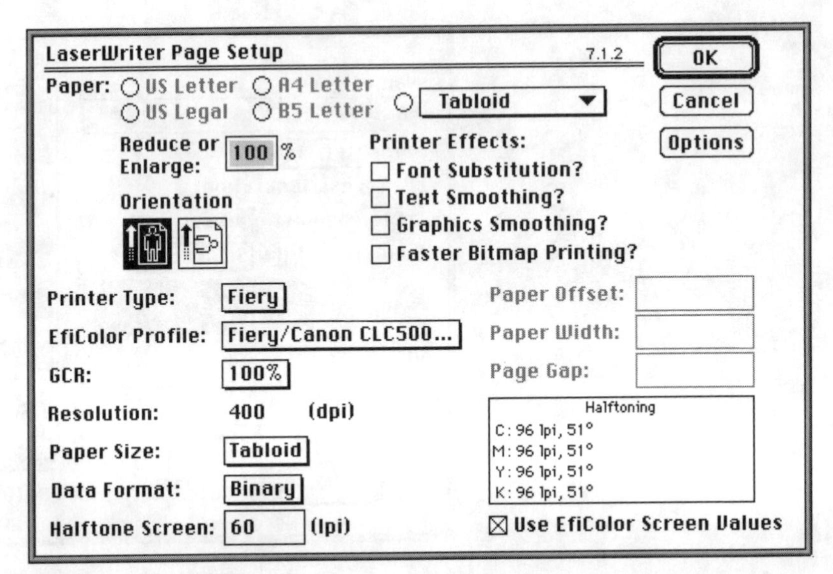

Figure 4.34 EfiColor Profile and GCR When outputting to a CMYK device, GCR is enabled and may be specified by selecting from the pop-up menu.

the combination of cyan, magenta, and yellow inks does not produce true black, adding black extends the gamut somewhat.

The level of GCR is set by selecting a percentage from the pop-up menu. It is somewhat disappointing that this field is not editable; you can't enter a value. You can choose among only the predefined entries (usually 0, 25, 50, 75, and 100%). EfiColor's GCR is different from traditional GCR in that the resulting color is independent of the level of GCR. Colors separated with 0% GCR match those separated with 100% GCR, as illustrated in this book's color plates.

Anyone who creates color separations knows how the angle and frequency of a halftone screen can effect color. EfiColor takes this into account by providing you with specific settings, displayed in the lower right-hand corner of the Page Setup dialog. These angles may be overridden by unchecking the Use EfiColor Screen Values check box. Given that the EfiColor Profiles were created based on these settings, it makes sense to leave this box checked.

Profile Usage

Like the Font and Picture Usage dialogs, the Profile Usage dialog is useful for making sure you have all of the necessary ancillary files before outputting a document. Also, like Font and Picture usage, EfiColor will warn you when opening or printing a document that specifies a profile that is not currently available (Figure 4.35).

The Profile Usage dialog lists the profiles used in the current document, the objects (types of color) that they affect, and whether the profile is OK, modified, or missing. When you select a profile, the three buttons at the bottom of the dialog become active. The first button is Show First. Selecting this option will find the first object for which the selected profile is used and display the name of the object and its specified rendering style in the Picture Info section of the dialog. After showing the first object, the name of the button changes to Show Next. Selecting this button will cycle through each object that uses the selected profile. The name of the button will return to Show First when the last object with the selected profile is selected.

The Replace All button allows you to substitute any selected profile with any other available profile of the same type (color model). This option also allows you to specify the rendering style for all objects that use the selected profile. This feature is useful for making global changes to your documents.

The Replace button allows you to apply a new profile and rendering style to the selected object without affecting other objects that use the same profile. The Show First/Next button and the Profile List allow you to navigate through all of the color objects used in a document so that you can change these settings.

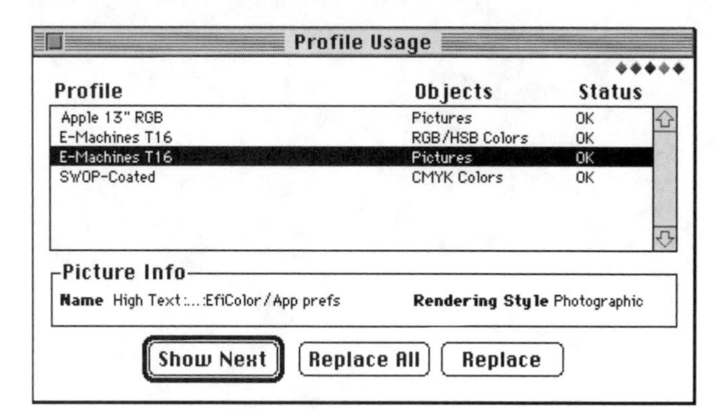

Figure 4.35 Profile Usage This dialog is similar to QuarkXPress' Font and Picture Usage dialogs. It allows the user to see which profiles are being used, where they're being used, and then to selectively change them.

Real-world EfiColor

EfiColor sounds great in theory, but how does it work in the real world? As we've discussed, there are several pitfalls that must be avoided, such as specifying colors outside the gamut of the target device and relying too heavily on the color shown on screen. It also presents us with an array of controls over color separation that we've never had before. Like most tools, it will take some playing around with these to get a good feel for how they work. For some examples, take a look at the color plates in this book; they contain comments on specific things we discovered while producing them.

Some users have complained about the cost of extra EfiColor profiles. If the profiles for your devices aren't included with the XTension, then you'll have to buy additional profiles from EFI. Profiles were originally priced between $129 and $250. However, EFI has announced a new package called EfiWorks, which will include the complete profile library and tools to let users modify profiles for there own devices. It's supposed to cost around $400, and it's scheduled to ship during the first quarter of 1994. Until then, you can purchase individual profiles for a flat price of $129 each; EFI has promised a $79 upgrade to EfiWorks to anyone who purchases a profile before EfiWorks ships.

5

Output

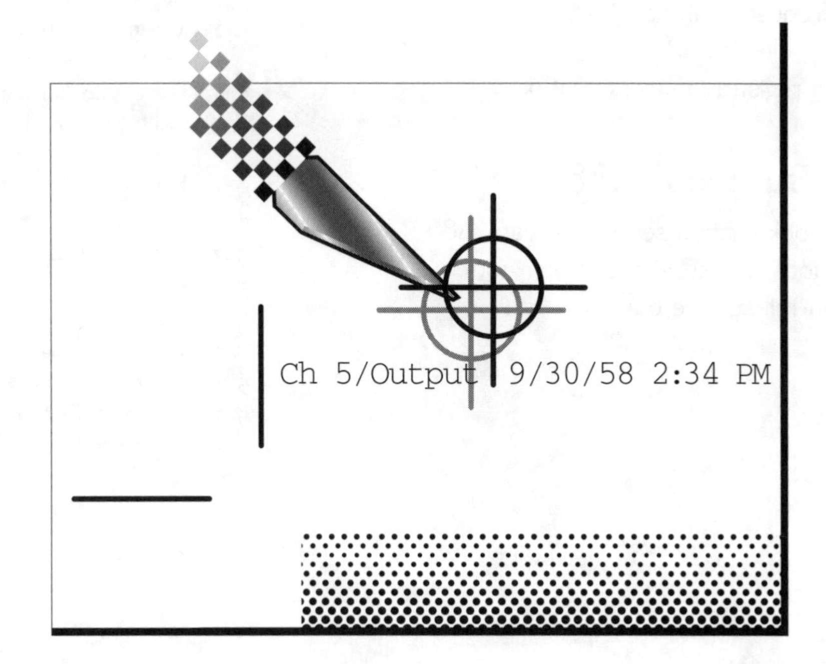

CHAPTER 5 CONTENTS

FIGURES

Perhaps the single greatest thing about desktop publishing is the control it gives you over your work. Unless you have an imagesetter, though, it probably feels like the final output of each job is beyond your control. Communication with both the service bureau and the printer is essential in order to get the output you desire. Jobs can fly through a service bureau and be happily accepted by a printer if an understanding of the printer's needs exists at the start of production.

This chapter starts with a summary of desktop output options, including a few ways to get more use out of black-and-white laser printers. That's followed by a discussion on trapping and other printing issues, such as screen frequencies and bleeding elements. The chapter concludes with ways to communicate with and distribute files to service bureaus.

Output options

There are a number of devices on which you can "proof" jobs. Proofing a job usually entails outputting an inexpensive—and lower resolution—printout. The goal is to save money by finding problems before sending the job to a more expensive output device. The most common proofing device is a black-and-white laser printer. Now that prices are coming down, color proofing from the desktop is becoming more common, too. And then there are the more traditional devices for creating Matchprint-like proofs.

Black-and-white laser printers

Most of us print our jobs a number of times on a black-and-white laser printer. In fact, you probably take your toner-based laser printer for granted—except when you run out of memory or need to print an image whose size is larger than the paper. Here are a few things you can do to get the most out of proofing jobs on a black-and-white laser printer.

Memory

By their very nature, laser printers usually print jobs at a resolution lower than the final output. If you have a 300 dot-per-inch (dpi) laser printer, only 90,000 dots are being imaged per square inch. A high-resolution imagesetter, however, images documents at millions of dots per inch: At 1270 dpi, 1,612,900 dots are generated per inch; at 2540 dpi, 6,451,600 are used. What this all adds up to is the fact that just because a document will print on a laser printer does not necessarily mean it will print on an imagesetter. And even if it does print on the imagesetter, if it's so complex that it adds appreciable time to the output, you may be billed overtime charges.

TIP Although QuarkXPress doesn't allow editing of the "flatness value" for any of its items, you can do so for images created by graphics programs such as Aldus FreeHand and Adobe Illustrator. Flatness refers to how many segments will be used to draw a curved object; the lower the flatness value, the smoother the curve. At the lowest flatness value, imagesetters will try to create a curve with far more segments than necessary. You—or your service bureau—should watch for "limitcheck" printing errors and increase the flatness value if these errors occur.

Print colors as grays

When working with spot colors, it's often helpful to print the different colors as unique shades of gray. This option, available in the Print dialog box, chooses a shade of gray for each color based on that color's darkness. This helps a client check the colors that have been assigned to each item, and it also aids in marking a proof for color breaks, which printing plants often require you to do before they'll accept a job.

TIP When colors are too close together in darkness, I often go into the **Edit→Colors** dialog box and edit one color's palette to distinguish it from another color. There's no harm done, as long as process color separations (cyan, magenta, yellow, and black) aren't being produced.

When editing a PANTONE color, I just change the model from PANTONE to CMYK, adjusting the black value up or down, depending on whether I want it to print darker or lighter. You should also watch out for colored type printing so light that it's unreadable.

As shown in the **Page Layout** chapter, it can also be a good idea to print a swatch of colors on each page so the client can keep track of which color is which (Figure 5.1). This is especially helpful if there are a large number of colors or if different shades of a color are used. The colors can be drawn in a margin on the master page or placed in an item that bleeds off the top, bottom, or outside edge of the page. If you make sure that the item touches the page but that none of its contents enter the page area, there's no harm in printing it at the service bureau, too. If the colors are drawn in the page area, the item containing the colors should have its printout suppressed in **Item→Modify** before sending the file to the service bureau.

Printing enlarged pages

It's awfully tough to check trapping—discussed at length later in this chapter—on laser printer output, since the trapping is generally tiny and 300-dpi output is so coarse. A good way to check trapping is to output part of the page at 400% enlargement. This way a quarter-point trap will be one point wide, which is much easier to see when you hold your separated output up to the window or desk lamp (if you're anything like me).

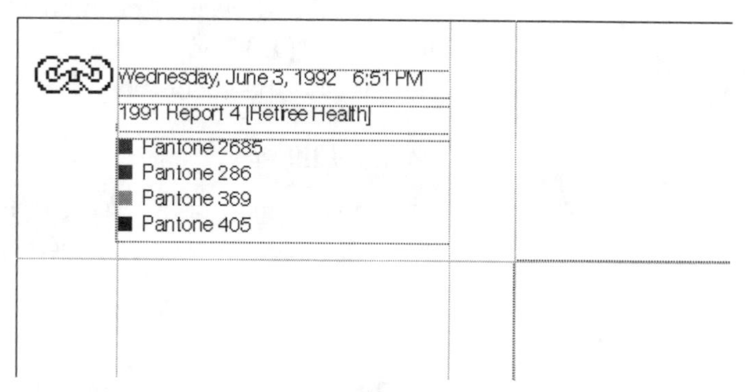

Figure 5.1 Color swatches on the master page I've shown swatches of all this job's PANTONE colors in an item on the master page. I had to twiddle a bit to get the PANTONE 2685 and 286 blues to look appreciably different from each other.

Automatic tiling

The term "tiling" refers to printing only part of a page. Generally, tiling is required when the output device uses paper smaller than the page size defined in QuarkXPress. Tiling also comes in handy when you want to enlarge the printing percentage in the **File→Page Setup** dialog box.

QuarkXPress can automatically tile oversize pages during output, but a little forethought and experimentation with this option's settings in the **File→Print** dialog can save you some time—and a lot of paper. The Automatic tiling option assumes that overlapping tiles are desired, and the default value for that overlap is a whopping 18 picas (Figure 5.2). With such a high setting, you may find that a lot of unnecessary tiles are generated. On the other hand, you may not have convenient overlaps if you don't use a large enough setting.

Optimally, you should set the automatic tiling overlap so that large areas of white space are included in the overlap. This will simplify piecing the tiles together into one large page. A few tests should prove useful—and necessary. Sets of corner marks are generated on each tile in order to show how to piece together the page (Figure 5.3). The sets appear in different sizes and orientations in order to aid alignment of the individual tiles. The largest corner marks indicate the outside edges of a tile, whereas the smallest set marks the section of the page that has been overlapped.

Automatic tiling also adds an element to the slug line generated when Registration Marks is turned on in the Print dialog box. The horizontal and vertical position of each tile is appended to the slug line, as in "(2,1)," where the first number is the horizontal position of the tile and the second number is the vertical position.

Manual tiling

The other option under Tiling in the Print dialog box is Manual. This type of tiling allows you to customize which part of a page will print. You define the printable area by changing the position of the docu-

Tiling: Automatic **Overlap:** 18p

Figure 5.2 Automatic tiling The tiling choices in the Print dialog box are: No, Manual, and Automatic. With the Automatic option, you need to define an overlap value.

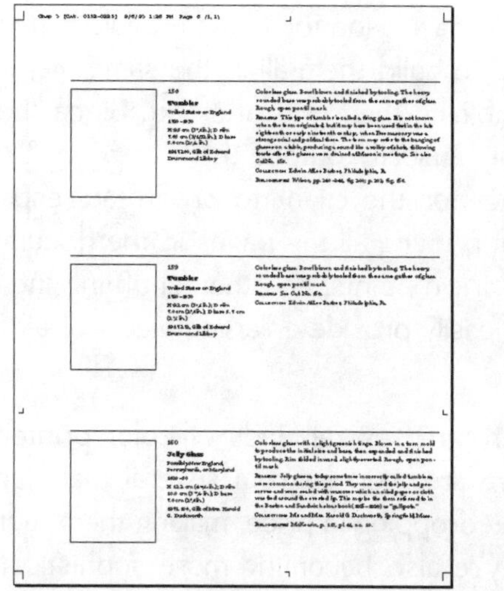

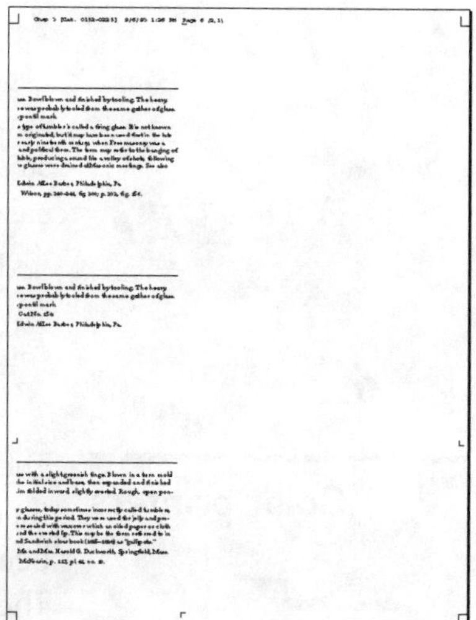

Figure 5.3 Overlapping tiles The small corner marks centered at the top and bottom of each tile for this page show where these tiles overlap.

ment's origin point, which is done by dragging the crosshairs from the corner of the document window—where the horizontal and vertical rulers meet (Figure 5.4).

Once the new origin point has been defined, turning on Manual tiling results in the printing of only the portions of the page that are below and to the right of the new origin. By giving you control over the origin point, Manual tiling lets you determine which parts of pages print on specific tiles. Clicking once in the crosshairs restores the origin point to its default position of the top-left corner of the page.

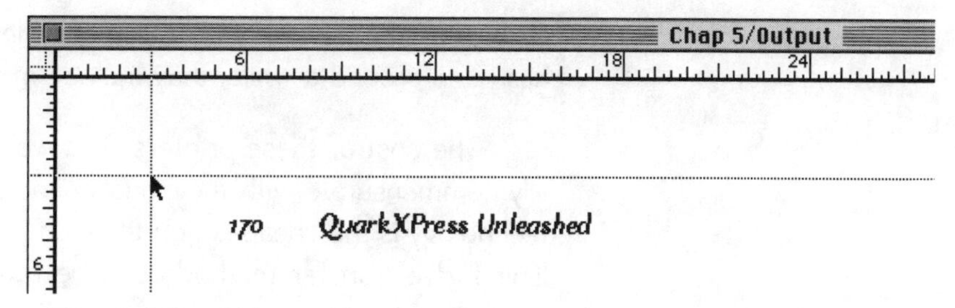

Figure 5.4 Manual tiling This document's origin point is being changed by clicking in the crosshairs and dragging them out onto the page—in this case, to 3 picas from the top and left of the page.

I have a job for which I regularly need to produce bar charts, and I like to build them all in the same file, usually four to a page, before combining them with the text. Since the type in the charts is pretty small, I usually output them at a 200% enlargement, making it a lot easier for the client to proofread, especially if I'm faxing them. By then printing all the pages in the document with each of four different origin points, and then shuffling the pages to restore the order, I can easily provide enlarged views of all the charts.

Color printers

There are several kinds of color printers, and within each category there are models from several manufacturers. These printers have been dropping in price, making them more affordable to more people. They're also becoming more sophisticated and powerful, and when you combine this new hardware with some rather ingenious calibration software, the quality of pages we can print today with Quark XPress has increased dramatically.

There are four kinds of color printers:

- Thermal wax—these use a crayon or ribbon to lay down color and are available from Tektronix, QMS, Calcomp, and Hewlett-Packard.

- Color laser—represented by the Canon Color Laser Copier (CLC500, CLC300 and the new CL150, which is not a copier, but actually a laser printer), and Xerox 5775.

- Subliminal dye transfer—producing some of the best looking color coming off the desktop; they include the Du Pont 4Cast, 3M Rainbow, Kodak XL77, SuperMac Proof Positive, and Raster Ops Correct Color.

- Inkjet—the new kids on the block, despite using technology that has been around a while; they include models available from Iris.

The cost of these printers—as well as their output—is generally commensurate with their quality and power. The old thermal wax technology is the cheapest; on the high end, calibrated inkjet and subliminal dye transfer methods can be rather pricey. As is often the case, the mid-range lasers from mainstream companies such as QMS and Hewlett-Packard are appearing with some amazing technology that is quite reliable.

TIP It's important to realize that no desktop proofing device will fully represent the relationship between film, the printing plate, and paper. Also, none of these devices will output anything but a round or square dot, neither of which will necessarily be what you get when generating output from an imagesetter.

Before purchasing or standardizing on a color printer, test each one that contains the desired feature set and is within your price range. Use real jobs that represent typical production work—preferably jobs that have already been completed and for which you still have Matchprints.

Matchprints

Folks in the prepress industry still refer to the output from desktop color proofing machines as "goofy proofs." For one thing, most of these machines still leave a fine gap between colors, a limitation in PostScript which is supposed to be fixed in Level 2, a new version of Adobe's page description language. But since you can't get a properly shaped dot out of these machines, color-critical jobs will still require Matchprints.

There are actually five different proofing technologies falling under the rubric of "matchprint." They all work by taking four-color (CMYK) film separations and exposing the negatives onto four photosensitive colored emulsions. Each emulsion is processed, washing away the unexposed areas. Some methods are water-based, while others require less ecologically friendly solvents. Then the four emulsions are laminated together to form a prepress proof.

I'm told that as long as the materials are kept fresh and the replenishment systems are kept clean (which is apparently a little more difficult with water-based systems), the output from various matchprint systems is indistinguishable. The five available types are 3M, Agfa, Fuji, Du Pont, and Pressmatch. Chances are you'll end up getting whichever one your service bureau or printing plant already uses.

Printing XTensions

Print Area and PrintArea

Both QuarkPrint, a commercial XTension from Quark, and PrintArea, from XTend, allow specific areas of pages to be printed. In both cases, the origin across and down as well as the width and height of the

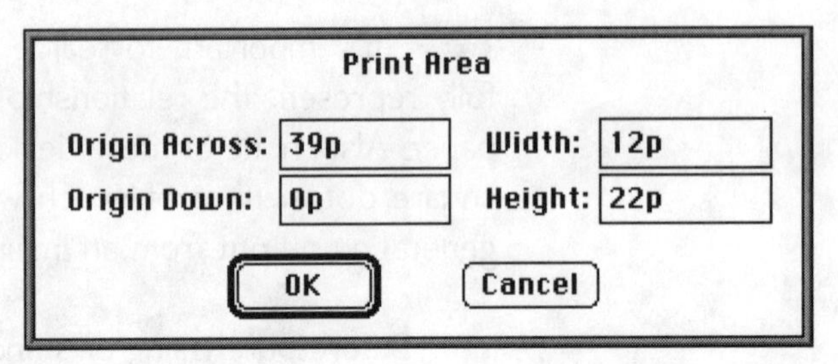

Figure 5.5 QuarkPrint A new Print Area option is added to the File menu as one of QuarkPrint's several features.

page area can be specified (Figure 5.5). The advantage to using such an XTension is that you can choose the point at which printing will cease; QuarkXPress' built-in tiling always prints a page area starting at the origin point and ending only when the paper ends.

QuarkPrint has an unnecessary and "big brother-ish" feature that keeps you from specifying a width and height that will take you beyond the edge of the page, making it unable to print bleeds; PrintArea doesn't suffer from this problem. On the other hand, of the two, only QuarkPrint recognizes the current position of the origin point; PrintArea always assumes that the origin point is in its default position.

The Display Print Job Dialog choice in PrintArea's dialog allows you to skip the Print dialog and start printing directly from the XTension (Figure 5.6). This feature would be more useful if you were also allowed to state which pages to print, or if you could choose an option to print only the currently displayed page. If you select one or more items on a page before calling up PrintArea, their total area will

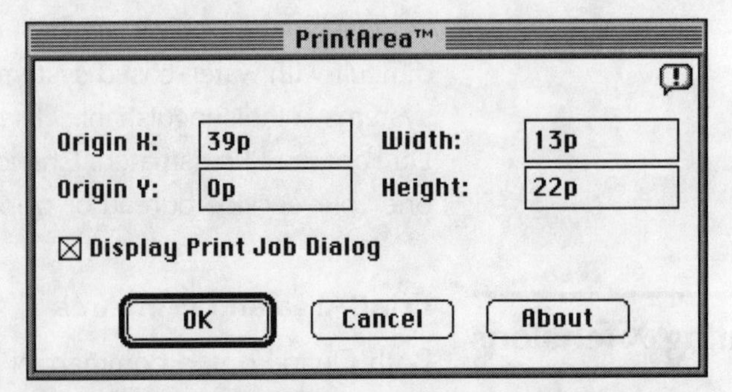

Figure 5.6 PrintArea This XTension has a few more features than the Print Area option of QuarkPrint, including the choice of bypassing the Print dialog box.

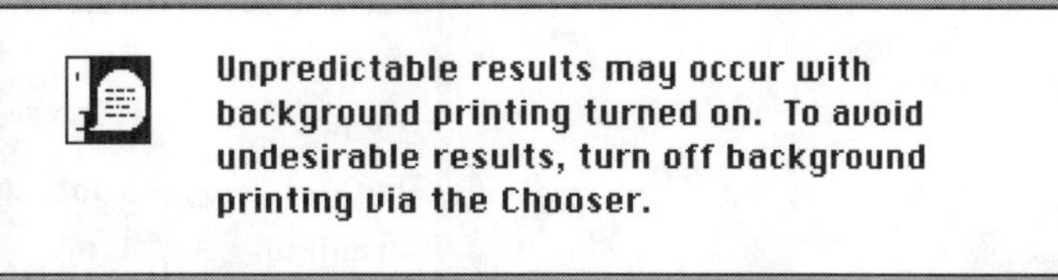

Unpredictable results may occur with background printing turned on. To avoid undesirable results, turn off background printing via the Chooser.

Figure 5.7 Background printing "Unpredictable results" is an understatement. Whatever area you've defined—with either QuarkPrint or PrintArea—will be stretched horizontally and vertically to fill the paper size if Background Printing is turned on.

already be displayed in PrintArea's dialog when you access it, which is a very nice feature.

Unfortunately, neither of these XTensions has a clue as to what to do when Background Printing is turned on in Macintosh's Chooser. Instead of politely printing the requested page area at the top left of the paper, they both stretch the image from edge to edge and from top to bottom of the paper. To its credit, XTend's PrintArea informs you of this if you click on the balloon in its dialog box (Figure 5.7).

PrintIT

The PrintIT XTension, from a lowly apprentice production, adds a new tool to the QuarkXPress Tool palette. This tool can be used to draw a marquee around the area of a page that you wish to print. Once the marquee is drawn, a dialog box appears, allowing further definition of the area to be printed (Figure 5.8). Like QuarkPrint and PrintArea,

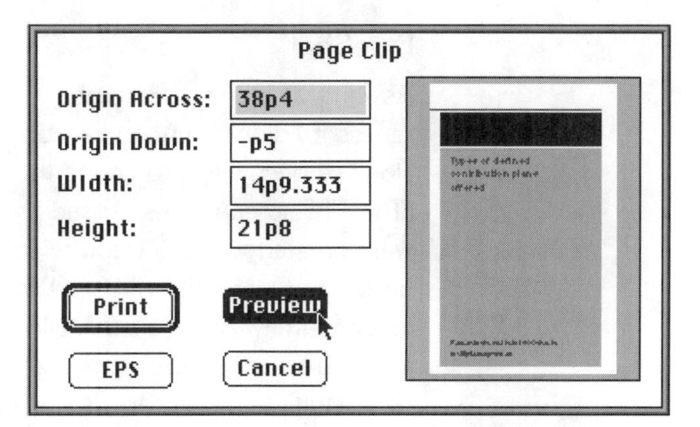

Figure 5.8 PrintIT Called Page Clip for some reason, PrintIT's dialog box adds a couple of features unavailable in QuarkPrint and PrintArea, such as a Preview and EPS.

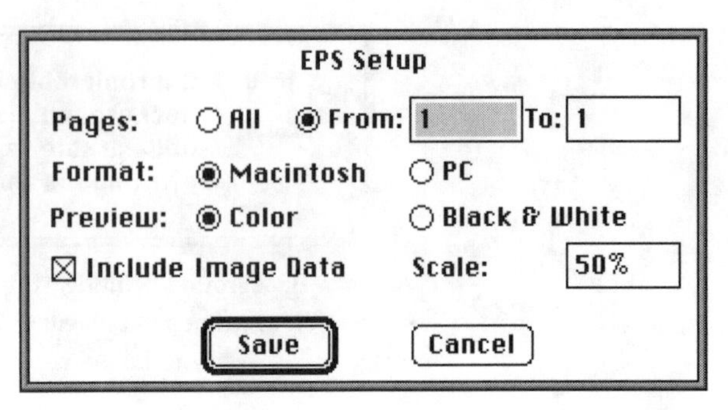

Figure 5.9 PrintIT's EPS choices Partial pages and ranges of pages can be saved as EPS images by clicking the EPS button in PrintIT's main (Page Clip) dialog box.

PrintIT has trouble with Background printing. However, it properly prints bleed elements.

PrintIT also has a Preview button in its dialog. Pressing the button generates a screen preview of the area of the page to be printed. If further adjustments are made to the origin across, origin down, width, or height, pressing the Preview button again will generate a new preview.

Parts of one or more pages can be saved as EPS images by pressing PrintIT's EPS button. It's important to note that EPS files created with PrintIT can include bleed elements, differentiating it from QuarkXPress' own Save Page as EPS command, which truncates its EPSs at the edge of the page. PrintIT can also save multiple pages at once, unlike QuarkXPress (Figure 5.9).

PageShot

As long as we're talking about saving pages as EPS images, I'd be remiss if I didn't mention PageShot, from Vision's Edge. It's the XTension I've been using to create the EPS screen shots used in this book. (The TIFF screen shots—used predominately for dialog box figures—were created with the Capture control panel.) PageShot adds a Resize button to QuarkXPress' Save Page as EPS dialog. When the button is clicked, a new dialog opens, allowing custom dimensions to be typed in (Figure 5.10). There's a demo of PageShot on this book's disk.

Multiple pages can also be saved as EPS images with PageShot. Like PrintIT, PageShot overcomes QuarkXPress' bias against printing

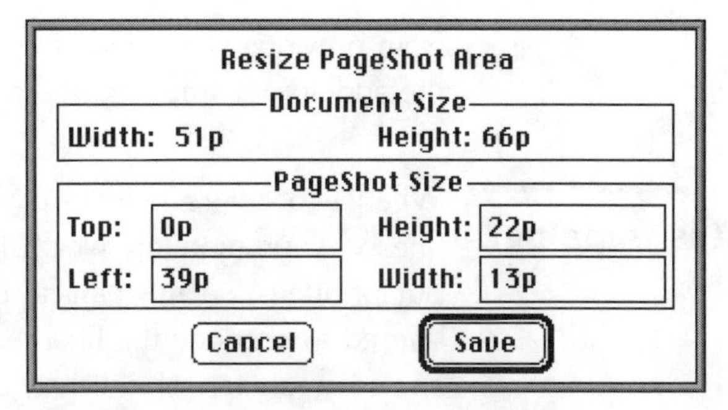

Figure 5.10 PageShot Specific areas of one or more QuarkXPress pages can be saved as EPS images with the PageShot XTension.

bleed elements. But be careful: PageShot doesn't recognize a moved origin point, so you'll need to reset the origin point if you want to refer to a selected item's position when filling in PageShot's dialog box. Additionally, PageShot adds a Box to EPS choice in QuarkXPress' Utilities menu that can be used to save individual items as EPS images.

TIP Prior to version 3.2, EPS images created by QuarkXPress were always shifted one point down and to the right. This meant that a tightly defined EPS capture would always have one point of extra space at the top and left of the image, and one point would be missing from the bottom and right side. PageShot must have been using some of the same routines as QuarkXPress, since they now both work properly.

Trapping

I've been doing spot-color trapping with QuarkXPress since the introduction of the Trap Information palette in version 3.1. Before that, I really couldn't understand what was going on with the program's trapping options. Once I could see—and set—individual traps with the Trap Information palette, I felt it worth exploring further. It has enabled me to save my clients money at the printer, in some cases. I have also been able to charge more for some jobs; on others, I was able to keep my prices constant even though the jobs were repeating from previous years and little or no setup was required—except for the addition of trapping.

What is trapping?

When two colors overlap or butt up against each other, they look fine on your monitor, which is electronically producing the colors. But printing is a mechanical process, and colors aren't necessarily layered to produce the final result. The printer generally doesn't want any color on top of another, since that will cause new colors to be created on the press.

QuarkXPress can automatically remove—or knock out—the background colors when two colors overlap. In the case of white type on a dark background, a simple knockout is all the printer needs. And when there's black type on top of a light background, it's okay for both colors to print; the black type is said to overprint the lighter color (Figure 5.11).

But when any other two colors overlap, the printer will require you to *partially* knock out the background, allowing a little more of the lighter color to be printed. The reason for this is that the printer has to register the printing plates that contain the two colors, and getting the different color plates to be precisely registered on a press is not always possible. It's not uncommon for color registration to be off by slight amounts, which means that the color of the paper may show between the ink colors.

Trapping is the process of printing a little more of the lighter color ink so that, if the press is misregistered, the paper color won't show through. If a lighter color is printed on top of a darker color, it is said to "spread" to the darker color; if the lighter color is behind the darker color, it is said to "choke" to the darker color (Figures 5.12a, b).

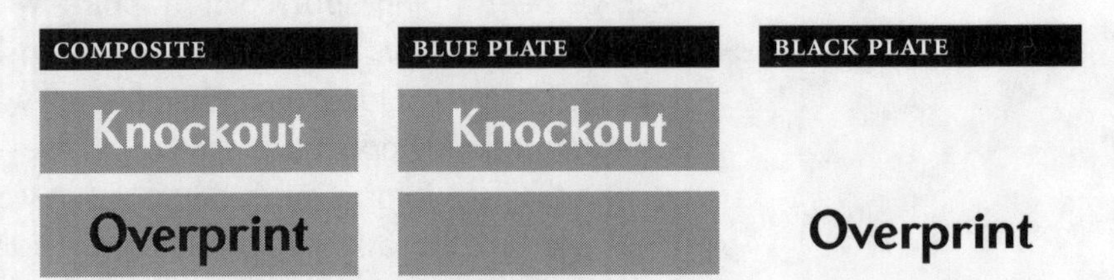

Figure 5.11 Knockout and overprint The white type is said to knock out the blue background, and the blue plate prints with a hole where the text would be. On the other hand, the black type overprints the blue background; both plates are completely printed.

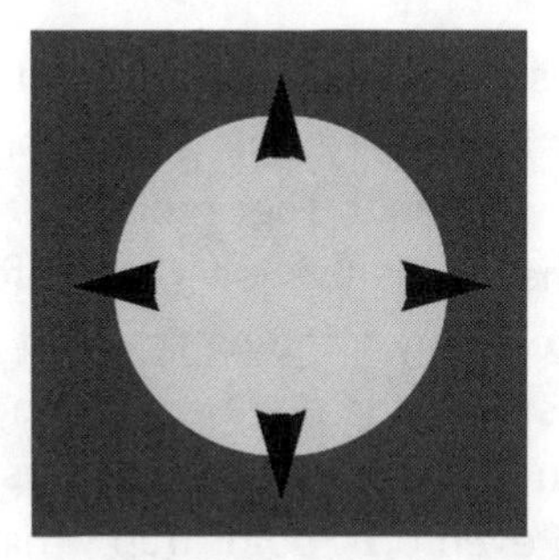

Figure 5.12a Spreading The lighter foreground color is spread out toward the darker background.

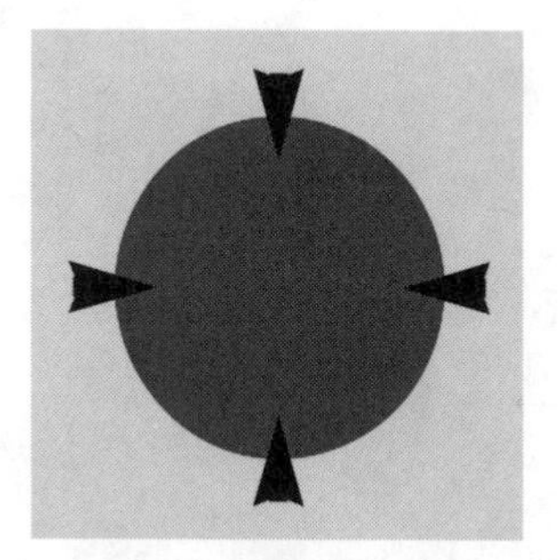

Figure 5.12b Choking The lighter background color is choked to the darker foreground.

Trapping Preferences

The Trapping Preferences dialog, whose values are document-based instead of application-based as of version 3.2, is the foundation of proper trapping in QuarkXPress. It is here that you define the default values that the other two trapping areas will refer to (Figure 5.13). The numbers in the Trapping Preferences dialog need to come directly from your printer, but a surprising amount of trapping can be done in a job before knowing what these values should be—as long as you rely on QuarkXPress' automatic trapping.

The values entered into the Auto Amount and Indeterminate fields will be determined by the press the job will be printed on. The printer will probably specify these numbers in thousandths of an inch.

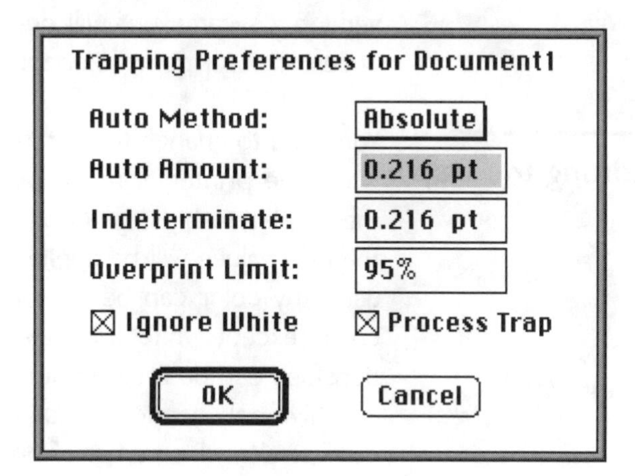

Figure 5.13 Trapping Preferences Available as a separate dialog box starting with version 3.2, these preferences—which should come directly from the press printing the job—will travel with the document.

QuarkXPress' default of 0.144 point is equal to 0.002 inch, and the 0.216 point that my regular printer prefers is the same as 0.003 inch. However, on one job I set recently, the client switched presses after I was finished with the job (but before we ran out the film, thankfully). Since all my trapping referred to the automatic values, all I had to do was switch the numbers in the prefs dialog. I'm told by my service bureau that some of the printers in New York City are starting to request an even 0.25 point trap, which simplifies things a bit.

If you don't want trapping to occur, change the Auto Amount to zero and change the Overprint Limit to 100%. Also, make sure you don't have any color pair specific traps defined in the **Edit→Colors** dialog box, as discussed in the next section. Although black will still overprint at 100%, you can even get rid of that by specifying that black knock out of every other color in the **Edit→Colors** dialog.

TIP Since the Trapping Preferences were saved only in the application and not in the document prior to version 3.2, you might expect that you could define new defaults with no documents open and that old documents would now open up using these new preferences. Oddly enough, this is not the case. Even if you used the Trap Preferences XTension that was distributed by Quark—which would carry the preferences with the document as long as any machines opening the document used the XTension—all old documents opened since version 3.2 came out will default to using QuarkXPress' old preferences of 0.144 point (0.002 inch). So be careful!

Editing the trap

You need to change the default trapping relationships between colors when the printer is not happy with QuarkXPress' determination of these relationships. If you change them in the **Edit→Colors** dialog, the new values will be applied wherever the edited color pairs are in use. Any color can be set to overprint, spread, or choke any other color (except white, which will always be overprinted), or the relationships can be reset to automatic (Figure 5.14).

I've only needed to use this dialog with one type of job: When I do charts in which a bar of one color crosses a grid of another color, I often have to override QuarkXPress' automatic trapping. Since my bar charts rarely extend above or to the right of the last grid line (depending on their orientation), the last line will appear thinner if the

PhotoCD

PANTONE 152 CVP (PROSIM)

Each head at the top of these color plates uses a different color matching system. The short bar in the head is shaded 100%; the long one is shaded 30%. All of the colors were converted to CMYK by the EfiColor XTension.

photo: Bruce Walrod

PhotoCD image (raw) The print of this photograph didn't look too bad, but the PhotoCD image clearly illustrates that the photo processor must have done some work before releasing the print. Here's the photo in all its unretouched glory.

photo retouch: Sam Merrell

PhotoCD image (retouched) Here's the same PhotoCD image after it was opened in Photoshop and retouched. If you use QuarkXPress' PhotoCD XTension, use professional—not amateur—photographs, or be prepared to electronically retouch them.

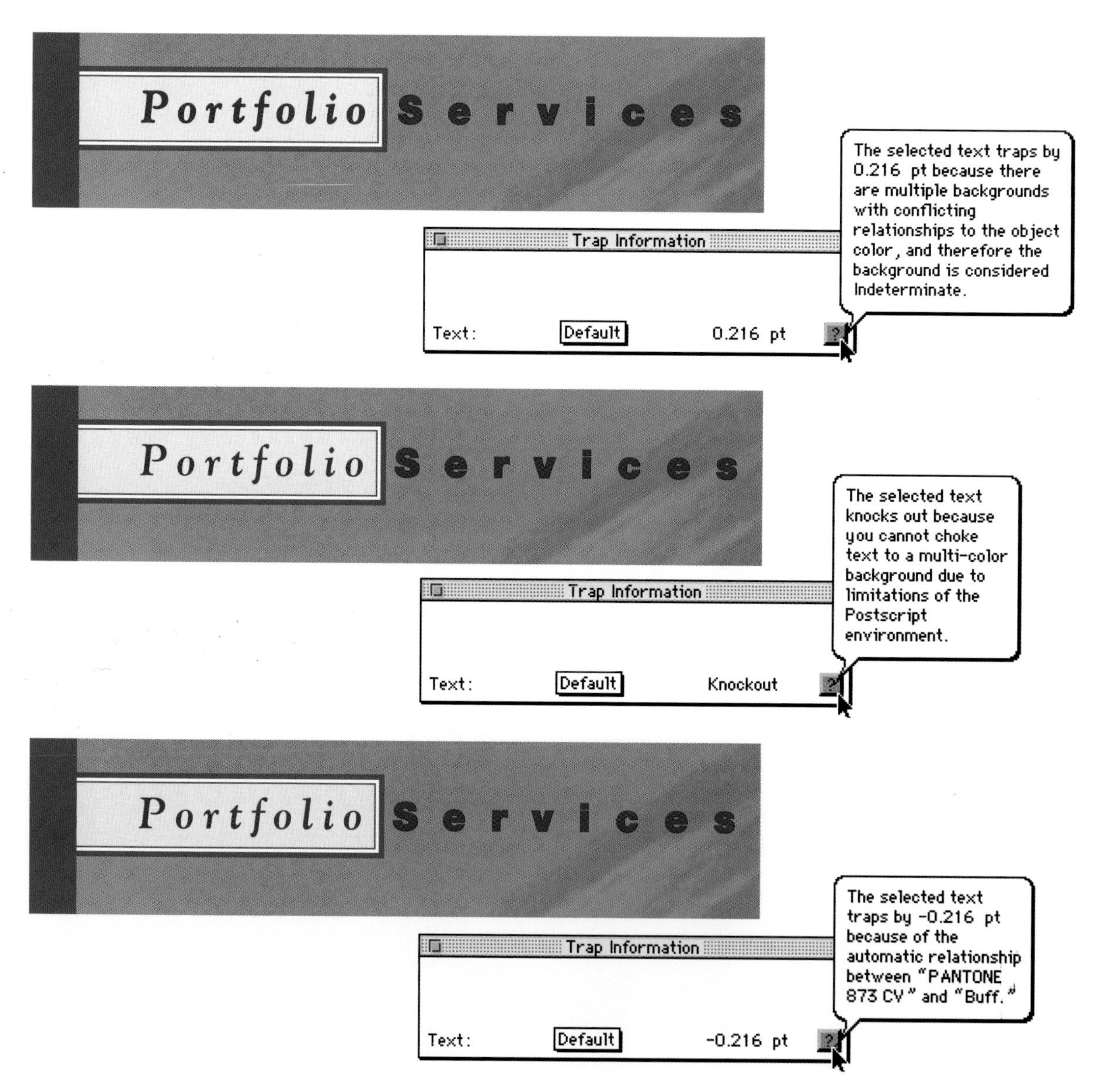

Trapping and text box sizes In the top illustration, both words of the headline are in one text box, and the box straddles multiple backgrounds. Since the text has different trapping relationships with each of the backgrounds, QuarkXPress automatically spreads the text. In the second illustration, the text box has been resized so that it's in front of both the "buff" background and its frame. The text should choke to both of those backgrounds, but to choke text, QuarkXPress strokes it in the background color. Since PostScript can't stroke type in two different colors, the text is simply knocked out. In the final illustration, the text box has been resized so that it's in front of only one color, and it chokes properly.

Trapping

PANTONE 327 CVU (uncoated)

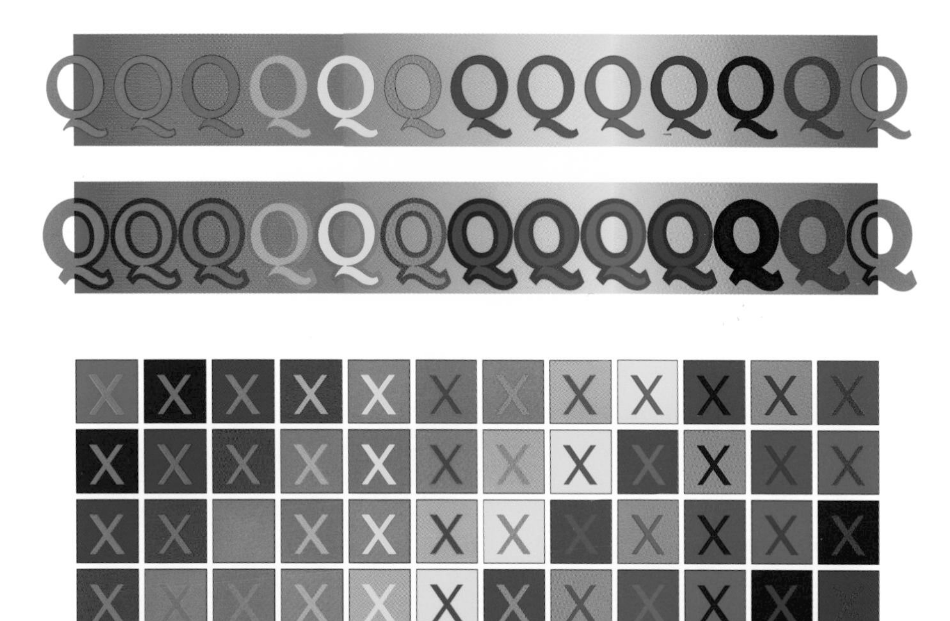

Unexpected colors from trapping When text is spread or choked, the overlapping colors sometimes create a noticeable third color. In the top row of Qs, each letter has a custom spread trap of .2 points. In the second row, a spread of 2 points has been designated to exaggerate the effect.

Proportional trapping The Xs are being trapped proportionally, rather than by an absolute amount, which has reduced the chance of unwanted color. The trapping shown above varies from −0.3 to 0.2 points, depending on the color of each X and its relationship to its background.

EfiColor XTension

TOYO 0836PC

EfiColor XTension/0% GCR

EfiColor XTension/50% GCR

EfiColor XTension/100% GCR

SWOP shortkey

EfiColor XTension/0% GCR

EfiColor XTension/50% GCR

EfiColor XTension/100% GCR

EfiColor and GCR The EfiColor XTension employs a method of gray component removal that preserves the colors of the picture while still transferring ink to the black plate. As you can see from the first three illustrations on the left, settings of 0%, 50%, and 100% GCR make no difference in the final four-color picture. However, the black plates from each separation, shown above, clearly illustrate the transfer of detail from the cyan, magenta, and yellow plates to the black plate. As a control, the bottom illustration on the facing page was generated from a professional color separation program using a standard printer's SWOP shortkey table. You should consult your printer before modifying GCR values, since increasing GCR will limit your printer's ability to control the press.

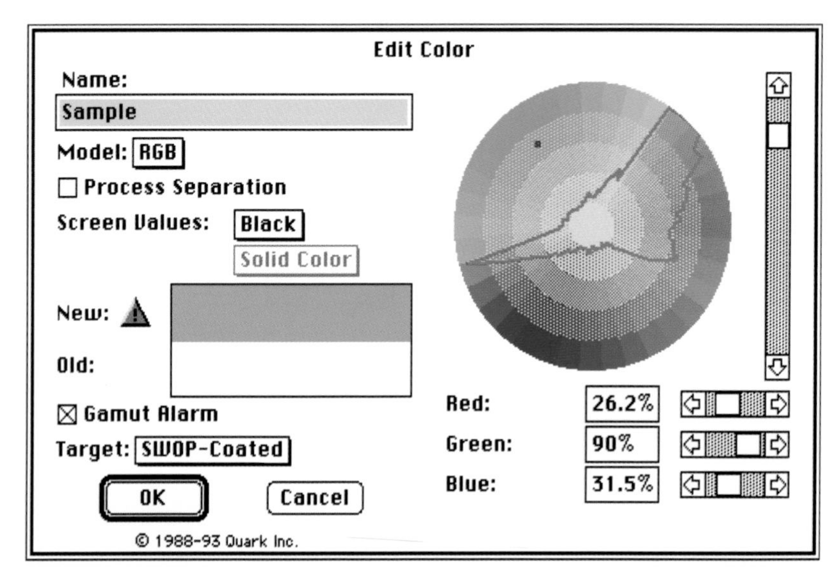

EfiColor Gamut Alarm/RGB When a color is created from the RGB or CMYK color wheel, the EfiColor XTension illustrates the selected target's color gamut by drawing an outline. Any color that falls outside the outline is considered out of gamut; when Gamut Alarm is checked, the exclamation mark in the triangle also appears.

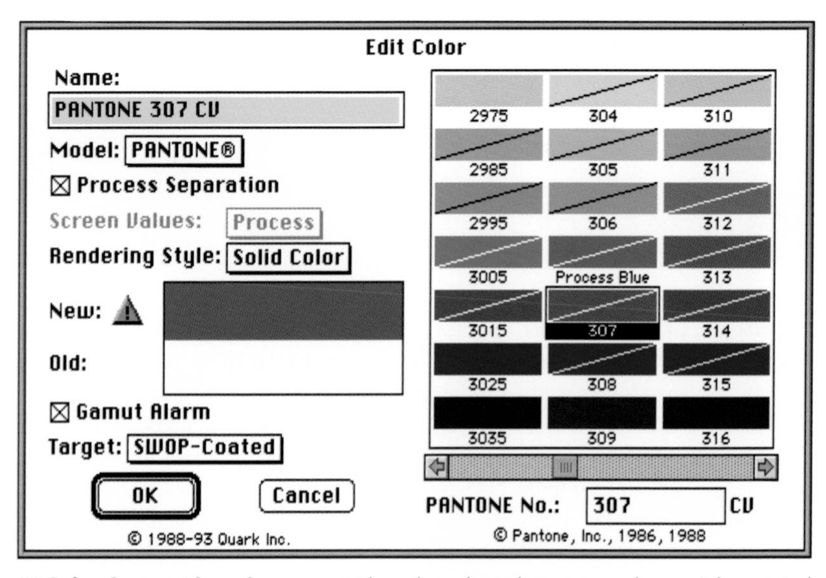

EfiColor Gamut Alarm/PANTONE When the selected PANTONE color can't be printed on a chosen target device, a slash is drawn through the color swatch.

Line screens

TRUMATCH 36-A1

150-line screen

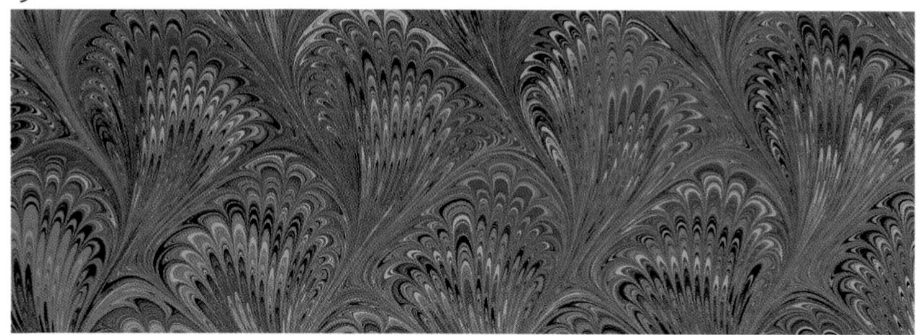

120-line screen

150-line screen

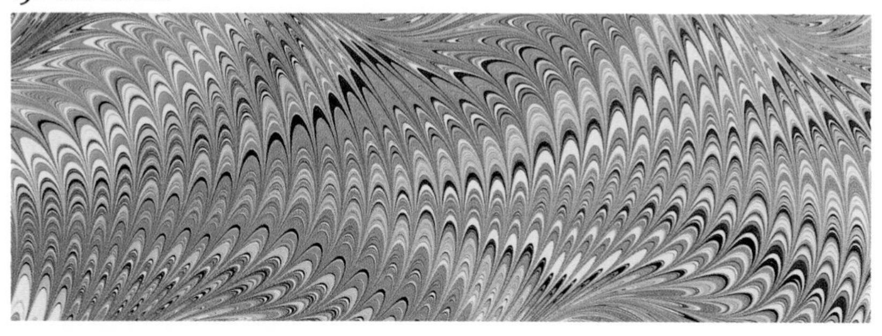

120-line screen

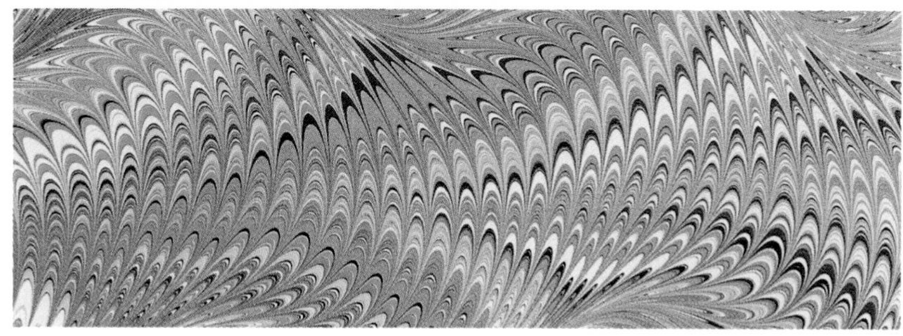

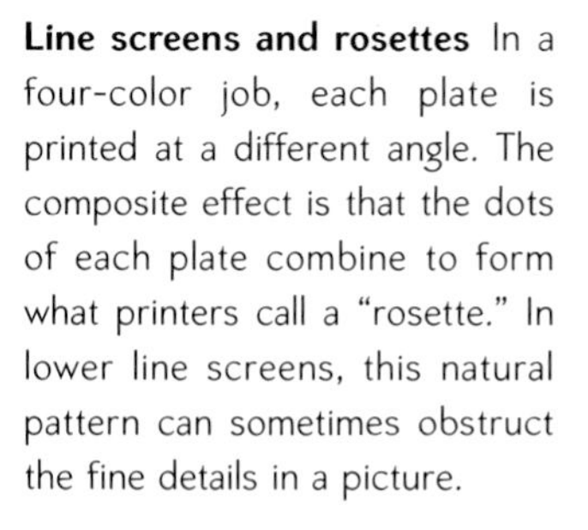

Line screens and rosettes In a four-color job, each plate is printed at a different angle. The composite effect is that the dots of each plate combine to form what printers call a "rosette." In lower line screens, this natural pattern can sometimes obstruct the fine details in a picture.

SXetch Pad and Taco Clipart

DIC 295P

UNLEASHED

Blending each letter The SXetchPad XTension is used here to apply a blend to each letter independently.

UNLEASHED

Blending entire word SXetchPad can also join all the letters so the blend applied is uniformly, which is necessary when all the letters aren't the same height.

UNLEASHED

Different strokes SXetchPad can stroke each letter any color you want.

Taco Clipart Company This is an example of the clip art coming out of Omaha, Nebraska these days. Taco donated this image to show how QuarkXPress on the Macintosh can easily open and separate files created on PCs.

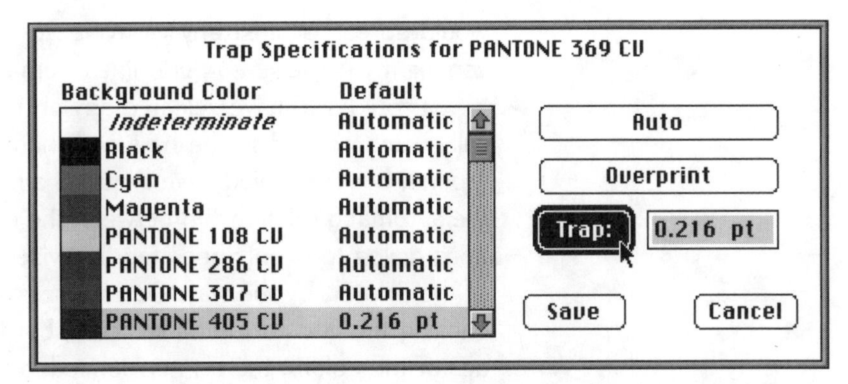

Figure 5.14 Trap Specifications Here I've edited the trap that occurs when PANTONE 369 is the foreground color and PANTONE 405 is the background color. This dialog would be a lot more useful if it stated the specific automatic relationship.

grid is choking to the bars (Figure 5.15). By changing the automatic relationship between the bar color and its background grid color, I can prevent the grid from only partially choking the bars.

When I first entered the Trap Specifications area in the **Edit→ Colors** dialog box, PANTONE 369 had the automatic trap setting when PANTONE 405 was behind it. I can't tell what that automatic relationship is from this dialog box, but by using the Trap Information palette, discussed next, I determined that when PANTONE 369 is the foreground color, a lightly shaded PANTONE 405 in the background would automatically choke. I edited the trap values for PANTONE 369 so that it

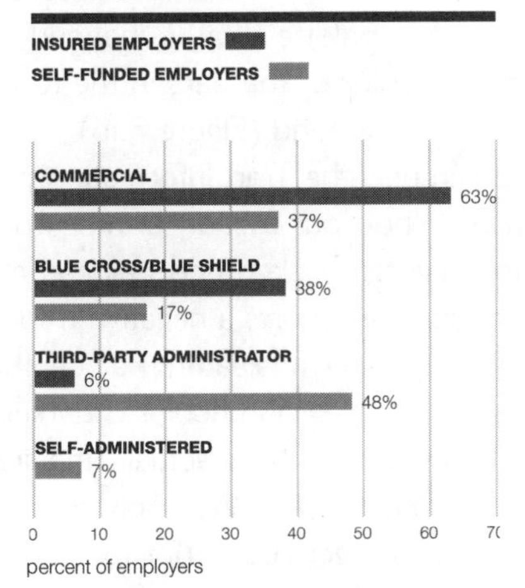

Figure 5.15 Overriding the automatic If I don't do something about the automatic trapping for these colors, all of the dark bars will choke to the light grid lines. Since the rightmost grid line is rarely touched by a dark bar, it will end up appearing thinner than the rest of the grid lines.

would spread against any PANTONE 405 backgrounds, thereby preventing my PANTONE 405 grid lines from appearing uneven.

I could also have selected any grid lines that weren't automatically being choked to the bars and then spread them to their background, but this would have required a lot of manual work. Changing the automatic relationship between the colors in the Trap Specifications dialog took only one step. I devised this plan with the blessing of the printer, by the way. QuarkXPress is doing the logical thing by choking the grid to the darker bars, but because of the relative values of the colors, the printer conceded that the job would still print okay. He also agreed that it was safer to automate the process than to constantly worry about the outermost grid line on each chart.

TIP The hardest part of talking to a printer about trapping is getting the terminology straight. On a press, you're always referring to a light color spreading or choking a darker color. But in QuarkXPress, you have to specify the trapping on the foreground color, whether or not it's the lighter of the two colors. So if a printer tells you to choke a yellow background to a blue foreground, you have to make sure that the trap value for the foreground color—the darker blue—is a negative value. This causes QuarkXPress to do just what the printer wants: Expand the size of the yellow background so that it overlaps the blue foreground.

Trap Information palette

Using the Trap Information palette to check automatic relationships between colors is essential. As discussed above, it was only after checking this palette that I changed the automatic relationship between the color of the bars in the foreground and the color of the grid in the background (Figure 5.16).

Remember, the Trap Information palette words things a bit differently from how our friendly printer would. Where the printer would refer to a lighter background color choking to a darker foreground color, the palette reports a negative trapping value for the foreground color. This is a bit misleading, since the darker color never really changes; if the foreground color is darker, the palette indicates that it will choke, even though it's actually the lighter color in the background that's doing the choking. We apply a negative value to the foreground color in order to get PostScript to make the knockout smaller.

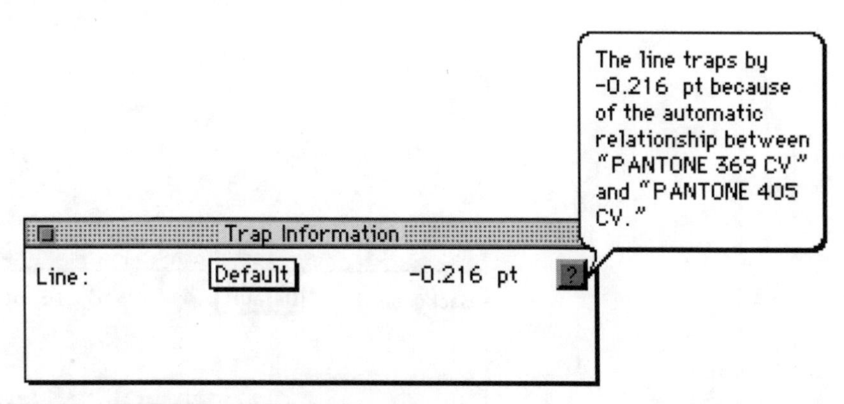

Figure 5.16 Before changing the Trap Specifications This is what the Trap Information palette reported about the relationship between the bar color (PANTONE 369) and the grid color (PANTONE 405) before I made any changes to the Trap Specifications.

Prior to QuarkXPress 3.3, if you customized the relationships between colors in the Trap Specifications dialog box, the Trap Information palette sometimes gave erroneous information (Figure 5.17). Whenever a background color did not completely surround a foreground color, the palette did not properly report edited traps as user-specified relationships. I suspect that this is because the palette thought that the foreground was in front of an indeterminate (multicolor) background, even though white was often the only other "color" in the background. This happened even when the Ignore White option was checked in the Trapping Preferences dialog, which made things needlessly confusing. If the foreground color was com-

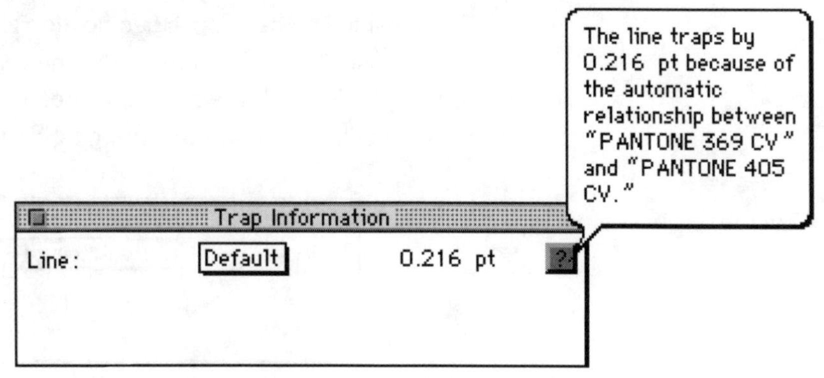

Figure 5.17 After changing the Trap Specifications After I edited the trap to make sure the PANTONE 369 bars wouldn't cause the PANTONE 405 grid to get thicker, the palette erroneously reported it as an "automatic relationship."

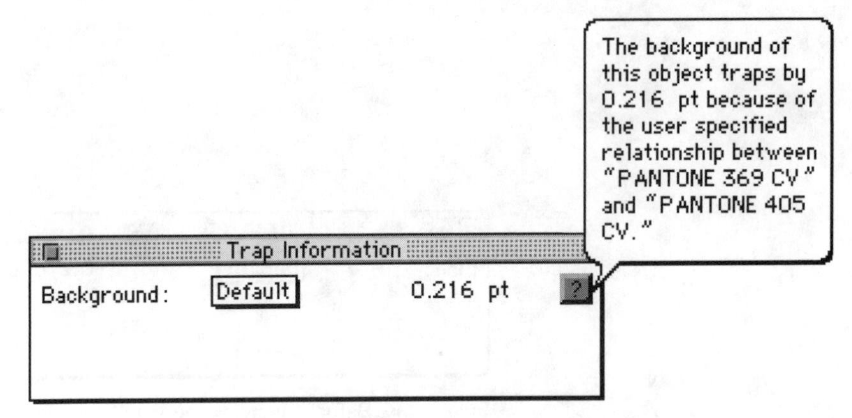

Figure 5.18 When the Trap Information palette works After changing the automatic relationship between colors in the Trap Specifications dialog box, this is the way the default setting in the Trap Information palette should read.

pletely surrounded by its background, then the palette correctly reported the user-specified relationship (Figure 5.18).

When neither the Trapping Preferences nor the Trap Specifications dialog box supplies the tools needed to make the necessary adjustments, making manual changes in the Trap Information palette is the last resort. Whenever possible, however, the palette should be used in a way that depends on the automatic values put forth in the Preferences and Specifications dialogs. For example, if instead of having only to worry about PANTONE 369 bars sitting in front of PANTONE 405 grid lines I also had to worry about other occurrences of this combination of colors, I might not have been able just to change their relationship in the Trap Specifications dialog. In that case, I would have chosen Auto Amount (+) in the palette instead of Default (Figure 5.19). Granted, it would have been a manual change, but at least it would still depend on the Trapping Preferences values for the actual

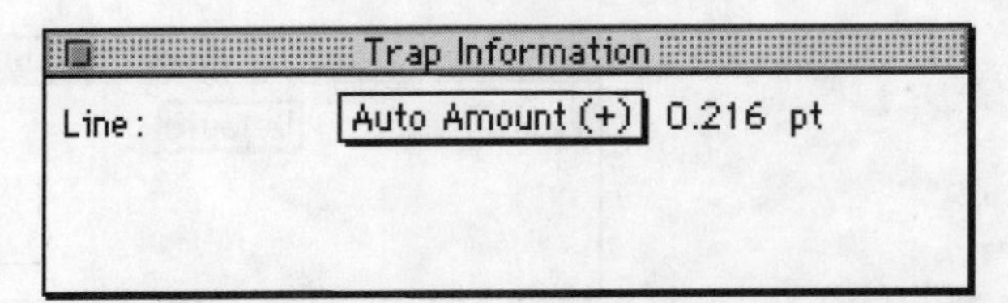

Figure 5.19 Using Auto Amount (+) If you choose either of the Auto Amount options in the Trap Information palette, the overall trapping can still be changed in the Trapping Preferences dialog and individual traps like this will change accordingly.

amount of the trap, meaning that if we had to change presses I'd still only have one document-wide value to change.

TIP QuarkXPress will allow you to select Auto Amount (–) or even a Custom negative trap—even when an element is in front of an indeterminate color. You are allowed to select the Auto Amount (–) because the object you're applying the trap to could be later moved over a background to which it can choke. The Trap Information palette *should* show a value of zero or Knockout in situations where the choke cannot occur, but that's not the case. Even though the value that the object will be trapped by is shown as a negative value, a knockout or overprint will still occur, since PostScript can't choke to an indeterminate color.

Trapping frames

The color applied to a frame is a "foreground" color in that it can be trapped to both the background color of its box and any color surrounding the box. Frames are unique in that you can specify trapping for a colored frame relative to both the inside background color and the outside background colors (Figure 5.20).

Only the first seven frames shown in **Item→Frame** can be trapped, since these frames are made with PostScript code. The last nine frames in the standard list—along with any frames created with the Frame Editor application—can't be trapped, since they are only bitmap frames.

Multi-line frames

Double- and triple-rule frames are made of solid lines separated by white space. On boxes for which an item runaround is specified, these frames are trapped in the same way as a solid frame except that the white areas are unaffected and knock out of all plates. If a

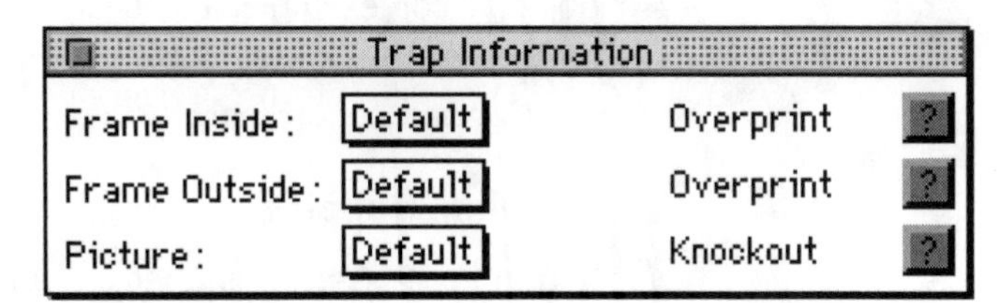

Figure 5.20 Inside and outside Frames can be trapped to both the background color of their box (inside) and the colors behind the box (outside).

runaround of None is specified, the background color prints in the space between the lines.

Trapping a frame to its background

When trapping a frame color to the background color of its box, the inside of the frame can be spread or choked. A frame can be spread to the contents (text or picture) of a box by giving the box background a minute percentage of a certain color and then spreading the frame to that color.

If a framed box is surrounded by items of different colors, the outside of the frame will trap according to the trapping relationship specified between the frame color and the Indeterminate color. If the frame color would normally spread to *all* of the background objects' colors, the frame will be spread; if it would normally be choked by *all* of the background colors, it will be choked.

Trapping process colors

When Process Trap is *unchecked* in **Edit→Preferences→Trapping**, QuarkXPress traps all four-color separation plates equally. It uses the automatic values for trapping and compares the foreground and background colors normally. When Process Trap is *checked*, trapping that's specified in the Trap Information palette may not be implemented as you expect when you print process separations; the trap value specified will actually be divided among plates.

Process trap

QuarkXPress individually traps each process separation plate when the Process Trap check box in **Edit→Preferences→Trapping** is checked and a page contains overlapping process colors. At the time that color separations are printed, the program compares the amount of each process color resident in both foreground and background objects. For example, the shade of cyan in the foreground color is compared to the shade of cyan in the background color. Then plates are trapped accordingly.

Absolute trapping

When Process Trap is checked and overlapping process colors have an Absolute trapping relationship, as defined in **Edit→Preferences→Trapping**, QuarkXPress divides the absolute value in half and applies it to the darker component on each plate. Dividing the value among plates apparently creates a smoother trap while providing the same area of overlap.

Proportional trapping

When abutting process colors have a Proportional automatic trapping relationship, QuarkXPress determines the amount of trapping by multiplying the Auto Amount value in **Edit→Preferences→Trapping** by the difference in darkness between the foreground and background colors. The resulting trapping value is then applied as explained above for colors with Absolute trapping relationships. Proportional trapping is illustrated in this book's color plates.

Trapping third-party pictures

QuarkXPress can use its trapping features only on objects that it generates. Any trapping that needs to be applied to imported graphics will have to be done manually in the programs that created them. Strangely enough, this also applies to EPS files created by Quark XPress: They can only carry the program's overprint trapping information with them.

TIP If you need to print both composite and separated proofs of QuarkXPress pages after trapped EPS images have been imported, you'll need to save a copy of the illustration without traps. Import the nontrapped version when printing composites, and bring the trapped version into the document only when separations are desired. This is because the traps are being created manually, so they will show up whether or not separations are requested.

Overprint and knockout

Colors can be applied only to certain types of graphics imported into QuarkXPress: PAINT; both line art and grayscale TIFFs and RIFFs; and black-and-white bitmap and grayscale bitmap PICTs. The only trapping options for pictures in these formats are overprint and knockout.

Pictures that have had colors applied in QuarkXPress can be made to overprint the background color of their graphic boxes by choosing Overprint for the picture in the Trap Information palette or by editing the trap in **Edit→Colors**. If you choose any other trap specification, the picture will knock out from the background color of its graphic box.

TIP When shading line art that has had the color black applied to it, the Overprint Limit specified in the Trapping Preferences dialog box will determine whether the picture will be allowed to knock out its background. If you're using the default value of 95% for the overprint limit, then the program will knock out the graphic box background only if the picture is shaded lighter than 95%.

To make imported EPS images—which can't be colorized—overprint their graphic box background, open the illustration in the program that created it, and use that program's tools to specify that the entire illustration should be overprinted. Make sure to add to the illustration at least one pixel of the same color that will be used as the graphic box background in QuarkXPress, or else this method won't work.

Merging TIFFs with their backgrounds

If you import a grayscale TIFF into QuarkXPress, its trapping relationship is determined by the background color of the picture box into which you are importing it. If you import it into a picture box with a background color of None, the grayscale will be left alone and the Trap Information palette will indicate that you have the option to either overprint or knock out the TIFF from any other background that might be present.

However, if you import the TIFF into a picture box with a background color other than None, the TIFF's grayscale is applied to the background color, in effect merging the two. Rather than getting a color range from 0 to 100% Black, the grayscale is converted to the same scale as the background color: A 50% gray will be transposed to a 50% of the background color. QuarkXPress can do this because it is relatively simple to merge together the values of the pixels of the grayscale and the background.

Once you have imported the grayscale TIFF into a picture box with a colored background, you will no longer have a Picture option in the Trap Information palette. This is because of the merging process that has taken place. QuarkXPress no longer views the TIFF as a separate item from its background, but rather views the two as one object for trapping purposes. You can still trap the background to objects behind it, but the TIFF itself has no trapping identity.

If you'd rather be able to knock out the TIFF from its background, there are two workarounds. The first would be to change the mode of the TIFF from grayscale to Indexed Color in PhotoShop or a similar program. QuarkXPress does not have the ability to merge files that contain Indexed (custom) color information, so it will not merge the TIFF with its background. You would then be able to set up the Picture trapping relationship manually from the Trap Information palette. The second workaround is to place the TIFF in a picture box with a background of None and in front of the background you wish to knock it out of. Since the picture box containing the TIFF has a background of None, the Picture menu will be available for trapping from the Trap Information palette.

TIP If you place a grayscale TIFF with a background of None over another background color in QuarkXPress 3.2, it will knock out of that background even if you set it up to Overprint from the Trap Information palette. The solution for the inability to overprint the TIFF would be to simply suppress the output of the graphic while printing the background color plate, and then unsuppress it to print the plate containing the graphic.

Spreading and choking EPS files

When an illustration is lighter than its graphic box background, an extra stroke has to be added to the illustration. Stroking the outside of the illustration will produce the spreading effect that the printer will require to compensate for press misregistration. If further trapping is required *within* the illustration, you will need to perform the same steps on individual elements of the illustration.

To spread in Adobe Illustrator, select the object that will be trapped and choose **Paint→Style**. If there's just a Fill value and no Stroke value, create a stroke that's the same color as the fill. Turn off Overprint for the fill and turn it on for the stroke. The weight of the stroke should be the same amount that you'll be using in QuarkXPress.

To spread in Aldus FreeHand, the same logic applies as above, only it's applied to **Attributes→Fill and line**. Because of the way Free-

Hand applies line weight—starting at the center of the line—its line value needs to be twice the amount that you'll be using in QuarkXPress.

Choking in Illustrator is a little more complicated, but not by much. A copy of the object to be choked will be made and moved to the back of the illustration, where a stroke will be applied to create the choke. Select the object that will be trapped and choose **Paint→Style**. Make sure the object has a Fill color specified, but no stroke. Check Overprint in the Fill area and click OK.

With the object still selected, choose **Edit→Copy** and then choose **Edit→Paste in Back**. Now, go back to **Paint→Style** and change the Fill value of this copy of the object to white, turning on the Overprint option. Create a stroke that's the same color as the background and make the weight of the stroke the same amount that you'll be using in QuarkXPress.

It's a little easier to create a choke in FreeHand than it is in Illustrator. Select the object that will be trapped and choose **Attributes→Fill and line**. Create a line that's the same color as the fill used in the background. Turn off Overprint for the fill and turn it on for the stroke. The weight of the stroke should be twice the amount that you'll be using in QuarkXPress, since the line is being drawn from the center.

To trap text against a background color in Freehand, select the text you want to trap and choose **Type→Effects→Fill and stroke**. Turn on Overprint for the Stroke and turn off Overprint for the Fill. To spread the text into the background, choose the same color for the stroke area as was used for the fill. To choke the background into the text, make sure that the color of the stroke is the same as the background color.

Trapping similar colors

You can always choose to split the trap between two objects in an illustration program if it's not obvious which one should be spread or choked. For example, if you normally create 0.25 point traps, create a 0.125 point choke of the background color and a 0.125 point stroke around the foreground object.

When producing process color separations, if the foreground and background colors share common process colors, press misregistration is not as much of a problem as it can be with spot colors and with illustrations made up of dissimilar process colors. You may not need to specify trapping when overlapping colors are created by one or more of the same process colors.

Specifying PANTONE colors in illustration programs

QuarkXPress is able to print spot and/or process color separations of PANTONE colors specified in either Illustrator or Freehand documents. To separate a PANTONE color contained in an imported EPS illustration, the color must be in the QuarkXPress document's color palette.

The PANTONE color can be added to the color palette manually, but the name must be spelled exactly the same as in the application that created the illustration. Also, the Process Separation area of the **Edit→Color** dialog box needs to be used to specify it as a spot or process color, depending on how the color was specified in the illustration application.

TIP As of version 3.3, any colors not already defined in QuarkXPress will be created automatically when an illustration is imported. This is fine if you haven't already created custom colors in the QuarkXPress document or if the colors in the illustration use the same spelling as used in the document. If you find instead that a lot of similarly-but-not-exactly-named colors are being created, either go back to the illustration application and rename the colors or use the Color-Change XTension, discussed in the **Graphics** chapter.

Other printing considerations

If you're "just" the production person on a job—you know, the one who does all the work and rarely gets a credit on the copyright page or in the masthead—you probably have never talked directly to the printing plant about a job. (And before you look, *I* did the production on this book; Random House used my company name, High Text Graphics, for the composition credit on the copyright page.) There are a few things that should be discussed with the printing plant before a job is started, however, whether it's you, the project manager, the art director, the editor, or the print broker who does the talking.

Screen frequency and angles

One of the nicest features of desktop publishing technology is the ability to assign shading values to type, frames, and item backgrounds. With that ability, however, comes the responsibility of knowing what line screen to use when printing high-resolution output. Assuming the printing plant is not also the service bureau, it's necessary for you to provide repro or film that is screened properly (Figure 5.21). Even if there are no photographs in a job, any use of shading will require knowing what screen frequency (lines per inch) the printer would use if he produced the screens traditionally. That value will be based, at least in part, on the paper stock the job will be printed on.

Setting up bleeds

When designers state that certain elements should bleed off the page, they're not requesting that you cut yourself and leave red marks all over the paper. (That's the proofreader's job.) Instead, what they're requesting is that part of the design print to the edge of the paper the job will be printed on. To get the effect of printing to the edge of a

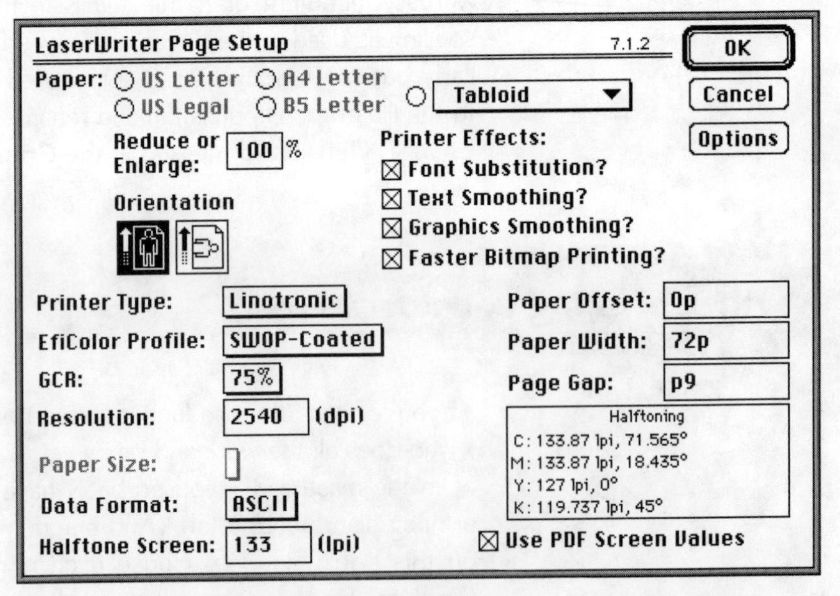

Figure 5.21 Halftone screen If you're outputting process color separations, it's interesting to note the screen frequency and angles built into an output device's printer description file (PDF).

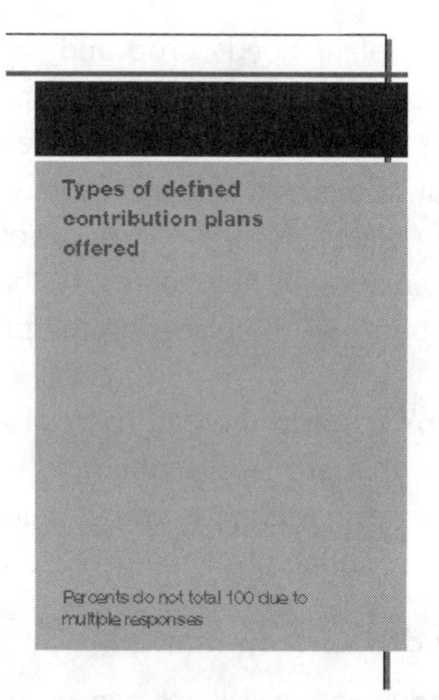

Figure 5.22 Bleeding The thick and thin rules and the text box all bleed off the edge of this page.

page, printers need to use larger paper and trim the pages back. And you'll need to provide them with repro or film that have elements that extend beyond the edge of the page (Figure 5.22). This compensates for the potential misregistration of the printing press. I usually bleed elements off the page by 9 points, which is the same as ⅛ inch.

Any element that at least partially touches a page in a Quark XPress document will print out. It is considered a bleeding element, whether or not any part of the element actually prints on the page. This makes for a handy way to add custom slug lines and other information that may fall within the crop marks but won't show up on press. Note, however, that if a page is exported using **File→Save Page as EPS**, all bleeding elements will be cropped at the page boundaries.

TIP There are a couple of reasons why you may need to keep bleeds when you save QuarkXPress pages as EPS images. Some imposition programs require EPS files to work, and you may want to bring a QuarkXPress page into another application. EPS Bleeder is a shareware utility that can help with this. It examines EPS files, determines whether or not it can enlarge the bleed area, and writes a new document with the enlarged bleed area. EPS Bleeder also allows batch processing of multiple EPS pages. I've included a copy on the disk in the back of the book.

Crop and registration marks

The printing plant needs crop and registration marks primarily for aligning color separations—whether spot color or process color separations. It's also a good idea to provide the marks on composite (normal) output, too, since crop marks can be used to position pages on the printing plates. Also, the information printed in the slug line next to the crop marks will help to ensure that pages printed without folios (page numbers) will be placed in the proper position.

TIP Don't get into the bad habit of using a letter-size page when setting jobs that are smaller than 8½ × 11 inches. Define the correct page size when creating a new document; the crop marks can be used by the printing plant to ensure proper placement.

Manually drawn crop marks

When producing small items like business cards, the printing plant may prefer that you provide them six-up, or six cards on a letter-size page. In that case, crop marks should be drawn for each card. You could do worse than to mimic QuarkXPress' crop mark defaults: lines 2p6 in length, 6 points from the edge of the printing area. Once the

Figure 5.23 Cropmark Incase The crop marks above were automatically generated by an XTension called Cropmark Incase, aka Logical XTension 1. Each of the eight marks is 7mm long and is spaced 3mm from the item.

first set of eight marks—two per corner—have been set up, group them and step-and-repeat them around the page. Use 0.25 point as the line width, and don't forget to color them Registration, the color that prints on all plates!

Cropmark Incase XTension

Crop marks around items can also be created with an XTension from the Electronic Studio called Cropmark Incase, aka Logical XTension 1. Crop marks can be generated by selecting any item and choosing the XTension; all the lines for the crop marks are drawn and automatically grouped together (Figure 5.23).

The PressMarks XTension

If you really want to knock your clients' socks off, check out the PressMarks XTension from Vision's Edge (Figure 5.24). It offers over 30 different registration marks and informational boxes that can be placed around the page, and you can save different templates for various page sizes and job types. It also allows you to add EPS images, such as a company logo or a custom color strip.

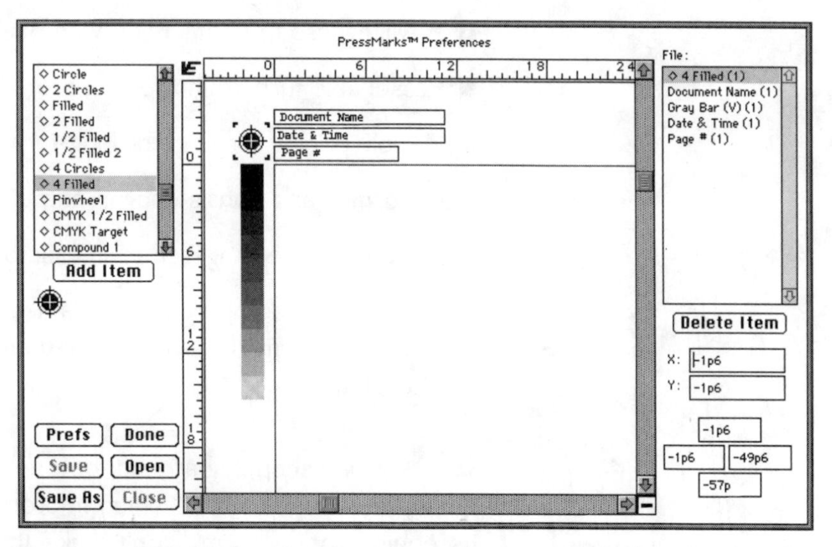

Figure 5.24 PressMarks All of the elements shown outside the "page" in the XTension's viewing area were individually chosen and arranged. Information boxes are automatically updated each time the job is printed.

Service Bureaus

The relationship you develop with a service bureau should be a partnership. The bureau will be part of a team dedicated to getting a job out the door in the best possible shape and with a minimum of hassles. If your first impression of a new service bureau is that they're dictatorial or uninterested in your business, there's a real good chance that it will be—or should be—a short relationship.

What to look for in a service bureau

Personally, I think the most important thing to look for in a service bureau is access to the people working on your job. This access need not be abused; there's no good reason to interrupt their work just to see if your job is ready. But when there's a problem getting a job out, passing technical information through a receptionist or salesperson is often inefficient and a waste of time.

Other important things to look for include:

- An organized way of accepting, running, and delivering jobs
- A willingness to contact you with questions
- Reasonable turnaround for nonproblematic jobs
- Flexible pricing for large or long-turnaround jobs
- Uniformity and consistency in output from job to job
- More than one imagesetter, in case of mechanical failure
- A system for archiving jobs for at least a month so that small corrections can be made—by you or them—without requiring you to send back the entire job

TIP When shopping around for a new service bureau, it's imperative that you run a small test job in order to see how the bureau and its equipment perform. Don't make this the "job from hell," both because that's not a fair test and because the service bureau may never want to see you again. The job should definitely reflect the type of work you would normally send, though, including a variety of fonts and some halftones. It should not be a time-sensitive production job, and it might be wise not to let on that it's only a test.

Calibration

One of the most important pieces of equipment at any service bureau is a densitometer for measuring halftone screens. If a bureau tries to tell you they don't need one, don't even bother continuing the conversation. Imagesetters and processors are greatly affected by the environment; changes in temperature and humidity can wreak havoc with these machines. Of course, the densitometer won't do anyone any good if it's not used; find out how often they take readings. If the machines are properly maintained, once a day should be acceptable.

Without proper calibration as measured by a densitometer, the bureau will have no way of guaranteeing that a true shade of gray will be generated on its equipment. Many service bureaus will print out a strip showing increments of gray percentages on every page or at the end of each job (Figure 5.25). Don't throw these away! Either you or the service bureau should file these strips, as they provide the only way to properly match densities between jobs that are either being partially re-run after corrections are made or that are being run out in pieces over several weeks.

Calibration is not an exact science, and even a shop that uses a densitometer will realize that a small density variation will occur from day to day. This isn't much of a problem with different jobs; matching parts of the same job is much more difficult.

TIP Note the 5% and 95% patches in the calibration strip shown in Figure 5.25. If there is any shift in density, it can be seen in the strip without the use of any special equipment. Normally, printers will say that an acceptable margin of error is ±3%. Any larger shift will turn the 5% patch to white or the 95% patch to black, depending on the direction of the shift.

Figure 5.25 Calibration slug If a service bureau provides a calibration slug—such as the one shown here from rhinoType in New York City—hold onto it for use in matching subsequent passes of the same job.

The service bureau you choose should make regular calibration checks. Its chemistry and film should be of the highest quality and very stable. There are some bureaus that even guarantee density. In fact, the technology is readily available—all shops should be able to maintain density whether in summer or winter, this year or next year. Remember, competition is fierce. Demand high-quality film, consistency of output, and ease of job submission from any service bureau you work with.

Sending jobs to a service bureau

Above and beyond what you should expect from a service bureau, there's the topic of what it should be able to expect from you. Any job sent to a service bureau without any printouts or documentation is liable to have problems—possibly serious ones. You may be working on no more than one or two jobs this week; the service bureau will be working on a number of different jobs every hour.

Sending printouts

Making sure that the service bureau gets hard copy (a printout) of every job is very important. Even though it's generally just a low-resolution laser printout, at least it gives the bureau an idea of what's expected to be on the pages they print. Bureaus can't check that their output matches yours without it. Checking their output against their screen is no good, since any problems that occur are usually caused *when* they open the file. Their output will reflect what they see on their screen.

Problems can crop up even when using industry-standard Adobe fonts. I recently had a problem with a job that I had been sending to my service bureau each month for three years. It's a newsletter that has a sidebar text box on the first page, and one month I happened to close up the box a little tighter than usual in order to get everything on the page to fit just so. Although I usually have a couple of points to play with under the last line in the box, this time I didn't have a whisper of extra space.

By checking the modification dates on each of our sets of screen fonts, we could tell that we had different versions of Futura. Further investigation showed that one set had only 10 and 12 point screen fonts in the suitcase, while the other one had the original sizes of 10, 12, 14, 18, and 24 points. I guess the characters that Adobe Type Manager generated on their machine differed slightly from mine, perhaps due to the different screen font sizes. The headline in the sidebar text box was a couple of tenths of a point lower when my bureau opened the file on their machines—just enough to push the last line of the sidebar into oblivion. Since I had faxed them a printout of my output, though, they had something to check their output against, helping to catch the problem in time.

For a job with a large number of pages, it's not always practical to send a complete set of printouts or to expect the service bureau to check each page. I usually send the first and last pages of each chapter of book projects, enough to show key items that will be on a different page if lines reflow. That at least gives them a chance to compare things somewhat.

TIP Although I recommend using the same version of QuarkXPress that your service bureau uses, this isn't necessarily as important as one might think. Changes occur in the way that QuarkXPress flows a document from version to version. But the program automatically recognizes the version that last saved the document and flows it according to that version's rules. The program can't go back in time indefinitely; version 3.3 won't know how to flow according to version 2.0 rules, but it will correctly flow files made with versions 3.2, 3.11, 3.1, and 3.0. It might even go back further, but if you're not using at least version 3.0 of QuarkXPress, you're probably not reading this book. By the way, when opening a file through the Open dialog box, holding down the Option (⌥) key will force the program to flow the file according to the rules present in the version you're using.

Giving instructions

Okay, so you've been sending jobs to the same service bureau for three years (like me), and they know you so well they remember your birthday, your kids' names, and your shoe size. No need to send them instructions on how to run your jobs, right? *Wrong.* In addition to including printouts of a job, it really is imperative that you give the bureau some sort of job order detailing what's needed for each job (Figure 5.26). Why make them look up last month's version of the job just to see whether the negatives need to be output with the emulsion side up instead of down or whether you need 120 or 133 lpi?

ELECTRONIC OUTPUT REQUEST

CLIENT INFORMATION
Contact Person: ____________
Company: ____________
Address: ____________
City, ST, Zip: ____________
Office Phone: ____________
Home Phone: ____________

DELIVERY INFORMATION
__ Deliver __ Hold For Pickup __ Call When Complete
Delivery Address: ____________
City, ST, Zip: ____________

TURNAROUND INFORMATION
__ Normal __ Rush __ Emergency

FONT INFORMATION
__ Adobe/Linotype __ Font Company __ Agfa Compugraphic
__ Bitstream __ Monotype __ ____

COPYRIGHT INFORMATION
All that appears on the enclosed medium (including, but not limited to, floppy disk, modem transmission, removable media) is unencumbered by copyrights. We, the customer, have full rights to reproduce the supplied content.
Signature: ____________
Date: ____________

OUTPUT MEDIA (CHECK ALL THAT APPLY)
__ Film __ RC Paper __ Color Proof
__ Laser Print __ Color Slides ____________
__ Negative -or- __ Positive
__ Emulsion Down -or- __ Emulsion Up

OUTPUT SPECIFICATION
__ Output All Pages
__ Output The Following Specified Pages…
From: ____________ To: ____________

CROP MARKS
__ Yes __ No

RESOLUTION/DPI
__ 1200/1270 __ 2400/2540 __ 3000+

SCREEN RULING/LPI
__ 65 __ 85 __ 120
__ 133 __ 150 __ ____

COLOR SEPARATION PLATES
__ Cyan __ Magenta __ Yellow __ Black
__ ____ __ ____ __ ____ __ ____

COLOR PROOF SPECIFICATION
__ Proof All Pages
__ Proof The Following Specified Pages…
From: ____________ To: ____________

LASER PROOF PROVIDED WITH JOB?
__ Yes __ No

OTHER INFORMATION
Type information about the job here.

Figure 5.26 Info for the service bureau Here's the first page of the output request template that came with QuarkXPress 3.2. It's a good model to follow when sending a job to the service bureau.

My service bureau does keep a database of all their clients' jobs, which I'm sure is especially handy when they're running jobs late at night. The database includes the file name, the job number, any descriptions, the date and time, the line screen and emulsion (up-down-pos-neg), which screening method (HQS-RT-B&W-none) was used, the number of pages, and the number of inches.

But, basically, the instructions on how to run a job are the customer's responsibility. I wouldn't blame a service bureau for refusing to take a job without adequate information, such as:

- Which pages to print
- What resolution and line screen to use

- Whether to print with registration marks
- What kind of media (repro, film positives, film negatives) to use
- Whether film emulsion is to be up or down (right-reading or wrong-reading)
- When to complete the job
- Where and how to deliver it

More often than not, the service bureau uses its own default settings if a client doesn't specify part of the above information. When running out film, if there's no line screen specified, they'll probably run it at 150 lpi—the standard line screen in most printed material today. On the other hand, if the job is being run out on repro paper, most likely they'll run it at 120 lpi—the tightest line screen that can be shot reliably in a stat camera.

Listing and sending the pieces

There are many pieces to the jigsaw puzzle that make up any Quark XPress file, and the service bureau has to put them all together properly in order to run a job. *Listing* all these pieces will make their job easier, which is good for everyone; not *sending* them all will definitely keep the job from running properly. Don't forget that EPS and TIFF images aren't actually moved into QuarkXPress when you use them: Only a screen image is placed in the file, along with a link to the actual graphic.

Introduced in version 3.2, the Collect for Output option under the File menu is an important innovation in QuarkXPress. It allows you to copy all the pieces of a job to any folder or disk. Many people find this a handy way to move large jobs to Syquest cartridges or other removable media. Even the most experienced user occasionally forgets to send an art file to the service bureau. (I did, while working on this chapter! I was so embarrassed.) But Collect for Output never forgets any of the artwork, no matter how deeply it is hidden in folders. The report that Collect for Output creates is too verbose for my needs, but it's a nice feature. I prefer to use the Document Statistics portion of the QuarkPrint XTension, available commercially from Quark (Figure 5.27).

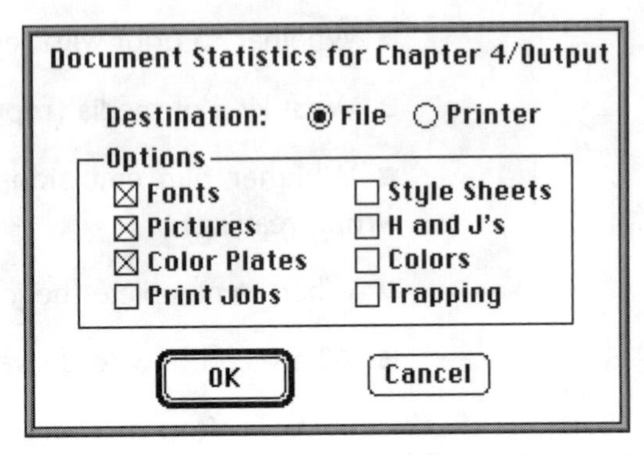

Figure 5.27 Document Statistics Part of the QuarkPrint XTension, Document Statistics lets you customize the report you send to the service bureau. I usually output to a file so that I can edit the report, adding my two cents where appropriate.

Greg Swann (1-602-756-2767) has written a drag-and-drop application that greatly simplifies the task of collecting information about files being sent to a service bureau. The program, called Bureaucrat, generates an order form that can be sent with a job. Bureaucrat files are saved as TeachText PICTs, meaning they can be read or printed from TeachText. But Bureaucrat will also save the information in the resource fork of the file so that when it opens one of its own files, it will reload all of the information in editable form. This way service bureaus can correct any mistakes in the order form prior to printing it out and running the job.

To generate the order form, you select the folder containing your job and drag-and-drop it onto Bureaucrat. The software sifts through that folder and any others nested within it looking for files. Each file it finds it interrogates for document, picture, font, and color information. This information is then placed in a customizable template. Everything that can reasonably be expected to remain consistent from job to job—such as your name and address and delivery instructions—can be saved as a preference. Imaging details particular to the job must be specified, but everything is organized to make this as painless as possible. The upshot is that the form is 80% done after the drag-and-drop, with the balance being quick and easy.

If your service bureau buys Bureaucrat, they can get it customized with their logo and can distribute it to their clients. There's also a personal edition of Bureaucrat that you can use to generate order forms for any service bureau you do business with.

Whether or not to send fonts

Fonts are not collected with the Collect for Output option. In fact, talking to the service bureau and reading font license agreements are both necessary steps in order to decide whether or not to send copies of your fonts with a job. A few font companies recognize the need to send fonts with a job for output; most of them license fonts for use with only one output device.

If you're using Adobe fonts and sending files to an established service bureau, chances are they already have all the fonts you're using. If you've standardized on fonts from another foundry, it's a good idea to seek out a service bureau that has also invested in these font libraries. A full-service bureau should have most or all fonts from the four major foundries: Adobe, Monotype, The Font Company, and Bitstream. These days, it's rare that an established service bureau doesn't at least have the entire Adobe library.

If you buy the latest and greatest font from Adobe, however, be sure to check with the bureau to see if they've got their copy yet. Many service bureaus are on a subscription service and are prepared for most requests; some have CD ROM drives containing a vendor's fonts and may need a couple of hours to obtain the decryption codes for the fonts in your job. But you may be able to buy the font by mail order faster than the bureau can receive font updates.

What fonts to send

When you need to send a job to a bureau that doesn't own the fonts the job uses, it's common practice to send along a copy of the screen (bitmap) and printer (outline) fonts. Discuss this with the bureau before doing so, making sure they realize that the fonts are meant to be used on this particular job and should be discarded after the job has been run. I can't recommend that you send your fonts, possibly violating your font software license agreement; I'm just stating what has been common practice in the DTP industry. Service bureaus often make it a matter of pride that they're better stocked on fonts than any one of their customers, though, so that works in your favor.

Both parts of a font have to be present in order for a job to print successfully, at least for industry-standard PostScript Type 1 faces. Screen fonts reside in a file that looks like a suitcase and has a nor-

Figure 5.28 Screen and printer fonts These are the icons used on the screen (bitmap) and printer (outline) fonts I used for this book.

mal-sounding name (Figure 5.28). The screen font file contains the font metrics (widths) and kerning information for each font style in the file. Printer fonts, which have a variety of icons, contain the mathematical descriptions of each character in the font. The name of a printer font file is made up of the first five letters of the first word in the font name, followed by the first three letters of all the rest of the words in the name. Include both types of font files—screen and printer—if you're sending fonts to a service bureau.

TIP Mac file icons are controlled by a bundle resource which resides in the application that created the file. Most files don't contain their own bundle resource, but rather have a couple of bytes describing their creator and type. The Finder reads that info, pulls the icon from the creating application, and puts it in the Desktop file for use in displaying files created by that application. If you don't have the application that created a file, you usually get a plain-paper document icon. Outline fonts are different in that the manufacturers assume you won't have the creating application, but they want the icons to look pretty. So they add a customized bundle resource to their outline fonts, and that's why printer fonts from different font manufacturers have unique icons.

An atypical font license

Following is the font licensing agreement that comes with the typeface used in this book, Clear Prairie Dawn. David Vereschagin, owner of Quadrat Communications and the designer of the face, has given me permission to reprint it here. If you don't want to read the whole thing—and who could blame you—please do take a peek at the last half of paragraph 2 and all of paragraph 3. It's rare to see a license speak both of installing fonts on more than one machine and of giving permission to send a font to a service bureau.

Quadrat Communications Typeface Software Licence Agreement

Please read this licence agreement before opening the diskette envelope. Opening of the envelope and use of the software on the diskette(s) indicates your acceptance of the terms of this agreement. If you do not agree to the terms below, please return the complete package, with the unopened diskette envelope and your receipt, for a full refund.

1 You are granted a non-exclusive licence for the use of the typeface software programs on the diskette(s) provided for your normal business or personal use.

2 This licence allows for the limited use of the software at a single worksite. A worksite is a single physical location used by a business, institution, organization or individual, which location is no greater than the premises specifically occupied by that business, institution, organization or individual in a single building. The software may be installed and used on up to six computers, along with their associated peripherals such as printers and monitors, at the worksite. These computers and peripherals may or may not be linked in a network. This licence also covers possible use on portable computers which, under normal circumstances, would be located at the worksite.

3 In addition to the worksite, the software may also be used at a single output site. An output site is a service or business located outside of the worksite which is used for high-resolution or other types of output which are required but cannot be accomplished at the worksite. The software may be temporarily installed and used at the output site provided all of it is promptly removed from the computer equipment at the output site upon completion of the immediate work for which it is required.

4 A single complete copy of the software may be made for normal archival purposes.

5 Copying, installation and use of the software at any other locations and under other circumstances than those detailed above is not allowed. For use at separate worksites or on more than six computers separate software packages must be purchased and licenced.

6 Title and ownership of the software included on the diskette is retained by Quadrat Communications. This extends to any and all copies of the software made regardless of form or media used. This licence does not include the sale of the original software programs or any portions of them. The software may not be altered except for your private use as outlined in this agreement.

7 This licence agreement is in effect as long as the software is in use or until it is breached by you. If this agreement is breached, all copies of the software

in use or possessed by you must be either destroyed or returned to Quadrat Communications.

8 This licence and a single complete copy of the typeface software may be transferred to a third party, provided that the third party agrees to abide by all the terms of this agreement and you destroy all copies of the software in your use or possession. Quadrat Communications must be promptly informed of any such transfer.

Less-than-full-service bureaus

I believe that it's important to send a service bureau fully editable files, since it's often more convenient to have them make the last few minor corrections and avoid the cost and time of sending the entire job again. However, low-cost service bureaus often accept only PostScript dumps, which are effectively uneditable. When sending a PostScript file to a service bureau, you take full responsibility for the job's Page Setup and Print dialog settings, as well as trapping, spot color separations, and halftone transfer curves. The bureau simply makes sure there's paper in the machine.

You can generate a PostScript file by choosing that option in the **File→Print** dialog box. The OK button changes to Save and, once you've decided to Save, you're offered the opportunity to name the file and choose where to save it (Figure 5.29). Don't use the default name of "PostScript" or it will be impossible to tell one PostScript file from another when you get back to the Finder.

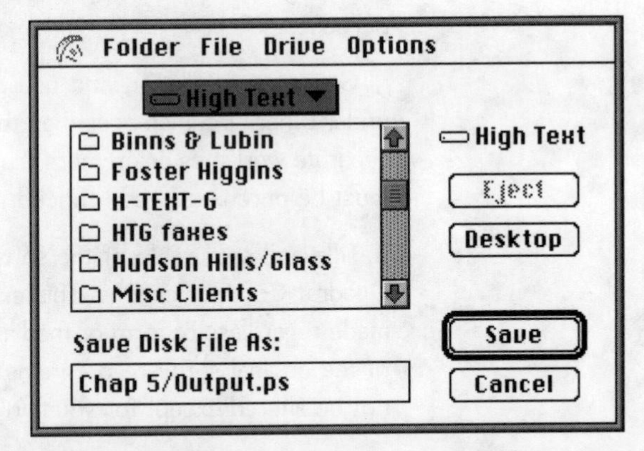

Figure 5.29 PostScript dumps Be sure to name the file so that it's easily recognizable and to save it in a logical place.

Besides all that, some imagesetters have special printer description files (PDFs) that must be used in order to properly print files. Consult with your service bureau on what all the settings should be, as well as what PDF file to use.

Printer description files

If you don't like the grayscale values you're getting out of your laser printer, try selecting a different printer type in **File→Page Setup**. Many applications do their own calibration based on what PDF has been selected. If you choose Linotronic or another imagesetter, for example, you may be able to make the application leave the grayscales alone.

TIP QuarkXPress doesn't download an entire TIFF file to most laser printers. Instead, it changes the printing resolution to the maximum the printer can produce. The Bobzilla XTension allows you to force QuarkXPress to download entire TIFFs with its Full Resolution Output option. Each TIFF has to have Full Resolution Output applied to it. Files will take longer to print when this feature is in use, but it may be the only way to get the resolution you need. The Bobzilla XTension is included on the disk in the back of the book.

Sometimes the PDF will also crop a page unnecessarily. Instead of letting the printer image the entire page, it'll include a cropping command. Even if you send the file to an imagesetter, it'll end up with a nonprinting margin—as if it were being printed on a laser printer. There are also several cases where the manufacturer got their own margin wrong. So if you don't like the results you're getting, try using a different printer selection. The biggest improvements come from selecting a more powerful printer than the one you've got, or selecting an imagesetter rather than a laser printer.

Some PDFs spit out device-specific PostScript that will not run on other devices. If a PDF has its own custom PostScript command, then a file created with that PDF might not run on another machine. If so, it's a case of sloppy PostScript coding on the part of the manufacturer. It's possible for manufacturers to write code that works on their machine but is safely ignored on other printers, making the file portable.

TIP As of version 3.3, QuarkXPress will support PostScript printer description (PPD) files. PPDs are similar to PDFs in that they store information about a particular output device, and applications can use this information when printing a file. QuarkXPress will always use a PDF file for a particular printer if it has one built-in or if one is loose in the QuarkXPress folder. However, if you remove a PDF from the QuarkXPress folder and add a PPD, the PPD can be selected in **File→ Page Setup** and you may get different results when you print.

6

Tables

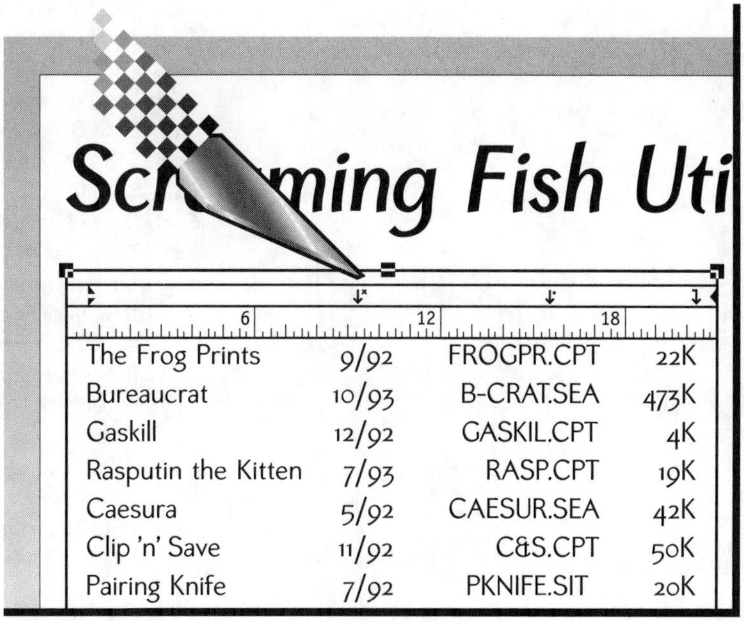

Scr ming Fish Uti

The Frog Prints	9/92	FROGPR.CPT	22K
Bureaucrat	10/93	B-CRAT.SEA	473K
Gaskill	12/92	GASKIL.CPT	4K
Rasputin the Kitten	7/93	RASP.CPT	19K
Caesura	5/92	CAESUR.SEA	42K
Clip 'n' Save	11/92	C&S.CPT	50K
Pairing Knife	7/92	PKNIFE.SIT	20K

CHAPTER 6 CONTENTS

FIGURES

The difficulty of setting tables in QuarkXPress both easily and accurately is one of the most often heard complaints from users at all skill levels. Exacerbating the problem is the fact that many people haven't used QuarkXPress' built-in table tools enough to be comfortable with them. But this is definitely one of the places where QuarkXPress most benefits from its open architecture, as XTension developers have created a number of solutions for this vexing problem.

This chapter starts with a brief discussion on how to build tables in QuarkXPress without any add-on products, and then we'll take an in-depth look at four table-making XTensions: fcsTableMaker, ProTabsXT, XTable, and Tableworks. In each case, ease of use will be compared with functionality, in an attempt to help you decide which XTension would make your table-making tasks more productive. Even if Quark adds stronger table-making capabilities to future versions, it's unlikely that they'll offer all the features available in these XTensions.

QuarkXPress tables

For most typesetters getting used to working in QuarkXPress, the biggest hurdle to leap is the difficulty in setting precise tables in a program that prides itself on its precision. Whereas typesetters are used to being able to define individual column widths and text orientations on their high-end systems, QuarkXPress' cute ruler with the funny shaped arrows just doesn't cut it.

The least frustrating method to use when setting tables with Quark XPress is to forget mathematical precision and just make the tables look good. This lesson was hard for me to learn, since I came from a traditional type background. If your table needs are light, though, the tools available in the program may be powerful enough, if used wisely.

Paragraph Tabs dialog box

The Paragraph Tabs dialog box is reasonably easy to use. Since tab settings are paragraph-based, clicking anywhere in a line with tabs is all that's required to start specifying the tabs. Call up the **Style→Tabs** dialog box (or type ⌘ ⇧ T), choose an alignment, type in a position, hit Apply; keep repeating the last three steps until finished, and then hit OK. Not too bad, so far.

Alignment

There are six choices available for alignment: Left, Center, Right, Decimal, Comma, and Align On. Left alignment means that all of the lines of text in that column will align on their left edges; center-aligned columns align on the middles of each of the lines; and right-aligned columns align on the right edges of the text lines. This is not at all unlike choosing a different paragraph alignment for individual columns of the table, except that Justified alignment is not an option.

I find that a lot of my students never use the Decimal, Comma, and Align On alignment options. Decimal alignment should always be used with columns of numbers, at least whenever there's a chance of decimal values (as in cents in a price) being used. In European typesetting, the decimal place may be represented by a comma, which is why there's a Comma alignment option.

The Align On option is the most flexible, since it allows any character to be defined as the alignment character (Figure 6.1). I mostly use this option for aligning percent signs (%) or closed parentheses. Both of these characters crop up a lot in financial work.

Any items in a column aligned on a particular character (including decimal- and comma-aligned columns) that don't contain the align-

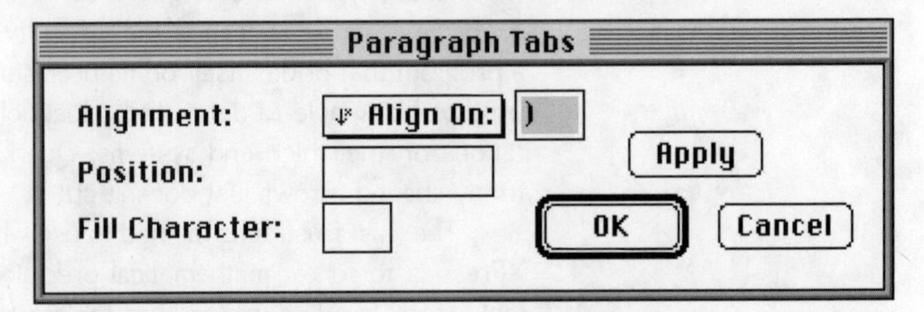

Figure 6.1 The Align On alignment Any character can be defined as the alignment character. Percent signs (%) and closed parentheses are probably the most commonly defined characters.

ment character will automatically be placed to the left of the point on the line where the character would logically appear. This way a column of numbers, for example, will always be aligned properly, even if some of them don't require decimal places.

Position

The toughest thing to get used to in the position portion of this dialog box is that with different alignments, the tab position will change meanings. If a tab position of 13 picas is chosen for a left-aligned column, all the text in that column will *start* at 13 picas. However, if the same value is assigned to a right-aligned tab, all the text in that column will *end* at 13 picas. And if a position of 13 picas is used for a center-aligned column, text will be *centered* on 13 picas. For some, this is perfectly intuitive; for others, especially the aforementioned typesetters, this is too bizarre for words.

Positions entered for the Decimal, Comma, and Align On alignments need to reflect the spot directly to the left of where the alignment character should sit (Figure 6.2). When aligning on a percent sign, for example, the value for the position will be the spot between the number in any column and the percent sign following it.

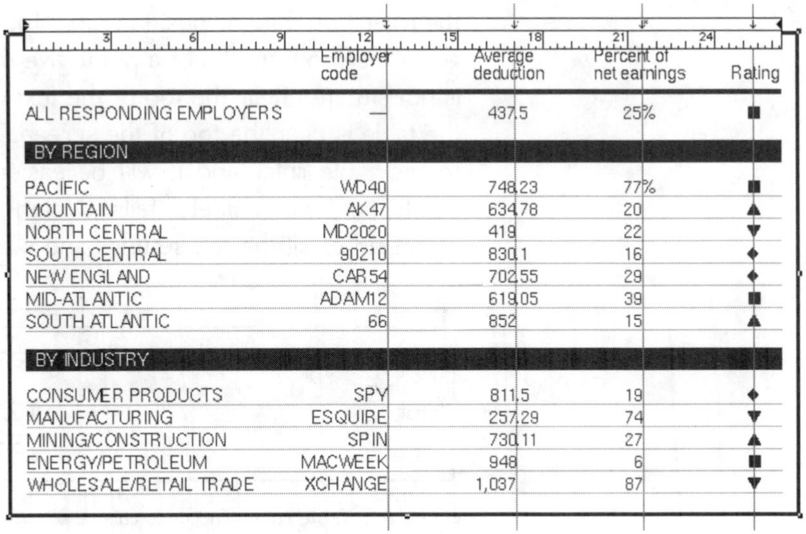

	Employer code	Average deduction	Percent of net earnings	Rating
ALL RESPONDING EMPLOYERS	—	437.5	25%	■
BY REGION				
PACIFIC	WD40	748.23	77%	■
MOUNTAIN	AK47	634.78	20	▲
NORTH CENTRAL	MD2020	419	22	▼
SOUTH CENTRAL	90210	830.1	16	◆
NEW ENGLAND	CAR54	702.55	29	◆
MID-ATLANTIC	ADAM12	619.05	39	■
SOUTH ATLANTIC	66	852	15	▲
BY INDUSTRY				
CONSUMER PRODUCTS	SPY	811.5	19	◆
MANUFACTURING	ESQUIRE	257.29	74	▼
MINING/CONSTRUCTION	SPIN	730.11	27	▲
ENERGY/PETROLEUM	MACWEEK	948	6	■
WHOLESALE/RETAIL TRADE	XCHANGE	1,037	87	▼

Figure 6.2 Tab position The position of the tab has everything to do with the alignment that's chosen for that tab. Ignoring the column heads, note how each of the alignment types used here (right, decimal, align on %, and centered) is positioned differently.

The table ruler

It's awfully tempting to try to determine tab settings by using page guides, writing down the numbers, and then entering them as the position in the Paragraph Tabs dialog box. But unless the page's origin point is aligned with the left edge of the text box containing the table, this is often fruitless. Add to that the fact that the table ruler takes into account any text inset used for the box, and it quickly becomes apparent that moving numbers from the page to the dialog is a tough way to go (Figure 6.3).

It's usually considerably easier to just click on the table ruler to specify the desired tab position. When you click on the ruler, an arrow indicating the alignment appears there and a number is placed in the position box. If you don't let go of the mouse, you can slide the alignment arrow along the ruler until you get the desired position. If you do let go of the ruler, you can just click again on the arrow to start sliding again. One common mistake people make is to click on an already existing alignment arrow and then type a number in the position box. All this does is create a new tab; it doesn't edit the one that was just selected.

TIP Iif you want to see whole numbers in the **Style→Tabs** dialog box, it's very important to be in Actual Size or 200% view when using the ruler to create or position tabs. Too many tabs with positions that go to the thousandths of a point give me a headache. Also, if a table is not situated near the top of the text box, move the page up so that the table is near the top of the screen. This will move the table closer to the table ruler and it will be easier to make fine-tuning adjustments. And when all else fails, Option-Click (⌥ ↖) in the table ruler to get rid of all the tab settings and start over again.

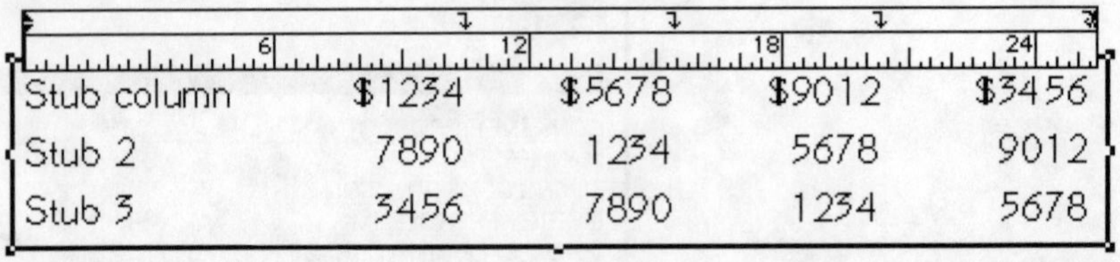

Stub column	$1234	$5678	$9012	$3456
Stub 2	7890	1234	5678	9012
Stub 3	3456	7890	1234	5678

Figure 6.3 Table ruler The table ruler takes into account any text inset in a text box by truncating the tab ruler on both the left and right sides. This makes it especially difficult to establish tab values on the page and transfer them into the dialog.

Style sheets and tab settings

Although the Tab ruler is available when defining style sheets, this is not the greatest place to assign tab settings. This is mostly due to the fact that there's no Apply button available when creating a style sheet. It's great *having* tab settings in a style sheet, but *assigning* them there is crazy. Another frustrating aspect of creating or editing tabs in a style sheet is the small ruler that QuarkXPress provides. To access numbers larger than 30 picas on this ruler, click anywhere on the ruler and drag to the right. The ruler will then scroll and you can access the higher numbers. Be sure to delete the bogus tab that gets created in the process by dragging it above or below the ruler until it disappears.

Better yet, instead of doing all that, set up a table that will be used frequently and then create a new style sheet that will use those settings. First create the table, then create the new style sheet in the **Edit→Style Sheets** dialog box. As long as you don't base the new style sheet on any other, QuarkXPress will automatically pick up all of the character and paragraph specs from the spot where the cursor is sitting in the document.

Editing tabs in style sheets

When—and notice that I didn't say "if"—the tab settings in that style sheet need to be edited, first play around with the settings directly in the document. Record the desired changes on a piece of paper, and then edit the style sheet and make the change based on your experiments. This procedure gives you the convenience of working on tabs within the document as well as the security of having all tables using that style sheet automatically updated when the changes are saved in the style sheet.

TIP Since the release of QuarkXPress 3.2, there's another way to make changes to a style sheet containing tab settings. Instead of writing down changes you've made in the document and then transferring them to the style sheet, create a brand new style sheet with your new tab settings. Now delete the old style sheet, and when prompted for the name of the style sheet that should be used as a replacement, choose the newly created style sheet.

Borrowing tab settings

Once tab positions have been assigned to a paragraph, it's relatively easy to copy those settings to other paragraphs, even if the tab settings aren't part of a style sheet. All that needs to be done is to select a number of paragraphs, making sure that the paragraph with the proper tabs is at the top of the selection, and then go into the Paragraph Tabs dialog box and click OK. The tab position assignments will be added to all the paragraphs that are selected.

Another method of doing this is to copy paragraph attributes from one paragraph to another. To do this, first click in the paragraph that the settings will be copied to. Then Option-Shift-Click (⌥ ⇧ ↖) in the paragraph that the settings will be copied from. Be careful, though, as this will copy *all* of the paragraph settings from paragraph to paragraph, including a style sheet if it has been applied.

fcsTableMaker

This is the first of the table-making XTensions we'll be talking about, and although it has the fewest features, it is the easiest to use. And it works as advertised—a nice feature in any XTension. fcsTableMaker specializes in creating evenly divided grids for pages or tables, and all of its features are available from a small palette (Figure 6.4). In many cases, this XTension may not be adequate to complete a table, but it will take much of the drudgery out of the setup of tables.

TIP In an interesting twist, the developer of fcsTableMaker actually encourages the widespread distribution of this commercial XTension. Since it's "keyed" to a particular QuarkXPress serial number, it won't fully work on another machine, but it can be used in any one-page

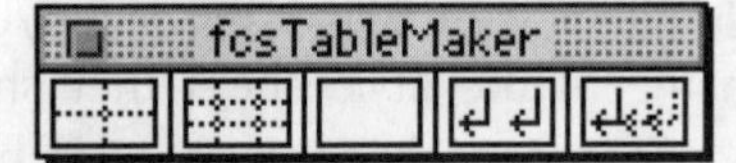

Figure 6.4 fcsTableMaker palette A handy palette allows for easy access to all of fcsTableMaker's features.

documents, which should give anyone a good idea of whether they'll be able to use it for production work. I've included a copy of the fcsTableMaker XTension on the disk in the back of the book.

Creating simple tables

fcsTableMaker's main dialog box is simple to use. It allows you to define the number of columns, the left and right margins of the table, and the alignment of all the columns in the table (Figure 6.5). That's right: *All* the columns have to have the same alignment. That's not as bad as it sounds at first, though, since the XTension only uses Quark XPress' tab setting and indent commands, making it easy to edit the table after it's set up.

The left and right margin settings in the main dialog box refer to the positions where fcsTableMaker should start and stop computing the column widths. In the table shown in Figure 6.6, for example, a 6 pica left margin ensured that there would be enough room to clear the stub (first) column, which is not preceded by a tab. Unfortunately, fcsTableMaker doesn't take into account any text insets in use in a text box, so a little extra work may be involved in setting a table like the one shown. I quickly got around it by reducing the width of my text box by the thickness of the frame plus the text inset, creating the table, and then stretching the table's text box back out to its full width.

Vertical rules between columns

Perhaps fcsTableMaker's strongest feature is its capability to create vertical rules between columns. Just tell the XTension what thickness

Table maker

Columns: 4 Left Margin: 6p Right Margin: 0p

☒ Tabs Distance to rules: p5 ☒ Create rules

○ Left Rule thickness: 0.5 pt

○ Centered ☐ Create Style sheet Rule height:

◉ Right ◉ Box

○ Decimal ○ Text

○ Comma

○ Align On: Test Do it Cancel

Figure 6.5 fcsTableMaker This XTension has few options, which makes it easy to use. The Test button is the same as an Apply button; Do It means the same as OK.

Stub column	$1234	$5678	$9012	$3456
Stub 2	7890	1234	5678	9012
Stub 3	3456	7890	1234	5678

Figure 6.6 fcsTableMaker in action This table was created using the settings shown in the dialog box in Figure 6.5.

to use for the rules and how far they should be set from the text, and the XTension does the rest. Rules can run from the top to the bottom of the currently selected text box, or they can be aligned with the top and bottom of the text. When aligning with text, there's also an option for extending the rules a user-definable number of points above or below the text. The XTension automatically groups the vertical rules together, which is a nice touch!

Moving columns

fcsTableMaker also has an option—called Tab mover—that allows tab columns to be moved after they've been set up. Ranges of columns can be moved left or right as a group, or they can be moved closer together or farther apart from each other (Figure 6.7). Had I decided to move the text instead of the rules in Figure 6.6, I could have used this feature to easily move all the columns an equal amount at one time.

Creating grids and guides

In addition to its table-making features, fcsTableMaker also offers the ability to split pages into grids made of guidelines (Figure 6.8). This feature would be especially useful for catalogue work; while experimenting with it I couldn't help but think of those real estate magazines

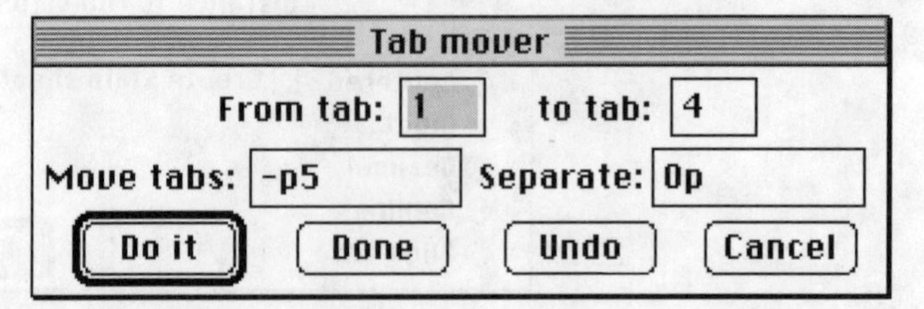

Figure 6.7 Tab mover The Move tabs option will move all the specified columns one direction or the other, whereas the Separate option moves the specified columns in relation to each other.

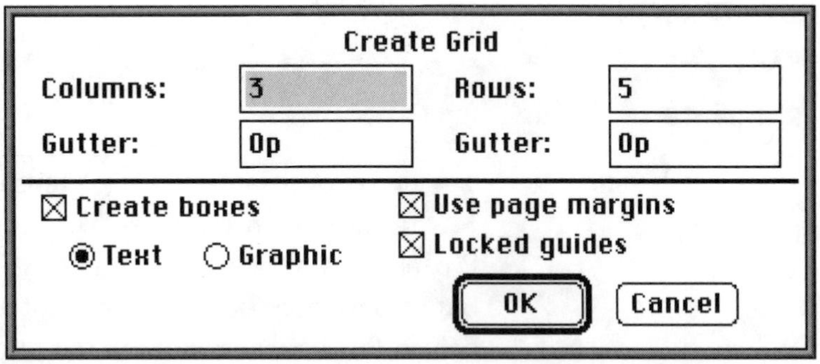

Figure 6.8 Create Grid A page's type area or page area can be subdivided into grids, with or without text or graphic boxes drawn.

that have three columns and three rows of pictures boxes showing houses. The XTension can optionally create text or graphic boxes within the grid, too.

It would be nice if the XTension could link all the text boxes it creates in this manner. In fact, if it could do that, it could be used to create "cells," or intersections of columns and rows, where each cell could have multiple lines of text wrapping as need be. If the developer also added the ability to split a selected text box into a grid of smaller text boxes—instead of only working on the entire page—one of the key features of Tableworks, discussed later in this chapter, could be simulated with this XTension.

The Centered guides feature just draws locked or unlocked guides in the middle of the page or margins (Figure 6.9). I wouldn't load this XTension just to use this feature, but if it was already loaded I'd definitely prefer drawing centered guides this way. If you want a relatively cheap, easy-to-use table-making XTension that takes the drudgery out of splitting columns evenly and drawing vertical rules, fcsTableMaker is a nice step up from QuarkXPress' built-in table tools.

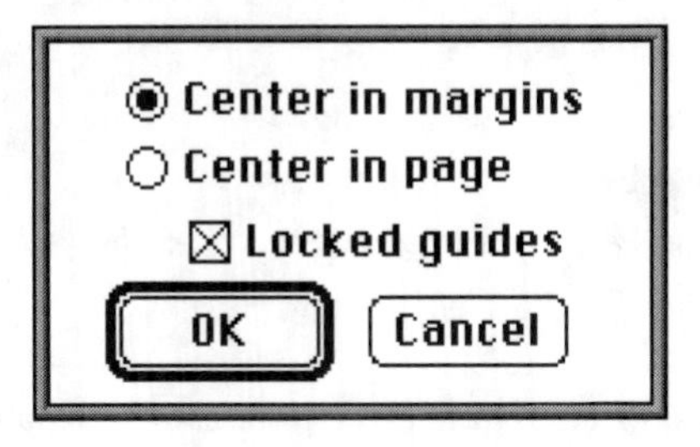

Figure 6.9 Centered guides This fcs-TableMaker feature creates guides that are horizontally and vertically centered in the margins or the page.

ProTabsXT

Our second table-making XTension, ProTabsXT, has many more features than fcsTableMaker but will take a bit longer to learn. ProTabsXT was sold as a commercial XTension for a couple of years, but its developer decided to make it a shareware product a few weeks before this book was sent to the printer. The disk in the back of the book contains the XTension and its documentation. I have used ProTabsXT for a number of jobs in which a lot of manual calculations were required, and I've been very happy with the results.

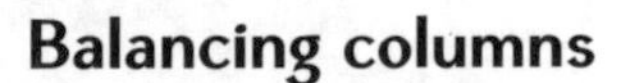

Balancing columns

ProTabsXT refers to the act of calculating column widths and tab settings as "balancing," which is an apt description. At the very least, properly typeset tables need to have equal space placed between the columns. That space is calculated by determining the longest line of each column, adding these together, subtracting the result from the total white space available, and dividing that by the number of gutters. This is an arduous task when done with paper and pencil; as soon as some real-world variables get thrown into the equation, it becomes quite a mind-numbing proposition.

The first variable that's often thrown into the equation is column heads. Are they consistently longer than the text columns? Should they figure into the calculations for white space, or should they be treated separately? And do they need to start and end in the same place in each table? ProTabsXT offers a few different solutions—depending on the answers to these questions.

Vitamin A	3000 IU	2000 IU	2500 IU
Vitamin B-1	4 mg	2 mg	7.5 mg
Vitamin B-2	4 mg	2 mg	12.5 mg
Vitamin B-6	4 mg	2 mg	15 mg
Vitamin B-12	3 mcg	3 mcg	6 mcg
Vitamin C	150 mg	150 mg	600 mg

Figure 6.10 Fixed gutters In this example, ProTabsXT uses a fixed gutter of 1p6 between all the columns. All the extra space was placed to the right of the table.

Vitamin A	3000 IU	2000 IU	2500 IU
Vitamin B-1	4 mg	2 mg	7.5 mg
Vitamin B-2	4 mg	2 mg	12.5 mg
Vitamin B-6	4 mg	2 mg	15 mg
Vitamin B-12	3 mcg	3 mcg	6 mcg
Vitamin C	150 mg	150 mg	600 mg

Figure 6.11 Variable gutters Here I wanted all the extra space to be evenly divided among all the gutters between the columns.

Fixed gutters

When setting small tables, it's not uncommon to want to keep the gutter size consistent between columns and add all the extra space to the left or right of the table (Figure 6.10). Since ProTabsXT calculates the longest entry in each column, it's perfect for this task. The XTension can also center the table by leaving half of the extra space on either side.

Variable gutters

On the other hand, sometimes all the extra space in a table should be evenly divided between all the columns, in which case the XTension needs to be assigned a variable instead of a fixed space value for the gutter size. This allows it to add all the extra space to the gutters after calculating the longest lines of each column (Figure 6.11).

Proportional gutters

Lastly, variable spacing in the gutters can be assigned proportions. For example, by asking ProTabsXT to give twice as much space between the first and second columns as it gives between all subsequent columns, we can proportionally distribute the white space (Figure 6.12).

Vitamin A	3000 IU	2000 IU	2500 IU
Vitamin B-1	4 mg	2 mg	7.5 mg
Vitamin B-2	4 mg	2 mg	12.5 mg
Vitamin B-6	4 mg	2 mg	15 mg
Vitamin B-12	3 mcg	3 mcg	6 mcg
Vitamin C	150 mg	150 mg	600 mg

Figure 6.12 Proportional gutters In this example, there is twice as much space in the gutter between the first and second columns as there is in the other two gutters.

This is a feature that has long been available on high-end typesetting systems, yet unavailable in QuarkXPress until now.

Setting up the table

Now that some of the terms have been defined, let's tackle the creation of a somewhat complex table, one with heads and a mixture of fixed and variable columns and gutters. I'll give a detailed explanation of the setup for each column, with illustrations. In this table, our heads will all be wider than the columns of text below them, our stub column will be a fixed size, and the heads will need to start and stop at a fixed point. Since the columns of text consist only of one- and two-digit numbers, the client has decreed that the gutters between them should equal each other, with inconsistent spacing used between the column heads.

TIP ProTabsXT is the only table-making XTension to recognize the fact that a table's heads and body need to be treated independently when it comes to the distribution of white space. When the body of a table is made up of columns that have a variety of widths, it's okay for the heads to be included in the gutter computations. But when working with long, skinny columns of numbers, for example, white space that varies greatly from gutter to gutter—due to the assuredly inconsistent widths of the column heads—will make the table look out of balance.

The first column

Our stub column for this example will always measure 10p6. There's no need to type a tab at the start of each line in this case, since the column's alignment will be left. Other alignments would require the typing of a tab in front of the first character in each line. The first thing to do when entering ProTabXT's dialog box is to define the number of columns, and in this case that number is 7 (Figure 6.13).

Ignoring much of this dialog for now, we see that the column number is already set to 1, meaning that all the following information is specific to that column. Note that we have fixed and variable options for both the column and its gutter; the gutter is always defined as the space to the left of a column in ProTabsXT. We can also choose an alignment for the column, followed by Gutter and Column Entry fields that have been given values of zero picas and 10p6, respectively.

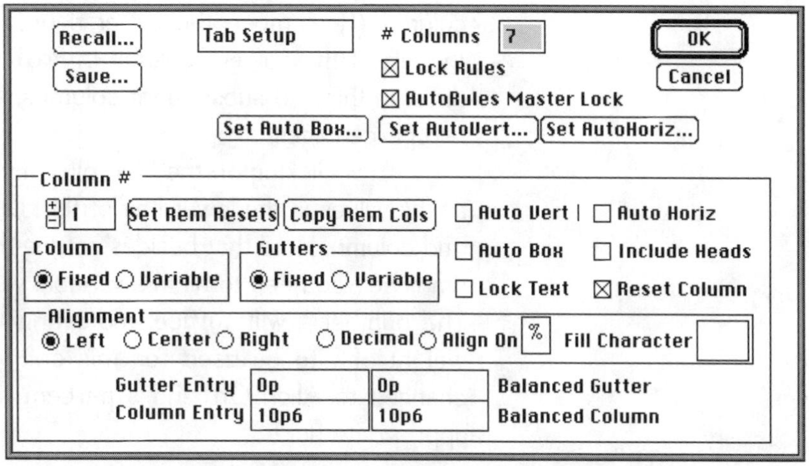

Figure 6.13 The stub column Our first column has been assigned fixed values for both the column and gutter size, as well as an alignment of Left.

TIP The Balanced Gutter and Balanced Column fields reflect the actual measurements of gutters and columns after the table has been balanced; they provide a great way of seeing what values ProTabsXT calculated.

The second column

Our second column differs from the stub column in a couple of important ways. For one thing, we don't know the length of the longest entry in this column, so we want to define the column as variable and let ProTabsXT figure it out (Figure 6.14). We still want a gutter of zero picas, however, so as to maintain our fixed space of 10p6 for the stub

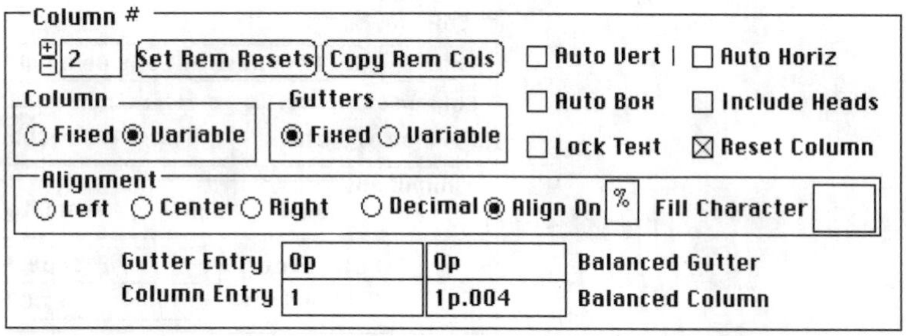

Figure 6.14 The second column Our second column will have a variable column width but a fixed gutter width (of zero picas), as well as an alignment of Align On (%).

column. (Remember, the gutter figures always refer to the space to the left of the current column in ProTabsXT.) But our alignment will differ in this and subsequent columns, since these columns will contain percentages.

After clicking on the little plus sign next to the column number, all the values in the lower half of the dialog box now refer to the second column. Note that besides setting the variable option for the column, we also need to fill in a variable value in the Column Entry field. The number 1 will suffice, indicating that we want a proportional weight of 1 to be used for this column. The alignment has been changed to Align On, and a percent sign has been typed into the appropriate field.

Subsequent columns

The third through seventh columns will all have the same setup. They will all require both variable columns and gutters, and they'll all align on the percent sign (Figure 6.15). By assigning a variable value to the gutter to the left of the third through seventh columns, we're letting ProTabsXT know that it should split up the extra white space into these areas. Once we've defined the third column to have a variable column and gutter, an alignment of Align On (%), and Gutter and Column Entries of 1, we can click the Copy Rem Cols button in order to copy these settings to the remaining columns in the table.

Column heads

Now that the table has been set up, ProTabsXT needs to be told one more thing before we can set it loose on a table: how to handle the

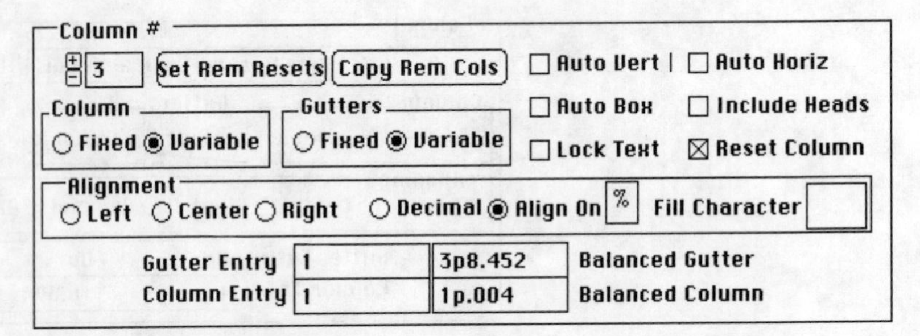

Figure 6.15 Subsequent columns The remainder of the columns all have the same variable settings and alignment.

Figure 6.16 The Tab palette ProTabsXT's Tab palette provides a convenient way to define column head and text alignment, as well as allowing table balancing, deletion of user-defined items, and accessing the Settings dialog box.

column heads. Two buttons in the XTension's Tab palette, shown in Figure 6.16, specifically refer to heads. By selecting our column heads and pressing the HL button, we tell it to align each head on the left edge of the longest line of text in the column below. Selecting HC makes the heads flush left, but centers them over the text in the column below. This latter setting is often referred to as Flush Left/ Centered among typesetters.

Once we've defined how our heads should be treated, we can go ahead and press the Balance button on the Tab palette. ProTabsXT will—based on the previously described table setup—measure all the entries in the table, position the first and last column heads, center their respective text columns below them, compute the spacing for all the gutters, and properly position the remaining text columns and column heads, in that order (Figure 6.17).

	Percentage of respondents* negotiating:					
	Turnaround time	Financial error rate	Administrative error rate	Percent of benefits paid in error	COB savings	Other
ALL RESPONDING EMPLOYERS	89%	47%	46%	27%	21%	8%
BY REGION						
PACIFIC	94%	51%	49%	29%	14%	9%
MOUNTAIN	88	33	38	25	25	8
NORTH CENTRAL	90	49	45	23	24	7
SOUTH CENTRAL	83	49	44	30	19	7
NEW ENGLAND	81	43	43	26	20	11
MID-ATLANTIC	89	48	46	29	24	7
SOUTH ATLANTIC	92	42	49	25	20	8

Figure 6.17 The finished product Note that all the rules in this table were generated by style sheets. ProTabsXT produces orthogonal lines, as drawn from the Tool palette, but I prefer to use QuarkXPress' paragraph rules.

Saving settings

Now that the table is all set up, what do we do about the other 20 or 30 tables that need to be typeset? Tables do tend to run in packs, it seems. There are options to both Save and Recall settings in ProTabs-XT's dialog box, and I would definitely save the settings for this table so that I can call them up when I need them again.

I hope this example has given you a taste of how ProTabsXT works, as well as how useful it can be. It used to take me anywhere from 30 to 60 minutes to set up a table like the one shown above, and now it takes no more than five minutes. Besides being more prof-itable to me, of course, I've been able to keep my rates constant and improve on turnaround time for my clients.

Xtable

Xtable—also known as Mathable when sold with its sibling, an equation-creating XTension called Xmath—combines the ease of use of fcsTableMaker and the computing power of ProTabsXT. Unlike those of the other table XTensions, tables made with Xtable don't need to reside in their own text boxes. The advantage of this is that tables can flow along with text without having to be placed in anchored text boxes. And since tables aren't in anchored boxes, text and graphic anchored boxes can be part of tables. (It's a big no-no to anchor a box within another anchored box. Prior to version 3.2 of QuarkXPress, it could be done, but results were said by Quark to be "unpredictable.")

The disadvantage of Xtable's tables being part of the text stream is that the XTension's tools can't be used to modify a table after the setup has been completed; the XTension only keeps track of a table's particulars while you're creating it. You can, however, still use Quark XPress' built-in table commands to edit a table created with Xtable.

Xtable intelligently accounts for any box frame thickness, text inset, or left indents in effect when calculating column and gutter widths, but these things should be decided upon before starting to set up the table; too drastic a change afterwards may necessitate starting the setup process from scratch. In Xtable's various dialog boxes, you're allowed to:

- Choose from one of seven established table styles
- Specify the target width for the table
- Assign fixed or flexible (variable) width gutters for the insides and outsides of the table, depending on the style chosen
- Select an overall text alignment for all the columns
- Specify characters for individual columns to align on
- Specify text that should be allowed to straddle columns
- Reposition (realign) individual cells, columns, rows, or heads after the table calculations have been made

Unfortunately, all these capabilities reside in four different dialog boxes. Xtable's developer would perform a great service to the user by combining all the pre-process dialog boxes—except perhaps the straddle head assignments—into the main dialog box. It would certainly help to ensure that all the necessary steps have been made in the proper order.

Seven styles of tables

The Xtable developers have deduced that tables tend to be set in one of seven different styles. I suspect that the person who came up with these seven styles is a bigger technonerd than even me; this many styles is needlessly confusing, with four styles probably being an optimum number for most folks to keep straight.

Style A

Although Xtable does not do any rule-drawing on its own, this style is designed to be used for tables that will require vertical rules. The size of inside and outside gutters are figured by the XTension—with no user input allowed—and exactly half of the space assigned to inside gutters will be given to the outside gutters (Figure 6.18). This makes sense because a properly ruled table should have equal white space on either side of all rules.

Number	Fax/Tel	Type	Company
01	1-212-929-7233	Fax	rhinoType, Inc.
02	1-614-841-3645	Fax	Macmillan Publishing
03	1-201-884-0169	Fax	LP Thebault
04	1-609-921-2611	Fax	Response Analysis

Figure 6.18 Style A table Specially designed to accommodate user-drawn vertical rules, Style A tables get twice as much space for inside gutters as they get for outside gutters.

Style B

This style offers the most options for user-defined inside and outside gutters. In fact, Xtable wisely defaults to Style B in its main dialog box. Style B is the only style that gives the user full and independent control over whether the inside and outside gutters are fixed or flexible (Figures 6.19a–d).

Style C

This is the easiest style to use when centering a table in the overall width of a text box. The user can specify *either* fixed inside or fixed outside gutters, but not both. Style C would commonly be used

Capacity	Model	Description	Access	Internal	External
240mb	M2637SA	2.5″ low profile	15ms	$499	$599
520mb	M2624SA	3.5″ low profile	9ms	$699	$759
1.2gig	M2694SA	3.5″ low profile	8.5ms	$1139	$1199
2.4gig	M2654SA	5.25″ full height	11.5ms	$2199	$2299

Figure 6.19a Automatic gutters The default setting of Style B tables gives equal, flexible gutters on the inside and no gutters on the outside.

Capacity	Model	Description	Access	Internal	External
240mb	M2637SA	2.5″ low profile	15ms	$499	$599
520mb	M2624SA	3.5″ low profile	9ms	$699	$759
1.2gig	M2694SA	3.5″ low profile	8.5ms	$1139	$1199
2.4gig	M2654SA	5.25″ full height	11.5ms	$2199	$2299

Figure 6.19b Fixed outside Xtable's Style B can also be told to maintain fixed outside gutters. All the rest of the white space is divided among the flexible inside gutters.

Capacity	Model	Description	Access	Internal	External
240mb	M2637SA	2.5″ low profile	15ms	$499	$599
520mb	M2624SA	3.5″ low profile	9ms	$699	$759
1.2gig	M2694SA	3.5″ low profile	8.5ms	$1139	$1199
2.4gig	M2654SA	5.25″ full height	11.5ms	$2199	$2299

Figure 6.19c Fixed inside Xtable moves all the extra white space to the right side of this Style B table when fixed inside gutters are specified.

Capacity	Model	Description	Access	Internal	External
240mb	M2637SA	2.5″ low profile	15ms	$499	$599
520mb	M2624SA	3.5″ low profile	9ms	$699	$759
1.2gig	M2694SA	3.5″ low profile	8.5ms	$1139	$1199
2.4gig	M2654SA	5.25″ full height	11.5ms	$2199	$2299

Figure 6.19d Fixed inside and outside All the extra space still ends up on the right side with fixed settings for the inside and outside gutters.

when treating tables like extracts, indented from both sides to set them off in running text (Figures 6.20a, b). An especially nice feature of this style is that left and right indents are established for all the lines in the table, thereby making it easy to generate properly sized paragraph rules.

	1/20 EM	1/200 EM
Increase kerning/tracking	⌘ ⇧ }	⌘ ⌥ ⇧ }
Decrease kerning/tracking	⌘ ⇧ {	⌘ ⌥ ⇧ {
Increase leading	⌘ ⇧ "	⌘ ⌥ ⇧ "
Decrease leading	⌘ ⇧ :	⌘ ⌥ ⇧ :

Figure 6.20a Fixed inside This Style C table has 2 picas of fixed *inside* gutters. Xtable automatically indented the left and right margins by approximately 3p9.

	1/20 EM	1/200 EM
Increase kerning/tracking	⌘ ⇧ }	⌘ ⌥ ⇧ }
Decrease kerning/tracking	⌘ ⇧ {	⌘ ⌥ ⇧ {
Increase leading	⌘ ⇧ "	⌘ ⌥ ⇧ "
Decrease leading	⌘ ⇧ :	⌘ ⌥ ⇧ :

Figure 6.20b Fixed outside This Style C table has 2 picas of fixed *outside* gutters. Xtable automatically generated inside gutters of approximately 3p9.

Styles D through G

These last four styles will probably be used less than the others, but in an effort to be complete I'll go ahead and show examples of each. Styles D and E are generally set to the right and left of the text box width, respectively, and their claim to fame is that the side at which the table does not rest is given an extra half-gutter of space (Figures 6.21a, b). These table styles can be used for tables that cross a page gutter, since the extra space will be absorbed by the binding. Both styles offer automatic gutter computation with no user input allowed.

Style F also sets to the right of the text box, but it doesn't have the extra half-gutter of space to the left shown in Style D. The user is also allowed to specify fixed gutters in this case (Figure 6.22). The

Filename	Size	Title
XPSEYB.CPT	37K	Mac QXP Scripting examples for use with Frontier
XPSUIT.CPT	6K	QuarkXPress Suite, script for use w/Frontier(Mac)
CAL32.SEA	293K	Calibration XT for use with Mac QuarkXPress 3.2
DSUPD.SEA	52K	Default Settings XT Updater for QXP 3.2

Figure 6.21a Style D This style table is automatically shifted to the right, with a gutter on the left equal to half of the inside gutters.

Filename	Size	Title
XPSEYB.CPT	37K	Mac QXP Scripting examples for use with Frontier
XPSUIT.CPT	6K	QuarkXPress Suite, script for use w/Frontier(Mac)
CAL32.SEA	293K	Calibration XT for use with Mac QuarkXPress 3.2
DSUPD.SEA	52K	Default Settings XT Updater for QXP 3.2

Figure 6.21b Style E This style table is automatically shifted to the left, with a gutter on the right equal to half of the inside gutters.

Filename	Size	Title
XPSEYB.CPT	37K	Mac QXP Scripting examples for use with Frontier
XPSUIT.CPT	6K	QuarkXPress Suite, script for use w/Frontier(Mac)
CAL32.SEA	293K	Calibration XT for use with Mac QuarkXPress 3.2
DSUPD.SEA	52K	Default Settings XT Updater for QXP 3.2

Figure 6.22 Style F Fixed inside gutters were specified for this Style F table. The remaining white space was automatically placed on the left side of the table.

Anytime	Sometimes	Seldom
All fruits & vegetables (except at right)	Avocado, guacamole	Coconut
	Dried fruit	Pickles
Applesauce	Canned fruit	Scalloped potatoes
Potatoes, white	Fruit juice	Au gratin potatoes

Figure 6.23 Style G Xtable gave the same widths to all the columns in this table. The width was based on the longest line in the entire table ("All fruits & vegetables").

columns in Style G tables are all set to be the width of the longest entry found in any of the columns. This Xtable style will effectively split up your table as if it was flowed into a multi-column text box, one column at a time (Figure 6.23).

Building a table

Throughout the previous examples, I've shown exactly what Xtable generates when asked to produce one kind of table or another. In this section, however, I'd like to take a real-world example—one that requires different alignments from column to column as well as a head that straddles multiple columns—and show the settings used to create it. The table shown in Figure 6.24 comes from the samples included with the XTension (except that I made it look better). It's a table that summarizes the different features available in the seven Xtable styles.

	Types of user-specified gutters permitted			
Style	Inside	Outside	Both	Comment
A	No	No	No	Use this style with vertical rules.
B	Yes	Yes	Yes	This style table fills the measure.
C	Yes	Yes	No	These tables center in the measure.
D	No	No	No	Flush right; half gutter in front.
E	No	No	No	Flush left; half gutter after last column.
F	Yes	No	No	Flush right; leftover space in front.
G	No	No	No	All columns same width.

Figure 6.24 Xtable for real The first four columns are centered below their heads, and the fifth column is flush left. A straddle head goes across the second through fourth columns.

Certain actions have to be performed in the correct order to get Xtable to produce the desired results, and I'll present them in the proper order in this section. It took me a couple of tries to make the table, since I didn't understand the order at first. No harm done, but I did waste a few minutes repeating already performed steps once I got back on track.

Set up the text box

If the text box in which the table will reside requires a frame or some text inset, define them before getting started. Xtable will factor these settings into its computations, so now's the time to assign them. (This is the step I left out when first creating the example.)

Define the straddle heads

Before Xtable can start calculating the column and gutter widths, it needs to know if there are any straddle heads. Otherwise it will treat the long straddle heads as if they need to fit in the column in which they start. This is a simple enough procedure: A piece of the straddle text is selected, a dialog box is opened, and the columns over which the head must straddle are specified (Figure 6.25).

Define the table

Next, I selected all the text in the table and opened up the New Table Specifications dialog box (Figure 6.26). This is where a table's target width, style, gutters, and column alignment are given. I used the defaults of "current box" for the width and "B" for the style, as well as "Automatic" gutters. I did change the column alignment from its default setting of "left," however, since I knew that most of my columns would need to be center-aligned.

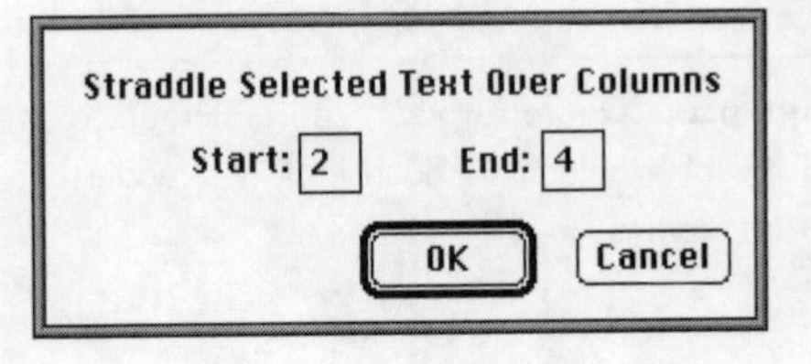

Figure 6.25 Straddle heads I selected each line of the straddle head (one at a time) and entered the start and end columns in this dialog box.

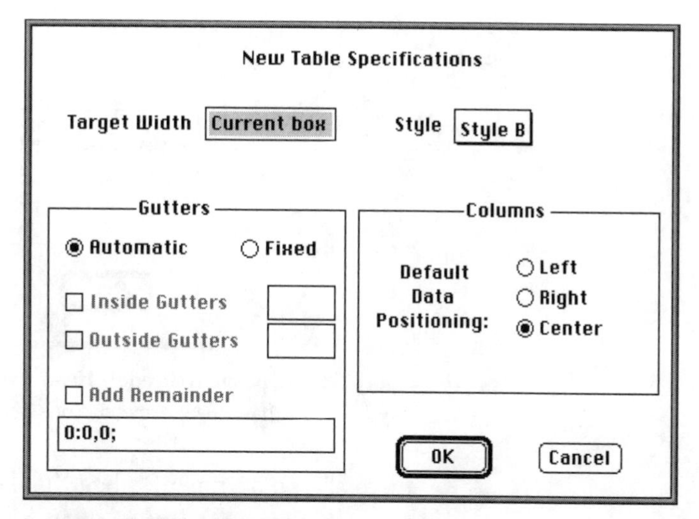

Figure 6.26 New Table Specifications The only thing I changed from the defaults in this dialog box was the column alignment.

Repositioning some columns

If you glance back at the finished table in Figure 6.24, you'll see that there were two places where I didn't want centered text: the last column and the straddle head. By clicking anywhere in the last column and calling up the Repositioning dialog box, I was able to choose to make the entire last column flush left (Figure 6.27).

I could have chosen to make just that cell a different alignment, or even the current row or the entire table. This is much easier than using fcsTableMaker and editing individual columns after it makes

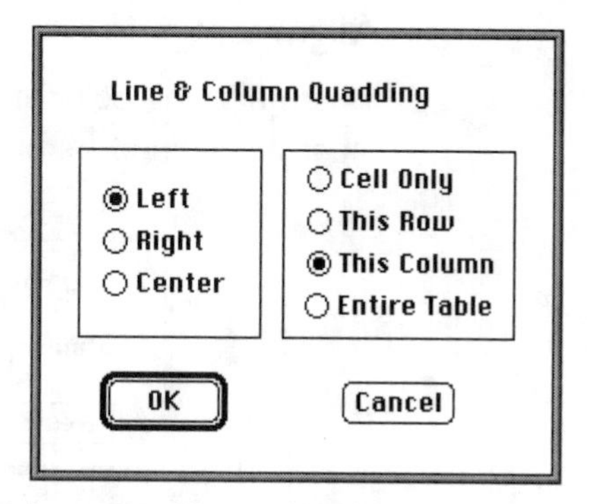

Figure 6.27 Line & Column Quadding When the cursor is in a regular column of text, the Repositioning command calls up this dialog box, with all choices available.

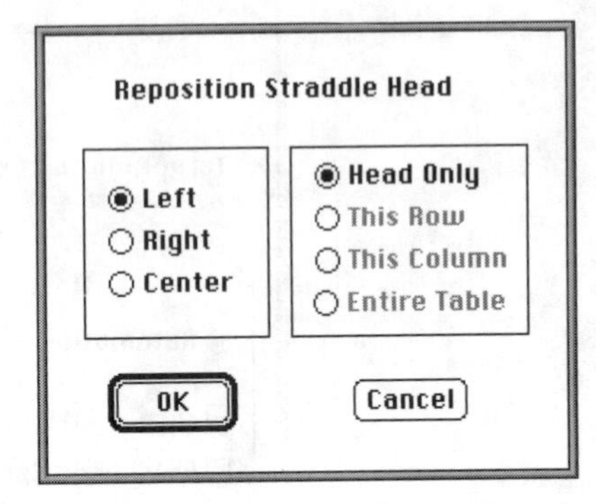

Figure 6.28 Reposition Straddle Head When the cursor is placed in a straddle head, the dialog box has a new name and one choice on the right: Head Only.

them all one alignment, since Xtable does all the work of choosing the new tab alignment and position on the Tab ruler (I peeked).

After fixing the alignment of the last column, I clicked in both lines of the straddle head—one at a time—and again chose Repositioning. This time the dialog box had a slightly different name and would only let me change the alignment of the head (Figure 6.28). Finally, I manually added a couple of paragraph rules to the table: one under all the column heads and another under the straddle head.

The rest of the story

There are a few other nice features in Xtable that I'd hate to leave out of this discussion. They have to do with choosing a character on which to align text in specific columns (before Xtable figures their widths), controlling the proportion of space Xtable adds to flexible gutters, and using anchored text and graphic boxes inside a table.

Alignment points

When aligning columns of numbers, the proper alignment character must be defined before Xtable measures the columns (Figure 6.29).

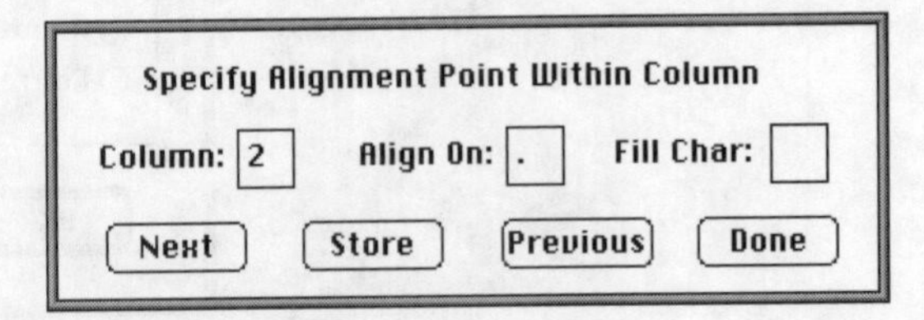

Figure 6.29 Specify Alignment Point Within Column The Next and Previous buttons can be used to select each column, and any changes are saved with the Store button.

Project	1991	1992
Scientific support	3,521,884	2,766,223
Public education	3,170,388	4,500,167
Legislative activities	57,975	187,222
Intern program	69,841	118,235

Figure 6.30 Before adding remainder This is a Style B table with fixed outside gutters; the rest of the white space is equally divided among the inside gutters.

This is because any cell that doesn't contain the alignment character will be shoved to the left of where the alignment character would be if it had one, thus potentially changing how Xtable figures the longest line in the column.

Add remainder

This wonderful feature makes Xtable's flexible gutters truly flexible, as it allows for a range of adjustments in each specified column. This option is available in Style B, C, and F tables, which are the ones that allow user-defined gutters.

Although the table in Figure 6.30 doesn't look bad, it doesn't look like most financial statements found in annual reports. To achieve such a look, we need to use another option available in the New Table Specifications dialog box: Add remainder (Figure 6.31). Its syntax is

```
gutter:maximum,minimum
```

where *gutter* is the gutter number, starting with the first gutter (between columns 1 and 2, in this XTension); *maximum* is the largest amount of space we want added to the fixed size of the gutter; and *minimum* is the least amount of space to add to the fixed gutter.

Gutters

○ Automatic ◉ Fixed

☒ Inside Gutters [2p]

☐ Outside Gutters [ ]

☒ Add Remainder

[1:0,0;]

Figure 6.31 Add remainder This excerpt from the New Table Specifications dialog box shows a special form of the Add Remainder command.

Project	1991	1992
Scientific support	3,521,884	2,766,223
Public education	3,170,388	4,500,167
Legislative activities	57,975	187,222
Intern program	69,841	118,235

Figure 6.32 After adding remainder The Add Remainder command has some trouble with maintaining outside gutters, so I cheated here and gave all the lines 6 points of indent on both the left and right sides before asking Xtable to compute the table.

To spread the columns as shown in Figure 6.32, I used a shortcut in defining the way Xtable should add the remaining space to the gutters. By typing "1:0,0" instead of explicitly stating maximum and minimum values, I've let Xtable know that it should put all the extra white space into the gutter following column 1.

Anchored boxes in tables

Since tables created with Xtable don't require their own text box, they can easily contain anchored text and picture boxes as cells inside the table. The columns and gutters won't be calculated based on the width of the contents of the anchored text boxes, of course, but rather on the width of the boxes themselves.

The type of table shown in Figure 6.33—where each table cell is actually a multi-line, anchored text box—is not practical if you're running a plain vanilla copy of QuarkXPress, since the program is unable to link anchored text boxes. But the Xtags XTension (discussed in the **Automating DTP** chapter) can create anchored text boxes around blocks of text when importing files into QuarkXPress, so such a table might be possible when using both Xtable and Xtags.

	8:00	8:30	9:00	9:30	10:00	10:30
❷	**Evening Shade:** Fontana despairs when only Evan can quiet baby Scott. (R) (CC)	**Major Dad:** A corporate head-hunter woos several marines. (R) (C)	**Murphy Brown:** Murphy fights Baldwain over a new studio set. (R) (C)	**Big Wave Dave's:** Marshall (Adam Arkin) feels out of place in Hawaii. (C)	**Northern Exposure:** An ill wind spurs fisticuffs, then intimacy between Maggie and Joel; Chris saves Maurice, who hates owing his life to anyone. (R) (C)	

Figure 6.33 Multi-line cells Using anchored text boxes, I created table cells containing wrapping paragraphs of text. Note that the last entry straddles two columns.

Tableworks

There are two versions of this XTension: Tableworks Shortcut and Tableworks Plus. Of the two, Tableworks Shortcut contains fewer features, is easier to use, and costs less, but it still has a number of powerful features not found in the other table XTensions. In this section, I'll show dialog boxes from and tables created with Tableworks SC. This should prove to be a good introduction to Tableworks' method of generating tables; at the end of the section I'll review the high-end features that are available only in Tableworks Plus.

Each cell in a table created with either version of Tableworks is a normal QuarkXPress text box, subject to the memory overhead of such text boxes. Any text box attribute—such as frame, background, and vertical alignment—can be applied individually to each cell. Since Tableworks creates these text box cells, they can be assigned attributes in logical groups, such as rows, columns, or the entire table. Neither version of Tableworks can create tables that dynamically flow with text, but Tableworks Plus can attach its tables to other anchored text boxes which can then control the positioning of the tables when a certain command is invoked.

Setting up a table

Tableworks adds its own icon to the Tool palette, which looks like this: [icon]. Tables are created by choosing this new tool and drawing a box. The box can be exactly or approximately the size of the table to be created, although the table's dimensions can also be defined in the New Table Setup dialog box (Figure 6.34). The Setup dialog automatically appears as soon as a box is drawn with the Tableworks tool.

The default values for all the fields in the Setup dialog box can be accepted, or the desired values can be filled in. A table's "style" can be set at this point, and text can be imported from a regular QuarkXPress text box. Both of these actions can be performed later, also, which is what I chose to do. After OK has been clicked in the Setup dialog, Tableworks creates all the text boxes that will be used as cells for the table, and it automatically activates the table (Figure 6.35). You can tell a table is activated when you can see the selection bars

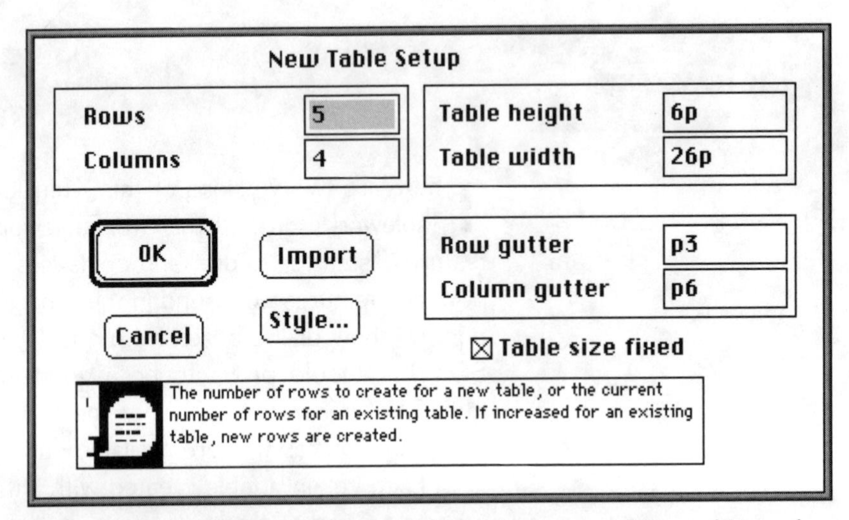

Figure 6.34 Setup dialog box I typed in the numbers shown above, and I turned on the "Table size fixed" option. Note the context-sensitive help in the box at the bottom.

at the top and side of the table; they indicate the columns and rows of the table.

Columns and rows

Each selection bar in an active table can be individually selected in order to work on all the cells in that column or row (Figures 6.36a, b). When a table is created, all columns are the same size, as are the rows.

Gutters

The gutters running between columns and rows can be specified in the Setup dialog box when creating or editing a table, or Tableworks can be trusted to make up some numbers. If not told otherwise, the

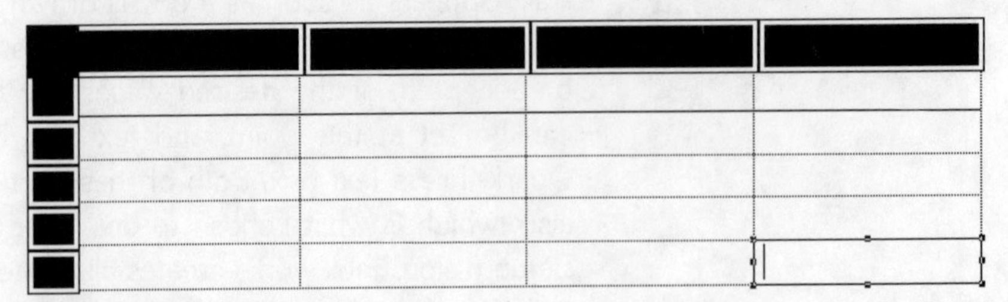

Figure 6.35 An empty table This is an activated, empty table, shown with **View→Show Guides** turned on. Each of the cells is a text box, and the last cell in the table is currently selected.

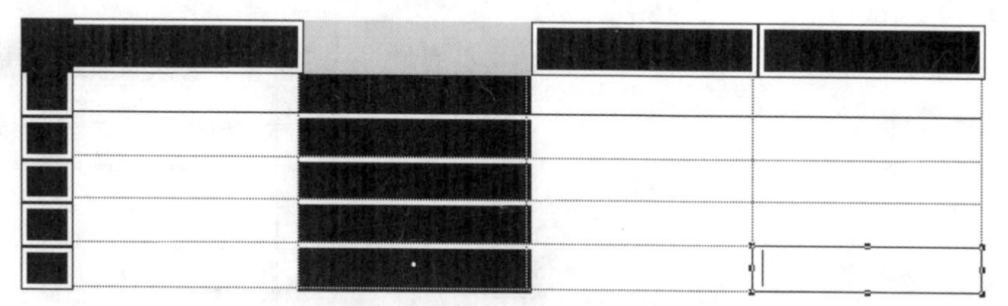

Figure 6.36a Selected column When the selection bar over the second column is clicked, all cells in that column are selected and the selection bar changes color.

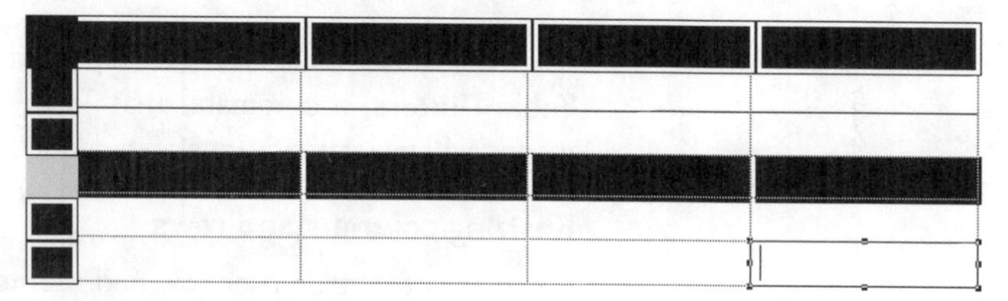

Figure 6.36b Selected row When the selection bar next to the third row is clicked, all cells in that row are selected and the selection bar changes color.

XTension will default to using 10% of the initial row size for row gutters and 10% of the column size for column gutters.

Tableworks generates gutters by adjusting the text inset of each cell, since a cell is just a text box. To get the proper size, half of the required gutter is applied as a text inset. If the gutters are different for columns and rows, you won't be able to confirm that by looking in QuarkXPress' Text Box Specifications dialog (**Item→Modify**), since that dialog only supports assigning and viewing text insets that are the same on all sides of a text box. The SetInset XTension, however, let's us see what Tableworks is up to (Figure 6.37).

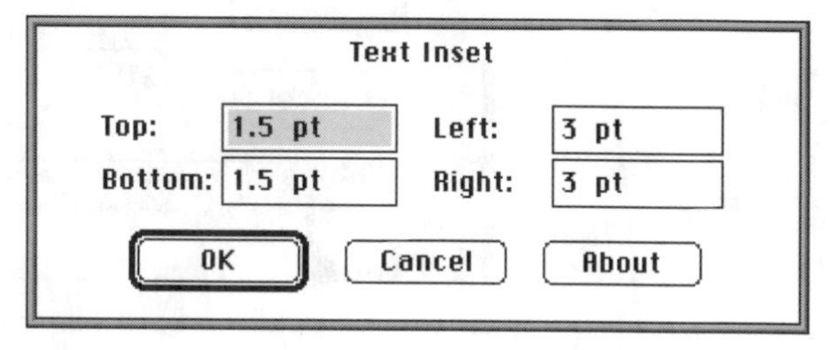

Figure 6.37 Gutter sizes Courtesy of the SetInset XTension, we can see that Tableworks has assigned half of the gutter space requested to each side of the cell text box.

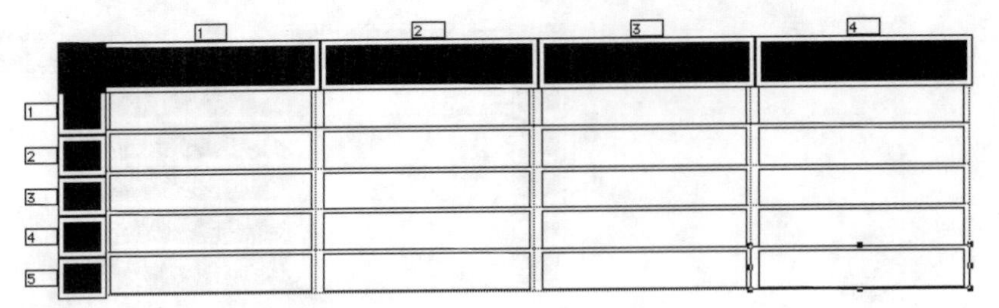

Figure 6.38 Show gutters Here's a visual representation of the actual live text areas of each cell after the gutters have been taken into account.

The gutters can also be inspected by choosing **View→Show Table Gutters**, a command that Tableworks adds to QuarkXPress' menus whenever the XTension is loaded (Figure 6.38).

Resizing columns and rows

If you select a column or row and reenter the Setup dialog box, you can assign new widths or heights to the selected column or row. The Setup dialog's name changes slightly—from New Table Setup to Current Table Setup (Figure 6.39). Also, the Table height and Table width fields are now called Column height and Column width. Note that only one dimension can be altered, depending on whether a column or row was selected before entering the dialog.

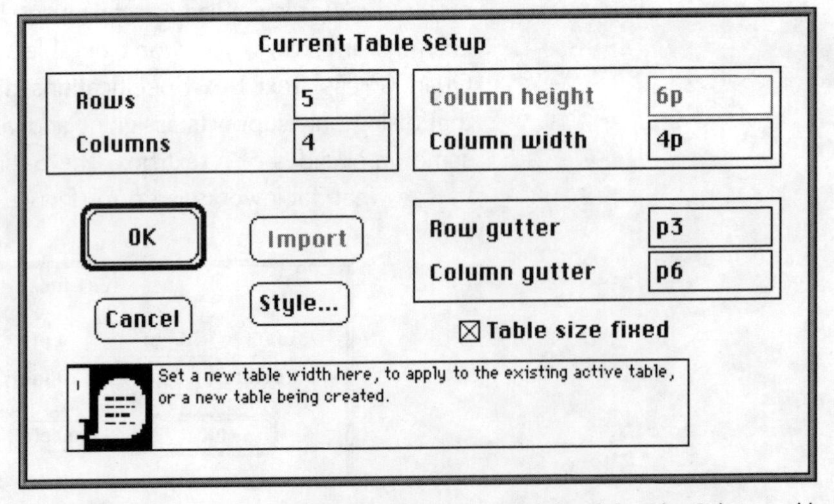

Figure 6.39 Changing the column size When I entered this dialog, the Column width field was shown as 6p6. I've changed it to 4p, and I've left "Table size fixed" turned on.

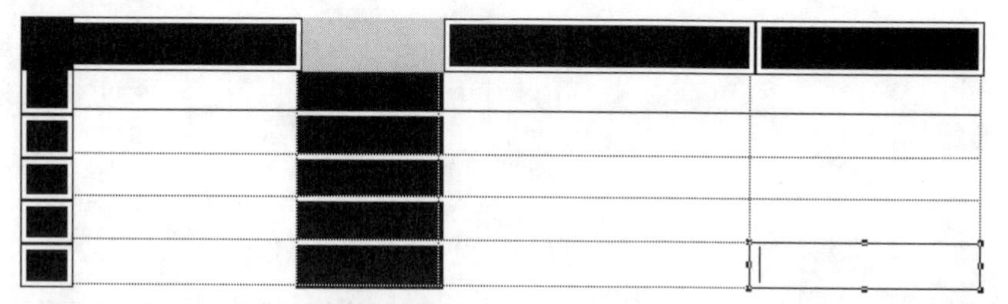

Figure 6.40 Changed column The width of the second column was reduced by the amount specified in Figure 6.39. Note that the third column got larger, since the table size is "fixed."

When the table size is marked as "fixed" in the Setup dialog, the column (or row) adjacent to the column being adjusted will also change, since Tableworks needs to get or put the extra space somewhere (Figure 6.40). If a fixed table size is not specified, all subsequent columns or rows will just move over (or up). Tableworks can also be instructed to resize columns and rows based on the contents of the cells, which I'll show after moving some text into the table.

Entering and formatting text

Text can be entered into a Tableworks table either before or after columns and rows are resized. It sometimes makes sense to resize them upfront when typing text directly into a table, so as to make sure you can see the text being typed.

Keying text inside a table

Tableworks has a nice option in its Preferences dialog called "Key through table." It makes it easy to key (type) in a table by interpreting the Tab key as an instruction to move to the next cell. Also, the Return key will move to the start of the next row.

Moving around the table

To move from cell to cell in a table, Tableworks provides a number of keyboard shortcuts. The Go To Cell (nice name) submenu in the Table menu that Tableworks adds to QuarkXPress shows that ⌘ 5 will move the cursor from the current cell to the one directly below; ⌘ 7 moves the cursor to the cell to the left; ⌘ 8 moves the cursor to the cell above; and ⌘ 9 moves the cursor to the cell to the right. (Don't ask me what happened to ⌘ 6.)

Parameter→ Fluke·5790A→ Fluke·792A→ Fluke·540B¶
Typical·transfer·time→ 4·sec·to·1·min→ 30·sec·to·1·min→ 1·min·to·30·min¶
Transfer·function→linear→ linear→ square·law¶
Voltage·ranges→ 2.2·mV·to·1·kV→ 2.2·mV·to·1·kV→ 0.5V·to·1·kV↵
Minimum·signal·→600·µV→2·mV→ 0.25V

Figure 6.41 Importing text Text to be imported into a Tableworks table need only have a tab between columns and a return at the ends of the lines. The New Line command at the end of the second to last line acts the same as a return.

Importing text into a table

Text can be imported into a table from regular QuarkXPress text boxes. The text should be typed with tab characters between columns and returns at the ends of rows (Figure 6.41).

To start the import procedure, simply select the text box that contains the text for the table, select the table itself, and then choose the Import option in the Setup dialog. Tableworks copies all the contents of the text box into the table, always starting with the first cell of the table (Figure 6.42). There's no point styling the text before importing it, since Tableworks will use whatever attributes are present in the current document's Normal style sheet. (Tableworks Plus is a little smarter than Tableworks Shortcut in this regard.)

Formatting the text

Since all the formatting was lost when the text was imported into the table, it could be expected that Tableworks would offer some way to reformat the text. This is true. Tableworks' Table Format dialog box can be used to apply certain item, paragraph, and character styling to a selected cell, column, or row, or to the entire table (Figure 6.43).

Parameter	Fluke	Fluke 792A	Fluke 540B
Typical trans-	4 sec	30 sec to 1 min	1 min to 30
Transfer	linear	linear	square law
Voltage	2.2 mV	2.2 mV to 1 kV	0.5V to 1 kV
Minimum sig-	600 mV	2 mV	0.25V

Figure 6.42 Imported text The imported text lost its character and paragraph styling, and the overset boxes in many cells show that the cells aren't big enough, yet.

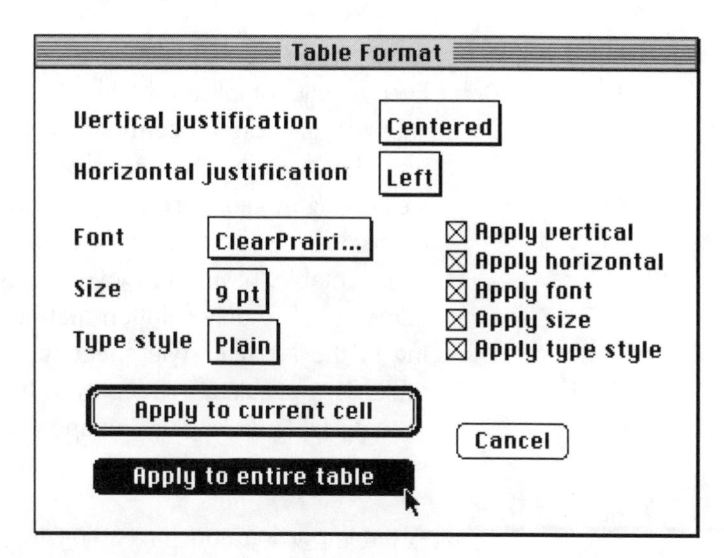

Figure 6.43 Formatting Only the attributes checked on the right side of the dialog will be applied to the cell, column, row, or entire table.

For character attributes, the choices are font, size, and style, which should be sufficient for most users' needs. Note that in addition to specifying the various characteristics, you must select the appropriate check box in the Format dialog for the style changes to take effect. Figure 6.44 shows the results of applying the styles specified in Figure 6.43.

The only Item characteristic that the Format dialog offers is vertical alignment, "mislabeled" as Vertical justification. The standard choices of top, centered, bottom, and justified are offered. The only paragraph characteristic available is horizontal alignment, mislabeled as Horizontal justification.

Parameter	Fluke 5790A	Fluke 792A	Fluke 540B
Typical transfer time	4 sec to 1	30 sec to 1 min	1 min to 30 min
Transfer function	linear	linear	square law
Voltage ranges	2.2 mV to 1	2.2 mV to 1 kV	0.5V to 1 kV
Minimum signal	600 mV	2 mV	0.25V

Figure 6.44 Formatting results Here's what the table in Figure 6.42 looks like after applying the style changes to the entire table. Note that two of the cells still overset.

TIP The fact that leading is not offered is a serious shortcoming. Even mildly complicated tables—which might require the features of Tableworks—often use more than one font or size in a line. And, as was shown in the **Typography** chapter, auto leading does not work well enough to support multiple fonts and sizes. Whereas changing an occasional character to a different font and size in an individual cell is acceptable, having to move through every cell to apply hard leading is not. The only solution that I can think of is to change the leading in the Normal style sheet to whatever value is required in the table. This problem exists only in the Shortcut version of Tableworks, though; Tableworks Plus can apply style sheets to or set attributes for selected cells from the Style menu.

Modifying the table

After importing and formatting the text, you will no doubt need to perform fine-tuning adjustments on the table. I've already shown how the Setup dialog can be used to resize a column or row by typing in the exact width or depth. Now let's look at how they can be resized by hand or even automatically.

The Resize cursor

Tableworks has a wonderful feature that is available when you pass the cursor over a row or column boundary while also holding down the Command (⌘) key. The cursor changes to an icon of two arrows pointing in opposite directions: either left and right, at column boundaries, or up and down, at row boundaries. In addition, a small dialog box opens and shows you how to use the Resize cursor (Figure 6.45).

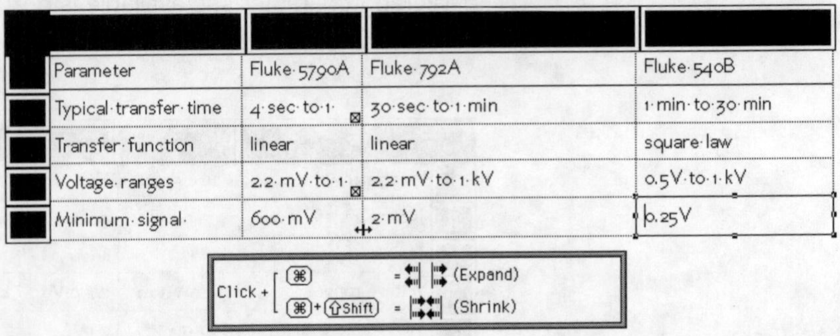

Parameter	Fluke 5790A	Fluke 792A	Fluke 540B
Typical transfer time	4 sec to 1	30 sec to 1 min	1 min to 30 min
Transfer function	linear	linear	square law
Voltage ranges	2.2 mV to 1	2.2 mV to 1 kV	0.5V to 1 kV
Minimum signal	600 mV	2 mV	0.25V

Click + ⌘ = (Expand)
⌘ + Shift = (Shrink)

Figure 6.45 Manually resizing The Resize cursor can be seen near the bottom of the table between the second and third columns. The dynamic dialog appears just below the table and explains how the command works.

Parameter	Fluke 5790A	Fluke 792A	Fluke 540B
Typical transfer time	4 sec to 1 min	30 sec to 1 min	1 min to 30 min
Transfer function	linear	linear	square law
Voltage ranges	2.2 mV to 1 kV	2.2 mV to 1 kV	0.5V to 1 kV
Minimum signal	600 mV	2 mV	0.25V

Figure 6.46 Results of resizing On my first try, I was able to open up the second column enough to see all the text in its cells. Note that the size of the third column was reduced, since this is a "fixed" table.

When you move a column or row boundary with just the Command key held down, one of the surrounding columns or rows is enlarged, depending on which direction you move the Resize cursor. When you hold down the Shift key in addition to the Command key, one of the columns or rows will be shrunk. If the table size has been set as "fixed" in the Setup dialog, the adjoining column or row will be reduced or enlarged to accommodate the change made with the Resize cursor (Figure 6.46). If the table size is not fixed, the rest of the columns or rows will just move over to accommodate the change.

Update from Contents

The Update from Contents menu command offers another way to resize columns. Choosing this command causes Tableworks to compute the column widths and row depths based on the text present in all the cells (Figure 6.47). The widest and deepest cell in each column and row will dictate the final size for each. Of course, gutters are figured into the computations.

Although Tableworks' generally excellent manual states that Update from Contents will ignore a "fixed table size" setting in the

Parameter	Fluke 5790A	Fluke 792A	Fluke 540B
Typical transfer time	4 sec to 1 min	30 sec to 1 min	1 min to 30 min
Transfer function	linear	linear	square law
Voltage ranges	2.2 mV to 1 kV	2.2 mV to 1 kV	0.5V to 1 kV
Minimum signal	600 mV	2 mV	0.25V

Figure 6.47 The updated table Each column and row size was adjusted to meet the needs of the contents of each cell, and no more.

Setup dialog, I found that what actually happens is that the update is ignored if this feature is turned on. If that setting is turned off, Update from Contents works as advertised. It makes sense that one or the other must be ignored, since by its very nature, Update from Contents will change the size of the table.

Resizing the entire table

After you use the Update from Contents command, the whole table may need to be returned to its original size. This can be done proportionally so as to keep the relative column widths and row depths that were established in the update. If you hold down the Command key and click in the upper left-hand corner—the intersection of the column and row selection bars—the table's base box is selected and standard item handles appear (Figure 6.48).

The text boxes that Tableworks creates for each cell in a table have a runaround of None, and they're all placed in front of a base box. This base box controls the text runaround for the table, and through some programming magic the base box can also be resized in a manner that will affect all the cells. Unfortunately, there's no way to tell the Shortcut version of Tableworks to avoid adding space to the end of the column at the right edge of the table (Figure 6.49). Tableworks Plus has an advanced feature that solves this problem, though.

Automatically sized cells

Since Tableworks creates a separate text box for each cell of a table, it only makes sense that more than one line of text can be placed in each cell. In fact, a table can be designated as "Auto sizing" in Tableworks' Preferences dialog (Figure 6.50). When auto sizing is turned

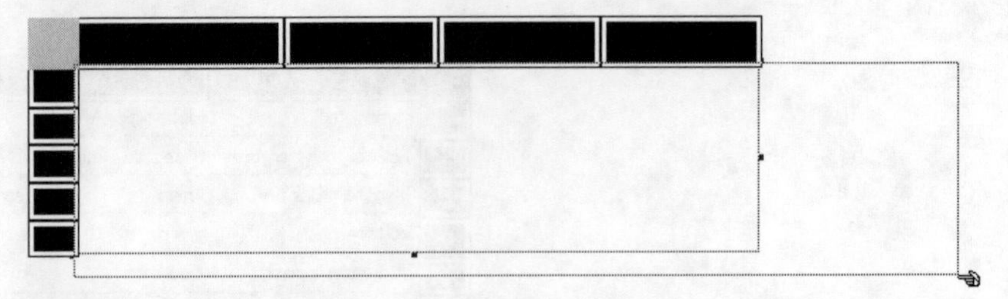

Figure 6.48 Resizing the base box By grabbing and pulling a handle from the table's base box, you can proportionally resize the table.

Parameter	Fluke 5790A	Fluke 792A	Fluke 540B
Typical transfer time	4 sec to 1 min	30 sec to 1 min	1 min to 30 min
Transfer function	linear	linear	square law
Voltage ranges	2.2 mV to 1 kV	2.2 mV to 1 kV	0.5V to 1 kV
Minimum signal	600 mV	2 mV	0.25V

Figure 6.49 Proportionally resized table The size of each column and row changed relative to the amount the base box was enlarged.

on, the upper left-hand corner of the table turns into an arrow which indicates the direction the table cells can automatically grow. If you need to change direction, just click on the arrow and the direction will be changed. Now any typing in a cell that would cause that cell to overset will instead cause the cell to expand (never contract) in the direction chosen (Figure 6.51).

Auto sizing also works when pasting text into a cell. Just be sure to format the text first, so as to avoid having to do a lot of manual resizing due to the cells' having grown too much after unformatted text is pasted in.

Moving a table

If the upper left-hand corner of the table is clicked with both the Command and Shift keys held down, the table's base box will be

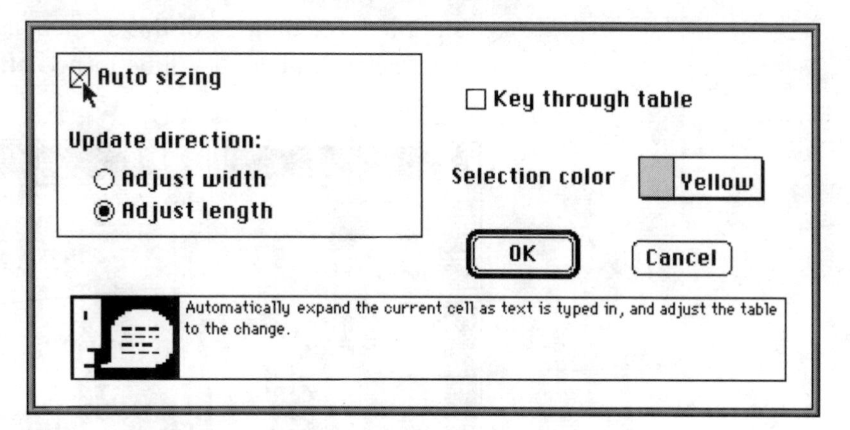

Figure 6.50 Auto sizing Tableworks' Preferences dialog box offers these choices, including Auto sizing. You can also choose to have either the length or width of cells adjusted, but not both.

Parameter	Fluke 5790A	Fluke 792A	Fluke 540B
Typical transfer time	4 sec to 1 min	30 sec to 1 min	1 min to 30 min
Transfer function	linear	linear	square law
Voltage ranges	2.2 μV to 1 kV	2.2 mV to 1 kV	Model 11: 1.0V to 1.2 kV Model 12: 2.4 μV to 240 μV
Minimum signal	600 μV	2 μV	0.25V

Figure 6.51 Auto-sized cells The selected cell grew automatically to the required depth when the extra text was added. [I also finally remembered to change (most of) the m's to μ's.]

selected in a way that allows it to be moved. Although tables can be moved from page to page, if they're created with Tableworks Shortcut they can't be moved to another document. Tables created with Tableworks Plus can be moved between documents.

Frames, lines, and shades

In its Current Table Style dialog box, Tableworks provides a variety of choices for framing cells, drawing lines between columns and rows, and shading rows. All of the Tableworks illustrations so far have been shown with **View→Show Guides** turned on for the sake of showing the white space in the tables. As with any job, guides should be turned off occasionally to see what the page will really look like when it's printed. For the rest of this section, the guides—as well as Tableworks' selection bars—will be turned off (Figure 6.52).

Parameter	Fluke 5790A	Fluke 792A	Fluke 540B
Typical transfer time	4 sec to 1 min	30 sec to 1 min	1 min to 30 min
Transfer function	linear	linear	square law
Voltage ranges	2.2 μV to 1 kV	2.2 mV to 1 kV	Model 11: 1.0V to 1.2 kV Model 12: 2.4 μV to 240 μV
Minimum signal	600 μV	2 μV	0.25V

Figure 6.52 Guides turned off Here's what our table looks like with the guides turned off. It should be obvious now that it needs more work.

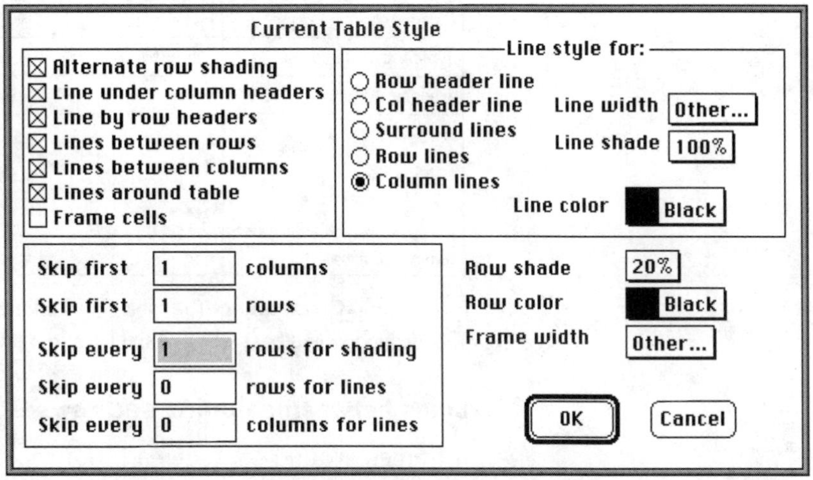

Current Table Style

☒ Alternate row shading
☒ Line under column headers
☒ Line by row headers
☒ Lines between rows
☒ Lines between columns
☒ Lines around table
☐ Frame cells

Line style for:
○ Row header line
○ Col header line
○ Surround lines
○ Row lines
◉ Column lines

Line width Other...
Line shade 100%
Line color Black

Skip first 1 columns
Skip first 1 rows
Skip every 1 rows for shading
Skip every 0 rows for lines
Skip every 0 columns for lines

Row shade 20%
Row color Black
Frame width Other...

OK Cancel

Figure 6.53 Style dialog box The options shown were turned on one or two at a time as I produced Figures 6.54 to 6.59. Only "Frame cells" was turned on for the next illustration; it was turned off after that.

The Style dialog box has four distinct sections (Figure 6.53). The first one controls what frame, line, and shading features are turned on. The second section allows for the setting of the line width, shade, and color for whichever line's radio button is clicked. After that there are two areas that allow the user to customize where lines and shades are to be placed as well as a few miscellaneous options having to do with the styling of shades and frames.

Frames around cells

Tableworks can frame cells in one of two ways: with a combination of lines between columns and rows and lines surrounding the table; and with a built-in cell framing feature. If the same line weight is desired in all places, the cell framing feature is easier to use and takes less memory in your QuarkXPress file (Figure 6.54).

With cell framing, Tableworks applies a frame around each of the text boxes it uses as cells. Although the manual says that the actual frame width given to each cell is one half the desired thickness—in order that adjacent cells together make up the full requested frame thickness—this is incorrect. Instead, each cell is made to overlap adjacent cells by one half the frame width. In any event, the option works just fine.

Parameter	Fluke 5790A	Fluke 792A	Fluke 540B
Typical transfer time	4 sec to 1 min	30 sec to 1 min	1 min to 30 min
Transfer function	linear	linear	square law
Voltage ranges	2.2 μV to 1 kV	2.2 mV to 1 kV	Model 11: 1.0V to 1.2 kV Model 12: 2.4 μV to 240 μV
Minimum signal	600 μV	2 μV	0.25V

Figure 6.54 Cell framing The table looks a lot better with framing around the cells. This method works best when all the lines in a table need to be the same weight.

Lines between columns and rows

If frames around each cell are not required (or desired), there are a number of other options available in the Style dialog. Lines can be independently generated between columns and between rows. They can be set to skip a user-specified number of columns and rows at the start of the table, for example, when such columns or rows are being used as headers for the table. Once in the table, they can be set to skip columns and rows there, too. In order to show the rest of the line options, cell framing has been turned off in Figures 6.55a–c.

Row shading

Tableworks can also generate background shading for selected rows. As with the "Lines between rows" feature, if a header is designated by skipping the first row, that row will be skipped for the shading (Figure 6.56). Then the number of rows to be skipped for shading within the table can be chosen, too.

Parameter	Fluke 5790A	Fluke 792A	Fluke 540B
Typical transfer time	4 sec to 1 min	30 sec to 1 min	1 min to 30 min
Transfer function	linear	linear	square law
Voltage ranges	2.2 μV to 1 kV	2.2 mV to 1 kV	Model 11: 1.0V to 1.2 kV Model 12: 2.4 μV to 240 μV
Minimum signal	600 μV	2 μV	0.25V

Figure 6.55a Header lines By telling Tableworks to skip the first column and row for lines, I've defined that column and row as headers. Turning on both the "Line under column headers" and "Line by row headers" options, I produced the above ruling.

Parameter	Fluke 5790A	Fluke 792A	Fluke 540B
Typical transfer time	4 sec to 1 min	30 sec to 1 min	1 min to 30 min
Transfer function	linear	linear	square law
Voltage ranges	2.2 μV to 1 kV	2.2 mV to 1 kV	Model 11: 1.0V to 1.2 kV Model 12: 2.4 μV to 240 μV
Minimum signal	600 μV	2 μV	0.25V

Figure 6.55b Column and row lines Here I've added the "Line between rows" and "Line between columns" options, using a different line weight so that headers still stand out.

Parameter	Fluke 5790A	Fluke 792A	Fluke 540B
Typical transfer time	4 sec to 1 min	30 sec to 1 min	1 min to 30 min
Transfer function	linear	linear	square law
Voltage ranges	2.2 μV to 1 kV	2.2 mV to 1 kV	Model 11: 1.0V to 1.2 kV Model 12: 2.4 μV to 240 μV
Minimum signal	600 μV	2 μV	0.25V

Figure 6.55c A framed table Finally, I've used the "Lines around table" option to completely surround the table with lines, in this case using the same weight as used for the headers.

Parameter	Fluke 5790A	Fluke 792A	Fluke 540B
Typical transfer time	4 sec to 1 min	30 sec to 1 min	1 min to 30 min
Transfer function	linear	linear	square law
Voltage ranges	2.2 μV to 1 kV	2.2 mV to 1 kV	Model 11: 1.0V to 1.2 kV Model 12: 2.4 μV to 240 μV
Minimum signal	600 μV	2 μV	0.25V

Figure 6.56 Shaded rows By skipping the first row and every other row for shading, I was able to put the finishing touches on this table.

Background color

A background color, shade, or blend can be applied to an entire table, but a little planning ahead is required. Although Tableworks applies a runaround of None to all of its cells, it leaves the color of the cells set to the document's default background color. For most of us, that means 100% white. If the default is changed to None *before* the table is created, then it's a simple matter to add a color, shade, or blend to the table's base box. Once again, Tableworks Plus overcomes this problem with one of its advanced features.

Messing with cells

In addition to all of the above styling features, there are a handful of important cell-manipulation features available in Tableworks. Included are the capabilities to rotate cells, merge two cells together, and split a cell. Entire columns and rows of cells can be deleted and duplicated, also.

Cell rotation

Tableworks can rotate any individual cells as well as entire columns or rows of cells by 90° or −90° (Figure 6.57). It refers to these rotations as "facing up" or "facing down."

Merging cells

Any cell in a Tableworks table can be merged with an adjacent cell, and an entire column or row can be merged into what the XTension calls a "title bar." Merging cells is Tableworks' way of creating straddle heads. It's important to understand the consequences of merging cells before attempting to do so.

In order to merge cells, a direction that the selected cell will "merge from" has to be chosen. If the table already contains text,

Parameter	Fluke 5790A	Fluke 792A	Fluke 540B
Typical transfer time	4 sec to 1 min	30 sec to 1 min	1 min to 30 min
Transfer function	linear	linear	square law
Voltage ranges	2.2 μV to 1 kV	2.2 mV to 1 kV	Model 11: 1.0V to 1.2 kV Model 12: 2.4 μV to 240 μV
Minimum signal	600 μV	2 μV	0.25V

Figure 6.57 Rotated cells I rotated the entire first row so that it was "facing down" and then I rotated the first cell back to "normal." I also used the Resize cursor to resize this row.

only the cell that's being merged from will survive the action. This is a little counterintuitive, since it might be more logical to assume that the selected cell contains the text that you care about. But in any case, make sure you have a copy of the text that's present in the selected cell if you need to preserve it for later use.

The effect that a "merge" action will have on the table's selection bars and grid lines will depend on whether the grid was created with column and row lines or with cell framing. The selection bars will be combined whenever two cells are merged, and anything requiring unique columns or rows, such as lines or shading, will be affected by the merge. Figure 6.58 shows what happens when two cells are merged and column lines (instead of cell framing) are in use.

On the other hand, if cell framing was used instead of column and rule lines, the selection bars are combined into one bar but the cell framing remains intact, and only the frames around the two cells merge into one frame (Figure 6.59).

An entire column or row can be merged into a title bar. In that case, the selection bars won't be affected. If text needs to be imported into a table, title bars are skipped over.

Splitting cells

Any cell in a table can be split into two, either horizontally or vertically. The new cell will have all the attributes of the original cell.

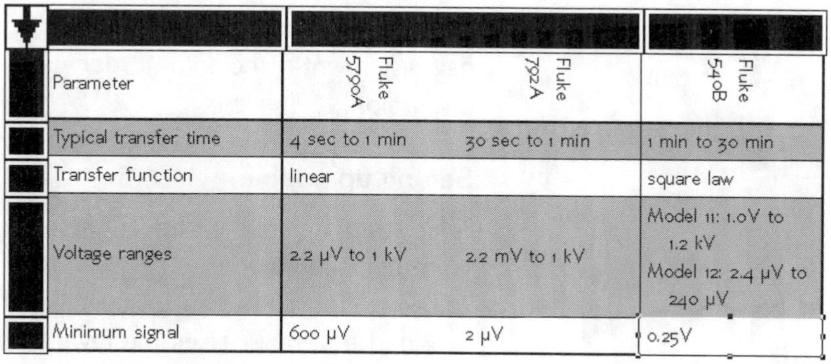

Parameter	Fluke 5790A	Fluke 792A	Fluke 540B
Typical transfer time	4 sec to 1 min	30 sec to 1 min	1 min to 30 min
Transfer function	linear		square law
Voltage ranges	2.2 μV to 1 kV	2.2 mV to 1 kV	Model 11: 1.0V to 1.2 kV Model 12: 2.4 μV to 240 μV
Minimum signal	600 μV	2 μV	0.25V

Figure 6.58 Merge with lines When I merged two cells in the middle of the table, I lost the line between the two columns, as well as the text in the second column, third row.

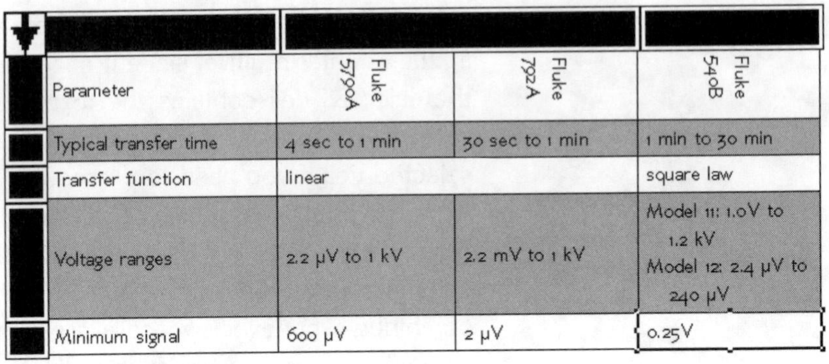

Parameter	Fluke 5790A	Fluke 792A	Fluke 540B
Typical transfer time	4 sec to 1 min	30 sec to 1 min	1 min to 30 min
Transfer function	linear		square law
Voltage ranges	2.2 μV to 1 kV	2.2 mV to 1 kV	Model 11: 1.0V to 1.2 kV Model 12: 2.4 μV to 240 μV
Minimum signal	600 μV	2 μV	0.25V

Figure 6.59 Merge with frames Although the selection bars still merged into one bar, the grid remained intact when I merged cells in a table that uses cell frames.

Deleting and duplicating columns and rows

Entire columns and rows can be deleted or duplicated in a Tableworks table. When deleting, you can dictate the direction that the table adjusts itself. When duplicating, all the attributes of the duplicated cells will be applied to the new cells, and any text in those cells will also be copied into the new cells.

Tableworks Plus

TableWorks Plus is the Cadillac of the table-making XTensions. Note that I didn't say it was a Ferrari; it's definitely an all-American, gas-guzzling hulk of a program, not a zippy Italian sportscar. But it has to be big, with all that it has under the hood. Tableworks Plus has all the features of Tableworks Shortcut plus everything listed on the next few pages, shown in the same order used in the above Tableworks Plus discussion.

Setting up a table

Table templates Table configurations and style settings can be saved in template libraries.

Tab rows Tab rows can be specified for a new table, or new rows added to a table. Uses the fewest number of boxes used per row.

Dynamic multi-page tables Tables automatically re-break across pages when the table size or structure changes; column headers are duplicated automatically.

Entable A table can be created out of a group of separately drawn text boxes.

"Virtual cells" A table can be made without text boxes.

Entering and formatting text

Palette-based Controls Controls for alignment, insets, style sheets, rotation, text styles, and numerical row and column selection can be accessed with the Tableworks palette.

More flexible text Import Text can be imported from a file and column-break and row-break delimiters can be chosen. Style settings of text being imported can be retained.

Table Publish/Subscribe When used with TextLinker XTension, an entire table can be specified as a Publisher or Subscriber. Table contents of a Subscriber table will be updated automatically when the source data changes.

Subscribe to Excel files Table Subscribers can be created from an Excel Publisher, with most Excel formatting preserved. Table row/ column configuration can be set automatically.

Interaction with the Style menu Typographic changes can be applied to selected row(s) or column(s), directly from the Style menu; also, style sheets can be applied.

Lock item/text style changes Any Item or text attributes of a selected column or row can be locked against changes subsequently applied from the other direction (row or column).

Modifying the table

Resize using grab handles A table can be resized with the mouse, or to an exact spec using the Measurements palette.

Copy table An entire table can be copied, within or across documents; all configuration, style settings, and contents will be duplicated.

Update from boxes Any number of cell boxes can be manually resized.

Picture cells Any selected table cells can be converted to picture cells (or back to text cells).

Rearrange rows and columns Any table row or column can be moved to a new location in the table using the mouse.

Cut/Copy/Paste rows and columns The standard Clipboard functions can be used on either complete rows or columns, or text only.

Justified table spacing The width of gutters between maximum text extents of adjacent columns can be automatically equalized.

Frames, lines, and shades

Apply Item attributes Any framing, shading, or color can be applied to any selected part of a table

Line scripts A much more flexible method of applying lines to a table, analogous to QuarkXPress style sheets, is available.

More global style controls For lines around table, lines on each table edge can be customized individually. Controls can enable/disable global cell framing and customize frame style.

"Snap to Corners" for added lines or boxes Text boxes can be added anywhere the same way as lines; automatically aligns endpoints of added custom lines or boxes.

Messing with cells

Slanted rows or columns Slant angles from –45° to 45° can be specified for any table row or columns.

Cell selection options A mode to allow selecting columns or rows that ignore straddle cells can be selected.

New cell selection and merging A new tool in the Tools palette can be used to drag around and select any area of table cells.

7

Automating DTP

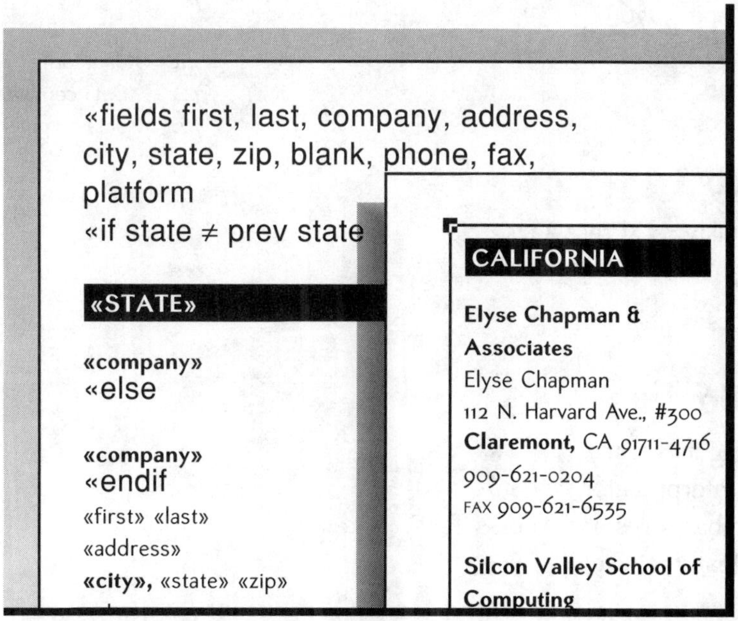

«fields first, last, company, address, city, state, zip, blank, phone, fax, platform
«if state ≠ prev state

«STATE»

«company»
«else

«company»
«endif
«first» «last»
«address»
«city», «state» «zip»

CALIFORNIA

Elyse Chapman & Associates
Elyse Chapman
112 N. Harvard Ave., #300
Claremont, CA 91711-4716
909-621-0204
FAX 909-621-6535

Silcon Valley School of Computing

CHAPTER 7 CONTENTS

FIGURES

As discussed in the **File Preparation** chapter, there are times when it makes more sense to perform tasks unrelated to layout before importing text into QuarkXPress. If the text needs a lot of "massage," doing so directly in the program can be time-consuming, inefficient, and frustrating. This chapter will discuss a handful of tools that will help to automate the massage of text files, either before they're brought into QuarkXPress or while they're on their way into a document.

The first half of the chapter concentrates on utility programs written by Greg Swann. Greg is a typesetter who learned to program in order to produce tools that he could use on his own work. Among other things, these tools are useful for converting formatted Microsoft Word files to XPress Tags format; automatically adding XPress Tags to files in order to enhance the typography of QuarkXPress documents; and performing powerful batch search-and-replaces.

In addition to generating XPress Tags, Greg's programs also can be used to add Xtags to text files. Xtags are a superset of XPress Tags developed by Chris Ryland. Chris writes XTensions that are especially useful for automating the creation of large, complex, or repetitive QuarkXPress documents. A discussion of both his Xtags and Xdata XTensions will make up the second half of the chapter.

Mark My Words

Up until now, when presented with formatted MS Word files, there were only two things that I felt could be done with them: Import them into QuarkXPress and manually clean out all the coding that isn't needed (and add the styling that didn't survive QuarkXPress' MS Word Filter); or open the files directly in MS Word, save them as

Text Only, and manually add XPress Tags. A third option would be to import the text files into QuarkXPress and manually add style sheets and character formatting, but this seems like the least efficient use of my time and this high-end page layout program.

Mark My Words, on the other hand, can automatically convert formatted MS Word files to XPress Tags or (Chris Ryland's) Xtags format. Its initial interface is pretty simple, but it expands to a full-featured interface for power users. It converts everything in Word files, including pictures and tables! There's a demo version of Mark My Words on the disk in the back of the book, and I encourage you to open the program and play with it while reading this section.

File settings

There are three choices for output file formats: Xtags, XPress Tags, or Text Only. Mark My Words is smart enough to generate Xtags- or XPress Tags–compliant coding, depending on which you choose. QuarkXPress' XPress Tags Filter will choke on some of Xtags' more complex coding, so it's important to choose the appropriate format type when starting to process files.

There are also eight choices for output file type: Mark My Words, BBEdit, MS Word (the logical choice, if you have MS Word in the first place), MacWrite, WriteNow, Nisus, Alpha, and Other (which allows you to enter the four-digit file creator code of your choosing). All of Mark My Words' options can be saved as personal preferences, and the program's defaults can be reverted to whenever needed (Figure 7.1).

Conversion settings

This is where Mark My Words really shines. Of course, the assumption here is that your clients have done some formatting in the MS Word files. Perhaps they have defined and applied style sheets, or maybe they manually applied various paragraph settings. They may have only changed an occasional word or phrase to italic or bold. In any case—no matter what level of coding was used—Mark My Words will be able to strip out codes or convert them to XPress Tags or Xtags.

Style sheets

Mark My Words can generate a style sheet definition—something I would *never* do by hand, or it can just place a style sheet name at the

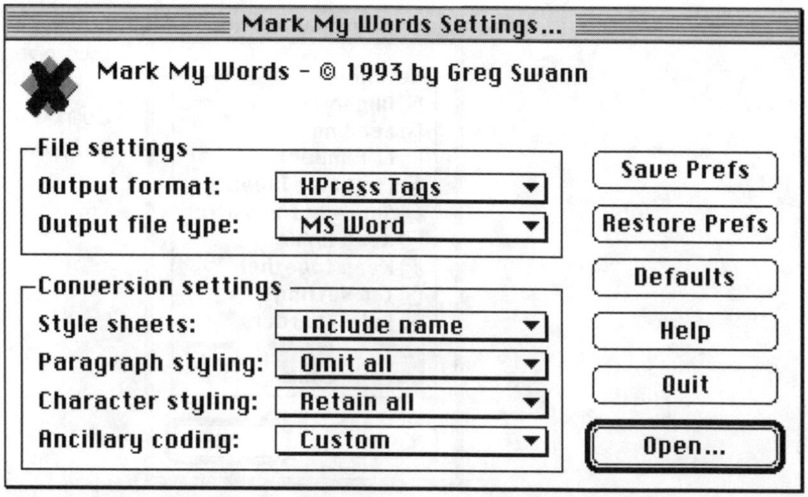

Figure 7.1 Mark My Words Although not the defaults the program comes with, this would be a good setup to use the first time you need to convert a formatted MS Word file to XPress Tags coding.

start of each paragraph. It can also change all paragraphs so that they use the Normal style sheet when imported into QuarkXPress, or it can completely ignore a client's application of style sheets.

Paragraph styling

Client-coded paragraph styling—those attributes that affect an entire paragraph, such as leading, indents, and alignment—can be retained completely, retained based on the default preferences, customized for a particular job, or completely omitted. I tend to completely omit paragraph-level styling, as I like to accomplish such styling through QuarkXPress style sheets. Besides, it's rare for clients to use the same paragraph styling in manuscripts that will be used in the typeset job.

However, sometimes I *will* let Mark My Words generate the paragraph-based XPress Tags codes *if* the client has added them in a consistent manner. In such a case, the resulting patterns of XPress Tags that Mark My Words creates can be searched for and replaced with style sheet names. Let's face it: When's the last time you received an MS Word file in which the client actually used Word's style sheets correctly? If they've consistently added paragraph styling manually, though, this option gives you a chance to get style sheets inserted in the right place.

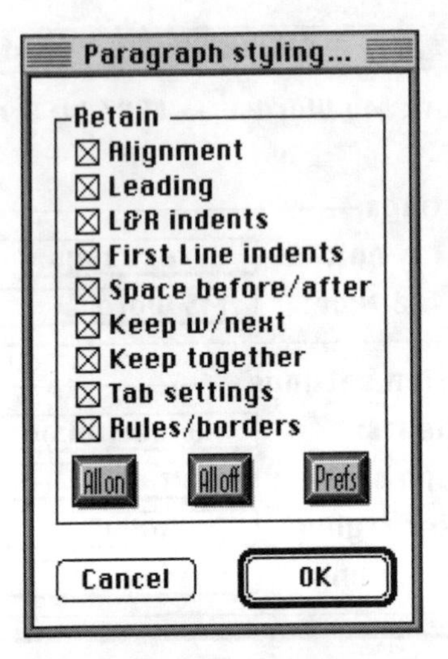

Figure 7.2 Paragraph styling Mark My Words goes to great lengths to convert all of MS Word's styling in a manner that can be duplicated in QuarkXPress. Especially difficult were the last two options: Tab settings and Rules/borders.

When the Custom option for Paragraph styling is chosen, Mark My Words offers the full gamut of styling options (Figure 7.2). If I choose to retain any of the settings, I'll often opt for just the first four or five, rather than the whole lot. The goal is to have the program generate only as many codes as are necessary to distinguish between different types of paragraphs, and no more.

TIP My jobs rarely contain any client-coded tables or rules, and I don't really care what lines of text a client thinks should be held together. But I can use the codes generated by Mark My Words to determine which paragraphs follow a head (no first line indent), are normal, or are meant to be set as extracts (left and right indents), so I may very well leave these options turned on.

Character styling

For styles that can individually be applied to selected characters, such as italics, Mark My Words offers the same four choices as for Paragraph styling—Retain all, Retain defaults, Custom settings, and Omit all. I definitely want the program to capture all the italics, even if the client has used underlining instead of italicization. I may want to ignore other specific styling, however, such as color or tracking changes.

Mark My Words will convert MS Word's character styling to the appropriate XPress Tags, so if clients are really savvy enough to specify their own colors or tracking values, it would be safe to keep them.

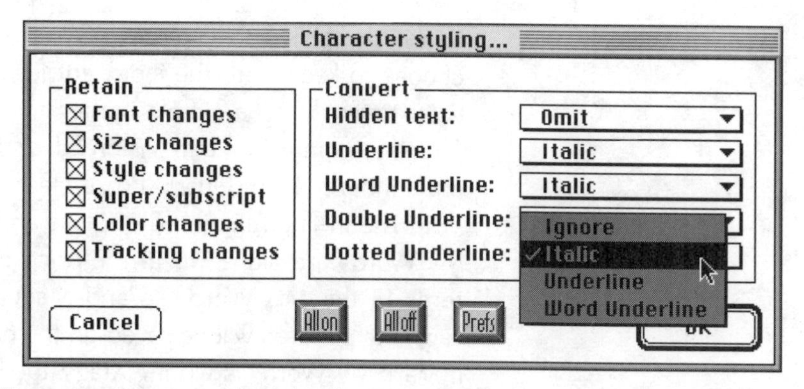

Figure 7.3 Character styling A wide variety of character styling choices can be made, allowing you to ignore some of the sillier formatting done by clients while still capturing, for example, all of the italicization they've done.

Or you can let the program generate XPress Tags and then search and replace the values that really need to be used.

Hidden text can be omitted or retained, shaded 0% or set as strike-through text, depending on whether it needs to be captured at all. All four of the underline conversions offer the same choices: Ignore, Italic, Underline, and Word Underline. More often than not, I leave them all set up to change underlining to italics (Figure 7.3).

Ancillary coding

This section has a number of miscellaneous options, including some of the file header and footer garbage that I would usually choose to ignore (Figure 7.4). One very exciting part of the Ancillary coding sec-

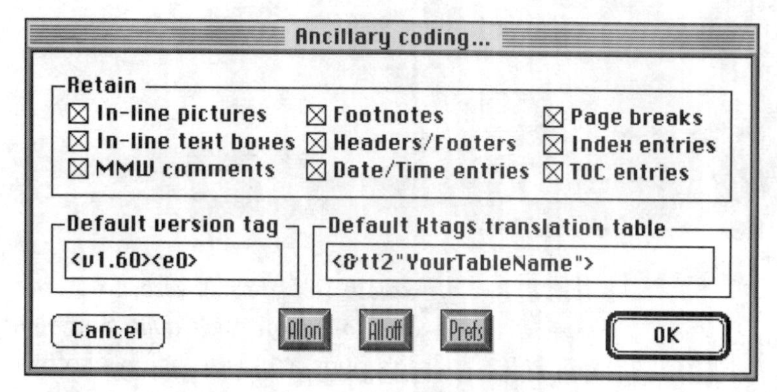

Figure 7.4 Ancillary coding With most jobs you can probably safely ignore (or "omit," to use Mark My Words' terminology) all of these options. Do remember to clear the translation table field if you're not using one with the Xtags XTension, though.

tion is the ability to capture MS Word's indexing commands. If you choose to keep both the index entries and hidden text (under Character styling), it's a simple matter to translate the resulting XPress Tags into commands that Vision Edge's IndeXTension can use to generate indexes from QuarkXPress files.

The in-line (anchored) picture and text box capabilities in Mark My Words are alone worth the price of admission. If there are pictures in the MS Word file and Mark My Words is writing XPress Tags, the pictures will be saved on the hard drive as Photoshop PICTs. If Mark My Words is writing Xtags, the pictures will still be saved, but the program will also generate an Xtags command that automatically creates an anchored picture box *and imports the picture* when the file is brought into QuarkXPress using the Xtags XTension.

With in-line text boxes chosen, either an Xtags code for anchored text boxes will be generated, where the anchored box is created and filled when importing the file to QuarkXPress with Xtags, or the text will appear properly styled in the text stream if you're using XPress Tags.

TIP I'm not trying to cover every single feature of these utilities and XTensions, but rather state enough of their traits to show how useful they can be in production work. Some form of on-line (electronic) documentation is included on the disk, and the XTensions talked about in this chapter come with very good manuals. I'm also not trying to act like a sales agent for Greg Swann and Chris Ryland, but I use these programs so often that I tend to get excited when extolling their virtues!

XP8

Expiate (ek′spē āt′), *verb,* to atone for; make amends or reparation for: *to expiate one's guilt.* Sometimes it's as much fun to figure out Greg's puns as it is to use his software! After using Mark My Words, the next step in massaging files to be brought into QuarkXPress is often to run them through XP8.

XP8 Confessional...

XP8 ©1993 by Greg Swann
Plain Text to XPress Tags File Translator

Select your options then pick a source file and a file to save as. Get Text (Include Style Sheets) on the new file.

Paragraphs...
◉ XP8's guess
○ Macintosh-like
○ MS-DOS-like

Character Set...
◉ Macintosh
○ MS-DOS
○ WordStar

Options... | Help... | Save Prefs | Quit | Start...

☒ Strip multi-returns
☒ Strip multi-tabs
☒ Strip underbars
☒ Strip leaders
☐ 3+ spaces to tabs
☒ Clean apostrophes

☐ Convert fractions
☐ Convert acronyms
☒ Convert faux bullets
☐ Kern around 1s
☒ Turn before dashes
☒ Widow control

Figure 7.5 XP8 Confessional... This is XP8's main window. Just a quick glance through these choices should give you a pretty good idea of how powerful it is.

This small but powerful utility reformats Macintosh and DOS text files, adding XPress Tags for typographic refinements and stripping out unwanted characters. The shareware version (1.0) of XP8 can be found on the disk, but in this section I'm showing the registered version (1.0.7), which has many enhancements (Figure 7.5). The documents that are included with the shareware version detail how you can upgrade to the registered version.

Cleaning up text

XP8 does a number of things to text files that we'd all like to do if we had the time. For example, as annoyed as I am when I see em dashes running into their surrounding characters, there's a good chance I won't bother to kern them unless they appear in a head. Without even being asked, XP8 adds 6 units of kerning on either side of em dashes (Figure 7.6). XP8 also adds a discretionary return after each em dash so that QuarkXPress will allow a line to break at that point. If you choose "Turn before dashes," XP8 will also add a discretionary return *before* em dashes, for those jobs where space is tight and the client won't mind such a break.

Speaking of kerning, another option in XP8's main window—the "XP8 Confessional"—is whether or not XP8 should "Kern around [ones]." Most fonts on the desktop use the same widths for all fig-

EM DASHES WITHOUT KERNING

Em dashes—often too close—can be fixed.

EM DASHES WITH KERNING

Em dashes—often too close—can be fixed.

Figure 7.6 Em dashes and XP8 Just a slight amount of adjustment—6 units of kerning—can prevent em dashes from running into their adjacent characters.

ures, so they look great in tables and bad in text, especially the ones and sevens. Amazingly, XP8 is smart enough to avoid kerning ones used in tables even when this option is turned on, since they should be left to align with the other numbers in the table. But the ones in text are given –11 units of kerning, which often makes them look much better (Figure 7.7).

Your mileage may vary with this option, since not all fonts require as much (or any) kerning around the number one; test this out before choosing to invoke it. Fonts in which the ones have a wide serif often need no kerning, and if you're using a font with old-style numbers, such as the font used in this book (Clear Prairie Dawn), the widths of the figures will differ, and they may already have kerning pairs built into them.

In addition to the above options, XP8 can also be told to strip out multiple returns. It's not uncommon for me to leave extra returns in a file while I'm manually cleaning it up—since it makes it easier for me to see what's going on—and then let XP8 take them all out at once. XP8 will also strip out multiple tabs, but be sure that you don't

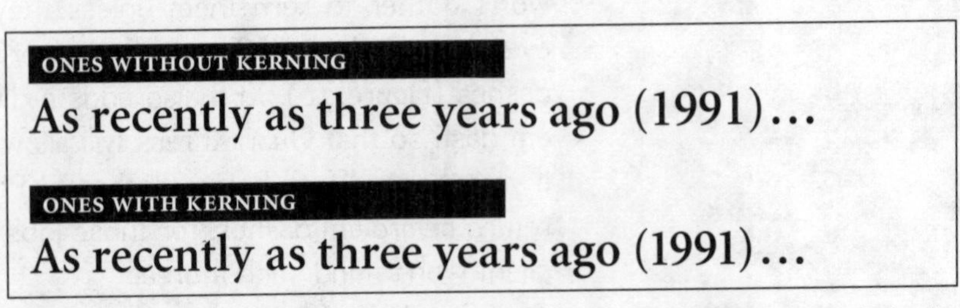

ONES WITHOUT KERNING
As recently as three years ago (1991)…
ONES WITH KERNING
As recently as three years ago (1991)…

Figure 7.7 Ones and XP8 In this case, a kerning of –11 units makes the ones look a lot better.

have any tables that need to keep their extra tab characters in order to show blank areas.

XP8 can strip out underbars (baseline rules) and leader dots, and it can be told to convert more than three spacebands in a row into a tab. It's important to read the documentation to learn the effect of turning on or leaving off these options. For example, when XP8 strips out underbars, it also inserts a tab character so that you can define a leader-fill tab in your QuarkXPress document and create a fill-in-the-blank rule.

XP8 also does a wonderful job cleaning up apostrophes. In fact, its quote-conversion algorithm is the best I've seen, intelligently recognizing apostrophes that are being used for open-ended contractions ('cause) instead of opening and closing quotations ('because'), unlike QuarkXPress' Convert Quotes option in the **File→Get Text** dialog box. XP8 also converts fractions, acronyms, and "faux" bullets (*, o). When asked, it will insert a discretionary hyphen in front of the last word of every paragraph to prevent partial-word paragraph widows. And XP8 *always* traps for XPress Tags errors that might result in missing text or document corruption.

Ligatures

Although QuarkXPress' ligatures option in Typographic Preferences is a real gem, there will still be times that ligatures cause grief. The first instance is when Expert Set ligatures need to be incorporated into a job; the second is when a file already has keyboard ligatures that need to be removed.

If "Ignore Ligs" is chosen in the XP8 Options dialog box (Figure 7.8), nothing will be done to ligatures or ligature candidates. On the other hand, if "Convert ffi/ffl" is chosen, XP8 will change "fi" and "fl" pairs to the characters residing in the Option-Shift-5 and Option-Shift-6 positions, respectively. "Ignore ffi/ffl" will only convert the "fi" and "fl" ligatures that don't follow another "f." I wouldn't recommend using either of these options anymore, now that we can get this much functionality right in QuarkXPress. The one exception to this is when setting a job that has two different faces, one of which requires ligatures to be turned off.

The "Expert Set—Monaco" choice changes all five ligatures (ff, fi, fl, ffi, and ffl) to the Monaco font and to the appropriate Adobe

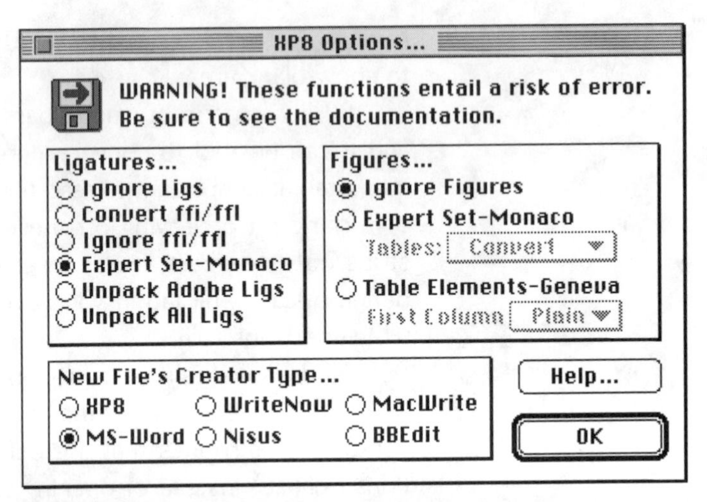

Figure 7.8 XP8 Options...Ligatures... Here's another example of where reading the documentation comes in real handy: those second and third ligature options don't really mean what they say!

Expert set character. This gives you the opportunity to use Quark XPress' Font Usage dialog box to change the Monaco characters to whichever Expert set you're using in the job, such as Adobe Garamond Expert or Minion Expert.

Lastly, if you're trying to get rid of ligatures, you can choose to "Unpack Adobe Ligs" to change Option-Shift-5 and Option-Shift-6 characters back to "fi" and "fl"; "Unpack All Ligs" will do the same, as well as convert the Expert set special characters back to "ff," "fi," "fl," "ffi," and "ffl."

Cleaning up figures and tables

If you've had the misfortune of setting a job that required all the numbers to be set as old-style figures from a different font, as in the Expert set of Adobe's Minion font, you'll really love the following features of XP8. Unless otherwise told, XP8 will ignore figures (numbers and punctuation), other than possibly kerning the ones. However, XP8 can also add XPress Tags for a font change to Monaco in front of all of the figures by choosing "Expert Set—Monaco" in the XP8 Options dialog box, again letting the proper font be applied with Font Usage once in QuarkXPress.

Figures in tables can either be skipped over, converted to Monaco, or converted to Geneva, this last option allowing a com-

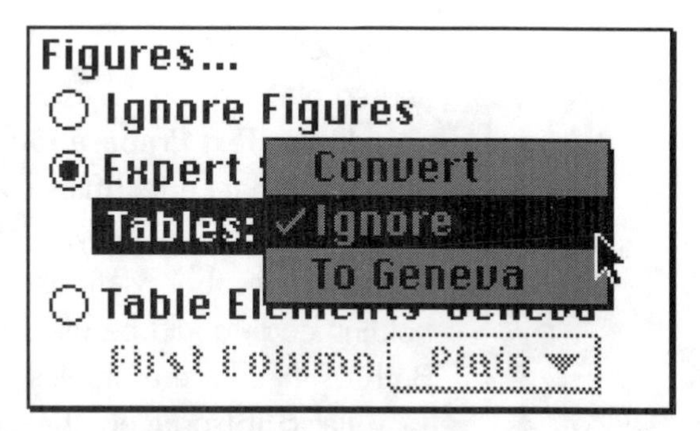

Figure 7.9 XP8 Options...Figures... XP8 offers a number of options regarding figures (numbers and punctuation) in and out of tabular settings.

pletely different font to be used in a Font Usage search for tabular figures (Figure 7.9). If you don't want any of your numbers in normal text disturbed, you can still choose "Table Elements—Geneva" and have all the numbers and punctuation in tables assigned a font different from that used in the stub (first) columns, which is all too often requested!

Torquemada the Inquisitor

I already discussed this curiously named search-and-replace utility in the **Text Preparation** chapter, but I just scratched the surface. Now I'd like to show some heavy duty uses of Torquemada the Inquisitor. If you start to get a headache trying to understand some of my examples, feel free to come back to this section when you're actually using Torquemada to prepare a job. But be sure not to skip the rest of the sections in this chapter; they're less headache-inducing to read, and they cover some important tools for a production environment.

Torquemada is a text-based search-and-replace program. The free version 1.1.0 that is found on this book's disk can be upgraded to the commercial program, which has some powerful additional features. With Torquemada, you can perform up to 640 search-and-replaces (32 sets of 20 searches each) on up to 128 files in a System 7 drag-and-drop batch—including wildcard searches that can distinguish between upper and lower case letters, numbers, punctuation, and so on.

In the **Text Preparation** chapter, I discussed how to use Torquemada to enhance text files by adding codes that would make it easier to typeset a job properly, such as nonbreakable spacebands before or after certain abbreviations. I also talked about how a simple placeholding code could be used to burst out long strings of XPress Tags. Both of these are examples of literal translations.

I also introduced the concept of wildcards, which are placeholders used to mask out characters surrounded by literal, specific characters. If you don't have a clue what I'm talking about (no insult intended), you might want to read that section again, since I'll be building onto those concepts now.

Typed wildcards

Untyped wildcards match (find) any character that's surrounded by the literal (specific) characters that you define. Typed wildcards, on the other hand, will only match certain types of characters, depending on the definition of the wildcard. Generally speaking, Greg Swann is the one doing the defining, although there is one instance where the user has that power. Figure 7.10 illustrates the different typed wildcards available in Torquemada.

Let's take the example of a text file that consists of a number of records from a database; each record is on its own line, with the fields separated by commas. A record would look something like this:

```
A2,Company,Address,City,State,Zip,Phone
```

The first field is a product category number which is always in the form of a capital letter followed by a one-digit number. Perhaps we would like to do something with that category code, such as making it bold or even deleting it. Obviously, doing either task manually could take a long time if we have more than a couple of dozen records. (The worst-case scenario would be 260 records: 26 letters of the alphabet times 10 numbers.) But using Torquemada's typed wildcards, the task would be a breeze. Referring to Figure 7.9, we see that the code "^+" will mask out any upper case letter and the code "^#" will do the same for numeric characters.

TYPED WILDCARDS
Match any one character of the following type:

Code	Meaning
^+	Upper case character (includes accented characters)
^-	Lower case character (includes accented characters)
^±	Character of either case (includes accented characters)
^&	Alphanumeric character (letter or number, not space or punct.)
^%	Tabular character (digit, space or punctuation; not alphabetical)
^$	Printable character (all characters *except* spaces)
^¢	Any character *except* return
^!	Punctuation character (includes high-ASCII punctuation)
^.	Sentence punctuation character (. , ; : ! ?)
^#	Numeric character (digits only)
^_	Space character (space, return, tab, option-space)
^¬	Space character (space, tab, option-space, but *not* return)

Figure 7.10 Torquemada's typed wildcards Some of the typed wildcards are similar to each other, like the ones for punctuation and sentence punctuation, but their subtle differences can be very powerful.

TIP There are a handful of characters that are used as "aliases" in Torquemada, partially due to the way the Macintosh deals with these characters in dialog boxes. Literal returns and tabs can't be typed in a dialog box, since they are equivalent to hitting an "OK" button and moving to another choice in the dialog, respectively. Instead, "^p" and "^t" are typed to get these characters in translations. The other three aliases that must be typed when their literal characters are desired are "^^" to get a caret symbol, since we're using "^" for all of our other coding; "^•" to get a raised solid dot, which is otherwise used by Greg to show a spaceband in the translation table dialog box; and "^°" to get a raised open dot, which Greg uses to show an en space.

To find the category codes in the example, lines starting with an upper case letter followed by a number will need to be searched for. In Torquemada-ese, this will look like

```
^p^+^#
```

The "^p" represents a return, so the next character must be the start of a new line. "^+" will only match upper case letters, and "^#" will only match numbers. Only occurrences of these three characters in a row will successfully match this search string.

If, after finding the category code, we want it to be set bold, we can replace the characters that this search found with

```
^p<B>^+^#<B>
```

If, on the other hand, we want to delete the category code, we will want to include the comma in the search (so that we're not left with a comma at the start of a line), either as a literal or as a wildcard. Since you already know how to type a comma, let's do it with the sentence punctuation wildcard instead:

```
^p^+^#^.
```

The only part of the search string that we want to keep is the return, so our replacement simply looks like

```
^p
```

That's really all there is to typed wildcards. As we continue, it should become apparent how we can use them to form much more complex search patterns.

Do-it-yourself wildcards

As I said earlier, Greg is usually the one defining what each wildcard searches for, but there is one instance where we can define our own wildcard. Taking the database record from above—which was sneakily chosen because I could build onto it and create more and more complicated translations—what would happen if the category code was always composed of a capital letter and *two* numbers? You might think of trying to search for

```
^p^+^#^#
```

and replacing it with

```
^p<B>^+^#^#<B>
```

But I guarantee that you'll only try it once. If you need to preserve whatever is found by a typed wildcard, you can only use it once per translation (search-and-replace pair). In the example above, the number that was found with the last use of the numeric wildcard (^#) will be used in both places that it's called out in the replacement side of the translation.

The do-it-yourself wildcard will let us get around this limitation, though, allowing us to define a second wildcard that can be used to mask out the second number. The form of this command is: ^«...», where the chevrons (« and ») are keyed with Option-Backslash (⌥\) and Option-Shift-Backslash (⌥⇧\), respectively, and the ellipsis is just meant to show where the definition is keyed. You can define any character or range of characters with this wildcard—you can even define what characters it should *not* find, but for now, let's just define a second numeric character. Our new search string would now look like this:

```
^p^+^#^«0-9»  or  ^p^+^#^«^#»
```

and the replacement would look like this:

```
^p<B>^+^#^«<B>
```

Note that only the beginning of the do-it-yourself wildcard (^«) should be specified in the replacement.

If we were instead looking for *only* one-letter, one-number category codes at the start of a line, we could use the do-it-yourself wildcard as in this search string:

```
^p^+^#«!#»
```

By placing the "!" in front of the "^#" inside the do-it-yourself wildcard, we're telling Torquemada that the translation string is only valid if it finds an upper case letter followed by a number that's *not* followed by another number; the "!" acts as a logical "not." I'd no doubt want to embellish that search string in a real job, since I suspect it would also find things that I didn't want, such as Canadian postal codes (e.g., S7H 2K6) at the start of a paragraph.

Wildstrings

The four Wildstrings built into Torquemada are very powerful masks that pick up multiple characters of any kind (unless further modified, as we'll discuss). Since wildstrings will pick up everything that's not nailed down, it's immensely important that unique patterns of literals and aliases be included as part of the search strings.

All four wildstring commands act the same; Greg has provided us with four of them so that we can mask out more than one section in the same search string of characters. The commands are

```
^*   ^~   ^?   ^@
```

Let's go back to the database record, but this time we'll use some real data from which we want to extract the category code and the company name:

```
X3,XChange,P.O. Box 270578,Fort Collins,
Colorado,80527,(303) 229-0656
```

We can continue to use the wildcard coding we already established in order to reformat or delete the category code, and we can feel confident that the next field is the company, but we don't know how many characters are used in the company's name. That's where wildstrings come in handy. This search string

```
^p^+^#,^*,
```

will pick up the category code at the start of the line (^p^+^#), the comma following the category code, and all of the characters up to and including the comma after the company (^*,). We can then replace these with:

```
^p<B>^+^#<B>^p<I>^*<I>
```

which carries over the return, adds XPress Tags to make the category code bold, deletes the comma after the category code (due to the fact that we left it out of the replacement string), adds a return so that the category code is on its own line, and adds XPress Tags to italicize the company. To tell the truth, I'd probably do my formatting with style sheets for each paragraph instead of loose character formatting, so the following replacement string would be more like what I would use:

```
^p@code:^+^#^p@comp:^*
```

Does that make sense? The wildstring (^*) is picking up everything between the two commas, and it's being moved to its own line and getting an XPress Tags style sheet callout added in front of it. This is not a completed translation, of course, since we haven't done anything with the rest of our record. We'll get to that soon.

Next we'll take advantage of the fact that we can use four wildstrings in one translation to format the data as a mailing label:

```
^p^*,^~,^?,^@,(
```

This will break the line up into these parts:

```
^p^*,     X3,
^~,       XChange,
^?,       P.O. Box 270578,
^@,(      Fort Collins,Colorado,80527,(
```

We have no need for any of the literals, so our replacement string can be as simple as this:

```
^p^~^p^?^p^@
```

Note that I've deleted the category code—which was captured with a wildstring (^*) instead of two wildcards this time—by not carrying it over to the replacement string. The commas between the company and address and between the address and city were also left out, and each of the three sections were moved to their own lines by adding a couple of returns. Again, this is not a completed translation, since I didn't do anything with the phone number. And I'd probably want to do another translation to add a spaceband before the commas that precede the state and zip code.

The wildstring modifier

The only problem with wildstrings is that they're sometimes too wild! But the wildstring modifier command—which, along with the do-it-yourself wildcard and a few of the regular wildcards, is only available in the commercial version of Torquemada—will constrain a given wildstring so that it only matches specific literals, aliases, or types of wildcards.

The format for the wildstring modifier is:

```
^<
```

where a literal, alias, or wildcard precedes the command, and any of the four wildstrings follows it, like this:

```
^#^<^*
```

This means "look for a sequence of one number followed by *zero or more* numbers and store them in this wildstring." The modifier itself won't need to be repeated in the replacement string, but the defining character and the wildstring will:

```
^#^*
```

Let's see if we can use the wildstring modifier to finally complete the translation of the database record. We'll revert to using wildcards for the category code, since our data contains five unique sections: category, company, address, city/state/zip, and phone. Here we go:

```
^p^+^#,^*,^~,^?,(^¢^<^@
```

Breaking it down to its component parts, we have:

```
^p^+^#,    X3,
^*,        XChange,
^~,        P.O. Box 270578,
^?,(       Fort Collins,Colorado,80527,(
^¢^<^@     303) 229-0656
```

with this last section reading: "a sequence of one nonreturn character (^¢) followed by zero or more nonreturn characters." In other words, we're reading everything up to the next return character, which starts our next record. If we're still looking to produce a mailing label, the replacement string would be

```
^p^*^p^~^p^?^p
```

wherein we leave out both the category code (^+^#) and the phone number (^¢^<^@), as well as all of the literal commas and the open parentheses. And what about those pesky spaceband-less commas after the city and state? Piece of cake:

```
,^&
```

which means "a comma followed by any character that's not a space or punctuation," gets changed to:

```
, ^&
```

which is the comma and a spaceband, followed by the nonspace character found in the search.

Markers

No discussion of Torquemada would be complete without covering the use of "markers," unique placeholders that can be temporarily inserted in the text stream to indicate that a certain translation has taken place. Sometimes they are used to prevent subsequent translations from occurring on the text; other times they can point to a spot where further translations need to occur.

The most common use for markers is to indicate the beginnings or ends of paragraphs. Granted, in most programs, a carriage return serves this purpose just fine. But Torquemada is unique in that its wildstrings can search beyond the boundaries of a single paragraph. You can use a wildstring modifier to define a wildstring that searches for all characters except a return, but that gets cumbersome, especially if you need to do it multiple times in one translation.

For instance, the database record problem that I've been using in all of these examples was originally much more complicated. Hugo Heriz-Smith left a message on CompuServe's Desktop Publishing Forum asking how he could translate the following records:

```
P14,T40,XYZ Company,999 Walnut Street,
Anytown,PA,19104,(333)123-4567

C71,ABC Cleaners,2000 Pine Blvd,Suite 200,
ThisTown,PA,19406,(333)345-4567
```

He wanted to find records that contained multiple category codes, move each of the category codes to its own record, and copy the company information to each of these new records. Greg Swann, who supports his programs in the DTP Forum, answered Hugo by typing a Torquemada translation set (table) into his reply. Hugo (and I) needed only to copy Greg's message into a text file and open the file in Torquemada, since the program can recognize any text file as a set (Figure 7.11).

Note that Greg uses markers a couple of times in this set. First, he looks for all instances of categories, where a category starts with an upper case letter (^+), a number followed by zero or more numbers (^#^<^*), and a comma. He then adds markers to both sides of all the categories (|). After that, he changes any occurrences of two markers (||) to a different marker (_), which will show the rest of the translations the spot where they have to do their stuff.

Since there can be up to six categories in a record, he runs the next translation six times, looking for the first new marker (_), every-

Multiple categories

<table>
<tr><td></td><td>Mark every category</td><td>_^?|^¢^<^~^p</td><td>^¢^<^~^p^?|^¢^<^~^p</td></tr>
<tr><td>^+^#^<^*,</td><td>|^+^#^*,|</td><td>_^?|^¢^<^~^p</td><td>^¢^<^~^p^?|^¢^<^~^p</td></tr>
<tr><td></td><td></td><td>_^?|^¢^<^~^p</td><td>^¢^<^~^p^?|^¢^<^~^p</td></tr>
<tr><td></td><td>Mark multiples</td><td></td><td></td></tr>
<tr><td>||</td><td>_</td><td></td><td>Leading 0 for sort order</td></tr>
<tr><td></td><td></td><td>^+^#,</td><td>^+0^#,</td></tr>
<tr><td></td><td>Split multiples 6 times</td><td></td><td></td></tr>
<tr><td>_^?|^¢^<^~^p</td><td>^¢^<^~^p^?|^¢^<^~^p</td><td></td><td>Lose marks</td></tr>
<tr><td>_^?|^¢^<^~^p</td><td>^¢^<^~^p^?|^¢^<^~^p</td><td>|</td><td></td></tr>
<tr><td>_^?|^¢^<^~^p</td><td>^¢^<^~^p^?|^¢^<^~^p</td><td></td><td></td></tr>
</table>

Open Set... ⌘O | Save Set... ⌘S | Clear All ⌘K | Wildcards ⌘? | OK

Figure 7.11 Torquemada's markers In this table (or "set") that Greg wrote, he makes judicious use of "markers," or placeholders that show spots that need further work. Here he uses the | and _ characters to great advantage.

thing up to the first old marker (|), and everything else up to the end of the paragraph (^¢^<^~^p). The contents of this final wildstring, which contains everything on the line after the last category (indicated by the only old marker on the line), is repeated so that it follows both the first and last categories on the line. After that, he does a single translation that will help Hugo sort the resulting records (adding a zero in front of any categories composed of an upper case letter, one number, and a comma), and then removes the remaining old markers.

Miscellaneous examples

If you're still with me at this point, take a moment to pull out that pocket protector and hold it high: You definitely belong to that hallowed group of technonerds who can make a killing in this business by chewing up large manuscripts and spitting out typeset files. Greg often jokes in the DTP Forum about "the four or five people" in the world who can use such-and-such a feature, and I guess that my goal in this chapter is to make sure that these numbers increase. I really hate the thought that I may be part of a species on the brink of extinction!

I took a look through some of my old Torquemada sets so that I could show some real examples of translations that have worked for me. In no particular order, here they are.

Chapter cleanup

This Torquemada set works on files that have already been processed through Mark My Words. The client had actually provided me with MS Word files that used style sheets, so I'm searching for the style sheet names and certain other patterns.

The heads were all marked either "@Subhead A:" or "@Subhead B:," and I needed to pay attention to what was on the line after the heads. This first translation in this set looks for Subhead A, picks up everything to the end of the line (^¢^<^*), as well as the two returns following it (^p^p) and the first character of the subsequent line (^1). This search string:

```
@Subhead·A:^¢^<^*^p^p^1
```

was used to find this text:

```
@Subhead·A:Bottle·Glasshouses·and·their·
Products¶
¶
After·window·glass,·bottles·and·other...¶
```

The translation replaces the text with with a new style sheet name and the rest of the first line (@ChapName:^¢^<^*^p), a text style sheet callout for the first paragraph after the chapter name (@Texto:), and an XPress Tag for changing the font for the drop cap (<f"ZapfBook">). Then the face is changed back and a new line command is added so that the drop cap sticks up by one line (<f$><\n>). Here's the replacement string:

```
@ChapName:^¢^<^*^p@Text0:<f"ZapfBook">^1<f$><\n>
```

that produces this new text:

```
@ChapName:Bottle·Glasshouses·and·their·
Products¶
@Text0:<f"ZapfBook">A<f$><\n>fter·window·
glass,·bottles·and·other...¶
```

Subhead B has two possible scenarios, the first of which looks for a catalog number and two returns after the head:

```
@Subhead·B:^¢^<^*^p(Cat.^~^p^p
```

and changes it to a new style sheet for the head, a style sheet for a subhead, and a style sheet for the first paragraph of text after a subhead:

```
@Head1:^¢^<^*^p@Head1a:(Cat.^~^p@Text1:
```

In the second Subhead B scenario, the head isn't being followed by a subhead, but rather by two returns:

```
@Subhead·B:^¢^<^*^p^p
```

so the text style sheet used is for the first paragraph of text after a head, instead of a subhead:

```
@Head1:^¢^<^*^p@Text1a:
```

Since the client keyed tabs at the start of all the rest of the paragraphs, I could easily search for them:

```
^p^t
```

and replace them with just the return and the proper style sheet, leaving out the tab:

```
^p@Text2:
```

And, lastly, the client was resourceful enough to add codes around the literally thousands of instances of small caps, but managed to screw that up by typing the small caps text in all caps:

```
[sc]^?[r]
```

No worries, since Torquemada has the most awesome set of case conversion tools I've ever seen. Everything between the "^L" and "^=" commands is automatically changed to lower case:

```
<H>^L^?^=<H>
```

Fractions and slashes

In the same job as above—a job that required four or five Torquemada sets, as I recall—I used Greg's text processing utility, XP8, to convert full-size fractions (3/4, 1-1/2, 2 2/3) into solidus fractions (¾). However, I still needed to do some additional manipulations—due as much to the idiosyncrasies of the font as to those of the client. XP8 changes "1-1/2" to the following XPress Tags when told to convert a fraction:

```
1<V>1<V>/<V->2<V->
```

In this first translation, I looked for any single number (^#) followed by the XPress Tag for superior (<V>). I then used a do-it-yourself wildcard as a wildstring modifier (^«^#»^<^~) to pick up one number followed by zero or more numbers up to the toggling superior tag:

```
^#<V>^«^#»^<^~<V>
```

which carries over the first number, adds a nonbreakable flex space (<\!q>) which I defined as a quarter of an en space, I believe, and the wildstring of numbers (^«^~):

```
^#<\!q><V>^«^~<V>
```

These next five translations show kerning values being added around the virgule (fraction slash), as determined by some tests that I ran:

SEARCH	REPLACE
7<V>/	<k-20>7<Vk0>/
<V>/<V->2	<Vk5>/<V-k0>2
<V>/<V->4	<Vk-10>/<V-k0>4
<V>/<V->8	<Vk5>/<V-k0>8
<Vk0>/<V->8	<Vk5>/<V-k0>8

Text trans

This table was for an entirely different job. It wasn't consistently keyed, to say the least, but it was well worth my time to go through the text files and make them as structured as possible. By spending 15 minutes per file manually cleaning it up, I was able to save hours that would have otherwise been spent applying style sheets and character styling on every other line.

Most of the time the client actually keyed the following pattern correctly, occasionally missing one of the hyphens, which I would add. By searching for a spaceband followed by the makeshift arrow, one space character followed by zero or more space characters

(^_^<^*), and one nonreturn character followed by zero or more nonreturn characters (^¢^<^~):

```
· --->^_^<^*^¢^<^~
```

I was able to insert an en space (<\f>), a color and font change (<c"PANTONE·328·CV"f"ZapfDingbats">), the proper character for an arrow, a return to the font used in the current style sheet (<f$>), a punctuation space and the Indent Here command (<\p\i>), the rest of the characters on the line (^¢^~), and a return to the color used in the current style sheet (<c$>):

```
<\f><c"PANTONE·328·CV"f"ZapfDingbats">'<f$>
<\p\i>^¢^~<c$>
```

This next translation simply searches for a baseline rule character at the start of a line, followed by a spaceband:

```
^p_·
```

and calls the appropriate style sheet for the paragraph plus all the character styling for a par symbol that starts the paragraph:

```
^p@par1:<c"PANTONE·328·CV"f"Universal-
NewswithCommPi">©<c$f$><\p>
```

And Quark wonders why we want character-based style sheets! (That's not exactly true, actually, since character-based style sheets have been promised for version 4.0 of QuarkXPress.)

The next two sets of searches depend on finding numbers at the start of a line, but the replacement strings differ depending on whether the numbers are followed by a spaceband or a tab character:

SEARCH	REPLACE
^p^#^<^~·	^p@side0:^#^~^p@side:•^t
^p^#^<^@^t	^p@que:^#^@^p@text:•^t<\i>

TIP Note that both replacement strings call two different style sheets on two different lines, with the second line starting with a bullet. This is a down and dirty way of getting character-based styling, since I let the XPress Tags filter apply the style sheets to these two "paragraphs" and then use **Edit→Find/Change** in

QuarkXPress to search for (and delete) any return/bullet pairs, recombining the two differently styled pieces of the same paragraph. If your job contains a legitimate use of a bullet at the start of a line, you should use some other unused character.

This final translation looks for any number of baseline rules:

```
_^<^?
```

and changes them to a set number of baseline rules, first reducing the point size and then changing it back:

```
<z6>______________________<z$>
```

This allows me to make sure that all the fill-in-the-blank rules in the file are of a consistent length and thickness, and that they'll actually be closer to residing on—instead of under—the baseline. Try it sometime.

DTP File cleanup

I've abbreviated this final example, but I believe it still shows how you can use markers to continue a translation. In this case, the first replacement filled Greg's limit of 256 characters, so I ended the replacement with a bullet, which I then used in the second search pair to continue the text. This actually runs through six translations to burst out an incredible 1,532 characters!

Search

```
list·*.*^p
```

Replace

```
CompuServe's·Desktop·Publishing·Forum^p^pThis
·is·a·complete·list·of·all·the·files·in·t
he·DTP·Forum's·libraries.·If·you·have·any·•
```

Search

```
•
```

Replace

```
questions·about·any·of·the·files·shown·here
,·please·leave·a·message·to·SYSOP·in·Secti
on·17·of·the·DTP·Forum·and·we'll·get·back
·to·you!^p
```

Other useful utilities

Shane the Plane

Get used to it: All of Greg's utilities have goofy names (although I'm sure he'd prefer the appellation "unique"). This first one is actually named after someone, Greg's primary beta (pre-release) software tester, Shane Stanley, of Nar Nar Goon, Victoria, Australia.

It should be noted here that Greg, Chris, Shane, and I all first "met" in the DTP Forum on CompuServe. I manage the forum, and the others are all distinguished members. Greg, Chris, and I have all met in person several times at various trade show dinners hosted by the DTP Forum; none of us has actually met Shane in person, but Greg says that mail sent to Shane in Nar Nar Goon is never returned, so we figure that's a good sign.

Shane the Plane is a utility that can change the creator and type of files, and/or their creation and modification dates and times (Figure 7.12). It also intelligently renames files and inserts the file name as a "slug" in text files, if desired. I usually use Shane the Plane to fix creator and type codes on StuffIt files improperly uploaded to CompuServe. A demo of version 2.0 can be found on this book's disk.

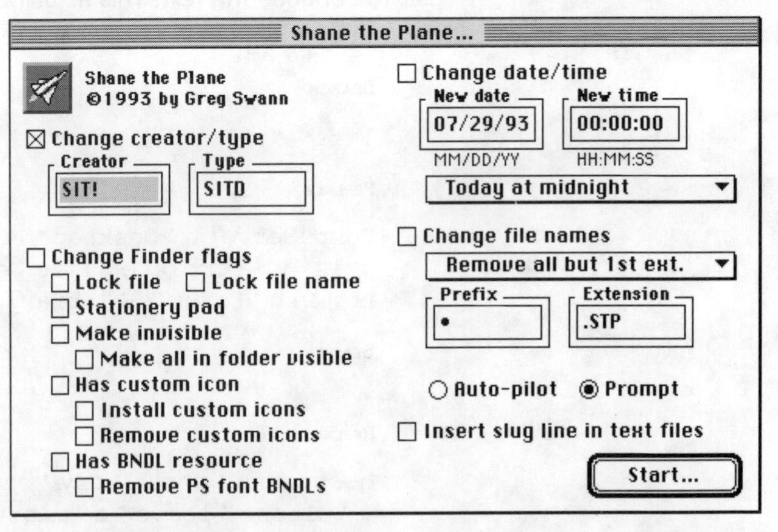

Figure 7.12 Shane the Plane As with most of Greg's utilities, there are a great number of options available, many of which you'll never need (but will be grateful to have when you do need them).

Shane the Plane can also perform batch editing of Finder attributes, including making files invisible/visible. It can make fonts behave like files—greatly reducing the time it takes to copy them between hard disks—by removing their BNDL resources. And it batch "pastes" custom Finder icons.

PixPex

This utility—whose name actually makes sense if you say it quickly enough (PixPex = PicSpecs = Picture Specs)—interrogates PICT, TIFF, and EPS files and creates an Xtags picture box specification for them. The specification is a string of codes describing the anchored picture box that will contain the picture.

PixPex can either create a new file containing the Xtags codes or simply leave them on the Clipboard for pasting into your word processing file. It's a drag-and-drop-only application, so it must be used with System 7. I'll wait to define the following Xtags-valid codes when I discuss Xtags later in the chapter, but here's what PixPex produced when I dragged a couple of sample images onto its icon in the Finder:

```
<&pb(155,103,B,0,K,0,1,K,0,0,M,100,100,0,0,0,0,
"High Text:QXP Unleashed:Ch. 1 art:Earth
according to Anne")>
```

```
<&pb(57,67,B,0,K,0,1,K,0,0,M,100,100,0,0,0,0,
"High Text:QXP Unleashed:Ch. 1 art:oil well")>
```

Figure 7.14 shows the anchored boxes that were automatically created and filled when I imported the above codes into QuarkXPress using the Xtags XTension. A free copy of PixPex is on this book's disk.

Figure 7.13 PixPex This is a drag-and-drop-only application, so there are no dialog boxes. But here's the Finder icon that Greg's daughter, Meredith, created.

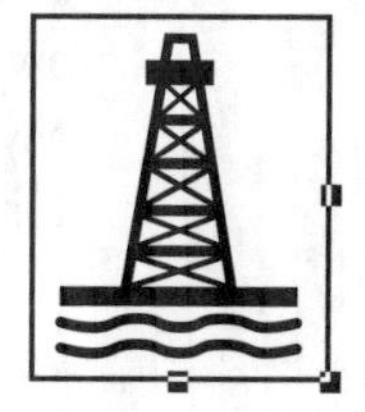

Figure 7.14 PixPex pictures When I imported the PixPex codes into a QuarkXPress document using the Xtags XTension, these anchored boxes were automatically created and the images were automatically imported.

MyEditor

Greg has announced plans to integrate Mark My Words, XP8, and Torquemada the Inquisitor—along with several of his other text processing utilities—into a stand-alone text editor. It will essentially be a word processor designed for desktop publishing text preparation, and he has code-named it MyEditor.

MyEditor is vaporware at this writing—it exists solely as a burgeoning design specification. As a text editor, it will give you the kind of interactive flexibility you have with MS Word or any other off-the-shelf word processing program. Simple character styling will be in "styled text"—words in italics will appear as "*italics*" rather than "<I>italics<I>." MyEditor will interpret tags to styled text on the fly and write XPress Tags when you save a file, so you can use familiar Macintosh menu commands or keyboard equivalents to add or remove text styling.

MyEditor will read files already containing XPress Tags, Xtags, and Aldus PageMaker Tags (if and when that language is promulgated); it will also be able to open files from both MS Word for Macintosh and Windows. Files will be saved as either XPress Tags, Xtags, or Aldus PageMaker Tags.

Torquemada the Inquisitor will provide the search-and-replace engine for MyEditor. Interactive searches will be run in a fashion similar to other find/change dialogs, or as Torquemada-like bulk searches. You'll be able to constrain search-and-replace operations to a particular selection range of text. XP8's transformations will be unbundled and placed in a menu for easy access.

As an interactive editor, MyEditor will possibly be better for desktop publishers than any other word processing program. But all of MyEditor's functionality will also be available in a scriptable, drag-and-drop, batch mode. A script will consist of a list of instructions, containing such things as import preferences, search-and-replace sets, and visits to the interactive editor. MyEditor will be AppleEvent-aware, so AppleScript or Userland Frontier will be able to deliver a MyEditor script—along with the files to be processed—to MyEditor for hands-off operation.

MyEditor has no projected shipping date at this writing, but a vocal noodge-corps campaigns for it regularly in the DTP Forum. Given Greg's track record, MyEditor (or whatever goofy name he gives it) should be worth the wait.

Xtags

Whenever I'm faced with a job that's highly repetitive—either in the number of files requiring similar setup or the frequency with which the job will be produced—I immediately think of Quark's powerful coding language, XPress Tags. With this language, I'm able to flow text into a QuarkXPress document with style sheets and character coding already in place, freeing me to concentrate on page layout.

However, XPress Tags falls short on a few key issues, not the least of which is error reporting. Enter Xtags, a powerful XTension from Chris Ryland of Em Software. This XTension enhances the XPress Tags language by:

- Adding more options for character and paragraph coding
- Allowing you to create—and fill—anchored text and graphic boxes automatically
- Applying different master pages as a document is flowed
- Translating client codes into Xtags codes while importing files

The Xtags Preferences dialog box is shown in Figure 7.15.

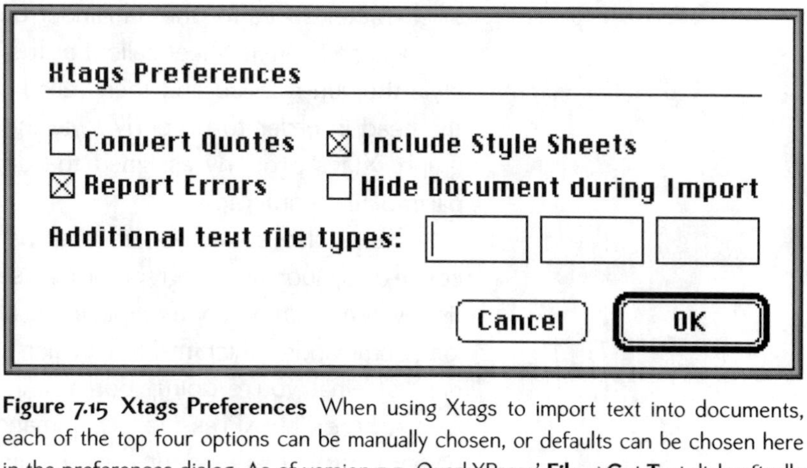

Xtags Preferences
Convert Quotes
Include Style Sheets
Report Errors
Hide Document during Import
Additional text file types:
Cancel
OK

Figure 7.15 Xtags Preferences When using Xtags to import text into documents, each of the top four options can be manually chosen, or defaults can be chosen here in the preferences dialog. As of version 3.3, QuarkXPress' **File→Get Text** dialog finally offers "sticky" Convert Quotes and Include Style Sheets buttons like Xtags.

There's a working demo of Xtags version 1.1 on the disk, limited only in the number of paragraphs it will process (30). The commercial version that should be shipping by the time you read this will include support for QuarkXPress 3.2 and 3.3. I'll be using examples from a book I typeset called *Cinematic Motion* (Michael Wiese Productions, 1992) throughout this discussion, as the production of this book really shows the power and versatility of Xtags.

Adding flexibility to XPress Tags

There are often times when I need to either change characteristics of text in relation to the text around it, or completely deviate from the normal character styling for part of a paragraph. Xtags allows both of these actions by permitting me to perform mathematical functions in tags as well as to call out more than one style sheet per paragraph.

If, for example, I need to make every occurrence of a particular phrase a couple of points larger than its surrounding text, but I don't know what its current size is going to be (since it may be part of a head, text, or even an extract), I can just use the Xtags command <z(.+2)> before the word or phrase. The normal XPress Tag <z$> would go after the word or phrase in order to return to the point size in use in the current style sheet. Relative sizing like this is available in the point size (<z__>), shading, (<s__>), horizontal scaling (<h__>), tracking (<t__>), and paragraph settings (<*p__>) commands.

In *Cinematic Motion* I had a number of run-in heads that required a certain font, style, and size, followed by a completely different set of character specs for the remainder of the paragraph. To accomplish this, I placed a style sheet callout at the beginning of the paragraph to style the run-in head and then called another style sheet right after the head in order to properly style the rest of the text in that paragraph. Xtags properly assigned the different specs to the different parts of the paragraph.

Xtags also allows you to omit parameters in long XPress Tags constructs, such as paragraph or rule settings, which can save a lot of time when creating codes. Spacing is also allowed inside those same long commands, which makes it easier to find errors and generally figure out what you're doing! Borrowing from the Xdata discussion to follow, here's an XPress Tags command for drawing a 6 point triple paragraph rule that's indented 130 points from the right, along with the paragraph settings for indenting the first line of text that's next to the rule by 279 points:

```
<*ra(6,133,"Black",100,0,130.0,0):
*p(0,279.0,0,12,0,0,g,"U.S. English")>
```

With Xtags, this command could be abbreviated to:

```
<*ra(6,133,,,,130.0)*p(,279.0,,12)>
```

Since the color, shade, indent from left, and offset of the rule, along with the left indent, right indent, space before, space after, lock to grid setting, and language code for the paragraph are all the same as the defaults, they can be left out, greatly simplifying the commands.

Anchored text and graphic boxes

I had to deal with both anchored text and graphic boxes in *Cinematic Motion,* so I used Xtags to make the process quite a bit less painful. That book—not unlike this one—required subheads to sit in a side column next to the text, and it also had illustrations that were related to keys and captions in the text. Both anchored text and graphic boxes can be created and filled automatically with Xtags (Figure 7.16).

Just to give you an idea of what the coding looks like, here's what was necessary to get the above head placed properly:

```
<&tb(156,96,a)>@subhead:Cars, buses and
planes<&te>@text2:At some time in his or
her....
```

Note that the <&tb(etc.)> command goes before the head, the <&te> command goes after the head, and the @subhead: and @text2: XPress Tags style sheet callouts exist happily within the line. I'll show an example of the automatic graphic box creation command when I talk about Xtags' translation capabilities in a few pages. I saved an enormous

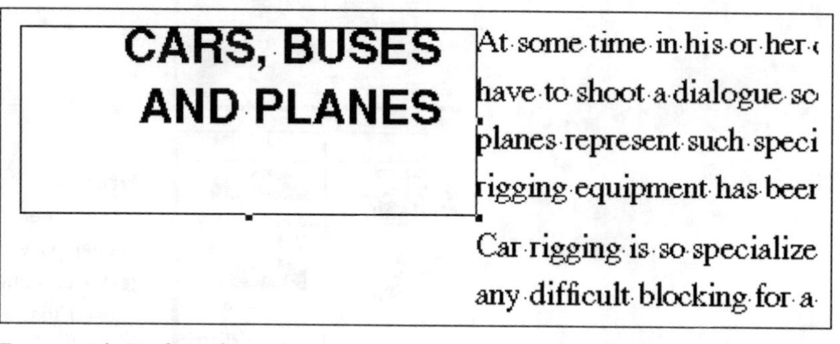

Figure 7.16 Anchored text boxes Xtags automatically created the above anchored text box and brought the text into it, too.

amount of time by having Xtags create and fill the anchored text and picture boxes in this job.

Applying a plethora of master pages

Each of the chapters in *Cinematic Motion* started with a unique chapter opener page, followed by one or more introductory text pages, something called a staging opener page, the subsequent staging spreads, and then back to text pages. I didn't look forward to applying all of those master pages to each page of the chapter, not to mention wondering about what would happen when I tried to apply new masters to such complex pages.

The Xtags codes <&mf___> and <&m___> handily took care of this dilemma for me, allowing me to address a particular master page—either by name or number. Xtags used the commands to apply the correct master page to each document page as text was being flowed into the QuarkXPress document (Figure 7.17). And since each

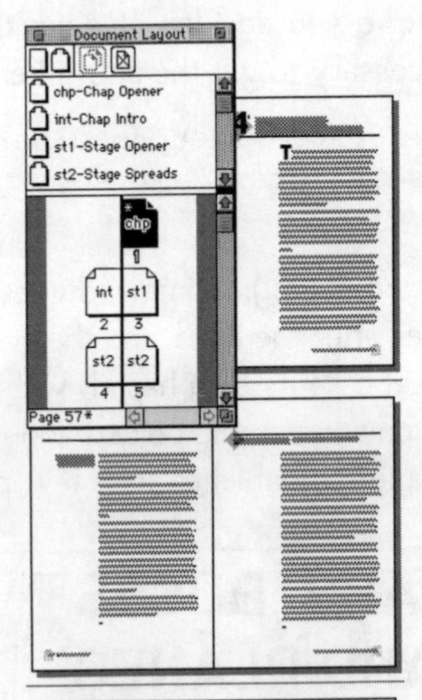

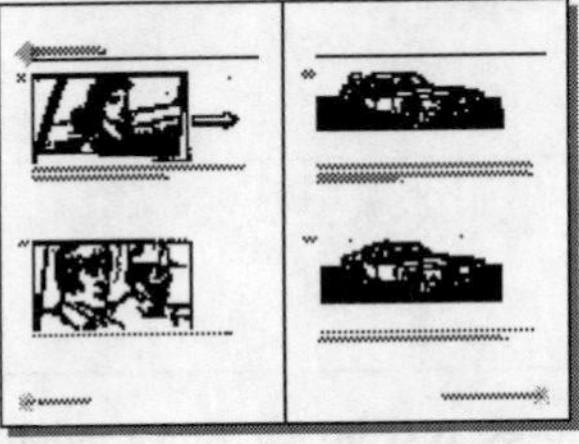

Figure 7.17 Applying master pages The significant heads on each of the five pages shown had Xtags' master page commands appended to them. As the text was brought into the document, the commands caused the appropriate master page to be applied to each document page.

of these master page changes took place at the start of a major head, I simply added the proper Xtags command every place one of these heads was called out.

Translating on import

As powerful as Torquemada the Inquisitor is at translating text files, there are times when it's more convenient to translate files on their way into QuarkXPress. For one thing, if a lot of XPress Tags or Xtags need to be added to the text files, sizes can grow rapidly. And if you need to do a very large number of translations—even more than the 640 total translations possible by dragging and dropping 32 Torquemada sets with 20 translations each—Xtags' translation capabilities may offer the solution you need.

Xtags performs its translations on text files when importing them. It's limited to simple, literal translations: no masks, wildstring modifiers, or any of that. But there's no practical limit to the number of translations you can perform with Xtags. The example I'm about to use had 1500 translations defined for a particular job. I only needed a couple of hundred per text file, but I didn't know which couple of hundred for which file. In any event, the translating didn't appreciably slow down the text input.

The scenario: To produce a directory of museum pieces, I needed to use Xtags to create anchored graphic boxes with 0.5 point frames, sized correctly and flowing with the text. The data: one long text file structured like this:

```
1,10p0,14p0
2,10p0,13p6
3,10p0,12p8
4,10p0,12p9
5,10p0,12p9
6,10p0,12p9
```

representing 1500 lines of data exported from a database, showing the catalogue number, the width of the picture, and the depth of the picture. By itself, reasonably useless to me. However, by "pre-processing" it through this Torquemada set:

SEARCH

```
^p^#^<^~,
```

Replace

```
^p@Number:^#^~\r^t@Picture:<&pb(
```

Search

```
@Number:^#^<^?\r^¢^<^*^p
```

Replace

```
@Number:^#^?\r^¢^*,a,.5)><\#13>@Number:^#^?
<\#13>^p
```

I ended up with a text file that looked like this:

```
@Number:1\r     @Picture:<&pb(10p0,14p0,a,.5)>
                <\#13>@Number:1<\#13>

@Number:2\r     @Picture:<&pb(10p0,13p6,a,.5)>
                <\#13>@Number:2<\#13>

@Number:3\r     @Picture:<&pb(10p0,12p8,a,.5)>
                <\#13>@Number:3<\#13>

@Number:4\r     @Picture:<&pb(10p0,12p9,a,.5)>
                <\#13>@Number:4<\#13>

@Number:5\r     @Picture:<&pb(10p0,12p9,a,.5)>
                <\#13>@Number:5<\#13>
```

Well, sort of like that. I'm hanging the above turnovers so they look better in this book's text width. But the upshot is that I converted the plain database output file into a valid Xtags translation table: a simple text file with the search string on the left and the replacement string on the right. The text files containing the actual job already had catalogue numbers preceded by an XPress Tags style sheet callout ("@Number:"), and when I translated them through the above file, the Xtags command for an anchored graphic box was added before each catalogue number.

The Xtags command that was required was pretty simple. In the case of catalogue number 5, the command says to create an anchored picture box that's 10p0 wide and 12p9 deep, align it on the ascender, and put a 0.5 point frame on the box (<&pb(10p0,12p9,a,.5)>). The other command (<\#13>) is simply the ASCII equivalent of a carriage return.

Figure 7.18 XPress Tags error No more surprises? Well, at least we're now notified when text is truncated, which is a step forward and should certainly be commended.

Error reporting

Even when I'm not using any Xtags-specific commands, I usually do my text importing with the Xtags XTension, mainly due to its wonderful error-reporting capabilities. When it comes to tag errors, the XPress Tags filter is pretty brain-dead—still. I remember when I did my first big database job with QuarkXPress, using version 2.0 in 1988; by then I had already discovered that it only took one glitch in the coding to lose substantial portions of data. The XPress Tags filter simply truncated any text after it encountered an error. Admittedly, the XPress Tags filter in version 3.3 will at least tell us if it encounters an error, but the remainder of the text is still ignored (Figure 7.18).

Since I often couldn't tell if I had lost data—the job resulted in an average of 3000 characters per page across 30 files of about 20 pages each—I instructed the data house to insert a special command at the end of the files. If I didn't see that command after importing a file, I knew that it was time to go hunting for a needle in the haystack. Asking for end-of-file codes is still a good procedure to follow, what with the various translations needed for jobs such as these. But I feel a lot more confident these days now that I can import text files with Xtags and get decent error reports (Figure 7.19).

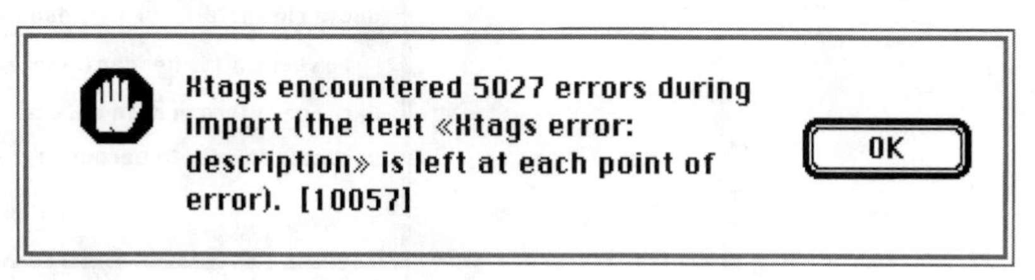

Figure 7.19 Xtags error reporting Xtags will insert «Xtags error» reports wherever it encounters problems. By the way, it was easy creating 5027 errors; I just changed a bunch of letters into the "<" character, which is reserved for starting commands.

Xdata

Xdata—another powerhouse XTension from Chris Ryland—allows for the importing and styling of structured text, such as text that comes from databases. All database programs have export functions, and most let you decide what format to use when exporting the data. Xdata, like the Xtags XTension and Quark's own XPress Tags filter, uses plain text (ASCII) files.

Database programs—which structure data as a series of records containing multiple fields of information—generally provide several choices for how the records and fields are delimited (separated) when exported to a text file. The most common record delimiter is a carriage return; commas or tabs are often used as field delimiters. Consider yourself blessed if a client actually asks you what to use as a delimiter before sending the job to you. Xdata's format preferences dialog box offers a wide variety of delimiters that it can accept (Figure 7.20).

The Xdata XTension can take the structured data exported from a database program and import it into QuarkXPress, styling the text

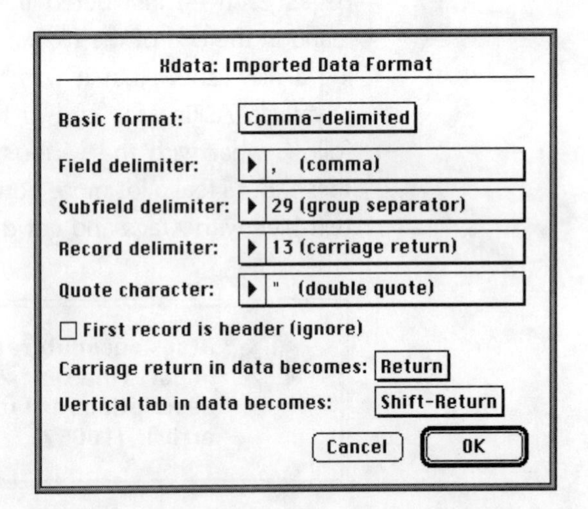

Figure 7.20 Xdata format preferences This is only one of the four preferences dialogs in Xdata. Here we can define which delimiter characters to expect from the data about to be imported.

and laying out pages based on a "prototype" that the user builds inside the QuarkXPress document. Xdata offers a number of preferences for how the data should be processed, including the definition of what record and field delimiters to expect. There's a working demo of Xdata on this book's disk, limited only in that it imports no more than 30 records at a time.

Simple mailing lists

This first example of Xdata in action may remind you of the address labels we made with Torquemada the Inquisitor a few sections back. This time, however, we won't do any processing of the data outside of QuarkXPress. Instead, we'll set up a prototype (example) of what we want the text to end up looking like. A simple list of names, addresses, and phone numbers may look like this when exported from a database program:

```
Crashaw,Richard,928 St. Teresa,Iconia,NM,72637,
373-291-2771

Greville,Fulke,876 Caelica Lane,Loredo,TX,56293,
747-828-2837
```

Note that in this example the records are delimited with a carriage return and the fields are delimited with commas.

The prototype is set up in QuarkXPress, with the first line reserved for defining the fields in each record. The field names don't have to be the same as those used in the original database program. In fact, they could simply be labeled "field1," "field2," and so on, but it makes things a lot easier in the long run if more descriptive names are used. Throughout our examples, the chevron characters (« and ») are used whenever referencing particular fields or Xdata commands.

After the fields are defined, the individual field names are styled and arranged in "placeholders" to show how the actual text should be typeset:

```
«fields lastname, firstname, address, city,
state, zip, phone

«firstname» «lastname»
«address»
«city», «state» «zip»
«phone»
```

Note that the order of the first two fields has been switched, and literal characters such as spacebands, commas, and carriage returns have been interspersed within the placeholders. In this case, the final output would look like:

```
Richard Crashaw
928 St. Teresa Terrace
Iconia, NM 72637
373-291-2771

Fulke Greville
876 Caelica Lane
Loredo, TX 56293
747-828-2837
```

Conditional interpretation of data

This above example doesn't even scratch the surface of what Xdata is capable of. Let's move on to a slightly more complicated situation, wherein the styling of the text depends on the first character found in each record. This example comes from the sample files Chris has included with the demo on the disk.

Our data is composed of fields containing part numbers, letters that indicate footnotes, and a couple of prices. Some records, however, will just contain a field indicating the classification that the following part numbers fall into. Also, note that some fields are empty, showing up as two comma delimiters in a row with nothing between them:

```
*Transmission
400102000,EF,3,74.50,37.25
400102001,A,9,86.50,43.25
400102002,,,60.00,30.00
400102003,B,1,34.50,17.25
400102004,H,,67.00,33.50
400102005,C,6,42.50,21.25
400102006,LB,,92.00,46.00
400102007,G,,51.50,25.75
400102008,KEB,9,30.00,15.00
400102009,L,1,63.50,31.75
400102010,JK,,74.00,37.00
400102011,FCJ,,22.00,11.00
400102012,G,6,41.50,20.75
```

The column heads shown in Figure 7.21 aren't actually part of the prototype; they're in a separate text box that's on the master page.

The protype, as always, starts off with the definition of the record, in this case naming the fields "partno," "note1," "note2," "list,"and "discount." Following that is an Xdata conditional statement that determines whether or not the first character of the first field is an asterisk («if char 1 of partno is "*"). Xdata commands tend to be pretty easy to read and understand, although Chris has provided shortcuts for some conditional statements that power users will want to take advantage of.

If the conditional statement ends up being true (i.e., the first character of the first field really is an asterisk), then the Xdata command "«char 2 to 500 of partno»" grabs all but the first character of the first field and styles it as white text in front of a black paragraph rule. If the conditional statement is false, Xdata knows to jump to the "«else" command and spit out the fields in their appropriate style and arrangement, in this case with tab characters added as needed.

This prototype uses a wonderful Xdata command called "«char" that lets us split a field by using only certain characters in the field. Since the part number field needs to have a hyphen added after the first three characters in that field, the field placeholders "«char 1 to 3

Part Number	Note 1	Note 2	List Price	Dicount Price

```
«fields partno, note1, note2, list, discount
«if char 1 of partno = "*"
«char 2 to 500 of partno»
«else
«char 1 to 3 of partno»-«char 4 to 20 of partno»
«note1»          «note2»   «list»«discount»
«endif
```

Figure 7.21 XData conditionals This prototype shows how Xdata can query the data as it's being imported and make decisions based on what it finds.

Part Number	Note 1	Note 2	List Price	Dicount Price
Transmission				
400-102000	EF	3	74.50	37.25
400-102001	A	9	86.50	43.25
400-102002			60.00	30.00
400-102003	B	1	34.50	17.25
400-102004	H		67.00	33.50
400-102005	C	6	42.50	21.25
400-102006	LB		92.00	46.00
400-102007	G		51.50	25.75
400-102008	KEB	9	30.00	15.00
400-102009	L	1	63.50	31.75
400-102010	JK		74.00	37.00
400-102011	FCJ		22.00	11.00
400-102012	G	6	41.50	20.75

Figure 7.22 Xdata output When the conditional statement found an asterisk as the first character of the first field, it acted differently on that record, styling the word "Transmission" as a category head.

of partno»-«char 4 to 20 of partno»" do so for us. Figure 7.22 shows what our file would look like after bringing in some of the data.

Merging database files and XPress Tags

My main use for Xdata has been as a glorified mail-merge utility. I do a job in which I have to produce a number of sets of rules that are used to compare survey results from different geographical regions. It's not uncommon for me to have to produce 50–60 of these data profiles per year, and the first few years I did them by drawing lines with QuarkXPress' orthogonal line tool. Needless to say, I needed a new method.

Further complicating matters was the fact that the data house could only provide me with "print image" files, meaning that I could get a real pretty text file from them with all the numbers lined up nicely, but with no unique delimiters between the fields. (I still don't understand the reasoning behind that one.) As of version 2.0 of Xdata, though, a command that would recognize a "word" as any number of nonspace characters surrounded by spacebands (or at the start or end of a line) was added, giving me the tool I needed to automate the interpretation of these print-image files.

This year the data house gave me text files with a head in the first field followed by numbers computed to show me how much to indent a paragraph rule from the right margin, how much to indent the first line of the paragraph so that I could set a number next to the rule, and the number itself. I then merged these numbers with XPress Tags that included Xdata field placeholders showing where to place each number. I've underlined both the actual data and the Xdata codes in the following examples so that you can follow them as they travel through the procedure. Here's the raw data:

```
COMPREHENSIVE      126.4      282.6     76
158.8      250.2      67     137.2      271.8      73
```

The numbers represent three sets of the data I described above: a right indent for a rule, a first line indent for the text, and the actual text. Here's my Xdata prototype, starting with a field definition that rightly throws up its hands and just defines the whole record as a field called "line:"

```
«fields line

@rule:<*ra(6,128,"Black",100,0,«word 1 of char
15 to 62 of line»,0)*p(0,«word 2 of char 15 to
62 of line»,0,12,0,0,g,"U.S. English")>«word 3
of char 15 to 62 of line»%

@rule:<*ra(6,0,"Black",100,0,«word 4 of char 15
to 62 of line»,0)*p(0,«word 5 of char 15 to 62
of line»,0,12,0,0,g,"U.S. English")>«word 6 of
char 15 to 62 of line»%

@rule:<*ra(6,133,"Black",100,0,«word 7 of char
15 to 62 of line»,0)*p(0,«word 8 of char 15 to
62 of line»,0,12,0,0,g,"U.S. English")>«word 9
of char 15 to 62 of line»%
```

Basically, the only thing changing from set to set is the code for the rule (128, 0 , or 133, for double, solid, and triple rules, respectively) and which "word" it picks up from the record (1 through 9). In all cases, the Xdata commands look through the same range of characters (15 through 62). As you may recall from the previous section in this chapter, had I been using Xtags at the time I set up this job I could have simplified these XPress Tags considerably by leaving out any default values, such as the hyphenation language.

After "merging" the Xdata prototype with the raw data, I had these XPress Tags which were used to call out the Rule style sheet, create a paragraph rule, and indent the first line of each paragraph:

```
@rule:<*ra(6,128,"Black",100,0,126.4,0)
*p(0,282.6,0,12,0,0,g,"U.S. English")>76%

@rule:<*ra(6,0,"Black",100,0,158.8,0):
*p(0,250.2,0,12,0,0,g,"U.S. English")>67%

@rule:<*ra(6,133,"Black",100,0,137.2,0):
*p(0,271.8,0,12,0,0,g,"U.S. English")>73%
```

Now all I have to do is choose Save Text from the File menu in order to export the above as a text file, and then do a Get Text with Include Style Sheets turned on to produce this:

76%

67%

73%

Other cool features

Some of the other features of Xdata that are hard to show as examples but are definitely worth mentioning are it's ability to:

- Import pictures into anchored graphic boxes
- Automatically create page headers and footers by placing Xdata commands on master pages
- Apply a specific master to a page based on the values it finds in imported fields
- Interpret XPress Tags codes imbedded in any fields
- Understand and process variables and integer math
- Generate a dialog box querying the user before continuing to process data.

Xdata 2.1, which I'm beta-testing now, adds string concatenation; word, line, and item counting and extraction; page-location sensitivity, case-conversion functions; and lots more.

8

Scripting

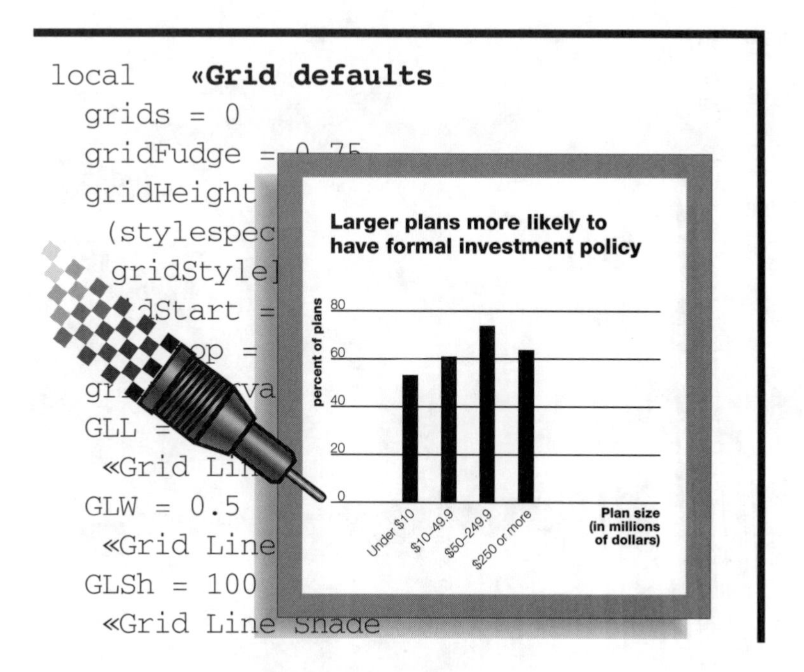
local «Grid defaults
grids = 0
gridFudge =
gridHeight
(stylespec
gridStyle]
GLL =
«Grid Lin
GLW = 0.5
«Grid Line
GLSh = 100
«Grid Line Shade
Larger plans more likely to
have formal investment policy
percent of plans
80
60
40
20
0
Under $10
$10–49.9
$50–249.9
$250 or more
Plan size
(in millions
of dollars)

CHAPTER 8 CONTENTS

FIGURES

Perhaps the biggest sleeper feature of QuarkXPress 3.2 was its Apple Events scripting support. Apple Events scripts can be written to automate tasks such as performing mail-merges or importing prices into a catalog, and to interact with other applications. Scripts can be created using Apple's AppleScript or UserLand Frontier. Both are commercial programs, but a runtime version of Frontier has been included with every version of QuarkXPress since 3.2.

The runtime version of Frontier will allow you to run the sample scripts that come with QuarkXPress, as well as any other Frontier scripts written by friends or consultants. Frontier scripts are also becoming available for downloading from electronic bulletin board services such as CompuServe. The script shown and discussed in the second half of this chapter can be found on the disk in the back of this book, along with a few scripts written by Scott Lawton; the runtime version of Frontier can be used to run these scripts.

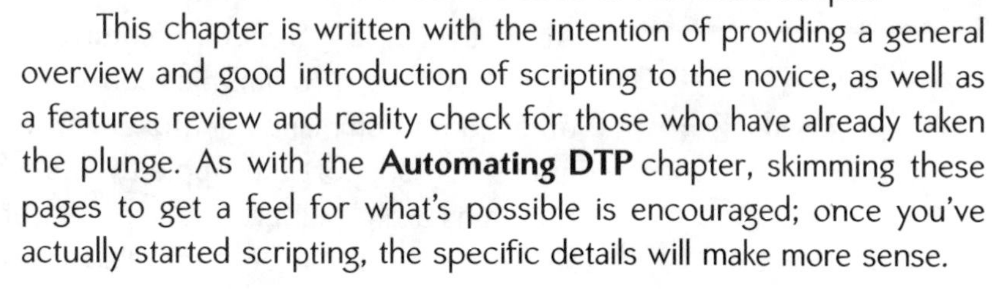

This chapter is written with the intention of providing a general overview and good introduction of scripting to the novice, as well as a features review and reality check for those who have already taken the plunge. As with the **Automating DTP** chapter, skimming these pages to get a feel for what's possible is encouraged; once you've actually started scripting, the specific details will make more sense.

Scripting basics

QuarkXPress 3.2's full support of Apple Events marks Quark's most important advance in open systems architecture since the introduction of XTensions. By sending Apple Events to QuarkXPress, you can automate almost everything you can do manually, as well as a few things that could be done up till now only with XTensions.

The documentation

What exactly are Apple Events and how can you benefit from Quark XPress' support of them? What are their limitations? What can be done manually in QuarkXPress and yet can't be automated with scripts? The answers to these and many other important questions lie within the "Apple Events Scripting with QuarkXPress" document buried in the "For Advanced Scripting" folder in your QuarkXPress folder. The file's location depends on whether you chose to include it when you installed the program. If not, you can find it on the Apple Events Scripting disk that came with QuarkXPress.

Except for one technical error—which I'll explain later—the scripting documentation is excellent. It's clear and concise, yet chock full of useful examples and surprisingly easy to read. Quark has gone beyond explaining *what* instructions can be sent to the program, telling us *how* the instructions need to be sent—from both AppleScript and Frontier. There is also information on how to optimize script performance as well as a detailed explanation of the "Document Construction" script that came with QuarkXPress 3.2. You really must read this documentation before starting to write any scripts.

Defining Apple Events

Apple Events is a System 7 feature that provides a mechanism for interapplication communication—letting programs talk to each other. Both commands and data can be sent and received by programs that support the Apple Events message protocol, even if the programs are on different computers on a network. Yes, entire networks of Macs can be controlled from a single workstation using Apple Events.

Using AppleScript or Frontier, it is possible to send and receive Apple Event messages to and from any application in logical sequences controlled by conditional statements and complex looping structures. These sequences of Apple Event messages, simply called scripts, can be set up to run in the background, starting at a certain date or time, or even when a file first appears in a folder. An Apple Event message may contain references to objects, events, and data. The rules that govern the use of Apple Events are defined in terms of an abstract object model.

The object model

An object model contains objects, the events that can be applied to them, their elements (objects which they can contain), reference forms, and their properties. The QuarkXPress object model is defined in chapter 4 of "Apple Events Scripting with QuarkXPress." This chapter is literally the key to scripting QuarkXPress through Apple Events.

Objects

Objects such as text and picture boxes are distinct items in an application. They are described in terms of "properties" such as bounds, angle, runaround mode, etc. Objects that share specific properties are said to be of the same class. Objects are arranged in a hierarchy that controls which objects can contain which other objects, if any. Objects that can contain other objects are known as "containers." Objects that can be contained by other objects are known as "elements" of their containers. Many objects are both elements of and containers for other objects.

For example, in QuarkXPress, a document can contain pages, a page can contain text boxes, a text box can contain a story, a story can contain paragraphs, a paragraph can contain lines, lines can contain words, and words can contain characters. Characters cannot contain any other elements—they are at the bottom of the hierarchy.

The hierarchy also specifies the "insertion points" where new objects may be placed within the container hierarchy. Objects may be inserted:

- At the beginning of a container
- At the end of a container
- After other objects of the same class within a container
- Before other objects of the same class within a container
- As a replacement for objects of the same class within a container

In QuarkXPress, the insertion point of an object determines whether it is "in front of" or "in back of" other objects. Thus you can control the layering of QuarkXPress items.

Objects may be referenced by index, name, range, relative position, or test. For example, you can search for the first text box on each page, or all of the picture boxes on pages 3 to 5 of a document. You can even search for paragraphs that have a particular style sheet applied to them.

Events

Events are actions that can be applied to objects, such as create, copy, paste, and delete. Objects and the verbs that manipulate them are grouped into suites that pertain to a particular task. The Quark XPress suite, for example, contains a single verb—doUpdates—which updates the screen display. All of the other events you need in order to script QuarkXPress are defined in the Required, Core, Miscellaneous, and Text suites from Apple. These are general-purpose suites intended for all applications.

Data

Data can be any information that you wish to send to or receive from an application, such as text to fill a text box or the name of a style sheet used in a document.

Scripting vs. XTensions

Are XTension developers upset that they had to pay for access to information that is now included with the program? Not necessarily. Even though more of QuarkXPress is revealed through Apple Events than is normally available to a user, not everything available to XTension developers is available through Apple Events. Scripts can't add items to any menu other than the Scripts menu, for example, nor can they add a tool to the Tool palette.

XTension developers can also enhance their current products so that they support Apple Events. This would make their XTensions more powerful, which might lead to increased sales. And in many cases, it may be much more efficient for developers to create a solution through a script rather than an XTension. The shorter time spent writing a script could mean more time for other programming assignments. Even though writing a script is significantly easier than writing an XTension, it's still not that easy; programming is programming. And XTensions run a lot faster than scripts, at least for now.

AppleScript vs. Frontier

AppleScript and Frontier are specialized applications which send and receive Apple Event messages. Both programs include a scripting language which provides conditional statements and looping structures, a script editor, and syntax checking. In addition, AppleScript includes the abilities to compile a script and record factored applications, as explained in the following section. However, with its object database and debugging features, Frontier provides a much more complete development environment.

The syntax (statement structure) of AppleScript is very much like that of HyperCard's HyperTalk: It's easy to learn but hard to live with, since it tends to be verbose. The syntax of Frontier's scripting language, UserTalk, is very similar to the C programming language, quite popular among Macintosh developers. C programming can be extremely concise, but it also allows you to be verbose whenever you want to be, usually for the sake of clarity.

TIP The features of both AppleScript and Frontier go far beyond those of any application with built-in scripting. They also have the advantage of being able to communicate with any application that supports Apple Events. This means that you don't have to learn an entirely new language in order to script each application; you just need to learn the object model of the application.

A small example

The QuarkXPress object model—mentioned above in the section on **Defining Apple Events**—describes every aspect of a QuarkXPress document in terms of objects and their properties. An object's properties include all of the settings normally available to a QuarkXPress user, as well as some options that were accessible only to XTension developers before the release of QuarkXPress 3.2. For example, while QuarkXPress normally allows only a uniform text inset, it's possible to set the top, left, bottom, and right insets independently through an XTension. Previously there was no other way to accomplish this. With scripting, it's a trivial matter to set independent insets. However, first you have to know a little bit about QuarkXPress' special datatypes.

Text inset is a property of text boxes that is represented by a special data type called a fixed rectangle. In order for QuarkXPress to set properties represented by special data types, the data has to be coerced into a format that the program can understand. Fortunately, there is a routine—called fixedrect—that performs this particular coercion for us. If you're using Frontier and you'd like to take a look at the fixedrect routine, you can find it in the Frontier object called QuarkXPress.Frontier; it's listed under QXP.defs. This is the code needed to create independent text insets using Frontier:

```
local
  frect = 0
  TopInset = 6
  LeftInset = 9
  RightInset = 12
  BottomInset = 0
frect = fixedrect ( TopInset, LeftInset,
                    BottomInset, RightInset )
set ( document[currentdocument].textbox[currentbox].
                    textinset, frect )
```

A new way of communicating

How can mere mortals deal with such power? It's really not as complicated as it looks; you just need to learn a new way of communicating with QuarkXPress. Maybe that doesn't sound so easy, but think back to when you first started using the application. You didn't know any of the keyboard shortcuts, so you were constantly pulling down menus looking for commands. Now I bet you know all of the shortcuts for commands that you use regularly, and you probably make extensive use of palettes. Apple Events scripting is just another way of doing the same thing—with the advantages of inter-application communication and a robust development environment that includes:

- **Information**—to give you a better understanding of the structure of QuarkXPress documents

- **Customizability**—the ability to create custom publishing solutions using off-the-shelf software

- **Access**—to built-in features previously only available through XTensions
- **Interapplication communication**—great for database publishing
- **Interactive processing**—for creating custom dialogs and functions
- **Batch processing**—to let you automate repetitive tasks
- **Automated processing**—agent scripts run unattended

The bad news...

With all of the work that was necessary to implement support for Apple Events within QuarkXPress, there wasn't enough time for Quark to implement everything they wanted to. Support for scripting Page Setup and Print settings wasn't added until version 3.3, for example. The current implementation of Apple Events still doesn't support libraries, groups, auxiliary dictionaries, hyphenation exceptions, box creation defaults, color pair trapping, blends, anchored boxes, or page sections. However, it seems obvious that these features were left out only because there was no time to implement them, and I expect to see them in future versions.

It's also important to note that, while some third-party developers have begun to add Apple Events support to their XTensions, Quark has not added Apple Events support to any of its XTensions. In the meantime, many of the features not covered in QuarkXPress' Apple Events support can be accessed by sending Apple Events to third-party utilities. These utilities can directly control QuarkXPress' menus and dialog boxes, and can often be used to control XTensions, too.

PreFab Player

PreFab Software has announced a product—called PreFab Player—that will allow you to fill in some of the missing pieces mentioned above. Many applications, desk accesories, and control panels still lack sufficient Apple Events support; PreFab Player will mimic user input, pulling down menus and selecting items in dialog boxes. PreFab Player will be a user interface–automation utility that can be integrated with standard system-level scripting products. Scripters won't have to learn a new language or leave their familiar scripting environment to create a workaround for missing Apple Events.

PreFab Player will at first add verbs to Frontier, and eventually AppleScript, that directly "play" or "drive" the user interface, choosing menus and intelligently selecting standard dialog items (radios, checkboxes, pop-ups, buttons). Unlike alternative solutions, PreFab Player won't force you to leave the familiar environment of your chosen system-level scripting product. For example, in the Frontier version, UserLand's outline-based editor, powerful debugger, and flexible object database will be available every step of the way. Both Frontier and AppleScript have rich, high-level script languages that offer unmatched power and simplicity. PreFab Player will add to these languages, rather than trying to duplicate their functionality. Within a single script, you'll be able to mix Apple Events–based verbs with verbs that "play" the user interface.

Since only a few applications and almost no desk accessories or control panels have any Apple Events support at all, by directly driving the Macintosh user interface from Frontier or AppleScript, PreFab Player sounds like it will be able to extend a script writer's reach far beyond what can be done with Apple Events alone.

PreFab Player will ship in 1994. PreFab Software can be reached at 617-628-9555 or on CompuServe at ID 70214,424.

Factoring applications

Apple is actively encouraging developers to "factor" their applications. Factoring is a means by which all the functions of an application are isolated from its interface such that all program functions are activated by sending and receiving Apple Events. In other words, Apple wants programs to talk to themselves using Apple Events.

Factoring has several advantages, including making programs instantly recordable. It adds the ability to watch a program as it runs and keep track of its actions. This can be used to create scripts that automate repetitive tasks or as a debugging tool. Imagine being able to recreate the exact series of actions that cause a program to crash, or better yet, all the actions that were performed between the last save and a crash!

Factoring does have its price, in that it reduces execution speed, but that may be more than made up for if it saves you hours of work. Factoring any application requires a lot of work, and QuarkXPress has not been factored—yet. It would make a lot of sense if Quark, Inc., made factoring an option in a future release.

An annotated script

You might think that creating bar charts in QuarkXPress is a ludicrous proposition, and you'd probably be correct. However, I have found that none of the programs that automatically generate bar charts give me the level of precise positioning and trapping control I need to meet my designer's specifications. Although each chart can take anywhere from one to two hours to produce, I've been manually creating bar charts in QuarkXPress for the past three years. But with the advent of scripting, it looks like this laborious task can be completely—or at least mostly—automated. And, as it turns out, it's not a bad example to show the power of scripting QuarkXPress.

The bar chart shown in Figure 8.1 required three pages of specifications. Before you write a script, you need to collect information on all the elements that the script needs to create; you also need to define the relationships between the elements. The chart below is composed of QuarkXPress text boxes and rules, and it includes separate elements for the grid key, bar key, and bar labels. All of the items are positioned relative to the origin of the chart and to each other. There's also quite a lot of math involved in figuring out the lengths of the bars. Although the computer will do the math, you still have to give the script the formulas for doing the math.

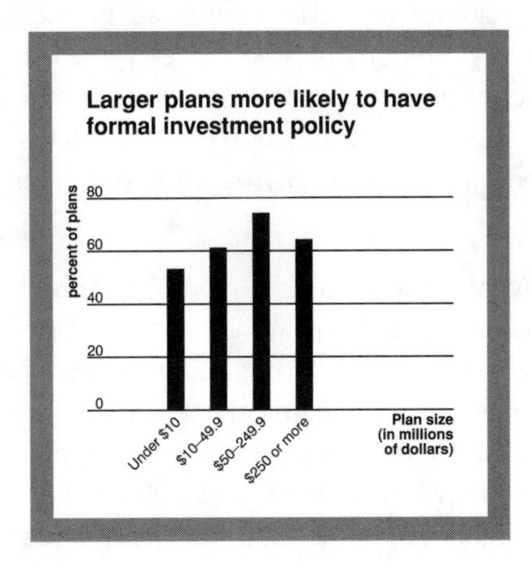

Figure 8.1 The chart This is the bar chart that I wanted to create with a script.

Fire, ready, aim

Perhaps the fastest way to learn most things is by doing them. In discussions about programming strategy, you'll often hear the phrase "fire, ready, aim." It means that you build a program that you think will solve the problem, examine why it does or doesn't work, and then build a better program. This is the strategy that I followed for my first script. I should also note that I chose to use Userland Frontier for the reasons listed earlier. Writing this script was a learning process, during which I had to figure out how to tell QuarkXPress what I wanted to do while at the same time learning the syntax of both UserTalk and the QuarkXPress object model. I didn't worry about program structure at all. This worked fairly well except that soon the script had grown unwieldy; I realized that I needed to simplify it before I became buried.

TIP If you really want to get serious about scripting, then you need to understand one fundamental principle of good programming—modularity. The concept of modularity is very simple—divide and conquer. If a complex problem can be broken down into smaller parts, it will be easier to handle. Create a module to handle each of the small parts, one at a time. When you've solved all of the small problems, then you can link the modules together to solve the larger problem.

It's easy to spot code that needs to be modularized. In this example, I needed to create several text boxes and lines. In the first version of my script I repeated the code to build a text box or line every time one needed to be created. For the second version of the script, I wrote separate routines for these tasks. Not only does this simplify the script, but those modules are now a lot more useful because they can be reused in other scripts.

Parental discretion advised

What follows is a dissection of a script. It contains graphic displays of advanced technology not suitable for all readers—parental discretion is advised. I'm not going to describe every detail of this script, since the scripting mechanics are covered very well in the examples in the QuarkXPress scripting documentation. What I will attempt to do is describe the logic and point out some of the more interesting aspects of Frontier and the QuarkXPress object model.

Initializing the variables

Because there are so many variables for this script, I've grouped them in separate local statements. A local statement is a local variable declaration. A local variable is one that is valid only in the indented script block within which they are defined. The same names can be used for local variables in different parts of a script.

```
On BuildChart()
  with QXP,QXP.charts,objectModel
    local «General Script defaults
      Custom = true «Interface control
      paramlist = 0
      firstGrid = 0
      lastGrid = 0}
```

Chart defaults

The next group of variables defines the properties of the text box that lays the foundation for the chart. The X and Y variables are particularly important because they represent the origin of the chart, from which all of the chart elements are relatively positioned.

```
    local «Chart defaults
      X = 72 «Horizontal Origin of Chart (the
                  distance from left edge of page
                  to left edge of chart)
      Y = 72 «Vertical Origin of Chart (the distance
                  from top edge of page to top
                  edge of chart)
      W = 168 «Width of Chart (168 pts = 14 p)
      H = 12 «Height of Chart (12 pts = 1 p)
      A = 0 «Box Angle
      FS = solidframe «Frame Style
      FC = "PANTONE 405 CV" «Frame Color
      FSh = 40 «Frame Shade
      FW = 8 «Frame Width
      TI = 12 «Top Text Inset
      LI = 12 «Left Text Inset
      BI = 6 «Bottom Text Inset
      RI = 12 «Right Text Inset
      VJ = topjustified «Vertical Justification
                  Style (topjustified, centered,
                  bottomjustified, or
                  fullyjustified)
```

```
  headLines = 2
  headHeight = 9
  headText = "Larger plans more likely to have
         formal investment policy"
  headTextStyle = "charthead"
  subheadLines = 0
  subheadHeight = 9
  subheadText = ""
  subheadTextStyle = "chartsubhead"
```

Bar defaults

The next group of variables defines the properties of the lines that represent the bars. Note that I only declare the properties that were given in the specification.

```
local «Bar defaults
  bars = 4
  barFudge = 0.25
  barLength = 0
  barWidth = 6
  barStart = 51
  barStop = 0
  barInterval = 15
  barColor = "Black"
  barShade = 100
```

Bar key defaults

The next group of variables defines the properties of the text box used for the bar key. At this point the variable names started getting a bit long, so I reverted to minimalism, using the initials of the chart element, followed by an abbreviation of the attribute it represents. For example, "BKFSh" holds the value of the Bar Key Frame Shade.

```
local «Bar Key defaults
  BKX = 120 «Bar Key Horizontal Origin
  BKY = 0 «Bar Key Vertical Origin
  BKW = 28 «Bar Key Box Width
  BKH = 23 «Bar Key Box Height
  BKA = 0 «Bar Key Box Angle
  BKFS = 0 «Bar Key Frame Style
  BKFW = 0 «Bar Key Frame Width
  BKFC = "Black" «Bar Key Frame Color
```

```
BKFSh = 0 «Bar Key Frame Shade
BKTI = 0 «Bar Key Top Text Inset
BKLI = 0 «Bar Key Left Text Inset
BKBI = 0 «Bar Key Bottom Text Inset
BKRI = 0 «Bar Key Right Inset
BKVJ = centered «Bar Key Box Vertical
              Justification
barKeyText = "Plan size (in millions of
              dollars)"
barKeyTextStyle = "chartkey"
```

Bar label defaults

The next group of variables defines the properties of the text boxes used for the bar labels. Again, I'm only declaring the properties given in the specifications.

```
local «Bar Label defaults
  BLX = 0 «Bar Label Horizontal Origin
  BLY = 0 «Bar Label Vertical Origin
  BLH = 10 «Bar Label Height
  BLW = 38.5 «Bar Label Width
  BLA = 0 «BarLabelAngle
  BLFS = solidframe «Bar Label Frame Style
  BLFW = 0 «Bar Label Frame Width
  BLFC = "Black" «Bar Label Frame Color
  BLFSh = 0 «Bar Label Frame Shade (percentage)
  BLTI = 0 «Bar Label Top Text Inset
  BLLI = 0 «Bar Label Left Text Inset
  BLBI = 0 «Bar Label Bottom Text Inset
  BLRI = 0 «Bar Label Right Text Inset
  BLVJ = topjustified «Bar Label Vertical
              Justification
  barLabelDisplacement = 36
  «This number is completely made-up. It's
              supposed to represent the
              vertical height of the bar label
              text boxes.
  BLVO = 14 «Bar Label Vertical Offset
  BLHO = 20 «Bar Label Horizontal Offset
```

Grid defaults

The next group of variables define the properties of the lines that make up the grid. "gridFudge" might sound like a snack food, but it's actually part of the specifications for this script. It spaces the grid lines just below the baseline of the grid labels.

```
local «Grid defaults
  grids = 0
  gridFudge = 0.75
  gridHeight = 18
  gridStart = 0
  gridStop = 80
  gridInterval = 20
  GLL = 128 «Grid Line Length
  GLW = 0.5 «Grid Line Width
  GLSh = 100} «Grid Line Shade
```

Grid key defaults

The next group of variables defines the properties of the text box for the grid key. Again, I'm only declaring the variables given in the chart specifications.

```
local «Grid Key defaults
  GKX = 10 «Grid Key Horizontal Origin
  GKY = 35 «Grid Key Vertical Origin
  GKW = 87 «Grid Key Box Width
  GKH = 10 «Grid Key Box Height
  GKA = 90 «Grid Key Box Angle
  GKFS = 0 «Grid Key Frame Style
  GKFW = 0 «Grid Key Frame Width
  GKFC = "Black" «Grid Key Frame Color
  GKFSh = 0 «Grid Key Frame Shade
  GKTI = 0 «Grid Key Top Text Inset
  GKLI = 0 «Grid Key Left Text Inset
  GKBI = 0 «Grid Key Bottom Text Inset
  GKRI = 0 «Grid Key Right Inset
  GKVJ = centered «Grid Key Box Vertical
              Justification
  gridKeyText = "percent of plans"
  gridKeyTextStyle = "chartkey"
```

"Extra" variables

The last group of variables defines the properties that are not user modifiable through this script, but I included them so that I could write a generic routine to build text boxes. In other words, I don't need to specify all of these properties to satisfy the chart specifications, but since my text box routine is designed to accept parameters for all of the properties normally available through **Item→Modify**, **Item→Runaround**, and **Item→Frame**, I added these "filler" variables to be passed to the text box building routine. If this doesn't make sense now, don't fret. It should become more obvious once you see the routine that builds text boxes and how it's called.

```
local «The following variables are defaults,
                i.e. they are not user
                modifiable. This may change...
  IR = itemrunaround «Runaround Mode Item
  NR = nonerunaround «Runaround Mode None
  SP = false «Suppress Printing
  BC = "White" «Box Background Color
  BSh = 0 «Box Background Shade
  S = 0 «Box Skew
  C = 1 «Number of Columns in a Text Box
                 (0 < Integer ≤ 30)
  G = 3 «Width of Gutter between Columns in a
                Text Box (3 ≤ Points ≤ 288)
  O = 0 «Offset of First Baseline from Top of
                Text Box
  min = 0 «Minimum Offset of First Baseline from
                Top of Text Box (Cap Height, Cap
                + Ascent, or Ascent Height)
  max = 0 «Maximum Interparagraph Spacing in
                Vertically Justified Text Box
  LS = solidline «Line Style
  E = plainline «Line Endcap Style
```

The action begins

Now that I've initialized my variables, we'll begin to see some action. The first order of business is finding out if the user wants to cancel the script, build a demo chart using the built-in defaults, or build a custom chart with its own values. To poll the user, I present a simple dialog box that asks the user what action to take (Figure 8.2). If the user chooses to cancel the script, an error message is displayed, QuarkXPress is brought to the front, and the script is terminated. If the user chooses to build a demo chart, execution continues. If the user chooses to build a custom chart, the script generates more dialog boxes that prompt the user to enter the necessary data. If you want to follow along, you should start running the script now.

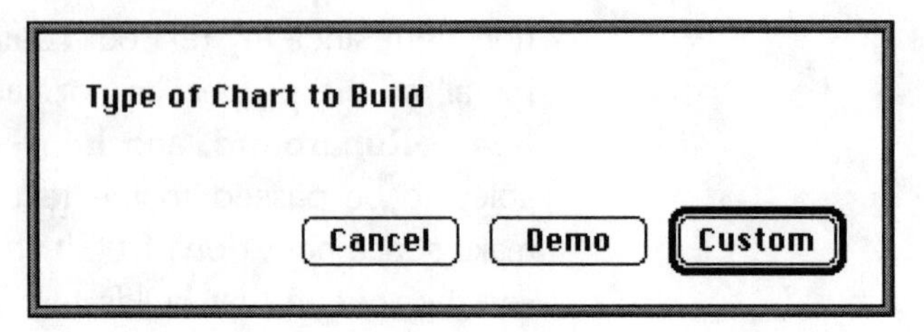

Figure 8.2 Type of chart This is the inital dialog you'll be presented with when you run the Build Bar Chart script included on the disk.

These actions are controlled through a "case" statement which allows the script to branch in one of many directions based on the value of a single variable. In this case, we're testing the value returned by the three-way dialog routine. If the value is "1," the user has selected "custom," so the script branches through a series of dialogs asking for the various chart settings. The first three dialogs are shown with their default values in Figures 8.3a–b and 8.4.

```
case dialog.threeWay("Type of Chart to
        Build","Custom","Demo","Cancel")
  1
    msg("Your wish is my command.")
    if !(dialog.getInt("X (in pts.)",@X))
      scriptError("Script canceled by User.")
    if !(dialog.getInt("Y (in pts.)",@Y))
      scriptError("Script canceled by User.")
    if !(dialog.ask("Head text",@HeadText))
      scriptError("Script canceled by User.")
    if !(dialog.ask("Subhead text",
            @SubheadText))
      scriptError("Script canceled by User.")
    if !(dialog.getInt("Grid starting value",
            @GridStart))
      scriptError("Script canceled by User.")
```

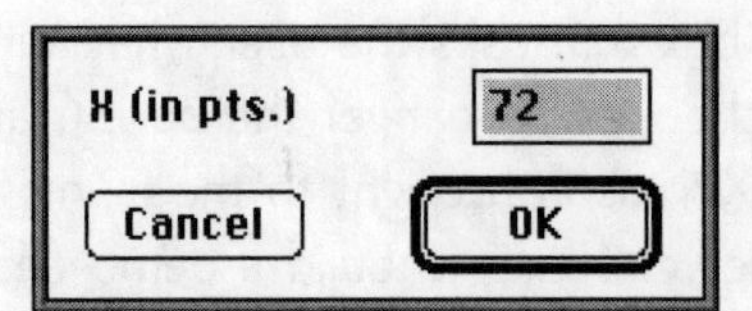

Figure 8.3a X position of chart The dialog box that asks how far from the left of the page the chart should start.

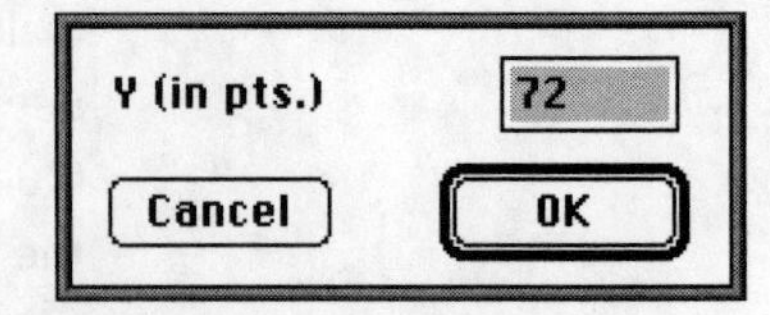

Figure 8.3b Y position of chart The dialog box that asks how far from the left of the page the chart should start.

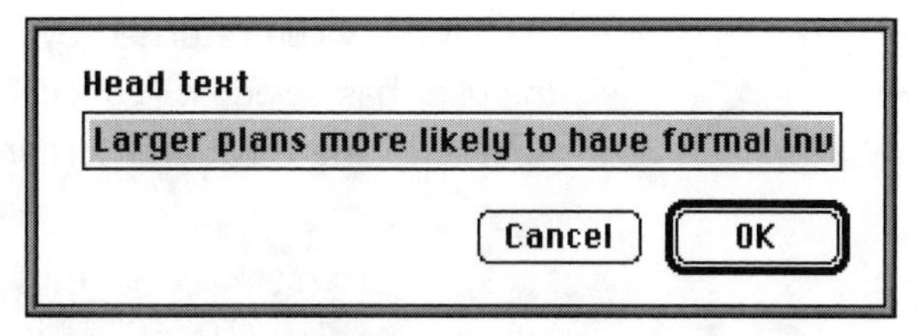

Figure 8.4 Head text for chart Most of the dialogs contain default text or numberic values. New data can be entered into the dialogs, too.

```
        if !(dialog.getInt("Grid ending value",
                @GridStop))
          scriptError("Script canceled by User.")
        if !(dialog.getInt("Grid increment",
                @GridInterval))
          scriptError("Script canceled by User.")
        while (GridInterval == 0)
          dialog.alert("Grid increment must be non-
                zero!")
          if !(dialog.getInt("Grid increment",
                @GridInterval))
            bringToFront()
            scriptError("Script canceled by User.")
        if !(dialog.ask("Grid Key text",
                @GridKeyText))
          bringToFront()
          scriptError("Script canceled by User.")
        if !(dialog.getInt("Number of Bars",@Bars))
          bringToFront()
          scriptError("Script canceled by User.")
        if !(dialog.ask("Bar Key text",@BarKeyText))
          bringToFront()
          scriptError("Script canceled by User.")
```

If the value returned by the three-way dialog routine is "2," then the user has selected "demo." Since all of the variables are initialized with the values of the demo chart, the script needs only to set a single variable signifying that the script is running in demo mode before continuing on.

```
    2
        msg("Aye, Captain! We'll give'em a show...")
        msg("they won't soon forget!")
        Custom = false}
```

If the value returned by the three-way dialog routine is "3," then the user has selected "cancel." In this case the script will bring Quark XPress to the front and terminate execution.

```
3
    msg("We've scuttled'em, Captain!")
    bringToFront()
    break
```

Figuring the chart depth

The real fun begins when we start figuring out the size and shape of the chart. This is where I figure out how many grid lines I'll need based on the starting and stopping values and the interval specified.

```
grids = (((gridStop - gridStart) / gridInterval)
          + 1)
```

And now I calculate the height of the chart, H, based on the number of grid lines found in the last calculation.

```
H = (FW * 2) + TI + (headLines * headHeight) +
                    (subheadLines * subheadHeight) +
                    (grids * gridHeight) +
                    barLabelDisplacement + BI
```

I call on my buildTextBox script (explained later) to build a text box on page 1 of document 1. I could just as easily specify a document name, or with a few additional lines, I could have the script bring up a standard file directory dialog and ask the user to specify the document in which to build the chart. You might want to run the script from within the QuarkXPress 3.2 document that's on the disk in the back of the book, since it contains a set of style sheets and a custom color used by the script. The file name is "Bar Chart template."

```
with document[1]
  with page[1]
    buildTextBox (X,Y,W,H,A,IR,SP,BC,BS,S,FS,FW,
                  FC,FSh,C,G,TI,LI,BI,RI,O,Min,
                  VJ,Max)
```

Generating text

Here I'm actually generating the text that goes in the main text box of my chart. I build the text backwards because of an idiosyncrasy of the way in which text is referenced. If you reference the last paragraph, then you get the last line contained in the box which has no return on the end of it. Since I didn't know how to insert a return into my text, it was necessary to create a new paragraph first, and then set the text and apply the appropriate style sheet to it. I've since learned that Frontier does include the carraige return among its several constants. Note that the "!=" coding seen in several of the following statements means "not equal." For example, if subheadText is not equal to nothing (meaning that it is equal to something), then put it in the chart. Figure 8.5 illustrates how the chart would look at the end of this routine, using the default values.

```
with textbox[1]
  if (Grids > 0)
    with story[1]
      local (GridLabel,j)
      for j = 0 to (Grids-1)
        GridLabel = string(GridStart +
            (GridInterval * j))
        create(paragraph,0,0,
            beginningOf(it))
        with paragraph[1]
          set(it,GridLabel)
          set(stylesheet,"chartgrid")
  if (SubheadText != "") «Create Subhead
    with story[1]
      create(paragraph,0,0,beginningOf(it))
```

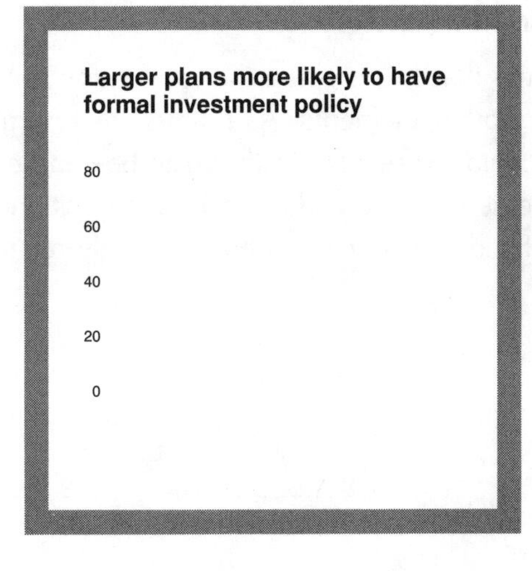

Figure 8.5 Main box and text This is what we've generated so far with the script.

```
          with paragraph[1]
            set(it,HeadText)
            set(stylesheet, "charthead")
            Subheadlines = count(it,line)
      if (HeadText != "") «Create Head
        with story[1]
          create(paragraph,0,0,beginningOf(it))
          with paragraph[1]
            set(it,HeadText)
            set(stylesheet, "charthead")
            Headlines = count(it,line)
```

Adjusting the chart depth

When I generated the text for the main box of my chart, you may have noticed that I was keeping track of how many lines were generated by each paragraph. This is so I can adjust the size of the chart to fit the amount of text. This next section of the script performs that adjustment.

```
if !SP «Adjust Chart Size to Fit Text & Grid
   H = (FW * 2) + TI + (headLines *
           headHeight) + (subheadLines *
           subheadHeight) + (grids *
           gridHeight) +
           (barLabelDisplacement) + BI
   frect = textRect (Y,X,Y + H,X + W)
   set(bounds,frect)
```

Creating the grid key

Now that I've created the foundation for the chart, I can move on to the other elements. As I stated before, all of the chart elements are positioned relative to the main box and each other. The first of these elements is the grid key, which is positioned horizontally relative to the left edge of our chart and vertically relative to the top gridline.

```
«Create Grid Key
GKX = GKX + X
GKY = GKY + (Y + FW + TI + (headLines *
              headHeight) + (subheadLines *
              subheadHeight) + gridHeight)
buildTextBox (GKX, GKY, GKW, GKH, GKA, NR, SP,
              BC, BS, S, GKFS, GKFW, GKFC,
```

```
                    GKFSh, C, G, GKTI, GKLI, GKBI,
                    GKRI, O, Min, GKVJ, Max)
```

Once the box is created, the text can be inserted and the appropriate style sheet applied.

```
«Create Text Box for Grid Key
with textBox[1].story[1]
  set(it,gridKeyText)
  set(paragraph[1].stylesheet,"chartkey")
```

Creating the grid lines

The grid lines are positioned horizontally relative to the left edge of our chart and vertically relative to the top edge of the chart, the width of the frame, the top text inset, the head height, and the subhead height (if any). Figure 8.6 shows how the chart looks after the grid key and grid lines have been generated.

```
«Create Grid Lines
if Grids > 0
  local «Set Horizontal Value for both
            Endpoints
    X1 = X + FW + LI
    Y1 = 0
    X2 = X1 + GLL
    Y2 = 0
  For i = 1 to grids
```

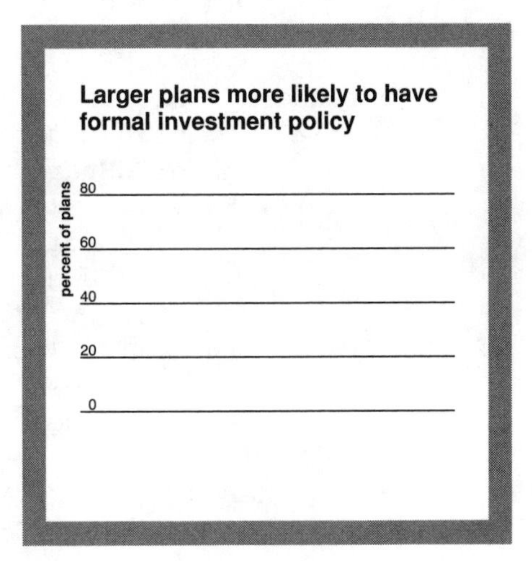

Figure 8.6 Grid key and lines The chart looks like this after adding the grid key and grid lines.

```
Y1 = Y + FW + TI + (headLines *
        headHeight) + (i * gridHeight) +
        gridFudge
Y2 = Y1
buildLineBox(X1,Y1,X2,Y2,A,NR,SP,LS,GLSh,
        GLW,E)
```

Creating the bars and bar labels

Since I have yet to figure out how to use arrays in Frontier, I have grouped the creation of bars and bar labels together so that I can loop through the routine, gathering data as I need it and quickly discarding it. The bars and bar labels are positioned horizontally relative to the left edge of our chart and vertically relative to the bottom gridline. Note that if the script is running in demo mode, it generates random values for the bars.

```
«Create Bars w/Labels
local(barLength,barValue)
for i = 1 to bars
  if custom
    dialog.getInt("Value for Bar
          #"+i,@barValue)
  else
    barValue = random(gridStart,gridStop)
```

Here I calculate the length of the bars based on the value given and the height of the grid. The height of the grid is dependent on the range and interval of the grid lines.

```
barLength = (barValue * ((grids - 1) *
        gridHeight))/(gridStop -
        gridStart)
Y1 = Y + FW + TI + (headLines * headHeight)
        + (grids * gridHeight) +
        gridFudge - barLength
X1 = X + barStart + ((i -1) * barInterval)
Y2 = Y + FW + TI + (headLines * headHeight)
        + (grids * gridHeight) +
        gridFudge - barFudge
X2 = X1
buildLineBox(X1,Y1,X2,Y2,A,NR,SP,LS,BSh,
        barWidth,E)
```

```
«Create BarLabel
BLY = Y2 + BLVO
BLX = X + BLHO + ((i - 1) * barInterval)
buildTextBox (BLX, BLY, BLW, BLH, BLA, NR,
              SP, BC, BS, S, BLFS, BLFW,
              BLFC, BLFSh, C, G, BLTI, BLLI,
              BLBI, BLRI, O, Min, BLVJ, Max)
«Create Text Box for Bar Label
with textBox[first]
  with story[1]
    if Custom
      dialog.ask("Text for Bar Label #" + i,
            @barLabelText)
    else
      barLabelText = string(i)
    set(it,barLabelText)
    set(paragraph[1].stylesheet,"chartbars")
```

Creating the bar key

The bar key is positioned horizontally relative to the left edge of the chart and vertically relative to the top edge of the chart, the width of the frame, the top text inset, the head height, the subhead height (if any), and the height of the grid.

```
«Create Bar Key
BKX = BKX + X
BKY = Y + FW + TI + (headLines * headHeight) +
              (subheadLines * subheadHeight) +
              (grids * gridHeight) + 1
BuildTextBox (BKX, BKY, BKW, BKH, BKA, NR, SP,
              BC, BS, S, BKFS, BKFW, BKFC,
              BKFSh, C, G, BKTI, BKLI, BKBI,
              BKRI, O, Min, BKVJ, Max)¬

«Create Text Box for Bar Label
with textBox[first].Story[1]
  set(it,barKeyText)
  set(paragraph[1].stylesheet,"chartkey")
```

Finishing up

Now that the chart is complete, the script makes sure that guides are not showing and then brings QuarkXPress to the front before terminating execution. Figure 8.7 shows the final result.

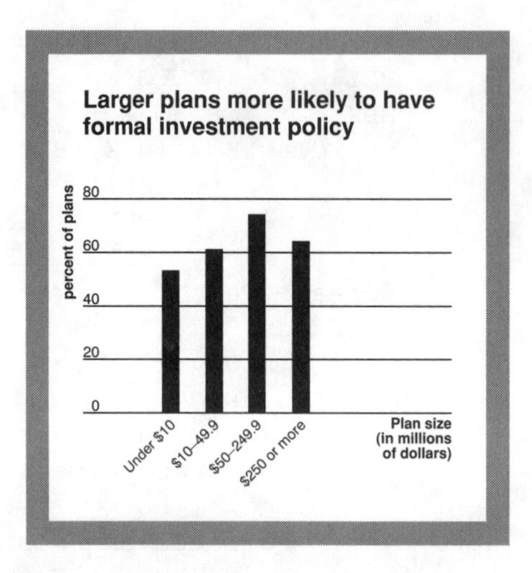

Figure 8.7 The finished chart The chart will look like this after the bars, the bar key, and the bar labels are added.

```
set(document[1].guidesShowing,false)
msg("All Done!")
bringToFront()
```

Building text boxes

While the specification is detailed, it doesn't specify properties such as trapping, flipping contents (horizontally and/or vertically), column gutter width (all of the text boxes used are single column), maximum interparagraph spacing for vertically justified text (only the grid key is vertically justified and it will never contain more than one paragraph), linking, skew, selection (as in, leave the box selected when the script finishes), or suppress printing. It doesn't need any of these features.

When I decided to write a generic script to build text boxes, I knew I wouldn't need all of these features, either. But to ensure the usefulness of the script, I created it to set all of the properties normally available through the **Item→Modify**, **Item→Runaround**, and **Item→Frame** dialogs. Once you've seen the ungodly list of parameters, you'll know why I limited the number.

TIP When you create a text box in a script, the position, height, and width are specified in terms of bounds, i.e., top, left, bottom, and right. Unfortunately, in the advanced scripting documentation included with QuarkXPress 3.2, the bounds are described as "how far from the top, left, bottom, and right side of the document page [that] the text box will be placed." This statement should read "how far from the top left-hand corner of the page that the top, left, bottom, and right sides of the text box will be placed."

Optimizing script performance

In the portion of the scripting documentation that concerns itself with script performance, one of the points stressed is that the initial properties should be set through the "create event," rather than setting the properties individually after the object has been created. To do this, I needed to build a list of properties to pass to the create event. This routine does just that.

However, there are some properties—such as background and frame colors—which rely on other objects, such as ColorSpecs. In my rush to complete this script, I've found it much easier to deal with setting these properties after creating the object. The reason for this is reliability. If I specify a color that doesn't exist, then the creation event will fail. I could also create the color specification through the script.

Passing variables between script modules

As I stated before, this routine sets all of the text box attributes found in the **Item→Modify**, **Item→Runaround**, and **Item→Frame** dialogs. These attributes are passed to the routine through the parameters shown in Figure 8.8. All units are points except where otherwise noted.

X	= Horizontal Origin	FC	= Frame Color (XPress color name)
Y	= Vertical Origin	FSh	= Frame Shade (percentage)
W	= Width	C	= Number of Columns (Integer)
H	= Height	G	= Gutter Width
A	= Angle of Rotation (degrees)	TI	= Top Text Inset
R	= Runaround Mode (enumerated)	LI	= Left Text Inset
SP	= Suppress Printing (True or False)	BI	= Bottom Text Inset
BC	= Background Color (XPress color name)	RI	= Right Text Inset
		O	= First Baseline Offset
BS	= Background Shade (percentage)	Min	= First Baseline Minimum Offset
S	= Angle of Skew (degrees)	VJ	= Vertical Justification Style (enumerated)
FS	= Frame Style (enumerated)		
FW	= Frame Width	Max	= Maximum Interparagraph Spacing

Figure 8.8 Script parameters All text box attributes are passed through these parameters.

Enumerated data types

Enumerated data types are variables for which QuarkXPress has defined the set of possible values. For example, the possible values for the runaround mode of a text box are "itemrunaround" or "none-runaround." All of the enumerated data types are defined in the advanced scripting documentation found in the Advanced Scripting folder on the Apple Events Scripting disk of the QuarkXPress 3.2 package.

```
on buildTextBox(X,Y,W,H,A,R,SP,BC,BS,S,FS,FW,FC,FSh,
                    C,G,TI,LI,BI,RI,O,Min,VJ,Max)
  with objectModel,QXP,QXP.defs
```

Box bounds

In the QuarkXPress object model, the position and size of a box are defined in terms of bounds—the distance from the top left corner of the page to the top, left, bottom, and right sides of the box. However, as a QuarkXPress user, I'm much more accustomed to thinking of boxes in terms of X-origin, Y-origin, width, and height, so I wrote this script to accept input in my terms and deliver output to QuarkXPress in its terms—hence, the local variables X2 and Y2. The local variable paramlist (parameter list) will hold the list of initial properties that I'll send with the create event.

```
local (paramlist,X2,Y2)
paramlist = 0
```

Error checking

Now I check each variable to make sure its value is of the proper type and within the proper range before adding it to my list of initial properties. If a value falls out of range, the user is notified of the problem with an appropriate message and then given a chance to either enter a new value or cancel the script.

```
while ((X < 0) or (X > 3456))
  dialog.alert("Horizontal Origin of Box must be
                    between 0 and" +
                    get(currentdocument.width)+".")
  if !dialog.getInt("X",@X)
    scriptError("Script canceled")
```

```
while ((Y < 0) or (Y > 3456))
  dialog.alert("Vertical Origin of Box must be
              between 0 and" +
              get(currentdocument.height) +
              ".")
  if !dialog.getInt("Y",@Y)
    scriptError("Script canceled")
while ((W < 0) or (W > (3456 - X)))
  dialog.alert("Width of Box must be between 0
              and 3456.")
  if !dialog.getInt("Width",@W)
    scriptError("Script canceled")
while ((H < 0) or (H > (3456 - Y)))
  dialog.alert("Height of Box must be between 0
              and 3456.")
  if !dialog.getInt("Height",@H)
    scriptError("Script canceled")
```

Coercing data

Here's where I do the conversion of the box bounds description from my terms (X-origin, Y-origin, width, height) to QuarkXPress' terms (top, left, bottom, right). Then I call the textRect routine. Note that I wanted to check the bounds against the document size, but ran out of time. So I fudged by checking against the largest document possible in QuarkXPress: 3456 points by 3456 points (48 x 48 inches). The "msg" statements are displaying pertinent data in Frontier's windoid for your viewing pleasure (and script debugging).

```
Y2 = Y + H
X2 = X + W
msg("Box Bounds = "+Y+", "+X+", "+Y2+", "+X2)
frect = textRect (Y,X,Y2,X2)
putAppleListItem(frect,bounds,@paramlist)
```

Revenge of the technonerds

I then continue checking the rest of the variables to make sure that they are valid text box properties. Note that I have arbitrarily restricted the acceptable range of some properties. QuarkXPress will let you set just about any angle, but I think it's absurd to specify more than 360 in either direction. Since I'm writing this script, I can define a subset of values which seem more logical to me.

```
while ((A < -360) or (A > 360))
  dialog.alert("Angle of Rotation must be
               between -360 and 360.")
  dialog.getInt("Angle",@A)
msg("Rotation = "+A+" °")
putAppleListItem(A,rotation,@paramlist)
```

Here's something that I found irritating. While it's fairly easy to specify one of the enumerated runaround modes, I've been unable to figure out how to specify the runaround offset. I don't think it has been implemented, but the documentation doesn't include it in the list of things scripts can't do.

```
while ((R != itemrunaround) and
               (R != nonerunaround) and
               (R != autorunaround) and
               (R != manualrunaround))
  dialog.alert("Runaround Mode must be
               itemrunaround, nonerunaround,
               autorunaround, or
               manualrunaround.")
  dialog.ask("Runaround Mode",@R)}
msg("Runaround = "+R+" pt(s)")
putAppleListItem(nonerunaround,runaround,
               @paramlist)
if ((SP != True) and (SP != False))
  SP = !(dialog.twoWay("Suppress
               Printout","False","True"))
msg("Suppress Printing = "+SP)
putAppleListItem(SP,suppressprinting,@paramlist)
while ((S < -360) or (S > 360))
  dialog.alert("Angle of Skew must be between
               -360 and 360.")
  dialog.getInt("Skew",@S)
msg("Box Skew = "+S+" °")
putAppleListItem(S,skew,@paramlist)
while ((C < 1) or (C > 30))
  dialog.alert("Number of Columns must be
               between 1 and 30.")
  dialog.getInt("Columns",@C)
msg("Columns = "+C)
putAppleListItem(C,columns,@paramlist)
while ((G < 3) or (G > 288))
```

```
    dialog.alert("Gutter Width must be between 3
                  and 288 points.")
    dialog.getInt("Gutter",@G)
  msg("Gutter = "+G+" pt(s)")
  putAppleListItem(G,gutter,@paramlist)
  msg("Text Inset = "+TI+", "+LI+", "+BI+", "+RI)
  frect = fixedrect (TI,LI,BI,RI)
  putAppleListItem(frect,textinset,@paramlist)
  while ((O < 0) or (O > H))
    dialog.alert("First Baseline Offset must be
                  between 0 and "+H+".")
    dialog.getInt("Offset",@O)
  putAppleListItem(O,firstbaselineoffset,
                  @paramlist)
```

First baseline minimum offset

The fact that the first baseline minimum offset is represented by something called a "vertical measurement" threw me at first. But I soon figured out that a vertical measurement is nothing more than a number; I haven't figured out the level of precision, but I would guess that it's a floating point number. I expected it to be another enumerated data type with the possible values normally listed in the pop-up menu in the Text Box Specifications dialog (cap height, cap, cap+ ascent, and ascent). If I can ever figure out how to get the cap and ascent height, then I'd like to add the ability to specify this property with those enumerated values.

```
  while ((Min != "capheight") and (Min != "cap")
                  and (Min != "capplusascent") and
                  (Min != "ascent") or ((Min < 0)
                  or (Min > H)))
  while ((Min < 0) or (Min > H)) {
    dialog.alert("First Baseline Minimum Offset
                  must be between 0 and "+H+".")
    dialog.getInt("Minimum",@Min)
  putAppleListItem(Min,firstbaselineminimum,
                  @paramlist)
  while ((VJ != topjustified) and (VJ != centered)
                  and (VJ != bottomjustified) and
                  (VJ != fullyjustified))
    dialog.alert("Vertical Justification must be
                  topjustified, centered,
```

```
                    bottomjustified, or
                    fullyjustified.")
  dialog.ask("Vertical Justification",@VJ)
putAppleListItem(VJ,verticaljustification,
                    @paramlist)
while ((Max < 0) or (Max > H)) {
  dialog.alert("Maximum Interparagraph Space
                    must be between 0 and "+H)
  dialog.getInt("Maximum",@Max)
putAppleListItem(fixed(Max),interparamax,
                    @paramlist)
```

Creating the text box

Once my list of initial properties is complete, I call the create event and ask it to build a box—with my list of initial properties—at the "beginning of it." The "beginning of it" tells QuarkXPress to place the box on the lowest layer of the page, sort of like using the Send to Back command. Now that I'm writing this, I wish I had put it on the top layer, just in case there are any boxes in the way of the chart. I guess that will be implemented in version 1.1 of the script!

```
msg("Conjuring Text Box...")
create(textbox,0,paramlist,beginningOf(it))
```

Setting the background color

Now that I've created this box, I need to set its background color and frame settings.

```
with textbox[1]
  msg("Background Color = "+BC)
```

Here's another minor hole I have yet to plug—I haven't quite figured out how to check the current QuarkXPress color palette for the requested color. Instead, I've used a nice feature of UserTalk called a "try" statement. The advantage of this is that if the set event fails, the script will recover gracefully, notifying the user, applying the default background color, and continuing to execute.

```
while ( BC != (get(current.doc.ColorSpec[all]
                    )))
  dialog.alert("Background Color '"+BC+"' has
                    not been defined!")
```

```
  dialog.ask("Background Color",@BC)
try
  set(color,BC)
else {
  dialog.alert("Background Color '"+BC+"' has
               not been defined! Box will be
               created with default color.")
msg("Background Shade = "+BS+" %")
while ((BS < 0) or (BS > 100))
  dialog.alert("Background Shade must be
             between 0 and 100.")
  dialog.ask("Background Shade",@BS)
set(shade,BS)
```

Oops!

I'm somewhat embarrassed to admit that in my haste I didn't take time to figure out why this section of the script wouldn't work and just "commented it out." I will come back and fix this later.

```
msg("Frame Style = "+FS)
local(dataCheck = false)
«while dataCheck == false
  «case FS
    «solidframe
      «dataCheck = true
      «break
    «doubleframe
      «dataCheck = true
      «break
    «thinthickframe
      «dataCheck = true
      «break
    «thinthickthinframe
      «dataCheck = true
      «break
    «thickthinthickframe
      «dataCheck = true
      «break
    «thinthinthinframe
      «dataCheck = true
      «break
  «else
```

```
        «dialog.alert("Frame Style must be
                  solidframe, doubleframe,
                  thinthickframe,
                  thinthickthinframe,
                  thickthinthickframe, or
                  thinthinthinframe.")
        «dialog.ask("Frame Style",@FS)
    «while ((FS != solidframe) and (FS !=
                  doubleframe) and (FS !=
                  thinthickframe) and
                  (FS != thinthickthinframe) and
                  (FS != thickthinthickframe) and
                  (FS != thinthinthinframe))
      «dialog.alert("Frame Style must be
                  solidframe, doubleframe,
                  thinthickframe,
                  thinthickthinframe,
                  thickthinthickframe, or
                  thinthinthinframe.")
       «dialog.ask("Frame Style",@FS)
```

After this, I continue to check for errors, this time in the frame specifications.

```
try
  set(frame.style,FS)
msg("Frame Width = "+FW+"pt(s)")
while (FW < 0)
  dialog.alert("Frame width cannot be
               negative")
  dialog.getInt("Frame Width",@FW)
try
  set(frame.width,FW)
else
  dialog.alert("Frame width setting failed
               default width applied")
msg("Frame Color = "+FC)
try
  set(frame.color,FC)
else
  dialog.alert("Frame Color '"+FC+"' has not
                 been defined! Frame will be
                 created with default color.")
msg("Frame Shade = "+FSh+" %")
```

```
    while ((FSh < 0) or (FSh > 100))
      dialog.alert("Frame Shade must be between 0
                   and 100.")
      dialog.ask("Frame Shade",@FSh)
    try
      set(frame.shade,FSh)
    else
      dialog.alert("Frame shade setting failed
                   default shade applied")
```

Building rules

The following script creates a rule with the parameters passed to it. These parameters include all of those normally available through the **Item→Modify**, **Item→Runaround**, and **Item→Frame** dialogs. Like the buildTextBox script, it accomplishes this as efficiently as possible by building a list of properties and using that list to set the initial properties of the rule, rather than setting the properties individually. It also includes the same type of data verification that was built into buildTextBox.

```
on buildLineBox(X1,Y1,X2,Y2,A,R,SP,LS,LSh,LW,E)
  with objectmodel,QXP,QXP.defs
    local (paramlist,fp)
    local (debug = true)
    paramlist = 0
    while ((X1 < 0) or (X1 > 3456))
      dialog.alert("Horizontal component of left
                   endpoint must be between 0 and"
                   +get(currentpage.width))
      dialog.getInt("X1",@X1)
    while ((Y1 < 0) or (Y1 > 3456))
      dialog.alert("Vertical component of left
                   endpoint must be between 0 and"
                   +get(currentpage.height))
      dialog.getInt("Y1",@Y1)}
    if debug
      msg("Left Endpoint: X = "+X1+" Y = "+Y1)
    fp = fixedPt(Y1,X1)
    putAppleListItem(fp,leftpoint,@paramlist)
    while ((X2 < X1) or (X2 > (3456 - X1))) « 3456 =
                   48 * 72, i.e. the maximum page
                   width in QXP
```

```
  dialog.alert("Horizontal component of left
               endpoint must be between 0 and"
               +get(currentpage.width))
  dialog.getInt("X2",@X2)
while ((Y2 < Y1) or (Y2 > (3456 - Y1))) « 3456 =
               48 * 72, i.e. the maximum page
               height in QXP
  dialog.alert("Vertical component of left
               endpoint must be between 0 and"
               +get(currentpage.height))
  dialog.getInt("Y2",@Y2)
fp = fixedPt(Y2,X2)
putAppleListItem(fp,rightpoint,@paramlist)
while ((A < -180) or (A > 180))
  dialog.alert("Angle of Rotation must be
               between -180 and 180.")
  dialog.getInt("Angle",@A)
putAppleListItem(A,rotation,@paramlist)
while ((R != itemrunaround) and (R !=
               nonerunaround) and (R !=
               autorunaround) and (R !=
               manualrunaround))
  dialog.alert("Runaround Mode must be
               itemrunaround, nonerunaround,
               autorunaround, or
               manualrunaround.")
  dialog.ask("Runaround Mode",@R)
putAppleListItem(nonerunaround, runaround,
               @paramlist)
if ((SP != True) and (SP != False))
  SP = !(dialog.twoWay("Suppress Printout",
               "False", "True"))
putAppleListItem(SP,suppressprinting,@paramlist)
while ((LS != solidline) and (LS != dashedline)
               and (LS != denselydashedline)
               and (LS != dottedline) and (LS
               != doubleline) and (LS !=
               thinthickline) and (LS !=
               thickthinline) and (LS !=
               thickthinthickline) and (LS !=
               thinthinthinline))
  dialog.alert("Style must be solidline,
               dashedline, denselydashedline,
               dottedline, doubleline,
```

```
                     thinthickline, thickthinline,
                     thickthinthickline, or
                     thinthinthinline.")
  dialog.ask("Line Style",@LS)
putAppleListItem(LS,style,@paramlist)
while ((LSh < 0) or (LSh > 100))
  dialog.alert("Line Width must be between 0 and
                     100.")
  dialog.getInt("Line Shade",@LSh)
putAppleListItem(LSh,shade,@paramlist)
while ((LW < 0) or (LW > 3456))
  dialog.alert("Line Width must be between 0 and
                     3456.")
  dialog.getInt("Line Width",@LW)
putAppleListItem(LW,width,@paramlist)
while ((E != plainline) and (E != rightarrow)
                     and (E != leftarrow) and (E !=
                     rightfeatheredarrow) and (E !=
                     doublearrow))
  dialog.alert("Style must be plainline,
                     rightarrow, leftarrow,
                     rightfeatheredarrow, or
                     doublearrow.")
  dialog.ask("Endcap Style",@E)
  msg("Endcap Style = "+E)
putAppleListItem(E,endcaps,@paramlist)
  msg("Conjuring Line...")
create(linebox,0,paramlist,beginningOf(it))
```

So, that's about it. I do have plans to continue enhancing this script so that it can handle batch processing and a variety of chart styles. If you're interested in this script, or just scripting in general, check out the "Automating DTP" section of the Desktop Publishing Forum on CompuServe (GO DTPFORUM). There you'll find lots of knowledgeable people asking questions and giving answers about scripting. Dave Winer, president of Userland, has been known to post messages there!

Appendixes

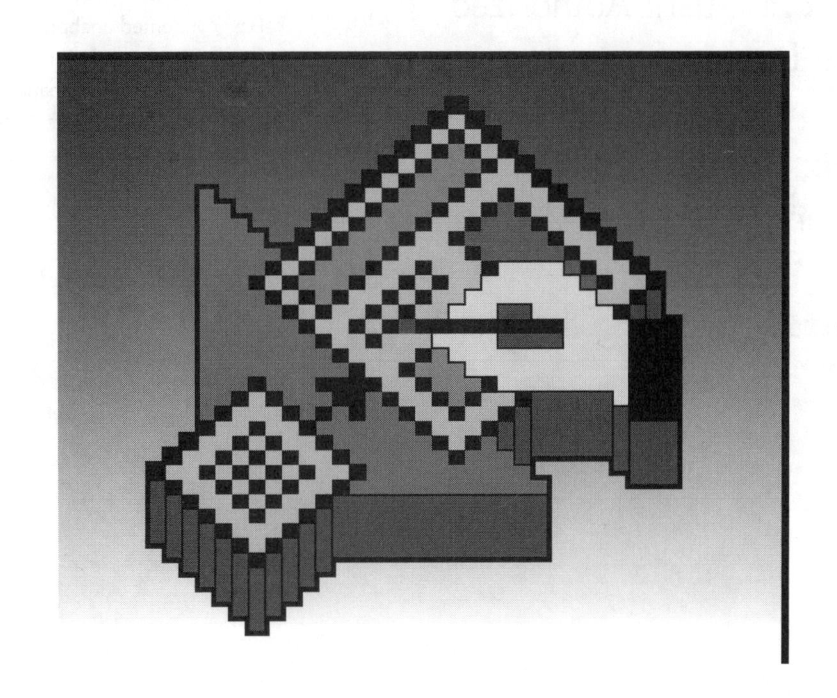

APPENDIXES CONTENTS

FIGURES

Appendix A: New features in QuarkXPress 3.2

Here's a list of the new features that were included in QuarkXPress version 3.2. Even though this book already incorporates many of these features in its text, I thought it would be worthwhile to include this list and mention some of my own experiences with the features. The sections of this appendix are in the same order as the chapters of this book. I hope you find things in this list that you weren't aware of—and can make use of what you find!

Text preparation

Drag-and-drop editing

If you're used to doing drag-and-drop text editing in a word processing program—such as Microsoft Word—then you'll love this feature. If you haven't had the pleasure, this feature may take some getting used to. I know that I still haven't trained myself to use it, and instead find it getting in the way. (But I'm persistent.)

Selected text can now be clicked and dragged around a text box. While you're moving it around, the cursor changes to an arrow attached to a rectangular box (). The box represents the characters being moved. Wherever you rest the arrow cursor, an insertion cursor starts flashing to show you where the text will be placed if you let go of the mouse. Additionally, if the Shift key is held down when you click on the text, the selection will be cut from its current position when you drop it elsewhere. Remember: Unshifted, the text is copied; shifted, the text is moved. If you change your mind about copying or moving selected text, just drag the arrow cursor so that it's back over the selected text and let go. Nothing will change.

Next Style

I've really enjoyed this feature since I moved the writing of this book over to version 3.2. For each style sheet defined, a pointer can be made to the next style sheet that should be used. When a return is typed at the end of a paragraph, the next style is automatically applied to the new paragraph.

In this book, for example, the third-level heads, such as "Next Style" above, are styled as Head3. After typing one of these heads and hitting a return, I'm automatically in the unindented text style (Text3) that follows these heads. When I finish typing that paragraph, a return puts me into the normal text style, creatively called Text.

Unfortunately, this feature cannot yet be used in conjunction with XPress Tags. Adding its capabilities to the XPress Tags filter would greatly improve productivity, since it would make coding text files much simpler. I can think of a number of jobs where I could add XPress Tags to subheads and not have to code the intervening paragraphs—*if* XPress Tags recognized the Next Style command.

Flag local formatting

Quark, Inc., calls this the Show Local Overrides feature, but it would have to be a little more useful before I'd agree that it's "showing" the "overrides." Prior to version 3.2, if a style sheet had been applied to a paragraph, clicking in that paragraph would cause the style sheet's name to be highlighted in the Style Sheets palette. Now the style sheet name will also have a plus sign (+) next to it if the paragraph contains local (manually applied) formatting (Figure A.1).

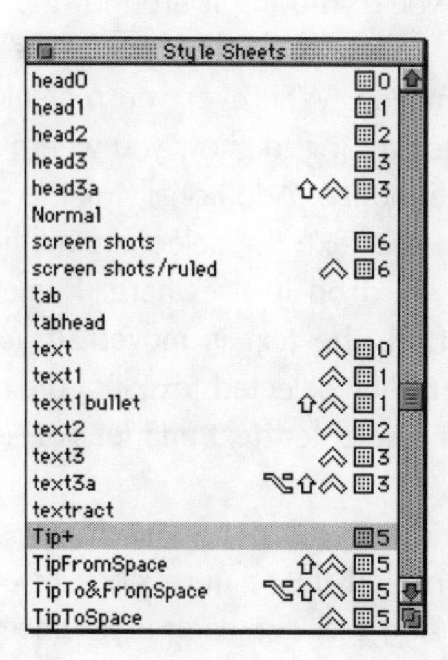

Figure A.1 Local formatting I added a point of leading (temporarily) to one of this book's Tip paragraphs to show how the plus sign gets appended to the style sheet name when local formatting has been applied.

TIP The same character (+) is appended to the style sheet name whether the local formatting is paragraph- or character-based. Since you may be trying to figure out just what formatting has been manually applied—in order to determine whether or not it should be overridden, for example—there are a few things that can help. First, local character formatting will cause a plus sign to be added to the style sheet name only if the cursor is to the right of a formatted character, or if formatted characters are included in a text selection. On the other hand, local paragraph formatting will append the plus sign to the style sheet name no matter where the cursor is sitting in a paragraph.

An even nicer implementation of this feature exists in the Xstyle XTension, from Em Software. Paragraph-based formatting will also append a plus sign to the style sheet name shown in Xstyle's Character/Paragraph palette, but local character formatting will show up with an ellipsis (...) appended to the name, too (Figures A.2a, b). If a selection has both character and paragraph local formatting, both characters are appended to the name. Xstyle lets you choose between appending the characters at the start or at the end of a style sheet name, which is handy for those times when you have style sheet names that are very long. And with Xstyle's Character/Paragraph

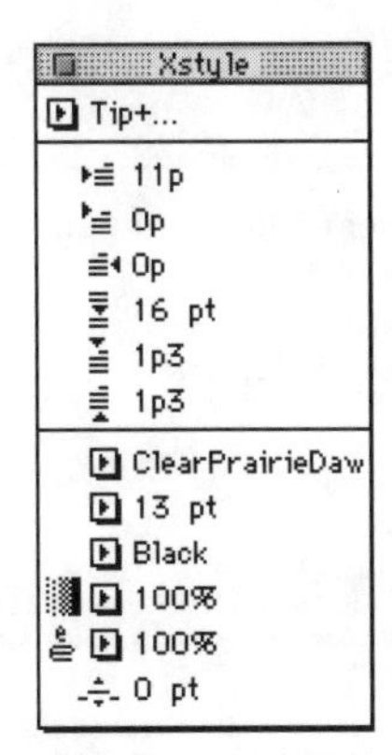

Figure A.2a Vertical Xstyle I changed both a paragraph and character style attribute in a Tip paragraph to show how Xstyle flags both changes independently with a plus sign and an ellipsis. This is Xstyle's Character/Paragraph palette shown in its vertical orientation.

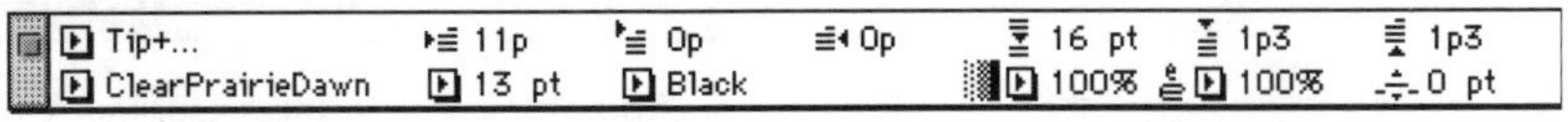

Tip+... 11p 0p 0p 16 pt 1p3 1p3
ClearPrairieDawn 13 pt Black 100% 100% 0 pt

Figure A.2b Horizontal Xstyle This is Xstyle's Character/Paragraph palette shown in its horizontal orientation.

palette open, most of the common character and paragraph attributes can be viewed without entering the menus!

When applying a style sheet with either a keyboard equivalent, from the **Style→Style Sheets** menu, or by clicking in the Style Sheets palette, local formatting is not overridden. But by holding down the Option key when selecting a style sheet in the palette, You can override local formatting. The Xstyle XTension also adds the capability to apply only the character attributes of a style sheet to selected text by holding down the Command key when a style sheet is applied from its Character/Paragraph palette. Holding down the Command key while clicking in QuarkXPress' Style Sheets palette causes you to jump into the **Edit→Style Sheets** dialog box with the clicked-on style sheet already selected.

Append styles and resolve name conflicts

Style sheets, colors, and H & Js could be appended from other Quark XPress documents in earlier versions, but if any of the names were the same, you were stuck with the existing styles. With QuarkXPress 3.2, new style sheets, colors, and H & Js being appended to a document can be renamed if their name is already in use (Figure A.3). You can instead ignore the new style, choosing to use the existing styles. Conflicting imported styles automatically get an asterisk (*) appended to their names.

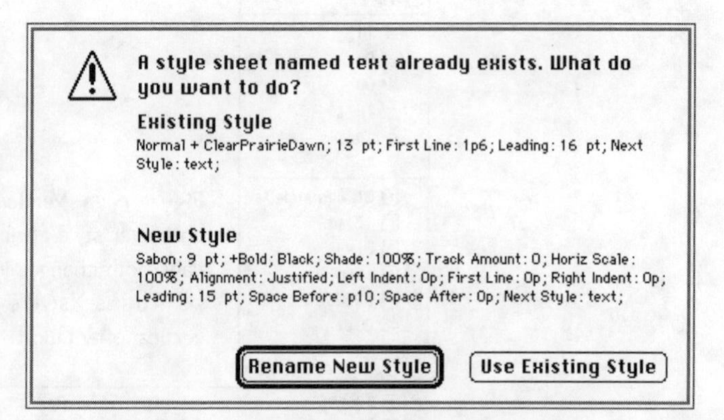

Figure A.3 Append styles In this case, the text style being imported has specs different from the one already present in the document. I could choose to import the new version with a different name, or ignore it completely.

Replace style sheets, colors, H & Js

When you try to delete a style sheet, color, or H & J in QuarkXPress 3.2, you'll be prompted to change any existing uses of the style to any other style that has been defined in the document (Figure A.4). It's a real shame that appending *and* replacing style sheets, colors, and H & Js can't be done in one step. If you're trying to append styles to a document because you want to update older versions, you have to do the following:

- When appending the styles, choose to rename each style that's going to be updated.
- Save the new styles.
- Re-enter the appropriate style dialog box.
- Delete each old style and select the new style to replace it.

When you click on the pop-up menu to choose which style should be used for the replacement, you'll notice that the name of the style sheet you're deleting will be grayed out. This makes sense, since you don't want to replace a deleted style with itself. But if you're deleting styles that were appended and renamed, this also serves as a handy way to tell which style should be chosen as the replacement. The first name below the grayed-out name will often be the one you want, since it will have the same name plus the appended asterisk. My own experience shows that this trick only works for the first 32 styles in a document, though, since after that the graying-out ceases to occur.

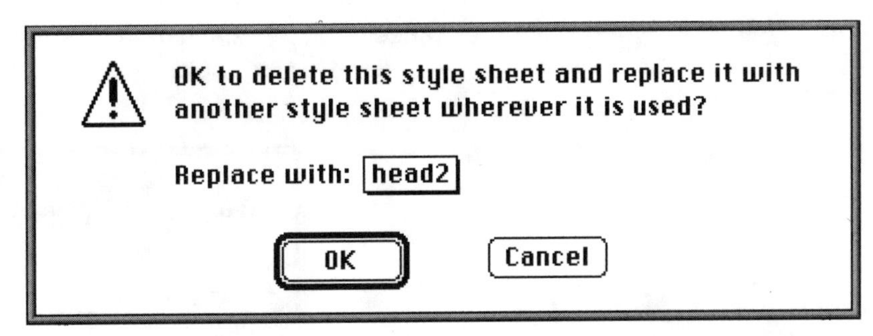

Figure A.4 Replacing styles Whenever a style sheet, color, or H & J is deleted, a dialog box similar to this will prompt you to choose which style to replace it with.

Typography

Interactive text scaling

Text can be resized interactively by selecting the box, holding down the Command key, and dragging a text box handle. If a corner handle is dragged, the point size, leading, and horizontal scale of the text in the box is dynamically changed. The side handles can be dragged if scaling in only one direction is desired, and adding the Shift key constrains the scaling to a square box.

Scaling can be done proportionally—so that the width and height change by the same percentage—by holding down the Option and Shift keys in addition to the Command key. If you want to see the text being scaled, wait half of a second before moving the handle. The box can't be scaled more than 400%, but the program will let you make a change larger than 400% temporarily. When you let go of the handle the box will snap back to the maximum size, though. This feature doesn't work on linked text boxes, but it will work on the automatic text box in a one-page document.

Vertical character scaling

QuarkXPress 3.2 allows users to compress or expand characters vertically as well as horizontally from 25 percent to 400 percent of their normal height or width. You can only scale in one direction at a time, and you choose which direction in the **Style→Horizontal/Vertical Scale** dialog box (Figure A.5). The keyboard shortcuts for scaling always work in the horizontal direction only, and, in fact, reset the scaling direction back to horizontal in the dialog box.

Accents for All Caps

If the Accents for All Caps option is turned on in the Application Preferences dialog box, QuarkXPress will stop removing accents from letters when the All Caps style is applied. This option is only available

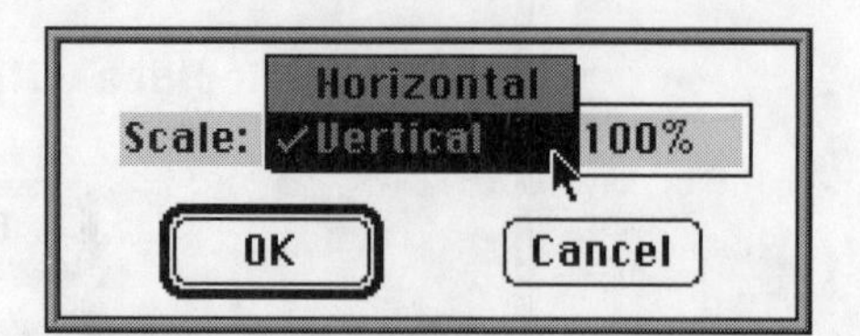

Figure A.5 Character scaling This pop-up menu let's you choose which direction to scale characters.

for documents created in version 3.2 or above; when an older file is opened, the option is grayed out. Text with the Small Caps style applied to it will also retain its accents when this option is turned on. Be sure to check the style rules for whatever language you're working in, though. Accents are usually used when Spanish is capitalized; they come off in French and stay on in Quebecois, although I'm told that European French is beginning to retain the accents as well.

Standard em space

A standard typesetter's em space character can be used instead of the double-zero width that QuarkXPress has always employed to represent an em space. With the Standard em space option enabled in the Typographic Preferences dialog box, em spaces will be equivalent to the point size being used. Two en spaces (Option-Space) still have to be typed to get an em space, unfortunately. All kerning and tracking calculations are based on units of an em, so they will also be adjusted when this feature is turned on. By all means, don't experiment with this option after a job has been completed, since text may very well reflow when this change is made.

TIP There actually is a way to get an em space in QuarkXPress without having to type two en spaces. The Flex Space Width setting in Typographic Preferences refers to a percentage of the en space, so changing it to 200% effectively creates an em space. To access the flex space from the keyboard, type Option-Shift-Space. I prefer to use the flex space as a thin space with a custom width based on the job I'm working on, and continue to type two en spaces to get an em space.

Nonbreaking space options

With the introduction of System 7.1, some folks are having trouble getting the nonbreaking spaces in QuarkXPress to work. Adding Command to any spaceband keystroke is supposed to change it to a nonbreaking space, meaning that the characters on either side of the space will be kept together at the ends of lines. But Command-Space is used to switch scripts or keyboard layouts at the system level now. If you have two or more scripts or layouts installed, Command-Space combinations won't work.

QuarkXPress 3.2 lets you type Control in place of Command when keying spacebands, so now you can use these shortcuts to get nonbreaking spaces:

SPACE	BREAKING	NONBREAKING
Spaceband	#	⌃ #
Punctuation space	⇧ #	⌃ ⇧ #
En space	⌥ #	⌃ ⌥ #
Flexspace	⌥ ⇧ #	⌃ ⌥ ⇧ #

Automatic typographer's quotes

The Smart Quotes feature in the Application Preferences dialog box can be used to substitute typographer's quotation marks (single and double) for the single and double tick marks on the keyboard. If this option is switched on and tick marks are desired (for whatever reason), they can be typed by holding down the Control key and typing the tick mark keys. The following quotation mark pairs can be chosen: “ ”/” ”/„ “/« »/» «. Single quotation marks (‘/’) always set the same.

TIP Please don't make the same mistake as QuarkXPress' documentation by confusing tick marks with foot and inch marks. The Symbol font has prime and double-prime characters that I use as foot and inch marks, simply because they're so easy to access. Just type Command-Shift-Q to access the Symbol font followed by Option-4 for the prime (′) and Option-Comma for the double prime (″). (It's easier to do than to read about.) And if the Symbol characters are too angled for your taste, you can use the Universal News and Commercial Pi font's 8 (′) and 9 (″) characters to get true foot and inch marks. You'll probably want to use Find/Change or XPress Tags to access them, since there's no keyboard shortcut for switching to the Universal News and Commercial Pi font.

Drop caps of up to 16 lines

If you're using drop caps this large, don't forget that you can kern the drop cap (or the first character in any paragraph) into the left margin by preceding it with a spaceband and then manually kerning between the spaceband and the drop cap. Since the spaceband will be considered the first character in the paragraph, your drop cap definition will have to call for two characters in order to pick up the first printing character. The spaceband can also be selected and tracked smaller, if you prefer that method.

Forced Justify

The Forced Justify alignment option forces the last line of a paragraph to be justified along with the rest of the paragraph, as well as justifying any single line. With the regular justified option, single lines and the last lines of justified paragraphs are always set flush left. The Forced Justify alignment option can be chosen from the Measurements palette or the **Style→Alignment→Forced** menu item.

Font mapping

When you open up a document whose fonts aren't open, Quark XPress 3.2 will display a dialog box warning you of the situation (Figure A.6). If you click the List Fonts button in this dialog, you'll get a list of all the missing fonts. If you don't want to open the missing fonts, you can substitute fonts right from this dialog box (Figure A.7).

Unfortunately, this feature goes a little overboard, warning you of missing fonts that aren't actually used in the document but that are present in the document's style sheets. Before going crazy replacing all the fonts shown in this dialog, it might make sense to open the file, see how it looks, and then make the font replacements from the Font Usage dialog box.

Multiple Master font support

The Multiple Master Utilities XTension—aka MMU 3.2—needs to be loose in the QuarkXPress folder or in the XTensions folder to achieve

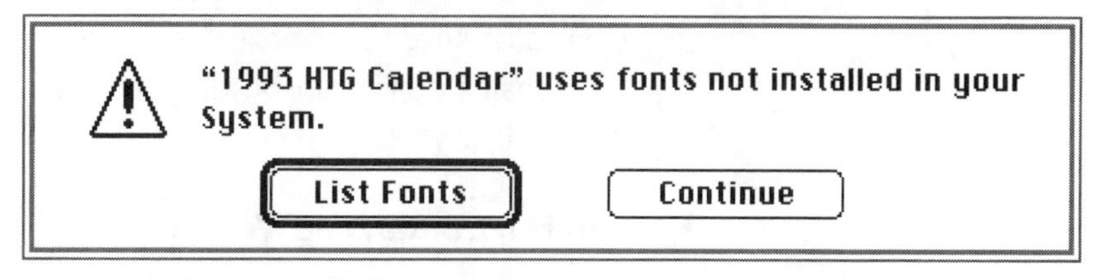

Figure A.6 Fonts not installed This new dialog box comes up when the document being opened uses fonts that you haven't opened yet.

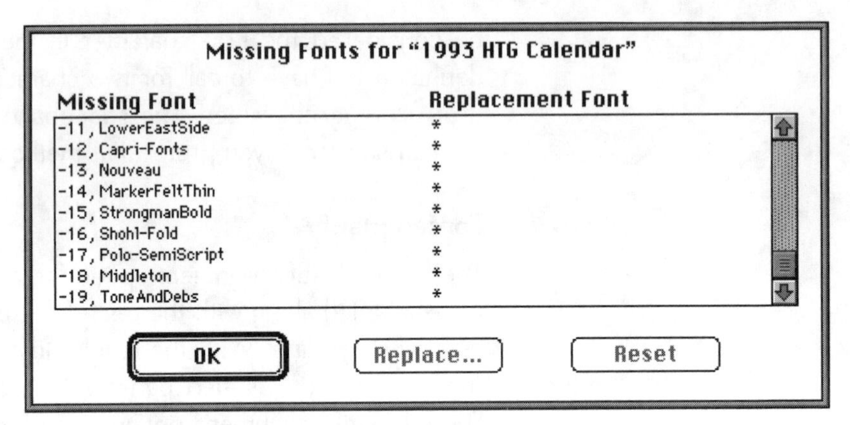

Figure A.7 Missing fonts This dialog box lists all the fonts used in the document *and its style sheets* that aren't open on your system.

full Multiple Master font support. You also need Adobe Type Manager 3.0 or higher and the Multiple Master INIT that ships with those fonts.

When you open a document that has Multiple Master font instances (variations) not already present in your system, Quark XPress will create them. Also, if EPS files contain any such instances, they will be created at print time. The Font Creator application that comes with Adobe Multiple Master fonts can be opened from within QuarkXPress, too. Font Creator can be used to make your own instances of a Multiple Master font.

Page layout

Duplicate and copy linked text boxes

You can now duplicate or copy a chain of linked text boxes, and the new copy will retain its links. You can also duplicate or copy one text box that's part of a linked chain, in which case the new copy will contain the text that was in the copied box as well as all the text that was in subsequent boxes of the chain. You can't duplicate or copy more than one linked box, though, unless you're copying the whole chain. Chains of linked text boxes—as well as individual boxes that are part of a chain—can also be dragged from document to document and into a library.

Flip Horizontal/Flip Vertical

The contents of text and picture boxes can now be flipped horizontally and/or vertically so that the text and art appear as mirror images

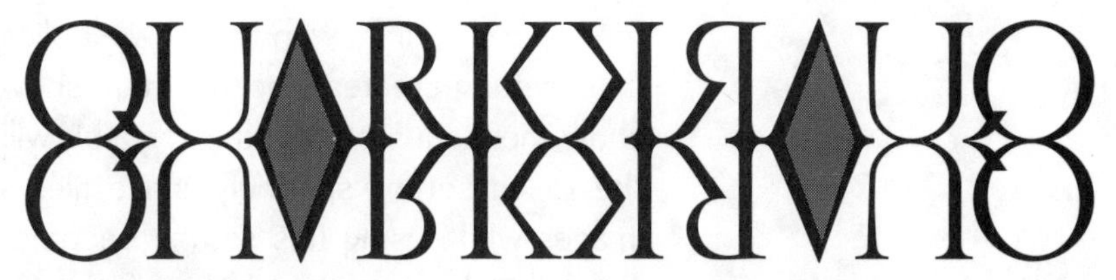

Figure A.8 Flip horizontal/vertical This familiar logo was flipped horizontally, vertically, and both horizontally and vertically in order to create these reflections.

of the original (Figure A.8). Either select the appropriate commands in the Style menu or click the two new arrow icons in the Measurements palette. Flipped boxes are still fully editable, and flipping works in anchored boxes!

Box Skew

Text boxes can now be skewed from –75 degrees to 75 degrees in 0.001 degree increments. This is especially useful for creating elongated shadows for display text (Figure A.9). The skew value is given in **Item→Modify**. Frames can be applied to skewed boxes, too.

Graphics

EfiColor for QuarkXPress

With the EfiColor Color Management System integrated into Quark XPress, colors will match more closely from scanned input to output on a variety of monitors, digital proofing printers, and offset presses. In addition, EfiColor for QuarkXPress supports Metric Color Tags (MCT) to read color information from TIFF and RGB images created or color-corrected in EFI Cachet and Adobe Photoshop. See the EfiColor XTension section in the **Graphics** chapter for more information.

Color TIFFs display

As discussed in the **Graphics** chapter, you can control the number of colors QuarkXPress will use when creating the PICT screen preview

Figure A.9 Text box skew After duplicating and shading the text in the backmost text box, I skewed it by –45°.

for imported TIFFs with this new Application Preferences setting. The 8-bit setting creates a preview that shows up to 256 colors; 16-bit will show thousands of colors and 32-bit will show millions of colors. Use the 32-bit setting sparingly, since files saved with even a handful of images while using this setting become quite large. The only way to get full-color images to print from QuarkXPress to a QuickDraw printer is to use the 32-bit setting, however, since only the PICT screen preview is sent to such devices.

Image resolution

The Low Resolution option for importing images is no longer available from a dialog box. All images are now brought in at 72 dpi unless you hold down the Shift key when opening them. The Shift key causes images to import with a screen resolution of only 36 dpi.

Image scaling and positioning

If you type horizontal and vertical scale and offsets into the Measurements palette or the **Item→Modify** dialog box while an empty graphic box is selected, a newly imported image will use those settings. For this to be a truly useful feature, QuarkXPress should offer a method whereby an image can be deleted from a graphic box and the settings remain. I made a lot of alternate screen shots when producing this book, and I can't count the times I wanted to replace an image with a newer version. Had I been able to import the new version maintaining the settings used for the old version, it would have saved a lot of time. Had I been willing, I realize that I could have given the new version the same name as the old one and updated the graphic box in the Picture Usage dialog box, but that became cumbersome when dealing with as many screen shots as I have in some chapters.

Color Swatch Drag

The Color Swatch Drag feature provides an easy way to apply colors to frames, box backgrounds, and lines by simply dragging the swatch over the frame, line, or box. Select any item (so that the Colors palette becomes available), click on the color swatch in the Colors palette, and drag the color until it's over any item (Figure A.10). If the item's

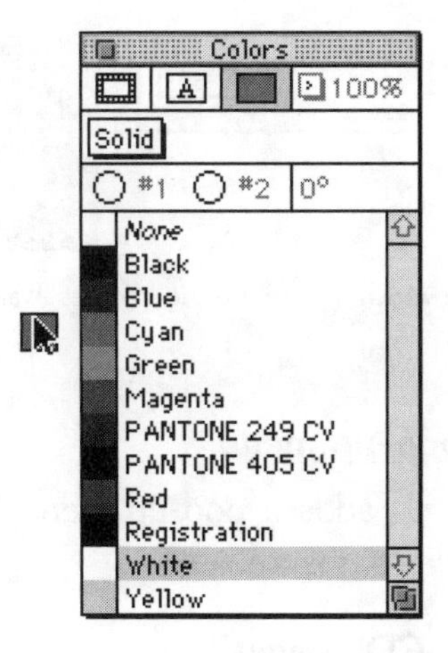

Figure A.10 Swatch drag Dragging on a color swatch breaks off a piece of that color. The swatch can be dragged onto an item to change its background color.

background shade is less than 100%, holding down the Option key when clicking on the color will force the shade to 100% when the color is applied.

Cool Blends XTension

The Cool Blends XTension adds five new blends that can be used as backgrounds for picture boxes and text boxes: Mid-Linear, Rectangular, Diamond, Circular, and Full Circular. These are discussed (and shown) in the **Graphics** chapter.

PANTONE Matching System models

If the Pantone Colors file is present in the QuarkXPress folder, there will now be a total of four PANTONE color models available in **Edit→ Colors** dialog box:

- **PANTONE**—PMS solid colors for use when printing on coated paper stock
- **PANTONE Uncoated**—PMS solid colors for use when printing on uncoated paper stock
- **PANTONE Process**—PANTONE's three process colors mixed with black to produce more than 3000 colors
- **PANTONE ProSim**—Simulations of PANTONE colors made with four-color separation settings to ensure that the colors will print on four-color presses

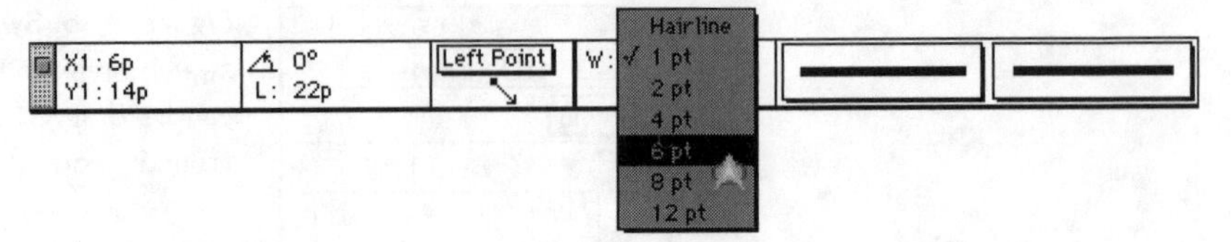

Figure A.11 Line width These are the choices available on the new Line width pop-up menu.

Line width pop-up menu

QuarkXPress 3.2 adds a pop-up menu for line widths to the Measurements palette (Figure A.11).

Import PhotoCD images

QuarkXPress 3.2 comes with a PhotoCD XTension that can be used to import Kodak PhotoCD images directly into documents. Please see the **Graphics** chapter for more information on PhotoCD. Also, the color plates in this book contain a PhotoCD image brought directly into QuarkXPress with this XTension and the same image after a professional photographer worked on it in Photoshop.

Import images from PCs

QuarkXPress 3.2 can import Windows Metafile vector images and BMP raster images created on PCs. Windows Metafile images are converted to PICTs when imported into QuarkXPress; the type of PICT created will control what Style menu options are available for each image.

Output

Save Page as EPS options

You can now save QuarkXPress 3.2 pages in color or black and white, in Mac or PC, or as DCS 1.0 or 2.0 formats. The DCS (Desktop Color Separation) option actually saves five files, one each for the process colors (cyan, magenta, yellow, and black) and one preview file linked to the other four. The specs for DCS 2.0 allow for additional plates to be composed, such as extra plates for spot colors or varnishes.

Trapping Preferences

Trapping Preferences are now saved with each document and are available in a separate preferences dialog box. There's plenty more on trapping in the **Output** chapter.

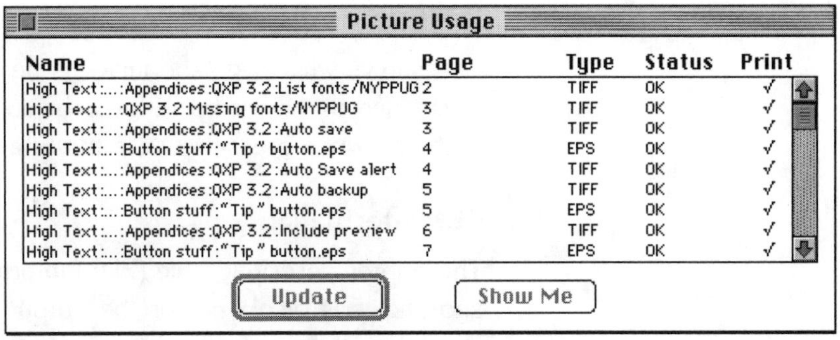

Picture Usage

Name	Page	Type	Status	Print
High Text:...:Appendices:QXP 3.2:List fonts/NYPPUG	2	TIFF	OK	√
High Text:...:QXP 3.2:Missing fonts/NYPPUG	3	TIFF	OK	√
High Text:...:Appendices:QXP 3.2:Auto save	3	TIFF	OK	√
High Text:...:Button stuff:"Tip" button.eps	4	EPS	OK	√
High Text:...:Appendices:QXP 3.2:Auto Save alert	4	TIFF	OK	√
High Text:...:Appendices:QXP 3.2:Auto backup	5	TIFF	OK	√
High Text:...:Button stuff:"Tip" button.eps	5	EPS	OK	√
High Text:...:Appendices:QXP 3.2:Include preview	6	TIFF	OK	√
High Text:...:Button stuff:"Tip" button.eps	7	EPS	OK	√

Update   Show Me

Figure A.12 Picture suppression All pictures can now be suppressed (or unsuppressed) in the Picture Usage dialog box.

Suppress pictures

Individual pictures can now be suppressed from the Picture Usage dialog box. Just click to remove the checkmark next to the picture name, and the picture will be suppressed (Figure A.10). If you want to enable printing, click in the last column in the dialog box to add a new checkmark. This feature works just like the Suppress Picture Printout feature in the Picture Box Specifications dialog box (**Item→Modify**). Unlike the the full-blown Suppress Printout feature in **Item→Modify**, suppressing the printout in the Picture Usage dialog box does not suppress the printout of a picture box's frame.

To suppress or unsuppress more than one picture in this dialog box, either Shift-Click to select a range of pictures or Command-Click to select discontiguous pictures and then click in the Print column. All the selected pictures will be either suppressed or unsuppressed.

Updating multiple pictures

If you tell the program to update one picture using the Picture Usage dialog box and there are other missing or modified pictures in the same folder, QuarkXPress will let you update all those pictures at the same time.

Low Resolution printing

If this Output method is chosen in the **File→Print** dialog box, a picture's low-resolution preview is printed instead of the high-resolution file it's linked to.

Print status display

This shows what page and image is being downloaded to the printer or spooled to the hard disk. It can be suppressed by holding down the Shift key when pressing OK in the **File→Print** dialog.

PDF information

The printer description file (PDF) information on screen frequencies and angles is displayed for the output device chosen in the **File→ Page Setup** dialog box.

Collect for Output

The Collect for Output feature copies QuarkXPress files, pictures, and documents into a user-specified folder for delivery to a service bureau for high-resolution output. I've discussed this feature in greater detail in the section on sending jobs to a service bureau in the **Output** chapter. Documents need to be saved just before this command is chosen, and if you haven't done so, you'll get a warning that forces you to either save the document or cancel the process.

I'm going to use the Collect for Output feature when I move all of this book's files to the Syquest cartridge that I'm going to give to the printer. I could just drag the appropriate folders to the Syquest, but almost all the art folders for my chapters have artwork that I didn't end up using; Collect for Output will only copy the art that was used in each document.

Automating DTP

Auto Save

The Auto Save feature is indispensible and should be turned on immediately (Figure A.13). It saves a temporary copy of the document currently being worked on so that if you crash, you'll lose less work. *It does not overwrite the file you're working on.*

Figure A.13 Auto Save setup This portion of the Application Preferences dialog box needs to be activated in order for Auto Saves to be performed.

If you crash after the program has done an Auto Save but before you've done a "hard" save (from the File menu or by typing ⌘ S), the next time you open the document you'll get a dialog box telling you that the Auto Saved version is being used (Figure A.14). If you don't want that version for any reason, you can immediately choose Revert to Saved from the File menu and your document will be back to the state it was in when you last did a hard save.

TIP If you find yourself occasionally avoiding a hard save while experimenting on a page, you may not be sure whether to keep the Auto Saved version or Revert to Saved after a crash. Do not make the the mistake of assuming—as I once did—that you can get back to the Auto Saved version once you've reverted. It doesn't work that way: You only get one chance to use the Auto Saved version. If you aren't sure which version to use, let the Auto Saved version open and proceed to save it under a different name; then open the hard saved version normally and decide which version you want to keep.

The program performs these Auto Saves at the interval specified in the Applications Preferences dialog box. Don't forget that you won't be able to recover work performed between the last Auto Save or hard save—whichever came last—and a system crash. But if you have a time increment of 5 minutes specified, the most work you could lose is 4 minutes and 59 seconds' worth. Quark, Inc., could have done us an even greater service by having an Auto Saved file open to the page

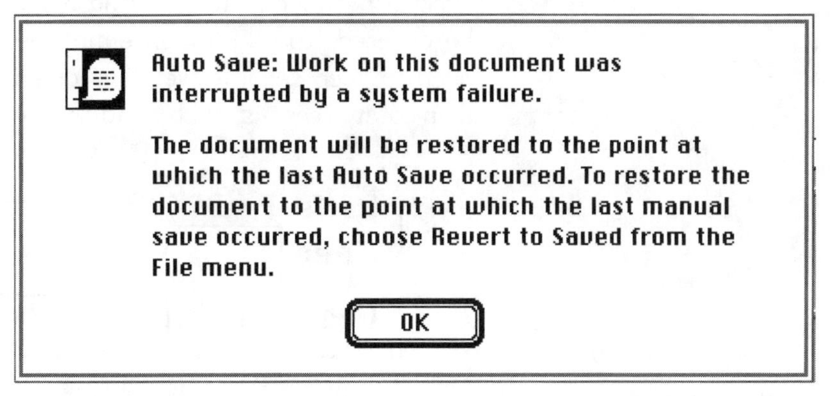

Auto Save: Work on this document was interrupted by a system failure.
The document will be restored to the point at which the last Auto Save occurred. To restore the document to the point at which the last manual save occurred, choose Revert to Saved from the File menu.
OK

Figure A.14 Auto Save restore This is the warning you'll get when opening a document that was last saved automatically with QuarkXPress 3.2's Auto Save feature.

where you were last working when the Auto Save was performed. Too bad they didn't think of it.

Auto Backup

This feature makes a copy of the previously saved version of a document each time you do a hard save (from the File menu). If this is turned on and left with its default settings, you may soon find that you have no hard disk space left. The default setting—five revisions—may be too high, especially if you're working with large files.

Each revision will be given the same name as the original file with a number sign (#) and the revision number added to the end of the name. When the program has made as many revisions as you've asked, it will start deleting old backups, starting with the oldest one. The numbers appended to the names of backup versions continue to grow, however; as of the moment I'm writing this sentence, the latest backup of this appendix is #154!

TIP It can't be stressed enough that Auto Backup files are always at least one revision old. Do not use this feature as a replacement for a solid backup routine. And if you find that your original document is damaged and you need to use an Auto Backup revision, keep in mind that you'll have to re-do any work performed between the time of the Auto Backup revision and the time of the last hard save.

I usually keep just one revision of each file (Figure A.15), figuring that between Auto Save and one Auto Backup revision I should be covered from losing an entire file due to a system crash. If I need to keep separate versions of a document for anything other than safety reasons, such as to keep different page designs that I'll

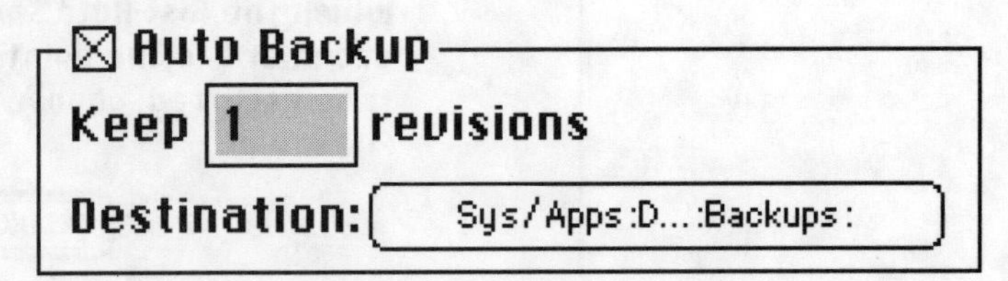

Figure A.15 Auto Backup setup You'll need to turn on Auto Backup in the Application Preferences dialog box, too. The number of revisions and the location of the backup folder need to be defined.

need to show a client, I just use the Save As command under the File menu.

As for the destination, I highly recommend against keeping the default setting of Document Folder. If you let your backup revisions pile up all over the hard drive, there's a good chance that you'll just be wasting space for little reason. Instead, I created a folder on my Desktop called Backups, and I save all Auto Backup revisions there. That way I can easily clean it out once in a while—usually when I need hard disk space! (While making the copyedits on this paragraph, I realized that I hadn't checked my Backups folder recently. I found over 9 megabytes of stuff that could be trashed; had the backups been spread out over all my hard drives, recovery of that 9 megabytes of space would have been much more difficult.)

Speed Scroll

The Speed Scroll feature—available in the Application Preferences dialog box—greeks pictures and color blends, enabling you to scroll quickly through a document without waiting for the screen to redraw each element. When the scrolling stops, the elements are once again visible.

There are two other scrolling options in Application Preferences (Figure A.16). The first is a scroll speed sliding bar that goes from slow to fast. I've noticed that newly updated copies of QuarkXPress 3.2 tend to have this set at a very slow speed. This feature adjusts the speed the document scrolls when you use the scroll bars at the bottom and side of QuarkXPress' main window. The Live Scroll check box lets you see the page scrolling when you drag the boxes in the scroll bars, instead of just refreshing the screen when scrolling ceases. Holding down the Option key while dragging the bars will temporarily toggle this setting.

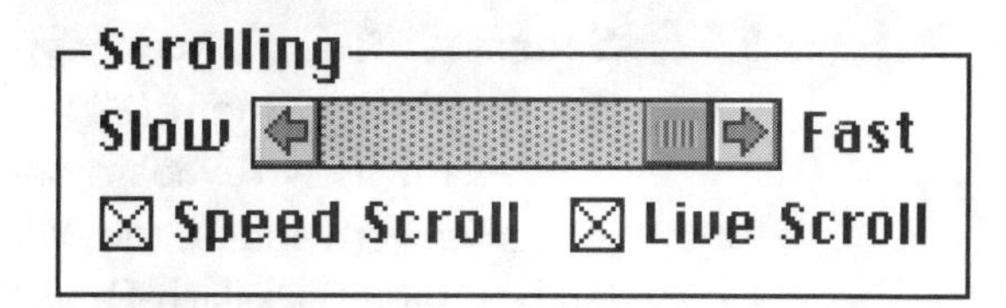

Figure A.16 Scrolling options As you can see, I crank up the scrolling speed, turn on Speed Scroll (for greeking pictures during scrolls), and turn on Live Scroll, too.

Window stacking and tiling

By holding down the Shift key and clicking on the name of the document that's at the top of the active document window, you can choose whether to stack or tile all open documents, as well as switch which document is active. Stacking is the normal way that QuarkXPress displays multiple documents on the screen, offsetting each newly opened document slightly below an already open document. Tiling resizes all the windows of open documents so that each one can be seen.

If you have two or three documents open, they will be tiled from top to bottom. If more than three documents are open, the program will put some documents next to each other. And if the Tile to Multiple Monitors option is turned on in Applications Preferences, the tiling will take advantage of all monitors connected to the same computer when configuring the tiles.

New—and newly visible—keyboard shortcuts

For the first time, all of the menu commands that are accessible from the main keyboard are shown in the menus. I don't know if there was some programming problem keeping the Option (⌥) key out of the menus prior to version 3.2, but if there was, it has been solved. The method used to solve the problem does conflict with version 4.0 of Now Menus, though, so you won't be able to use shortcuts created with that utility in conjunction with QuarkXPress' new shortcuts. QuicKeys seems to work fine, and if you've used any of the same key sequences as QuarkXPress uses, QuicKeys' sequences will take precedence.

QuarkXPress also has a number of new shortcuts. Since you can easily see the menu commands by clicking on the menus, there's no point in my listing them all here. I will say, however, that after a couple of months of using version 3.2, I've found that my favorite new shortcuts are **File→Save Text** (⌘ ⌥ E), **File→Document Setup** (⌘ ⌥ ⇧ P), **Item→Space/Align** (⌘ ,), and **Utilities→Check Spelling→Document** (⌘ ⌥ ⇧ L).

A few new keyboard shortcuts that handle things not available in menus were added, too. When using the **Edit→Find/Change** dialog box, type Backslash-Period (\.) to search for a punctuation space and Backslash-f (\f) to find a flex space. An en space can still be searched for by typing its normal shortcut, Option-Space (⌥ #).

Text can now be scaled horizontally by 1 percent increments with keyboard shortcuts. Command-Option-[(⌘ ⌥ [) will decrease scaling; Command-Option-] (⌘ ⌥]) will increase scaling. And whereas the Fit in Window menu command and keyboard shortcut (⌘ 0 [zero]) display an entire page spread in the document window, adding an Option to that sequence (⌘ ⌥ 0) fits the spread *and* the left and right pasteboards into the window. This is a great way to zip through a book while viewing one or more page spreads at a time.

TIP There has been a slight but welcome change to the way the keyboard shortcuts work when switching for one character to the Symbol and Zapf Dingbats fonts. Prior to version 3.2, you had to key the shortcuts (⌘ ⇧ Q for Symbol and ⌘ ⇧ Z for Zapf Dingbats) *before* typing the one character you wanted to access from those fonts. That still works, but now you can also select one or more characters and type the shortcuts to change the typeface of all the selected characters. If they'd just add a third shortcut that can be customized to change to a user-defined font, I'd be a happy camper!

QuarkXPress 3.2 shipped with a laminated card showing all the keyboard shortcuts, but be careful when using it, since there are a few errors on it. On the Productivity panel of the card, for instance, the section on highlighting characters with the arrow keys is messed up. Here are the correct commands:

	PREVIOUS	NEXT
Character	⇧ ←	⇧ →
Word	⌘ ⇧ ←	⌘ ⇧ →
Line (to line)	⇧ ↑	⇧ ↓
Paragraph	⌘ ⇧ ↑	⌘ ⇧ ↓
	START	**END**
Line (to margin)	⌘ ⌥ ⇧ ←	⌘ ⌥ ⇧ →
Story	⌘ ⌥ ⇧ ↑	⌘ ⌥ ⇧ ↓

If you'd like to start using these shortcuts but have a hard time remembering them, here's a suggestion. Concentrate on the two most useful (in my opinion) shortcuts: Select Word (⌘ ⇧ ← and ⌘ ⇧ →) and Select Paragraph (⌘ ⇧ ↑ and ⌘ ⇧ ↓). Then all you have to remember is the Command and Shift keys; you can poke all the arrows until you get the selection you want.

For those of us with extended keyboards containing the full complement of function keys, there are also a number of new shortcuts for accessing palettes, dialog boxes, and menu commands. It's a good thing that version 3.2 shipped with a keyboard template, since the positioning of the function key commands seems very illogical to me. For one thing, all the gaps in the function key layout seem disconcerting, especially when you consider that a number of other useful shortcuts could have been added, such as changing to different views. At least one built-in shortcut was left off the template, by the way: Shift-F8 toggles back and forth between the Item and Contents tools.

Arithmetic operators

Beyond the addition and subtraction that has been possible for a while now, QuarkXPress 3.2 supports the use of multiplication and division operators when entering values in numerical fields, such as those in some dialog boxes and the Measurements palette. The asterisk (*) is used for multiplication and the slash (/) is used for division.

Although parentheses can't be used to form complex equations, QuarkXPress does honor standard mathematical order of precedence. For example, if you want to reduce an item's width to 6 points less than half of its current width—something I've been doing a lot when creating some of the narrow screen shots shown in this book—you should append "/2-p6" to the item's width field in the Measurements palette (or in **Item→Modify**).

If you tried appending "-1p/2" in the hopes that it would subtract the 1 pica and then divide the result by 2, you would be disappointed. In this case, 1 pica would first be divided in half and the resultant 6 points would be subtracted from the current width. Being able to type the equations with parentheses to control the order of the operations would have saved me a lot of time in the past.

Change document scale on-screen

Typing Control-V places the cursor in the scale field at the lower-left corner of the main document window. To change the scale, type a new number in the field and press Return. If you type a "T" in this field, you'll be shown a thumbnail view of your pages.

Open up to 25 documents at one time

We can now open up to 25 documents at once. I've been pretty happy with being able to open up just seven documents prior to version 3.2, but this new feature will be especially handy when using the Finder to set up a large job with many files to print overnight.

Network support for templates

QuarkXPress 3.2 features network support for templates, which gives users their own local copies of documents from a template on a shared volume. Multiple users can open the template and a single user can open the same template multiple times. When the template is opened, it's automatically named "Document1."

Previews saved with documents

A preview of the first page of a document can now be saved with a document as well as with a template (Figure A.17). This feature gives the user a visual cue to the file's contents as well as its name.

Cross-platform compatibility

QuarkXPress 3.2 provides full compatibility with QuarkXPress 3.1 for Windows. Documents created on either platform can now be ex-

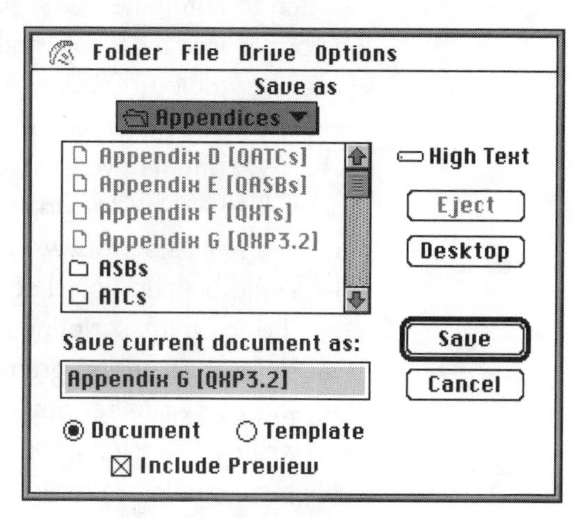

Figure A.17 Include Preview Now previews can be saved for the first page of any document, not just templates.

changed easily. You'll need QuarkXPress 3.3 on both platforms to exchange that version's files.

When moving files between platforms, keep in mind the various file-naming conventions. Mac files being sent to PCs should have their names changed to reflect the eight-character name and three-character extension restriction on PCs. QuarkXPress documents should use ".qxd" as the extension; templates need to have a ".qxt" extension.

QuarkXPress on the Mac recognizes these extensions even when a file is brought over from the PC. If a file from a PC doesn't have the right icon when viewed on the Mac, try appending one of the extensions to the file name and open up the file through the **File→Open** dialog box.

Cross-platform font mapping

To speed cross-platform document conversion, QuarkXPress 3.2 will automatically apply the correct Macintosh PostScript fonts when users open a document created with QuarkXPress for Windows. If any font names are different, QuarkXPress will substitute the correct Macintosh font name.

Scripting

Support for Apple Events scripts

Perhaps the biggest sleeper feature of QuarkXPress 3.2 is its phenomenal Apple Events scripting support. AppleEvents scripts can be written to automate tasks, such as performing mail merges or importing prices into a catalog, and to interact with other applications. You'll have the choice of using AppleScript or UserLand Frontier. AppleScript is the simpler of the two languages, but Frontier is more powerful. A "runtime" version of Frontier was included with version 3.2 that will allow you to run the sample scripts that came with the program as well as scripts written by friends and those downloaded from electronic bulletin board services.

I don't think scripting is for everybody, by any means; it's not all that different from programming. I think there's a real niche for people who can write scripts, including people who may not have gotten into writing XTensions, for whatever reason. Please see the **Scripting** chapter for much more information about QuarkXPress 3.2's support of Apple Events.

Undocumented features

The Quark Martian

By adding the Option key to your normal method of deleting items—either typing Command-K, pressing Delete when the Item tool is chosen, or choosing Delete from the Item menu—a multicolored "Martian" will appear on your screen and incinerate your items with its ray gun. This keyboard shortcut was changed in version 3.3 so that the Martian will appear only if you have the Item tool chosen and you hold down the Option and Shift keys while pressing the Delete key to remove an object.

Screen redraw interrupt

If you hold down Command-Period (⌘ .) when the screen is redrawing, it will stop. On simple pages, you have to be pretty quick to see this work, and you may just get beeped at if the page has been redrawn before you type the command. But on complicated pages, you'll see how the redraw freezes and waits for the next command.

If I need to both change views and hide the guides, I'll ask for the new view, type Command-Period, and then hit the F7 function key to toggle the guides. As soon as the function key is pressed, the redraw is started again, but with guides off. Instead of waiting for a complete redraw for both the view and guides change, I only wait for a little more than one redraw. I've also used this when going to a new page and wanting to see a different view size, as well as going to a new page and wanting to toggle the guides simultaneously.

Updating the text flow

Since most new versions of QuarkXPress change the way text flows in a document, the program maintains logic for at least the last few versions. This way, you can open an old document and make corrections without worrying about it reflowing due to any new flow logic. If you hold down the Option key when opening a file through the **File→Open** dialog box, you will force the program to flow the file according to the rules present in the version you're using. This is fine when you don't care if lines rebreak, or if you want to take advantage of some new feature in the program (such as Accents for All Caps), but should be avoided if a job's line breaks have already been seen and approved by a client.

Figure A.18 The development team A picture of the QuarkXPress 3.2 for Macintosh development team can be accessed in the QuarkXPress Environment window.

QuarkXPress 3.2 development team

You can see a picture of the QuarkXPress 3.2 development team when in the QuarkXPress Environment window, accessed by typing Option-Help. Hold down the Command, Option, and Shift keys while clicking anywhere in the window. The script shown in the **Scripting** chapter was written by the guy in the back right corner of the picture, the one with his left elbow sticking out (Figure A.18). His name is Jeff Cheney, and at the time the picture was taken he was the product specialist for the Macintosh version of QuarkXPress.

QuarkXPress 3.2 patcher

If you're not ready to move QuarkXPress 3.3 into production, you should know that there is a patcher available for QuarkXPress 3.2. The patcher fixes several minor problems that you may have encountered with version 3.2.

TIP The Preferences file from the patched version of QuarkXPress 3.2 is incompatible with the Preferences file of the unpatched version. You must patch all copies of QuarkXPress 3.2 at your site. This is particularly important to maintain the correct version of preferences in a networked environment.

The QuarkXPress 3.2 patcher—available directly from Quark—fixes the following problems.

Crash in large networks

When a computer was connected to very large networks (more than 512 zones), QuarkXPress would occasionally freeze when launched.

DCS clipping

If a picture box with a transparent background contained an imported DCS picture with clipping information, the knockout area on spot color plates was incorrect (the box, rather than the clipping area of the picture, knocked out of the plate).

Document Layout palette crash

In a document with four or more master pages, creating a new document page by dragging a master page icon to the document area of the Document Layout palette could cause a crash.

Fonts, installed but not available

Apple font specifications establish font ID ranges for various alphabets (or "scripts"). Roman alphabet font IDs, as dictated by Apple, are not to exceed 16383. Those that exceeded that range were not recognized by QuarkXPress. In some instances, fonts that did not exceed the ID range were not available in the unpatched version of Quark XPress 3.2. This occurred when two or more fonts with IDs beyond 16383 were installed.

With the Roman alphabet system installed, all font IDs are recognized by the patched version of QuarkXPress 3.2. With multiple alphabet systems installed, font IDs will be matched to their appropriate alphabet system. In such cases, some Roman alphabet fonts with IDs greater than 16383 may not be available in the U.S. English version of QuarkXPress.

Polygon XTension incompatibility

Under some circumstances, third-party XTensions could cause QuarkXPress to crash when polygon picture boxes were manipulated.

Printing to printers connected to the printer port

When a computer was connected to a LaserWriter Select 310 via the printer port (but not necessarily to a network), users could receive an "unable to access network" error and not be able to print.

TIP To verify the patch level of your QuarkXPress 3.2 application, open the QuarkXPress environment dialog box (hold down the Option key while selecting About QuarkXPress from the Apple menu). After running the Patcher, you should be at Patch Level 2.

Appendix B: New features in QuarkXPress 3.3

QuarkXPress 3.3 has a number of interesting features, many of which I used in the composition of this book. Some of the following things will sound like bug fixes, and that's fine. Folks that work at Quark maintain a narrow definition of what constitutes a bug, to wit: *If it does what the engineers told it to do, it ain't a bug.* I'm sure that works for them, and I hold them no grudge. On the other hand, a user's definition of a bug is probably something like this: *If it doesn't do what it makes sense for it to do, it's a bug.* Once you're over that hump, I'm sure you'll enjoy these new features and feature enhancements, grouped and presented in the same order as the chapters of this book.

Text preparation

Indent Here command works across text boxes

The Indent Here command (⌘\) allows you to align the remainder of a paragraph with whatever character immediately follows the command. Prior to version 3.3, if you used the command in a paragraph that flowed from one column to another in a multi-column text box, the indent was continued. But if part of the paragraph flowed into the next linked text box, the indent was canceled. I'm thrilled to report that in version 3.3, the Indent Here command now remains in effect in all cases. Since I used this command to align paragraphs that were next to my side column heads—such as Text Preparation, above—I was quite happy to have the feature in time to paginate this book.

Keep with Next ¶ and Keep Lines Together improved

The Keep with Next ¶ and Keep Lines Together commands in the **Style→Formats** dialog box have been enhanced to handle subheads that are paragraphs of two or more lines. The lines of such subheads will be kept together and kept with the next paragraph when a column break would otherwise separate them. Prior to version 3.3, a multi-line subhead—even when all its lines were being kept together—would often split in half when it was kept with the following paragraph and it fell near the bottom of a column or page.

Keep with Next ¶ also now enables you to string several paragraphs together. In this book, for example, I have a head that's actually composed of two paragraphs—one that just draws a paragraph rule with a 27p right indent, followed by another that has a non-indented paragraph rule and the text of the head. Those two paragraphs have to be kept with the first five lines of the next paragraph, which contains a 2-line drop cap. This works flawlessly in 3.3.

New method for calculating text indents

Indents applied to paragraphs of text will now repel only from the edges of the box containing those paragraphs, but not from other obstructions. Prior to version 3.3, if you positioned any item (other than those with a runaround of None) within the area of a paragraph's indent, the paragraph would indent an additional amount equal to the amount of the overlap between the item and the paragraph's text box. Paragraph indents continue to honor the text inset assigned to the boxes they're in.

This change is very good news for those of us who use anchored text and picture boxes in indented copy. As shown in Figure B.1, prior

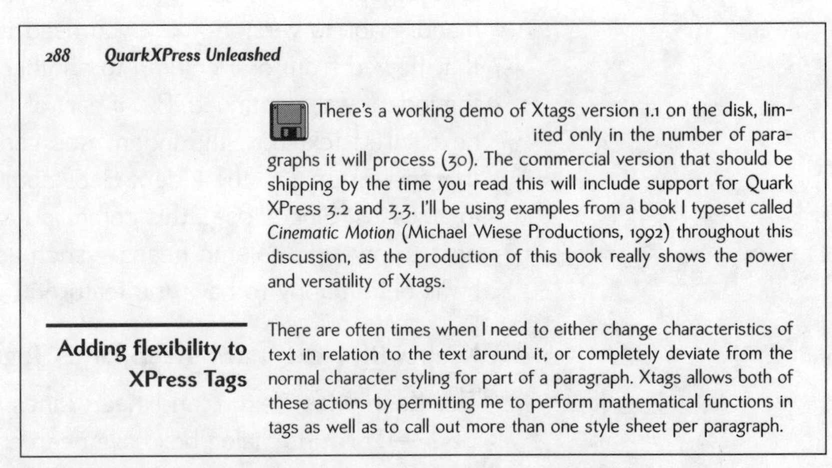

288 *QuarkXPress Unleashed*

There's a working demo of Xtags version 1.1 on the disk, limited only in the number of paragraphs it will process (30). The commercial version that should be shipping by the time you read this will include support for Quark XPress 3.2 and 3.3. I'll be using examples from a book I typeset called *Cinematic Motion* (Michael Wiese Productions, 1992) throughout this discussion, as the production of this book really shows the power and versatility of Xtags.

Adding flexibility to XPress Tags

There are often times when I need to either change characteristics of text in relation to the text around it, or completely deviate from the normal character styling for part of a paragraph. Xtags allows both of these actions by permitting me to perform mathematical functions in tags as well as to call out more than one style sheet per paragraph.

Figure B.1 Indented anchored box in 3.2 This is the way an ascender-aligned anchored box would look when pasted into indented text prior to version 3.3.

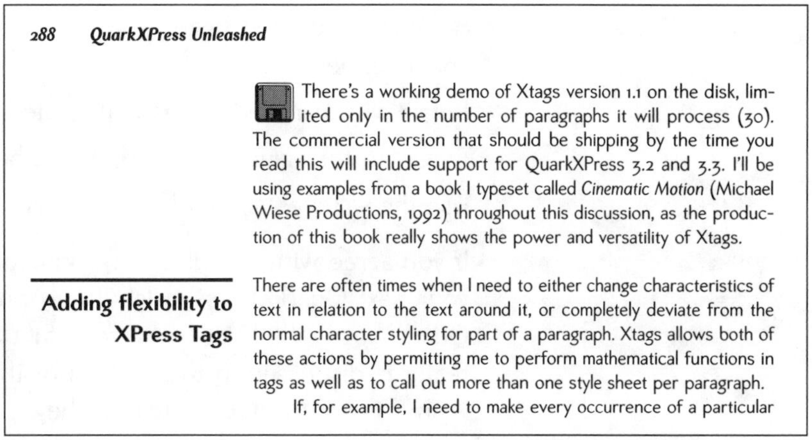

288 *QuarkXPress Unleashed*

There's a working demo of Xtags version 1.1 on the disk, limited only in the number of paragraphs it will process (30). The commercial version that should be shipping by the time you read this will include support for QuarkXPress 3.2 and 3.3. I'll be using examples from a book I typeset called *Cinematic Motion* (Michael Wiese Productions, 1992) throughout this discussion, as the production of this book really shows the power and versatility of Xtags.

Adding flexibility to XPress Tags

There are often times when I need to either change characteristics of text in relation to the text around it, or completely deviate from the normal character styling for part of a paragraph. Xtags allows both of these actions by permitting me to perform mathematical functions in tags as well as to call out more than one style sheet per paragraph.

If, for example, I need to make every occurrence of a particular

Figure B.2 Indented anchored box in 3.3 No more unsightly indents! Since paragraph indents are no longer affected by other items, I could have placed my disk icons within indented paragraphs when paginating the book in QuarkXPress 3.3.

to version 3.3, anchored boxes didn't work very well in indented text. Now that paragraphs are indented only from the edges of their boxes, anchored text and pictures can be used a lot more easily in indented text (Figure B.2).

Things aren't perfect yet in anchored box-land, however. To get the proper spacing next to the anchored picture box in Figure B.2, I had to apply a two-line drop cap to the paragraph, type a spaceband next to the anchored box, and kern –42 units between the box and the spaceband. I had to do this because anchored boxes still can't contain independent text outsets on all four sides. Instead, whatever text outset was in effect for the top of a box before it was anchored will be applied to all four sides once anchored. I wanted 6 points of space to the right of the anchored box, but there's no way that I could have had 6 points all around without messing up the text above and below the anchored box. Here's the way I'd like text outsets to work with anchored boxes:

- Anchored boxes should have all the runaround options as other items, including None, Item (with independent outset on all sides), Automatic, and Manual (the latter two for pictures, of course).

- When anchored boxes are first anchored, they should retain (and use) the outsets that were in place when they were copied/cut.

- When anchored boxes are duplicated (to unanchor them), they should either:

  Retain all runaround values that existed when they were anchored

  Revert to the values that were in use before they were anchored

  Use the value established in the Tools preferences

If you agree with me, please include some variation of the above on your next QuarkXPress "wish list." And don't be shy about sending Quark those wish lists. I know for a fact that most—if not all—of the features discussed in this section of the chapter were contained in wish lists sent to Quark. I know they were on mine!

Two characters can be specified as tab fills

You can now enter any two printing characters in the Fill Character field in the **Style→Tabs** dialog box. These characters will alternate to fill the space between the point at which you press the Tab key and the defined tab stop. For example, to increase the amount of space between the dots used in a dot leader, you could enter a period and a spaceband. In a line indented a few picas in from the width of this paragraph, such a tab fill would look like this:

. . . .

For even more space between the periods, you could use a period and an en space:

.   .   .   .

I couldn't get a punctuation space or a flex space to work with this feature, which is a shame; a flex space defined as 12.5–25% of the en space would have produced much nicer spacing for the leader dots. Other characters work, too. Here's an em dash and an angle bracket:

TIP The XPress Tags Filter has been updated in order to handle two-character tab fill characters in XPress Tags. Make sure you're using the XPress Tags Filter that came with QuarkXPress 3.3 if you need to use this feature for creating style sheets or customizing paragraphs with XPress Tags.

Overriding local formatting works for same style sheet

In QuarkXPress 3.2, if you applied local character or paragraph formatting to a paragraph that had a style sheet applied to it, you could only override the local formatting when applying a *different* style sheet. The trick of overriding the formatting by holding down the Option key and selecting a style sheet in the Style Sheets palette only worked if you were choosing a new style sheet. In 3.3, you can reapply the same style sheet to a paragraph and have its local formatting overridden properly.

Convert Quotes and Include Style Sheets buttons get "sticky"

The Convert Quotes and Include Style Sheets check boxes in the **File→Get Text** dialog box are now "sticky." This means that the program will leave the boxes checked or unchecked, depending on how you last used them. This is a handy enhancement, since it's not too hard to forget to check or uncheck one of these buttons when you're in the middle of importing a lot of text files.

Kern pairs that include spaces are allowed

You can now specify kerning pairs that consist of a character and a spaceband or en space using the Kern/Track Editor. These pairs are used just like other kerning pairs. To enter an en space in the Pair field of the Kerning Values dialog box, you must first enter the space in a QuarkXPress text box, copy it, and then paste it into the field.

TIP A new Kern/Track Editor came with version 3.3. Make sure that you're using it if you need to access this feature. The Kern/Track Editor can be placed in either the same folder as QuarkXPress or in the XTension folder that the QuarkXPress 3.3 installer (or updater) creates inside your QuarkXPress folder.

Page layout

New Document Layout palette

The Document Layout palette was revamped (again) in this latest version of QuarkXPress. There's lots to like in this latest incarnation, shown in Figure B.3. You can now apply a master page to a single document page in the palette in either of two ways. First, the "3.1 way": Drag the master page icon over the document page icon and

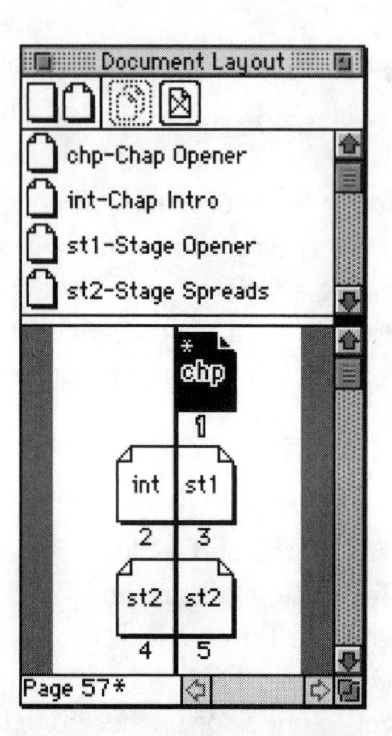

Figure B.3 Document Layout palette The 3.3 version of this palette offers a combination of the features that were available independently in versions 3.1 and 3.2.

release it once the document page icon is highlighted. Second, the "3.2 way": Highlight a document page icon in the palette, hold down the Option key, and select the desired master page. Both methods can be used to replace one master page with another.

TIP If you want to apply the same master page to more than one document page, you can do so by selecting ranges of contiguous or noncontiguous pages before holding down the Option key and selecting the desired master page. To select contiguous document pages in the Document Layout palette, select the first page in the range, hold down the Shift key, and select the last page in the range. All pages between the first and last in the range will be selected, also. To select noncontiguous pages, select one page and then hold down the Command key while clicking on one or more other pages. Only pages explicitly selected will be included in the noncontiguous range.

Two new buttons at the top of the Document Layout palette replace the words DUPLICATE and DELETE that were present in version 3.2. They enable you to copy and delete selected document and master pages. To make a duplicate of a master page, select the icon for a master page that you want to duplicate and click the first button (the overlapping pages). This option is available only when you have the icon for a master page selected. To delete a document or master page, select the icon of the page you want to delete and click the second button (the page with an X through it). An alert is displayed that asks you to confirm the deletion. To avoid the alert, hold down the Option key before clicking on the delete icon.

The area in the lower left corner of the palette displays the folio (printed page number) of the document page whose icon is selected in the palette. This marks the return of a much-loved feature, available prior to version 3.2 but mysteriously removed from that version. With this feature, you no longer have to display a document page in order to know its folio. This saves a lot of time when you want to use the palette to navigate around a document. If you click in the folio display while a document page icon is selected in the palette, the **Page→Section** dialog box will immediately open.

To move to a page via the Document Layout palette, you can either double-click on the page's icon or single-click on the small number that's under the page icon—your choice.

Variable-shaped text boxes

You can now create text boxes in any of five standard shapes plus polygons (Figure B.4). To create a variable-shaped text box, first create a rectangular text box as usual. With the text box active, choose any of the shape options from the **Item→Box Shape** submenu. To create a polygon text box, choose the polygon option from the submenu. To reshape the polygon text box, make sure that the **Item→Reshape Polygon** command is checked. Note that the controls in the Vertical Alignment area of the **Item→Modify** dialog box are not available for variable-shaped text boxes. Polygon-shaped text boxes behave just like polygon picture boxes; handles and line segments can be added, deleted, or moved.

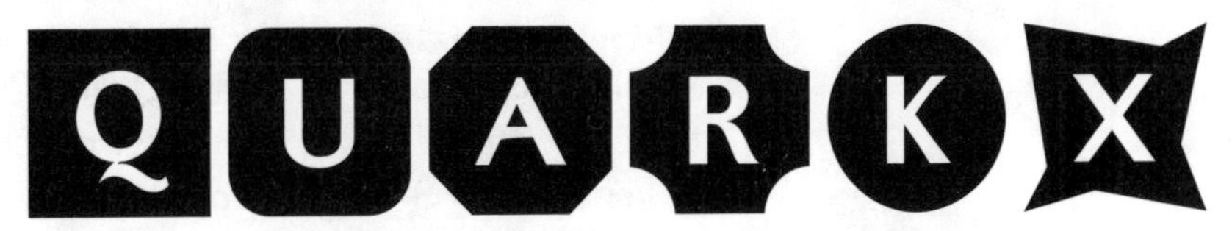

Figure B.4 New text box shapes These are the six shapes now available for text boxes. Each of the letters is in its own text box.

Multiple-item deletions can be undone

QuarkXPress 3.3 allows you to undo the deletion of any group or multiple-selected items. There are two things to watch out for, though. When the deleted items contain a text box that was part of a linked chain—but not every text box in the chain was deleted—the links to and from the deleted text box will be lost when the deletion is undone. Also, layering relationships will be lost when items from different layers are deleted simultaneously; undoing such a deletion places all the deleted items one layer below the layer that the topmost deleted item came from.

Items can be deselected from the keyboard

If you have one or more items selected, they can be deselected by pressing the Tab key—but only if the Item tool is chosen. This is especially nice for those times that you have guides turned off and would like to see what a page looks like without the framing effect caused by selected text and graphics boxes. No more searching for a piece of the pasteboard on which to click, in other words. And don't forget that it you have just one item selected with the Content tool, a quick press of the Command, Shift, and Tab keys will get you to the Item tool, from which you can hit the Tab key to deselect the one item. On extended keyboards, Shift–F8 also toggles between the Item and Content tools.

Graphics

EPS spot colors are automatically added

When you import an EPS (Encapsulated PostScript) picture that contains spot colors not already defined in the document, Quark XPress 3.3 automatically adds the colors to the **Edit→Colors** dialog box and the Colors palette. These colors will also be displayed in the Plate pop-up menu in the **File→Print** dialog box. If you edit the name of a color created this way, the program will not be able to separate the renamed color onto the correct plate when printing separations. The name of the QuarkXPress color and the name of the color stored in the EPS must match exactly. To prevent colors in imported EPS images from being being created in a document, hold down the Command key as you click Open in the **File→Get Picture** dialog box.

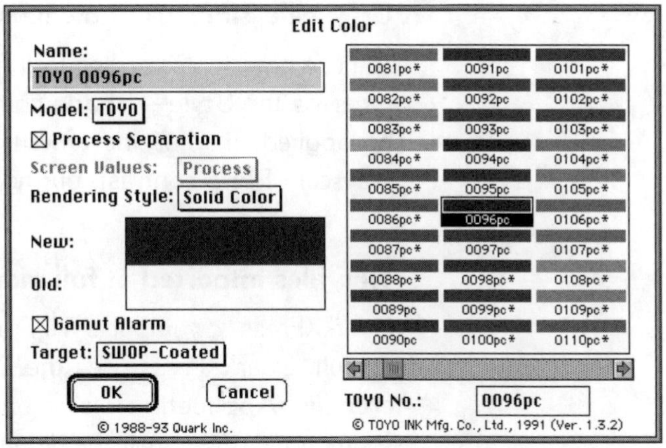

Figure B.5 Toyo spot colors A Toyo color is shown in a head on the color plates.

Toyo and DIC spot color models added

Two new spot color models, Toyo and DIC, have been added to the Model pop-up menu in the **Edit→Colors** dialog box (Figures B.5 and B.6). These are both Japanese color matching systems, and are used the same as any of the PANTONE, TRUMATCH, OR FOCOLTONE matching systems already included in the program. An asterisk next to a Toyo or DIC color name is supposed to indicate that the color preview seen on screen won't exactly match the actual printed color. Two asterisks—in the case of metallic colors, for example—indicate that the screen preview is significantly different from the printed color.

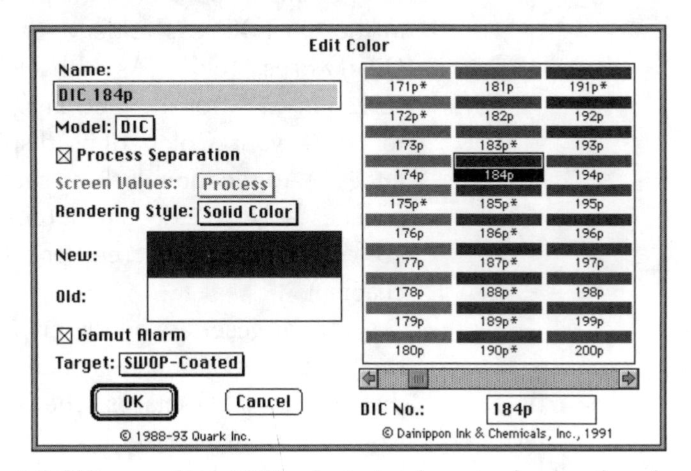

Figure B.6 DIC spot colors A DIC color is also shown in a head on the color plates.

Grayscale TIFFs can now be shaded

You can now apply shading to the gray elements of grayscale TIFF pictures via the **Style→Shade** command. Shades from 0% to 100% can be applied, in 0.1% increments. Prior to 3.3, you could adjust a grayscale TIFF's contrast, but not its shade.

TIFF files imported at full monitor resolution

QuarkXPress 3.3 imports TIFF images at full monitor resolution by default. QuarkXPress uses the Display DPI value in the **Edit→Preference→Application** dialog box as the default monitor resolution. To import a TIFF at half the default resolution, hold down the Shift key while importing it.

JPEG images can now be imported into QuarkXPress

The JPEG filter enables you to import graphics files saved in the JPEG (Joint Photographic Experts Group) format. Several image-editing applications, such as Adobe Photoshop, can generate JPEG files. Color clip art is also starting to be distributed more and more in this format. JPEG is a "lossy" compression standard, meaning that it intelligently (one hopes) loses image detail in order to compress files at a much higher rate than the traditional "lossless" compression utilities, such as Compact Pro.

To import JPEG files, the JPEG Import XTension must be present in the QuarkXPress folder—or in the XTension folder inside the QuarkXPress folder. As with TIFF images, QuarkXPress creates a screen preview for the JPEG image as it's being imported, so be sure to check your Color TIFFs display preference in **Edit→Preferences→Application**. If that's set at 32-bit, you might end up with an unnecessarily large document (due to the fact that QuarkXPress does not compress 32-bit screen previews, as discussed in the **Graphics** chapter).

All imagesetters and laser printers—whether they're based on PostScript level 1 or 2—should be able to output QuarkXPress files that contain JPEG images. The XTension is "required," though; files won't run from your service bureau's machines, for example, unless the XTension is loaded.

TIP QuarkXPress can now locate and run XTensions that are stored in the XTension folder within your program folder. This folder is created automatically when you install QuarkXPress 3.3. You can still leave XTensions loose in your QuarkXPress folder, but you should store any XTensions that you don't want to run in a subfolder with any name other than XTension.

PCX images can also be imported into QuarkXPress

The PCX Filter enables you to import graphics files saved in the bitmap-based PCX format used by many PC-based applications.

Output

Enhanced PDF/PPD Support

QuarkXPress now supports PPDs (PostScript Printer Descriptions, version 4.0 or greater) in much the same way that it supports PDFs (Printer Description Files). PDFs and PPDs contain PostScript printer-specific information that QuarkXPress uses to output pages correctly. PDFs can contain more information than PPDs, such as dot-gain calibration information. If you have both a PDF and a PPD for the same printer, QuarkXPress will always use the PDF.

QuarkXPress looks for PDFs in the PDF folder within the program folder, and in the QuarkXPress folder itself. The program looks for PPDs in the Printer Descriptions folder in the System folder, as well as a PPD folder in the program folder. Under System 7.x, the Printer Descriptions folder is contained in the Extensions folder within the System folder; you should store PPDs there so they are available to other applications. At startup, QuarkXPress reads the information from a PPD or PDF and adds the printer name specified in the file to the Printer Type pop-up menu in the **File→Page Setup** dialog box.

QuarkXPress now contains only three built-in PDFs, which are listed in the Printer Type pop-up menu. They are Generic B&W, Generic Color, and Generic Imagesetter. Use one of these new generic options if there is no specific PDF for your output device. PDFs for all printer types built into previous versions are automatically installed in the PDF folder.

OPI 1.3

QuarkXPress 3.3 generates OPI (Open Prepress Interface) comments with the most recently published specification, version 1.3.

Scripting

New scripting capabilities

QuarkXPress 3.3 comes with a couple of addendums to the scripting documentation. You should print these pages and insert them in the appropriate place in the documentation that came with version 3.2. One exciting addition to the QuarkXPress object model is the print record. This record contains all of the settings found in the Page Setup and Print dialogs, thus giving Apple events scripts full control over QuarkXPress printing. Before this addition, scripts could only print documents with the default Page Setup and Print settings.

Undocumented features

View-sensitive guides

This feature is not really new with version 3.3, but I just learned about it. If you hold down the Shift key when you drag a guide from a ruler and place it on a page, that guide will only be visible when viewing the page at or above the viewing percentage that was in effect when the guide was created. This means that you could create a set of guides that only appear when you zoom in on a page. You could make a main set of guides that is viewable at Actual Size or above, as well as subsets of guides that appear at only larger views. The Snap to Guides feature—which works whether guides are shown or hidden—will work only on guides that are usually viewable at the current view size.

Increasing system heap to avoid crashes

This is hardly a feature, of course, but I wanted to make sure to mention it somewhere in the book. One trick that cures a lot of Quark XPress crashes is to increase your system heap allocation. One of the preferences in the Startup Manager utility that is part of Now Utilities can do this, as can a free utility called Bootman, which is included on this book's disk. Crashes due to system heap problems are not really QuarkXPress' fault; it's more the fault of the way the system works.

The QuickDraw toolbox uses temporary memory to do its job, and that memory comes out of the system heap. The application making the QuickDraw calls—in this case, QuarkXPress—has no control over or knowledge of this system heap usage. The theory is that QuarkXPress, being an exceedingly heavy user of QuickDraw, is requiring lots of extra system heap to avoid crashing due to QuickDraw internal failures for lack of memory.

Appendix C: XPress Tags, Xtags, and ProTagsXT

Code-based typesetting has been around for ages, and anyone who has worked at a type shop will be familiar with its use. Those of you with experience in only WYSIWYG systems—or layout boards—may find the following codes daunting at first. I encourage everyone to at least skim these pages in order to see the formatting power available to QuarkXPress users.

For starters, you may find one or two codes that will greatly speed up your production workflow. For example, if you find yourself manually re-italicizing words and phrases after word processing files have been brought into QuarkXPress, you might be able to use some of the utilities discussed in the **Automating DTP** chapter—in conjunction with XPress Tags—to automate that process.

On the other hand, you may be an avid XPress Tags user already, so much so that you find yourself stretching XPress Tags to their limits. In that case, please take a look at the tags available through the use of two XTensions: Chris Ryland's Xtags and Bob Shevlin's ProTagsXT. These XTensions have their individual strengths, but both strongly enhance the XPress Tags coding language.

Whether using Quark's XPress Tags, Xtags, or ProTagsXT, the tags shown below will need to be added to plain text files; the codes are only interpreted when the text files are imported into a Quark XPress document.

XPress Tags

The industry-standard ASCII file exchange format makes it possible to share text among different computer systems and programs. Text entered on a dedicated word processing system, for example, can be saved as ASCII text and imported into other programs running on different computer systems. QuarkXPress can import and save text in the ASCII file format, enabling you to exchange text with many different programs.

The ASCII format does not support character attributes or paragraph formats. However, the XPress Tags XTension included with QuarkXPress enables you to import and export character attribute and paragraph format information with ASCII text. When entering text in another program, you can include XPress Tag codes that specify attributes and formats. When you import an ASCII file with embedded XPress Tag codes into QuarkXPress, the program translates the codes and converts them to actual character attributes and paragraph formats.

QuarkXPress also enables you to embed XPress Tag codes in saved text automatically. When you save text, QuarkXPress gives you the option of saving it with XPress Tag codes or as plain ASCII text without any coding information. XPress Tag codes enable you to specify in ASCII text all the character attributes and paragraph formats available in QuarkXPress. Only QuarkXPress can convert XPress Tag codes.

Generating tagged text in a word processor

To include XPress Tag coding information in a text file you generate using another program, precede the text with the codes you want. Save the text you generate in the ASCII file format. If an XPress Tag code specifies a paragraph format, you must enter the code at the beginning of the paragraph. Codes that specify only character attributes should immediately precede the text to which you want to apply them.

All XPress Tag–formatted files must have a version tag as the first thing in the file. Use version 1.7 for 3.3 files; for example, <V1.7>. An XPress Tag code must begin with a left angle bracket (<) and end with a right angle bracket (>). For example, the XPress Tag code for bold text is <B>.

You can combine codes by entering more than one code between the angle brackets. For example, the code for bold italic text can be <BI>. Separate <B> and <I> commands can be used, too.

Generating tagged text in QuarkXPress

To include character attribute and paragraph format information as embedded XPress Tag codes automatically when you save Quark

XPress text as a text file, choose XPress Tags from the Format pop-up menu in the **File→Save Text** dialog box. The XPress Tags Filter must be in the QuarkXPress folder (or in the XTension folder in the QuarkXPress folder, starting with version 3.3) when you start up the program for it to be available in the Format pop-up menu. Use the controls in the Save Text dialog box to name the ASCII text file you create and to specify the volume and folder in which you want to save it.

To import an ASCII text file that contains embedded XPress Tag codes into a QuarkXPress document, choose **File→Get Text**. To convert XPress Tag codes into actual character attributes and paragraph formats, check Include Style Sheets in the Get Text dialog. If you don't check Include Style Sheets in the Get Text dialog before importing tagged text, QuarkXPress will not convert XPress Tag codes to character attributes and paragraph formats. Instead, the program imports the codes as text characters. The imported text takes on the attributes and formats of the text insertion point when you import the text.

Character Attributes

As mentioned, XPress Tag codes for character attributes must be placed immediately preceding the characters to which you want to apply the attributes. When you apply a character attribute using an XPress Tag code, the attribute remains in effect until you disable it or until you apply a different style sheet. You can cancel an attribute by respecifying its code following the last character to which you want it applied or by entering the code for plain text, <P>. This is the list of type style codes:

<P> Plain
<B> Bold
<I> Italic
<O> Outline
<S> Shadow
<U> Underline
<W> Word Underline

</> Strikethru
<K> All Caps
<H> Small Caps
<+> Superscript
<-> Subscript
<V> Superior
<$> Use type style of current style sheet

When any of the following commands are followed by a $ (for example, <f$>), the attributes are set to the values specified in the current style sheet. If a style sheet is not currently applied, the Normal style sheet is used. A # character in this list indicates a numeric value.

<f"font name">	Change text font
<z###.##>	Change text font size (in points)
<c"color name">	Change text color
<cC>	Change text color to cyan
<cM>	Change text color to magenta
<cY>	Change text color to yellow
<cK>	Change text color to black
<cW>	Change text color to white
<s###>	Change text Shade (in percentage of shade)
<h###>	Horizontally scale text (in percentage of scale)
<y###>	Vertically scale text (in percentage of scale)
<k###.##>	Kern the next two characters (in 1/200 em space)
<t###.##>	Track the text that follows until another Track command (in 1/200 em space)
<b###.##>	Set Baseline Shift (in points); preceding the value with a hyphen will produce a downward shift

Paragraph Formats

XPress Tag codes for paragraph formats must be placed at the beginning of a paragraph. Formats specified by XPress Tag codes remain applied until you specify other values at the beginning of a subsequent paragraph or until you apply a different style sheet. These are the paragraph alignment commands:

<*L>	Left-align paragraph
<*C>	Center-align paragraph
<*R>	Right-align paragraph
<*J>	Justify paragraph
<*F>	Force Justify paragraph

If a $ replaces any or all format codes in the next two commands (for example, <*t$>), the current style sheet values are used. All numeric values in these two commands are measured in points.

<*t(##.#,#,"character")>
Set tab stops (position, alignment, fill character) e.g., <*t(36,1,".")>

<*p(##.#,##.#,##.#,##.#,##.#,##.#,G or g>
Set paragraph formats (left indent, first line indent, right indent, leading, space before, space after, lock to baseline grid (G = lock to baseline grid, g = do not lock to baseline grid), for example, <*p(18,0,18,12,9,9,g>.

<*h"specification name">
Set Hyphenation & Justification style

To specify one of the first four alignment options (Left, Center, Right, or Decimal) from the Alignment pop-up menu in the Paragraph Tabs dialog box (Style menu), enter the number that corresponds to the alignment option in the pop-up menu: 0 = Left, 1 = Center, 2 = Right, 3 = Decimal. For example, the codes to specify a right tab stop 72 points from the left indent with a dot leader would look like this: <*t(72,2,".")>. For the remaining two options: "," = Comma, and "any single printing character" = Align On. (For example, "/" would specify alignment on the "/" character.)

Any or all of the format codes for the commands Rule Above, Rule Below, Drop Caps, and Keep Together can be replaced by a **$** to use the current style sheet's definition, or by a 0 (zero) to specify no rule (for example, <*ra$> and <*ra0>).

<*ra(##,#,"color name","#,##,##,## or ##%)>
Paragraph rule above (width, style, "color name", shade, from left, from right, offset)

<*rb(##,#,"color name","#,##,##,## or ##%)>
Paragraph rule below (width, style, "color name", shade, from left, from right, offset)

<*d(character count, line count)>
Drop cap

<*kn1> or <*kn0>
Keep with Next ¶ (1 = keep with next, 0 = don't keep with next)

<*kt(A)> or <*kt(#,#)>
Keep Together (A = all; #,# = start line number, end line number)

Special Characters

Placing a ! before the hyphen or any of the space commands in this group (Standard, En/figure, Punctuation, Flex) makes the hyphen or space nonbreaking (for example, <\!s>).

<\n>	Return
<\d>	Discretionary new line
<\->	Hyphen
<\h>	Discretionary hyphen
<\i>	Indent here
<\t>	Right indent tab
<\s>	Standard space
<\f>	En/figure space
<\p>	Punctuation space
<\q>	Flex space
<\h>	Discretionary hyphen
<\2>	Previous text box number character
<\3>	Current text box number character
<\4>	Next Page text box number character
<\c>	New column
<\b>	New box

In the following command, the "#" symbol is part of the code. Placing a "!" before the command makes the character nonbreaking.

<\#decimal val**>**	Decimal ASCII code for a character

One of the following three extended character set indicators is automatically placed at the top of an XPress Tags file you create using the Save Text command (File menu).

<e0>	Macintosh character set
<e1>	Windows DTP character set
<e2>	ISO Latin 1 character set

To use as text certain characters that XPress Tags would otherwise consider to be part of specific codes, use the following special characters:

Code	Character
<\@>	@
<\<>	<
<\>>	>
<\\>	\

Style Sheet Definition

For XPress Tag code commands that enable you to specify more than one value (for example, paragraph formats), you can enter a **$** in place of an actual value. When QuarkXPress encounters a **$** code, the program will substitute the value specified in the currently applied style sheet. (If no style sheet is currently applied, the value of the Normal style sheet is used.) For example, you may want a paragraph to contain all the formats specified in the applied style sheet, but you want to apply 18 points of leading instead of the value specified in the style sheet. The code for this would be <*p(**$**,**$**,**$**,18,**$**,**$**,**$**)>.

To apply the Normal style sheet (whose attributes are defined in the QuarkXPress document) to paragraphs, begin the first paragraph to which you want to apply it with the code "@**$**:". To specify that a specific style sheet be applied to paragraphs, begin the first paragraph to which you want to apply it with the code "@StyleName:". To specify that no style sheet be applied to paragraphs, begin the first paragraph you want to disassociate from any style sheet with the code "@:".

When you are specifying a style sheet for a paragraph, you have the option of basing that style sheet on another, existing style sheet. The code for this is "@stylesheetname=[s"based on name"]definition of style sheet." When you apply a style sheet to a paragraph using XPress Tags, the style sheet remains applied to subsequent paragraphs until another style sheet is applied or until No Style is applied using the code "@:".

You can apply attributes to characters within a paragraph to which you have applied a style sheet. These attributes remain applied until you cancel them or until you apply a different style sheet. You can define a style sheet's character attributes and paragraph formats using XPress Tag codes. To define a style sheet using XPress Tag codes, begin the first paragraph to which you want to apply it with the code "@StyleName=<paragraph format and character attribute codes>".

If you import text tagged with style sheet names that the Quark XPress document already contains, the program automatically applies the character attributes and paragraph formats specified in their style sheets. The following characters cannot be used in style sheet names: ", :, =, and @.

You can override a character attribute or paragraph format applied via a style sheet at any time. If you do so, you can then use a **$** to revert to the style sheet's assigned value. If no user-defined style sheet is applied, the value contained in the Normal style sheet is used.

XPress Tags Guidelines

Font names, style sheet names, or colors must be single words when you specify them using XPress Tag codes. Names you specify as XPress Tag codes must be preceded and terminated by a ditto mark (") character. Typesetter's quotation marks will cause errors. For example, if you want to specify the font Palatino, use the code <f"Palatino">.

To enter an XPress Tag code sequence on multiple lines, enter a colon followed by a Return where you want the line to break. You cannot split an individual code with a colon and Return; you must split code sequences between individual codes.

When specifying a font using style tag codes, you can enter a partial font name within the code (for example, you can enter helv to specify the font Helvetica). When QuarkXPress applies a font to imported text per the XPress Tag code you specify, the program will apply the first font in the Font submenu whose name matches the characters you specified in the XPress Tag code.

Colors and H & J specifications must be defined within the QuarkXPress document before you import tagged text that specifies them. If you specify a color name using an XPress Tag code and QuarkXPress cannot locate it in the document's color list, it is replaced with the color Black. If you specify an H & J specification as an XPress Tag and QuarkXPress cannot locate it in the document's list of H&J specifications, the Standard H & J specification is substituted. The maximum length for style sheet, H & J specification, or color names is 63 characters.

Style Tags

Prior to QuarkXPress 3.0, QuarkXPress employed style tags to embed character attributes and paragraph formats. It used a Style Tags filter. If you have files containing text saved with style tags, you can use the Style Tags filter that came with your copy of QuarkXPress 3.1 to import that text. As of version 3.2, QuarkXPress no longer ships with a Style Tags Filter.

If you have text saved with style tags that you use regularly, you should import them into a QuarkXPress document and then resave the text using XPress Tags. When you import or export tagged text, be sure that only one of these filters (Style Tags or XPress Tags) is active (that is, in the same folder as your QuarkXPress program) at any time. Store the other filter in a subfolder within your QuarkXPress program folder. Otherwise, text may not import or export correctly.

Xtags

Xtags provides an enhanced version of the XPress Tags language supported by QuarkXPress. Both XPress Tags and Xtags allow you to import plain text files into QuarkXPress as fully formatted text, using special formatting codes embedded in the text files. Xtags supports all XPress Tags constructs and also provides several new tags, enabling you to:

- Create and fill anchored text and picture boxes
- Apply master pages
- Translate user-defined tags into standard Xtags constructs (or into anything else, as this is a general translation facility)

Xtags further provides an optional error-reporting facility; in any case, at each error, it forges ahead as best it can, unlike XPress Tags (which stops at the first sign of trouble). Xtags was discussed at length in the **Automating DTP** chapter, and there's a demo version of this XTension on the disk in the back of the book.

Anchored box tags

These commands can be used to create anchored boxes automatically while text files are being imported into QuarkXPress. Anchored text boxes can be filled with the appropriate text, and anchored picture boxes can be made to import their pictures automatically. Although each command has a lot of parameters, Xtags provides very logical defaults and allows you to type only a comma when a parameter's default is to your liking. And you don't have to fill in a bunch of commas at the end of the command; they can be left off once you've filled in all of your custom parameters. Here are both the text box and picture box commands, with all of their parameters.

<&tb(width, height, text align, frame width, frame color, frame shade, frame style, background color, background shade, text outset, columns, gutter, text inset, baseline offset, baseline minimum, vertical alignment, interparagraph maximum**)>**...Text to be placed in the box, normally containing other tags... **<&te>**

<&pb(width, height, text align, frame width, frame color, frame shade, frame style, background color, background shade, text outset, placement, horizontal scale, vertical scale, horizontal offset, vertical offset, angle, skew, picture, pathname**)>**

Master page tags

<&m"masterpage"**>**

<&mf"masterpage"**>**

The Xtags codes <&mf___> and <&m___> allow you to apply specific master pages—either by name or number—while text is being imported into a document. I usually add the command right before major heads that signify a change of page style. The command parameter is either the number of the master page (A = 1, B = 2, etc.) or the name of the master page, as typed in the Document Layout palette.

If more than one <&mf command falls on a page, the first one is used; if more than one <&m command falls on a page, the last one is used. And if one or more of each of the commands falls on a page, the last <&m command is the one used to apply a master page.

Translation tags

<&tt2"table name"**>**

Xtags can perform translations on text files when importing them.

It's limited to simple, literal translations: no masks, wildstring modifiers, or any of that. But there's no practical limit to the number of translations you can perform with Xtags. The "table name" parameter signifies the name of the text file which contains your translation strings.

XPress tags enhancements

Xtags enhances XPress Tags in a number of ways, including letting you specify relative values for some of the character styles. Instead of using the XPress Tags code "<z12>" to change text size to 12 points, you could use the Xtags code "<z(.+2)>" to increase the current text size by 2 points. This allows for much more flexibility in coding, since the same translation could conceivably be used for every occurrence of a particular word or phrase, regardless of its surrounding text.

Relative values can also be used for text shading, tracking, and scaling. In addition to adding relative values, you can decrease them (<s(.-20>)>), multiply them (<t(.*3>)>), and divide them (<h(./2>)>).

Other nice enhancements that Xtags adds to XPress tags include the ability to omit parameters and use spaces within long command constructs, as well as use whatever numbering system you want. For example, the XPress Tags paragraph command has seven parameters, making it one of the hardest to create and debug. The XPress Tags command <*p(132,24,0,14,0,0,g)> can be simplified to the Xtags command <*p(11p, 2p, , 14)>.

Xtags also allows you to use style sheet callouts to apply character formatting to partial paragraphs. I often need to style run-in heads in a typeface, point size, and style that's different from the remainder of the paragraph. If I import my text files into QuarkXPress using Xtags, I can type "@run:" at the start of a paragraph, followed by the run-in head, then the style sheet needed for the rest of the paragraph, such as "@text:." The run-in head will have the character styles of the style sheet named "run," while the rest of the paragraph will have the character and paragraph attributes of "text."

ProTagsXT

ProTagsXT is an enhanced version of XPress tags. It supports all of the importing features of XPress Tags and has more than 60 additional tag commands. ProTagsXT is a shareware XTension, and it's supported on CompuServe's Desktop Publishing Forum (GO DTPFORUM). Pro-

TagsXT also includes merge tags which allow for the merging of text with preset control data.

With ProTagsXT it is possible to create and perform all of the item modifications on boxes and lines including their shading, color, framing, sizing, orientation, and positioning. The following information is extracted from the documentation that comes with the XTension; the XTension and its documentation can be found on the disk in the back of this book, along with some sample files. You certainly won't be able to use ProTagsXT from reading the following lists of commands, but I hope that they serve as a printed reference for you if you choose to take advantage of this shareware XTension.

ProTagsXT Terminology

Tag An import command embedded within character delimiters. Some Tags may be appended within the same <>.

Box A standard QuarkXPress item.

Line A standard QuarkXPress item.

ID Box Stored parameters for creating boxes. 120 maximum per Grid.

Segment Subdivisions of an ID Box, which define starting and ending points for lines and boxes. 60 maximum per Grid.

Grid An array of Boxes and Lines as a single entity and addressed by a common Label.

Label An addressable name given to a Grid.

Text All imported ASCII data not delimited by <>. It will be flowed into the last created Box.

Horizontal Orientation of ID Box.

Vertical Orientation of ID Box.

Depth y dimension of Horizontal ID Box; x dimension of Vertical ID Box.

Boxes are standard QuarkXPress boxes and may be generated relative to a main text box, relative to the last box generated, or relative to a prior grid row or column. Grids can be predesigned by tags or specified by a setup table under ProTagsXT menu items. If Pro-

TagsXT is used with ProTabsXT, the setup capabilities of ProTabsXT may be used.

Standard QuarkXPress Lines may be generated with all the capabilities available from the QuarkXPress menus and dialog boxes. As with Boxes, Lines may be generated with respect to the main text box or relative to column and row specified points. QuarkXPress documents that have text boxes labeled by ProTagsXT or ProTabsXT can be addressed by tags, and further tag operations will be directed to that labeled text box. Several tags can be used as left/right page sensitive, adding logic capability to ProTagsXT.

Linked Text boxes in a QuarkXPress document can have boxes overflow from one linked box to another. Head Rows and columns from the prior linked box may be replayed at the start of the linked box. Running boxes may be appended to the starting data so that the last visible running box may be at the head of the linked page. 2000 tag characters may be saved in a buffer for processing at the end of the box that oversets. This storage makes it possible to justify the total grid within the page text box boundaries (see **<Tj>**).

Head Tag

<THProTags> This tag is required at the start of the file selected with Get Text in QuarkXPress.

Label Tag

<TLanyLabel> This tag addresses a labeled box within a Quark XPress Document. <TL> with no label is used to indicate the end of ProTagsXT importation.

Immediate/Global Tags

<TRT> This tag causes all box tags to be limited in scope in the current box.

<TRF> This tag causes all box tags to be effective on all subsequent boxes until terminated by a subsequent <TRT> tag.

Box Generation Tags

Note that depth always refers to the variable dimension (initial value) of either a Row (horizontal) or Column (vertical). It usually is the narrower of the box dimensions.

<TAn> Set Box Runaround in current box. This must follow a <TB...> command.

<Tan,v> Add variable expansion to ID Box n. v = points.

<Ta,v> Add variable expansion to current ID Box. v = points.

<Tbn> This tag calls for predefined box row or column parameters. These are parameters that are set using ProTagsXT setup menu selections or execution of tags that set or modify row or column parameters. The Orientation of the box determines whether it is a row (Horizontal <Th>) or a column (Vertical<Tv>). This command cannot be combined with others and must precede the generation of text boxes in a new row (horizontal Orientation) or column (vertical Orientation). <Tb> advances to the next sequential row or column.

<TDn,w> Set ID box Variable dimension to w. If n = Blank then ID Box = Current.

<Tgn,v> Set gap before box n. If n blank then before current box.

<Tkfn> Set all Boxes generated with ID Box n to be of fixed Depth. If n is missing then current ID Box is set.

<Tkvn> Set all Boxes generated with ID Box n to be of Variable depth. If n is missing then current ID Box is set.

<TDn,w> Set initial depth of ID Box n to value w.

<Thn> Set ID Box n to Horizontal Orientation. If <Th>, then current box is affected.

<Tin> This tag sets initial segment to start next box generation.

<TKv> Set Box Skew. v = percent.

<Tkfi> Set BoxID i to Fixed.

<Tkvi> Set BoxID i to Variable.

<Tkf> Set Current ID Box to fixed depth.

<Tkv> Set Current ID Box to variable depth.

<Tln> Set Box Lock.

<TVn> Set Box ID n to variable depth.

<Ten> This tag sets the number of segments that the next generated box will contain. See ProTagsXT setup and <Tw...> command for setting segment values.

<TE> This tag executes the generation of a box to the initial values set by prior tags.

<Tb><Tkv><Th><TD,10><Ti0Te2TE> This series of tags would create a Row (horizontal) box starting at the beginning of the row and extending over segments 1 and 2 with an initial depth of 10 points. Subsequent data would be set in this box and it would grow vertically to contain the data.

<TBiXnHwXdXcT> Identifies Row in Labeled Box and number of segments to Straddle. The Number of Segments starts at the last segment. If the Row Identifier is different than the last, the Starting Segment is Set to 0. X is terminator for Sequential Strings. i = Box ID (Box contains only Dimensions). n = Number of segments to generate a Box over. H = Orientation (can be H or V). w = weight of Border (0 = No border). d = Shade of Box (Percentage). c = color of Box (Menu Position). T = alignment of Text Within Box (can be T, C, B, or J).

<Tfl,t,w,d,p> Create Fixed Box. l = left edge, t = top edge, w = width, d = depth, p = optional entry for left right page control.

Box Attribute Tags

<*j> Box Align justify

<*T> Box Align top

<*B> Box Align bottom

<*c> Box Align center

<TC"color"> This selects a Frame Border Color

<Tc"color"> Set Box Color

<TGv> Set Gutter value for current box (v = points)

<TIv> Set Current Box Inset (v = points)

<TOv> Set Box Angle (v = angle in degrees)

<Ton> Set number of columns in current Box (n = column count)

<TSv> Set Frame Shade (v = percent, including fractions)

<Tsv> Set box Shading (v = percent)

<TTv> Set Frame Thickness (v = points and fractions of a point)

<Ttn> Sets Background of Box to be Opaque or Translucent

<TYn> Set Frame Style (n = valid position number under Item Menu)

Line Generation Tags

<TNFh1,v1,h2,v2> Sets a Fixed Line length and position (values are points with respect to labeled Box; h1 = horizontal start; v1 = vertical start; h2 = horizontal end; v2 = vertical end)

<TNVs,w> Sets a Rule of line length of cumulative length of variable boxes, with position starting at end of current box and at segments (w = weight of rule). Current values for color shade, width, background color and runaround are used.

Line Attributes Tags

<Tdv> Set Line shade

<Tnc> Set Line noncolor c

<Trn> Set current Line color

<TWv> Set Line thickness

Document Tags

<TFw> Set Expand Value per new line (w = expand value). Default = current point size p = r = right pages = odd pages.

<TJ> Set to expand boxes that are overset.

<Tj> Expand variable boxes to fit main box.

<TManyLabel> anyLabel identifies a command file to merge with the import text that contains this command. The file anyLabel will be accessed immediately if it is in the folder ProTags, which should be a subfolder of the QuarkXPress folder. If it is not there, an Open dialog box will be presented to the user to select the appropriate file. All further data will come from that file until it encounters a <Tmt> command, at which point control will revert to the import text file—until a <Tmc> command switches it back to the command file. If anylabel is blank then this is a single file merge and this is the first call to text.

<Tmc> Revert control to the command file selected with a <TM...> command. This command must reside in an import text file or text portion of single file.

<Tmt> Revert control to the import text file. This command must reside in a command file that was called with a <TM...> command from the same import text file or the command portion of a single file.

<TPa> Append Text up to <TPe> to Prior <TPb> or <TPs>. Prior Append is overwritten.

<TPb> Save Text being Processed for overflow head.

<TPe> End saving of Text.

<TPs> Save Text but do not process until overflow and start of linked box.

<TPsb> Save Text but do not process until overflow and end of current linked box.

<Tuf> Reset Unlinking of Boxes.

<Tut> Unlink boxes when grids overflow from one box to another.

<Tvn> Set Box ID n to Vertical Orientation.

<Twn,w,v,v,v,v,...> Set Segment Width Values. Can be used instead of Tab Setup. If v < 10 it is considered a variable and will be computed by remaining width after subtracting Fixed Values. There can be up to 60 values set. n = number of segments in box ID, w = Grid width.

<TXw1,w2,p> Starting dimensions for relative boxes (w1 = Y or depth; w2 = x or Width; p is optional and is used to select only l (left) or r (right) pages for this command.

<Txi,p> Starting ID for Relative Boxes. p is optional and is used to select only l (left) or r (right) pages for this command. If i is absent then the current Box ID will be used. p = optional right left page selection. l = left pages (even), r = right pages (odd).

ProTagsXT demonstration

The examples included with the ProTagsXT demonstration consist of pairs of files that are used together to create a complete QuarkXPress document. Some pairs required linked text boxes for grids or tables that extend over more than one page.

To run each pair, open the QuarkXPress document and select the text box on page 1. Using the **File→Get Text** dialog, select the associated text file. You will notice that is of type TABX. The text will flow into the document and the table or grid will be created. Each of the text files are commented using the tag <TZ...>.

It is necessary to label the text boxes that tagged data is to flow into. This has been done in the associated QuarkXPress documents using the set rows and columns submenu item (under the ProTagsXT menu item, which is under the ProXT menu).

When creating your own text files with editors such as Teach Text or QUEDM (or any editor capable of generating an ASCII file), it will be necessary to change the file type using a resource tool such as ResEdit. Software XTensions will be releasing a utility to do this with version 1.1 of ProTagsXT.

The proper procedure for creating your own document pairs is to create your QuarkXPress document first, creating pages and text boxes. In each text box (for linked boxes, only the first) use the Protags Set Segments & ID Boxes menu item to bring up the Tag setup dialog box. Each Grid has two dimensions, Horizontal and Vertical.

Grid Boxes are individual boxes within the grid whose dimensions are controlled by an ID Box and segment values. ID Boxes may be Horizontally or Vertically Oriented. If the Orientation is Horizontal, then the depth dimension is vertical and may be variable. If the Orientation is Vertical then the depth dimension is horizontal and may be variable. Segments are created within ID Box Space. It is important to understand that both ID Boxes and Segments represent measurements only, and that the actual creation of boxes is controlled by tags. Examine the commented examples to see how various grids are generated.

Appendix D: Quark Authorized Training Consultants

The following pages contain a list of all of the Quark Authorized Training Consultants and Training Centers. They are sorted first by state, then by city, and finally by company name. To aid you in finding ATCs in your city, I've styled the city names in **bold**.

If you're looking for local support for QuarkXPress, including classroom or personal instruction, you may want to give one of these ATCs a call.

ALABAMA

MacAdvice
Terry Martin
2021 Trammell Chase Dr.
Birmingham, AL 35244
205-733-0079
FAX 205-733-8340

The Idea Source College
Chris Simpkins
PO Box 236
Mobile, AL 36601-0236
205-343-5011
FAX 205-452-4201

ALASKA

Computerland
Becky Landon
4240 Old Seward Hwy 7
Anchorage, AK 99503
907-561-5191
FAX 907-562-4151

ARIZONA

Computer Support Professionals
Michelle Peterson
5201 N. 7th St., #207
Phoenix, AZ 85014
602-285-0655
FAX 602-285-1425

Bowne of Phoenix, Inc.
Jerry Brown
2345 E. Thomas Rd., #100
Phoenix, AZ 85016
602-468-1012
FAX 602-957-1860

Pima Community College
Stephen Romaniello
1255 N. Stone Ave.
Tucson, AZ 85703-0027
602-884-6424
FAX 602-884-6201

The Art Center
Kirk Van Gilder
2525 N. Country Club Rd.
Tucson, AZ 85716
602-325-0123
FAX 602-325-5535

ARKANSAS

Complete Computing
Shawn Shuffield
400 West 7th
Little Rock, AR 72201-4212
501-372-3379
FAX 501-372-7832

CALIFORNIA

Elyse Chapman & Associates
Elyse Chapman
112 N. Harvard Ave., #300
Claremont, CA 91711-4716
909-621-0204
FAX 909-621-6535

Silicon Valley School of Computing
Lee Porter
780 Sea Spray Lane, #310
Foster City, CA 94404
415-341-6656
FAX 415-570-5098

Applied Graphics Technologies
Marie Pence
110 Marsh Dr., #105
Foster City, CA 94404
415-578-8333
FAX 415/578-0599

The Joule Group (dba Master Trainers' Consortium)
Jaye L. Towne
10428 Apache River Ave.
Fountain Valley, CA 92708
714-968-8902
FAX 714-963-3343

California State Univ., Fullerton
Jim Mavity
800 N. State College Blvd.
Fullerton, CA 92634
714-773-2797
FAX 714-339-7055

AlphaBet
Betty Marchese
318 E. Glenoaks Blvd., #101
Glendale, CA 91207-2012
818-246-5306
FAX 818-246-0425

Mountain View Press
Jerome W. Lilly
RR2 - Box 429; 19500 Skyline
LaHonda, CA 94020
415-851-2791

The Acacia Group
Jeff Kozuch
681 Mira Mar Ave.
Long Beach, CA 90814-1621
213-437-7690

Bradley Group
James Bradley
3603 Seneca Ave.
Los Angeles, CA 90039
213-953-0700
FAX 213-953-0800

RAPAX aka Action 2
John Feld
16644 Johnson Dr.
Los Angeles, CA 91745
818-855-1232
FAX 818-855-1240

Zerovnik & Company
Greg Zerovnik
4650 Arrow Hwy., Suite G-24
Montclair, CA 91763
714-625-6086
FAX 714-626-7794

Palo Alto Design, Inc.
Connie Veraldi
640 Waverley St.
Palo Alto, CA 94301
415-322-9675
FAX 415-322-0117

Synergy Computer Training
Ed Woodhull
225 South Lake Ave., Suite 401
Pasadena, CA 91101
818-356-0380
FAX 818-356-0283

The IconoClass
Mel Ryan-Roberts
2125 19th, #207
Sacramento, CA 95818
916-443-2527
FAX 916-443-2931

Platt College
Sharon Varley
6250 El Cajon Blvd.
San Diego, CA 92115
619-265-0107
FAX 619-265-8655

Photo Metro Magazine
Henry Brimmer
17 Tehama St.
San Francisco, CA 94105-3109
415-243-9917
FAX 415-243-9919

Automatrix
William Buckingham
530 Hampshire, #401
San Francisco, CA 94110
415-864-7592
FAX 415-864-7594

Landor Associates
Peter Mack
1001 Front St.
San Francisco, CA 94111
415-955-1400
FAX 415-956-5436

Ciber Training Service
Jill Pappenheimer
514 Bryant St.
San Francisco, CA 94107
415-974-7204
FAX 415-974-7140

Caldwell Communications
Donna Caldwell
15260 Dickens Ave.
San Jose, CA 95124
408-377-4618
FAX 408-879-0492

Mentor Training
Paul Switzer
2880 Zanker Rd., #205
San Jose, CA 95134
408-433-0990
FAX 408-267-7981

Mission College
Rhona Sturges
2261 Sunny Vista Dr.
San Jose, CA 95128
408-554-9436

Bay Area Computer Training
Ken Dickinson
4340 Redwood Hwy, D-311
San Rafael, CA 94903-2125
415-507-0384
FAX 415-507-0385

Tom Buhl Imaging Center
Tom Buhl
621 Chapala St., Suite A
Santa Barbara, CA 93101
805-963-8841
FAX 805-962-1314

Stieglitz Design
Carol Stieglitz
938 3rd St., #203
Santa Monica, CA 90403
213-395-5978
FAX 213-395-3008

Lee Jordan & Associates
Lee Jordan
3015 Main St., #390
Santa Monica, CA 90405
310-450-7941
FAX 310-450-1069

The Textur Group
Scott Prewett
13546 Riverside Dr.
Sherman Oaks, CA 91423
818-907-5579
FAX 818-907-7801

Client Center Training
Carole A. Crone
1717 N. California Blvd., #2-A
Walnut Creek, CA 94596-4132
510-939-9569
FAX 510-947-6742

COLORADO

21st Century Graphics
Tim Meehan
9723 W. 83rd Ave.
Arvada, CO 80005
303-420-4344
FAX 303-421-0087

Arts & Letters
Jay Nelson
1332 Pearl St.
Boulder, CO 80302
303-444-5757
FAX 303-449-1136

Culver & Callahan
Dan Culver
4350 Chippewa Dr.
Boulder, CO 80303
303-494-8028
FAX 303-494-8028

Inside Triathlon
Joy Siegel
1830 N. 55th St.
Boulder, CO 80301-2703
303-440-0601
FAX 303-444-6788

Grey Stone Systems Inc.
Toni Tregear
632 N. Sheridan Ave.
Colorado Springs, CO 80909
719-635-0263
FAX 719-635-0069

Pike Computing Resources
Sharon Pike
1821 Blake St., #1-C
Denver, CO 80202-1287
303-293-3840

Training Access
Cheryl Brumbaugh
8000 E. Iliff Ave.
Denver, CO 80231
303-752-5006
FAX 303-752-5102

PageWorks & Tri Design
Michael Guzofsky
7535 E. Hampden Ave., Suite 350
Denver, CO 80231
303-337-7770
FAX 303-337-7780

Compuskills
Tony Stubbs
1510 York St.
Denver, CO 80206
303-329-6666
FAX 303-399-0477

Intron Computer Training
John Gargano
6746 South Revere Pkwy., Suite 125
Englewood, CO 80112
303-649-1114
FAX 303-649-1113

SYNAPSE
William Mount
980 Simms, #9-154
Golden, CO 80401
303-973-0808

Grafik Solutions
Jeff C. Anderson
6899 S. Yukon Court
Littleton, CO 80123
303-933-9148
FAX 303-933-9148

Teel & Company
Ben Teel
2120 Abeyta Ct.
Loveland, CO 80538
303-667-9882

Computer Training Associates
Peter Richardson
4550 Wadsworth Blvd., #122
Wheat Ridge, CO 80033-3323
303-433-3851
FAX 303-650-1700

CONNECTICUT

ProMac Consulting & Support
Rick Burg
99 Pinepoint Dr.
Bridgeport, CT 06606
203-373-0200
FAX 203-373-0201

AM Computer Products
Jeff Ostroff
410 Prospect St.
East Hartford, CT 06108
203-528-1656
FAX 203-528-4695

Shoreline Computers, Inc.
Donna Vaccaro
545 Main St.
East Haven, CT 06512
203-467-0191
FAX 203-467-9523

Computer SuperCenter/ Greenwich
Vincent Vodola
103 Mason St.
Greenwich, CT 06830
203-661-1700
FAX 203-661-1730

Our Studio
Nancy-jo Funaro
23 Katherine Dr.
Hamden, CT 06514
203-248-8194
FAX 203-248-2773

MicroTraining Plus
David Knise
98 East Ave.
Norwalk, CT 06851
203-853-1011
FAX 203-831-5124

CPCE, Inc.
Diana Chevrette
One Corporate Dr., #310
Shelton, CT 06484
203-925-0400
FAX 203-925-0156

Sys-Ed Microcomputer Learning Centers
Harriet Simon
3001 Summer St.
Stamford, CT 06905
203-356-1230
FAX 203-358-8055

SoftKare
Steven Goethner
191 Post Rd. West
Westport, CT 06880
203-221-2881
FAX 203-661-7972

DC

Future Enterprises, Inc.
Judi George
1331 Pennsylvania Ave. NW, Suite 1301
Washington, DC 20004
202-662-7676
FAX 202-662-7606

Thomas J. Piwowar & Assoc., Inc.
Thomas J. Piwowar
1500 Mass. Ave. NW, Suite 34
Washington, DC 20005
202-223-6813
FAX 202-223-5059

Studio Services
Charles McNeill
1700 K St. NW, #1201
Washington, DC 20006
202-785-9605
FAX 202-785-9609

Advanced Laser Graphics
Rylan Winslow
1101 30th St. NW
Washington, DC 20007
202-342-2100
FAX 202-331-1115

DELAWARE

McGann Design Company
Debbie Heaton
5108 Christiana Meadows
Bear, DE 19701
302-322-6680
FAX 302-322-6680

Online Consulting
Bonnie Dasher-Andersen
913 Market St. Mall, 6th floor
Wilmington, DE 19801
302-658-3018
FAX 302-658-4051

FLORIDA

RBL Publications
Beki Levantini
PO Box 2566
Boca Raton, FL 33427
407-482-2024
FAX 407-482-2024

Warren M. Exmore
Warren Exmore
22368 Boyaca Ave.
Boca Raton, FL 33433
407-488-4743
FAX 407-488-4743

Photo Associates, Inc.
Kym Martinez
5205 NW 33rd Ave.
Fort Lauderdale, FL 33309
305-733-9400
FAX 305-486-0188

Rick Bush Consulting
Rick Bush
1909 SW 48th Ave.
Gainesville, FL 32608
904-374-1517
FAX 904-374-1501

Mac Institute
Mark Miller
3200 N. 29th Ave.
Hollywood, FL 33020
305-920-3899

Mac Generation, Inc.
Janine A. Fertig
6627 Skipper Terrace
Margate, FL 33063
305-970-8950

Miami-Dade Community College
David Smith
11380 NW 27th Ave, Rm. 3213
Miami, FL 33167
305-237-1186
FAX 305-237-1620

Access Corporation
Lina Lopez
10661 N. Kendall Dr., Suite 112
Miami, FL 33176
305-271-0309
FAX 305-271-4030

I.D.E.A.S.
David Creamer
853 Vanderbilt Beach Rd., #3
Naples, FL 33963
813-566-3091
FAX 813-566-3091

Computer Training Group
Douglas Mitchell
8 Cinnamon Dr.
Orlando, FL 32825-3680
407-823-8000
FAX 407-823-8111

Primary Design Workstation
Maurice Eagle
4985 N. Palm Ave.
Winter Park, FL 32792
407-677-1747
FAX 407-657-8002

Winter Park Adult Vocational Center
Geraldine Dixon
901 Webster Ave.
Winter Park, FL 32789
407-647-6366 x233

T. D. Graphics, Inc.
Tim Doucette
1386 San Luis Ct.
Winter Springs, FL 32708
407-365-3060

GEORGIA

Atlanta Desktop
Fill Scroggs
75 14th St., #2500
Atlanta, GA 30309
404-873-4357
FAX 404-881-8424

On-Line Design, Inc.
Greg Weil
1006 North Crossing Way
Decatur, GA 30033
404-325-2977
FAX 404-325-5142

Momentum Imaging Solutions
Sterling Ledet
5865 Jimmy Carter Blvd.
Norcross, GA 30093
404-903-0465
FAX 404-903-0467

HAWAII

Connecting Point
Kelly Ann M. Fukuhara
1613 Nuuanu Ave.
Honolulu, HI 96817
808-523-0040
FAX 808-531-5244

Image Management
Kelly Ann M. Fukuhara
909 Kahikolu Pl.
Honolulu, HI 96818
808-833-8978
FAX 808-833-8978

Solid Concepts
Craig T. Tokumura
1279 Honokahua St.
Honolulu, HI 96825
808-396-6070
FAX 808-396-6070

IDAHO

Computerland Learning Center
Jackie Liddell
4795 Emerald, Suite A
Boise, ID 83706
208-345-8024
FAX 208-338-1783

ILLINOIS

Sharon Borstein
Sharon Borstein
1075 Beechwood Rd.
Buffalo Grove, IL 60089
708-541-1805

LaRue Graphics
Larry V. Gilbert
317 S. Garfield
Champaign, IL 61821
217-356-2376

Digital Resources, Inc.
Angela Dixon
165 North Canal St., #40
Chicago, IL 60606
312-258-4200
FAX 312-258-0617

Electronic Publishing Resources, Inc.
Kenneth W. Gortowski
445 West Erie St., #208
Chicago, IL 60610
312-787-6847
FAX 312-787-6097

Central Photo Engraving
Cheryl Boncuore
1712 S. Prairie
Chicago, IL 60616
312-427-5370
FAX 312-427-7836

Seneca Design and Consulting
Anne-Marie Concepcion
3540 N. Leavitt
Chicago, IL 60618
312-248-3531
FAX 312-248-6596

Computing Solutions, Inc.
Laura Kew
118 N. Clinton, #403
Chicago, IL 60661
312-902-9900
FAX 312-902-9904

Bentley, Barnes & Lynn
Marie Kahle
420 N. Wabash, 3rd floor
Chicago, IL 60611
312-321-5864

Columbia College
Chris Koules
600 S. Michigan Ave.
Chicago, IL 60605
312-663-1600 x678

DDB Needham Chicago
William Hertel
303 E. Wacker Dr.
Chicago, IL 60601
312-552-2414
FAX 312-552-2371

Productivity Point International
Joe Kelleher
208 S. LaSalle
Chicago, IL 60604
312-332-3865
FAX 708-920-2138

Automated Images, Inc.
Peter Paulsen
855 Sunset Court
Deerfield, IL 60015-4057
708-735-8517
FAX 708-735-8510

Technical Learning Center
Howard Manthei
1441 Branding Ln., #310
Downers Grove, IL 60435
708-971-0600
FAX 708-971-0610

Computer Workshop Inc.
Donna Clavey
1020 31st St., Suite 110
Downers Grove, IL 60515
708-971-0004
FAX 708-971-0065

CompUSA
Ann McGinley
3000 Finley Dr.
Downers Grove, IL 60515
708-241-5713
FAX 708-241-5725

Electronic Business Equipment
Russ Armstrong
4430 Kennedy Dr.
East Moline, IL 61244
309-792-5550
FAX 309-792-5557

Electronic Business Equipment
Steve Bratcher
4430 Kennedy Dr.
East Moline, IL 61244
309-792-5550
FAX 309-792-5557

Scott Foresman
Nancy Jo Yundt
1900 E. Lake Ave.
Glenview, IL 60025
708-486-2725
FAX 708-729-8721

Screaming Color, Inc.
Jill Schwartz
125 N. Prospect Ave.
Itasca, IL 60143
708-250-9500
FAX 708-250-8729

MJS Graphics
Michele Struchil
1041 Douglas
Naperville, IL 60540
708-355-6099
FAX 708-355-6192

Illinois State University
James L. Toppen, Ph.D.
Turner 211
Normal, IL 61790-5100
309-438-2737
FAX 309-438-3776

Publishing Consultants
Clinton Funk
3465 Bayberry Dr.
Northbrook, IL 60062
708-272-3829
FAX same

Applied Computer Services
Diane Wilczak
15511 S. 70th Court
Orland Park, IL 60462
708-614-4900
FAX 708-614-4919

ECP Computer Consulting
Edward Peters
648A N. NW Highway, #305
Park Ridge, IL 60068
708-692-4682
FAX 708-825-6047

Flying Color Graphics
Frank Brunacci
1001 W. North St.
Pontiac, IL 61764
815-842-2811
FAX 815-844-1044

Livingston Area Vocational Center
Joe Brettnacher
1100 Indiana Ave.
Pontiac, IL 61764
815-844-6113
FAX 815-844-6116

Desktop Staffing, Inc.
Cindy Caravello
3705 Bluebird Lane South
Rolling Meadows, IL 60008
708-255-1197

Donna's House of Type
Donna Aschenbrenner
217 West Cook
Springfield, IL 62704
217-522-5050
FAX 217-522-9673

J. S. Computer Training Center
Jay Saffarzadeh
716 Elm St.
Winnetka, IL 60093
708-501-4944

INDIANA

Pemberton Design
Gene Pemberton
1999 East Dutcherman Dr.
Bloomington, IN 47401
812-824-7206
FAX 812-334-0210

Creative Services Network
Richard Crow
7520 Valley Meadows Dr.
Ft. Wayne, IN 46815
219-493-4898

LMB Microcomputers
Karen Zwick
6330 E. 75th St.
Indianapolis, IN 46250
317-849-4999
FAX 317-576-5975

Productivity Point International
Tyran Hahn
10585 N. Meridian St., #300
Indianapolis, IN 46290
317-573-2320
FAX 317-573-2360

The Printing Company/Americolor
Vincent Freeman
2820 N. Shadeland
Indianapolis, IN 46219
317-543-2380
FAX 317-547-0839

Kokomo Lithographic Co., Inc.
Jerry Hammal
100 E. Broadway
Kokomo, IN 46903-0824
317-459-8081
FAX 317-457-5111

Desktop Media Consulting
Catherine Brosseau Indiano
PO Box 1016
Noblesville, IN 46060
317-877-0495
FAX 317-877-0495

Valparaiso University
Marlane C. Steinwart
AC-CC 30
Valparaiso, IN 46383
219-464-5153
FAX 219-464-6742

IOWA

Compu-T.E.A.C.H.
Sandy Johnson
515 28th St., Suite 104
Des Moines, IA 50312
515-283-0824
FAX 515-283-0430

Maharishi International University
Rick Archer
1000 N. 4th St.
Faculty Mail Box 1097
Fairfield, IA 52557
515-472-5031 x4182
FAX 515-472-1189

Iowa Computer Solutions
Martin Tschofen
155 Marion Blvd.
Marion, IA 52302
319-377-8688
FAX 319-377-7566

KANSAS

Direct Digital Design
Eric I. Owen
1100 W. Cambridge Circle Dr., #400
Kansas City, KS 66103
913-371-4333
FAX 913-371-6382

MacSource
Sheila Soetaert
9083 Metcalf Ave.
Overland Park, KS 66212
913-383-3111
FAX 913-383-9053

Haddock Computer Services
Christan Baumer
2020 N. Woodlawn, #460
Wichita, KS 67208
316-683-5211
FAX 316-686-5914

KENTUCKY

Magna Graphic
David Salyer
2528 Palumbo Dr.
Lexington, KY 40509
606-268-1211
FAX 606-268-9546

Cobb, Inc.
Tom Bell
901 Monmouth St., PO Box 368
Newport, KY 41071
606-291-1146
FAX 606-291-1182

MAINE

Searls Design, Inc.
Karen Searls
166 Main St., Suite 201
Rockland, ME 04841-3312
207-596-6008
FAX 207-596-6008

MARYLAND

PageSmiths, Ltd
Dixie Lea Smith
8341 Liberty Rd
Baltimore, MD 21244
410-655-1480

The Maryland Institute, College of Art
Lew Fifield
1300 W. Mt. Royal Ave.
Baltimore, MD 21217
410-225-2239
FAX 410-669-9206

Microcomputer Center/ Connecting Point
Marge Smith
7668 Belair Rd.
Baltimore, MD 21236
410-668-2600
FAX 410-668-0194

Clockface & Creole
Stephen Kaufman
7801 Norfold Ave., Suite 1
Bethesda, MD 20814
301-718-0612
FAX 301-718-6204

Alvin Rosenbaum
Alvin Rosenbaum
3107 Rolling Rd.
Chevy Chase, MD 20815
301-654-1988
FAX 301-654-1994

MASSACHUSETTS

Mac Resource
Will McNaughton
7 Coach Lane
Amherst, MA 01002
413-253-7223

Bit by Bit Computer Training
Lance A. Robinson
20 Park Plaza, Suite 1101
Boston, MA 02116
617-277-6455
FAX 617-423-4642

MacPro Boston
Robert Thornton
1599 Washington St.
Braintree, MA 02184
617-848-6622
FAX 617-848-6224

Agawam Productions
Andrew Lindsay
5 Old England Rd.
Ipswich, MA 01938
508-356-0437
FAX 508-356-9860

Schmidt Publishing Services
Jay Schmidt
PO Box 601
Mansfield, MA 02048
508-261-9779

The Corps
Mary Jane Forbes
30 Green St.
Newburyport, MA 01950
508-462-4778
FAX 508-462-2315

Computers Etc Superstore
Ken Zindler
216 Newbury St.
Peabody, MA 01960
508-535-5252
FAX 508-535-8171

TriMac
Bob Trikakis
52 Maple Circle
Shrewsbury, MA 01545
508-842-3759

Software & Systems, Inc.
Joseph R. Grimes
100 Grove St., 4th floor
Worcester, MA 01604
508-752-8930
FAX 508-754-9250

MICHIGAN

Sequoia Diversified
Deborah Foy
70 S. Grey Rd.
Auburn Hills, MI 48326
313-299-4220
FAX 313-852-2045

Bell & Associates
Leisha Bell
1355 Edgewood
Holland, MI 49424
616-399-8165
FAX 616-399-8166

Lansing Community College
Sharon Wood
315 N. Grand Ave.
Lansing, MI 48901
517-483-1476
FAX 517-483-9781

Midland Computer Shoppe
Carman Minarik
244 E. Main St.
Midland, MI 48640
517-631-5440
FAX 517-832-0907

The McKay Press
Pam Anderson
215 State St.
Midland, MI 48640
517-631-2360
FAX 517-835-4581

Quebecor/Pendell Printing, Inc.
Cheryl Cromer
1700 James Savage Rd.
Midland, MI 48640
517-496-3333
FAX 517-496-9165

Lanista Corporation
Genevieve Skory
1000 Town Center, Suite #215
Southfield, MI 48075-1218
313-350-3322
FAX 313-350-3397

MacTraining & Design
Terry White
15900 W. 10 Mile Rd., #106
Southfield, MI 48075
313-557-0750
FAX 313-557-0758

Butler Graphics
Beth Moss
294 Town Center Dr.
Troy, MI 48084
313-528-2808
FAX 313-528-0588

Meteor Photo & Imaging
Michael Thomas
1099 Chicago Rd.
Troy, MI 48007
313-597-1639
FAX 313-588-8727

MINNESOTA

Art Direction
Beth Travis-Betts
5009 Oakley St.
Duluth, MN 55804
218-525-6561
FAX 218-525-6561

Inacomp Computer Centers
Lori Weed
10371 W. 70th St.
Eden Prairie, MN 55344
612-828-9550
FAX 612-828-9555

Hennepin Technical College
Ralph Schmidtke
9200 Flying Cloud Dr.
Eden Prairie, MN 55347
612-944-2222
FAX 612-550-3143

Scott Franze Associates
Scott Franze
3151 Dean Court, #302
Minneapolis, MN 55416
612-927-9478

South Central Technical College
Bob Williams
1920 Lee Blvd.
North Mankato, MN 56002-1920
507-625-3441
FAX 507-388-9951

Connecting Point
Duane Kuss
2870 7th St., North
St. Cloud, MN 56303
612-252-7753
FAX 612-251-1336

Litho Specialties, Inc.
Barbara Bear
1280 Energy Park Dr.
St. Paul, MN 55108
612-644-3000

Kennedy Business Systems
Bryan Olson
111 Main St.
Winona, MN 55987
507-454-6705
FAX 507-454-6836

MISSISSIPPI

Eagle Graphics, Inc.
Dan Westphal
2750 Bienville Blvd.
Ocean Springs, MS 39564
601-872-1680
FAX 601-872-7298

MISSOURI

Mike's Litho
Michael Congemi
525 Aubuchon St.
Florissant, MO 63031
314-921-1412

Empower Trainers & Consultants, Inc.
Caroline Yescavage
4717 Grand Ave., Suite #220
Kansas City, MO 64112
816-753-8880
FAX 816-753-8885

Armadillo Computer Services
Ken Reiss
301 Sovereign Ct., Suite 209
Manchester, MO 63011
314-256-0824
FAX 314-256-0856

TSI Graphics, Inc.
Karl Schoenefeld
1035 Hanley Industrial Ct.
St. Louis, MO 63144
314-968-6800
FAX 314-968-2739

Brown Graphics
Gregory Dean
2320 Pine St
St. Louis, MO 63103
314-241-2214
FAX 314-241-0821

Productivity Plus, Inc.
Loire Kroeger
655 Craig Rd., Suite 324
St. Louis, MO 63141
314-569-2901
FAX 314-569-2911

Advanced Systems and Peripherals
John Gallina
1854 Craig Park Court
St. Louis, MO 63146
314-576-2727
FAX 314-576-1587

NEBRASKA

Desktop Cafe
Tim Lillethorup
5011 Decatur St.
Omaha, NE 68104
402-558-2812
FAX 402-341-8375

Omaha Graphics, Inc.
David Kahn
3115 So. 61st Ave.
Omaha, NE 68106
402-556-0335
FAX 402-556-4203

Orent Graphic Arts, Inc.
Mark Tindell
4805 G St.
Omaha, NE 68117
402-733-6400
FAX 402-733-2083

Holigraphic, Inc.
Gerry Holiday
8311 Spring Plaza
Omaha, NE 68124
402-391-2961
FAX 402-391-1816

NEVADA

DBK Training
Diane Kennedy
2685 Lakeridge Shores West
Reno, NV 89509
702-825-2349
FAX 702-825-9073

DeskTop ComPosition Services
Gary J. Duarte
336 Greenbrae Dr.
Sparks, NV 89431
702-355-7588

NEW HAMPSHIRE

Datalex Corporation
Keith Thompson
7 Lord Jeffrey Dr., PO Box 1209
Amherst, NH 03031
603-672-6544
FAX 603-673-3575

NEW JERSEY

World of Computers
Lisa Petronaci
520 Main St.
Boonton, NJ 07005
201-335-1470
FAX 201-335-4562

American Business Products
Judd Grayzel
155 N. Dean St.
Englewood, NJ 07631
201-569-0853
FAX 201-569-1297

Peifer Design
Sabine Peifer
36 Veranda Ave.
Little Falls, NJ 07424-0106
201-256-2758
FAX 201-256-2758

New Century Graphics
Gil Poulsen
70 Park St.
Montclair, NJ 07042
201-744-0174

Mobius Associates
Laura Leach
7 Century Dr., #202
Parsippany, NJ 07054
201-292-1289
FAX 201-326-1776

The Computer Training Center of Princeton
Kathleen Unick
401 Wall St.
Princeton, NJ 08540
609-921-7900
FAX 609-921-6908

Imageworks, Inc.
Ivan Boden
400 B Lake St.
Ramsey, NJ 07446
201-327-6692
FAX 201-327-3730

TransNet Corporation
Wendi Becker Hoak
45 Columbia Rd.
Somerville, NJ 08876
908-253-0500 x1110
FAX 908-253-0601

Dow Jones Training Services
Kenan Van Vranken
Rt. 1 & Ridge Rd.
South Brunswick, NJ 08852
609-520-5269
FAX 609-520-5479

Design On Disk, Inc.
Mary Cicitta
10131 Teaneck Rd.
Teaneck, NJ 07666
201-837-7171
FAX 201-837-7087

Voltex Corporation
Suzanne Thomas
41 Knollwood Dr.
Tinton Falls, NJ 07724
908-842-7699
FAX 908-842-5889

J&D Associates
John Arcoleo
2816 Morris Ave.
Union, NJ 07083
908-964-0006
FAX 908-964-9159

Cardinal
Ken Jackson
180 Coolidge Terrace
Wyckoff, NJ 07481
201-444-3050
FAX 201-444-3050

NEW YORK

Educational Research & Mktg., Inc.
Mark Hendriks
1461 Lakeland Ave., #1
Bohemia, NY 11716
516-589-4000
FAX 516-589-4082

Imtech
Kara Lynn Murrell
401 Sackett St.
Brooklyn, NY 11231
718-643-1079

Spectragraphic, Inc.
Joan Reiss
4 Brayton Ct.
Commack, NY 11725
516-499-3100
FAX 516-499-5255

DiPalma Design
Gary DiPalma
9 Manor Hill Dr.
Fairport, NY 14450-2519
716-425-4637

Computer Graphic Arts Services
Mara Sachs
127 Woodshire North
Getzville, NY 14068
716-688-3058
FAX 716-688-3058

Kenmore-Town of Tonawanda Schools
Amanda Veazie
3200 Elmwood Ave.
Kenmore, NY 14217
716-874-8512
FAX 716-874-8621

Leapfrog, Inc.
David Didato
4 Gilder St., Suite #2
Larchmont, NY 10538
914-834-8292
FAX 914-834-2587

Donald Norkett
Donald Norkett
28 N. Babylon Turnpike
Merrick, NY 11566
516-868-4932

High Text Graphics
Brad Walrod
350 Bleecker St., Suite 3G
New York, NY 10014-2631
212-645-6965
FAX 212-645-9584

Microcomputer Publishing Center
David Cammack
150 Fifth Ave., Suite 500
New York, NY 10011
212-463-8585
FAX 212-366-0458

Steven Gorney
Steven Gorney
280 Riverside Dr., 2E
New York, NY 10025
212-866-2373

Marie Babcock
Marie Babcock
625 Main St., Suite 320
New York, NY 10044
212-486-0226

RGB New York, Inc.
Joshua Masur
18 West 27th, 6th floor
New York, NY 10001
212-889-0400
FAX 212-696-9676

Microsystems, Inc.
M. Leo West, Jr.
900 Broadway, #900
New York, NY 10003
212-388-1900
FAX 212-614-0724

Michael Meyerowitz & Co.
Michael Meyerowitz
175 Fifth Ave.
New York, NY 10010
212-353-1561
FAX 212-353-1567

The Future Now
Stacey Czerniawski
111 8th Ave., 5th floor
New York, NY 10017
212-229-6773

Electronic Directions
Ron Lockhart
220 E. 23rd St., Suite 503
New York, NY 10010
212-213-6500
FAX 212-213-0599

Macology
Neal Spitzer
799 Greenwich St., #6N
New York, NY 10014
212-989-1595

Novaworks Computer Sys., Inc.
Maggie Soffer
630 3rd Ave.
New York, NY 10017
212-557-9199
FAX 212-949-1878

Erie Community College-South
Kathy Catalino
4140 Southwestern Blvd.
Orchard Park, NY 14127
716-851-1800
FAX 716-648-9953

Christopher Meadows
Christopher Meadows
59 Edgewood Rd.
Port Washington, NY 11050
516-883-7260
FAX 516-944-6665

Digitech Publishing, Inc.
Brad Saunders
478 Thurston Rd.
Rochester, NY 14619-1719
716-436-3100
FAX 716-436-3627

Lazer Photo Engraving, Inc.
Carl M. Palmer
2099 Mt. Read Blvd.
Rochester, NY 14615
716-254-6050
FAX 716-254-4497

Cohber Press, Inc.
Steve Kangas
1000 John St.
PO Box 93100
Rochester, NY 14692
716-475-9100
FAX 716-475-9406

Computer Confidence, Inc.
JennyLee Smallman
1200 Jefferson Rd.
Rochester, NY 14623
800-724-1366
FAX 716-292-9995

J & J Computing, Inc.
John Sagaria
400 Rella Blvd., #130
Suffern, NY 10901
914-357-6381
FAX 914-357-0658

Imagecraft
Larry Pacilio
1402 Genesee St.
Utica, NY 13502
315-797-7816
FAX 315-797-9816

NORTH CAROLINA

Amano Consulting
Taka Amano
112 Duchess Lane
Chapel Hill, NC 27514
919-493-0264
FAX 919-419-0412

University Directories
Jeff Luttrell
100 Europa Dr., #330
Chapel Hill, NC 27514
919-968-0225
FAX 919-968-8513

dTT, Inc.
Taz Tally, Ph.D.
5100 N. I-85, #5,
University S. Center
Charlotte, NC 28206
704-598-7402
FAX 704-597-5094

Pharus Corporation
Wanda L. Little
6302 Fairview Rd., #100
Charlotte, NC 28210
704-362-7720
FAX 704-362-7778

Macintosh Design, Training & Consulting
Dennis Hermanson
3432 Sandy Creek Dr.
Durham, NC 27705
919-489-3674

Computer Decisions, Inc.
Debbie Kinsey
2950 Gateway Centre Blvd.
Morrisville, NC 27560
919-460-0071
FAX 919-460-6354

Conrad Design
Barbara Conrad
3131 Eton Rd.
Raleigh, NC 27608
919-783-5563

Solutions!
William Block
4526 Fountain Dr.
Wilmington, NC 28403
919-395-0233
FAX 919-392-5829

NORTH DAKOTA

Team Connecting Point
Chris Kjorven
2600 DeMers Ave.
Grand Forks, ND 58206
701-775-5512

Desktop Training Professionals
Deborah Hancock
670 N. Commercial St.
Manchester, NH 03101
603-626-5551
FAX 603-669-7456

OHIO

Carpec Graphics
Marty Davis
221 Beaver St.
Akron, OH 44304-1965
216-434-2288
FAX 216-434-8562

All Systems Color, Inc.
Victoria Webber
7333 Paragon Rd.
Centerville, OH 45459
513-433-5054
FAX 513-433-8992

The Future Now
Deb Tyson
2722 E. Kemper Rd.
Cincinnati, OH 45241
513-771-7110
FAX 513-771-5495

Antonelli Institute
Jim Slouffman
124 E. 7th St.
Cincinnati, OH 45202
513-241-4338

Kreber Graphics, Inc.
Patrick Grady
670 Harmon Ave.
Columbus, OH 43223
614-228-3501
FAX 614-228-2115

Transcontinental Communications
Andrea Stein
678 Fairfield Yellow Springs Pike
Fairborn, OH 45324
513-879-5678
FAX 513-878-5283

Richland Graphics Systems
Laura Crowther
140 Park Ave. East
Mansfield, OH 44902
419-525-3760
FAX 419-524-6494

Owens Technical College
Sally Welch
Oregon Rd., PO Box 10
Toledo, OH 43699-1947
419-666-0580

OKLAHOMA

Linda Jenkins
Linda Jenkins
1115 W. Austin
Broken Arrow, OK 74011
918-455-7978

MacSpec, Inc.
Carol Barber
10712 Dorothy Dr.
Oklahoma City, OK 73162
405-720-9622

Louise Broda Consulting
Louise Broda
1809 N. Villa
Oklahoma City, OK 73107
405-946-7328
FAX 405-946-8143

Epic, Inc.
Wes Caves
4860 S. Lewis Ave., #101
Tulsa, OK 74105-5171
918-744-1118
FAX 918-744-1543

Graphics Universal, Inc.
Carol Purkey
6580 E. Skelly Dr.
Tulsa, OK 74145
918-665-6633

Oral Roberts University
Douglas Latta
7777 South Lewis Ave.
Tulsa, OK 74171
918-495-6613

PENNSYLVANIA

Berkeley Corporation
Sandy Mayer
2 Bala Plaza, Suite 504
Bala Cynwyd, PA 19004
215-664-3880
FAX 215-664-5269

Visual Sound
Mary Malinconico
485 Parkway South
Broomall, PA 19008
215-544-8700
FAX 215-544-3385

Busy Bytes
Suzanne Gillstrom
949 Cornwallis Dr.
Chester, PA 19380
215-696-5925

PC Support Group
Wanda Eck
757 Springdale Dr.
Exton, PA 19341
215-524-6665
FAX 215-524-9455

R.R. Donnelley & Sons
Angel L. Rivera
216 Greenfield Rd.
Lancaster, PA 17601
717-293-2172
FAX 717-293-2371

Morgan's Computer
Bob Morgan
1694 Citation Dr.
Library, PA 15129
412-653-0836

SpectraComp
Jeff Fackler
5170 E. Trindle Rd.
Mechanicsburg, PA 17055
717-697-8600
FAX 717-691-0433

EPS Associates
Alan Lasdon
720 Montgomery Ave.
Narberth, PA 19072
215-660-0325
FAX 215-664-0649

Graphic Arts Technical Foundation
Daniel J. Makuta
4615 Forbes Ave.
Pittsburgh, PA 15213-3796
412-621-6941
FAX 412-621-3049

Ziff Technologies
Tracey Syrylo
1265 Drummers Lane, Suite 102
Wayne, PA 19087
215-293-4631
FAX 215-293-4602

RHODE ISLAND

CompUSA
Therese Strik
945 Bald Hill Rd.
Warwick, RI 02886
401-827-5150
FAX 401-827-5198

SOUTH CAROLINA

Midlands Technical College
Alan Clayton
PO Box 2408
Columbia, SC 29202
803-822-3361
FAX 803-822-3422

À La Carte Advertising/Design
Mark Bazil
210 Altamont Rd.
Greenville, SC 29609
803-370-9503
FAX 803-235-6954

MicroAge Computers/SC
Janet Swindell
314 Moss Creek Village
Hilton Head, SC 29926
803-837-6570
FAX 803-837-6571

SOUTH DAKOTA

McInally Associates, Inc.
Dan Claymore
115 St. Joseph, Suite #3
Rapid City, SD 57701
605-343-0934
FAX 605-343-1049

TENNESSEE

Professional Computer Training
Theresa Emmert
101 Westpark Dr., #100
Brentwood, TN 37027
615-373-4771
FAX 615-373-4766

InterSYS, Inc.
Tommy Gascon
5211 Linbar Dr., Suite 508
Nashville, TN 37211
615-331-6000

Critical MASS
Tony Crowder
1705 Charlotte Ave.
Nashville, TN 37203
615-320-9400
FAX 615-320-9674

NEC, Inc.
Donna Arnold
1504 Elm Hill Pike
Nashville, TN 37210
615-367-9110
FAX 615-360-7952

TEXAS

Trafton Printing
Vickie Bryant
109 S. Fillmore
Amarillo, TX 79105
806-376-4347
FAX 806-374-6831

Krazy Kat Studio
Kathryn E. Kroll
2035 Oakwood Ct.
Arlington, TX 76012
817-277-2015

MBA Seminars, Inc.
Michael Cox
1950 Stemmons Fwy., Suite #2045
Dallas, TX 75207
800-966-6873
FAX 214-746-5256

Capstone Communications, Inc.
Rich Bussen
1950 Stemmons, Suite 3043
Dallas, TX 75207
214-746-4855
FAX 214-746-4329

Characters & One Works
Carla Berger
2501A Central Parkway
Houston, TX 77092
713-683-6666
FAX 713-681-6501

Unlimited Ink
James Tucker
532 S. Academy
New Braunfels, TX 78130
210-629-7483
FAX 210-629-7483

SRW Institute, Inc.
Warren Hill
8025 Rice Dr.
Rowlett, TX 75088-6699
214-918-9967
FAX 214-918-9968

UTAH

Lettersetters
Laurie C. Cook
836 South State
Orem, UT 84058
801-224-6990
FAX 801-224-1784

Salt Lake Community College
Lana Hall
4600 S. Redwood Rd.
Salt Lake City, UT 84130
801-967-4004
FAX 801-965-8008

VERMONT

LaserImage, Inc.
Patricia Torpie
187 St. Paul St.
Burlington, VT 05401
802-863-1884
FAX 802-863-5526

VIRGINIA

EEI
Sally Smith
66 Canal Center Plaza, #200
Alexandria, VA 22314-1538
703-683-0683
FAX 703-683-4915

Catapult, Inc.
Jennifer Dickerson
2011 Crystal Dr., #608
Arlington, VA 22202
703-271-9800
FAX 703-271-0036

Falcon Microsystems
Thomas Fuhr
1745 Jefferson Davis Hwy.
Arlington, VA 22202
703-412-8060
FAX 703-412-8064

1st Step Computers/ MicroAge
Kathy Sutter
4925 W. Broad St.
Richmond, VA 23230
804-358-5881
FAX 804-355-7208

Imagetech
Michael Fountain
7275 Glen Forest Dr., #206
Richmond, VA 23226
804-288-0628
FAX 804-285-7480

Vaz-Yor DTPublishers
Pedro Vazquez
10400 Hunt Country Lane
Vienna, VA 22182
703-281-6552

Type & Graphics, aka Dougherty & Assoc.
Michael Dougherty
815 Dryden St.
Virginia Beach, VA 23462
804-671-8837
FAX 804-671-8837

Morse Computer Graphics, aka The MCG Group
Charles Morse
1915 Pocahantas Trail
Williamsburg, VA 23185
804-229-9969
FAX 804-220-9098

WASHINGTON

Infotec Training Institute
Lia Cicuto
2310 130th Ave. NE, #B101
Bellevue, WA 98005
206-869-4080
FAX 206-869-4065

Sound Partners, Inc.
Becky L. Milmoe
P.O. Box 27577
Seattle, WA 98125
206-488-7781
FAX 206-828-2149

Graphic Acrobatics, Inc.
Michael Friend
7302 Bowlyn Place South
Seattle, WA 98118
206-725-7250
FAX 206-723-6720

Seattle Central Community College
Michael Doane
The City Collegian, 1701 Broadway
Seattle, WA 98125
206-587-6960

Connecting Point Computers
Cathleen Brown
E. 200 Second Ave.
Spokane, WA 99202
509-455-5255
FAX 509-455-6611

WISCONSIN

Fox Valley
Jim Reinke
1825 N. Bluemound Dr.
Appleton, WI 54913
414-735-2579
FAX 414-735-4771

Fox Valley Technical College
Doug Paape
1825 N. Bluemound Dr.
Appleton, WI 54913
414-735-2427
FAX 414-735-2582

Scan Graphics
Bob Galica
14540 W. Greenfield Ave.
Brookfield, WI 53005
414-786-1365
FAX 414-786-6483

Byte Shop
Sue Ann Sanders
4840 S. 76th St.
Greenfield, WI 53220
414-281-7004
FAX 414-423-7571

Widen Technologies, Inc.
Lisa Brehm
2614 Industrial Dr.
Madison, WI 53713
608-222-1296
FAX 608-222-8346

D&D Computer Consulting
Dennis Brault
6320 Monona Dr., #209
Madison, WI 53716
608-222-6422
FAX 608-272-4916

Computerland
John McLaughlin
6688 Odana Rd.
Madison, WI 53719
608-833-0777
FAX 608-833-0539

Imagesetter, Inc.
Bill Howard
2423 American Lane
Madison, WI 53704
608-244-6243
FAX 608-244-1541

Inacomp
Beth Lunstrum
6406 Odana Rd.
Madison, WI 53719
608-277-8000

Four Lakes Colorgraphics, Inc.
Rick Pietrykowski
4230 Argosy Court
Madison, WI 53714
608-221-9500
FAX 608-221-7574

Macro Resources
Diana Leonard
180 Main St.
Menasha, WI 54952
414-722-6960
FAX 414-722-9163

Graphic Composition, Inc.
Sally Hyde
1435 Midway Rd.
Menasha, WI 54952
414-739-3152
FAX 414-739-4066

JWP Information Services
Karen Fowler
9163 N. 76th St.
Milwaukee, WI 53223-1905
414-357-4650
FAX 414-357-0525

London Litho
Russ Brock
16900 W. Cleveland Ave.
New Berlin, WI 53151-3535
414-784-8700
FAX 414-784-4081

Technical Support Services, Inc.
Loretta Koscak
8311 West Bluemound Rd.
Wauwatosa, WI 53213
414-276-4165
FAX 414-258-7116

North Shore Computers
Peter Nelson
11310 W. Theo Trecker Way
West Allis, WI 53211
414-475-6500
FAX 414-475-6897

CANADA

The Babel Fish Corporation
John Bohaychuk
Edmonton, AB T5H 3B2
403-944-9964

Phoenix Studios, Inc.
Richard Mayer
205-4882 Delta St.
Delta, BC V4K 2T8
604-946-6445
FAX 604-946-1450

Advantage Computers Ltd.
Lorna Krassie
150-4011 Viking Way
Richmond, BC V6V 2K9
604-231-5700
FAX 604-244-0437

Lazer Fare Media Services
Tracey Reid
602-491 Portage Ave
Winnipeg, MB R3B 2E4
204-786-8615
FAX 204-783-9120

Desktop Computer Systems
Robert Campbell
134 South Albion St.
Amherst, NS B4H 2X3
902-667-7603
FAX 902-667-4364

VectorGraphics
Gary Biesinger
351 Town Line Rd.
Barrie, ON L4M 4S7
705-734-3699
FAX 705-734-9124

MacTutor
Alan Rubenstein
61 Alness St., #205
Downsview, ON M3J 2H2
416-665-1050
FAX 416-665-9693

Kathryn Dunne Graphics
Kathryn Dunne
1467 McLarenwood Terrace
London, ON N5W 1X8
519-680-1782

Fuji Graphic Systems
Maureen Brown
333 Consortium Court
London, ON N6E 2S8
519-681-5913
FAX 519-681-9866

TechnoPlus, Inc.
Scott Gerard
461 N. Service Rd. West
Oakville, ON L6M 2V5
416-847-1934

Fuji Graphic System Canada, Inc.
Simon Hooper
2160 Thurston Dr.
Ottawa, ON K1G 4V4
613-738-2929
FAX 613-738-9262

Desktop Publishing Associates
Michael Kieran
1992 Yonge St., #301
Toronto, ON M4S 1Z7
416-480-1376
FAX 416-480-0192

Southside Publishing Studios, Inc.
Cathy Zivot
1133 Yonge St.
Toronto, ON M4T 2Z3
416-920-2500
FAX 416-920-9150

Synesis, Inc.
Harold Sookman
1929 de Maisonneuve West, 3rd
Montreal, PQ H3H 1K3
514-937-2433
FAX 514-937-4661

MEXICO

Color y Autoediciòn Nitida S.A. de C.V.
Juan Lauro Aguirre
Ave. Alfonso Reyes 4520-2
Monterrey Nuevo Leòn , Mexico 64850
52-83-49-3668
FAX 52-83-65-4077

Appendix E: Quark Authorized Service Bureaus

The following pages contain a list of all of the Quark Authorized Service Bureaus. They are sorted first by state, then by city, and finally by company name. Due to space constraints, each entry contains only the company name, city, state, zip code, and phone number.

If you're looking for someone to send your jobs to, consider calling one of these bureaus. Quark provides technical support to them, so they should be able to hand even your most challenging jobs.

ALABAMA

Communication Arts, Inc.
Birmingham, AL 35222
205-251-6642

Comp-U-Type
Birmingham, AL 35205
205-323-8898

The Graphic Zone, Inc.
Birmingham, AL 35223
205-870-5300

Mobile Color House
Mobile, AL 36804
205-476-7400

Williams Printing & Office Supply Inc
Montgomery, AL 36106
205-265-9658

ALASKA

Visible Ink, Inc.
Anchorage, AK 99517
907-562-3825

ARIZONA

VisionSetter Commercial Lithographers, Inc.
Mesa, AZ 85201
602-844-2294

Bowne of Phoenix
Phoenix, AZ 85016
602-468-1012

Central Graphics
Phoenix, AZ 85016 7122
602-265-5555
or 207-3000

Just My Type
Phoenix, AZ 85027
602-581-5900

Phoenix PhotoType, Inc.
Phoenix, AZ 85013-3079
602-248-TYPE

Subia Corporation
Phoenix, AZ 85034
602-275-6565

Typography Unlimited, Inc.
Phoenix, AZ 85017
602-266-2445

ArtSetters
Tempe, AZ 85283
602-820-0647

Ben Franklin Press, Inc.
Tempe, AZ 85281
602-968-7959

ARKANSAS

Peerless Engravers
Little Rock, AR 72201
501-375-8266

Royal Graphics
Little Rock, AR 72201
501-375-8255

CALIFORNIA

Southern California PrintCorp
Altadena, CA 91001
818-398-3501

On The Ball Typesetting
Anaheim, CA 92805
714-978-9057

Aptos Post, Inc.
Aptos, CA 95001
408-688-7474

Hagar Typography
Berkeley, CA 94710
415-843-1358

Hunza Graphics
Berkeley, CA 94704
510-549-1766

Graphic Design Services
Brea, CA 92621
714-529-7003

Graphics Two
Burbank, CA 91506
818-841-4922

The Network Forty
Burbank, CA 91502
818-955-4040

Grafica EPS (Electronic Publishing Solutions)
Canoga Park, CA
91303-2006
818-712-0071

Viking Lithograph
Canoga Park, CA 91304
818- 882-8396

Pacific Color
Carlsbad, CA 92009
619-438-8933

Page Printing Services
Chatsworth, CA 91311
818-341-6033

Highpoint Imaging
Claremont, CA 91711
714-625-7785

Via Type Corporation/ Inland Imaging Services
Claremont, CA 91711
909-626-8973

PM Graphics, Inc.
Costa Mesa, CA 92626
714-556-2890

Universal Printing and Graphics
Costa Mesa, CA 92626
714-662-6800

Abrash Typografix
Culver City, CA 90230
310-838-4995

Graphics Plus
Culver City, CA 90232
310-559-7444

Dean Enterprises Typography
El Cajon, CA 92020
619-449-0574

Artype
Emeryville, CA 94608
510-547-8418

Headline Graphics
Encinitas, CA 92024
619-436-0133

Applied Graphics Technologies
Foster City, CA 94404
415-578-8333

Graphic Types
Fresno, CA 93727
209-252-9177

Hayden Design & Production
Fullerton, CA 92635
714-255-9377

KBN Desktop Service Bureau
Fullerton, CA 92632
714-738-3047

Crestec Los Angeles, Inc.
Gardena, CA 90247
213-532-8880

Applied Graphics Technologies
Glendale, CA 91201
213-245-4111

Dynamedia Design & Graphics, Inc.
Glendale, CA 91205
818-243-1114

Insight Communications
Glendale, CA 91201
818-507-8730

TRI Graphics
Glendale, CA 91204
818-548-0003

Treasure Chest Advertising
Glendora, CA 91740
818-852-3017

Alternative Graphics
Goleta, CA 93117
805-964-8875

Comp Set, Corp.
Hawthorne, CA 90250
310-644-6639

Raging Fingers
Hollywood, CA 90028
213-462-0575

Blake Typography—AlphaQueue
Irvine, CA 92718
714-727-0711

Omnipage Design & Imaging
Irvine, CA 92718
714-727-3339

Page One
Irvine, CA 92715
714-851-1530

Phoenix Press
Irvine, CA 92714
714-261-0333

Primary Color
Irvine, CA 92714
714-660-7080

Integrated Graphic Media
Irwindale, CA 91706
818-963-7545

Blue Book Publisers, Inc., dba Coastal Graphics
La Jolla, CA 92037
619-454-7939

Matthews International
La Palma, CA 90623
714-523-5511

CameraGraphics, Inc.
Lafayette, CA 94549
510-273-2473

Prep Graphics
Laguna Hills, CA 92653
714-586-5305

Desktop Publishing, Inc.
Larkspur, CA 94939-1802
415-258-9090

Versa Type, Inc
Long Beach, CA 90802
310-432-4086

Glazener Typesetting
Los Alamitos, CA 90720
310-594-9373

Access Publishing Network
Los Angeles, CA 90036
213-938-8973

Adage Graphics
Los Angeles, CA 90045
213-216-2828

Aldus Type Studio, Ltd.
Los Angeles, CA 90036-4208
213-934-1179

The Art Director
Los Angeles, CA 90036
213-933-9668

ASUCLA Typography
Los Angeles, CA 90024
310-206-0891

Desktop Studio
Los Angeles, CA 90024
213-474-9544

Electric Pencil
Los Angeles, CA 90046
213-852-9665

Electronic Publishing Specialists/EPS
Los Angeles, CA 90068
813-874-6141

G2 Graphic Service, Inc.
Los Angeles, CA 90028
213-467-7828

The Graphic Studio of Reynolds & Kasai
Los Angeles, CA 90025
310-477-4717

Graphics Etc. L.A., a division of Stats, Etc., Inc.
Los Angeles, CA 90057
213-384-1300

GTS Graphics, Inc./ Graphics Typesetting
Los Angeles, CA 90040
213-888-8889

Hi-Rez Graphics
Los Angeles, CA 90035-4549
213-838-8448

Icon West
Los Angeles, CA 90048
213-938-3822

Litho West
Los Angeles, CA 90035
213-939-2620

PrePress Studio
Los Angeles, CA 90036
213-938-3956

Taft Printing
Los Angeles, CA 90036-2501
213-933-9138

The Trunk Line
Los Angeles, CA 90034
310-204-2853

Typographic Service Company
Los Angeles, CA 90015
213-749-8383

Cal Sierra
Martinez, CA 94553
415-372-4200

A&A Printers
Menlo Park, CA 94025
415-365-1919

MarinStat, Inc.
Mill Valley, CA 94941
415-381-1188

Ridgecrest Graphics
Modesto, CA 95354
209-526-9778

Gary Walton Graphics, Inc.
Mountain VIew, CA 94043
415-961-0778

Graphic Express
Mountain View, CA 94043
415-962-9900

TLC Graphics
Mountain View, CA 94043
415-965-8524

San Diego Type and Graphics/DeFrance Printing
National City, CA 91950
619-474-8683

Paul Baker Printing, Inc.
North Highlands, CA 95660
916-485-2128

ImageSetters
North Hollywood, CA 91607
818-760-6595

OakCreek Typography
Northridge, CA 91325
818-773-2060

Spartan Typographics
Oakland, CA 94604 2333
415-836-0933

The Typesetting Shop, Inc.
Oakland, CA 94618
510-654-5404

Creative Graphics
Orange, CA 92667-5535
714-633-5770

Graphic Center
Palm Desert, CA 92211
619-340-1933

Computer Corners
Palmdale, CA 93551
805-943-2771

American Printing and Copy
Palo Alto, CA 94301
415-325-2322

Consultex
Palo Alto, CA 94306
415-322-3999

Design Spectrum
Palo Alto, CA 94301
415-329-1844

Metagraphics, Inc.
Palo Alto, CA 94301
415-327-8200

The Typemasters
Palo Alto, CA 94301
415-329-8973

Z Typography
Palo Alto, CA 94301
415-327-8671

The Castle Press
Pasadena, CA 91103
818-798-0858

Robert Meyers Studio
Pasadena, CA 91107
818-405-0922

Golden Pacific Systems, Inc.
Petaluma, CA 94952
707-579-3528

ImageSetters/ Pleasanton
Pleasanton, CA 94588
510-460-8462

InfoMania
Rancho Cordova, CA 95670
916-635-0201

Archetype Typesetting & Service Bureau
Riverisde, CA 92507
909-369-8058

ImageStation
Riverside, CA 92507
714-781-7337

Transnational Printing Services, Inc.
Rocklin, CA 95765
916-632-5888

Hal Hammond Graphics
Sacramento, CA 95816
916-452-6840

Lithographics
Sacramento, CA 95814
916-447-3219

Palmer Photographic
Sacramento, CA 95816
916-441-3305

Precision Graphic Arts
Sacramento, CA 95827-1706
916-364-1882

Beta Pacific (Beta Graphics)
San Diego, CA 92101
619-239-2382

Central Graphics
San Diego, CA 92101
619-234-6633

Clear Image Graphics
San Diego, CA 92126
619-566-8482

Graphic Communications, Inc.
San Diego, CA 92103
619-296-8171

ImageSetters West, Inc.
San Diego, CA 92111
619-576-2171

Laser Express
San Diego, CA 92111
619-694-0204

Lorilee Art Services
San Diego, CA 92106
619-223-0478

So Cal Graphics
San Diego, CA 92111
619-292-4919

Thompson Type, Inc.
San Diego, CA 92106
619-224-3137

VIVID Graphics and Typesetting, Inc.
San Diego, CA 92126
619-578-4843

Access Typography
San Francisco, CA 94107-3425
415-824-8973

Andresen Typographics
San Francisco, CA 94111
415-421-2900

Bay Area Prep
San Francisco, CA 94107
415-495-6085

Circus Lithograph Company, Inc.
San Francisco, CA 94105-3090
415-777-0575

Design & Type
San Francisco, CA 94107
415-495-6280

Imagewrights
San Francisco, CA
94107-1699
415-543-5035

Jessie's Graphics
San Francisco, CA 94105
415-543-3422

Krishna Copy Center
San Francisco, CA 94108
415-986-6161

Litho Graphic Services
San Francisco, CA 94103
415-863-2641

Lithographic Consultants
San Francisco, CA 94124
415-648-0329

MasterType
San Francisco, CA 94111
415-781-1351

Octagon Graphics, Inc.
San Francisco, CA 94107
415-777-9889

Omnicom
San Francisco, CA 94111
415-398-3377

Prepress Assembly, Inc.
San Francisco, CA 94103
415-621-8970

Rapid Lasergraphics
San Francisco, CA 94111
415-982-6071

ZesTop Publishing
San Francisco, CA 94114
415-863-1877

AdType
San Jose, CA 95126
408-297-3834

Coast Engraving Company
San Jose, CA 95112
408-297-2555

Prototype
San Jose, CA 95123-1353
408-226-8973

Tintype Graphic Arts
San Luis Obispo, CA
93401
805-544-9789

Lazertouch
San Mateo, CA 94401
415-348-7010

Top Hat Typography
San Mateo, CA 94402
415-344-3802

California Graphics
San Rafael, CA 94901
415-454-3494

Andresen Graphic Services
Santa Ana, CA 92705
714-250-4450

Imagination Graphics
Santa Ana, CA 92704
714-662-3114

Orange County Typesetting
Santa Ana, CA 92630
714-541-2288

Porter Graphics, Inc.
Santa Ana, CA 92705
714-558-1947

Graphic Traffic
Santa Barbara, CA
93101-2545
805-965-2372

Grayphics Typesetting and Design
Santa Barbara, CA
93101-3107
805-899-2387

In-Color Graphics
Santa Barbara, CA 93101
805-568-0800

Tom Buhl Imaging Center
Santa Barbara, CA 93101
805-963-8841

Andresen Typographics, Inc.
Santa Monica, CA 90405
310-452-5521

Digi-Type, Inc.
Santa Rosa, CA 95403
707-527-0873

Graphis Imaging Systems
Santa Rosa, CA 95407
707-571-8855

Just Your Type, Inc.
Santa Rosa, CA 95401
707-579-3528

Metrotype and Communication Arts
Sausalito, CA 94965
415-331-8393

Express Color & Imaging (Express Type, Co.)
Simi Valley, CA 93063
805-583-5512

RTS
South Pasadena, CA 91030
818-799-1610

CBM Type
Sunnyvale, CA 94086
408-739-0460

Alphabet City
Torrance, CA 90501
310-787-7580

Image Communications
Torrance, CA 90503
213-533-8911

The Type Factory, Inc.
Tustin, CA 92680
714-730-0990

Western Laser
Valencia, CA 91355
805-295-8797

Eureka + Avalon
Van Nuys, CA 91406
818-609-7274

West Coast Graphics/ SelectGraphics
Van Nuys, CA 91406
818-781-5336

West Coast Type & Color
Van Nuys, CA 91406
818-787-5600

PCC
Venice, CA 90291
213-823-8322

Cal Central Press
West Sacramento, CA 95691
916-373-0973 X02201

COLORADO

Color Print Imaging Center
Aurora, CO 80011
303-366-2642

Frederic Printing
Aurora, CO 80011
303-371-7990

Brown Graphics, Inc., dba Just Your Type
Boulder, CO 80302
303-938-9888

The Dot Ranch
Boulder, CO 80301
303-442-8244

Image Systems International, Inc.
Boulder, CO 80303
303-444-6162

Johnson Printing Company
Boulder, CO 80301
303-443-1576

WESType
Boulder, CO 80302
303-444-7009

Advanced Graphics & Publishing, Inc.
Colorado Springs, CO 80903
719-632-8142

Campro Systems, Ltd.
Denver, CO 80204
303-698-2125

Capitol Color Imaging
Denver, CO 80223
303-777-7550

Knudsen Printing Company
Denver, CO 80216
303-399-1144

LaserWriting, Inc.
Denver, CO 80204
303-592-1144

Lineaux, Inc.
Denver, CO 80218
303-333-5466

Mel Typesetting, Inc.
Denver, CO 80210
303-777-5571

Pageworks & TriDesign
Denver, CO 80231
303-337-7770

Publication Design, Inc.
Denver, CO 80203
303-830-0118

T & R Engraving
Denver, CO 80211
303-458-0626

Type etc., Inc.
Denver, CO 80231-4928
303-369-5600

Cottrell Printing Company
Englewood, CO 80227
303-790-4600

Interrobang
Englewood, CO 80111
303-937-9030

Precise Reprographics, Inc.
Englewood, CO 80111
303-850-7574

TeleTech
Ft Collins, CO 80524
303-493-0138

Colorado Printing Company
Grand Junction, CO 81501
303-242-3312

Colorline Photographics
Lakewood, CO 80227
303-986-7730

Mile-Hi Publishers
Lakewood, CO 80227
303-985-3825

Elegant Graphics
Steamboat Springs, CO 80477
303-879-4334

CONNECTICUT

Lumascan
Bloomfield, CT 06002
203-243-0700

Cyber Chrome, Inc.
Branford, CT 06405
203-488-9594

RMR Graphics/RM Reynolds, Inc.
Brookfield, CT 06804
203-740-7400

High Tech Type
Danbury, CT 06811
203-744-3280

Marketing Design Group, Inc.
Deep River, CT 06417
203-526-4357

Maximize
East Haddam, CT 06423
203-873-2665

AlphaCom, Inc.
Greenwich, CT 06830
203-625-0242

Icons & Images, Inc.
Greenwich, CT 06830
203-661-4469

Production Typographers, Inc.
Greenwich, CT 06830
203-531-4600

C.o.m.p.o.s.e., Inc.
Guilford, CT 06437-1314
203-855-9944

U-Design, Inc.
Hartford, CT 06109
203-278-3648

Information Designs
Marlborough, CT 06447
203-295-8111

Graphic Hearts
Milford, CT 06460
203-874-1305

Graphic Image, Inc.
Milford, CT 06460
203-877-8787

Alpha Typsetting
Monroe, CT 06468
203-261-1302

Graphix Group, Inc.
Monroe, CT 06468
203-261-7665

Phoenix Press
New Haven, CT 06513-0347
203-498-1055

Northeast Graphics
North Haven, CT 06473
203-288-2468

Computertech Design
Stamford, CT 06901
203-358-0003

Petco Photo & Design
Stamford, CT 06905
203-327-6554

Planetwide Productions, Inc.
Stamford, CT 06906
203-967-8808

Stamford Typesetting Corporation
Stamford, CT 06902
203-327-1441

Rainbow Press
Torrington, CT 06790
203-482-9388

Digital Imaging Service, Inc.
Trumbull, CT 06611
203-452-1901

Type House
Wallingford, CT 06492
203-284-8737

PrePress Computer Works, Inc.
West Hartford, CT 06110
203-232-1595

DC

Advanced Laser Graphics, ALG Electronics Publishing Center
Washington, DC 20007
202-342-2100

Applied Graphics Technologies
Washington, DC 20037-1153
202-832-9800

Aurora Color
Washington, DC 20002
202-546-3311

Automated Graphic Imaging/Copy Center
Washington, DC 20005-3305
202-371-5484

Studio Services, Inc.
Washington, DC 20006
202-785-9605

DELAWARE

Desktop Express, Inc.
Wilmington, DE 19809
302-762-3342

Firenze & Company, Inc.
Wilmington, DE 19801
302-571-8973

Modern Press, Inc.
Wilmington, DE 19804
302-998-9000

Technigraphics, Inc.
Wilmington, DE 19808
302-994-7782

Wm. N. Cann Graphics, Inc.
Wilmington, DE 19806
302-656-8260

FL

Falkinburg Typesetting, Inc.
Boca Raton, FL 33487
407-997-0704

The Set Up, Inc.
Cape Coral, FL 33904
813-542-4142

Blackhawk Color
Clearwater, FL 34622
813-535-4641

Norel Service Bureau
Coral Gables, FL 33146
305-444-9393

Peninsular Printing
Daytona Beach, FL 32117
904-274-4837

World Venture Corporation
Daytona Beach, FL 32127
904-767-6284

World Ventures Corporation
Daytona Beach, FL 32129
904-767-6284

Romax Communications
Fort Lauderdale, FL 33311-1527
203-324-4260

Typographical Service
Fort Lauderdale, FL 33309-5940
305-772-4710

Resolutions
Ft Lauderdale, FL 33301
305-763-4205

Pro-Creations Inc.
Gainesville, FL 32606
904-371-0832

Central Press
Hialeah, FL 33014
305-825-1212

Paramount Miller Graphics, Inc.
Jacksonville, FL 32207
904-448-1700

Progressive Printing
Jacksonville, FL 32210
904-388-0746

The Type House
Jacksonville, FL 32223
904-730-2934

Warecraft Press, Inc.
Jacksonville, FL 32211
904-355-3829

GCS/LaserTech—Graphic Composing Systems
Miami, FL 33172-2313
305-633-8548

Precision Imaging
Miami, FL 33169
305-653-5460

Palm Beach Typography
North Palm Beach, FL 33408
407-625-0276

Central Repro Inc
Orlando, FL 32801
407-843-0707

Ewasko Color
Orlando, FL 32805
407-425-6747

Lanman Lithotech
Orlando, FL 32805
407-293-3980

Linographics, Inc., dba Central Florida Typgraphics
Orlando, FL 32801
407-425-4824

Magna Graphic South, Inc.
Orlando, FL 32809
800-333-7880

Mechanical Art Graphics
Orlando, FL 32810
407-298-6384

Quebecor Orlando
Orlando, FL 32822
407-851-3681

Creative Images of Brevard, Inc.
Palm Bay, FL 32905
407-725-6006

MTM Publishing
Palm Beach Gardens, FL 33410
409-627-0035

Graphic Dynamics, Inc.
Pompano Beach, FL 33069
305-979-6212

Kall Graphics
Pompano Beach, FL 33060
305-942-5255

Printing Dimensions, Inc.
Sarasota, FL 34238
813-924-1351

Extra! Extra! Graphics
St. Petersburg, FL 33710
813-341-2700

Laser Image
St. Petersburg, FL 33716-1820
813-578-2661

The Type House
St. Petersburg, FL 33704
813-812-1726

Rex Three, Inc.
Sunrise, FL 33326
305-452-8301

Rapido, Inc.
Tallahassee, FL 32301
904-222-3136

Hall Type & Imaging Services
Tampa, FL 33609
813-870-1862

Hillsboro Printing
Tampa, FL 33629
813-251-2401

Action Printers
Vero Beach, FL 32960
407-567-4377

Great Impressions Printing
Winter Haven, FL 33880
813-294-7441

GEORGIA

Americas Performance Group, Inc.
Atlanta, GA 30339-5927
404-984-9444

The Graphic Forum
Atlanta, GA 30309
404-876-9902

Ogilvy & Mather Atlanta
Atlanta, GA 30309
404-888-5247

PST, Inc.
Atlanta, GA 30308
404-873-1200

Station to Station
Atlanta, GA 30318
404-609-7820

Tandem Services
Atlanta, GA 30341-5020
404-321-7676

TR Graphics, Inc.
Atlanta, GA 30045
404-633-8335

Treasure Chest Advertising Co.
Atlanta, GA 30354
404-761-2100

Type Direction
Atlanta, GA 30336
404-696-1537

Williams Printing Company
Atlanta, GA 30309
404-875-6611

Powerhouse Color, Inc.
Augusta, GA 30901
706-722-4773

Church Street Type & Publishing
Decatur, GA 30030
404-373-5360

Graphic Art Service, Inc.
Marietta, GA 30060
404-422-5500

Matthews International, Inc.
Marietta, GA 30067
404-984-9610

Graphic Production Center, Color US
Norcross, GA 30071
404-691-3201

Savannah Color Separations, Inc.
Savannah, GA 31401
912-233-8053

Copy Preparation
Tucker, GA 30084
404-939-2002

HAWAII

Belknap Publishing & Design
Honolulu, HI 96813
808-533-2999

PrintPrep of Hawaii
Honolulu, HI 96813
808-521-8268

Quality Graphic Service, Inc.
Honolulu, HI 96814
808-536-1718

Tongg Publishing
Honolulu, HI 96819
808-847-5310

Typehouse Havaii
Honolulu, HI 96817
808-842-4442

Electronic Publishing Services
Kahului, HI 96732
808-871-6224

IDAHO

Color Ad Corp.
Boise, ID 83706
208-375-6965

Spectra Printing and Graphics
Boise, ID 83702
208-322-1122

Typestyle
Boise, ID 83702
208-342-6563

DigiType, Division of BTGraphics, Inc.
Coeur d'Alene, ID 83814
208-667-8973

IOWA

Compo Arts Printing
Cedar Rapids, IA 52404
319-362-1646

Type 2
Cedar Rapids, IA 52402
319-366-6411

Typecraft, Inc.
Davenport, IA 52807
319-355-2500

The Printing Station
Des Moines, IA 50309
515-243-8144

Type-O-Graphics Two, Inc.
Des Moines, IA 50311
515-274-9231

Typeco, Inc.
Des Moines, IA 50309
515-282-8973

Waddell's Computer Graphic Center
Des Moines, IA 50309
515-282-0000

McCullough Graphics, Inc.
Dubuque, IA 52001
319-556-2392

Tursso Companies, Inc.
Ft Dodge, IA 50501
515-573-4393

ILLINOIS

ABS Graphics
Addison, IL 60101
708-495-2400

3E Litho
Arlington Heights, IL 60004
708-398-8677

Davis Litho Arts, Inc.
Bensenville, IL 60106
708-860-2009

Micro Link
Bensenville, IL 60106
708-860-1661

Design Typographers Corporation
Berkeley, IL 60163-1041
708-449-5200

Input/Output
Bloomington, IL 61701
309-662-1848

Color and Beyond
Carol Stream, IL 60188
708-462-4990

Glenbard Graphics, Inc.
Carol Stream, IL 60188-0026
708-653-4550

CPM Typesetting
Carpentersville, IL 60110
708-426-9244

Precision Graphic Services, Inc.
Champaign, IL 61820
217-359-6655

AnzoGraphics Computer Typographers
Chicago, IL 60610
312-642-8973

Chicago Art Production Services
Chicago, IL 60610
312-644-2740

Continental Graphics, Inc.
Chicago, IL 60605
312-987-1800

Davidson Group
Chicago, IL 60606
312-559-8973

Henderson Typography, Inc.
Chicago, IL 60610
312-951-8973

Image & Likeness, Inc.
Chicago, IL 60601
312-263-0900

InfoComm
Chicago, IL 60610
312-751-1220

Lakeshore Typographers, Inc.
Chicago, IL 60607
312-666-6606

Liberty Engraving
Chicago, IL 60605
312-786-0600

Master Typographers, Inc.
Chicago, IL 60610
312-661-1733

Matthews International
Chicago, IL 60618
312-539-7000

Noral Color Corporation
Chicago, IL 60630
312-775-0991

The Photographic and Reprographic Group, Inc.
Chicago, IL 60610
312-329-9600

Publishers Imageset/ Publishers Typesetting, Inc.
Chicago, IL 60630
312-283-3340

Shore Typographers, Inc.
Chicago, IL 60622
312-944-6650

Stats-It, Inc.
Chicago, IL 60611
312-988-9095 x101

Sunrise Hitek Service (Chicago Multi-Lingua Graphics)
Chicago, IL 60641
312-777-8708

Transet Graphics, Inc.
Chicago, IL 60611
312-670-6810

The Typesmiths Inc.
Chicago, IL 60610
312-787-8200

Liberty Lithographers, Inc.
Chicago Heights, IL 60411
708-754-6644

Black Dot Graphics, Inc.
Crystal Lake, IL 60014
815-459-8520

Lightning Graphic Services, Inc.
Des Plaines, IL 60018
708-298-1616

Booklet Publishing Company
Elk Grove Village, IL 60007
708-364-1544

Lehigh Press-Colortronics
Elk Grove Village, IL 60007
708-364-8000

The Type Studio, Ltd.
Evanston, IL 60201
708-328-8244

Crown Color Corporation
Fox Lake, IL 60020
708-587-2177

Tukaiz Innovative PrePress
Franklin Park, IL 60131
708-455-1588

The Complex
Glen Ellyn, IL 60137
708-858-4575

Lasercom, Inc.
Glenview, IL 60025
708-724-2490

PRI
Glenview, IL 60025
708-724-0182

Brown Kow Graphics
Hillside, IL 60162-0696
708-547-8383

Laser Graphics, Inc.
Hillside, IL 60162
708-449-2090

Screaming Color, Inc.
Itasca, IL 60143
708-250-9500

Graphics Plus, Inc.
Lisle, IL 60532
708-968-9073

TechGraphic, Ltd.
Milan, IL 61264
309-787-8324

Alpha Omega Color Graphics Inc
Mt. Morris, IL 61054
815-734-6066

Jackson County Printing/Jackson Printing and Publishing
Murphysboro, IL 62966
618-687-2432

Comply Enterprises, Inc.
Naperville, IL 60563
308-717-5566

StudioNorth
North Chicago, IL 60064
708-473-4545

The Fontworks, Inc.
Northbrook, IL 60062-5241
708-392-8973

Publishing Technologies, Inc.
Northbrook, IL 60062-7905
708-498-5633

Vision Art Type
Northbrook, IL 60062
708-272-1902

Computer Publishing Services
Palos Heights, IL 60463
708-448-1900

Typographics Plus
Park Ridge, IL 60068
708-292-8973

Coventry Creative Graphics
Peoria, IL 61615
309-692-0364

Chief City Graphics
Pontiac, IL 61764
815-844-3114

Steven James LaMont
Prospect Heights, IL 60070
708-520-1210

Royal Printing Co.
Quincy, IL 62306
217-222-0617

Fairchild Graphics
Rockford, IL 61104
815-398-8788

Lundquist Graphics, Inc.
Rockford, IL 61112
815-332-5540

Professional Graphics, Inc.
Rockford, IL 61109
815-226-9422

H & S Graphics
Rolling Meadows, IL 60008
708-506-9800

Melís Litho Service
Roselle, IL 60172
708-894-8440

Exacto Type & Design
Schaumburg, IL 60173
708-882-7225

Color Imetry Corporation
Skokie, IL 60077
708-679-5757

Graphic Electronics
Spring Valley, IL 61362
815-664-2371

JB Typesetting Company
St. Charles, IL 60174
708-377-1966

Barnaby Printing
Sycamore, IL 60178
815-895-6555

Graphic Arts Services
Villa Park, IL 60181
708-629-7770

Laser Colour, Inc.
Wood Dale, IL 60191
708-860-9292

The Typegroup, Inc.
Wood Dale, IL 60191
708-595-4949

INDIANA

Fine Light, Inc.
Bloomington, IN 47404
812-339-6700

Photo Comp Corporation
Brownsburg, IN 46112
317-852-4377

Impressions, Inc.
Elkhart, IN 46615-0007
219-294-3445

The Crown Press Corporation
Evansville, IN 47713
812-424-3724

Schwindel Graphics, Inc.
Evansville, IN 47711
812-422-6094

Greencastle Offset Printing
Greencastle, IN 46135
317-653-4026

Alexander Typesetting
Indianapolis, IN 46201
317-634-2206

Channing Graphics, Inc.
Indianapolis, IN 46219
317-259-4513

Douglas & Gayle, Ltd.
Indianapolis, IN 46205
317-924-5460

Repro Electronic Imaging
Indianapolis, IN 46241
317-243-2711

Rheitone, Inc.
Indianapolis, IN 46202
317-925-3543

RPS Printing Service
Indianapolis, IN 46225
317-464-0261

Shepard Poorman Communications Corporation
Indianapolis, IN 46278
317-293-1500

Weimer Graphics, Inc.
Indianapolis, IN 46225
317-267-0565

The Woodfield Group
Indianapolis, IN 46278
317-290-0559

The Image Center Inc.
Michigan City, IN 46360
219-874-6243

Ludwick Graphics, Inc.
South Bend, IN 46628
219-233-2165

Mossberg & Company, Inc.
South Bend, IN 46624-0210
219-289-9253

Rink Riverside Printing, Inc.
South Bend, IN 46617
219-232-7935

The Image Group
Syracuse, IN 46567
219-457-3111

KANSAS

Direct Digital Design
Kansas City, KS 66103
913-371-4333

Commercial Arts Services
Lenexa, KS 66215
913-894-9391

Graphics Four Inc
Lenexa, KS 66214
913-268-1200

Marketing Resources America
Overland Park, KS 66212
913-648-6789

Ottmar's Laser Printing
Overland Park, KS 66204
913-381-7409

Boelte-Hall Litho, Inc.
Roeland Park, KS 66205
913-432-0900

National Electronic Type, Inc.
Topeka, KS 66611-1167
913-357-6331

KPN Typographics, Inc.
Wichita, KS 67203
316-265-4231

The Typesetter, Inc./ COLORations
Wichita, KS 67211
316-267-5001

KENTUCKY

Beau Graphics
Lexington, KY 40575-1398
606-259-1899

Clark Typesetting
Lexington, KY 40504
606-254-5302

Image Printer, Inc.
Louisville, KY 40269
502-491-8201

QC, Inc.
Louisville, KY 40202
502-584-8973

Cobb Type
Newport, KY 41071
606-291-1146

Image Graphics
Paducah, KY 42002-6163
502-442-6163

LOUISIANA

K & W PrePress, Inc.
Baton Rouge, LA
70809-2524
504-927-8872

The Slide Source
Baton Rouge, LA 70806
504-925-8278

Spectrum Press, Inc.
Baton Rouge, LA 70809
504-292-1450

Fontenette Enterprises, Inc.
Kenner, LA 70065
504-467-6081

Hanson Graphics of New Orleans
Metairie, LA 70001
504-834-4864

Sistematik Graphics, Inc./Pagemasters
Shreveport, LA
71103-3660
318-222-0075

MAINE

High Resolution, Inc.
Camden, ME 04843-0397
207-236-3777

ImageSet Design
Portland, ME 04101
207-775-4738

MARYLAND

Alpha Graphics, Inc.
Baltimore, MD 21202
301-727-1400

GKV Design
Baltimore, MD 21202
301-685-3770

Monotype Company
Baltimore, MD 21211
301-467-3300

Spectrum Arts, Ltd.
Baltimore, MD 21217
301-462-6900

M & M Communications
Berwyn Heights, MD
20740
301-441-9119

The Bluemont Company
Bethesda, MD 20814
301-657-8315

Litho Composition Services, Inc.
Bethesda, MD 20814
301-657-2990

Type Foundry
Bethesda, MD 20814
301-656-0025

Peake Printers, Inc.
Cheverly, MD 20781
301-341-6540

Columbia Type & Art, Inc.
Columbia, MD 21044
410-997-3351

Harlowe Typography, Inc.
Cottage City, MD 20722
301-277-8311

Publishing Solutions, Inc.
Derwood, MD 20855
301-424-3942

Bladen Lithographics, Inc.
Gaithersburg, MD 20879
301-948-9600

Frank Gumpert Printing Company
Gaithersburg, MD 20877
301-948-1000

Copy-Quik Services
Hagerstown, MD 21740
301-791-7400

Corporate Press, Inc.
Landover, MD 20785
301-499-9200

Nebel Printing, Inc.
Rockville, MD 20852
301-881-4016

In Tandem Design
Towson, MD 21204
410-832-8706

Pubtek International, Inc.
Waldorf, MD 20602
301-843-2423

Automated Graphic Systems
White Plains, MD 20695
301-843-1800

MASSACHUSETTS

WE Andrews Co., Inc.
Bedford, MA 01730
617-275-0720

Allison Associates
Boston, MA 02215
617-267-2100

Capital Typographers (Dynograt)
Boston, MA 02127
617-268-1900 x205

Matthews International
Braintree, MA 02184
617-848-8220

TeleTypesetting
Brookline, MA 02146
2906
617-734-9700

CGI Inc
Burlington, MA 01803
617-229-2345

CIS Graphic Communications
Cambridge, MA 02139
617-491-3010

Pageworks
Cambridge, MA 02141-1117
617-374-6000

ABC Publications, Inc.
Canton, MA 02021-1404
617-575-9915

Graphic Traffic Co.
Duxbury, MA 02331
617-934-9036

Treasure Chest Advertising
East Longmeadow, MA 01028
413-525-8552

ILS Business Services
Feeding Hills, MA 01030
413-789-4555

Larry Cron Design
Framington, MA 01701
508-820-7773

Diversified Business Systems
Haverhill, MA 01831-1111
508-373-4748

Custom Printing & Design, Inc.
Leominster, MA 01453
508-537-8095

Vision Graphics, Inc.
Ludlow, MA 01056
413-589-9551

SPV Teletype Graphics
Medford, MA 02155
617-396-3017

Crockergraphics
Needham, MA 02194
617-444-7020

Imagepoint
Newton Highlands, MA 02161
617-965-6788

ImageResolutions, Inc.
Norwell, MA 02061
617-659-7023

United Lithograph
Somerville, MA 02143
617-776-6400

Berkeley Typographers, Inc.
South Boston, MA 02127
617-269-6160

MicroPrint
Waltham, MA 02154-1026
617-890-7500

WrapArounds, Inc., Division of Power-Vu Graphics
West Springfield, MA 01089
413-781-5447

Boston Business Graphics
Woburn, MA 01801
617-938-6525

WordTech Corporation
Woburn, MA 01801-2008
617-933-5550

COMP Associates, Inc.
Worcester, MA 01603
508-754-1179

MICHIGAN

Desktop Technologies, Inc.
Ann Arbor, MI 48103
313-663-3320

Goetzcraft Printers, Inc.
Ann Arbor, MI 48108
313-973-7604

ImageSet
Ann Arbor, MI 48104
313-971-7030

Total Type & Graphics, Inc.
Ann Arbor, MI 48107-7341
313-994-6166

Typographic Insight
Ann Arbor, MI 48103
313-994-3904

Unitech Graphics, Inc.
Ann Arbor, MI
48108-2417
313-973-8939

Key-Tech
Birmingham, MI
48301-3158
313-644-4993

Ad Gravers, Inc.
Detroit, MI 48207
313-259-3780

North American Graphics, Inc.
Detroit, MI 48216
313-962-6970

T.P.H. Graphics, Inc.
Detroit, MI 48202
313-875-1950

Milbrook Printing Company
Grand Ledge, MI 48837
517-627-4078

D & D Printing Co.
Grand Rapids, MI 49503
616-454-7710

The Electronic Publishing Center
Grand Rapids, MI
49548-7832
616-698-9890

Rhombus Design
Grand Rapids, MI 49504
616-235-0030

Trade Typographers, Inc.
Grand Rapids, MI 49546
616-956-6901

Holland Litho Service
Holland, MI 49423
616-392-4644

SSG Image & Design Group
Kalamazoo, MI
49009-9451
219-295-7467

Superior Typesetting Service
Kalamazoo, MI 49001
616-349-9741

Number One Graphics
Lansing, MI 48912
517-332-6231

Pendell Printing Inc.
Midland, MI 48640
517-496-3333

Words and More, Inc.
Royal Oak, MI 48067-4111
313-547-8650

Tark Graphics, Inc.
South Field, MI 48075
313-557-6004

Applied Laser Graphics, Inc.
Spring Lake, MI 49456
616-846-0770

Type House, Inc.
St. Joseph, MI 49085
616-983-7704

Diversified Type
Traverse City, MI 49684
616-947-2117

Butler Graphics, Inc.
Troy, MI 48084
313-528-2808

VuCom Graphicsystems
Troy, MI 48084
313-362-4212

MINNESOTA

Quality Imaging
Baxter, MN 56425
218-828-0264

Schmidt Printing, Inc.
Byron, MN 55920-1386
507-288-6400

Duluth Publishing and Pre-Press Services, Inc.
Duluth, MN 55812
218-728-6897

Horizon Graphics
Eden Prairie, MN 55344
612-941-0757

May Typography
Eden Prairie, MN 55344
612-829-7475

The Hart Press, Inc.
Long Prairie, MN 56347-1935
612-732-2121

MGA Graphics, Inc.
Mankato, MN 56001
507-387-7953

7•30 Productions
Minneapolis, MN 55403
612-333-2322

A. G. Johnson Imaging Corporation
Minneapolis, MN 55401
612-332-2122

AlphaGraphics Group, Inc.
Minneapolis, MN 55426
612-525-1005

Apache Print, Inc.
Minneapolis, MN 55421
612-789-1000

Bolger Publications/ Creative Printing
Minneapolis, MN 55414
612-645-6311

Colorhouse, Inc.
Minneapolis, MN 55441
612-550-3640

CTS Creative Graphics
Minneapolis, MN 55415
612-339-0531

Dahl & Curry, Inc.
Minneapolis, MN 55403
612-338-7171

Electric Graphics
Minneapolis, MN 55402
612-339-2227

Gopher State Litho
Minneapolis, MN 55406
612-724-3600

Great Faces, Inc.
Minneapolis, MN 55411
612-522-3223

Image Arrangers
Minneapolis, MN 55439
612-831-1444

Jodee Kulp Graphic Arts
Minneapolis, MN 55401
612-824-7712

Printing Arts, Inc.
Minneapolis, MN 55422
612-588-0863

Smart Set, Inc.
Minneapolis, MN 55401
612-339-7725

T D Type & Design, Inc.
Minneapolis, MN 55423
612-861-7409

Type House-Duragraph, Inc.
Minneapolis, MN 55411
612-588-7511

Weston Engraving
Minneapolis, MN 55418
612-789-8514

GS Graphics, Inc.
New Hope, MN 55428
612-533-2275

GV Graphics, Inc.
New Hope, MN 55427
612-542-8330

Continental Press, Inc.
St. Cloud, MN 56302
612-251-5875

As Soon As Possible, Inc.
St. Louis Park, MN 55410
612-926-4735

Master Graphics
St. Louis Park, MN 55416
612-927-9260

Bob's Litho
St. Paul, MN 55107-1217
612-227-4037

Computer Chrome, Inc.
St. Paul, MN 55114
612-646-2442

The Electronic Easel
St .Paul, MN 55114-1820
612-659-2424

NWprintcrafters
St. Paul, MN 55107
612-227-7721

Sexton Printing, Inc.
St. Paul, MN 55118
612-457-9255

Tursso Companies, Inc.
St. Paul, MN 55107
612-222-0376

Villager Graphics
St. Paul, MN 55116
612-699-1462

Nordell Graphic Communications, Inc.
Staples, MN 56479
218-894-3591

Brown Printing Company
Waseca, MN 56093
507-835-2410

PrePress Services and Technology, a division of Brown Printing
Waseca, MN 56093
507-835-0491

Virtual Image
Winona, MN 55987-0030
507-454-6657

MISSISSIPPI

Heritage Graphics, Inc.
Jackson, MS 39206
601-981-2161

Blackwell Lithographers, Inc.
Richland, MS 39218
601-932-7422

Ringier America
Senatobia, MS 38668
601-562-5252

MISSOURI

Media Graphics
Columbia, MO 65201
314-449-0002

Connell-Zeko Type & Graphics
Kansas City, MO 64131
816-842-1484

Digital Illusions, Inc.
Kansas City, MO 64127
816-483-4446

Fontastik, Inc.
Kansas City, MO 64105
816-474-4366

Graphic Services, Inc.
Kansas City, MO 64111
816-561-5313

The Lowell Press, Inc.
Kansas City, MO 64108
816-753-4545

Bass Lithocolor, Inc.
Springfield, MO 65802
417-866-4929

Type Center, Inc.
Springfield, MO 65806
417-865-6805

Network Color Technology
St. Charles, MO 63301
314-949-5300

The Composing Room, Inc.
St. Louis, MO 63110
314-773-2400

Focus Graphics
St. Louis, MO 63132
314-991-1698

Jamik Laser Graphics
St. Louis, MO 63119-2702
314-962-5860

Matthews International
St. Louis, MO 63132
314-423-9800

Repco Printers & Lithographers, Inc.
St. Louis, MO 63144
314-647-8100

TSI Graphics, Inc.
St. Louis, MO 63144
314-968-6800

Type Gallery, Inc.
St. Louis, MO 63139
314-645-3084

Type Two
St. Louis, MO 63144
314-647-8880

MONTANA

Speedy Print, Inc.
Bozeman, MT 59715
406-587-3233

NEBRASKA

Petersen Typographers
Lincoln, NE 68505
402-476-2816

Custom Typographers, Inc.
Omaha, NE 68105
402-422-0240

Graphic Technologies, Inc.
Omaha, NE 68137-1105
402-334-4455

Holigraphic, Inc.
Omaha, NE 68124
402-391-2961

Micro Graphics
Omaha, NE 68108-3504
402-339-1250

Omaha Graphics, Inc.
Omaha, NE 68106
402-556-0335

NEVADA

Laser Image Reprographics, Inc.
Binghamton, NV 13905
607-723-2145

Beehive Images, Inc.
Carson City, NV 89706
702-883-3961

Graphic Services
Carson City, NV 89706
702-885-0101

The Imagesetters, Inc.
Henderson, NV 89015
702-564-8888

LaserPrint, Inc.
Las Vegas, NV 89119
702-736-4064

Suburban Graphics, Inc.
Las Vegas, NV 89109
702-735-1212

ETGIN Co.
Reno, NV 89502
702-322-0627

Reno Typographers, Inc.
Reno, NV 89501
702-322-7366

NEW HAMPSHIRE

Eastern Rainbow, Inc.
Derry, NH 03038
603-432-2547

LaserLab
Hanover, NH 03755
603-643-1900

Type II
Lebanon, NH 03766-1272
603-448-3988

Whitman Communications Group
Lebanon, NH 03766
603-448-2600

Winzeler Group Ltd.
Manchester, NH 03104
603-668-0036

Media Solutions, Inc.
Merrimack, NH 03054
603-429-8300

GraphPro
Portsmouth, NH 03801
603-436-3868

NEW JERSEY

Another Way, Inc.
Berlin, NJ 08009
609-768-6340

Deputy Crown, Inc.
Camden, NJ 08103
609-365-2110

Applied Graphics Technologies
Carlstadt, NJ 07072
201-935-3200

GS Imaging Services
Carlstadt, NJ 07072
201-933-8585

Printers' Choice, Graphic Innovations
Cherry Hill, NJ 08003-2600
609-751-1188

Spectracolor
Cherry Hill, NJ 08002-2990
609-663-8642

Old Stone Graphic Services, Inc.
Cinnaminson, NJ 08077-0095
609-829-1878

JRI Graphic Communications
Clifton, NJ 07011
201-340-0170

Mates Graphics
Clifton, NJ 07012
201-778-3110

Weinrich Associates, Inc.
Clifton, NJ 07013
201-473-6643

Whitman Studio
Clifton, NJ 07013
201-472-0990

Graphic Connexions, Inc.
Cranbury, NJ 08512
609-655-8970

CDI/Maikron Publishing Center
Florham Park, NJ 07932
201-765-0303

ROP Digitek
Harrison, NJ 07029
201-482-8000

Express Press/Harvill Communications
Hightstown, NJ 08520
609-443-5900

Tristin, Inc.
Kendall Park, NJ 08824
908-297-6900

Desktop Dynamics
Lakewood, NJ 08701
908-364-2111

Midland Park Graphics
Midland Pk, NJ 07432
201-445-8816

CompuLith, Inc.
Moonachie, NJ 07074
201-804-7654

Line & Tone Group, Inc. (Desktop Productions, Inc.)
Mountain Lakes, NJ 07046
201-263-0410

C. J. Piparo Associates, Inc.
North Brunswick, NJ 08902
908-297-8780

Newark Trade Typographers
Orange, NJ 07050
201-674-3727

Armstrong Graphic Services
Pennsauken, NJ 08109
609-486-4846

American Impressions
Plainfield, NJ 07060
908-757-2600

Imageworks, Inc.
Ramsey, NJ 07446
201-327-6692

OnLine Design
Ramsey, NJ 07446-1223
201-825-4499

QPL, Inc.
Ramsey, NJ 07446
201-825-7777

Riverside Imagesetters, Inc.
Red Bank, NJ 07701
908-758-1133

The Color Bureau, a division of Yvey/Lonier, Inc.
Ridgewood, NJ 07446
201-670-0338

Dimensional Graphics
Roselle, NJ 07203
201-241-6900

Quality Graphics Center, Inc.
Roselle, NJ 07203
908-245-7300

Granite Graphics
Rutherford, NJ 07070
201-438-7398

L&B Typo, Inc.
Scotch Plains, NJ 07076
908-232-7770

Parker Color Company
Trenton, NJ 08618
609-394-8151

NEW MEXICO

Copygraphics, Inc.
Santa Fe, NM 87501
505-988-1438

NEW YORK

Alternative Ink Ltd.
Albany, NY 12205
518-458-9000

Associated Graphic Services, Inc.
Albany, NY 12210
518-465-1497

Word Management
Albany, NY 12205
518-482-8659

CompuPrint Graphics & Marketing Corp.
Baldwin, NY 11510-3354
516-223-2270

Regional Typographers, Inc.
Bellmore, NY 11710
516-785-4422

Niles & Phipps/ The TypePeople
Binghamton, NY 13901
607-722-6435

Olson Typographic, Inc.
Brewster, NY 10509
914-279-7586

Computer Imaging Center
Buffalo, NY 14225
716-896-7601

ImageCore Ltd.
Buffalo, NY 14215 0244
716-832-3402

Printing Prep/ Color Copy Center
Buffalo, NY 14203
716-852-5011

Rapid Service Engraving Company, Inc.
Buffalo, NY 14211
716-895-4555

Computer Composition Service
Cheektowaga, NY 14225
716-632-0300

Meritís Laserset
Floral Park, NY 11001
516-352-5060

Online Ontime
Hauppauge, NY 11788
516-348-6914

Ilsand Typographers, Inc.
Hicksville, NY 11802
516-931-2282

Atlantic Digital Typesetting
Latham, NY 12110
518-783-6170

Rolf Krauss, Inc.
Mt. Kisco, NY 10549
914-241-3145

All Union Press, Inc., dba MetroGrafik
New York, NY 10001
212-741-0047

Art-Pro Graphics
New York, NY 10003
212-473-4100

The Artistic Group
New York, NY 10001
212-255-7087

Autographica, Inc.
New York, NY 10010
212-675-1265

Axiom Design Systems
New York, NY 10011
212-989-1100

Boro Typographers, Inc.
New York, NY 10010
212-475-7850

Brilliant Image
New York, NY 10001
212-736-9661

Cardinal Communications Group
New York, NY 10036
212-489-1717

City Offset Services
New York, NY 10010
212-929-7083

Colortec Graphic Production, Inc.
New York, NY 10017-5102
212-431-6565

DBS Services, Inc.
New York, NY 10017
212-972-7513

Digital Pre-Press
New York, NY 10001
212-924-7661

Enterprise Press
New York, NY 10014
212-741-2111

ExpoGraphics, Inc.
New York, NY 10036
212-819-0045

Graphic Art Service, Inc.
New York, NY 10019
212-582-9541

Graphics Corporation of America
New York, NY 10010
212-684-0909

Image Assemblers, Inc.
New York, NY 10001
212-741-2280

Impressive Prepress, Inc.
New York, NY 10001
212-564-4948

Integrated Software
New York, NY 10016-6901
312-545-0110

JCH Group, Ltd.
New York, NY 10010
212-532-4000

Katz Graphics, Inc.
New York, NY 10016
212-725-8500

Leonardo Studio, Inc.
New York, NY 10011
212-645-7844

Line & Tone Typografix Corp.
New York, NY 10018
212-921-8333

LinoGraphics Corporation
New York, NY 10011
212-727-3070

Manhattan Graphic Productions, a division of The Ace Group
New York, NY 10001
212-255-6687

Microcomputer Publishing Center
New York, NY 10011
212-463-8585

Micropage
New York, NY 10003
212-533-9180

New York Review
New York, NY 10107
212-757-8070

O'Sullivan Typographers
New York, NY 10012
212-226-3481

Oh Jackie!, Inc.
New York, NY 10017
212-986-9538

Quad Right, Inc.
New York, NY 10025
212-222-1220

rhinoType, Inc.
New York, NY 10014
212-929-1134

Sarabande Press
New York, NY 10012
212-473-0888

Seth Meredith Concepts
New York, NY 10014
212-675-4666

Spectra Desktop Solutions
New York, NY 10014
212-366-6777

The Stat Store, Inc./ Digital Exchange
New York, NY 10011
212-929-0566

Typogram, Inc.
New York, NY 10003
212-505-1640

Typographic Images
New York, NY 10011
212-645-6100

Print-Crafters, Inc.
North Merrick, NY 11566
516-489-0691

Your Type
North Tonawanda, NY 14120
716-694-7472

Arc-O-Type Graphics, Inc.
Oyster Bay, NY 11771
516-624-6703

Graphic Laser Networks, Inc.
Peekskill, NY 10566
914-737-0938

Nassau Typographers
Plainview, NY 11803
516-433-0100

Profile PS, Inc.
Plainview, NY 11803
516-293-0480

AB Typesetting
Poughkeepsie, NY 12603
914-473-3220

All Pro Printers
Rochester, NY 14606
716-247-1430

Digitech Publishing International, Inc.
Rochester, NY 14619-1719
716-436-3100

Lazer Photo Engraving
Rochester, NY 14615
716-663-9000

Master Typography
Rochester, NY 14614
716-232-9230

R. A. Ellis Corporation
Rochester, NY 14609
716-288-8820

Rochester Empire Graphics
Rochester, NY 14623
716-272-1100

Rochester General Graphics
Rochester, NY 14612
716-663-0689

Rochester Monotype
Rochester, NY 14605
715-546-1690

Sentry Color Labs, Ltd.
Rochester, NY 14620
716-262-2030

Discus, Inc.
Scotia, NY 12302
518-377-4692

J & J Computing, Inc.
Suffern, NY 10901
914-357-6381

Associated Graphic Enterprises
Syosset, NY 11791
516-681-6060

Imaging International, Inc.
Syosset, NY 11791-3044
212-255-1110

Infinity/USA
Syosset, NY 11791
516-496-3900

Communications & Energy Corp.
Syracuse, NY 13220
315-452-0709

Dupli Graphics, Inc.
Syracuse, NY 13201 1302
315-472-1316

George Monagle/ Graphic Partners
Syracuse, NY 13203
315-426-0513

ImPress, Inc., dba The Image Press
Syracuse, NY 13203
315-422-8984

GW Canfield & Son Lithographers
Utica, NY 13502
315-735-5522

E & M Graphics
Wantagh, NY 11493
516-826-0759

Computer Design and Publishing
White Plains, NY 10606
914-949-4655

NORTH CAROLINA

Craftsman Printing Co.
Charlotte, NC 28273
704-588-2120

ICCA Graphics
Charlotte, NC 28209
704-523-7219

Letter-Perfect, Inc.
Charlotte, NC 28217
704-523-6730

RareType
Charlotte, NC 28203
704-372-6646

Raven Type
Charlotte, NC 28203
704-376-0064

Azalea Typography
Durham, NC 27705
919-286-2091

Marathon Typography Service, Inc.
Durham, NC 27713
919-544-1087

Desktop Publishing Services
Greensboro, NC 27409
919-855-0400

Douglas Graphics, Inc.
Greensboro, NC 27407
919-299-4621

Types, Inc.
Greensboro, NC 27401
919-275-1326

Furniture City Color, Inc.
High Point, NC 27262
919-883-7314

EyeBeam
Morrisville, NC 27560
909-469-3859

Image Associates, Inc.
Raleigh, NC 27609
919-876-6400

Modular Graphic Services
Wilmington, NC 28401
919-763-2012

PrePress Graphics, Inc.
Winston Salem, NC 27101
919-722-4604

AdType, Inc.
Winston-Salem, NC 27101
919-727-0309

Southern Graphics, Inc.
Winston-Salem, NC 27127
919-727-0640

Walt Klein & Associates
Winston-Salem, NC 27101
919-727-4900

Theo Davis Sons, Inc.
Zebulon, NC 27597
919-269-7401

OHIO

Enterprise Information Services
Akron, OH 44311
216-762-2222

TypeWorks
Akron, OH 44333-4034
216-864-2027

Life Systems, Inc./ The Graphics Center
Beachwood, OH 44122
216-464-3297

All Systems Color
Centerville, OH 45459
513-433-5054

Harlan Typographic
Cincinnati, OH 45225
513-751-5700

Jala Advertising, Inc.
Cincinnati, OH 45240
513-742-4102

Precision Digital Images, Inc.
Cincinnati, OH 45203-1892
513-784-1555

Robin Color Lab
Cincinnati, OH 45214
513-381-5116

RPI Color Service, Inc.
Cincinnati, OH 45204
513-471-4040

Studio Art Services
Cincinnati, OH 45202
513-421-8040

Lithokraft Plate Company, Inc.
Cleveland, OH 44103
216-881-3838

TSI Typesetting Service, Inc.
Cleveland, OH 44115
216-241-2647

Cardinal Type, Inc.
Columbus, OH 43214
614-261-8973

Columbus Typographic Co., Inc.
Columbus, OH 43215
614-221-1544

Harlan Type
Columbus, OH 43215
614-486-9641

LaserPrep, Inc.
Columbus, OH 43235
614-792-0888

Lithokraft II
Columbus, OH 43228-9416
614-771-4848

Concept Imaging Group
Dayton, OH 45439
513-293-2555

Laser Graphics, Inc.
Dayton, OH 45459
513-434-8805

Type One Graphics, a division of Dayton Tech Art Company
Dayton, OH 45404
513-461-4720

Andrew's Graphics
Fairlawn, OH 44333
216-864-4192

Richardson Printing Corporation
Marietta, OH 45750
614-373-5362

Carey Color, Inc.
Medina, OH 44256
216-725-5637

Medina Printing Company
Medina, OH 44256
216-723-3686

Toledo Engraving Company
Toledo, OH 43602
419-241-5155

Robin Enterprises Company
Westervile, OH 43081
614-891-0250

Bestgen Publications
Willoughby, OH 44094
216-946-0700

OKLAHOMA

Be-Graphics
Oklahoma City, OK 73116
405-840-9999

Art's Graphic Services, Inc.
Tulsa, OK 74104-1711
918-592-5758

Cat Tail Type
Tulsa, OK 74105
918-747-7947

Epic, Inc.
Tulsa, OK 74105
918-744-1118

Graphics Universal, Inc.
Tulsa, OK 74145
918-655-6633

Rodgers Litho Company
Tulsa, OK 74107
918-587-8165

Tulsa Litho Company
Tulsa, OK 74107 3203
918-582-8185

US Graphics, Inc.
Tulsa, OK 74119
918-584-5860

OREGON

Pride Printing Company
Albany, OR 97321
503-928-3322

Phoenix Digital PrePress, Graphics Plus
Beaverton, OR 97006
503-629-0587

TechnaPrint, Inc.
Eugene, OR 97401-3247
503-244-4062

Accuprint
Gresham, OR 97030
503-667-3100

Award Design & Desktop Service, Inc.
Medford, OR 97501-5923
503-772-2971

B & W Typography, Inc. and Graphics Service Bureau
Portland, OR 04101
207-761-2815

Color Magic, Inc.
Portland, OR 97220
503-253-3237

Harrison Typesetting, Inc.
Portland, OR 97214
503-238-9891

JV Hollingsworth Company
Portland, OR 97209
503-223-8181

L Grafix
Portland, OR 97209
503-248-9713

Portland Ad Type
Portland, OR 97204
503-294-1400

Premier Press
Portland, OR 97209
503-223-4984

Wy'east Color
Portland, OR 97201
503-228-7053

Advanced Typographics, Inc.
Salem, OR 97301
503-364-2100

Precision Photography NW Inc./Precision Imagesetting
Tigard, OR 97223
503-620-9229

PENNSYLVANIA

Kingswood Advertising (Digital Arts)
Ardmore, PA 19003
215-896-9260

Desktop Technologies, Inc.
Boyertown, PA 19512
215-367-7599

The Graphics Link
Camp Hill, PA 17011
717-737-2650

On Trak Graphics, Inc.
Cedars, PA 19423
215-584-8973

PHP Typography
Conshohocken, PA 19428
215-940-1044

Creative Image & Design
Dickson City, PA 18519
717-383-2295

Easton Printing Company
Easton, PA 18044-0228
215-253-4171

Harmony Press
Easton, PA 18042-6301
215-559-9800

International Computaprint Corporation
Fort Washington, PA 19034-2792
215-641-6000

Harrisburg Graphic Arts Shop
Harrisburg, PA 17111
717-939-0411

Town & Country Press
Hellertown, PA 18055
215-838-0356

Kalnin Graphics, Inc.
Jenkintown, PA 19046
215-887-6970

Centennial Graphics, Inc
Lancaster, PA 17605-0067
717-397-8863

Lancaster Ultra Graphics
Lancaster, PA 17601
717-393-5188

Red Rose Graphics, Ltd.
Lancaster, PA 17604-4576
800-633-7673

Bucks County Type & Design
Langhorne, PA 19047-1748
215-757-3600

The LaserTouch, Inc.
Malvern, PA 19355
215-993-9911

Spectra Comp
Mechanicsburg, PA 17055
717-697-8600

Michael Typography, Inc.
Media, PA 19063
215-565-1683

Alphabet Graphics, Inc.
Mountville, PA 17554
717-285-7105

Computer Assisted Graphics Network
Murrysville, PA 15219-1317
412-471-6231

Adams Graphics, Inc.
Philadelphia, PA 19107
215-557-7376

Cage Graphic Arts
Philadelphia, PA 19129-1299
215-843-2243

Composing Room, Inc.
Philadelphia, PA 19107
215-829-9611

Fels Printing
Philadelphia, PA 19111
215-342-1106

Regency Typographic Services
Philadelphia, PA 19134
215-425-8810

Stallone Typography Services, Inc.
Philadelphia, PA 19107
215-568-631

Today's Graphics, Inc.
Philadelphia, PA 19103
215-567-0332

The Type Connection
Philadelphia, PA 19102
215-963-0800

Copyrite Printing
Pittsburgh, PA 15237
412-367-3220

Eagle Typography, Inc.
Pittsburgh, PA 15216-3004
412-344-4114

Electronic Images
Pittsburgh, PA 15219
412-481-7600

Filmet Color Labs, Inc.
Pittsburgh, PA 15218
412-351-3510

Image & Ink
Pittsburgh, PA 15222
412-765-1010

Keystone Graphics Services, Inc.
Pittsburgh, PA 15233
412-321-1755

Mangis & Associates
Pittsburgh, PA 15219
412-261-0596

Matthews International
Pittsburgh, PA 15230
412-788-2111

New Image Press
Pittsburgh, PA 15224
412-683-1300

Robert Anthony Casey and Associates, Ltd.
Pittsburgh, PA 15222
412-765-1470

TaskMasters DeskTop Productivity Center
Pittsburgh, PA 15222
412-338-8600

Sewickley Graphics & Design
Sewickley, PA 15143
412-741-3777

Digital Grafix Center, a division of West Lawn Communications
Sinking Spring, PA 19608
215-678-2640

Data-Matic Systems Company
Souderton, PA 18964
215-723-8500

Phase One Graphic Resources
Sunbury, PA 17801
717-286-1111

Walker & Naylor, Inc.
Warrington, PA 18976
215-491-9970

Centre Grafik
Wayne, PA 19087
215-688-2949

York Graphic Services, Inc.
York, PA 17404
717-792-3551

RHODE ISLAND

Blazing Graphics
Cranston, RI 02920
401-946-6100

Aquidneck Graphics, Inc.
Middletown, RI 02840
401-849-8900

Faces Typography, Inc.
Providence, RI 02903
401-273-4455

ForeMost Printers—RI Division
Providence, RI 02904
401-351-1540

Prime Graphics, Inc.
Providence, RI 02903
401-455-0650

Printers' Service & Supply, Inc.
Providence, RI 02908
401-421-5652

Typesetting Service Corporation/ Sprintout Corporation
Providence, RI 02903-3885
401-421-2264

SOUTH CAROLINA

DEK & Company, Inc., dba Cole & Company
Columbia, SC 29205
803-254-3889

D G & F Typography, Inc.—Graphic Communications
Columbia, SC 29205
803-799-9140

ACME Imaging Services
Greenville, SC 29609
803-242-5924

Dynagraphics
Greenville, SC 29602
803-233-4317

Creative Media Concepts
Myrtle Beach, SC 29577
803-236-3208

Sumter Printing Co., Inc.
Sumter, SC 29151-0606
803-775-8326

Granby Typesetting
West Columbia, SC 29169
803-796-8263

TENNESSEE

Capper, Inc.
Knoxville, TN 37919
615-584-0168

Hart Graphics, Inc.
Knoxville, TN 37922
615-675-1600

Adron Graphics, Inc.
Memphis, TN 38103
901-521-0706

Graphic Arts Associates, Inc.
Memphis, TN 38118
901-795-8973

Hanson Graphics
Memphis, TN 38116
901-396-4350

HOT Graphics & Printing, Inc.
Memphis, TN 38134
901-387-1717

Mercury Printing
Memphis, TN 38132
901-345-8480

The Alphabet Shop
Nashville, TN 37212
615-383-3949

Arcata Graphics/ Baird Ward
Nashville, TN 37204
615-386-6175

Colorcopy, Inc.
Nashville, TN 37203-2527
615-321-5740

Goeser & Goeser
Nashville, TN 37203
615-255-8973

The MacFactory
Nashville, TN 37203
615-327-3437

NEC, Inc.
Nashville, TN 37210
615-367-9110

The Omni Art Supply Corp.
Nashville, TN 37215
615-327-1600

TEXAS

MicroPublish
Austin, TX 78704 3360
512-440-7242

RJL Graphics
Austin, TX 78731
512-453-8989

Wallace Engraving Company
Austin, TX 78760
512-444-2244

Simpson Graphics
Avinger, TX 75630-0100
201-334-8000

Alphabet Soup, Inc.
Beaumont, TX 77702
409-835-6484

Precision Printing Company
Conroe, TX 77305
409-756-3738

Associated Graphics
Dallas, TX 75240
214-233-0330

Chiles & Chiles
Dallas, TX 75243
214-690-4606

The Color Connection
Dallas, TX 75207
214-742-4700

Creative Type & Graphics
Dallas, TX 75202
214-969-0424

Electronic Publishing Services
Dallas, TX 75231
214-368-3997

EPS, Electronic Publishing Services
Dallas, TX 75231
214-367-3997

The Graphics Group
Dallas, TX 75226
214-749-2222

Image Reproductions
Dallas, TX 75247
214-634-7427

Matthews International
Dallas, TX 75247
214-638-7520

RG Color
Dallas, TX 75247
214-630-1001

StatCat, Inc.
Dallas, TX 75201
214-720-0606

The Type & Stat Place
Dallas, TX 75240-4346
214-951-0341

Typography Plus, Inc.
Dallas, TX 75235
214-630-2800

Printerís, Inc.
El Paso, TX 79936
915-598-8747

Fort Worth Linotyping Company
Fort Worth, TX 76104
817-332-4070

RS Graphics
Fort Worth, TX 76110
817-921-6266

Type Case, Inc.
Fort Worth, TX 76104
817-332-7563

South Press, dba Hicks Press
Garland, TX 75041
214-840-2682

Central Desktop
Houston, TX 77009
713-869-8749

Characters & One Works, Inc.
Houston, TX 77092
713-683-6666

Desktop Service Bureau
Houston, TX 77027
713-621-0799

DTPros, Inc.
Houston, TX 77027-4298
713-237-8387

Houston DeskTop Graphics
Houston, TX 77058
713-488-5577

ImageSet
Houston, TX 77006
713-528-6600

MicroType
Houston, TX 77098-2106
713-963-8717

Perfection Typographers, Inc.
Houston, TX 77008
713-863-1700

Typografiks, Inc.
Houston, TX 77007
713-861-2290

Visual Impact Advertising
Irving, TX 75038
214-580-8433

ABC Printing
Longview, TX 75606
903-753-8421

Hudson Printing
Longview, TX 75607-7010
903-758-1773

Chaparral Press, Inc.
Lubbock, TX 79408-5505
806-745-9292

New Tex Graphics, Inc.
Mesquite, TX 75150
214-270-8877

Laser Expressions!, Inc., dba Laser XPress
San Antonio, TX 78249
210-699-8007

LISAT
San Antonio, TX 78228
512-736-6400

New Century Graphics Corporation
San Antonio, TX 78212
210-829-7515

River City Silver
San Antonio, TX 78212
512-734-2020

Woodlands Printing/ Prototype Graphics
The Woodlands, TX 77380
713-367-8771

TypeGraphics/Digital PrePress Imaging
Tyler, TX 75701
214-561-0093

UTAH

Document Systems Corporation, dba TypeTech
Odgen, UT 84401
801-394-4162

Lettersetters
Orem, UT 84058
801-224-6990

On-Line Graphics
Orem, UT 84058
801-225-3825

Scitran
Provo, UT 84601
801-377-4115

Blake Typographers
Salt Lake City, UT 84101-1212
801-359-8973

Color Litho Lab
Salt Lake City, UT 84104
801-972-1056

Interwest Graphics, Inc.
Salt Lake City, UT 84119
801-973-6720

RepliColor Computer Services
Salt Lake City, UT 84111
801-328-0271

Whipple/White—DTP Connection
Salt Lake City, UT 84111
801-322-0455

VIRGINIA

Murad Enterprises, Inc., TA/The Publishers Service
Alexandria, VA 22302
703-824-8022

Signal Corporation, Award Publications Division
Alexandria, VA 22312
703-354-1600

VIP Systems, Inc.
Alexandria, VA 22314
703-548-2164

Publication Technology Corporation
Fairfax, VA 22030
703-591-0687

Sans Serif Graphics
Fairfax, VA 22030-7271
703-802-0334

Composition Systems, Inc.
Falls Church, VA 22044
703-237-1700

American Press, Inc.
Gordonsville, VA 22942
703-832-2253

Sir Speedy Printing
Hampton, VA 23666
804-838-5500

The Design Group
Lynchburg, VA 24504
804-528-4665

Deadline Typesetting, Inc.
Norfolk, VA 23517
804-625-5883

Beatley & Gravitt, Inc.
Richmond, VA 23230
804-355-9151

Imagetech—Graphic Imaging Technologies, Inc.
Richmond, VA 23226
804-288-0628

Lewis Creative Technologies
Richmond, VA 23220
804-648-2000

Mobility Imagesetting Division, Inc.
Richmond, VA
23228-2839
804-264-9031

Richmond Engraving Company
Richmond, VA 23220
804-643-0563

Riddick Advertising Art, Inc.
Richmond, VA 23219
804-780-0006

Moody Graphic Color Services
Roanoke, VA 24014
703-344-6423

VERMONT

Americomp, American-Stratford Graphic Services, Inc.
Brattleboro, VT 05304
802-254-6073

Ampersand/RAD Type Systems
Burlington, VT 05401
802-658-1497

The Lane Press
Burlington, VT 05402
802-863-5555

StereoType, Inc.
Burlington, VT 05401
802-864-5495

Meriden Stinehour
Lunenburg, VT 05906
802-328-3057

WASHINGTON

New Tech, Inc.
Bellevue, WA 98007
206-747-5450

The Typesetter
Bellevue, WA 98005
206-883-3337

Wy'east Color
Bellevue, WA 98004-3822
206-454-8006

I/O Communications
Bellingham, WA
98226-4815
206-671-7851

Northwest Graphics
Mount Vernon, WA
98273
206-856-6062

Designers Service Bureau
Olympia, WA 98501
206-943-7964

Word Graphics, Inc.
Redmond, WA 98052
206-882-2626

Sir Speedy Printing
Renton, WA 98055
206-251-8680

Art-Foto Typography, Inc.
Seattle, WA 98121
206-448-2122

CMYK Digital Prepress
Seattle, WA 98103
206-284-2695

Nikko Media Center
Seattle, WA 98104
206-343-0942

Seattle ImageSetting, Inc.
Seattle, WA 98104-0085
206-382-1633

Thomas & Kennedy Typographers, Inc.
Seattle, WA 98101-1153
206-622-0918

Wizywig
Seattle, WA 98121
206-283-3069

Type Plus
Spokane, WA 99201
509-328-6102

Kehler & Company Imaging Center
Sumas, WA 98295-8000
604-850-2286

Graphic Services, Inc.
Tacoma, WA 98402
206-627-8495

KwiKolor, Inc.
Tumwater, WA 98512
206-753-8728

Spritzer Type and Design
Vancouver, WA 98663
206-694-8973

WISCONSIN

Burczyk Creative Group, Inc.
Brookfield, WI 53005-2427
414-327-1710

National Graphics, Inc.
Brookfield, WI 53005
414-781-5888

Ries Graphics, Ltd.
Butler, WI 53007
414-781-5720

Web Tech, Inc.
Butler, WI 53007
414-781-8805

Independent Printing Company, Inc.
De Pere, WI 54115
414-336-7731

Hot Dot Images
Delevan, WI 53115
414-728-8899

Accuracy Typesetting
Green Bay, WI 54303-2786
414-432-9299

Smits Typo/Graphics
Green Bay, WI 54311
414-465-1522

Graphic Innovation
Greenfield, WI 53228
414-529-4090

Cross Advertising
Kenosha, WI 53140
414-657-4737

Four Lakes Colorgraphics
Madison, WI 53714
608-221-9500

Images Unlimited
Madison, WI 53713
608-273-8588

ImageSetter, Inc.
Madison, WI 53704
608-244-6243

MacPherson Ltd.
Madison, WI 53704-6030
608-241-6633

Madison Graphic Services, Inc.
Madison, WI 53715-2072
608-257-2431

Port to Print, Inc.
Madison, WI 53713
608-273-4887

TypeTronics
Madison, WI 53703
608-257-2939

Widen Colourgraphics, Ltd.
Madison, WI 53713
608-222-1296

Graphic Composition, Inc.
Menasha, WI 54952
414-739-3152

Northwestern Colorgraphics
Menasha, WI 54952
414-722-3375

Image Systems, Inc.
Menomonee Falls, WI 53051-1629
414-255-3300

Reindl Printing Inc
Merrill, WI 54452
715-536-9537

Bulfin Printers/Type A
Milwaukee, WI 53202
414-271-1887

Color Network, Inc.
Milwaukee, WI 53215
414-384-8980

Desktop Publishing Centers, Inc.
Milwaukee, WI 53202
414-223-4333

Image Tech, Inc.
Milwaukee, WI 53217
414-352-8575

Peter A. Alterhofen Typographers, Inc.
Milwaukee, WI 53223
414-352-3590

Trade Press Publishing Corporation
Milwaukee, WI 53209
414-228-7701

Zahn-Klicka-Hill, Inc.
Milwaukee, WI 53202
414-276-0136

Directions, Inc.
Neenah, WI 54956
414-725-4848

Crossmark Graphics
New Berlin, WI 53151-3627
414-821-1343

Merit Printing Company, Inc.
New Berlin, WI 53151
414-782-9200

St. Croix Press
New Richmomd, WI 54017
715-246-5811

Parkwood Composition Service, Inc.
New Richmond, WI 54017
715-243-7542

Design North, Inc.
Racine, WI 53402
414-762-1320

Olson+Fabel Electronic Design, dba OFAD Corp.
Racine, WI 53403-1029
414-632-7800

Tru Line Lithographing, Inc.
Sturtevant, WI 53177
414-554-7300

Marathon Press Company, Inc.
Wausau, WI 54401
715-845-4231

City Press, Inc.
Wauwatosa, WI 53213
414-475-0255

PUERTO RICO

The Studio Inc.
Hato Rey, PR 00919
809-753-8590

Artex
Puerto Nuevo, PR 00920
809-751-4848

CANADA

Creative Thinking Enterprises, Inc.
Calgary, AB T2E 7L9
403-291-6414

La Da Com Corporation
Calgary, AB T2R 0B8
403-237-6224

Resolution Graphics Limited
Calgary, AB T3C 0H9
403-233-2266

Skye Communications, Inc.
Calgary, AB T2P 3N2
403-233-7593

HeatWave Productions
Kelowna, BC V1V 1N2
604-762-6300

Interior Pacific Litho, Inc.
Kelowna, BC V1X 4J8
604-861-5519

Leno Whimster Printing, Ltd.
Nelson, BC V1L 4H7
604-352-2622

Alphagraphics
Richmond, BC V6X 3K8
604-270-2679

Prestige Words & Graphics, Inc.
Surrey, BC V3W 3N3
604-599-9410

Artisdean Graphics Repro, Inc. (aka Atristat)
Vancouver, BC V6B 1H6
604-688-8141

ChromaTech, Inc.
Vancouver, BC V6P 3J9
604-324-8324

G. T. Laserís Edge, Inc.
Vancouver, BC V6E 2S1
604-662-3774

High-Res Text and Graphics Management Ltd.
Vancouver, BC V5T 1E1
604-873-8398

Stellar Graphics Ltd.
Vancouver, BC V6B 1L8
604-688-7835

U & I Type Services, Inc.
Vancouver, BC V6J 4R7
604-734-2373

WYSIWYG Graphics, Inc.
Vancouver, BC V6B 1Z3
604-684-5466

Zenith Graphics Limited
Vancouver, BC V6B 3B3
604-682-4521

Alston Graphic Services, Ltd.
Victoria, BC V9A 3K9
604-382-4291

Camera Ready Graphics
Victoria, BC V8V 3P4
604-382-7228

Laserís Edge Desktop Publishing, Ltd.
Victoria, BC V8W 1E1
604-360-2466

Perfect Form Typesetting
Victoria, BC V8P 3K8
604-385-3676

Addison Graphics Ltd.
White Rock, BC V4B 3Z5
604-531-4411

Beth Crescent Design Co.
White Rock, BC V4B 3X7
604-572-5161

Designtype
Winnipeg, MB R3B 1L4
204-943-7596

Embassy Graphics
Winnipeg, MB R3B 1S2
204-772-8977

Triad—Colour 4 Graphic Systems Ltd.
Winnipeg, MB R2J 3W6
204-661-8548

Typoplate
Winnipeg, MB R3B 1S2
204-944-8181

Centennial Print & Litho Ltd.
Fredricton, NB E3B 4Z9
506-453-1310

VectorGraphics
Barrie, ON L4M 4S7
705-734-3699

Henderson Printing, Inc.
Brockville, ON K6V 5V5
613-345-0441

BPS Group
Cambridge, ON N1R 7R7
519-740-3051

Dobbie Graphics
Cambridge, ON N3H 4V6
519-653-1650

Victor Beitner Systems Ltd.
Concord, ON L4K 1L7
416-738-8874

Anagram Creative, Inc.
Etobicoke, ON M8Y 3H8
416-253-2260

Bianca Imagesetting, Inc.
Etobicoke, ON M8Z 1R7
416-259-2345

Scurr Design Associates, Inc.
Kitchener, ON N2C 1K9
519-748-6494

Bogdan Graphics, Inc.
London, ON N6C 2E4
519-438-9003

Corp-Text Graphics, Inc.
Markham, ON L3R 3A3
416-940-6711

Revelations/Whittaker Graphic Systems, Inc.
Markham, ON L3R 9R7
416-477-8830

Barker Cambria Press
Mississauga, ON L5T 1S8
416-670-7100

DAB Typographics Ltd.
Mississauga, ON
L5A 2W9
416-273-7521

Desktop Lino Services
Mississauga, ON L5N 1P6
416-279-2949

Desktop Publishing & Design, Inc.
Mississauga, ON L5B 1M3
416-279-2949

Toronto Business Communications, Inc.
Mississuaga, ON
L4W 2A1
416-238-0530

Artext Electronic Publishing, Inc.
Ottawa, ON K1P 5M9
613-232-9942

Graphic Partners, Inc.
Ottawa, ON K2P 0N8
613-235-3033

Hadwen Imaging Technologies
Ottawa, ON K1G 4Z3
613-736-1380

Imagraph
Ottawa, ON K1K 2C5
613-744-5102

Design Graphics, Inc.
Peterborough, ON K9J 7R7
705-876-1311

Acuity Computer Services
Richmond Hill, ON
L4B 3L8
416-731-9765

778809 Ontario Limited, operating as Colour Systems, Inc.
Toronto, ON M5A 2K1
416-922-7589

Ampersand Typographers
Toronto, ON M5A 1K3
416-864-9039

Ampersand Typographers
Toronto, ON M3H 1H1
416-422-1444

Artistat Canada, Ltd.
Toronto, ON M5R 1B9
416-923-0822

BTT Typesetting, Inc.
Toronto, ON M4S 2Z7
416-481-4037

Crocker Bryant, Inc.
Toronto, ON M5E 1W1
416-863-1413

Cyber Images
Toronto, ON M5V 1Y6
416-777-9409

Lazerline Desktop Publishing and Design, Inc.
Toronto, ON M5T 1S2
416-924-8726

Linotext, Inc.
Toronto, ON M5A 1E3
416-368-5466

Moveable Type, Inc.
Toronto, ON M6K 3E3
416-532-5690

Rhino Lino
Toronto, ON M5A 1V1
416-366-5466

TriGraph, Inc.
Toronto, Ontraio
M4G 3V2
416-425-3818

Litho Plus
WillowDale, ON M2J 4H1
416-495-8293

Impression laser interface, inc.
Mirabel, PQ J0N 1K0
514-277-6983

Caractera Production Graphique
Montreal, PQ G1N 4K8
418-687-4434

Dessie, Inc., Computer Division
Montreal, PQ H4C 1G7
514-939-6399

MP Photo Reproductions
Montreal, PQ H2Z 1V8
514-861-9281

Photocomp RB Ltd.
Montreal, PQ H3G 1S8
514-933-8154

Servi-Typo, Inc.
Montreal, PQ H4S 1H3
514-335-2400

Typo Express, Inc.
Montreal, PQ H3H 2N4
514-933-3629

Typographie Compoplus
Montreal, PQ H2Z 1N3
514-861-1488

Interscript
Quebec, PQ G1K 4A3
418-694-0857

Novel-Shant, Inc.
St. Laurent, PQ H4T 1A7
514-733-1833

Louban Graphics Ltd.
Regina, SK S4N 0E7
306-359-3445

Accell Laser Image Center
Saskatoon, SK S7K 6M1
306-933-4227

Distinctive Imagesetting, Inc.
Saskatoon, SK S7K 1P1
306-244-8973

Appendix F: Quark and third-party XTensions

The following pages contain a list of XTensions for QuarkXPress. The XTensions are sorted by name. Each entry includes the name of the developer and a short description of the XTension. I'm providing the list to give you an idea of the different XTensions available, and also to provide a means to look up more info on an XTension you may hear of. All of these XTensions are available from XChange, Inc. They can be reached at 1-800-788-7557 or 1-303-229-0620.

AccentMaster
Linographic
AccentMaster is an indispensable utility for those setting body text in European languages. Some European and Baltic alphabets contain characters which have accents and other figures which do not normally appear in English-language text. AccentMaster gives users the ability to set foreign styled accents, umlauts, and other special characters otherwise impossible to place with QuarkXPress.

Ad Director
Managing Editor Software, Inc.
Ad Director is a full-featured, automated advertising dummying program that builds runsheets, electronic dummies and provides an accurate overview of where your ads are at any time. Dummying (positioning advertisements) a publication used to be a time-consuming process that would take production and advertising managers hours or days to complete. Ad Director takes your list of advertisements and places them in your publication in seconds.

AdMeasure
GreyStone Computer Management Systems
This powerful tool is a must for those who work with co-op advertisements. When building ad pages, it's important to charge the correct amount for the proportion of space occupied by each vendor. AdMeasure calculates the amount of co-op dollars to charge each vendor based on your production cost estimates. You can have several publications with different close dates all accounted individually.

AgencyFIT: Volumes 1 & 2
Monotype Typography, Inc.
Tune your type with AgencyFIT from Monotype Typography. AgencyFIT con-

sists of Macintosh screen fonts with over 1200 kerning pairs per font. All the popular Adobe and Monotype fonts have been meticulously kerned "tight not touching" to reduce the manual kerning required to achieve optimal typography results in QuarkXPress.

AutoLib

Vision's Edge, Inc.

Have you ever wanted to create a library of the art work that you use in QuarkXPress but you don't have the time to import each file into a library? Now there is an easier way. Using AutoLib, you can quickly create graphics libraries by selecting the folder of graphics and AutoLib does the rest. AutoLib creates the library, inserts the graphics in the selected folder into the library, and saves the library when it's done. After AutoLib has created the library, the library can be renamed and moved to another folder if desired.

AutoXTract

Vision's Edge, Inc.

AutoXTract is an XTension for Quark XPress version 3.1 which scans preselected folders for QuarkXPress documents, opens the documents, and exports all of the text from those documents to a user-selected folder as a text file. The text stories are exported in order from left to right and from top to bottom. With AutoXTract, it becomes easy to set up an archiving routine which will run automatically. This XTension allows the user to choose when the text files will be automatically exported. The files can be processed as often as every minute, or they can even be set to process once every twenty-four hours. It also allows the user to run the text to be exported manually at any time.

Azalea UPC-EAN XT

azalea software, inc.

This QuarkXPress XTension lets users create bar codes for any use right in QuarkXPress. Many types of bar codes can be chosen.

BackTrack

DPN

BackTrack solves the problem of managing multiple iterations! Install this XTension and you have precise control over when, where, and how your documents are saved. This is not just an auto-save mechanism. Instead of performing a normal save function, you can set BackTrack to keep as many iterations (versions of your document) on disk as necessary. The XTension automatically deletes the oldest copies from your backup folder.

Bar Code Pro XT

Synex

Bar code and bar code readers have become the standard means for entering data in the manufacturing and sale of products—in the creation of product literature, inventory control and management, shipping, and even in sales and marketing. And anyone who is remotely involved in retail trade will encounter the use of bar code. Therefore, it is becoming more and more important that those of us working with desktop systems adapt to this rising need.

BlendBuilder

XTend, Inc.

Blending new colors from within QuarkXPress during the design or production process is not always an easy task. That task becomes even more difficult when you must complement existing colors which are based on different color matching systems. Tightly integrated with the QuarkXPress user-interface, BlendBuilder allows users to add colors to their current document or the QuarkXPress application directly.

The Bundler

CompuSense

The Bundler XTension focuses on the problems encountered when users are dealing with increasing numbers of mobile QuarkXPress documents. The Bundler creates a copy of the document, all the graphic files, and all the screen and printer fonts, in such a way that anybody opening the Bundle on a different Mac at a different time and/or place can be as certain as possible that they will find exactly the same environment and resources, and therefore the same as when it was saved.

BureauManager

CompuSense

The BureauManager XTension is the definitive and ultimate tool that allows you to easily and completely prepare a job for delivery to a Service Bureau. It quickly extracts information from the original document to determine which fonts (screen and printer) and high resolution graphics are required to be copied.

ColorChange

Vision's Edge, Inc.

The ColorChange dialog utilizes Quark XPress' familiar find/change interface. Users can check how colors are used in a document, and then change them based on specific type of usage. Even shading percentages can be changed document wide with a click of the mouse. The utility allows you to segregate color changes to text, frames, background, and picture colors.

Color Usage

Vision's Edge, Inc.

This utility from Vision's Edge lists the colors in a given document in a dialog box that indicates where and how the color is used. Colors are sorted by page number, with additional information on whether process separation is selected for the color. Color Usage shows background or line color, frame color, picture color, and text character color. When you select a color from the dialog list, the RGB and CMYK values as well as a screen display sample of the color are shown.

ColorManager

CompuSense

ColorManager weaves power and simplicity into a "must have" XTension if you do any color work with Quark XPress. This 3.1 only program allows you to identify, control, and easily manipulate any color used within your document. It provides a tool that makes the production of any color job less arduous and more efficient in terms of money and time.

ColorSnap 32+

Computer Friends

ColorSnap 32+ is a 24-bit, frame capture board. Files are captured in 24-bit color but can be stored in a variety of formats. Particular care has been taken to enhance the quality of the image captured. Images can be printed in full color using a thermal or a color ink jet-printer, or they can be color-separated. They can also be printed on a common LaserWriter. The ColorSnap 32+ XTension is a hardware/software combination. The board is installed in any nubus slot, and is System 7 and QuickTime compatible.

Combs XT
Durrant Software Limited
Combs XT Lets you quickly and easily add data "combs" to your QuarkXPress layouts. Combs are those convenient to use, but impossible to create grids for facilitating completion of forms and applications.

Copy & Apply
Vision's Edge, Inc.
QuarkXPress allows you to copy paragraph attributes from one paragraph to another in the same text chain. But what if you need to copy those attributes from a paragraph in one text chain to a paragraph in another? Or even from text on one page to another? And what if you want to copy the character attributes as well as the paragraph attributes?

CopySet
Vision's Edge, Inc.
CopySet helps QuarkXPress users find and correct overset and underset text boxes. It includes a palette which lists overset and underset text boxes for the active document, allowing the user to determine how much text is affected in each story, and giving the user the option of naming the individual text boxes for easy identification in complex documents.

CopySpecs
Frank Kubin
ColorSpecs makes it easy to copy and paste type specs anywhere within a paragraph. Special "List" function lets you select sections of text anywhere in your document and change the specs of all sections simultaneously. Similar to using a style sheet but it works on text anywhere within a paragraph.

CROPS + REGISTRATIONS
Publishing Solutions, Inc.
This great new XTension from Publishing Solutions, Inc. adds professional, multiple crops and registration marks to any QuarkXPress page element or group. Just draw a picture box that crops your layout the way you wish, and tell C&R to do the rest. You'll instantly have high quality crops, registrations and CMYK indicators. And there is no limit to the number of crops/registrations on an QuarkXPress page.

CursorPos
Kytek, Inc.
CursorPos provides users with a floating palette to continuously display the position of the cursor. When the cursor is located in a text box, the CursorPos palette will display the horizontal and vertical position of the cursor in the current horizontal and vertical units of your document. The position is continually updated as you move the cursor through the text.

Dashes
CompuSense
The Dashes XTension provides high-quality Hyphenation for your Quark XPress text. Its aim and purpose is to

provide a tool that improves the appearance and readability of a user's page by inserting hyphens which are inconspicuous, so as not to disturb the flow of meaning in the story.

Data Link XTension

Techno Design

The Data Link XTension gives you the ability to place variable fields in a normal QuarkXPress textstream. These fields contains references to fields in a database file.

Demo Pak

XChange

XChange has put together a Demo Pak of over 30 XTension demos. Try them out on your own QuarkXPress documents. The Demo Pak includes: CursorPos, XSize, DoubleSave, IndeXTension, Managing Editor XT, AdMeasure, The Perfect XTension, Kerning Palette, Printer's Spreads, TableWorks Plus, SE XT, CompuSense Demos (5), Xdata, The Last Word Demos (6), Xtags, Special Effects, DPN Demos (3), TimeLogger, FCS Demos (3), XState, Navigator XT, and XMacro.

Design Tools

Integrated Software, Inc.

A collection of quality XTensions for design professionals, Celler "step and repeat" creates a grid of boxes identical to the original. "Divide and repeat" creates a grid of boxes inside the frame of the original box.

Dingbats

Adept Solutions

Rather than accessing dingbats through the tedious Keycaps utility, just open the Dingbat palette, and select the character desired. Choose an element from the Dingbat palette to replace a character in the desired text, and it will retain the character's size and attributes. The procedure may also be reversed.

DoubleSave

TechnoDesign

Save on! With this new product, also from TechnoDesign, an extra backup of your document is created after a standard save command. This extra copy can be stored anywhere, even on a fileserver. The DoubleSave XTension has been developed for those who require saving their documents locally, as well as an archived copy on their fileserver.

EasyType

Artemis Systems

This new XTension from Artemis Systems displays a small floating palette containing 36 characters from the extended ASCII set. EasyType allows the user to define sets of frequently used characters and save the configurations for use on other documents. You can select which characters are displayed in your palette and enter them into your document by simply clicking on the symbol in the palette. The selected character appears wherever the cursor is located or replaces any selected text.

Exposé

Vision's Edge, Inc.

Here's another great XTension from Vision's Edge, Inc. With Exposé, creating a catalog of graphic files is simple. Your catalog can look just like you want it to, because you build a QuarkXPress master page which will be used for each page of the catalog. Through the Exposé preferences, choose whether to include the full path name, the date the graphic was most recently modified, the file size, the file type (EPS, Paint, Pict, TIFF, RIFF, or Scitex CT) and fonts imbedded in any EPS files. You may also optionally elect to have the graphic scaled to fit the box in the catalog.

EXPRESSWAY Rules

JJCS

Since QuarkXPress does not have a floating rule feature, rules will not move with text as characters are added or deleted. QuarkXPress' default rules are page attributes and thus are positioned directly on a page. When text is modified on the page, or elements are moved, QuarkXPress rules stay put.

EXPRESSWAY Notes

JJCS

EXPRESSWAY Notes allows you to embed notations directly into the text of a QuarkXPress story. This means editors (and just about anyone else) can place notes at any spot in the text. With this XTension, it is now possible for copy editors to leave an audit trail of what was changed, and for layout editors to leave behind any text that was cut.

faceIt

a lowly apprentice production

faceIt allows you to set up special faceIt styles which will affect only the character attributes of a selected range of text. Now you can change the attributes of text embedded inside paragraphs without changing the entire paragraph. All standard QuarkXPress character attributes can be set with faceIt, including font, size, color, style, tracking, and horizontal scale. Use familiar QuarkXPress dialog boxes to create, edit, or delete faceIt styles. Change the character specification of any faceIt style, and the changes will be applied to any text to which that style has been set. Changes may be global or document specific.

FCSLock

F.C.S., S.A.

FCSLock is a QuarkXPress XTension designed specifically for large Quark XPress installations. This XTension will allow an administrator to disable any feature of QuarkXPress so that other users will not be able to modify certain aspects of QuarkXPress documents. FCSLock can disable any menu item of QuarkXPress, the measurements palette, or any creation tool.

FCSPrint

F.C.S., S.A.

From the developers of FCS TableMaker comes this new XTension created specifically for Service Bureaus. FCSPrint will automatically set all the options of the Setup and Print dialog boxes to save as much film as possible and to avoid ever-costly human errors. Service Bureaus who have been testing this product for over a year report incredible savings in time and errors.

FCS TableMaker

F.C.S., S.A.

FCS TableMaker is a collection of functions designed to facilitate the production of simple tables of data in Quark XPress. Though succinct in function, FCS TableMaker provides a large portion of the functionality needed by most users. The XTension includes functions for building gridlines, establishing an exact centerpoint on a page, building a grid of either text or graphics boxes, and several tab functions. TableMaker also contains a function for creating grouped sets of horizontal and vertical rules, using the default rule style set for the orthogonal line tool in the QuarkXPress Tool palette. Additionally, "Create Style Sheet" will define a new text style with the name you select, and apply all tab settings built in TableMaker.

FileManager
CompuSense
FileManager allows users to easily label, categorize, search for, move and otherwise control all their QuarkXPress documents The FileManager XTension is a powerful yet simple to use, add–on software module for QuarkXPress. It is an essential tool for administering your QuarkXPress documents, either on stand-alone or networked Macintoshes. It provides a valuable tool to help any QuarkXPress user who creates many documents of nonstandard sizes as well as anyone that needs to transfer their documents to different locations such as Service Bureaus.

FlexScale
Vision's Edge, Inc.
Another new XTension from Vision's Edge, this utility allows a document to be scaled when output to a printer. Vertical and horizontal scaling percentages can be assigned independent from one another to create rudimentary flexography. The document can be scaled between 50% and 150% vertically and horizontally. To activate this XTension, the user simply holds down the option key while selecting the Print command. Then, the desired scaling percentages are entered into the FlexScale dialog. The scaling percentages are accurate to two decimal places, i.e., 102.87%. After selecting the Print button, the printing process continues normally except that the output is scaled.

Fontasy
Vision's Edge, Inc.
The Fontasy XTension from Vision's Edge is elegantly simple. It contains a character viewing area with a horizontal scroll bar so that you can scroll through all characters in the selected font, including the extended character set. Just scroll to the character you want to use and click on it. Fontasy inserts the character at the cursor position in the document.

ƒXT
KyTek, Inc.
ƒXT automates the placement and numbering of footnotes within QuarkXPress documents. The XTension uses footnote references that are tied to the corresponding footnotes with hidden markers. References can be marked interactively within QuarkXPress via the fXT floating palette or with markup codes placed into the text either before or after importing text into QuarkXPress.

GraphXChange
Equilibrium
GraphXChange is the perfect utility for anyone who needs to import "alien" graphics formats into QuarkXPress. This XTension will allow you to read in graphics file formats not previously

supported by QuarkXPress. These documents can then be printed in your document, eliminating the need to translate the graphics with another application.

Grid Layout
J. Michael Marriner
The Grid Layout 1.1 XTension creates uniform snap-to guides for easy alignment of design elements. Choose the number of columns and rows in your layout grid, type in the numbers, and the guides appear. Grids will start at the edge of the page or margins, and can apply to a single page or across page spreads.

Grid Master
Vision's Edge, Inc.
Grid Master makes it easy to create a grid of boxes to fit within a given area. First, create a text or picture box. Then activate the Grid Master dialog, set the number of boxes and gutter for both across and down, and set the radio button to Divide. When the user clicks the Make button, boxes are created to fill the area defined by the original box, using the preferences indicated in the Grid Master dialog.

GridLock
Mousedown Productions
GridLock adds an option to the Utilities menu that brings up a dialog box into which you can put exact numerical definitions for gridline positions—including multiples. For instance, you can enter 10*75 for 75 guides at 10 point offsets. GridLock guides can be a different colour from those applied by hand, and can be locked and saved in sets.

Headers & Footers
Barry Palmer Development
Now you can produce running Headers/Footers quickly and easily. With this XTension, you simply tag the text items either on screen with your mouse or during origination on another device. After loading the text into a document, you then hide the tags so they don't produce readable text anymore, but are still recognized by the XTension. There are three types off output available: first headline text of the actual page, last headline of the actual page, and previous headline if the new headline is not at the start of the actual page.

HyphenSet
Vision's Edge, Inc.
Some of the most significant tools when it comes to fine-tuning your text in QuarkXPress are the Hyphenation & Justification settings. The HyphenSet XTension makes the intensive work of getting letter spacing and word spacing less stressful by saving you some steps. With HyphenSet, applying H & J settings is as effortless as a click of the mouse button, using the convenient HyphenSet palette. This palette displays a list of all of the current document's H & J settings; all you have to do is click on the one you want. HyphenSet makes it easier than ever to produce professional-looking documents with QuarkXPress.

ImPress
XTend, Inc.
Introducing ImPress from XTend, the new XTension for QuarkXPress which automates the task of stripping pages into signatures. ImPress provides the

tools and support necessary to impose your QuarkXPress documents into a variety of saddle-stitched or perfect-bound books.

IndeXTension
Vision's Edge, Inc.
Another product from Vision's Edge, Inc., IndeXTension provides a quick and easy utility for creating simple indices in QuarkXPress.Using hidden text technology in QuarkXPress, IndeXTension allows you to quickly "mark" words or phrases using a menu selection or keyboard command. You can generate index listings for general phrases which do not form part of the text, but are a general theme. Index markers can be turned off and on for convenience and accuracy of line endings.

INposition
DK&A
The time-consuming task of imposition ordering has just become vastly easier thanks to INposition. This revolutionary XTension is the missing link in the electronic pre-press process: It does both signature creation and publication building, and it enables you to impose your entire publication on any PostScript imagesetter. So, whether you are building a 600-page technical manual or simply creating a 16-page corporate brochure, INposition will handle all of your imposition needs.

InsertSpace
XTend
InsertSpace provides a means for "justifying" multiple blocks of text on a line. This is accomplished by distributing the leftover white space at one or more locations within the line. This ability is commonly found only on today's dedicated typesetting systems. InsertSpace provides results that are more accurate than those achieved manually in a fraction of the time. Users maintain full editing capabilities and the ability to modify up to 21 blocks of text when using InsertSpace.

Kerning Palette
Clearface, Inc.
The Kerning Palette gives you control of character spacing that formerly required dedicated, stand-alone programs—without leaving QuarkXPress. Use of kerning tables is guaranteed to improve the quality and the value of the type you produce dramatically; and the better it gets, the less time you need to spend on it. The Kerning Palette makes the process of creating and maintaining kerning tables as simple and convenient as it can be; it's positively the best tool for the job.

Keyliner
DataStream Imaging Systems, Inc.
Keyliner is a professional stripping station XTension which allows QuarkXPress users to input graphic elements and build page geometry from conventional art boards and documents. These QuarkXPress documents can be formatted quickly and precisely. Keyliner supports all QuarkXPress features.

KitchenSink
a lowly apprentice production
It's all just one click away with KitchenSink. KitchenSink does everything but the dishes! Featuring Command Pad and the Co-Pilot palette, this XTension pro-

vides one-click access to nearly every QuarkXPress menu item, plus some of QuarkXPress' other commonly used features. For example, one click opens a document; you show or hide the Measurements palette with a click, scroll to any part of the page with one click, click to check spelling, and so on.

LayerManager 2.0
a lowly apprentice production
LayerManager 2.0 comes equipped with the ability to move elements up or down even one level at a time, all with a simple click of the mouse. No longer will you have to navigate your way up and into the menus just to bring an element forward, or send one back a few levels.

Line Count XT (LcXT)
Kytek, Inc.
LcXT provides a convenient way to estimate the line count of a range of text based on the character count of the range. The LcXT Options dialog allows you to specify the number of characters which constitute a line, whether to include hidden text in the character count and whether to include overflow text in the character count.

LinkUp
MC Research
LinkUp allows you to invisibly connect your Quark publications to an externally maintained database, making it simple to produce updated documents without having to manually correct information held in the database. The nature of the information is entirely dependent on the user—it might be prices for a catalogue, a list of telephone numbers, or even the results of the latest football league. If you can store the information in a database, then LinkUp can update it in your publication. Also included is a facility for producing an Index and Table of Contents from either single or multiple documents, without having to rely on text within the document.

Logical XTensions I (Crop Marks; InCase Tools)
Alphalogic
Logical XTensions I is a bundle of two utilities: Crop Marks and InCase Tools. Crop Marks provides a considerably more flexible system of creating and manipulating crop marks than those provided by Quark. Text Tools provides a set of tools for manipulating the case of text runs.

Logical XTensions V (Data Pipeline)
Alphalogic
Data Pipeline is a text file database utility that allows a Quark user to insert multiple records of information into a QuarkXPress document, with automatic formatting. The source is a text file with user configurable delimiters for records and fields. Each field can be assigned a different font, size, and style. After choosing the database file and setting up a format the Quark user can simply type in the unique identifier of a record and issue a menu command to have the text inserted. The text file would normally be exported from a conventional database and placed on the operator's machine for production use.

Logical XTensions II (Kern-Ease)
Alphalogic
Kern-Ease is an XTension for Quark XPress that enables the operator to have a very precise control over the

kerning of any selection of text. The XTension provides a manual kerning palette which allows the operator to add or remove kerning to a selection of text as easily as tracking. Unlike tracking, using Kern-Ease to change the kerning of a run of text does not destroy the kerning inherent in the font—rather it adds a specified kern to that which naturally exists within the font.

LogX

Vision's Edge, Inc.

Do you have volumes of QuarkXPress documents and would like to be able to tell what fonts or graphics are used in those documents without having to manually open each file and check? LogX can quickly gather this information for you. LogX is a cataloging program which provides an easy way to create catalogs of QuarkXPress documents. Catalogs can be made which describe a single document, a folder of document, or even all of the QuarkXPress documents on a single drive.

LTD_XS

Trias

This XTension is a managing editor's dream. With LTD_XS, you decide which functions within the QuarkXPress interface will be available to users. Text editing functions can be restricted to editors, and manipulation of graphics available only to designers or production personnel.

Magpie

Show-Ads Omega Group

Magpie is a QuarkXPress XTension that allows the user to quickly and easily archive or prepare a job for delivery to a service bureau. By examining the original QuarkXPress document, Magpie determines which fonts and high-resolution graphic files are required by the document, makes a copy of those elements in a new "job" folder, and places a copy of the original document in that folder as well. This folder can be placed on a floppy disk or removable cartridge for delivery to a service bureau.

Managing Editor XT

Managing Editor Software, Inc.

This XTension from Managing Editor Software, Inc. functions as a Finder-like runsheet (document item list) in Quark XPress, bypassing the standard Quark XPress import interface to allow users to quickly select and drag text and graphic files into an QuarkXPress document. Managing Editor XT not only facilitates locating the files you need, it remembers what you've already placed, and where.

MarkIt

a lowly apprentice production

MarkIt is a high-powered output alternative to QuarkXPress' standard registration and crop marks. Using MarkIt is no different from setting up a Quark XPress style sheet, but rather than appending styles, you can import or export MarkIt Styles to a physical disk file. As an added bonus, MarkIt Styles provide a graphical preview.

MasterMenus

Vision's Edge, Inc.

MasterMenus from Vision's Edge provides an easy way for you to have commonly used menu items as close as a mouse click on a user-customizable palette. The MasterMenus preferences dialog provides a quick, intuitive interface for the user to add or remove menu items from the palette.

Mathable
York Graphics, Inc.
Mathable is an integrated typographic enhancement for QuarkXPress that combines the features of York's XMath and XTable XTensions. Mathable has all the features of XMath and XTable, and allows users to create tables of equations and math problems for technical journals and exercise sections of textbooks.

Mimic
Mediamatic
Mimic is an efficient tool for duplicating box and text specifications quickly. Useful for applying many characteristics at once, Mimic can transmit background color, text style and formatting information, frame color and size, and box size attributes—all with the click of a mouse.

The Missing Link
Vision's Edge, Inc.
This XTension deserves a commendation! How often have you wished you could "freeze" the links in a text chain to facilitate special editing, drag-copying from document to document, or placement in a library?

MS Word DOS Filter
DPN
The MS Word DOS XTension enables users to import the text from MS Word DOS documents, including the character specifications. All MS Word DOS text with default character settings will be translated to the user's default QuarkXPress style. Other character specifications in text are are supported by a user configurable mapping of the MS Word DOS characters to the appropriate Macintosh font. Paragraph specifications are translated to Quark XPress style sheets with the inclusion of a new style sheet tag that can be placed in an MS Word DOS style tag.

MultiStyle
Techno Design
This XTension is especially useful for setting ads, tables, and other types of repetitive, complex formatting tasks. MultiStyle easily copies multiple character or paragraph-based text style variations and analyzes them during the Copy Style function. When the copied style is "pasted" onto selected text, that text assumes the formatting of the copied style. This means that if text is formatted differently for different tab stops in a document, MultiStyle will analyze the pattern and apply the local formatting to any other similarly formatted text. MultiStyle can also be used to only copy character-based information for application to an unlimited number of destinations in the document.

Navigator XT
Vision's Edge, Inc.
Here's another great Xtension to help you sail through your QuarkXPress documents. Navigator XT presents a palette that allows you to navigate through a QuarkXPress document effortlessly. The palette offers a thumbnail view of the page or spread, either displaying an actual miniature of the page or wireframe geometry. Clicking on a point in the thumbnail immediately takes you to that point on the document page. This can be invaluable when working on docu-

ments with layers or when the document is magnified.

Nouveau II

Vision's Edge, Inc.

Nouveau II gives the familiar New document dialog in QuarkXPress a facelift, adding several features. One feature is the ability to save multiple new document settings. Any time the Nouveau II dialog is on the screen, the user can choose to add the current settings to a pop-up menu of stored preferences. This means that commonly used document settings can be conveniently saved and accessed.

OnTap

Mousedown Productions

OnTap is for QuarkXPress users who like keyboard shortcuts. The XTension gives you the ability to assign easy-to-remember keystrokes to 50 or so Quark XPress menu commands. It adds an option to the Utilities menu that brings up a scrolling list of functions and commands normally accessed only by mouse or pull-down menus. Any key combination can be assigned to these functions.

Overset!

North Atlantic Publishing Systems, Inc.

Overset! saves you time fitting text to boxes. When you click on an overset mark within a text box, Overset! creates a temporary text box which allows you to view overset copy. You can then edit your copy or adjust your text box size in order to get the fit you want. The temporary text box will disappear when the text fits. If there is no actual copy, the temporary text box will turn on and off, signaling you that the overset mark is due to a return. When a document is stored, the temporary text box is automatically removed. Now you can get to an exact fit with ease.

Page Director

Managing Editor Software, Inc.

Page Director is a publication management and production system, encompassing everything from organizing the various page elements, to sizing content, to configuring color and paginating the layout. And Page Director allows for multiple users to work on different pages or sections, with the ability to merge all the documents into one issue.

PageShot

Vision's Edge, Inc.

PageShot allows users to select multiple, noncontiguous pages for saving as EPS files. Pages can be saved in color, B&W and in PC, DCS and DCS 2 formats, with or without EPS and TIFF OPI information. Users can also elect to save only a specified area of a specific page or pages by entering top, left, height and width coordinates—PageShot EPS can be created that actually captures information up to 72 points outside the printable area of the page.

The Perfect XTension

TechnoDesign

The Perfect XTension from TechnoDesign enables you to import text created in WordPerfect (versions 2.0 and 2.1) into QuarkXPress documents quickly and easily. TechnoDesign created the XTension in consultation with a large number of QuarkXPress users who regularly import sizable amounts of text created in word processors.

Picture Dæmon
Vision's Edge, Inc.
Picture Dæmon allows you to search for a graphic by name, accepting a full or partial file name to search for. Additionally, a convenient pop-up menu lets you choose to search for all graphic types or only for a particular kind of graphic such as as an EPS or TIFF. If you use Picture Dæmon on a graphic box which already contains a picture, the XTension allows you to search for graphic files which are newer than the file which was originally imported into the box.

Picture Reunion
DK&A
Picture Reunion is a QuarkXPress XTension that automates the linking of picture files when they are reported missing. You can search for files in a folder, folders, or even a whole volume.

Picture Tools
Vision's Edge, Inc.
Vision's Edge has created another utility —Picture Tools—with a variety of enhancements for working with pictures. Features include: Picture Suppression —performed via a dialog that lists all pictures in the document. Users can set the suppression by selecting a picture in the list and then setting the picture or box suppress check boxes. The suppression for every picture can be set using a global command.

PictureManager
CompuSense
The PictureManager XTension is a must for QuarkXPress users who work with graphics in their documents. It incorporates a comprehensive credits management utility that allows you to create caption boxes for graphics with ease. It also has an automatic picture updating facility. This module will search through user-specified volumes or folders anywhere on the network for missing and modified files and will update all as required. Other features of the XTension help to streamline tedious graphic-related production tasks from the initial importing of the picture to finally delivering the document to a service bureau.

PictureMate
Cheshire Group
With the press of a button, the high performance search utility in PictureMate automatically links pictures. You can search for files in a folder, folders, or even a whole volume.

PinpointXT
Cheshire Group
Can you afford to lose time trying to print? PinPointXT will save you hours debugging printing problems. No more having to rely on obscure screen messages or, worse, no message at all.

PiXTrix
Sparking Mad Software
PiXTrix charts new territory in Quark XPress with its unique picture-handling ability. PiXTrix will convert text to picture boxes so you can put pictures through type; place the same photo across multiple picture boxes, maintaining the picture's relative position. It will allow pictures placed across multiple boxes to be moved, sized, rotated, and skewed in real-time in an edit dialog and then applied to the original layout. It will break any picture box containing an image into multiple picture boxes

each containing a piece of the original image and create custom starburst picture shapes, including angled spikes and cogwheels and a buzzsaw.

PlaceMat

NPath Software, Inc.

PlaceMat adds a set of handy object manipulation functions into your Quark XPress environment. These functions give you a way of "linking" boxes and lines for resizing, so that changing the size of one causes corresponding changes to the sizes of the others.

Press2Go Jump Document

Atex

Press2Go Jump Document is the XTension for anybody who makes publications in Quark with stories which jump between various Quark documents. Just as Quark lets the user form links between story areas on different pages of the same Quark document, Jump Document produces dynamic links between story areas in separate Quark files. The process is simple. Open the different documents on your screen and use the Jump Document tool to chain between the various story areas. Text flowed into the first shape will then flow between the pages completing the link. Edits made in any of the components can be distributed throughout all affected pages by pressing the update button.

Press2Go Smart Shapes

Atex

Press2Go Smart Shapes makes grouped objects in QuarkXPress (like logos or story shapes) flexible and scalable—intelligently. At the moment, once several objects have been grouped together in QuarkXPress, they cannot be re-sized. To change any of the objects or the overall size of the group involves tedious and time-consuming "tweaking" of the component parts.

PressMarks

Vision's Edge, Inc.

Until PressMarks, users had to be content with QuarkXPress' default crop and registration marks, and the default plate information generated by QuarkXPress during output. These consist of a fixed-size and placement set of crop marks, a fixed-design registration mark, and a fixed-position text slug indicating the file name, time of output, and plate color. PressMarks changes all of that.

Preview Editor

Vision's Edge, Inc.

Users can attach a PICT preview to any QuarkXPress page, as well as a description of the document and keywords which might be used when searching for the document. This makes it convenient to catalog QuarkXPress documents in image browsing applications.

PrintArea

XTend, Inc.

PrintArea provides the ability to print specific items or a portion of a page. This feature proves invaluable during the process of designing and proofing a document. Changes to a document are made more efficiently since the user isn't required to print entire pages.

Printer's Spreads

Corder Associates, Inc.

Printer's Spreads was created by Corder Associates, Inc. to aid printers and desktop publishers in composing saddlestitched publications. Printer's

Spreads installs easily and allows the user to quickly convert QuarkXPress documents from reader's spread format to printer's spread format.

PrintIt

a lowly apprentice production

This XTension not only permits users to designate multiple pages for saving as EPS files, or to save a selected text or picture box as an EPS, but actually allows for defining a printable area of the page by dragging a marquee around the desired elements.

PuzzleMaker

DPN

Quickly, accurately, and easily create puzzle grids with this great new design XTension. Crosswords, Wordsearches, and Trailblazer puzzles can now be produced in a fraction of the time it previously took.

QSpool

Baseview

QSpool adds high-speed document spooling to QuarkXPress. Users can place a Quark or NewsEdit document in a specified folder—typically one that resides on the network file server. QSpool continually scans the folder looking for documents to print. If it finds a QuarkXPress document, QSpool opens it, prints it, and deletes it. If it finds a NewsEdit document, QSpool creates a template according to the specifications embedded in the file. QSpool flows text into the template, prints the document, and then deletes the text and template file from the folder—or moves it to a "Done" folder. QSpool gives every user the power of QuarkXPress without the cost.

QTools 2.0

Baseview Products, Inc.

New features found in QTools 2.0 include Fix Fractions, Smart Keys, a 600,000-synonym Thesaurus, and dozens of other improvements. This new version can change all the fractions in a document from a "pseudo-fraction" like 1 1/2 to a real fraction like 1½. You can design the look of the fractions yourself, so they fit your style.

QuarkPrint

Quark, Inc.

This printing productivity tool for QuarkXPress power users boasts four utilities to make your prepress process a breeze. Print Job saves time and reduces the probability of printing related errors by letting you save and apply frequently used settings from the Print and Page Setup dialog boxes. You can also specify custom CMYK screen angles and frequencies and print nonsequential pages and ranges. Document Statistics lets you print a list of all elements in an QuarkXPress document—even if the document is closed. No more guessing about formats, fonts, or other critical unknown elements in a document. The third utility, Print Area, lets you print just a portion of a page. With this feature you can now drag out a box to print page elements for faster editing and proofing, and Printer Calibration allows you to adjust screen output to compensate for dot gain on various printers—especially useful for color separations.

QXEdit

Baseview Products, Inc.

QXEdit allows you to "lift" blocks of text from the QuarkXPress screen for quick editing in a larger, more readable format. QXEdit works by creating a window into which the text of selected blocks can be placed. Most text style attributes, such as bold and italic, will be displayed in the window, along with line and paragraph justification. Other attributes, such as style sheet, font, and point size, are displayed in a pallet similar to the Quark measurements pallet.

Red, Hot & Publish

Quark, Inc., CompuSense, Vision's Edge, Inc., XChange, SuperMac Technology, HSC Software

A concerned group of computer publishing companies has joined together to help the Red Hot Organization in its efforts to raise awareness and funds for AIDS research and relief. Red, Hot & Publish includes: QuarkPresents—a wonderful slide-show generator—from Quark, Inc., PictureInfo from CompuSense/XChange, SepsChange from Vision's Edge/XChange, a discount from SuperMac Technology, and Photoshop plug-ins from HSC Software.

RefleXTion

Vision's Edge, Inc.

This nifty new XTension not only saves time, but can give you a striking mirrored effect for a change to your Quark XPress document design. While recreating a polygon upside-down might be next to impossible if you try it by hand, RefleXTion can quickly flip a polygon horizontally or vertically. Equally as frustrating would be trying to reflect a group of boxes manually, especially if the group has been rotated. This XTension gives you the option to try the effect quickly to decide whether or not it fits your design. You can even reflect an entire page horizontally or vertically with a single command.

ReLink

North Atlantic Publishing Systems, Inc.

Have you ever had a series of linked boxes all laid out in QuarkXPress, filled them with text, and then decided to switch the order of the text boxes—only to discover that you have to go back and use the Link Tool to relink the boxes in their new order? With North Atlantic Publishing System's ReLink XTension, you can automatically reflow the text in the proper order for you new design.

Resize XT 2.0

Vision's Edge, Inc.

Resize XT 2.0 allows all the elements of a group, which could include all the contents of a page or spread, to be scaled from 20 to 400% of the original size. Just check off the attributes you wish to be scaled in the Resize XT dialog. Resize XT also adds a new tool to the tool palette. The Resize Tool is the alternate way to resize groups of boxes.

ScaleIT

a lowly apprentice production

Use this XTension to resize an item or items and its content(s). Scaling can be done either as a percentage of the current size or by an absolute amount. Proportional or anamorphic scaling is possible using ScaleIT, and the actual scaling process is extremely fast.

Scitex XTensions

Scitex Corporation Ltd.

Scitex Corporation Ltd. has released Scitex XTensions—twelve powerful XTensions that provide for increased creativity, precision, and productivity in QuarkXPress. With Scitex XTensions, you can create multiple-color blends, silhouette images, produce detailed document reports, proof image-intensive documents quickly, and more. All Scitex XTensions feature the Scitex Launchpad, a floating palette from which the XTensions are easily accessed. The Scitex Launchpad also provides on-line help, and tells you which Scitex XTensions are currently in use.

Scitex Align & Measure

Choosing Align from the Align & Measure palette enables you to align the top of a picture box with a text baseline, or center a line on a box, or a box on a page. Align any two points vertically, horizontally, or both. Specify alignment points as selection handles or center points of boxes or lines, as text baselines, or as any point on a page. You can also align two points by an offset amount.

Scitex Blends

With Scitex Blends, you can create straight-line or radial blends of up to 14 colors. You can specify CMYK colors or pick them from the document's color palette, control the blend rate between pairs of colors (linear or logarithmic), and draw blend paths at any angle. When sent to a PostScript RIP, Scitex Blends produces standard PostScript-quality blends. When sent to a Scitex RIP, Scitex Blends generates Scitex degradés with "noise" to eliminate banding.

Scitex Document Reports

Scitex Document Reports enables you to extract information from a Quark XPress document and prepare a report. You can choose from over three dozen document attributes on which to report, including page geometry, style sheets (character, format, tabs, rules), fonts (and fonts in imported graphics), text boxes, picture boxes, pictures, colors, and trapping.

Scitex Fractions

Scitex Fractions enables you to fine-tune the appearance of fractions. You can specify numerators and denominators of up to three characters, and independently adjust the size, position and kerning of the numerator, denominator, and divisor.

Scitex Grids & Guides

Scitex Grids & Guides is a powerful set of tools for creating and editing grids and guides. You can define guides one at a time, specifying their numerical coordinates, color, and the view at which they appear.

Scitex Image Tools

Scitex Image Tools includes four XTensions for working with pictures and graphic elements.

Scitex Layers

Scitex Layers enables you to create and name up to 31 layers for viewing and printing. You can show or hide layers, and print only visible layers. Use Scitex Layers to organize electronic mechanicals with revisions or foreign-language versions, or just separate different elements for more efficient viewing and proofing.

Scitex Lock

Scitex Lock enables you to globally lock text boxes, picture boxes, lines, or any combination of the three. Locked items cannot be moved accidentally with the Item tool, but they can be moved using the Measurement palette or Modify command. The contents of locked items can also be locked. Scitex Lock protects text from designers, and designs from editors!

Scitex Nudge
With Scitex Nudge, you can move a selected item in user-definable increments. Scitex Nudge works with Scitex Zoom, so you can nudge an item displayed at 1600% for highly accurate placement.

Scitex Picture Scaling
Have you memorized all the keyboard shortcuts for "live" picture scaling? With the Scitex Picture Scaling palette, you can scale a picture interactively in 1%, 10%, or continuous increments, and center or fit a picture within its picture box—without entering numbers in palettes or dialog boxes, or remembering keyboard shortcuts.

Scitex Precision Tools
Scitex Precision Tools consist of four XTensions for creating electronic mechanicals quickly and accurately.

Scitex Silhouettes
With Scitex Silhouettes, you can quickly silhouette a picture using straight-line or smooth-cut techniques. Scitex Silhouette may be used for comps, and, depending on image complexity and quality requirements, for production masks as well. In a Scitex production workflow, Scitex Silhouettes can be used for automatic mask substitution—the automatic swapping of the Scitex silhouette for a high-resolution mask cut on a Scitex production system.

Scitex Quick Proof
When you need a quick look at an image-intensive document, use Scitex Quick Proof. This XTension prints the smaller PICT screen previews of EPS and TIFF images, giving you a fast proof with 72-dpi images in position. No need to suppress the printout of individual pictures one at a time—and then guess where the pictures should be when you look at the proof!

Scitex Zoom
When you need a closer look, use the Scitex Zoom palette to enlarge a selected area of the page to views ranging from 100% to 1600%. Simply specify the view you want, drag the selection marquee onto the page, and the selected area appears in the palette's window. Used with Scitex Align & Measure, Scitex Zoom is a powerful tool for fine-tuning production details such as alignment and serif weights.

Script XT
XSoft
This new XTension enables QuarkXPress to respond to Apple Events sent by either a scripting environment or another application. It allows you to ask QuarkXPress questions or to tell it to take certain actions. This is not a macro program. With Script XT, you actually talk to the application.

SetInset ii
XTend, Inc.
SetInset II permits a user to specify text inset values for QuarkXPress text boxes. Modifications to the text inset value

were previously limited to one value for all sides of a text box. SetInset II allows the user to design pages with much more flexibility when used in conjunction with existing features such as text indent, vertical justification, and tabs. SetInset II allows the user to enter a value using the unit of their choice and offers decimal precision similar to that found in QuarkXPress.

Shadow Master
Vision's Edge, Inc.
Shadow Master is a quick and easy way to create shadow effects for objects without leaving QuarkXPress. Drop shadows are a breeze when you use Shadow Master. A dialog lets you choose the shadow's offset as well as its color and shade. Three-dimensional shadows, which are time-consuming when created by hand, are easy with this utility. Just set the offset and color, then use the convenient shadow orientation box to select which way the shadow should fall. Shadow Master even allows you to create shadows with gradient blends.

Shortline Eliminator (SeXT)
Kytek, Inc.
SeXT detects and corrects paragraphs with short last lines. You may specify what constitutes a short last line in terms of character count and/or a hyphenated last word.

Sonar Bookends
Virginia Systems, Inc.
Sonar Bookends can index an Quark XPress document quickly with flexible formatting, indexing of word/phrase lists, or automatic indexing of keywords. The user can then print the index directly or bring it back into QuarkXPress for editing.

Sonar TOC
Virginia Systems, Inc.
Sonar TOC makes Quark's style sheets become automatic markers for a multi-level table of contents. Sonar TOC also lets you specify text selections for special indexing.

Special Effects!
Trias
This fun utility allows for the easy creation of round corners on boxes around text blocks, instant creation of breaks (a block of text perfectly centered on the top of the current text box), and the creation of rules inside gutters.

SpectreScan QX
PrePress Technologies
SpectreScan QX lets you make scans from within QuarkXPress, using any of the most popular desktop scanners, in B&W, grayscale, or color. You can make color corrections to a low-resolution preview scan, then scan a high-resolution corrected image into an active picture box or directly to disk as a 1-, 8-, or 24-bit TIFF file. Capturing a high-quality image onto a QuarkXPress page has never been easier.

SpectreSeps QX
PrePress Technologies
A Color Separation XTension that lets you make high-quality color separations of QuarkXPress documents, including continuous-tone images. Includes sophisticated control over color-correction and separation parameters, and lets you use custom halftone screening information as well.

SpellBound
CompuSense
The SpellBound spell checker XTension enables you to check the spelling of a single word, of an active story, of an entire document, or of the text on master pages. It provides functionality and features not found in the internal Quark XPress spellchecker.

Step & Flex-It
DataStream Imaging Systems, Inc.
Step & Flex-It performs specialized functions, such as automatic compensation for plate distortion, label bleed, and step-and-repeat, which effectively customize QuarkXPress for the needs of flexography. It brings to QuarkXPress all the features needed to make flexographic film quickly and economically.

Stylin'
Vision's Edge, Inc.
The Stylin' XTension from Vision's Edge allows QuarkXPress users to apply specific elements of style sheets to a selected range of text. Accessed from a floating palette similar to the Style Sheets palette, Stylin' presents a dialog that allows any or all paragraph or character-based attributes to be included or omitted from the selected text. This effectively permits the creation and application of style sheet subsets, without having to create the hundreds of new style sheets required to handle all the slight variations and special circumstances that arise in the layout process.

The Super Tabs XTension
Techno Design
The Super Tabs XTension gives you ultimate control over tab positions in QuarkXPress. This powerful design tool adds a floating palette to QuarkXPress with which you can control your tabs with ease.

SXetch Pad
Datastream Imaging Systems, Inc.
SXetch Pad, an exciting XTension from DataStream Imaging Systems, Inc., lets you create open and closed Bezier curves, polygonal shapes and wrap text to a curve. Additionally, you can fill closed objects with a multicolor blend, and convert Type 1 PostScript fonts into editable outlines. And all SXetch Pad's functions use QuarkXPress' built-in trapping capabilities.

Tableworks Plus
Npath
Tableworks Plus creates a professional table editing environment in Quark XPress. Easily change the size and position of rows or columns, either visually or to exact specs. Apply any typographic or style settings to rows, columns, or the entire table. Table shading and rules are maintained automatically. Import data in any file format available in QuarkXPress, or from another part ofyour document. Use table template libraries to save all customized configuration, style, and color settings.

Text Tools 2.0
Vision's Edge, Inc.
This XTension is actually a package of several utilities for working with text in QuarkXPress documents.

TextLinker
Npath Software, Inc.
TextLinker adds System 7 Publish/Subscribe capability for text to Quark

XPress. Publish/Subscribe allows data to be "linked" between documents and different applications. With TextLinker, you can "Publish" text from your QuarkXPress document, to be used in other documents, or "Subscribe" to text from other documents. The documents you link to can be documents produced by QuarkXPress any other applications that support Publish/Subscribe, such as Microsoft Word 5.0 and Excel 4.0.

Textractor

Vision's Edge, Inc.

With this comprehensive text extraction XTension, users can export all of the text in a document or selected portions of the text using any filter currently available to QuarkXPress.

Thesaurus Rex

Vision's Edge, Inc.

Thesaurus Rex XTension allows you to find the right word for your thought without taking your hands off the keyboard or your eyes off the screen. Just place the cursor anywhere in the word you want to look up and open the thesaurus. A window with a list of synonyms from the 220,000-word thesaurus will appear. Select the synonym you want, then select the Replace button. The new word replaces the old word in the document. Of course, you can choose to leave the original word in your document, using Thesaurus Rex to check spelling and meaning.

TIFFormation

Vision's Edge, Inc.

We all know QuarkXPress allows you to place TIFF files in your documents, but only minimal information about an imported TIFF is available from within QuarkXPress. The TIFFormation XTension displays detailed information about imported TIFFs including the resolution, compression, and the embedded description in a convenient palette. The information in the palette may be printed out for easy reference at any time. The Copy button transfers the text in the scrolling description field to the clipboard so it can be pasted into a text box in the document for use in a caption.

The Time Log XTension

Techno Design

Aren't you curious about how many hours you have spent on a job with QuarkXPress. Time log gives you the answer. This cost effective utility, from Techno Design, is the time registration option for QuarkXPress.

Time Logger

Trias

Time Logger adds a new menu item to the Utilities menu called, appropriately, Time Logger. The item remains grayed until you have opened a document. Upon selecting the new item from the Utilities menu, a dialog is displayed which provides the user with information on when the document was created, when it was last saved, and the total time spent on the document. Unbelievably valuable to those who have contractors, multiple users contributing, or just want an estimate for a budget or proposal.

TimeStamp

Vision's Edge, Inc.

The TimeStamp XTension allows the user to apply unlimited time stamps to any document. Automatically updated whenever the document is saved, the time stamps allow the user to easily and accurately determine when a document was last revised.

TruPack
Durrant Software Limited
TruPack is made up of two XTensions that enhance existing functions in QuarkXPress. TruNew replaces the standard QuarkXPress New dialog box with a much improved version adding several new options.

TypeMaster
Sparking Mad Software
This XTension from Sparking Mad Software offers users the chance to manipulate type the way they've always wanted to do it—by clicking and dragging it to the right position. The interface couldn't be easier or more intuitive. Highlight the text you want to work on with the content tool, and select TypeMaster... from the Utilities menu.

Verbaytum
Vision's Edge, Inc.
Verbaytum allows the user to link the stories to their original text files at the time they are imported, or the link can be established afterward. Once the story is linked, Verbaytum makes sure the imported story stays current. User options include automatically updating modified stories as well as notifying the user of missing and modified stories when a document is opened.

Vision Contents
Vision's Edge, Inc.
This flexible table of contents creator allows users to set preferences for the table and then automatically creates the table following the user-defined preferences. A table of contents can be created to describe a single document, or the batch processing feature makes it possible to quickly generate a table of contents for any number of chapters which are broken up into multiple QuarkXPress document files.

Vision Utilities
Vision's Edge, Inc.
This collection of utility functions includes a feature which draws grids of page guides, a utility which counts all of the words in the currently selected text, a function which fits a picture to its picture box so that it entirely fills the box, and a paragraph sorting utility which alphabetizes paragraphs.

Vision's Edge Utility Pack
Vision's Edge, Inc.
This utility pack includes several XTensions—a palette to open and close other palettes, a palette for setting vertical text alignment and text insets, and a pop-up menu that allows document preferences to be stored and accessed when creating a new document. Opening palettes at desired locations and closing them again is as simple as clicking a button. The top six icons on the Palette Manager represent the six built-in QuarkXPress palettes.

VJ
Trias
Do you frequently find yourself being asked to fill out underset or squeeze overset text into QuarkXPress text boxes or linked story chains? VJ (for Vertical Justification) makes the tedious job of copyfitting a breeze. Based on

parameters that you define, this XTension examines the selected text box/chain and determines what it can change to make it fit.

Wang WP/PC Filter

DPN

The Wang WP/PC XTension enables users to import Wang WP/PC documents directly into a QuarkXPress document, without using any additional conversion software. The XTension also enables the user to include style tags in the Wang WP/PC document and convert these directly to appropriate Quark XPress layout specifications.

WordPerfect DOS Filter

DPN

The WordPerfect DOS XTension enables users to import documents created in WordPerfect DOS versions 4.2 and 5.1 directly into a QuarkXPress document, without using additional conversion software.

XactHeight

Artemis Systems

This new XTension is a must for designers and other QuarkXPress users who need to produce headline and display text to a precise visual size. XactHeight allows type sizes to be specified by stating the visual height of capital letters or of the lowercase x-height.

XChar!

Schnittstelle

XChar! gives you a faster and more convenient way to insert special characters into your text! Special characters are already available from the Key Caps DA or by pressing the appropriate keyboard letter while holding down one or more of the Shift, Option, Control, or Command keys. Pressing Command-9 or selecting XChar! from the Utilities menu displays a neatly arranged chart showing all the special characters from any available font. Select a character by clicking on it once, and an enlarged version appears in the upper right of the table. Double-clicking on the character—or pressing the Insert button—inserts the desired special character in the desired font at your current cursor position, leaving surrounding characters unchanged.

Xdata

Em Software, Inc.

Unleash the power of QuarkXPress on your data. Xdata is the best-selling XTension that brings the full typographic and picture publishing power of QuarkXPress to bear on all your data-driven repetitive publishing tasks: catalogs, directories, form letters, financial summaries, tables, labels, lists of all sorts, and more. Completely integrated with QuarkXPress, Xdata automatically formats data exported from your Macintosh or PC database and spreadsheet applications, or downloaded from your corporate information systems, freeing you from endless manual formatting. Xdata can also import related pictures (of any type supported by QuarkXPress) into boxes anchored in the textual data.

XMacro

Schnittstelle

XMacro enables the user to structurally capture data from foreign systems. Simply, shortkeys are given for the recording of the data, which XMacro automatically translates into user-defined

XTag syntax. XMacro inserts the converted text directly into a selected QuarkXPress text box.

XMath

York Graphics, Inc.

XMath is a professional mathematical typography enhancement available for QuarkXPress that enables users to build complex equations right in an Quark XPress document. And since XMath is an XTension, you can take advantage of all the functionality of QuarkXPress.

Xnotes

Vision's Edge, Inc.

This XTension permits the user to assign electronic Post-Its to a Quark XPress document, or to individual items within that document. These notes can be up to 2,550 characters each, and are hidden away within the document until needed. They can be used for a multitude of tasks, from editing or commenting layouts to giving explicit instructions on an element by element basis to your service bureau.

XSize

Schnittstelle

XSize has been especially designed for the professional positioning of picture data. With this module, the size and the sector of a picture can be chosen depending on the selected QuarkXPress picture box. Magazines and other publications that require close cooperation between layout and picture processing will find XSize most useful.

XState

Markzware

XState is the XTension for QuarkXPress 3.2 that enables you to open all of your Quark document and library files to precisely the place you worked on them when they were last closed. This new "electronic bookmarker" easily opens any QuarkXPress file to its last screen position, window size, and page number. Also, selected objects and highlighted text still remain selected when reopened. Additionally, XState is able to clock the time you worked on Quark documents and provide a project report. This convenient and very useful feature can prove beneficial for your business.

XStyle

Em Software, Inc.

Xstyle is the accelerator for Quark XPress style use and reporting. The XTension greatly simplifies and accelerates the use of QuarkXPress style sheets and character and paragraph settings, whether you're a "QuarkXPress demon" or an enthusiastic beginner.

The XT-Batch XTension

TechnoDesign

If you have orders that normally are produced automatically with a traditional typesetting system and you want to make it with QuarkXPress and you want a fast production solution for this kind of job, XT-Batch is the answer. This powerful batch utility, from Techno Design, is a (command) macro language for QuarkXPress.

XTable

York Graphics, Inc.

XTable is a professional table composition tool for QuarkXPress. And since XTable is an XTension, users can take advantage of all the functionality afforded by QuarkXPress when setting type that is destined to be made into a table. XTable will calculate the tab stops, indentations, etc. to compose the table to the user's specifications.

XTags

em software, inc.

Xtags supports the full QuarkXPress Tags language, plus several major enhancements designed for data publishing, classified ad building, and input code translation.

XTension Manager

DK&A

This is the XTension every QuarkXPress user should have.This powerful tool lets you enable and disable XTensions when launching QuarkXPress. No longer will you have to shuffle XTensions in and out of your application folder. XTension Manager will take care of this mundane housekeeping for you.

XTensions from Quark, Inc.

Quark, Inc.

These disks include all the free XTensions Quark, Inc. has released for Quark XPress.

XT_Edit

Trias

This great new product from Trias is actually a stand-alone text editor designed exclusively to work with Quark XPress' powerful typographical features, and an XTension that brings the preformatted and styled text into Quark XPress via the Get Text dialog.

XyWrite Filter

North Atlantic Publishing

The XyWrite Filter allows XyWrite Plus III files to be imported and exported for layouts in QuarkXPress for the Macintosh. The XyWrite Filter translates XyWrite formatting commands that have QuarkXPress equivalents. Some of those styles included are screen modes, paragraph alignment, indents, leading and tabs. Commands that have no QuarkXPress equivalent are ignored.

Appendix G: Installing the disk

The various free, shareware, and demonstration utilities and XTensions found on the disk in the back of the book are discussed throughout the pages of *QuarkXPress Unleashed.* Wherever the book refers to something on the disk, a small floppy disk icon appears in the margin of the page.

The utilities on the disk are grouped into folders that represent the chapters of the book (for example, both fcsTableMaker and ProTabsXT are discussed in the Tables chapter, so they are in the Tables folder). Each folder is compressed into a Compact Pro self-extracting archive. Just move the archive to your hard disk and double-click on it to decompress the folder.

Each folder is listed below, followed by the names of the utilities and XTensions that can be found in that folder, along with a very brief description of each of the utilities and XTensions. See the **Index** to find out which pages discuss each utility, or check out the tables of contents that appear in each chapter of the book.

Text Preparation

■ WordLess Plus—a free utility that converts formatted Microsoft Word files to XPress Tags

Typography

■ Bobzilla—a free XTension from Quark that lets you search for loosely justified lines, send full-resolution TIFF images to a printer, and more

■ FeaturesPlus—a free XTension from Quark that adds a value converter palette, applies tracking on word spaces, removes manual kerning, creates fractions, and a whole lot more

- Pairing Knife—a free utility that analyzes a file and reports on the frequency of kerning pair combinations

Page Layout

- DocStamp—a free XTension that lets you "stamp" master pages with the name of the document and automatically updates the stamp if the file name is changed
- GuideLiner—a free XTension that allows you to numerically place guidelines on QuarkXPress pages
- Xstyle—a demo XTension that lets you view most of the character and paragraph attributes that can be applied to text

Graphics

- ColorChange—a demo XTension that lets you search and replace colors in a document, including colors applied to text and as backgrounds and frames in text and picture boxes
- Picture Tools—a demo XTension that adds handy graphics-related keyboard shortcuts for working with graphics in QuarkXPress
- TIFFormation—a demo XTension that provides interesting and useful information about TIFF images that have been imported into Quark XPress

Output

- EPS Bleeder—a shareware utility that extends the edges of bleed elements that get truncated when using QuarkXPress' Save Page as EPS feature
- PageShot—a demo XTension that can be used to save page ranges or partial pages in QuarkXPress as EPS images

Tables

- fcsTableMaker—a demo XTension that automates the creation of simple tables in QuarkXPress
- ProTabsXT—a shareware XTension that can be used to create complex tables in QuarkXPress

Automating DTP

■ Mark My Words—Wordless Plus's big brother, this demo utility lets you completely customize which Microsoft Word character, paragraph, and page styling gets converted to XPress Tags or stripped out of a file

■ PixPex—a free utility that interrogates graphic files and creates coding that can be used by the Xtags XTension to generate and fill anchored picture boxes

■ Shane the Plane—a demo utility that lets you change many characteristics of files in the finder, among other things

■ Torquemada the Inquisitor—the free version of a commercial utility that does batch search-and-replace on text files

■ XP8—a demo utility that cleans up text files and adds XPress Tags to automate typographic fine-tuning before a file is imported into QuarkXPress

■ Xtags—a demo XTension that adds new and powerful XPress Tags that can be used to automatically create and fill anchored text and picture boxes as well as apply master pages while text is being imported into QuarkXPress

■ Xdata—a demo XTension that can be used to format structured data on its way into QuarkXPress

Scripting

■ Build Chart—a free script that illustrates the power of scripting in QuarkXPress by building a complex, customizable bar chart

■ Save Range as EPS—a free script that allows entire ranges of non-contiguous pages to be saved as EPS

Appendix C

■ ProTagsXT—a shareware XTension that adds over 60 tags to the XPress Tags language and gives you unprecedented control over the creation and manipulation of QuarkXPress items while text is being imported

Colophon

It was discussions in CompuServe's Desktop Publishing Forum that got designer David Vereschagin interested in creating Clear Prairie Dawn, the text and display font used throughout this book. "Kathleen Tinkel put the idea in my head that I, too, could be a type designer," says David, "since the software tools now available have democratized type creation." The more he thought about it, the more appealing the idea was, at least as an experiment.

The decision of what kind of typeface to create did not prove too difficult, as he had been struck by the lack of humanist sans serif faces. "At the time I started, around three years ago, you could only name a few humanist sans: Optima, Frutiger, Gill Sans, Stone Sans and Lucida. There were a few others, but not in common usage. It seemed like a good field to explore."

Optima, Gill and Frutiger were examined closely, along with Stone, to a lesser extent, to look at how they were constructed. But the actual basis for Clear Prairie Dawn ended up being David's own handprinting. The font also has one deliberate eccentricity which the others do not: an angled axis. "I felt that a non-perpendicular axis would create a 'warmer' face. So, CPD is more of an 'oldstyle sans,' if such a thing could be said to exist."

The font was originally called Millenium, and a sample was uploaded to the DTP Forum (and is probably still there) in order to get some feedback. The characters were rendered in Adobe Illustrator at first, and then later completed in Altsys Fontographer. "As I developed the plain style of the face," says David, "it became obvious that the original designs were too lively to make a good text face—there were too many curves and angles." But as it turns out, many of the flourishes that didn't make it into the plain style were able to be included in the italic style.

Index

C

F

G

H

I

N

O

P

Q

R

S

T

U

V

W